THE JESUITS

1534-1921

A History of the Society of Jesus from Its
Foundation to the Present Time

BY

THOMAS J. CAMPBELL, S.J.

NEW YORK
THE ENCYCLOPEDIA PRESS

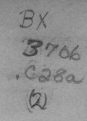

Permissu superiorum

NIHIL OBSTAT: ARTHUR J. SCANLAN, D.D., *Censor*
IMPRIMATUR: PATRICK J. HAYES, D.D., *Archbishop of New York*

PREFACE

Some years ago the writer of these pages, when on his way to what is called a general congregation of the Society of Jesus, was asked by a fellow-passenger on an Atlantic liner, if he knew anything about the Jesuits. He answered in the affirmative and proceeded to give an account of the character and purpose of the Order. After a few moments, he was interrupted by the inquirer with, " You know nothing at all about them, Sir; good day." Possibly the Jesuits themselves are responsible for this attitude of mind, which is not. peculiar to people at sea, but is to be met everywhere.

As a matter of fact, no Jesuit has thus far ever written a complete or adequate history of the Society; Orlandini, Jouvancy and Cordara attempted it a couple of centuries ago, but their work never got beyond the first one hundred years. Two very small compendiums by Jesuits have been recently published, one in Italian by Rosa, the other in French by Brucker, but they are too congested to be satisfactory to the average reader, and Brucker's stops at the Suppression of the Society by Clement XIV in 1773. Crétineau-Joly's history was written in great haste; he is often a special pleader, and even Jesuits find him too eulogistic. At present he is hopelessly antiquated, his last volume bearing the date of 1833. B. N. (Barbara Neave) published in English a history of the Society based largely on Crétineau-Joly. The consequence of this lack of authoritative works is that the general public gets its information about the Jesuits from writers who are prejudiced or ill-informed or, who, perhaps, have been hired to defame the Society for political purposes.

Other authors, again, have found the Jesuits a romantic theme, and have drawn largely on their imagination for their statements.

Attention was called to this condition of things by the Congregation of the Society which elected Father Martín to the post of General of the Jesuits in 1892. As a result he appointed a corps of distinguished writers to co-operate in the production of a universal history of the Society, which was to be colossal in size, based on the most authentic documents, and in line with the latest and most exacting requirements of recent scientific historiography. On the completion of the various parts, they are to be co-ordinated and then translated into several languages, so as to supply material for minor histories within the reach of the general public. Such a scheme necessarily supposes a very considerable time before the completion of the entire work, and, as matter of fact, although several volumes have already appeared in English, French, German, Spanish and Italian, the authors are still discussing events that occurred two centuries ago. Happily their researches have thrown much light on the early history of the Order; an immense number of *documents inédits*, published by Carayon and others, have given us a more intimate knowledge of the intermediate period; many biographies have been written, and the huge volume of the " Liber sæcularis " by Albers brings the record down to our own days. Thus, though much valuable information has already been made available for the general reader the great collaborative work is far from completion. Hence the present history of the Jesuits.

TABLE OF CONTENTS

CHAPTER I

ORIGIN

CHAPTER II

INITIAL ACTIVITIES

CHAPTER III

ENDS OF THE EARTH

Contents

Contents

PAGE

CHAPTER VIII

The Asiatic Continent

CHAPTER IX

Battle of the Books

CHAPTER X

The Two Americas
1567–1673

Contents

CHAPTER XI

CULTURE

CHAPTER XII

FROM VITELLESCHI TO RICCI
1615–1773

CHAPTER XIII

CONDITIONS BEFORE THE CRASH

Contents · xi

Contents

Contents

WORKS CONSULTED ·

Institutum Societatis Jesu.
JOUVANCY — Epitome historiæ Societatis Jesu.
JOUVANCY — Monumenta Societatis Jesu.
CRÉTINEAU-JOLY — Hist. relig., pol. et litt. de la Comp. de Jésus.
B. N.— The Jesuits: their foundation and history.
ROSA, I Gesuiti dalle origini ai nostri giorni.
MESCHLER, Die Gesellschaft Jesu.
BÖHMER-MONOD — Les Jésuites.
FEVAL, Les Jésuites.
HUBER — Der Jesuitenorden.
DUHR — Jesuiten-Fabeln.
BROU — Les Jésuites et la légende.
BELLOC, Pascal's Provincial Letters.
FOLEY — Jesuits in Conflict.
FOUQUERAY — Histoire de la compagnie de Jésus en France.
BOURNICHON — La Compagnie de Jésus en France: 1814–1914.
ALBERS — Liber sæcularis ab anno 1814 ad annum 1914.
TACCHI-VENTURI — Storia della compagnia di Gesù in Italia.
MONTI — La Compagnia di Gesù.
DUHR — Geschichte der Jesuiten in den Ländern deutschen Zunge.
KROESS — Geschichte der böhmischen Provinz der Gesellschaft Jesu.
ASTRAIN — Hist. de la Comp. de Jesús en la asist. de España.
HUGHES — History of the Society of Jesus of North America.
ALEGRE — La Compañía de Jesús en la Nueva España.
FRIAS — La Provincia de España de la compañía de Jesús, 1815–63.
POLLARD — The Jesuits in Poland.
HOGAN — Ibernia Ignatiana.
TANNER — Societas Jesu præclara.
Lives of Jesuit Saints.
Menologies of the Society of Jesus.
SOUTHWELL — Bibliotheca Scriptorum Societatis Jesu.
SOMMERVOGEL — Bibl. des écrivains de la comp. de Jésus.
CHANDLERY — Fasti breviores Societatis Jesu.
MAYNARD — The Studies and Teachings of the Society of Jesus.
DANIEL — Les Jésuites instituteurs.
WELD — Suppression of the Society of Jesus in Portugal.
DE RAVIGNAN — De l'existence et de l'institut des Jésuites.
DE RAVIGNAN — Clément XIII et Clément XIV.
THEINER — Geschichte des Pontifikats Klemens XIV.
ARTAUD DE MONTOR — Histoire du pape Pie VII.

CARAYON — Documents inédits concernants la Compagnie de Jésus.
BERTRAND — Mémoires sur les missions.
BROU — Les Missions du xixᵉ siècle.
SEAMAN — Map of Jesuit Missions in the United States.
MARSHALL — Christian Missions.
BANCROFT — Native Races of the Pacific States.
CAMPBELL — Pioneer Priests of North America.
CHARLEVOIX — Histoire du Japon.
CHARLEVOIX — Histoire du Paraguay.
CHARLEVOIX — Histoire de la Nouvelle-France.
CRASSET — Histoire de l'église du Japon.
AVRIL — Voyage en divers états d'Europe et d'Asie.
THWAITES — Jesuit Relations.
BOLTON — Kino's Historical Memoir.
JANSSEN — History of the German People.
LAVISSE — Histoire de France.
RANKE — History of the Popes.
LINGARD — History of England.
TIERNEY-DODD — Church History of England.
POLLEN — The Institution of the Archpriest Blackwell.
HAILE-BONNEY — Life and Letters of John Lingard.
POLLOCK — The Popish Plot.
GUILDAY — English Catholic Refugees on the Continent.
MACGEOGHEGAN — History of Ireland.
FLANAGAN — Ecclesiastical History of Ireland.
O'REILLY — Lives of the Irish Martyrs and Confessors.
ROCHEFORT — Histoire des Antilles.
EYZAGUIRRE — Historia de Chile.
TERTRE — Histoire de St. Christophe.
ROHRBACHER — History of the Church.
HÜBNER — Sixte-Quint.
HUC — Christianity in China, Tartary and Tibet.
ROBERTSON — History of Charles V.
SHEA — The Catholic Church in Colonial Days.
PACCA — Memorie storiche del ministero.
SAINTE-BEUVE — Causeries.
PETIT DE JULLEVILLE — Histoire de la littérature française.
GODEFROY — Littérature française.
SCHLOSSER — History of the Eighteenth and Nineteenth Centuries.
CANTÜ — Storia universale.
The Cambridge Modern History, Vols. VIII, XII.
The Month.
The Catholic Encyclopedia, passim.
The Encyclopedia Britannica, passim.
Realencyclopädie für protestantische Theologie und Kirche, passim.

THE JESUITS
1534-1921

CHAPTER I

ORIGIN

The Name — Opprobrious meanings — Caricatures of the Founder — Purpose of the Order — Early life of Ignatius — Pampeluna — Conversion — Manresa — The Exercises — Authorship — Journey to Palestine — The Universities — Life in Paris — First Companions — Montmartre First Vows — Assembly at Venice. Failure to reach Palestine — First Journey to Rome — Ordination to the Priesthood — Labors in Italy — Submits the Constitutions for Papal Approval — Guidiccioni's opposition — Issue of the Bull *Regimini* — Sketch of the Institute — Crypto-Jesuits.

THE name " Jesuit " has usually a sinister meaning in the minds of the misinformed. Calvin is accused of inventing it, but that is an error. It was in common use two or three centuries before the Reformation, and generally it implied spiritual distinction. Indeed, in his famous work known as " The Great Life of Our Lord Jesus Christ," which appeared somewhere about 1350, the saintly old Carthusian ascetic, Ludolph of Saxony, employs it in a way that almost provokes a smile. He tells his readers that " just as we are called Christians when we are baptized, so we shall be called Jesuits when we enter into glory." Possibly such a designation would be very uncomfortable even for some pious people of the present day. The opprobrious meaning of the word came into use at the approach of the Protestant Reformation. Thus, when laxity in the observance of their rule began to show itself in the once fervent followers of St. John Columbini — who were called Jesuati, because of their frequent use of

the expression: " Praised be Jesus Christ "— their
name fixed itself on the common speech as a synonym
of hypocrisy. Possibly that will explain the curious
question in the " Examen of Conscience " in an old
German prayer-book, dated 1519, where the penitent
is bidden to ask himself: " Did I omit to teach the
Word of God for fear of being called a Pharisee, a
Jesuit, a hypocrite, a Beguine? "

The association of the term Jesuit with Pharisee and
hypocrite is unpleasant enough, but connecting it with
Beguine is particularly offensive. The word Beguine
had come to signify a female heretic, a mysticist, an
illuminist, a pantheist, who though cultivating a saintly
exterior was credited with holding secret assemblies
where the most indecent orgies were indulged in. The
identity of the Beguines with Jesuits was considered
to be beyond question, and one of the earliest Calvinist
writers informed his co-religionists that at certain
periods the Jesuits made use of mysterious and
magical devices and performed a variety of weird
antics and contortions in subterraneous caverns, from
which they emerged as haggard and worn as if they
had been struggling with the demons of hell (Janssen,
Hist. of the German People, Eng. tr., IV, 406–7).
Unhappily, at that time, a certain section of the association of Beguines insisted upon being called Jesuits.
There were many variations on this theme when the
genuine Jesuits at last appeared. In Germany they
were denounced as idolaters and libertines, and their
great leader Canisius was reported to have run away
with an abbess. In France they were considered
assassins and regicides; Calvin called them *la racaille*,
that is, the rabble, rifraff, dregs. In England they
were reputed political plotters and spies. Later, in
America, John Adams, second President of the United
States, identified them with Quakers and resolved to

suppress them. Cotton Mather or someone in Boston denounced them as grasshoppers and prayed for the east wind to sweep them away; the Indians burned them at the stake as magicians, and the Japanese bonzes insisted that they were cannibals, a charge repeated by Charles Kingsley, Queen Victoria's chaplain, who, in " Westward Ho," makes an old woman relate of the Jesuits first arriving in England that " they had probably killed her old man and salted him for provision on their journey to the Pope of Rome," No wonder Newman told Kingsley to fly off into space.

The climax of calumny was reached in a decree of the Parliament of Paris, issued on August 6, 1762. It begins with a prelude setting forth the motives of the indictment, and declares that " the Jesuits are recognized as *guilty of having taught at all times, uninterruptedly, and with the approbation of their superiors and generals*, simony, blasphemy, sacrilege, the black art, magic, astrology, impiety, idolatry, superstition, impurity, corruption of justice, robbery, parricide, homicide, suicide and regicide." The decree then proceeds to set forth eighty-four counts on which it finds them specifically guilty of supporting the Greek Schism, denying the procession of the Holy Ghost; of favoring the heresies of Arianism, Sabellianism, and Nestorianism; of assailing the hierarchy, attacking the Mass and Holy Communion and the authority of the Holy See; of siding with the Lutherans, Calvinists and other heretics of the sixteenth century; of reproducing the heresies of Wycliff and the Pelagians and Semi-Pelagians; of adding blasphemy to heresy; of belittling the early Fathers of the Church, the Apostles, Abraham, the prophets, St. John the Baptist, the angels; of insulting and blaspheming the Blessed Virgin; of undermining the foundations of the Faith; destroying belief in the Divinity of Jesus Christ;

casting doubt on the mystery of the Redemption;
encouraging the impiety of the Deists; suggesting
Epicureanism; teaching men to live like beasts, and
Christians like pagans (de Ravignan, De l'existence
et de l'institut des Jésuites, iii).

This was the contribution of the Jansenists to
the Jesuit chamber of horrors. It was endorsed by
the government and served as a weapon for the
atheists of the eighteenth century to destroy the
religion of France, and finally the lexicons of every
language gave an odious meaning to the name Jesuit.
A typical example of this kind of ill-will may be
found in the " Diccionario nacional " of Domínguez.
In the article on the Jesuits, the writer informs the
world that the Order was the superior in learning to
all the others; and produced, relatively at every period
of its existence more eminent men, and devoted itself
with greater zeal to the preaching of the Gospel and
the education of youth — the primordial and sublime
objects of its Institute. Nevertheless its influence in
political matters, as powerful as it was covert, its
startling accumulation of wealth, and its ambitious
aims, drew upon it the shafts of envy, created terrible
antagonists and implacable persecutors, until the
learned Clement XIV, the immortal Ganganelli,
suppressed it on July 21, 1773, for its abuses and its
disobedience to the Holy See. Why the " learned
Clement XIV " should be described as " immortal " for
suppressing instead of preserving or, at least, reforming
an order which the writer fancies did more than all
the others for the propagation of the Faith is difficult
to understand, but logic is not a necessary requisite
of a lexicon. " In spite of their suppression," he
continues, " they with their characteristic pertinacity
have succeeded in coming to life again and are at
present existing in several parts of Europe." The

" Diccionario " is dated, Madrid, 1849. In other words, the saintly Pius VII performed a very wicked act in re-establishing the Order.

Of course the founder of this terrible Society had to be presented to the public as properly equipped for the malignant task to which he had set himself; so writers have vied with each other in expatiating on what they call his complex individuality. Thus a German psychologist insists that the Order established by this Spaniard was in reality a Teutonic creation. The Frenchman Drumont holds that " it is anti-semitic in its character," though Polanco, Loyola's life-long secretary, was of Jewish origin, as were Laínez, the second General, and the great Cardinal Toletus. A third enthusiast, Chamberlain, who is English-born, dismisses all other views and insists that, as Loyola was a Basque and an Iberian, he could not have been of Germanic or even Aryan descent, and he maintains that the primitive traits of the Stone Age continually assert themselves in his character. In reading the Spiritual Exercises, he says, " I hear that mighty roar of the cave bear and I shudder as did the men of the diluvial age, when poor, naked and defenceless, surrounded by danger day and night, they trembled at that voice." (Foundations of the Nineteenth Century, I, 570.) " If this be true," says Brou in " Les Jésuites et la légende, " then, by following the same process of reasoning, one must conclude that as Xavier was a Basque, his voice also was ursine and troglodytic; and as Faber was a Savoyard, he will have to be classified as a brachycephalous *homo alpinus*." Herman Müller, in " Les Origines de la Compagnie de Jésus" claims the honor of having launched an entirely novel theory about Loyola's personality. " The ' Exercises' are an amalgam of Islamic gnosticism and militant Catholicism," he tells us; " but where did Ignatius become acquainted with these Mussulmanic congregations? We have nothing positive on that score, though we know that one day he met a Moor on the road and was going to run him through with his sword. Then too, there were a great many Moors and Moriscos in Catalonia, and we must not forget that Ignatius intended to go to Palestine to convert the Turks. He must, therefore, have known them and so have been subject to their influence." Strange to say, Müller feels aggrieved that the Jesuits do not accept this very illogical theory, which he insists has nothing discreditable or dishonoring in it.

Omitting many other authorities, Vollet in " La Grande Encyclopédie " (s. v. Ignace de Loyola, Saint), informs his readers that " impartial history can discover in Loyola numberless traits of fantastic exaltation, morbific dreaminess, superstition, moral obscurantism, fanatical hatred, deceit and mendacity. On the other hand, it is impossible not to admit that he was a man of iron will, of indomitable perseverance in action and in suffering, and unshakeable faith in his mission; in spite of an ardent imagination, he had a penetrating intelligence, and a marvelous facility in reading the thoughts of men; he was possessed of a gentleness and suppleness which permitted him to make himself all to all. Visionary though he was, he possessed in the supreme degree, the genius of organization and strategy; he could create the army he needed, and employ the means he had at hand with prudence and circumspection. We can even discover in him a tender heart, easily moved to pity, to affection and to self-sacrifice for his fellow-men." Michelet says he was a combination of Saint Francis of Assisi and Machiavelli. Finally Victor Hugo reached the summit of the absurd when he assured the French Assembly in 1850 that " Ignatius was the enemy of Jesus." As a matter of fact the

poet knew nothing of either, nor did many of his
hearers.

As far as we are aware, St. Ignatius never used the
term Jesuit at all. He called his Order the *Compañía
de Jesús*, which in Italian is *Compagnia*, and in French,
Compagnie. The English name Society, as well as
the Latin *Societas*, is a clumsy attempt at a translation, and is neither adequate nor picturesque.
Compañía was evidently a reminiscence of Loyola's
early military life, and meant to him a battalion of
light infantry, ever ready for service in any part of the
world. The use of the name *Jesus* gave great offense.
Both on the Continent and in England, it was
denounced as blasphemous; petitions were sent to
kings and to civil and ecclesiastical tribunals to have
it changed; and even Pope Sixtus V had signed a
Brief to do away with it. Possibly the best apology
for it was given by the good-natured monarch, Henry
IV, when the University and Parliament of Paris
pleaded with him to throw his influence against its
use. Shrugging his shoulders, he replied: "I cannot
see why we should worry about it. Some of my officers
are Knights of the Holy Ghost; there is an Order of
the Holy Trinity in the Church; and, in Paris, we have
a congregation of nuns who call themselves God's
Daughters. Why then should we object to Company
of Jesus?"

The Spaniards must have been amazed at these
objections, because the name *Jesus* was, as it still is,
in very common use among them. They give it to
their children, and it is employed as an exclamation
of surprise or fear; like *Mon Dieu*! in French. They
even use such expressions as: *Jesu Cristo*! *Jesu mille
veces* or *Jesucristo, Dios mio*! The custom is rather
startling for other nationalities, but it is merely a
question of *autre pays, autres mœurs*. A compromise

was made, however, for the time being, by calling the
organization " The Society of the Name of Jesus,"
but that was subsequently forbidden by the General.

As a rule the Jesuits do not reply to these attacks.
The illustrious Jacob Gretser attempted it long ago;
but, in spite of his sanctity, he displayed so much
temper in his retort, that he was told to hold his peace.
Such is the policy generally adopted, and the Society
consoles itself with the reflection that the terrible
Basque, Ignatius Loyola, and a host of his sons have
been crowned by the Universal Church as glorious
saints; that the august Council of Trent solemnly
approved of the Order as a " pious Institute;" that
twenty or thirty successive Sovereign Pontiffs have
blessed it and favored it, and that after the terrible
storm evoked by its enemies had spent its fury, one
of the first official acts of the Pope was to restore the
Society to its ancient position in the Church.   The
scars it has received in its numberless battles are not
disfigurements but decorations; and Cardinal Allen,
who saw its members at close quarters in the bloody
struggles of the English Mission, reminded them that
" to be hated of the Heretikes, S. Hierom computeth
a great glorie."

It is frequently asserted that the Society was
organized for the express purpose of combatting the
Protestant Reformation.   Such is not the case.   On
the contrary, St. Ignatius does not seem to have been
aware of the extent of the religious movement going
on at that time.   His sole purpose was to convert the
Turks, and only the failure to get a ship at Venice
prevented him from carrying out that plan.   Indeed it
is quite likely that when he first thought of consecrating
himself to God, not even the name of Luther had, as
yet, reached Montserrat or Manresa.   They were
contemporaries, of course, for Luther was born in

1483 and Loyola in 1491 or thereabouts; and their lines of endeavor were in frequent and direct antagonism, but without either being aware of it. Thus, in 1521, when Loyola was leading a forlorn hope at Pampeluna to save the citadel for Charles V, Luther was in the castle of Wartburg, plotting to dethrone that potentate. In 1522 when the recluse of Manresa was writing his " Exercises " for the purpose of making men better, Luther was posing as the Ecclesiast of Wittenberg and proclaiming the uselessness of the Ten Commandments; and when Loyola was in London begging alms to continue his studies, Luther was coquetting with Henry VIII to induce that riotous king to accept the new Evangel.

Ignatius Loyola was born in the heart of the Pyrenees, in the sunken valley which has the little town of Azcoitia at one end, and the equally diminutive one of Azpeitia at the other. Over both of them the Loyolas had for centuries been lords either by marriage or inheritance. Their ancestral castle still stands; but, whereas in olden times it was half hidden by the surrounding woods, it is today embodied in the immense structure which almost closes in that end of the valley.

The castle came into the possession of the Society through the liberality of Anne of Austria, and a college was built around it. The added structure now forms an immense quadrangle with four interior courts. From the centre of the façade protrudes the great church which is circular in form and two hundred feet in height. Its completion was delayed for a long time but the massive pile is now finished. At its side, but quite invisible from without, is the castle proper, somewhat disappointing to those who have formed their own conceptions of what castles were in those days. It is only fifty-six feet high and fifty-eight wide. The lower portion is of hewn stone, the upper part of brick. Above the entrance, the family escutcheon is crudely cut in stone, and represents two wolves, rampant and lambent, having between them a caldron suspended by a chain. This device is the heraldic symbol of the name Loyola. The interior is elaborately decorated, and the upper story, where Ignatius was stretched on his bed of pain after the disaster of Pampeluna, has been converted into an oratory.

The church looks towards Azpeitia. A little stream runs at the side of the well-built road-way which connects the two towns. Along its length, shrines have been built, as have shelters for travelers if over-taken by a storm. The people are handsome and dignified, stately in their carriage—for they are moun-taineers — and are as thrifty in cultivating their steep hills, which they terrace to the very top, as the Belgians are in tilling their level fields in the Low Countries. There is no wealth, but there is no sordid poverty; and a joyous piety is everywhere in evidence. Azpeitia glories in the fact that there St. Ignatius was baptized; and when some years ago, it was proposed to remove the font and replace it by a new one, the women rose in revolt. Their babies had to be made Christians in the same holy basin as their great compatriot, no matter how old and battered it might be.

Ignatius was the youngest of a family of thirteen or, at least, the youngest of the sons; he was christened Eneco or Inigo, but he changed his name later to Ignatius. His early years were spent in the castle of Arévalo; and, according to Maffei he was at one time a page of King Ferdinand. He was fond of the world, its vanities, its amusements and its pleasures, and though there is nothing to show that there was ever any serious violation of the moral law in his conduct, neither was he the extraordinarily pious youth such

as he is represented in the fantastic stories of Nieremberg, Nolarci, García, Henao and others. After the
fashion of the hagiographers of the seventeenth century
and later, they describe him as a sort of Aloysius who,
under the tutelage of Doña María de Guevara, visited
the sick in the hospitals, regarding them as the images
of Christ, nursing them with tenderest charity, and so
on. All that is pure imagination and an unwise attempt
to make a saint of him before the time.

Indeed, very little about the early life of Ignatius
is known, except that when he was about twenty-six
he gained some military distinction in an attack on
the little town of Najara. Of course, he was conspicuous in the fight at Pampeluna, but whether he was in
command of the fortress or had been merely sent to
its rescue to hold it until the arrival of the Viceroy
is a matter of conjecture. At all events, even after
the inhabitants had agreed to surrender the town, he
determined to continue the fight. He first made his
confession to a fellow-knight, for there was no priest
at hand, and then began what was, at best, a hopeless
struggle. The enemy soon made a breach in the walls
and while rallying his followers to repel the assault
he was struck by a cannon-ball which shattered one
leg and tore the flesh from the other. That ended the
siege, and the flag of the citadel was hauled down.
Admiring his courage, the French tenderly carried him
to Loyola, where for some time his life was despaired
of. The crisis came on the feast of St. Peter, to whom
he had always a special devotion. From that day, he
began to grow better. Loyalty to the Chair of Peter
is one of the distinguishing traits of the Compañía
which he founded.

It is almost amusing to find these shattered limbs
of Ignatius figuring in the diatribes of the elder Arnauld
against the Society, sixty or seventy years after the

siege. " The enmity of the Jesuits for France," he said, " is to be traced to the fact that Loyola took an oath on that occasion, as Hannibal did against Rome, to make France pay for his broken legs." An English Protestant prelate also bemoaned " the ravages that had been caused by the fanaticism of that lame soldier." Other examples might be cited. To beguile the tediousness of his convalescence, Ignatius asked for the romance " Amadis de Gaul," a favorite book with the young cavaliers of the period; but he had to content himself with the " Life of Christ " and " The Flowers of the Saints." These, however, proved to be of greater service than the story of the mythical Amadis; for the reading ended in a resolution which exerted a mighty influence in the history of humanity. Ignatius had made up his mind to do something for God. The " Life of Christ " which he read, appears to have been that of Ludolph of Saxony in which the name " Jesuit " occurs. It had been translated into Spanish and published at Alcalá as early as 1502. Thus, a book from the land of Martin Luther helped to make Ignatius Loyola a saint.

When sufficiently restored to health he set out for the sanctuary of Montserrat where there is a Madonna whose thousandth anniversary was celebrated a few years ago. It is placed over the main altar of the church of a Benedictine monastery, which stands three thousand feet above the dark gorge, through which the river Llobregat rushes head-long to the Mediterranean. You can get a glimpse of the blue expanse of the sea in the distance, from the monastery windows. Before this statue, Ignatius kept his romantic Vigil of Arms, like the warriors of old on the eve of their knighthood; for he was about to enter upon a spiritual warfare for the King of Kings. He remained in prayer at the shrine all night long, not however in the apparel of a cavalier but in the common coarse garb of a poverty-stricken pilgrim. From there he betook himself to the little town of Manresa, about three miles to the north, on the outskirts of which is the famous cave where he wrote the " Spiritual Exercises." It is in the face of the rock, so low that you can touch the roof with your hand, and so narrow that there is room for only a little altar at one end. Possibly it had once been the repair of wild beasts. It is a mistake, however, to imagine that he passed all his time there. He lived either in the hospital or in the house of some friend, and resorted to the cave to meditate and do penance for his past sins. At present it is incorporated in a vast edifice which the Spanish Jesuits have built above and around it.

Perhaps no book has ever been written that has evoked more ridiculous commentaries on its contents and its purpose than this very diminutive volume known as " The Spiritual Exercises of St. Ignatius." Its very simplicity excites suspicion; its apparent jejuneness suggest all sorts of mysterious and malignant designs. Yet, as a matter of fact, it is nothing but a guide to Christian piety and devotion. It begins with the consideration of the great fundamental truths of religion, such as our duty to God, the hideousness and heinousness of sin, hell, death, and judgment on which the exercitant is expected to meditate before asking himself if it is wise for a reasonable creature who must soon die to continue in rebellion against the Almighty. No recourse is had to rhetoric or oratory by those who direct others in these " Exercises," not even such as would be employed in the pulpit by the ordinary parish preacher. It is merely a matter of a man having a heart to heart talk with himself. If he makes up his mind to avoid mortal sin in the future, but to do no more, then his retreat is over as far as he is concerned. But to have even reached that point is to have accomplished much.

There are, however, in the world a great many people who desire something more than the mere avoidance of mortal sin. To them the " Excercises " propose over and above the fundamental truths just mentioned the study of the life of Christ as outlined in the Gospels. This outline is not filled in by the director of the retreat, at least to any great extent. That is left to the exercitant; for the word *exercise* implies personal action. Hence he is told to ask himself: "Who is Christ? Why does He do this? Why does He avoid that? What do His commands and example suppose or suggest?" In other words, he is made to do some deep personal thinking, perhaps for the first time in his life, at least on such serious subjects. Inevitably his thoughts will be introspective and he will inquire why the patience, the humility, the meekness, the obedience and other virtues, which are so vivid in the personality of the Ideal Man, are so weak or perhaps non-existent in his own soul. This scrutiny of the conscience, which is nothing but self-knowledge, is one of the principal exercises, for it helps us to discover what perhaps never before struck us, namely that down deep in our natures there are tendencies, inclinations, likes, dislikes, affections, passions which most commonly are the controlling and deciding forces of nearly all of our acts; and that some of these tendencies or inclinations help, while others hinder, growth in virtue. Those that do not help, but on the contrary impede or prevent, our spiritual progress are called by St. Ignatius inordinate affections, that is tendencies, which are out of order, which do not go straight for the completeness and perfection of a man's character, but on the contrary, lead in the opposite direction. The well-balanced mind will fight against such tendencies, so as

to be able to form its judgments and decide on its
course of action both in the major and minor things
of life without being moved by the pressure or strain
or weight of the passions. It will look at facts in the
cold light of reason and revealed truth, and will then
bend every energy to carry out its purpose of spiritual
advancement.

Such is not the view of those who write about the
" Exercises " without knowledge or who are carried
away by prejudice, an exalted imagination, an overwhelming conceit or religious bias or perhaps because
of a refusal to recognize the existence of any spiritual
element in humanity. It is difficult to persuade
such men that there are no " mysterious devices "
resorted to in the Exercises; no " subterraneous
caverns," no " orgies," no " emerging livid and haggard
from the struggle," no " illuminism," no " monoideism"
as William James in his cryptic English describes
them; no " phantasmagoria or illusions;" no " plotting
of assassinations " as the Parliament of Paris pretended
to think when examining Jean Chastel, who had
attempted the life of Henry IV; no " Mahommedanism"
as Müller fancies in his " Origins of the Society of
Jesus," nothing but a calm and quiet study of one's
self, which even pagan philosophers and modern poets
assure us is the best kind of worldly occupation.

Even if some writers insist that " their excellence
is very much exaggerated," that they are " dull and
ordinary and not the dazzling masterpieces they are
thought to be," or are " a Japanese culture of counter-
feited dwarf trees," as Huysmans in his " En Route "
describes them; yet on the other hand they have,
been praised without stint by such competent judges
as Saints Philip Neri, Charles Borromeo, Francis de
Sales, Alphonsus Liguori, Leonard of Port Maurice,
and by Popes Paul III, Alexander VII, Clement

XIII, Pius IX and Leo XIII. Camus, the friend of
St. Francis of Sales, thought " they were of pure gold;
more precious than gold or topaz;" ~ Freppel calls
them " a wonderful work which, with the ' Imitation
of Christ ' is perhaps of all books the one which gains
the most souls for God;" Wiseman compares the
volume to " an apparently barren soil which is found
to contain the richest treasures," and Janssen tells
us that " the little book which even its opponents
pronounced to be a psychological masterpiece of the
highest class, ranks also as one of the most remarkable
and influential products of later centuries in the field
of religion and culture in Germany......As a guide
to the exercises it has produced results which scarcely
any other ascetic writings can boast of " (Hist. of the
German People, VIII, 223).

Whatever may be thought of it, it is the Jesuit's
manual, the *vade mecum*, on which he moulds his
particular and characteristic form of spirituality. In
the novitiate, he goes through these " Exercises " for
thirty consecutive days; and shortly after he becomes
a priest, he makes them once again for the same period.
Moreover, all Jesuits are bound by rule to repeat them
in a condensed form for eight days every year; and
during the summer months the priests are generally
employed in explaining them to the clergy and religious
communities. Indeed the use has become so general
in the Church at the present time, that houses have
been opened where laymen can thus devote a few days
to a study of their souls. Even the Sovereign Pontiffs
themselves employ them as a means of spiritual
advancement. Thus we find in the press of today the
announcement, as of an ordinary event, that " in the
Vatican, the Spiritual Exercises which began on Sunday,
September 26, 1920, and ended on October 2, were
followed by His Holiness, Benedict XV, with the

prelates and ecclesiastics of his Court; during which time, all public audiences were suspended. After the retreat, the two directors and those who had taken part in it were presented to the Sovereign Pontiff, who pronounced a glowing eulogy of what he called the ' Holy ' Exercises."

St. Ignatius' authorship of these " Exercises " has been frequently challenged, and they have been described as little else than a plagiarism of the book known as the " Ejercitatorio de la vida espiritual," which was given to him by the Benedictines of Montserrat. It is perfectly true that he had that book in his hands during all the time he was at Manresa, and that he went every week to confession to Dom Chanones, who was a monk of Montserrat, but there are very positive differences between the " Ejercitatorio " and the " Spiritual Exercises."

In the first place it should be noted that the title had been in common use long before, and was employed by the Brothers of the Common Life, to designate any of their pious publications. Even Ludolph of Saxony speaks of the " Studia spiritualis exercitii." Secondly, the " Ejercitatorio " is rigid in its divisions of three weeks of seven days each, whereas St. Ignatius takes the weeks in a metaphorical sense, and lengthens or shortens them at pleasure. Thirdly, the object of the Benedictine manual is to lead the exercitant through the purgative and illuminative life up to the unitive; whereas St. Ignatius aims chiefly at the election of that state of life which is most pleasing to God, or at least at the correction or betterment of the one in which we happen to be. Finally, the " Ejercitatorio " does not even mention the foundation, the Kingdom, the particular examen, the Two Standards, the election, the discernment of spirits, the rules for orthodox thinking, the regulation of diet, the three degrees of

2

humility, the three classes or the three methods of
prayer.   Only a few of the Benedictine counsels have
been adopted, as in Annotations 2, 4, 13, 18, 19 and
20.   Some of thoughts, indeed, are similar in the first
week; but the three succeeding weeks of St. Ignatius
are entirely his own.   In any case, the " Ejercitatorio "
itself is nothing else than a compilation from Ludolph,
Gerson, Cassian, Saint Bernard, Saint Bonaventure
and contemporary writers.   (Debuchy, article " Spiritual Exercises of Saint Ignatius " in the " Catholic
Encyclopedia," XIV, 226.)

It would be much easier to find a source of the
" Exercises " in " The Great Life of Christ " by
Ludolph of Saxony, which as has been said, was one
of the books read by Ignatius in his convalescence.
It is not really a life but a series of meditations, and
in it we find a number of things which are supposed
to be peculiar to the Exercises of St. Ignatius, for
instance, the composition of place, the application of
the senses and the colloquies.   On the other hand
there is nothing of the " first week " in it, such as
the end of man, the use of creatures, sin, hell, death,
judgment, etc., besides many other things which are
employed as " Exercises " in the book of Ignatius.

It will be a surprise to many to learn that the famous
meditation of the " Kingdom " which is supposed to
be particularly Ignatian is only an adaptation.   Father
Kreiten, S. J., writing in the " Stimmen " traces it to
a well-known romance which had long been current
in the tales of chivalry, but which, unfortunately, is
linked with a name most abhorrent to Catholics;
William of Orange.   The medieval William, however,
is in no way identified with his modern homonym.
He was a devoted Knight of the Cross, indignant that
his prowess had not been recognized by his king and he
asked for some royal fief as his reward.   " Give me

Spain," he cries, "which is still in the power of the Saracens." The curious request is granted, whereupon William springs upon the table and shouts to those around him: " Listen, noble knights of France! By the Lord Almighty! I can boast of possessing a fief larger than that of thirty of my peers, but as yet it is unconquered. Therefore I address myself to poor knights,who have only a limping horse and ragged garments; and I say to them that if, up to now, they have gained nothing for their service, I will give them money, lands and Spanish horses, castles and fortresses, if together with me, they will brave the fortunes of war, in order, to help me to effect the conquest of the country and to reestablish in it the true religion. I make the same offer to poor squires, proposing, moreover, to arm them as knights." In answer to these words all exclaim " By the Lord Almighty! Sir William! haste thee, haste thee; he who cannot follow thee on horseback, will bear thee company on foot." From all parts there crowded to him knights and squires with any arms they could lay hold of, and before long thirty thousand men were ready to march. They swore fealty to Count William and promised never to abandon him, though they should be cut to pieces. St. Ignatius applies this legend to Christ in the " Exercises ".

Finally, the " Two Standards " is a picture of those who want to do more than obey the Commandments. Their " Captain," the Divine Redeemer, reveals to them the wiles of the foe, which they resolve to defeat.

What is emphatically distinctive in the " Exercises " is their coherence. With inexorable logic, each conclusion is deduced from what has been antecedently admitted as indisputable. Thus, at the end of the first " week ", it is clear that mortal sin is an act or condition of supreme folly; and in the course of the second, third, and fourth, we are made to see that

unless a man chooses that particular state of life to
which God calls him, or unless he puts to rights the
one he is already in, he has no character, no courage,
no virility, no gratitude to God, and no sense of danger.
The fourth " week ", besides enforcing what preceded,
may be regarded as intimating, though not developing,
the higher mysticism,

Throughout the " Exercises," the insistent consideration of the fundamental truths of Christianity, and the
contemplation of the mysteries or episodes of the life
of Christ so illumine the mind and inflame the heart
that we cannot fail, if we are reasonable, at least to
desire to make the love of Christ the dominating
motive of our life; and, in view of that end, we are
given at every step a new insight into our duties to
God, chiefly under the double aspect of our Creation
and Redemption; we are taught to scrutinize our
thoughts, tendencies, inclinations, passions and aspirations, and to detect the devices of self-deceit; we are
shown the dangers that beset us and the means of
safety that are available; we are instructed in prayer,
meditation and self-examination. The proper co-ordi-
nation of these various parts is so essential, that if
their interdependence is neglected, if the arrangements
and adjustments are disturbed and the connecting
links disregarded or displaced, the end intended by
Saint Ignatius is defeated. Hence the need of a
director. It may be noted that the " Exercises "
were not produced at Manresa in the form in which
we have them now. They were touched and retouched
up to the year 1541, that is twenty years after Loyola's
stay in the " Cueva ", but they are substantially
identical with the book he then wrote.

After spending about a year in the austerities of the
Cave, Ignatius begged his way to Palestine, but
remained there only six weeks. The Guardian of the

Holy Places very peremptorily insisted upon his withdrawal, because his piety and his inaccessibility to fear exposed him to bad treatment at the hands of the infidels. He then returned to Spain and set himself to the study of the Latin elements, in a class of small boys, at one of the primary schools of Barcelona. It was a rude trial for a man of his years and antecedents, but he never shrank from a difficulty, and, moreover, there was no other available way of getting ready for the course of philosophy which he proposed to follow at Alcalá. At this latter place, he had the happiness of meeting Laínez, Salmerón and Bobadilla, but he also made the acquaintance of the jails of the Inquisition, where he was held prisoner for forty-two days, on suspicion of heresy, besides being kept under surveillance, from November, 1526, till June of the year following. It happened, also, that as he was being dragged through the streets to jail, a brilliant cavalcade met the mob, and inquiries were made as to what it was all about, and who the prisoner was. The cavalier who put the question was one who was to be later a devoted follower of Ignatius; he was no less a personage than Francis Borgia. Six years after the establishment of the Society, Ignatius repaid Alcalá for its harsh treatment, by founding a famous college there, whose chairs were filled by such teachers as Vásquez and Suárez.

Ignatius had no better luck at Salamanca. There he was not even allowed to study, but was kept in chains for three weeks while being examined as to his orthodoxy. But as with Alcalá, so with Salamanca. Later on he founded a college in that university also, and made it illustrious by giving it de Lugo, Suárez, Valencia, Maldonado, Ribera and a host of other distinguished teachers. Leaving Salamanca, Ignatius began his journey to Paris, travelling on foot, behind a little burro whose only burden were the books of the driver. It was mid-winter; war had been declared between France and Spain, and he had to beg for food on the way; but nothing could stop him, and he arrived at Paris safe and sound, in the beginning of February, 1528. In 1535 he received the degree of Master of Arts, after "the stony trial," as it was called, namely the most rigorous examination. For some time previously he had devoted himself to the study of theology, but ill health prevented him from presenting himself for the doctorate. He lived at the College of Ste Barbe where his room-mates were Peter Faber and Francis Xavier. Singularly enough and almost prophetic of the future, Calvin had studied at the same college. The names of Loyola and Calvin are cut on the walls of the building to-day. In 1533 Calvin, it is said, came back to induce the rector of the college, a Doctor Kopp, to embrace the new doctrines. He succeeded, and, before the whole university, Kopp declared himself a Calvinist. Calvin had prepared the way by having the city placarded with a blasphemous denunciation of the Blessed Eucharist. A popular uprising followed and Calvin fled. In reparation a solemn procession of reparation was organized on January 21, 1535. There is some doubt, however, about the authenticity of this story.

Ignatius encountered trouble in France as he had in Spain. On one occasion he was sentenced to be flogged in presence of all the students; but the rector of the college, after examining the charge against him, publicly apologized. There was also a delation to the Inquisition, but when he demanded an immediate trial he was told that the indictment had been quashed. Previous to these humiliations and exculpations he had gathered around him a number of brilliant young men, all of whom have made their mark on history.

They afford excellent material for an exhaustive study of the psychology of the Saints.

Most conspicuous among them was Francis Xavier, who will ever be the wonder of history. With him were Laínez and Salmerón, soon to be the luminaries of the Council of Trent, the former of whom barely escaped being elevated to the chair of St. Peter, and then only by fleeing Rome. There was also Bobadilla, the future favorite of kings and princes and prelates, the idol of the armies of Austria, the tireless apostle who evangelised seventy-seven dioceses of Europe, but who unfortunately alienated Charles V from the Society by imprudently telling him what should have come from another source or in another way. There was Rodriguez who was to hold Portugal, Brazil and India in his hands, ecclesiastically; and Faber who was to precede Canisius in the salvation of Germany.

Each one of these remarkable men differed in character from the rest. Bobadilla, Salmerón, Laínez and Xavier were Spaniards; but the blue-blooded and somewhat " haughty " Xavier must have been tempted to look with disdain on a man with a Jewish strain like Laínez. Salmerón was only a boy of about nineteen, but already marvelously learned; and Bobadilla was an impecunious professor whom Ignatius had helped to gain a livelihood in Paris, but whose ebulliency of temper was a continued source of anxiety; Rodriguez was a man of velleities rather than of action, and his ideas of asceticism were in conflict with those of Ignatius. The most docile of all was the Savoyard Peter Faber, who began life as a shepherd boy and was already far advanced in sanctity when he met St. Ignatius. In spite, however, of all this divergency of traits and antecedent environment, the wonderful personality of their leader exerted its undisputed sway over them all, not by a rigid uniformity of direction, but by an adaptation to the idiosyncrasies of each. His profound knowledge of their character, coupled as it was with an intense personal affection for them, was so effective that the proud aloofness of Xavier, the explosiveness of Bobadilla, the latent persistency of Laínez, the imaginativeness and hesitancy of Rodriguez, the enthusiasm of the boyish Salmerón, and the sweetness of Faber, all paid him the tribute of the sincerest attachment and an eagerness to follow his least suggestion. Rodriguez was the sole exception in the latter respect, but he failed only twice. Two other groups of young men had previously gathered around Ignatius, but, one by one, they deserted him. All of the last mentioned persevered, and became the foundation-stones of the Society of Jesus.

On August 15, 1534, Ignatius led his companions to a little church on the hill of Montmartre, then a league outside the city, but now on the Rue Antoinette, below the present great basilica of the Sacred Heart. In its crypt which they apparently had all to themselves that morning, they pronounced their vows of poverty, chastity and obedience. Faber, the only priest among them, said Mass and gave them communion. Such was the beginning of the new Order in the Church. A brass plate on the wall of the chapel proclaims it to be the " cradle of the Society of Jesus." It is almost startling to recall that while in the University of Paris, not only Ignatius but also Francis Xavier and Peter Faber, who were to be so prominent in the world in a short time, were in destitute circumstances. They had no money even to pay for their lodging, and they occupied a single room which had been given them, out of charity, in one of the towers of Ste Barbe. It was providential, however, for in the same college, but paying his way, was a former schoolmate of Faber

and like him a native of Savoy. This was Claude Le
Jay, or Jay, as he is sometimes called. Of course he
had noticed Ignatius and the group of brilliant young
Spaniards, but he had little or nothing to do with
them until once, when Ignatius was absent in Spain,
Faber let him into the secret of their great plan of
converting the Turks. The result was that when next
year the associates went out to Montmartre to renew
their vows, Le Jay was with them as were also two
other university men: Jean Codure from Dauphiné and
the Picard, Pasquier Brouet, who was already a priest.

It had been arranged that in 1536 when their courses
of study were finished and their degrees and certificates
secured, they were to meet at Venice to embark for
the Holy Land. They were to make the journey to
Venice on foot. They set out, therefore, in two bands,
a priest with each, taking the route that passed by
Meaux and then through Lorraine, across Switzerland
to Venice. It was a daring journey of fifty-two days
in the dead of winter, over mountain passes, without
money to pay their way or to purchase food; with
poor and insufficient clothing, across countries filled
with soldiers preparing for war, or angry fanatics who
scoffed at the rosaries around their necks, and who
might have ill-treated them or put them to death;
they bore it all, however, not only patiently but
light-heartedly, and on January 6, 1537, arrived in
Venice, where Ignatius was waiting for them. To
them was added a new member of the association,
Diego Hozes, who had known Ignatius at Alcalá and
now came to him at Venice.

After a brief rest, which they took by waiting on
the poor and sick in the worst hospital of the city,
they were told to go down to Rome to ask the Pope's
permission to carry out their plans. This journey was
not as long or as dangerous as the one they had just

made, but the bad weather, the long fasts, the sickness of some of them, the rebuffs and abusive language which they received when they asked for alms, made it hard enough for flesh and blood to bear; however their devotion to the end they had in view, or what the world might call their Quixotic enthusiasm bore them onward. They were apprehensive, however, about their reception in Rome, not it is true, from the Father of the Faithful himself, but from a certain great Spanish canonist, a Doctor Ortiz, who happened to be just then at the papal court, making an appeal to the Sovereign Pontiff in behalf of Catherine of Aragon against Henry VIII.

Ortiz had met Ignatius in Paris and was bitterly prejudiced against him. That, indeed, was the reason why the little band appeared in the Holy City without their leader, but neither he nor they were aware that Ortiz had changed his mind and was now an enthusiastic friend. Hence when the travel-stained envoys from Venice presented themselves, they could scarcely believe their eyes. Ortiz received them with every demonstration of esteem and affection. He presented them to the Pope, and urged him to grant all their requests. Subsequently, Faber acted as theologian for Ortiz, when that dignitary represented Charles V at Worms and in Spain. Of course the Pontiff was overjoyed and not only blessed the members of the little band but gave them a considerable sum of money to pay their passage to the Holy Land. So they hurried back to Ignatius with the good news, and on June 24 all those who were not priests were ordained.

The custom that prevails in the Church, in our days, is for a newly-ordained priest to celebrate Mass on the morning following his ordination; but Ignatius and his companions prepared themselves for this great act in an heroic fashion. They buried themselves in caverns or in the ruins of dilapidated monasteries for an entire month, giving themselves up to fasting and prayer, preaching at times in some adjourning town or hamlet. It was on this occasion that the vacillating character of Rodriguez revealed itself. He and Le Jay had taken up their abode in a hermitage near Bassano where a venerable old man named Antonio was reviving in the heart of Italy the practices of the old solitaries of the Thebaid. Rodriguez fell ill and was at the point of death when Ignatius arrived and told him that he would recover. So, indeed, it happened, but singularly enough he was anxious to continue his eremitical life and, without speaking of his doubts to Ignatius, set out to consult the old hermit about it, but became conscience-stricken before he arrived. " O man of little faith, why did you doubt?" was all St. Ignatius said, when Rodriguez confessed what he had done. Nevertheless, that did not cure him, for the desire of leading a life of bodily austerity had taken possession of him and was at the bottom of the trouble which he subsequently caused in Portugal, and also when, in 1554, he wrote entreatingly to Pope Julius III for permission to leave the Society and become a hermit (Prat, Le P. Claude Le Jay, 32, note).

At the end of the retreat, they all returned to Venice, where they waited in vain for a ship to carry them to the land of the Mussulmans. It was only when there was absolutely no hope left, that they made up their minds to go back to Rome, and put themselves at the disposal of the Pope for any work he might give them. As this was fully twenty years after Martin Luther had nailed his thesis to the church door of Wittenberg, it is clear that Ignatius had no idea of attacking Protestantism when he founded the Society of Jesus.

Possibly this stay in Venice has something to do

with the solution of a question which has been frequently mooted and was solemnly discussed at a
congress of physicians at San Francisco as late as 1900,
namely, why did Vesalius, the great anatomist, go to
the Holy Land? The usual supposition is that it was
to perform a penance enjoined by the Inquisition in
consequence of some alleged heretical utterances by
the illustrious scientist. However, Sir Michael Foster
of the University of Cambridge, who was the principal
speaker at the Congress, offered another explanation.
" It is probable," he said, " that while pursuing his
studies in the hospitals of Venice, Vesalius often
conversed with another young man who was there at
the time and who was known as Ignatius Loyola."
Such a meeting may, indeed, have occurred, for Ignatius
haunted the hospitals, and his keen eye would have
discerned the merit of Vesalius, who was a sincerely
pious man. Hence, it is not at all unlikely that the
young physician may have made the " Spiritual
Exercises " under the direction of Ignatius, and that
his journey to the Holy Land was the result of his
intercourse with the group of brilliant young students,
who just then had no other object in life but to convert
the Turks.

On the journey to Rome Ignatius went ahead with
Faber and Laínez, and it was then that he had the
vision of Christ carrying the cross, and heard the
promise: " Ego vobis Romæ propitius ero " (I will
be propitious to you in Rome.) They were received
affectionately and trustingly by the Pope, who sent
Laínez and Faber to teach in the Sapienza, one lecturing
on holy scripture and the other on scholastic theology;
while Ignatius gave the " Spiritual Exercises " wherever
and whenever the opportunity presented itself. When
the other four arrived, they were immediately employed
in various parts of Rome in works of charity and zeal.

It was in Rome that Ignatius first came in personal contact with the Reformation. A Calvinist preacher who had arrived in the city had succeeded in creating a popular outcry against the new priests, by accusing them of all sorts of crimes. As such charges would be fatal in that place above all, if not refuted, the usual policy of silence was not observed. By the advice of the Pope the affair was taken to court where the complaint was immediately dismissed and an official attestation of innocence given by the judge. The result was a counter-demonstration, that made the accuser flee for his life to Geneva. As an assurance of his confidence in them, the Sovereign Pontiff employed them in several parts of Italy where the doctrines of the Reformation were making alarming headway. Thus, Brouet and Salmerón were sent to Siena; Faber and Laínez accompanied the papal legate to Parma; Xavier and Bobadilla set out for Campania; Codure and Hozes for Padua; and Rodriguez and Le Jay for Ferrara. It is impossible to follow them all in these various places, but a brief review of the difficulties that confronted Rodriguez and Le Jay in Ferrara may be regarded as typical of the rest.

In conformity with the instructions of Ignatius, they lodged at the hospital, preached whenever they could, either in the churches or on the public streets, and taught catechism to the children and hunted for scandalous sinners. An old woman at the hospital discovered by looking through a crack in the door that they passed a large part of the night on their knees. At this point Hozes died at Padua, and Rodriguez had to replace him; Le Jay was thus left alone at Ferrara. The duke, Hercules II, became his friend, but the duchess, Renée of France, daughter of Louis XII, avoided him. She was a supposedly learned woman, a forerunner, so to say, of the *précieuses ridicules* of Molière, and an ardent patron of Calvin, a frequent visitor at the court, along with the lascivious poet Clément Marot, who translated the Psalms into verse to popularize Calvin's heretical teachings. Another ominous figure that loomed up at Ferrara was the famous Capuchin preacher, Bernardo Ochino, a man of remarkable eloquence, which, however, was literary and dramatic rather than apostolic in its character. His emaciated countenance, his long flowing white beard and his fervent appeals to penance made a deep impression on the people. They regarded him as a saint, never dreaming that he was a concealed heretic, who would eventually apostatize and assail the Church. He was much admired by the duchess, who conceived a bitter hatred for Le Jay and would not even admit him to her presence. The trouble of the Jesuit was increased by the attitude of the bishop, who, knowing the real character of Ochino, looked with suspicion on Le Jay, as possibly another wolf in sheep's clothing; but his suspicions were soon dispelled, and he gave Le Jay every means in his power to revive the faith and morals of the city. The duchess, however, became so aggressive in her proselytism that the duke ordered her into seclusion, and when he died, his son and successor sent her back to her people in France where she died an obstinate heretic.

From Ferrara Le Jay hastened to Bagnorea to end a schism there, and though neither side would listen to him at first, yet his patience overcame all difficulties, and finally, everybody met everybody else in the great church, embraced and went to Holy Communion. Peace then reigned in the city. The other envoys achieved similar successes elsewhere throughout the peninsula; and Crétineau-Joly says that their joint efforts thwarted the plot of the heretics to destroy the

Faith in Italy. The winter of 1538 was extremely
severe in Rome, and a scarcity of provisions brought
on what amounted almost to a famine. This distress
gave Ignatius and his companions the opportunity of
showing their devotion to the suffering poor; and they
not only contrived in some way or other to feed, in
their own house, as many as four hundred famishing
people, but inspired many of the well-to-do classes to
imitate their example.

With this and other good works to their credit, they
could now ask the authorization of the Sovereign
Pontiff for their enterprise. Hence on September 3,
1539, they submitted a draught of the Constitution,
and were pleased to hear that it evoked from the Pope
the exclamation: " The finger of God is here." But
they were not so fortunate with the commission of
cardinals to whom the matter was then referred.
Guidiccioni, who presided, was not only distinctly
hostile, but expressed the opinion that all existing
religious orders should be reduced to four, and hence
he contemptuously tossed the petition aside. It was
only after a year that he took it up again — he scarcely
knew why — and on reading it attentively he was
completely converted and hastened to report on it as
follows: " Although as before, I still hold to the
opinion that no new religious order should be instituted,
I cannot refrain from approving this one. Indeed, I
regard it as something that is now needed to help
Christendom in its troubles, and especially to destroy
the heresies which are at present devastating Europe."
Thus it is Guidiccioni who is responsible for setting
the Society to undo the work of Martin Luther.

The Pope was extremely pleased by the commission's
report, and on September 27, 1540, he issued the
Bull " Regimini militantis Ecclesiæ," approving " The
Institute of the Society of Jesus." In this Bull and

that of Julius III, the successor of Paul III, we have
the official statement of the character and the purpose
of the Society. Its object is the salvation and perfection of the souls of its members and of the neighbor.
One of the chief means for that end is the gratuitous
instruction of youth. There are no penances of rule;
but it is assumed that bodily mortifications are practised
and employed, though only under direction. Great
care is taken in the admission and formation of novices,
and lest the protracted periods of study, later, should
chill the fervor of their devotion, there are to be
semi-annual spiritual renovations, and when the studies
are over, and the student ordained to the priesthood,
there is a third year of probation, somewhat similar
to the novitiate in its exercises. There are two
grades in the Society — one of professed, the other
of coadjutors, both spiritual and temporal.

All are to be bound by the three vows of poverty,
chastity and obedience, but those of the coadjutors
are simple, while those of the professed are solemn.
The latter make a fourth vow, namely, one of obedience
to the Sovereign Pontiff, which binds them to go
wherever he sends them, and to do so without excuse,
and without provisions for the journey. The Father-
General is elected for life. He resides in Rome, so as
to be at the beck of the Sovereign Pontiff, and also
because of the international character of the Society.
All superiors are appointed by him, and he is regularly
informed through the provincials about all the members
of the Society. Every three years there is a meeting
of procurators to report on their respective provinces
and to settle matters of graver moment. The General
is aided in his government by assistants chosen mostly
according to racial divisions, which may in turn be
subdivided. There is also an admonitor who sees that
the General governs according to the laws of the

Society and for the common good. Disturbers of the peace of the Order are to be sharply admonished, and if incorrigible, expelled. When approved scholastics or formed coadjutors are dismissed they are dispensed from their simple vows. The simple vow of chastity made by the scholastics is a diriment impediment of matrimony. Because of possible withdrawals or dismissals from the Society, the dominion of property previously possessed is to be retained, as long as the general may see fit, but not the usufruct — an arrangement which has been repeatedly approved by successive Pontiffs, as well as by the Council of Trent.

All ambition of ecclesiastical honors is shut off by a special vow to that effect. There is no choir or special dress. The poverty of the Society is of the strictest. The professed houses are to subsist on alms, and cannot receive even the usual stipends. Moreover, the professed are bound by a special vow to watch over and prevent any relaxation in this respect. The rule is paternal, and hence an account of conscience is to be made, either under seal of confession or in whatever way the individual may find most agreeable. A general congregation may be convened as often as necessary. Its advisability is determined at the meeting of the procurators. In the first part of the Constitution, the impediments and the mode of admission are considered; in the second, the manner of dismissal; in the third and fourth, the means of furthering piety and study and whatever else concerns the spiritual advancement, chiefly of the scholastics; the fifth explains the character of those who are to be admitted and also the various grades; the sixth deals with the occupations of the members; the seventh treats of those of superiors; the eighth and ninth relate to the General; and the tenth determines the ways and means of government. Before the Constitutions were promulgated, Ignatius submitted them to the chief representatives of the various nationalities then in the Order, but they did not receive the force of law until they were approved by the first general congregation of the whole Society. After that they were presented to Pope Paul III, and examined by four Cardinals. Not a word had been altered when they were returned. The Sovereign Pontiff declared that they were more the result of Divine inspiration than of human prudence.

For those who read these Constitutions without any preconceived notions, the meaning is obvious, whereas the intention of discovering something mysterious and malignant in them inevitably leads to the most ridiculous misinterpretations of the text. Thus, for instance, some writers inform us that St. Ignatius is not the author of the Constitutions, but Laínez, Mercurian or Acquaviva. Others assure their readers that no Pope can ever alter or modify even the text; that the General has special power to absolve novices from any mortal sins they may have committed before entering; that the general confessions of beginners are carefully registered and kept; that a special time is assigned to them for reading accounts of miraculous apparitions and demoniacal obsessions; that before the two years of novitiate have elapsed a vow must be taken to enter the Society; that all wills made in favor of one's family must be rescinded; that in meditating, the eyes must be fixed on a certain point and the thoughts centered on the Pater Noster until a state of quasi-hypnotism results; that the grades in the Society are reached after thirty or thirty-five years of probation, after which the applicant becomes a probationer; the professed are called " ours "; the spiritual coadjutors " externs." The latter do the plotting and have aroused all the ill-will of which the Society has been the object; whereas the professed devote themselves to prayer and are admired and loved.

There are also, we are assured, secret, outside Jesuits. The Emperors Ferdinand II and III, and Sigismund of Poland are put in that class, and probably also John III of Portugal and Maximilian of Bavaria; while Louis XIV is suspected of belonging to it. The Father-General dispenses such members from the priesthood and from wearing the soutane. "Imagine Louis XIV," says Brou, who furnishes these details, "asking the General of the Jesuits to be dispensed from wearing the soutane!" Unlike the other Jesuits, these cryptics would not be obliged to go to Rome to pronounce their vows. Again, it is said, Pope Paul IV had great difficulty in persuading the Jesuits to accept the dispensation from the daily recitation of the breviary. Perhaps the most charming of all of these "discoveries" is that the famous phrase *perinde ac cadaver*, "you must obey as if you were a dead body," was borrowed from the Sheik Si-Senoussi who laid down rules to his Senoussis in Africa, about two centuries after St. Ignatius had died. The authors of these extraordinary conceptions are Müller, Reuss, Cartwright, Pollard, Vollet and others, all of whom are honoured with a notice posted in the British Museum, as worthy of being consulted on the puzzling subject of Jesuitry, and yet the Constitutions of the Society and the explanations of them, by prominent Jesuit writers, can be found in any public library.

CHAPTER II

THE pent-up energy of the new organization immediately found vent not only in Europe but at the ends of the earth. Portugal gave its members their first welcome when Xavier and Rodriguez went there, the latter to remain permanently, the former only for a brief space. Araoz evangelized Spain and was the first Jesuit to enter into relations with Francis Borgia, Viceroy of Catalonia, who afterwards became General of the Society. A college was begun in Paris and provided with professors such as Strada, Ribadeneira, Oviedo and Mercurian. Faber accompanied Ortiz, the papal legate, to Germany; Brouet, Bobadilla, Salmerón, Codure and Laínez went everywhere through Italy; while Ignatius remained at Rome, directing their operations and meantime establishing orphanages, night refuges, Magdalen asylumns, shelters for persecuted Jews, and similar institutions. Strangely enough, Ignatius was not yet the General of the Society, for no election had thus far taken place. Strictly speaking, however, none was needed, for none of the associates ever dreamed of any other leader. However, on April 5, 1541, the balloting took place; those who were absent sending their votes by messenger. That of

Xavier could not arrive in time, for he had already
left Portugal for the East; indeed he had departed
before the official approval of the Order by the Pope —
two things which have suggested to some inventive
historians that Francis Xavier was not really a Jesuit.
They would have proved their point better, if they
could have shown Xavier had remained in Europe
after he had been ordered away. As a matter of fact;
he had been one of the collaborators of Ignatius in
framing the Constitutions and was still in Portugal
when the news arrived of Guidiccioni's change of mind.

In the election every vote but one went for Ignatius.
The missing one was his own. He was dissatisfied and
asked for another election. Out of respect for him,
the request was granted but with the same result —
Such a concession, it may be noted, is never granted
now. The one who is chosen submits without a word.
The office is for life but provisions are made for removal — a contingency which happily has never arisen.
As in the beginning, those elections are held at what
are called general congregations. The first one was
made up of all the available fathers but at present they
consist of the fathers assistant, namely the representatives of the principal linguistic groups in the
Society or their subdivisions — a body of men who
constitute what is called the Curia and who live with
the General; the provincials; two delegates from each
province; and finally the procurator of the Society.
With one exception, these congregations have always
met in Rome; the exception is the one that chose Father
Luis Martín in 1892, which assembled at Loyola in
Spain. That these elections may be absolutely free
from all external and internal influence, the delegates
are strictly secluded, and have no communication with
other members of the Society. Four days are spent in
prayer and in seeking information from the various

electors, but the advocacy of any particular candidate is absolutely prohibited. The ballot is secret and the voting is immediately preceded by an hour's meditation in presence of the crucifix. The electors are fasting, but the method of voting is such that a deadlock or even any great delay is next to impossible. Up to the time of the Suppression of the Society in 1773, there had been eighteen Generals. In the interim between that catastrophe and the re-establishment, there were three Vicars-General, who were compelled by force of circumstances to live in Russia. In 1802 on the receipt of the Brief " Catholicæ Fidei," the title of the last Vicar was changed to that of General. Since then, there have been eight successors to that post.

St. Ignatius was chosen General on Easter Sunday, 1541. After the election, the companions repaired to St. Paul's outside the Walls and there renewed their vows. On that occasion it was ordained that every professed father should, after making his vows, teach catechism to children or ignorant people for forty days; subsequently this obligation was extended to rectors of colleges after their installation. Ignatius acquitted himself of this task in the church of Our Lady of the Wayside at the foot of the Capitol.

In 1541 we find Salmerón and Brouet on their way to Ireland as papal nuncios. They had been asked for by Archbishop Wauchope of Armagh, when Henry VIII was endeavoring to crush out the Faith in England and Ireland. Wauchope is a very interesting historical character. He had been named Archbishop of Armagh after Browne of that see had apostatized. He was generally known as " the Scotch Doctor," and had been the Delegate of Pope Paul III at Spires where Charles V was striving in vain to conciliate the German princes. With him as advisers were Le Jay, Bobadilla and Faber. What made him especially conspicuous

then and subsequently, was the fact that he had risen
to the dignity of archbishop and of papal delegate
though he was born blind. This is asserted by a host
of authors, among them Prat in his life of Le Jay,
and Crétineau-Joly, MacGeoghegan and Moore in
their histories.

On the other hand we find in the " Acta Sanctæ
Sedis " (XIII) a flat denial of it by no less a personage
than Pope Benedict XIV. It occurs incidentally in
a decision given on March 20, 1880, in connection with
an appeal for a young theologian, whose sight was very
badly impaired at the end of his theological course.
The appellants had alleged the case of the Archbishop
of Armagh and the court answered as follows: " Nec
valeret adduci exemplum cujusdam Roberti Scoti, cui
quamvis cæco a puerili ætate, concessa fuit facultas
nedum ad sacerdotium sed etiam ad episcopatum,
ascendendi, uti tenent Maiol. (De irregularitate), et
Barbos (De officio episcopi). Respondet enim Bene-
dictus XIV, quod reliqui scriptores, quibus major fides
habenda est, Robertum non oculis captum sed infirmum
fuisse dicunt;" which in brief means: " Benedict XIV
declares that the most reliable historians say that
Scotch Robert was not blind but of feeble vision."
As Benedict XIV was perhaps the greatest scholar who
ever occupied the Chair of Peter, and as his extraordinary intellectual abilities were devoted from the
beginning of his career to historical, canonical and
liturgical studies, in which he is regarded as of the
highest authority, such an utterance may be accepted
as final with regard to the " Scotch Doctor's " blindness.

Codure was to have been one of the Irish delegates,
but he died, and hence Salmerón, Brouet and Zapata
undertook the perilous mission. The last mentioned
was a wealthy ecclesiastic who was about to enter the

Society and had offered to defray the expenses of the journey. In the instructions for their manner of acting Ignatius ordered that Brouet should be spokesman whenever nobles or persons of importance were to be dealt with. As Brouet had the looks and the sweetness of an angel, whereas Salmerón was abrupt at times, the wisdom of the choice was obvious. They went by the way of France to Scotland, and when at Stirling Castle, they received a letter from James V, the father of Mary Queen of Scots, bespeaking their interest in his people. Crétineau-Joly says they saw the king personally. Fouqueray merely hints at its likelihood. From Scotland they passed over to Ireland and found that the enemy knew of their arrival. A price was put upon their heads, and they had to hurry from place to place so as not to compromise those who gave them shelter. But in the brief period of a month which they had at their disposal before they were recalled by the Pope they had ample opportunity to take in the conditions that prevailed. They returned as they had gone, through Scotland and over to Dieppe, and then directed their steps to Rome, but they were arrested as spies near Lyons and thrown into prison — a piece of news which Paget, the English ambassador in France, hastened to communicate to Henry; Cardinals de Tournon and Gaddi, however, succeeded in having them released and they then proceeded to the Holy City to make their report.

Eighteen years later, Father Michael Gaudan was sent as papal nuncio to Mary Stuart. He entered Edinburgh disguised as a Scottish peddler and succeeded in reaching the queen. As a Frenchman could not have acted the part of a Scottish peddler, it is more than likely that Gaudan is a gallicized form of Gordon. Indeed, there is on the records a Father James Gordon, S. J., who had so exasperated the Calvinists by his

refutation of their errors that he was driven out of the
country. He returned again, however, immediately,
as he simply got a boat to take him off the ship which
was carrying him into exile, and on the following day
he stood once more upon his native heath, remaining
there for some years sustaining his persecuted Catholic
brethren (Claude Nau, Mary's secretary).

That the " blind Archbishop " also succeeded in
reaching his see is clear from a passage in Moore's
" History of Ireland " (xlvii), which tells how during
the reign of Edward VI two French gentlemen, the
Baron de Fourquevaux and the Sieur Montluc, afterwards Bishop of Valence, went to Ireland as envoys
of the French king and were concealed in Culmer
Fort on Loch Foyle. They kept a diary of their
journey which may be found, we are assured, in the
" Armorial-général ou registre de la noblesse de France."
The diary relates that while at the Fort " they received
a visit from Robert Wauchope, better known by his pen
name as Venantius, a divine whose erudition was the
more remarkable as he had been blind from birth and
was at the time, titular Archbishop of Armagh."
He did not, however, remain in Ireland. MacGeoghegan says " he returned to the Continent and died
in the Jesuit house at Paris in the year 1551. Stewart
Rose in her " Saint Ignatius Loyola and the Early
Jesuits " tells us it was at Lyons, but that was
impossible, for there was no Jesuit establishment in
Lyons until after the great pestilence of 1565, when
the authorities offered the Society the municipal
college of the Trinity as a testimonial of gratitude to
Father Auger. The generosity of this offer, however,
was not excessive. The Fathers were to take it for
two years on trial. They did so and then the provincial insisted that the gift should be absolute or the
staff would be withdrawn. After some bickering on

the part of a number of Calvinist échevins or aldermen, the grant was made in perpetuity and confirmed by Charles IX in 1568.

Meantime, Faber had been laboring in Germany. He was to have been the Catholic orator at Worms in 1540, but conditions were such that he made no public utterance. Melanchthon was present, but whether Faber and he met is not clear. In 1541 Faber received an enthusiastic welcome at Ratisbon from the Catholics, especially from Cochlæus, the great antagonist of Luther. Among his opponents at the Diet were Bucer and Melanchthon; the discussion, as usual, led to no result. In one of his letters he notes the inability of the Emperor to prevent the general ruin of the Faith. From Ratisbon he went to Nuremberg, but as the legate had been recalled, Faber's work necessarily came to an end. Le Jay and Bobadilla succeeded him in Germany. The former addressed the assembly of the bishops at Salzburg, preached in the Lutheran churches, escaped being poisoned on one occasion and drowned on another; he failed, however, to check the flood of heresy, which had not only completely engulfed Ratisbon, but threatened to invade Catholic Bavaria, although Duke William maintained that such an event was impossible. Ingolstadt had already been badly damaged, both doctrinally and morally; and Bobadilla was despatched thither by the legate to see what could be done.

Faber had, meantime, returned to Germany. In spite of attacks by highwaymen, imprisonment, ill-treatment at the hands of disorderly bands of soldiers and heretics, he reached Spires and completely revived the spirit of the clergy. From there he hastened to Cologne, but in the midst of his work he was sent off to Portugal for the marriage of the king's daughter. By the time he reached Louvain, he was sick and exhausted, so that the order to proceed to Portugal had to be rescinded. He then returned to Cologne, where he again met Bucer and Melanchthon, who were endeavoring to induce the bishop to apostatize. Apprehensive of their success, he had them both expelled from the city. Again he was summoned to Portugal, and in 1547 the king, at his instance, gave the Society the college of Coimbra. Similar establishments were begun about the same time in Spain — at Valencia, Barcelona and Valladolid, chiefly through the influence of Araoz.

Le Jay, meanwhile, had been made professor of theology at Innsbruck, on the death of the famous Dr. Eck, and the university petitioned the Pope to make his appointment perpetual; but he was clamored for simultaneously by several bishops, and we find him subsequently at Augsburg, Salzburg, Dillingen and elsewhere, battling incessantly for the cause of the Faith. He succeeded in inducing the bishops assembled at Augsburg to prohibit the discussion of religion at the Diet, and a little later he assisted at the ecclesiastical council of the province. With him at this gathering was Bobadilla, who, says the chronicler, "resembled him in energy and zeal but was altogether unlike him in character." Le Jay was gentle and persuasive; Bobadilla, impetuous and volcanic. Bobadilla's fire, however, seems to have pleased the Germans. He strengthened the nobles and people of Innsbruck in their faith, was consulted by King Ferdinand on the gravest questions, scored brilliant successes in public disputes, and was made socius of the Apostolic nuncio at Nuremberg, where, it was suspected, a deep plot was being laid for the complete extirpation of the Faith. At the king's request, he attended the Diet of Worms, and by his alertness and knowledge rendered immense service to the Catholic party. He was shortly afterward summoned by the king to Vienna where he preached to the people incessantly and revived the ecclesiastical spirit of the clergy. He was again at Worms for another diet, and persuaded both the emperor and Ferdinand to oppose the Lutheran scheme of convoking a general council in Germany. At the suggestion of St. Ignatius, an appeal had been made to the bishops, through Le Jay, to establish seminaries in their dioceses. They all approved of the project; and several immediately set to work to carry it out.

When the Diet adjourned, Le Jay left Germany to take part in the Council of Trent, while Bobadilla remained with the king as spiritual adviser to the court and general supervisor of the sick and wounded soldiers of the royal armies. In the latter capacity he acquitted himself with his usual energy — his impetuosity of character often bringing him into the forefront of battle, where he merited several honorable scars for his daring. He also succeeded in falling a victim to the pestilence which was ravaging the country; he was robbed and maltreated by marauders, but came through it all safely, and we find him at the Diets of Ratisbon and Augsburg, everywhere showing himself a genuine apostle, as the Archbishop of Vienna informed Ignatius. The king offered him a bishopric, but he refused. He was soon, however, to know Germany no more.

The Council of Trent had already been in session for three years, when Charles V issued an edict known as the Interim, which forbade any change of religion until the council had finished its work; but at the same time he made concessions to the heretics which angered the Catholics both lay and clerical. Bobadilla was especially outspoken in the matter and in a public discourse was imprudent enough to condemn the imperial policy. Clearly he had not yet acquired the characteristic virtue of his great leader. Not only did he not mend matters by his intemperate eloquence, but he created an aversion for the Society in the mind of Charles V, which lasted till the time of St. Francis Borgia. Besides, he virtually blasted his own career. He was ordered to Naples by St. Ignatius and forbidden to present himself at the Jesuit house as he passed through Rome. He appears only once later and then in a manner scarcely redounding to his credit: objecting to the election of Laínez as vicar, although he had previously voted for him and obeyed him for a year. Happily the brilliant services of his fellow Jesuits who were at the Council of Trent and elsewhere, as well as his own splendid past, averted any very great damage to the Society.

Although Ignatius had been invited to be present at the sessions in Trent, he sedulously avoided the prominence which that would have given him personally; moreover, absence from his post as General of the newly-formed Institute would have materially interfered with the task of preparing successors to the great men who were already at work. Thus, Salmerón and Laínez were the Pope's theologians and Father Faber was summoned from his sick bed in Portugal to assist them, but he arrived in Rome only to die in the arms of Ignatius and never appeared at the council. Le Jay was present as theologian of the Cardinal Archbishop of Augsburg; Cavallino represented the Duke of Bavaria; and later Canisius and Polanco were added to the group. The coming of Canisius was due more or less to an accident. He had been laboring at Cologne to prevent the archbishop, Herman von Weid, from openly apostatizing; when the concessions to Melanchthon and Bucer had become too outrageous to be tolerated, he had hurried off to meet the emperor and King Ferdinand to ask for the deposition of the prelate. With the king he met Truchsess, the great Cardinal of Augsburg, and had no difficulty in gaining his point, but the Cardinal was so fascinated by the ability of the young pleader that he insisted on taking him to Trent as his theologian in spite of the protests of the whole city of Cologne.

Naturally, many of the Fathers of the Council had their suspicions of these new theologians. They were members of a religious order which had broken with the traditions of the past, and they might possibly be heretics in disguise. Moreover, they were alarmingly young. Canisius was only twenty-six, Salmerón thirty-one, Le Jay about the same age, and Laínez, the chief figure in the council, not more than thirty-four. But the indubitable holiness of their lives, their amazing learning, and their uncompromising orthodoxy soon dissipated all doubts about them. Laínez and Salmerón were especially prominent. They were allowed to speak as long as they chose on any topic. Thus, after Laínez had discoursed for an entire day on the Sacrifice of the Mass, he was ordered to continue on the following morning. Entire sections of the Acts of the council were written by him; and by order of the Pope both he and Salmerón had to be present at all the sessions of the council, which lasted with its interruptions from 1545 to 1563. Bishoprics and a cardinal's hat were offered to Laínez; and, at the death of Paul IV, twelve votes were cast for him as Pope. Indeed one section of the cardinals had made up their minds to elect him, but when apprised of it, he fled and kept in concealment until the danger was averted. He was at that time General of the Society.

After the first adjournment of the council, these men whose stupendous labors would appear to have called for some repose were granted none at all. Thus, we find Laínez summoned by the Duke of Etruria to found a

college in Florence. The Pope's vicar wanted him to look
after the ecclesiastical needs of Bologna, whither he
repaired with Salmerón, while Le Jay was working at
Ferrara and elsewhere in the Peninsula.   The most
remarkable of them all, however, in the matter of work
during these recesses was undoubtedly Peter Canisius
(Kanness, Kanys or De Hondt, as he was variously
called.)   One would naturally imagine that he would
have been sent back to Cologne to the scene of his
former triumphs.   On the contrary, he was ordered to
teach rhetoric in the newly-founded college of Messina
in Sicily.   He was then recalled to Rome, where he
made his solemn profession in the hands of St. Ignatius;
after this he started with Le Jay and Salmerón to
Ingolstadt, where he taught theology and began his
courses of catechetical instructions which were to
restore the lost Faith of Germany.

On the way to the scene of his labors, he received a
doctor's degree at Bologna. In 1550 he was made
rector of the University of Ingolstadt, but was nevertheless, sent to Vienna to found a new college. He
was simultaneously court preacher, director of the
hospitals and prisons, and, in Lent, the apostle of the
abandoned parishes of Lower Austria.   He was offered
the See of Vienna, but three times he refused it, though
he had to administer the diocese during the year 1557.
Five years prior to that he had opened colleges at
Prague and Ingolstadt, after which he was appointed
the first provincial of Germany.   He was adviser of
the king at the Diet of Ratisbon, and by order of the
Pope took part in the religious discussions at Worms.
He began negotiations for a college at Strasburg, and
made apostolic excursions to that place as well as to
Freiburg and Alsace.   While taking part in the general
congregation of the order in Rome, he was sent by
Pope Paul IV to the imperial Diet of Pieterkow in

Poland. In 1559 he was summoned by the emperor
to the Diet of Augsburg, and had to remain in that
city from 1561 to 1562 as cathedral preacher; during
this time it is recorded that besides giving retreats,
teaching catechism and hearing confessions, he appeared
as many as two hundred and ten times in the pulpit.
In 1562 he was back again as papal theologian at Trent,
where he found himself at odds with Laínez, then
General of the Society, on the question of granting the
cup to the laity — Laínez opposing this concession,
which he advocated. He remained at the council only
for a few sessions, but returned again after having
reconciled the Emperor with the Pope. The Emperor's
favor, however, he lost later when he changed his
views about Communion under both species, and also
by reason of an unfounded charge of revealing imperial
secrets which had been made against him.

In that year Canisius opened the college of Innsbruck
and directed the spiritual life of Magdalena, the saintly
daughter of Ferdinand I. In 1564 he inaugurated the
college of Dillingen and became administrator of the
university of that place; he was also constituted secret
nuncio of Pius IV to promulgate the decrees of the
council in Germany. His mission was interrupted by
the death of the Pope, and although Pius V desired
him to continue in that office, he declined, because it
exposed him to the accusation of meddling in politics.
In 1566 he was theologian of the legate at the Diet
of Augsburg and persuaded that dignitary not to issue
a mandate against the so-called religious peace. He
thus prevented another war and gave new life to the
Catholics of Germany. In 1567 he founded a college
at Wurzburg, and evangelized Mayence and Spires.
At Dillingen he received young Stanislaus Kostka into
the Society conditionally and sent him to Rome; he
settled a philosophical dispute at Innsbruck and

established a college at Halle. At last in 1569 at his
own request he was relieved of his office of provincial,
which he had held for thirteen years; in 1570 he was
court preacher of the Archduke Ferdinand II; in 1575
he was papal envoy to Bavaria, and theologian to the
papal legate at the Diet of Ratisbon. He introduced
the Sodality of the Blessed Virgin at Innsbruck, and
at the command of the Pope built a college at Freiburg,
where he remained for the rest of his life.

For years Canisius had urged his superiors and had
also pleaded at the Council of Trent for the establishment of colleges of writers in various countries to
defend the Faith. He was in constant touch with the
great printers and publishers of the day, such as
Plantin, Cholm and Mayer; he brought out the first
reports of foreign missions, and induced the town
council of Freiburg to establish a printing-press. All
this time he was actively writing, and the list of his
publications covers thirty-eight quarto pages in the
" Bibliothèque des écrivains de la C. de Jésus." He was
commissioned by Pius V to refute the Centuriators of
Magdeburg — the society of writers who, under the
inspiration of Flacius Illyricus, had undertaken to
falsify the works of the early Fathers of the Church,
century by century, so as to furnish a historical proof
in support of Luther's errors. In 1583 he united in
one volume the two books which he had previously
issued in 1571 and 1577, styling them " Commentaria
de Verbi corruptelis," having in the meantime published
the genuine texts of Saints Cyril and Leo.

His " Catechism " was his most famous achievement.
It consisted of two hundred and eleven, and later, of
two hundred and twenty-two doctrinal questions, and
was intended chiefly for advanced students; but there
were annexed to it a compendium for children, and
another for students of the middle and lower grades.

4

It is recognized as a masterpiece even by Protestant writers such as Ranke, Mezel, Kawerau and others. Two hundred editions of it in one form or another were published during his lifetime in twelve different languages. "I know my Canisius" became a synonym in Germany for "I know my catechism." In brief, he did more than any other man to save Germany for the Church, and he is regarded as another St. Boniface. He died on November 21, 1597 and was beatified by Pius IX on April 17, 1864. The Catechism appears to have been first suggested by Ferdinand I to Le Jay who took up the work enthusiastically. But instead of crowding everything into one volume, he divided it into three: the first, a summa of theology for the university; the second, a volume for priests engaged in the ministry; while the third was for school teachers. He laid the matter before St. Ignatius, who assigned the first part to Laínez and the second to Frusius, then rector of Vienna. But as Frusius died, and Laínez was made General of the Society, Canisius undertook the entire work.

Apparently, it was from Le Jay also that the idea came of founding the Collegium Germanicum in Rome, though Cardinal Morone claims it as his conception. Le Jay, indeed, had discussed the matter with him, but had previously made a much more serious study of the question with Cardinal Truchsess, Archbishop of Augsburg. As the purpose of the Collegium was to supply a thoroughly educated priesthood to Germany, Truchsess could appreciate the need of it more than Morone, whose ideas about the need of good works, the vital question in Germany at the time, were extremely curious, according to his own account of a stormy interview he had with Salmerón on that topic. He reproached Salmerón for making too much of good works. Indeed Morone had been at one time

under the surveillance of the Inquisition on account
of certain utterances. His orthodoxy, however, must
have been above suspicion, because of the exalted
position he occupied.

Le Jay was broken-hearted when Maurice of Saxony,
the leader of the imperial troops, swung his whole
army over to the very Lutherans whom he had just
defeated at Muhlberg. The awful condition of religion
in the Empire preyed upon his mind to such a degree
that he died at Vienna on Aug. 6, 1552, at the age of
fifty-two. Canisius, who preached the funeral oration,
said that he was "a worthy successor of Faber, and that
his instinct was so correct that the character he gave
to the college of Vienna over which he presided was
adopted as the model throughout Germany." Ranke
might be quoted on that point also. He points out
that "at the beginning of 1551 the Jesuits had no
fixed place in Germany — Le Jay was appointed
rector only in June of that year — but in 1566 they
occupied Bavaria, Tyrol, Franconia, a great part of
the Rhine Province and Austria, and had penetrated
into Hungary and Moravia. It was the first durable
anti-Protestant check that Germany had received."

Under normal conditions, Spain would of course,
have received these distinguished sons of hers with
open arms; but, unfortunately, a deplorable state of
affairs prevailed in the highest circles both of Church
and State, almost as open and as shameless as in
other parts of Europe. Princes and nobles held the
titles of bishops and archbishops and appropriated the
revenues of dioceses. That alone made any effort in
the way of reform impossible. Added to this, Bobadilla's indiscretion in attacking the policy of Charles V
in Germany had, as we have already said, predisposed
that monarch, and consequently many of his subjects,
against the whole Society; but as the Emperor did

not openly interfere with them they established colleges in Barcelona, Gandia, Valencia and Alcalá, as early as 1546; but two years later, when they made their appearance in Salamanca, they found an implacable foe in the person of the distinguished Dominican theologian, Melchior Cano.

From the pulpit and platform and in the press Cano denounced and decried the new religious, not only as constituting a danger to the Church, but as being nothing else than the precursors of Antichrist. His own Master-General wrote a letter eulogizing the Society and forbidding his brethren to attack it; but this had no effect on Melchior, nor did the fact that the new Order was approved by the Pope avail to keep him quiet. Finally, in order to mollify him he was made Bishop of the Canaries, but he actually resigned that see in order to return to the attack. His hostility continued not only till his death, but after it; for, before he departed, he left in the hands of a friend a document which was of great service to the enemies of the Society at the time of the Suppression. " God grant," he wrote, " that I may not be a Cassandra, who was believed only after the sack of Troy. If the religious of the Society continue as they have begun, there may come a time, which I hope God will avert, when the Kings of Europe would wish to resist them but will be unable to do so." One of the reasons of Cano's hostility to the Society was that the Fathers urged Catholics to frequent the sacraments (Suau, Vie de Borgia, 136). This opposition of Cano was backed by the Archbishop of Saragossa, who was Francis Borgia's uncle. Bands of street children carrying banners on which hideous devils were painted marched to the new church of the Society and pelted it with stones. Then the mob drove the luckless Fathers out of the city; when Borgia's sister sheltered the exiles in her castle her uncle, the archbishop, excommunicated her. But that was the way of the world in those days. Even the illustrious Cardinal Carranza was kept in the prison of the Spanish Inquisition for seventeen years, because of something discovered in his writings by his brother Dominican Melchior Cano (Suau, *op. cit.*, 136).

Little by little, however, the prejudices were dissipated, and both Alcalá and Salamanca called Strada to lecture in their halls. Nevertheless, each new success only raised a fresh storm. Thus it was bad enough when the rector of the University of Salamanca, Anthony of Córdova, who was just about to be made a cardinal, entered the Society; but the excitement became intense when, in 1550, Francis Borgia, who was Duke of Gandia, Viceroy of Catalonia, a friend of the Emperor, a soldier who had distinguished himself in the invasion of Provence, and whose future usefulness was reckoned upon for the service of his country, let it be known that he, too, was going to become a Jesuit. To prevent it, the Pope was urged to make him a Cardinal, but Borgia, who was then in Rome, fled back to Spain. When, however, he finally appeared as a member of the Order, houses and colleges were erected wherever he wished to have them: at Granada, Valladolid, Saragossa, Medina, San Lucar, Monterey, Burgos, Valencia, Murcia, Placentia and Seville. In 1556 Charles V was succeeded by Philip II, who asked that the cardinal's hat should be given to Borgia, but the honor was again refused. On three other occasions the same offers and refusals were repeated.

By the time Francis Borgia became General of the Order it had already developed into eighteen provinces, with one hundred and thirty establishments, and had a register of three thousand five hundred members.

Besides attempting to convert the Vaudois heretics, the Society maintained the missions of Brazil and the Indies and established new ones in Peru and Mexico; by the help of the famous Pedro Menéndez, who is the special object of hatred on the part of American Protestant historians, it sent the first missionaries to what is now Florida in the United States. Segura and his companions were put to death on the Rappahannock; and Martínez was killed further down the coast, while Sánchez, a former rector of Alcalá, reached Vera Cruz in Mexico in 1572 with twelve companions to look after the Spaniards and natives and to care for the unfortunate blacks whom the Spaniards were importing from Africa.

When Pius V was elected Pope, there was a general fear that he would suppress the Society; but the Pontiff set all doubts at rest when, on his way to be crowned at St. John Lateran, he called Borgia to his side and embraced him. He also made Salmerón and Toletus his official preachers, and gave the Jesuits the work of translating the " Catechism " of the Council of Trent and of publishing a new edition of the Bible. He was, however, about to revoke the Society's exemption from the office of choir; but Borgia induced him to change his mind on that point, and even obtained a perpetual exemption from the public recitation of the Office, as well as the revocation of the restriction of the priesthood to the professed of the Society. Moreover, when there was danger of a Turkish invasion, Borgia was sent with the Pope's nephew to Spain and France to organize a league in defence of Christendom, while Toletus accompanied another cardinal to Germany.

Philip II had asked for missionaries to evangelize Peru, and hence at the end of March, 1568, Portillo and seven Jesuits landed at Callao, and proceeding to

Lima established a church and college there on a
magnificent scale. It was easy to do so, however,
for the Spanish colonists were rolling in wealth. At
the same time, the Indians and negroes were not
neglected. In 1569 twelve new missionaries arrived,
and one of them, Alonzo de Barzana, to the amazement
of every one, preached in the language of the Incas as
soon as he came ashore. He had been studying it
every moment of the long journey from Spain. In
1574 a college was established at Cuzco, in an old
palace of the Incas, and another in the city of
La Paz.

At this stage of the work the first domestic trouble
in the New World presented itself. Portillo, the provincial, was admitting undesirable candidates into the
Society, and placing the professed in parishes, thus
flinging them into the midst of the civil and ecclesiastical
turmoil which then prevailed. In spite of his abilities,
however, he was promptly recalled to Spain. It is
very gratifying to learn that outside the domestic
precincts, no one ever knew the reason of this drastic
measure. Freedom from parochial obligations left the
Fathers time for their normal work, and they forthwith
established schools in almost every city and town of
Peru. The training school on Lake Titicaca, especially,
was a very wise and far-seeing enterprise, for there
the missionaries could devote themselves exclusively
to the study of the native language and to historical,
literary and scientific studies. The result was that
some of the most eminent men of the period issued
from that educational centre. It is said that the
printing-press they brought over from Europe was the
first one to be set up in that part of the New World.
Titicaca flourished as late as 1767, but at that time
Charles III expelled the Jesuits from Peru and Titicaca
ceased to be.

The Society had a long and desperate struggle, before it could gain an educational foothold in France. Possibly it was a preparation for the future glory it was to win there. Its principal enemies were the University of Paris and, incidentally, the Parliament, which came under the influence of the doctors of the Sorbonne. The first band of Jesuits arrived under the leadership of Domenech, who had been a canon in Spain but had relinquished his rich benefice to enter the Society — an act which seemed so supremely foolish in the eyes of his friends that they accused Ignatius of bewitching him. Later, he became a sort of Saint Vincent de Paul for Italy. He found Palermo swarming with throngs of half-naked and starving children, and immediately built an asylum for them. He established hospitals, Magdalen asylums, refuges for the aged, and went round the city holding out his hand for alms to repair the dilapidated convents of nuns, whom the constant wars had left homeless and hungry. Giving the Spiritual Exercises was one of his special occupations.

In the group, also, was Oviedo, the future Patriarch of Abyssinia, who was to spend his life in the wilds of Africa. There too was Strada, orator, poet and historian, who was to be one of the most illustrious men of his time; he taught rhetoric for fifteen years in the Roman College, was the official preacher and the intimate friend of Popes Clement VIII and Paul V, and wrote a "History of the Wars of Flanders," which met with universal applause. Finally, there was the famous young Ribadeneira, then only a boy of fourteen; he had left one of the most brilliant courts of Europe— that of Cardinal Farnese, the brother of princes and popes — and later became famous as a distinguished Latinist, a successful diplomat, the chosen orator at the inaugural ceremonies of the Collegium Germanicum,

an eminent preacher at Louvain and Brussels, and an
envoy to Mary Tudor in her last illness. He was
provincial, visitor and assistant under Borgia and
Laínez, the great champion of the Society in Spain
against Vásquez and his fellow-conspirators, and an
author whose works in his native Castilian are ranked
among the classics of the language.

Their staunch friend was du Prat, the Bishop of
Clermont, who gave them the palace which had been,
up to that time, his residence when visiting the
metropolis. Before that shelter was assured to them,
they had lived as boarders, first in the Collège des
Trésoriers and then in the Collège des Lombards,
not as Jesuits, but as ordinary students whose
similarity of taste in matters of piety seemed to
the outside world to have drawn them together. Of
course, their real character soon became known, and
then their troubles began. A college was attempted
at Tournon in the following year, with Auger as rector,
but the civil war was raging and before a twelve-
month, Adrets, the most bloodthirsty monster of the
Huguenot rebellion, whose favorite amusement was to
make his prisoners leap off the ramparts to the rocks
below, put an end to everything Catholic in Tournon.

Crétineau-Joly is of opinion that the recognition
of the Society in France was retarded by its refusal
to admit the famous Guillaume Postel in its ranks.
It seems absurd, but it happened just then that France
had gone mad about Postel; and Marguérite de
Valois used to speak of him as the " Wonder of the
World." He was indeed a very remarkable personage.
Though only self-instructed, he knew almost every
language; he had plunged in the depths of rabbinical
and astrological lore; to obtain an intimate knowledge
of the Orient, he had accompanied the Sultan in an
expedition against the Persians; he had spent vast

sums of money in purchasing rare manuscripts; he was sought for by all the universities; he drew immense crowds to his lectures, and wrote books about every conceivable subject, but at the same time with all his genius he was undoubtedly insane. So that when he went to Rome and told about his spiritual communications with the mythical Mère Jeanne, and how he proposed to unite the whole human race, by the power of the sword or the word, under the banner of the Pope and the King of France, who, he said, was a lineal descendant of the eldest son of Noe, the perspicacity of a Loyola was not needed to understand his mental condition. His rejection ought to have been a recommendation rather than a reproach.

When established in their new house, the Jesuits received scholars and asked for affiliation to the university, but the request was peremptorily refused, for the alleged reason that they were neither secular priests nor friars, but a nondescript and novel organization whose purpose was mysterious and suspicious. Besides, they were all Spaniards — a genuine difficulty at a time when Charles V and Francis I were threatening to go to war with each other. It happened also that the Archbishop of Paris, du Bellay, was their avowed enemy; he denounced them as corrupters of youth, and expelled them from the little chapel of Saint-Germain-des-Prés, which a Benedictine abbot had put at their disposal. Finally, when the war seemed imminent, the foreigners were sent away, some to Lyons and some to Louvain. For a time, those who remained were shielded by the papal nuncio at Paris, but he was recalled. Then the Archbishop of Rheims and the Cardinal of Lorraine appeared as their protectors. They had even secured the grant of a charter for the college and were very hopeful of opening it, but, as the concession had to be passed on by the Parliament

before it became effective, they were as badly off as
ever. Besides this, their lack of friends had left the
college without funds, for the teaching given in their
house was gratuitous — a practice which formed the
chief educational grievance alleged by the university.
Evidently a staff of clever professors who taught for
nothing constituted a menace to all other institutions.
Conditions became so desperate that at one time there
were only four pupils at Clermont. Nevertheless, with
an amazing confidence in the future success of the
Society in France, it was just at this moment that St.
Ignatius established the French province, and sent the
beloved Pasquier Brouet as superior.

Brouet had already given proofs of his ability in
dealing with difficulties; for with Salmerón he had
faced the danger of death in Ireland, and when there
was question of creating a Patriarch of Abyssinia or
Ethiopia, another place of prospective martyrdom, he
was the first choice, though Oviedo was ultimately
selected, probably because of his nationality. Shortly
after his arrival, a new college was attempted at Billom,
but Father de la Goutte who was appointed rector was
captured by the Turks and died on an island off the
coast of Tunis. A substitute, however, was appointed,
and in a few years the college had five hundred students
on its roll. Applications were made also for establishments at Montarges, Périgueux and elsewhere. In 1560
the first friend of the Society in France, the Bishop
of Clermont, died, leaving rich bequests in his will to
the colleges at Paris and Billom, but they were disal-
lowed by the courts because the Society was not an
authorized corporation. For, in spite of the fact that
not only the sanction of Henry II but also that of
Francis II had been given, yet the university and the
Archbishop of Paris had contrived by all sorts of
devices to delay the complete official recognition of the

establishment.   In the long fight that ensued against
this injustice, Father Cogordan, who was the procurator
of the province, distinguished himself by his resource-
fulness in facing and mastering the various situations.

The opposition finally collapsed in a very dramatic
fashion.   Charles IX was on the throne, but the reins
of government were in the hands of his mother,
Catherine de' Medici, who, contrary to the express wish
of the Sovereign Pontiff, had consented to the demands
of the Huguenots for a general assembly, where the
claims of the new religion might be presented to
the representative Catholics of the kingdom.   The
Colloquy, as it was called, took place at Poissy in 1561.
The experience of Germany in permitting such gather-
ings had shown very clearly that, instead of conducing
to religious peace, they only widened the breach between
Catholics and Protestants.   For the calm statement
of dogmatic differences was ignored by the appellants,
and the sessions were purposely turned into a series
of disorderly and virulent denunciations and recrimina-
tions.

The Colloquy in this instance was very imposing.
The queen mother, Charles IX and the whole court
were present.   There were five cardinals, forty bishops
and a throng of learned divines from all parts of
France.   Cardinal de Tournon presided; Hôpital was
the spokesman for the crown; while the King of
Navarre and the Prince de Condé represented the
Huguenot party.   Among the Protestant ministers
were Theodore Beza and Peter Martyr, the ex-friar.
Eight days had gone by in useless squabbles when into
the assembly came James Laínez, who was then General
of the Society, and had been sent thither by the Pope
to protest against the Colloquy.   Beza had already
been annihilated by the Cardinal of Lorraine, and
Peter Martyr was speaking when Laínez entered.

The great man who had held the Council of Trent enthralled by his leaning and eloquence listened for a while to his unworthy adversary and then arose. Addressing the queen, he said: "It may be unseemly for a foreigner to lift his voice in this presence, but as the Church is restricted to no nation, it cannot be out of place for me to give utterance to the thoughts that present themselves to my mind on this occasion. I will first advert to the danger of these assemblies and will especially address myself to what Friar Peter and his colleague have advanced."

The use of the name "friar" publicly pilloried the apostate. He writhed under it, but he could not escape. It recurred again and again as the tactics of Beza and his associates were laid bare. Then, turning to the queen, Laínez said: "The first means to be taken to avoid the deceits of the enemy is for your Majesty to remember that it is not within the competency either of your Majesty or any other temporal prince to discuss and decide matters pertaining to the Faith. This belongs to the Sovereign Pontiff and the Councils of the Church. Much more so is this the case when, as at present, the General Council of Trent is in session. If these teachers of the new religion are sincerely seeking the truth, let them go there to find it."

After adding his authority to the splendid reply already uttered by the Cardinal of Lorraine, Laínez said: "As Friar Peter has asked us for a confession of faith, I confess the Catholic Faith, for which I am ready to die; and I implore Your Majesties, both you, Madame, and your son, the Most Christian King, to safeguard your temporal kingdom if you wish to gain the Kingdom of Heaven. If on the contrary you care less for the fear and love of God than the fear and love of man, are you not running the risk of losing your earthly as well as your heavenly kingdom? I trust that this calamity will not fall upon you. I expect, on the contrary, that God in his goodness will grant you and your son the grace of perseverance in your faith, and will not permit this illustrious nobility now before me, and this most Christian kingdom, which has been such an example to the world, ever to abandon the Catholic Faith or be defiled by the pestilential touch of these new sects and new religions."

This discourse was a particularly daring act, on the part of Laínez. According to a recent authority (Martin, Gallicanisme et la Réforme, 28, note 4), Du Ferrier, the government delegate at Trent, circulated a note which said among other things: "As for Pius IV we withdraw from his rule; whatever decisions he may have made we reject, spit back at him (*respuimus*) and despise. We scorn and renounce him as Vicar of Christ, Head of the Church and successor of Peter." Far from reprehending his ambassador for these furious words, Charles IX and, of course, Catherine praised the ambassador unreservedly. Catherine had busied herself previous to this in trying to persuade the different governments to have a council in which the Pope should have nothing to say, one whose object would be, not to define dogma or enforce discipline, but, to draw up a formula of reconciliation which would satisfy Protestants. Even the French bishops, though admitting that the Pope was a supreme power in the Church, denied that he had supreme power over it, and refused to acknowledge " his plenitude of power to feed, rule and govern the Universal Church." The separation of France from the Church was at that time openly advocated. Since such were the conditions in France at that time, it is clear that Catherine never expected an attack of the kind that Laínez treated her to. She burst into tears and withdrew from the Colloquy. There was never

another public session. Crétineau-Joly says that
Laínez told Condé: " The queen's tears are a bit of
comedy; " but such an utterance from a man of the
character of Laínez and in such surroundings, where
the insult would have been immediately reported to
the queen, is simply inconceivable. He could never
have been guilty of such an unpardonable indiscretion.

Meantime, the bishops and archbishops of France
had been meeting during the recesses of the Colloquy
to consider the question of legislation for the Jesuit
colleges. With the exception of Cardinal de Châtillon
and the Archbishop of Paris, they were all anxious to
put an end to the proscription to which the Society had
been so long and so unjustly subjected. As it
happened that Cardinal de Châtillon, the brother of
the famous Admiral Coligny, the patron saint of the
French Calvinists, was just then on the point of apostatizing and taking a wife and as the scandal was of
common knowledge it evidently would not do for the
Archbishop of Paris to be ranged on his side. That
and, probably, the fact of his being tired out by the
long fight which had been protracted only because of
his natural stubbornness, made him give way, and the
Society was legalized in France. No doubt the
presence of Laínez and his closing up of the Colloquy
by his audacious discourse had helped largely to bring
about that result. Some disagreeable restrictions were
appended to the grant, it is true, but they were cancelled a few years later by a royal decree. Parliament
finally yielded and signed the charter of the College on
January 14, 1562. Laínez saw the queen frequently
after the Colloquy, and remained in France for some
time, striving unweariedly to win back to the Faith
such men as Condé, the King of Navarre and others,
and continuing to warn the queen that her unwise

toleration would result in disaster to the realm. Unfortunately he was not heeded.

While all this was going on, another college had been established at Pamiers, which was in the heretical territory of Navarre. Its founders were none others than the rector of the Roman College, Jean Pelletier, and Edmond Auger. But in the beginning the inhabitants were suspicious and refused the commonest hospitality to the new comers, so that their first dwelling had the advantage of being like the Stable of Bethlehem — a hut with no doors and no windows. Finally, however, their sermons in the churches captivated the people and the " Jezoists," as they were called, succeeded in getting a respectable house and beginning their classes. This was in 1559, but before the end of 1561 the " Jezoists " were expelled by the excited Huguenots, and were compelled to take refuge in Toulouse.

The Edmond Auger just mentioned was perhaps the most eloquent man of that period in France. He was called the Chrysostom of his country. Wherever he went, crowds flocked to hear him, fanatical Calvinists as well as devoted Catholics. His first sermon was in Valence, where the bishop had just apostatized and the Huguenots were in complete possession. A furious outbreak resulted, and he was seized and sentenced to be burned to death. While standing at the stake, he harangued the people before the torch was applied, and so captivated the mob that they clamored for his release. His devotedness to the sick in a pestilence at Lyons won the popular heart and a college was asked for. At various times he was chaplain of the troops, confessor of Henry IV, rector and provincial; but unfortunately he was so outspoken in his denunciation of the League that the people of Lyons, who once admired him, were wrought up to fury by his

utterances on the political situation, and were on the
point of throwing him into the Rhône. His unwise
zeal had thus seriously injured the Society.

When the council of Trent had concluded its sessions,
Canisius was sent back to Germany by the Pope to
see that the decrees were promulgated and enforced.
He labored for five years to accomplish this task, but
failed completely. With the exception of some bishops
like Truchsess of Augsburg, very few paid any attention
to the Pope's wish, the reason being that they were
mostly scions of the nobility, who were accustomed
to live in luxury and had adopted the ecclesiastical
profession solely because of the rich revenues of the
sees to which their relatives had had them appointed.
At that very time fourteen of them, it is said on the
best authority, were wearing their mitres without even
having notified the Pope of their election or asking
his approbation. They, more than Martin Luther,
were responsible for the loss of Germany. Their lives
were such that Canisius forbade his priests to accept
the position of confessor to any of them. Of course,
such men turned a deaf ear to the papal decree about
establishing diocesan seminaries; and those who desired
them were prevented by their canons, some of whom
were not even priests. It was for this reason that
Canisius begged the Pope to establish burses in foreign
seminaries, where worthy ecclesiastics might be trained
whose lives would be in such contrast with the general
depravity and ignorance of the clergy that the bishops
would perhaps be shamed out of their apathy.

The establishment of burses, however, was only
a temporary expedient; for the few secular priests they
might furnish could scarcely support the strain to
which they would be subjected in the terrible isolation
which their small number would entail. They would
not have the compact organization of a religious order

5

to keep them steady, and yet they would be the victims of the same kind of persecution as Canisius and his associates had to undergo. From this difficulty arose the idea of the Collegium Germanicum already referred to, an establishment in Rome under the direction of the Jesuits, to which young Germans distinguished for their intellectual ability and virtue could be sent and trained to be apostles in their native land. It was the Collegium Germanicum that saved to the Faith what was left of Germany and won back much that was lost.

"The German College at Rome," said a Protestant preacher in 1594 (Nothgedrungene Erinnerungen, Bl. 8), "is a hotbed singularly favorable for developing the worst kind of Jesuitry. Our young Germans are educated there gratuitously; and at the end of their studies they are sent home to restore papistry to its former place and to fight for it with all their might. You find them exercising the ministry in a great number of collegiate churches and parishes. They become the advisers of bishops and even archbishops; and we see these Jesuits under our very eyes defending the Catholic cause with such zeal that we Evangelicals may well ask ourselves in what lands and in what towns such fervent zeal for the beloved Gospel is found among our own party. They seduce so many souls from us that it is too distressing even to enumerate them." Martin Chemnitz, the Protestant theologian, said that if the Jesuits had done nothing but found the German College, they would deserve to be regarded for that one achievement as the most dangerous enemy of Lutheranism. "These young men," said another Protestant controversialist in 1593, "are like their teachers in diabolical cunning, in hypocritical piety, and in the idolatrous practices which they propagate among the people. They preach frequently, pretending to be good Christians, they frequent hospitals

and visit the sick at home, all out of a pure hypocrisy
saturating the very hides of these wretches.   They are
again persuading the simple and credulous people
to return to their damnable papistry " (Janssen, op.
cit., IX, 323, sqq.).

Echsfeld, Erfurt, Aschaffenburg, Mayence, Coblentz,
Trèves, Würzburg, Spires and other places soon felt
the effects of the zeal of these students of the Collegium
Germanicum.   Their manner of life meant hardship
and danger of every kind; assaults by degenerate
Catholics and infuriated heretics; vigils in miserable
huts and pest-laden hospitals, resulting sometimes in
sickness and violent death; but " these messengers
of the devil," as the preachers called them, kept
at their work and soon won back countless numbers
of their countrymen to the Faith.   Similar establishments also grew up at Braunsberg, Dillingen, Fulda,
Munich and Vienna.   Representatives of other religious
orders entered into the movement and gave it new life
and vigor.   Janssen (IX, 313) informs us that the
foundation of seminaries for poor students also was due
to Canisius and his fellow-workers.   At their suggestion Albert V founded the Gregorianum at Munich
in 1574; and Ingolstadt, Würzburg, Innsbruck, Halle,
Gratz and Prague soon had similar establishments.
As early as 1559 Canisius assumed the responsibility
for two hundred poor students, and by having them
live in common was able to supply all their needs.
After each of his sermons in the cathedral, he went
around among the great personages assembled to hear
him, to ask for alms to keep up his establishments.
Father Voth, following his example forty years later,
collected 1400 florins in a single year for the same
purpose.

The work of regeneration was not restricted to the
foundation of ecclesiastical seminaries.   Janssen (l. c.)

gives us an entire page of the names of colleges taken from the " Litteræ annuæ," in some of which there were nine hundred, one thousand, and even thirteen hundred scholars. Between 1612 and 1625 Germany had one hundred Jesuit colleges. In all of them were established sodalities the members of which besides performing their own religious exercises in the chapel, visited the hospitals, prisons and camps and performed other works of charity and zeal. On their rosters are seen the names of men who attained eminence in Church and State — kings, princes, cardinals, soldiers, scholars, etc. These sodalities had also established intimate relations with similar organizations all over Europe. Naturally, this intense activity aroused the fury of the heretics. Calumnies of every kind were invented; and in 1603 a preacher in Styria announced that the most execrable and sanguinary plots were being formed to drown the whole Empire in blood in order to nullify the teaching of the Evangel. " O poor Roman Empire!" he exclaimed, " your only enemies, the only enemies of the Emperor, of the nation, of religion are the Jesuits." Janssen adds: " The facts told a different story."

Father Peter Pázmány figures at this period in a notable fashion. He was a Hungarian from Nagy Várad, also known as Grosswardein. His parents were Calvinists, but at the age of sixteen Peter became a Catholic and entered the Society at Rome, where he was a pupil of such scholars as Bellarmine and Vásquez. He taught in the college of Gratz, which had been founded by the Jesuits in 1573 with theological and philosophical faculties. The Archduke Ferdinand enriched it with new buildings and furnished it with ample revenues, giving it also ecclesiastical supremacy in Carinthia and other estates of the crown. Pázmány became the apostle of his countrymen, both by his

books and his preaching. He was a master in his
native tongue, says Ranke (History of the Popes, IV,
124), and his spiritual and learned work " Kalaus,"
produced an irresistible sensation. Endowed with
a ready and captivating eloquence, he is said to
have personally converted fifty of the most distinguished families, one of which ejected twenty ministers
from their parishes and replaced them by as many
Catholic priests. The government was also swung
into line; the Catholics had the majority in the Diet
of 1625, and an Esterhazy was made Palatine.
Pázmány was offered a bishopric which he refused,
but finally the Pope, yielding to the demand of the
princes and people, appointed him primate and then
made him a cardinal. His " Guide to Catholic Truth "
was the first polemic in the Hungarian language. He
founded a university at Tyrnau which was afterwards
transferred to Buda. The Hungarian College at Rome
was his creation, as was the Pazmaneum in Vienna.
His name has been recently inserted in the Roman
Breviary in connection with the three Hungarian
martyrs, two of whom were Jesuits, Pongracz and
Grodecz, who were put to death in 1619.

Italy exhibited a similar energy from one end to the
other of the Peninsula. Chandlery in his " Fasti
Breviores " (p. 40) tells us that " the first school of
the Society was opened in the Piazza Ara Cœli in 1551,
and soon developed into the famous Roman College.
In 1552 it was removed to a house near the Minerva;
in 1554 to a place near the present site; in 1562 to
the house of Pope Paul IV; and in 1582 to the new
buildings of the Gregorian University." It was in
this college on March 25, 1563, that the Belgian
scholastic, John Leunis, organized the first sodality of
the Blessed Virgin. Fouqueray, however, contests this
claim of the Ara Cœli school, and asserts that the first

college was at Messina, and was begun in 1547, and that St. Ignatius determined to make it the model of all similar establishments. Its rule was based on the methods that prevailed in the colleges of the University of Paris, with changes, however, in its discipline and religious direction. Its plan of studies was the first " Ratio studiorum." It had two sessions of two or three hours each daily; Latin was always employed as the language of the house, but both Hebrew and Greek were taught. Vacation lasted only fifteen days for pupils in humanities and the higher grades; and only eight days or less for those in the lower classes. The students went to confession every month and assisted daily at Mass. Nearly all the cities of the peninsula had called for similar colleges. In what is now Belgium there were thirty-four colleges or schools, an apparently excessive number, but the fact that they were, with two exceptions, day-schools and that small boys were excluded will explain the possibility of managing them with comparatively few professors. Six or seven sufficed for as many hundred pupils. Moreover, something in the way of a foundation to support the school was always required before its establishment.

In 1564 the Roman Seminary was entrusted to the Society; and in 1578 the Roman College. Five years previously, the Collegium Germanicum, after Canisius had presented a memorial to Gregory XIII on the services it was expected to render, obtained a subsidy for a certain number of students. The Bull, dated August, 1573, exhorted the Catholics of the German Empire to provide for a hundred students of philosophy and theology. The Pope gave it the palace of St. Apollinaris, the Convent of St. Sabas and the revenues of St. Stephen on Monte Cœlio. Over and above this, he guaranteed 10,000 crowns out of the revenues of

the Apostolic Treasury. In 1574 it had one hundred
and thirty students and in a few years one hundred and
fifty. The philosophers followed a three years' course,
the theologians four. Between 1573 and 1585 the
Pope disbursed for the Collegium Germanicum alone
about 235,649 crowns — equivalent to about a quarter
of a million dollars. Besides this, as early as 1552
St. Ignatius had obtained from Julius III a Bull
endowing a college for the study of the humanities,
in which young Germans could prepare themselves
for philosophy and theology. In its opening year it
had twenty-five students, and in the following twice as
many. Under Paul IV when the establishment was
in dire want, St. Ignatius supported it by begging, and
he told Cardinal Truchsess that he would sell himself
into slavery rather than forsake his Germans. It was
while engrossed in this work that Ignatius died. His
memory is tenderly cherished in the Collegium Germanicum to this day. When his name is read out in
the Martyrology on July 31, the students all rise, and
with uncovered heads listen reverently to the announcement of the feast of their founder.

CHAPTER III

ENDS OF THE EARTH

Xavier departs for the East — Goa — Around Hindostan — Malacca — The Moluccas — Return to Goa — The Valiant Belgian — Troubles in Goa — Enters Japan — Returns to Goa — Starts for China — Dies off the Coast — Remains brought to Goa — Africa — Congo, Angola, Caffreria, Abyssinia — Brazil, Nobrega, Anchieta, Azevedo — Failure of Rodriguez in Portugal.

WHEN John III of Portugal asked for missionaries to evangelize the colonies which the discoveries of Da Gama and others had won for the crown in the far east, Bobadilla, Rodriguez and Xavier were assigned to the work. Bobadilla's sickness prevented him from going, and then His Majesty judged that he was too generous to his new possessions and not kind enough to the mother country; so it was decided to keep Rodriguez in Portugal, his native land, and send Xavier to the Indies.

Xavier arrived at Lisbon in June, 1540, and waited there eight months for the departure of the vessel, during which time he and Rodriguez effected a complete reformation in the morals of the city. He then began a series of apostolic journeys which were nothing less than stupendous in their character, not only for the distances covered during the eleven years to which they were restricted, but because of the extraordinary and often unseaworthy craft in which he traversed the yet uncharted seas of the East, which were swept by typhoons and infested by pirates, and where there was constant danger of being wrecked on inhospitable coasts and murdered by the savage natives. Three times his ship went to pieces on the rocks, and on one occasion he had to cling to a plank for days while the waves swept over him. Several times he came near being poisoned, and once he had to hide in the bush for a long time to escape the head-hunters of the Moluccas. The distances he traversed can only be appreciated by having an atlas at hand while perusing the story.

Leaving Europe, his course lay along the west coast of Africa, rounding Cape of Good Hope and then making for far away Mozambique. From there he pointed across the Arabian Sea to Goa on the west coast of Hindostan. Shortly afterwards, he continued down the coast to Cochin and Cape Comorin and across to Ceylon, then along the eastern side of the peninsula to the Pearl Fisheries, and back to Goa. Soon after, he is sailing across the Bay of Bengal to distant Malacca, which lies north of Sumatra; from there he penetrates into the Chinese Sea, and skirting Borneo and the Celebes, he arrives at the Molucca Islands, going through them from north to south and back. Returning to Goa, he again makes for Malacca and points north to Japan, passing the Philippines on his way, though it is claimed that he landed at Mindanao. From Japan he returns to Goa and then sets out for China. He reached an island opposite Canton, pined away there for a month or so, as no one dared to carry him over to the coast. He then took his flight to heaven, which was very near.

It was a great day for Lisbon when, on April 7, 1541, which happened to be his birthday, Xavier set sail for India. He was papal nuncio and King John's ambassador to the Emperor of Ethiopia. Nevertheless the princes and potentates whom this poorly clad ambassador met on 'his way must have gazed at him in wonder; for in spite of his honors, he washed and mended his own clothes, and while on shipboard refused the assistance of a servant and scarcely ate any food. The crew were a rascally set, as were most of the sea-rovers of those days; but this extraordinary papal nuncio and ambassador passed his time among them, always bright, approachable and happy, nursing them when they were sick, and gently taking them to task for their ill-spent lives. All day long he was busy with them, and during the night he was scourging himself or praying. By the time the ship reached its destination it was a floating church.

Goa was the capital of Portuguese India. It was not yet the golden Goa of the seventeenth century; but it had churches and chapels and a cathedral, an inchoate college and a bishop and a Franciscan friary. Mingled, however, with the Christian population was a horde of idolaters, Mussulmans, Jews, Arabians, Persians, Hindoos and others, all of them rated as inferior races by the Portuguese who were the hidalgos or fidalgos of Goa, even if they had been cooks and street-sweepers in Lisbon or Oporto. They were now clad in silks and brocades, and wore gold and precious gems in profusion; they delighted in religious displays; but in morality they were more debased than the worst pagans they jostled against in the streets. There were open debauchery, concubinage, polygamy and kindred crimes.

The coming of the papal nuncio was a great event, but he refused all recognition of his official rank. He lived in the hospital, looked after the lepers in their sheds, or the criminals in the jails, taught the children their catechism, and conversed with people of every class and condition. He got the secrets of their conscience; and in five months, Goa, at least in its Christian population, was as decent in its morals as it had formerly been corrupt and depraved. At the end of the peninsula, but beyond Cape Comorin, were the Pearl Fisheries, where lived a degraded caste who had been visited

by the Franciscans and baptized some years before;
but they had been left in their ignorance and vice, and
no one in Goa now ever gave them a thought. Thither
Xavier betook himself with his chalice and vestments
and breviary, but with no provisions for his support.

On his way he passed Salsette, where Rudolph
Aquaviva was martyred in later days; and he saw
Canara and Mangalore and Cananon, where there
was a mission station. He then went to Calicut and
Cranganore and Cape Comorin, where the goddess
Dourga was worshipped, and finally arrived at the Fisheries, where he found a people who were wretchedly
poor, with nothing to cover them but a turban and a
breech-clout, and who lived in huts along the shifting
sands near the cocoanut-trees. With their tiny boats
and rafts they contrived to get a livelihood from the sea,
but they were shunned by the other Hindoos; for
baptism had made them outcasts, and they were also
the helpless victims of the pirates who were constantly
prowling along the coast. Xavier lived in their filthy
houses, talked with them through interpreters, gave
them what instructions they were capable of receiving,
and baptised all who had not yet become Christians.
He remained two years with them, and after getting
Portuguese ships to patrol the Sea, sent other missionaries to replace him when he had built catechumenates
and little churches here and there. Although Xavier
appears to have justified these rapid conversions by
the precedent of 3000 people becoming Christians
after the first sermon of St. Peter, yet Ignatius, while
not blaming his methods, wrote him later that the
instructions should precede and not follow baptism,
and that quality rather than quantity should be the
guide in accessions to the Faith.

Xavier returned thence to Goa, but we find him in
the last days of September, 1545, abandoning India

for a time and going ashore near the Portuguese
settlement on the Straits of Malacca. It was a dangerous post, for it swarmed with Mohammedans. There
were fierce *écumeurs de mer*, or sea-combers, on the
near-by coasts of Sumatra, and on the island of Bitang
the dethroned sultans were waiting for a chance to
expel the Portuguese, while all through the interior
were fierce and unapproachable savage tribes. Besides
all this, the whites who had settled there for trade
were a depraved mob; it is recorded that Xavier spent
three whole days without food hearing their confessions, and passed entire nights praying for their
conversion. In spite of all this accumulation of labor,
he contrived to write a catechism and a prayer-book
in Malay. In 1546 he went further east, past Java
and Flores, and reached the Moluccas after a month
and a half. He was on sociable terms everywhere,
with soldiers and sailors and commandants of posts
as well as cannibals, and made light of every hardship
and danger in his efforts to win souls to God. Up and
down the islands of the archipelago he travelled,
meeting degeneracy of the worst kind at every step.
But he established missionary posts, with the wonderful
result that ten years later, De Beira, whom he sent
there, had forty-seven stations and 3000 Christian
families in these islands. Xavier spent two years
in the Moluccas to prepare the way, and was back
again in Goa in 1548.

During his absence, a number of missionaries,
making in all six priests and nine coadjutor brothers,
had been sent from Portugal. With them were a
dozen Dominicans. Among the Jesuits were Fernandes
and Cosmo de Torres, who, later on, were to be along
with Xavier the founders of the great mission of
Japan. There came also Antonio Gomes, a distinguished
student of Coimbra, a master of arts, a doctor of

canon law, and a notable orator. But, except as an orator, he was not to have the success in Goa that he had won in Lisbon. Likewise in the party was Gaspard Baertz, a Fleming, who had had a varied career, as a master of arts at Louvain, a soldier in the army of Charles V, a hermit at Montserrat, a Jesuit in Coimbra, and now a missionary in India. It was Baertz's capacity for work that prompted Xavier's famous petition: "Da mihi fortes Belgas" (Give me sturdy Belgians). Criminali, the first of the Society to be martyred in the East, had arrived previously, as had Lancilotti, a consumptive, who seemed to be particularly active in writing letters to Rome complaining of Xavier's frequent absences from Goa.

Gomes was appointed rector of the nondescript college, which belonged to the Bishop of Goa, and which had been partly managed by Lancilotti up to that time. The new superior immediately proceeded to turn everything upside down, and his hard, authoritative methods of government immediately caused discontent. According to Lancilotti, he was utterly unused to the ways of the Society in dealing not only with the members of the community but with the native students. His idea was to make the college another Coimbra — a great educational institution with branches at Cochin, Bacaim and elsewhere. However, the plan was not altogether his conception. Something of that kind had been projected for India in connection with a great educational movement which was agitating Portugal at that time. In writing to Lisbon and Rome about this matter, Xavier incidentally reveals his ideas on the question of a native priesthood. He required for it several previous generations of respectable Christian parents. The division of castes in India also created a difficulty, for the reason that a priest taken from one caste was never allowed intercourse with those who belonged to another; and, finally, he pointed out that for a Portuguese to confess to a native was unthinkable.

Meanwhile, although domestic matters were not as satisfactory as they might have been, Xavier was planning his departure for Japan. He first visited several posts and settled the difficulties that presented themselves. Gomes was his chief source of worry, and there is no doubt that he would have been removed from his post as rector on account of the dissatisfaction he had caused, had it not been for his wonderful popularity in the city as a preacher. Just then a change might have caused an outbreak among the people and a rupture with the bishop. Xavier contented himself, therefore, with restricting the activities of Gomes to temporal matters; and assigned to Cypriano the care of the spiritual interests of the community. He could have done nothing more, even if he had remained at Goa.

These repeated absences of Francis Xavier from Goa have often been urged against him as revealing a serious defect in his character; a yielding to what was called "Basque restlessness," which prompted those who had that strain in their blood to be continually on the road in quest of new scenes and romantic adventures. The real reason seems to have been his despair of doing anything in Goa, with its jumble of Moslems and pagans and corrupt Portuguese, and its string of military posts where every little political commandant was perpetually interfering with missionary efforts. It could never be the centre of a great missionary movement. "I want to be," he said, "where there are no Moslems or Jews. Give me out and out pagans, people who are anxious to know something new about nature and God, and I am determined to find them." He had heard something about Japan, as verifying these conditions; and, though he had travelled much already and was aware of the complaints about himself, he resolved to go further still; so, taking with him de Torres and Fernandes, besides a Japanese convert, Xaca, and two servants, he set his face towards the Land of the Rising Sun. He was then forty-three years of age.

He was at Malacca from May 31 to June 24, 1549, and found that the missions he had established there were doing remarkably well, as were the others in the Moluccas. The latter, however, he did not visit. He started for Japan in a miserable Chinese junk, three other associates having joined him meantime,— a Portuguese, a Chinaman, and a Malay. It took two months before he saw the volcanoes of Kiu Siu on the horizon, and it was only on August 15, 1549, that he went ashore at Kagoshima, the native city of his Japanese companion. The day was an auspicious one. It was the anniversary of his first vows at Montmartre.

Xavier began studying the language of the country and remained for a time more or less in seclusion; with the help of Xaca, or Paul as they called him, a short statement of the Christian Faith was drawn up. With that equipment, after securing the necessary permission, he, Fernandes and Xaca started on their first preaching excursion. Their appearance excited the liveliest curiosity. In the eyes of the people Xavier was merely a new kind of bonze, and they listened to him with the greatest attention. The programme adopted was first for Xaca to summon the crowd and address them, then Xavier would read his paper. They were always ready to stop at any part of the road or for any assembly and repeat their message. Soon their work rose above mere street preaching. They were invited to the houses of the great who listened more or less out of curiosity or

for a new sensation. When they had accomplished
all they could in one place, they went to another,
always on foot, in wretched attire, through cities and
over snow-clad mountains, always, however, with the
aim of getting to the capital of the empire, both to
see the emperor and to reach the great university,
about which they had heard before they set out for
Japan. Naturally, the teaching of this new religion
brought Xavier into conflict with the bonzes, who
were a grossly immoral set of men, though outwardly
pretending to great austerity. The people, however, understood them thoroughly and were more
than gratified when the hypocrites were held up to
ridicule.

By this time he discovered his mistake in going
about in the apparel of a beggar, and henceforward
he determined to make a proper use of his position
as envoy of the Governor of the Indies and of the
Bishop of Goa. He, therefore, presented himself to
the Daimyo of Yamaguchi in his best attire, with
his credentials engrossed on parchment and an abundant
supply of rich presents — an arquebus, a spinnet,
mirrors, crystal goblets, books, spectacles, a Portuguese
dress, a clock and other objects. Conditions changed
immediately. The Daimyo gave him a handsome
sum of money, besides full liberty to preach wherever
he went. He lived at the house of a Japanese nobleman at Yamaguchi, and crowds listened to him in
respectful silence as he spoke of creation and the
soul — subjects of which the Japanese knew nothing.
His learning was praised by every one, and his virtue
admired; soon several notable conversions followed.
After remaining at this place for six months, Xavier
went to the capital, Meaco, the present Kioto, but
apparently he made little or no impression there.
Then news came from Goa which compelled him to

return to India. So leaving his faithful friends, de
Torres and Fernandes, to carry on the work which
was so auspiciously begun, he started for Goa, somewhere between 15 and 20 November, 1551. He had
achieved his purpose — he had opened Japan to
Christianity.

On the ship that carried him back to Goa, Xavier
made arrangements with a merchant named Pereira
to organize an expedition to enter China. Pereira
was to go as a regularly accredited ambassador of
the Viceroy of the Indies, while Xavier would get
permission from the emperor to preach the Gospel,
and ask for the repeal of the laws hostile to foreigners
and, among other things, for the liberation of the
Portuguese prisoners — dreams which were never
realized, but which reveal the buoyant and almost
boyish hopefulness of Xavier's character. On his
way back he heard of the tragic death of Criminali
at Cape Comorin — the first Jesuit to shed his blood
in India. It occurred in one of the uprisings of the
Badages savages against the Portuguese. Later a
brother was killed at the same place. Success, however, had attended the labors of Criminali and his
associates; for according to Polanco and an incomplete
government census, there were between 50,000 and
60,000 Christians at that point in 1552. It was well
on in February of that year when Xavier stepped
ashore at Goa.

During his absence, the missions had all achieved
a remarkable success. Among them was a new post
at Ormuz off the coast of Arabia where Mussulmans
of Persia, Jews from far and near, even from Portugal,
Indian Brahmans and Jains, Parsees, Turks, Arabians,
Christians of Armenia and Ethiopia, apostate Italians,
Greeks, Russians and a Portuguese garrison met for
commerce, and for the accompanying debauchery of

6

such Oriental centres. The Belgian missionary, Baertz, had transformed the place. All this was satisfactory; but the college at Goa where Gomes presided was in disorder. Before that imprudent man could have possibly become acquainted with the ways of the new country, he had let himself be duped by one of the native chiefs who pretended to be a convert, but who was in reality a black-hearted traitor. He had also nullified the authority of his associate in the government of the college, and had been acting almost as superior of the entire mission. Among the people he had caused intense irritation by changing the traditional church services; he had dismissed the students of the college and put novices in their stead; he had appropriated a church belonging to a confraternity and, in consequence, had got both himself and the Society embroiled with the governor-general. But in spite of all this, it was still difficult to depose him on account of his popularity and because he was looked upon as an angel by the bishop. Unfortunately, Gomes refused to be convinced of his shortcomings and even disputed the right of his successor, who had already been appointed. Hence popular though he was, he was given his dimissorial letters. He appealed to Rome, and on his way thither was lost at sea. It is rather startling to find that Francis Xavier not only used this power of dismissal himself but gave it even to local superiors (Monumenta Xaveriana, 715-18). Possibly it was because of the difficulty of communication with Rome that this method was adopted, but it would be inconceivable nowadays.

When all this was settled, Xavier appointed Baertz, vice-provincial, and, on April 17, 1552, departed for China. On arriving at Cochin, he heard that one of the missionaries had been badly treated by the natives, that the mission was in dire want, and that

Lancilotti was in sore straits at Coulam. But all
that did not stop him. He merely wrote to Baertz to
remedy these evils, and then continued on his journey.
Of course it would be impossible to judge such
missionary methods from a mere human standpoint.
For Xavier's extraordinary thaumaturgic powers, his
gifts of prayer and prophecy easily explain how he
could not only convert multitudes to the Faith, in
an incredibly short space of time, but keep them firm
and constant in the practice of their religion, long
after he had entrusted the care of them to others.
The memory of his marvellous works, which are
bewildering in their number, would necessarily remain
in the minds of his neophytes, while the graces which
his prayers had gained for them would give them a
more intelligent comprehension of the doctrines he
had taught them than if they had been the converts
of an ordinary missionary.

Up to the time of his departure for China his apostolic
career had been like a triumphal progress. He was
now to meet disaster and defeat, but it is that dark
moment of his life which throws about him the greatest
lustre. His friend, Pereira, had been duly accredited
as ambassador of the viceroy and had invested the
largest part of his fortune in the vessel that was to
convey Xavier as papal nuncio to the court of the
Emperor of China. It was the only way to enter
the country and to reach the imperial court; but the
Governor of Malacca defeated the whole scheme.
He was a gambler and a debauchee, and wanted the
post of ambassador for himself to pay his debts.
Hence, in spite of the entreaties of Xavier and the
menace of the wrath both of the king and the Pope
he confiscated the cargo and left the two envoys
stranded, just when success was assured. The result
was that Pereira had to remain in hiding, while Xavier

shook the dust from his feet, not figuratively but actually, so as to strike terror into the heart of Don Alvaro. He embarked on his own ship, " The Holy Cross," which was now converted into a merchantman and packed with people. In that unseemly fashion he started for China.

A landing was made on the island of Sancian which lay about thirty miles from the mainland, on a line with the city of Canton. Trading was allowed at that distance, but any nearer approach to the coast meant imprisonment and death. That island was Xavier's last dwelling-place on earth; there he remained for months gazing towards the land he was never to enter. There were several ships in the offing, but he was shunned by the crews, for fear of the terrible Alvaro who was officially " master of the seas " and could punish them for being friends of his enemy. At least the Chinese traders who had come over to the island were approachable, and Xavier succeeded in inducing one of them for a money consideration to drop him somewhere on the coast — he did not care where. But no sooner was the bargain known than there was an uproar among the crews of the ships. If he were caught, they would all be massacred, and so he agreed to wait till they had sailed away.

Slowly the weeks passed, as one by one the vessels hoisted sail and disappeared over the horizon. Xavier's strength was failing fast, and he lay stretched out uncared for, under a miserable shed which had been built on the shore to protect him from the inclemency of the weather. With his gaze ever turned towards the coast which he had so longed to reach, he breathed his last on December 2, 1552, with the words on his lips: " In thee, O Lord, have I hoped, let me not be confounded forever." He was but forty-six years old; eleven years and seven months had elapsed since he sailed down the Tagus for the Unknown East. Only four people were courageous enough to give him the decencies of a burial, the others looked on from the gunwales of the ship, while his grave was being dug on shore. His body was placed in a box of quicklime so that the flesh might be quickly consumed, and the bones carried back to Goa; having lowered it into a grave which was made in a little hillock above the sea, the small party withdrew.

Two months later, when the ship was about to leave, the box was opened, and to the amazement and almost the terror of all, not only was the flesh found to be intact, but the face wore a ruddy hue, and blood flowed from an incision made below the knee. It was a triumphant ship's-crew that now carried the precious freight to Malacca. They were no longer afraid, for their ship was a sanctuary guarding the relics of a saint. The ceremonies were impressive when they reached Malacca, though Don Alvaro scorned even to notice them; but when the vessel entered the harbor of Goa the splendor of the reception accorded the dead hero surpassed all that the Orient had ever seen. Xavier rests there yet, and his body is still incorrupt. It was a proper ending of the earthly career of the greatest missionary the world has known since the days of the Apostles. In 1662 he was canonized with his friend Ignatius by Pope Alexander VII.

In striking contrast with all this glory is the failure of every one of the missions on the Dark Continent of Africa. Between 1547 and 1561 the Congo and Angola had been visited, but no permanent post had been established. In Caffreria, Father Silveira and fifty of his neophytes were martyred. In 1555 Nunhes, Carnero and Oviedo were sent to Abyssinia, the first as patriarch, the others as suffragans. The patriarchate subsequently passed to Oviedo, who was the only one

to reach the country. He was well received by the
Negus, Asnaf, and permitted to exercise his ministry,
but, in 1559 the king was slain in battle, and his
successor drove the missionary and his little flock
out into the desert of Adowa, a region made famous,
in our own times, by the disastrous defeat of the
Italian troops when they met Menelik and his Abys-
sinians. Oviedo continued to live there during twenty
years of incredible suffering. In 1624 Paez, one of
his successors, succeeded in converting the Emperor
Socimos, and in getting Abyssinia to abjure its Euty-
chianism, but when Basilides mounted the throne in
1632 he handed over the Jesuits to the axe of the
executioner. After that, Abyssinia remained closed to
Christianity until 1702.

The most curious of these efforts to win Africa to
the Faith occurred as early as 1561, when Pius IV,
at the request of the Patriarch of Alexandria, sent
a delgation to the Copts, in an endeavour to re-unite
them to the Church. Among the papal representatives
was a Jesuit named Eliano, who was a converted
Jew. He had been brought up as a strict Hebrew,
and when his brother became a Christian he had
hurried off to Venice to recall him to Judaism. The
unexpected happened. Eliano himself became a
Christian and, later, a Jesuit. As he had displayed
great activity in evangelizing his former co-religionists,
he was thought to be available in this instance, but unfortunately on arriving at Alexandria, he was recognized
by the Jews, who were numerous and influential there,
and a wild riot ensued, the voice that shrieked the loud-
est for his blood being that of his own mother. It was
with great difficulty that his friends prevented his
murder. He returned to Europe and his last days
were spent in Rome where he was the friendly rival
of the great Cardinal Farnese in caring for the poor

of the city. They died on the same day, and their tombs were regarded as shrines by their sorrowing beneficiaries.

In the western world, the first Jesuit missionary work was begun in the Portuguese possession of Brazil. After Cabral had accidentally discovered the continent in 1500, a number of Portuguese nobles established important colonies along the coast; and when subsequently some French Calvinists, under Villegagnon, attempted a settlement on the Rio Janeiro, Thomas da Sousa was commissioned by the king to unite the scattered Portuguese settlements and drive out the French intruders. He chose the Bay of All Saints as his central position, and there built the city of San Salvador. Fortifications were thrown up; a cathedral, a governor's palace and a custom house were erected, and a great number of houses were built for the settlers. Unlike France and England, Spain and Portugal lavished money on their colonies. With da Sousa were six Jesuit missionaries, chief of whom was the great Nobrega. They were given an extensive tract of land some distance from San Salvador, and there in course of time the city of São Paolo arose. There was plenty to do with the degenerate whites in the various settlements, but the savages presented the greatest problem. They were cannibals of an advanced type, and no food delighted them more than human flesh. To make matters worse, the white settlers encouraged them in their horrible practices, probably in the hope, that they would soon eat each other up.

Nobrega determined to put an end to these abominations, he went among the Indians, spoke to them kindly, healed their bodily ailments, defended them against the whites, and was soon regarded by these wild creatures as their friend and benefactor. At

last, concluding that the time had come for a master
stroke, he one day walked straight into a group of
women who were preparing a mangled body for the
fire, and with the help of his companions carried off
the corpse. This was sweeping away in an instant
all their past traditions, and as a consequence the whole
tribe rose in fury and swarmed around the walls of
the city determined to make an end of the whites.
But Sousa called out his troops, and, whether the
Indians were frightened by the cannon or mollified
by the kind words of the governor, the result was that
they withdrew and promised to stop eating human
flesh. This audacious act had the additional effect
of exciting the anger of the colonists against Nobrega
and his associates. The point had been made, however,
that cannibalism was henceforth a punishable offence
and great results followed. Tribe after tribe accepted
the missionaries and were converted to Christianity.
But it was very hard to keep them steady in their
faith. A pestilence or a dearth of food was enough
to make them fall into their old habits; and they were
moreover, easily swayed by the half-breeds who,
time and time again, induced them to rise against
the whites. But da Sousa was an exceptional man,
and had the situation well in hand. He pursued the
Indians to their haunts, and, as his punitive expeditions
were nearly always headed by a priest with his uplifted
cross he often brought them to terms without the
shedding of blood.

Another obstacle in this work of subjugation was
found in the remnants of Villegagnon's old French
garrison. At one time they had succeeded in uniting
all the savages of the country in a league to exterminate
the Portuguese. Villegagnon's supposedly impreg-
nable fort was taken and battle after battle was won
by the Portuguese, but the war seemed never to end.

At last Nobrega took the matter in his own hands.
"Let me go," he said, "to see if I cannot arrange
terms of peace with the enemy." It was a perilous
undertaking, for it might mean that in a few days
his body would be roasting over a fire in the forest,
in preparation for a savage banquet. But that did
not deter him. He and his fellow-missionary Anchieta
set out and found the Indians wild with rage against
the whites. Plea after plea was made, but in vain.
At last, he got them to make some concession, and
then returned to explain matters to the governor,
leaving Anchieta alone with the Indians. They did
him no harm, however; on the contrary, he won their
hearts by his kindness and amazed them by his long
prayers, his purity of life, his prophecies and his
miraculous powers. Month after month went by and
yet there was no news from Nobrega. Finally the
governor, accepting the conditions insisted on by the
Indians, yielded, and peace was made.

It is interesting to learn that the lonely man who
had stayed all this while in the forest, José Anchieta,
was a perfect master of Latin, Castilian and Portuguese;
besides being somewhat skilled in medicine, he was
an excellent poet and even a notable dramatist. He
composed grammars and dictionaries of the native
language, after he returned to where pen and ink
were available; and it is said he put into print a long
poem which he had meditated and memorized during
his six terrible months of captivity. He died in 1597;
but before departing for heaven, he saw the little
band of six Jesuits who had landed with Nobrega
increased to one hundred and twenty, and when his
career ended one hundred more rushed from Portugal
to fill the gap.

As for Nobrega, the day before he died, he went
around to call on his friends. "Where are you going?"

they asked him. " Home to my own country," he answered, and on the morrow they were kneeling around his coffin. Southey says that " so well had Nobrega and Anchieta trained their disciples that in the course of half a century, all the nations along the coast of Brazil, as far as the Portuguese settlements extended, were collected in villages under their superintendence " (History of Brazil, x, 310). " Nobrega died at the close of the sixteenth century," says Ranke, " and in the beginning of the seventeenth we find the proud edifice of the Catholic Church completely reared in South America. There were five archbishoprics, twenty-seven bishoprics, four hundred monasteries and innumerable parish churches." Of course, with due regard to Ranke, all that was not the work of Jesuits, but men of his kind see " Jesuit " in everything. It may be said, however, that they contributed in no small degree to bring about this result.

In 1570 Azevedo conducted thirty-nine Jesuits from Madeira to Brazil. Simultaneously, thirty more in two other ships set sail from Lisbon for the same destination. But the day after Azevedo's party had left Madeira, the famous Huguenot pirate, Jaques Soria, swooped down upon them, hacked them to pieces on the deck, and then threw the mangled remains to the sharks. The amazing Southey narrates this event as follows: " He did by the Jesuits as they would have done by him and all their sect:— put them to death." When the news reached Madeira, the brethren of the martyrs sang a Te Deum which Southey informs us, " was as much the language of policy as of fanaticism." Four days later, one English and four French cruisers which Southey fails to tell us were commanded by the Huguenot Capdeville, caught the other missionaries and did their work so effectually, that of the sixty-nine splendid men whom

Azevedo started out with, only one arrived in Brazil. The struggle did not end with the massacre. Sixty years afterwards the same enemy attacked the missions of Pernambuco in Brazil where, " one hundred and fifty tribes "— a Protestant annalist calls them " hordes "— had been brought into alliance with the Portuguese, and were rapidly making progress both in Christianity and civilization; on Good Friday in the year 1633 the freebooters, passing at midnight through the smoking ruins of Olinda, attacked Garassu in the early morning, while the inhabitants were assembled at Mass, with the result, says Southey, that " the men who came their way were slaughtered, the women were stripped, and the plunderers with cruelty tore away ear-rings through the ear-flap, and cut off fingers for the sake of the rings that were upon them. They then plundered and burnt the town."

Similar heroism was shown in other parts of the world about this time. Thus in 1549 Ribeira was poisoned at Amboina; a like fate overtook Gonzales in 1551 at Bazaim, India; in 1555 three Jesuits were wrecked on a desert island while on their way to the East, and died of starvation; in 1573, Alvares, the visitor of Japan and four companions were lost at sea; and in 1575 another Jesuit died at Angola in Africa after fourteen years' cruel imprisonment.

Over all this splendor, however, there rests a shadow. Simon Rodriguez, who was so to speak the creator of all this apostolic enthusiasm, came very near being expelled from the Society. He was the idol of Portugal and the intimate friend and adviser of King John III, who was untiring in promoting missionary enterprise in the vast regions over which he held sway, both in the Eastern and Western world. This association, however, involved frequent visits to the court, and the attractions of the work soon grew on Rodriguez,

though with his characteristic unsteadiness he was
writing to Xavier and others to say that he was longing
to go out to the missions, a longing he never gratified.
Moreover, his judgment in the choice of missionaries
was of the worst.   Untrained novices were sent out
in great numbers and were naturally found unfit for
the work with the result that they had to return to
Europe.   Meantime another influence was effacing the
real spirit of the Society from the soul of this chosen
man whom Ignatius himself had trained.   A craze
for bodily mortifications had swept over Portugal,
and Brou in his " Vie de St. François Xavier " tells us:
that it was not uncommon to see eight or ten thousand
flagellants scourging themselves as they walked processionally through the streets of Lisbon.   The Jesuits
there were naturally affected by the movement, with
the result that although intense fervor was displayed
in the practice of this virtue, domestic discipline
suffered.   The supreme fact that obedience was the
characteristic trait of the Society had never been
thoroughly appreciated or understood by Simon Rodriguez, although he was one of the first companions
of St. Ignatius.

Astrain in his " Historia de la Compañía de Jesús en
la Asistencia de España ", does not mince matters on
this point (I, xix).   Indeed, the provincialship of
Rodriguez in Portugal almost brought about a tragedy
in the history of the Society.   Yielding to the popular
craze for public penances, his subjects paid little
attention to mortification of the will, with the result
that the defections from the Society in that country,
both in number and quality, amounted to a public
scandal.   Finally, the removal of Rodriguez became
imperative, but, unfortunately, his successor, Father
Miró, was deplorably lacking in the very elements of
prudence.   Disregarding the advice of Francis Borgia

and of the official visitor, de Torres, who were sent with him as advisers, he went alone into Portugal and abruptly removed Rodriguez from his post. As Rodriguez was almost adored then by the people of Portugal and was very much admired and beloved by King John III and by the whole royal family, they should have been first approached and the reason of the change explained. To pass by such devoted friends who had lavished favors on the Society and who could do so much harm, if alienated, was not only highly impolitic but grossly discourteous. Anyone else but John III might well not only have driven them from Portugal but have withdrawn them from Brazil and the Indies, with the result that the Society would probably never have had an Anchieta or a Francis Xavier. Happily such a calamity was averted. Miró's subsequent administration was in keeping with his initial act, and when at last the visitor arrived and restored normal conditions in the province no less than one hundred and thirty-seven members of the province had either left the Society or had to be dismissed.

Rodriguez was summoned to Rome and might have been pardoned immediately had he avowed his fault, but he demanded a canonical trial. Several grave fathers were, therefore, appointed and their sentence was extremely severe, but Ignatius made them reconsider it again and again, and make it milder. He even modified their final verdict. Rodriguez never went back again to Portugal in an official capacity.

This humiliating episode is somewhat slurred over by Crétineau-Joly, but the Jesuit historians like Jouvancy, Brou, Astrain, Valignano, Pollen make no attempt to conceal or palliate it. The failure of Rodriguez only illustrates the difficulty that St. Ignatius had in making his followers grasp the fundamental idea of the Society.

Paulsen, the German Protestant historian, is shocked to find that in Jesuits, generally, there exists " something of the silent but incessant action of the powers of nature. Without passion, without appeals to war, without agitation, without intemperate zeal, they never cease to advance, and are scarcely ever compelled to take a step backward. Sureness, prudence and forethought characterize each of their movements. As a matter of fact, these are not lovable qualities," he says, "for whoever acts without some human weakness is never amiable." The " step backward " made by Rodriguez, in this instance, ought to satisfy Paulsen's requirements for that amiability which, according to him, is associated with " human weakness." One need not be reminded that it is a curious psychology that can find amiability in a disease or a deformity. The amiability is in the person who puts up with it, not in the offender. Henri Joly in his " Psychologie des Saints," furnishes another example of this disregard of facts which so often affects the vision of a man in pursuit of a theory. To prove the marvellous power which Ignatius exerted over men, he tells us that when Rodriguez was summoned to Rome " the only sentiment in his mind was that of almost delirious joy, at again seeing the companion of his youth, his friend and master." The facts narrated above would imply that there was anything but delirious joy in the mind of Rodriguez before, during or after his trial, and the facts also show that sometimes it takes more than the marvellous power of a St. Ignatius to control even a holy man under the influence of 'a passion or a delusion.

This incident also disposes of the hallucination that Jesuits are all run in the same mould and hence easily recognizable as members of the Order. This is far from being the case. It is true that as the Society is governed to a certain extent on military principles, cheerful and prompt obedience is its characteristic. The General is supreme commander and is in touch with every member of the organization; he can tell in a moment where the individual is, what he is doing and what are his good qualities and defects.   He can assign him to any country or any post; refusal to obey is absolutely out of the question.   Such is the special trait of the Society, but apart from this, it is an aggregation of as disparate units as can possibly be imagined. Men of all races, conditions, dispositions, aspirations and attainments, Americans, English, French, Italian, Spanish, Syrians, Hungarians, Hindoos, Chinese, Japanese, Malgache, and others live in the same house, follow the same rules, and maintain absolute peace with each other.   All infractions of brotherly love are frowned upon and severely punished, and continued dissension or rebellion means expulsion.   These men, from the highest to the lowest, do not shirk danger — like genuine soldiers they covet it; nor are they depressed by the repeated exiles, expulsions, spoliations and persecutions, to which the Society has been always subject.   Taught by experience of the past, they know that they will emerge from the struggle stronger and better than before and will win further distinction in the battle for God.

CHAPTER IV

CONSPICUOUS PERSONAGES

Ignatius — Laínez — Borgia — Bellarmine — Toletus — Lessius — Maldonado — Suárez — Lugo — Valencia — Petavius — Warsewicz — Nicolai — Possevin — Vieira — Mercurian.

St. Ignatius died on July 31, 1556. During his brief fifteen years as General, he had seen some of his sons distinguishing themselves in one of the greatest councils of the Church; others turning back the tide of Protestantism in Germany and elsewhere; others again, winning a large part of the Orient to the Faith; and still others reorganizing Catholic education throughout regenerated Europe, on a scale that was bewildering both in the multitude of the schools they established and the splendor of their success. Great saints were being produced in the Society and also outside of it through its ministrations. Meantime, its development had been so great that the little group of men which had gathered around him a few years before had grown to a thousand, with a hundred establishments in every part of the world.

Magnificent as was this achievement he did not allow it to reflect any glory upon himself personally. On the contrary, he withdrew more and more from public observation, and devoted to the establishment of his multiplied and usual charities, among the humblest and most abandoned classes of the city of Rome, what time was left him from the absorbing care of directing, advising, exhorting and inspiring his sons who were scattered over the earth in ever changing and dangerous situations. The palaces of the great rarely, if ever, saw him, and he was the most positive and persistent antithesis of what he is so commonly accused of being: a schemer, a plotter, a politician, a poisoner of public morality and the like.   Nor was he seeking to exercise a dominating influence either in the Church or State, as he is calumniously charged with doing. The glory of God and the advancement of the spiritual kingdom on earth was his only thought, and so far was he from imagining that the Society was an essential factor in the Church's organization that he did not hesitate to say that if it were utterly destroyed, or as he expressed it, " if it were to dissolve like salt in water," a quarter of an hour's recollection in God would have been sufficient to console him and restore peace to his soul, provided the disaster had not been brought about by his fault.

He was not, as he has often been charged with being, stern, severe, arbitrary, harsh, tyrannical; on the contrary, his manner was most winning and attractive. He was fond of flowers; music had the power of making him forget the greatest bodily pain, and the stars at night filled his soul with rapturous delight.   He would listen with infinite patience to the humblest and youngest person, and every measure of importance before being put into execution was submitted to discussion by all who had any concern in it.   He would show intense and outspoken indignation, it is true, at flagrant faults and offences, especially if committed by those who were in authority in the Society; his wrath, however, was vented not against the culprit, but against the fault.   Moreover, while reprehending, he kept his feelings under absolute control.   Indeed, his longanimity in the cases both of Rodriguez and Boba- dilla is astounding, and it is very doubtful if St. Francis Xavier, whom he wanted to be his successor, would have been as tolerant or as gentle.   In his directions for works to be undertaken he was not meticulous nor

7

minute, but left the widest possible margin for personal initiative; nor would he tolerate an obedience that was prompted by servile fear. He continually insisted that the only motive of action in the Society was love of God and the neighbor.

The gentle Lionel Johnson, poet though he was, gives us a fairly accurate appreciation of the character of Saint Ignatius. " In the Saints of Spain," he says, " there is frequently prominent the feature of chivalry. Even the great Saint James, apostle and Patriarch of Spain, appears in Spanish tradition and to Spanish imagination as an *hidalgo*, a knight in gleaming mail who spurs his white war horse against the Moor. And of none among them is this more true than of the founder of the Society of Jesus. Cardinal Newman, describing him in his most famous sermon, finds no phrase more fitting than ' the princely patriarch, St. Ignatius, the Saint George of the modern world with his chivalrous lance run through his writhing foe.' He was ever a fighter, a captain-general of men, indomitable, daunt-less. The secret of his character lies in his will; in its disciplined strength; its unfailing practicality; its singleness and its power upon other wills. It was hardly a Francisan sweetness that won to him his followers who from the famous six at Montmartre grew so swiftly into a great band; it was not supremacy of intellect or of utterance; it was not even the witness of his intense devotion and self-denial. It was his unequalled precision and tenacity of purpose; it was his will and its method. But we can detect no trace of that proud personal ambition and imperiousness often ascribed to him. He simply had learned a way of life that was profitable to religion which was all in all to him, and he could not be lukewarm in its service. *Noblesse oblige*, and a Christian holds a patent from the King of kings. The Jesuit A. M. D. G. was his ruling principle. The former heroic soldier of Spain was still a soldier, a swordsman, a strategist, but in a holy war. His eyes were always turned towards the battle; but he was far from forbidding, harsh, grim. He was tender and stern and like Dante kept his thoughts fixed on the mysteries of good and evil."

His death was in keeping with his life. There was no show, no ostentation, nothing " dramatic " about it, as Henri Joly imagines in his " Psychologie des Saints." There was no solemn gathering of his sons about his bedside, no parting instruction or benediction, as one would have expected from such a remarkable man who had established a religious order upon which the eyes of the world were fixed. He was quite aware that his last hour had come, and he simply told Polanco, his secretary, to go and ask for the Pope's blessing. As the physicians had not said positively that there was any immediate danger, Polanco inquired if he might defer doing so for the moment, as there was something very urgent to be attended to; whereupon the dying Saint made answer: " I would prefer that you should go now, but do as seems best." These were his last words. He left no will and no instructions, and what is, at first, incomprehensible, he did not even ask for Extreme Unction — possibly because he was aware that the physicians disagreed about the seriousness of his malady, and he was unwilling to discredit any of them; possibly, also, he did so in order to illustrate the rule that he laid down for his sons " to show absolute obedience in time of sickness to those who have care of the body." When at last they saw that he was actually dying someone ran for the holy oils, but Ignatius was already in his agony.

For one reason or another, he had not designated the vicar, who, according to the Constitution, was to govern the Society, until a General was regularly elected.   Hence, as the condition of the times prevented the assembling of the professed from the various countries of Europe, the fathers who were in Rome elected Laínez.   He, therefore, summoned the congregation for Easter, 1557, but it happened just then that Philip II and the Pope were at odds with each other, and no Spaniard was allowed to go to Rome.   Because of that, Borgia, Araoz and others sent in a petition for the congregation to meet at Barcelona.   This angered the Pope, and he asked Laínez, who put the case before him: " Do you want to join the schism of that heretic Philip?"   Nevertheless, when the papal nuncio at Madrid supported the request of the Spanish Jesuits, his holiness relented somewhat, and said he would think of it.

The situation was critical enough with a Pope who was none too friendly, when something very disedifying and embarrassing occurred.   The irrepressible Bobadilla who had not only voted for the election of Laínez as vicar, but had served under him for a year, suddenly discovered that the whole previous proceeding was invalid, and he pretended, that, because St. Ignatius had failed to name a vicar, the government of the Society devolved on the general body of the professed. The matter was discussed by the Fathers and he was overruled, but he still persisted and demanded the decision of Carpi, the cardinal protector of the Society. When that official heard the case, he decided against Bobadilla who forthwith appealed to the Pope.   This time the Cardinal assigned to investigate was no other than the future St. Pius V.   He took on the situation at a glance and dismissed Bobadilla almost with contempt.   There was another offender, Cogordan, who does not appear to have objected to Laínez personally but who sent a written communication to his holiness saying that Laínez and some others really wanted to

go to Spain, so as to be free from Roman control.
This so incensed the Pope that Laínez, though greatly
admired by Paul IV, obtained an audience only with
the greatest difficulty, and was then ordered to hand
over the Constitutions for examination. Fortunately,
the same holy Inquisitor was sent, and Cogordan never
forgot the lesson he received on that occasion for daring
to suggest such a thing about Laínez.   In the meantime,
Philip had allowed the Spanish Jesuits to go to Rome,
and Laínez was elected General on July 2, 1558. As
has been said in speaking of Rodriguez, this incident
is another illustration of the tremendous difficulty of
the task St. Ignatius undertook when he gathered
around him those unusually brilliant men, who were
accustomed to take part in the diets of the Empire,
to be counsellors of princes and kings and even popes.
He proposed to make them all, as he said " think the
same thing according to the Apostle." He succeeded
ultimately.

The splendid work performed by Laínez at the
Council of Trent had naturally made him a prominent
figure in the Church at that time. Personally, also
he was most acceptable to the reigning Pontiff, Paul IV;
nevertheless, owing to outside pressure, there was
imminent danger on several occasions of serious
changes being made in the Constitutions of the Society.
The Pope had been dissuaded from urging most of
them, but he refused to be satisfied on one point,
namely the recitation of the Divine Office. He insisted
that it must be sung in choir, as was the rule in other
religious orders. Laínez had to yield, and for a time
the Society conformed to the decision, but the Pope
soon died, and in the course of a year, his successor,
Pius IV, declared the order to be merely the personal
wish of his predecessor and not a decree of the Holy
See.

During this generalate there were serious troubles in various parts of Europe. Thus, in Spain, when Charles V withdrew into the solitude of Yuste he was very anxious to have as a companion in retirement his friend of many years, Francis Borgia. It was hard to oppose the expressed wish of such a potentate as Charles, but Laínez succeeded, and Borgia continued to exercise his great influence in Spain to protect his brethren in the storm which was then raging against them. There were troubles, also, throughout Italy. A veritable persecution had started in Venice; an attempt was made to alienate St. Charles Borromeo in Milan; in Palermo, the rector of the college was murdered. The General himself had to go to France to face the enemies of the Faith at the famous Colloquy of Poissy; Canisius was continuing his hard fight in Germany; there were the martyrdoms of two Jesuits in India where, as in Brazil, the members of the Society were displaying the sublimest heroism in the persecution of their perilous missionary work.

Laínez died in 1565, and was succeeded by Francis Borgia, who for many years had been the most conspicuous grandee of Spain. He was Marquis of Lombay, Duke of Gandia, and for three years had filled the office of Viceroy of Catalonia. His intimacy with the Emperor Charles V, apart from his great personal qualities, naturally resulted in having every honor showered upon him. Astrain, in his history of the Society in Spain, notes the difference in the point of view from which the Borgia family is regarded by Spaniards and by other mortals. The former always think of the saintly Francis, the latter see only Alexander VI. It is not surprising, however, for it is one of the weaknesses of humanity to exult in its glories and to be blind to its defects. Francis Borgia was the great-grandson of Alexander on the paternal,

and of King Ferdinand on the maternal, side; there
are, however, bar sinisters on both descents that are
not pleasant to contemplate, and Suau says, " he was
unfortunate in his ancestry."

Born on October 28, 1510, Borgia began his studies
at Saragossa, interrupting them for a short space to be
the page of the Infanta Catarina, daughter of Joanna
the Mad. At eighteen, he was one of the brilliant
figures of the court of Charles V. At nineteen, he
married Eleanor de Castro, who belonged to the highest
nobility of Portugal, and at that time he was made
Marquis of Lombay. When he was twenty-eight, the
famous incident occurred, which has been made the
subject of so much oratorical and pictorial exaggeration — his consternation at the sight of the corrupting
remains of the beautiful Empress Isabella, and his
resolution to abandon the court and the world forever.
Astrain in speaking of this event merely says: " he was
profoundly moved;" Suau, in his " Histoire de Saint
François de Borgia," makes no mention of any perturba-
tion of mind and ascribes Borgia's vocation rather to
subsequent events. The Bollandists do not vouch for
the story of his consternation, but note that he was
the only one who dared to approach the coffin, the
others keeping aloof on account of the odor. They add
that his biographers make him say: " Enough has been
given to worldly princes." As a matter of fact, later
on, he willingly accepted the office of major domo to
Prince Philip, who was about to marry the Infanta of
Portugal. As the King and Queen of Portugal, however, refused to accept him in that capacity, he was simply disgraced in the eyes of all diplomatic Europe and
was compelled to keep out of the court of his own sovereign, for three whole years. " This and other serious
trials, at that period," says Suau, " probably developed
in him the work of santification begun at Granada."

Borgia was thirty-six years of age when his wife died in 1546, and he then consulted Father Faber, who happened to be in Spain at the time, about the advisability of entering a religious order. He made the Spiritual Exercises under Oviedo, and determined to enroll himself as one of the members of the Compañía founded by Ignatius, with whom he had been for some time in communication. He was accepted and given three years to settle his wordly concerns. By a special rescript, the Pope allowed him to make his vows of profession immediately. In January, 1550, he was allowed to present himself for ordination to the priesthood whenever he found it feasible. On August 20 of the same year, he obtained the degree of doctor of theology and ten days later, set out for Rome with a small retinue. Accompanying him were nine Jesuits, among whom was Father Araoz, the provincial. In every city he was officially received, the nobility going out to meet him at Rome. He was sumptuously lodged in the Jesuit house, part of which St. Ignatius had fitted up at great expense to do honor to the illustrious guest. Soon, however, it was rumored that he was to be made a cardinal, whereupon he took flight, making all haste for Spain, without any of the splendor or publicity which had surrounded him three months before. His only purpose was to escape observation. Arriving in Spain, he visited Loyola, the birthplace of Ignatius, and then fixed his residence at the hermitage of Oñate, where, after receiving the Emperor's leave, he renounced all his honors and possessions in favor of his son Charles. He was ordained priest on May 23, 1551.

After six months spent in evangelizing the Basques, Borgia was sent to Portugal to put an end to the troubles caused by Simon Rodriguez, but did not reach that country until 1553. Meantime, sad to say,

Father Araoz astounded every one by displaying an intense jealousy of Borgia, who had been made independent of all superiors except Ignatius himself, and he demanded that his former friend and benefactor should show himself less in public and give evidence of greater humility. His complaints were incessant, and unfortunately an accidental unpopularity involving the whole Borgia family which just then supervened gave some color to the charges. In the meanwhile the Pope had again insisted on bestowing the cardinalitial honor upon Borgia, and for a moment Nadal, the Commissary General of Spain, was afraid that it might be accepted, not out of any ambition on the part of Francis, but because of his profound reverence for the will of the Sovereign Pontiff, especially as he had not as yet pronounced the simple vow of the professed against the reception of ecclesiastical dignities. Whereupon, Ignatius sent an order for him to make the vow, and from that forward his conscience was at rest on the question of running counter to the desires of the Pope.

In 1554 he was made commissary general in place of Nadal, who had been summoned to Rome to assist Ignatius, now in feeble health. The appointment of Borgia to such a post was most extraordinary for the reason that he had been but such a short time in the Society, and had never been in a subordinate position. The difficulty of his task was augmented by the fact that he had been commissioned to divide the Spanish section of the Society into four distinct provinces, and to assume in this and other matters the duties and functions of an office which had no defined limitations, and which would inevitably bring him into conflict with other superiors. As a matter of fact, the commissariate was such a clumsy contrivance that it had soon to be done away with.

Araoz had previously been at odds with Nadal, but he found it still more difficult to get along with Borgia. This disedifying antagonism continued for some time, and it is said that the old worldly superiority of the viceroy showed itself occasionally in Borgia. His dictatorial methods of government, his resentment of interference with his plans, even when Nadal spoke to him, showed that he was not yet a Jesuit saint. As if he still possessed unlimited revenues he established no less than twenty new houses; and, when there were not sufficient resources to carry them on, he expected his subjects to live in a penury that was incompatible with general content and fatal to the existence of the institutions. Moreover, his old propensity for great mortifications manifested itself to such an extent that there was danger of the Jesuits under him becoming Carthusian in their mode of life. Indeed, he was of opinion that the old monastic prison and stocks should be introduced into the Society, and he sent a *postulatum* or petition to that effect to the congregation which elected Laínez. The result was that a spirit of revolt began to mainfest itself in Spain, and Nadal, who was temporarily there, was happy when recalled to Rome.

How all this can be reconciled with the admittedly remarkable prudence of St. Ignatius and his profound knowledge of the character of those he had to deal with is difficult to say. Had he perhaps received some divine intimation of what Borgia was yet to be? On the other hand, it must be borne in mind that these isolated instances of impatience, authoritativeness, resentment and the like, naturally attract more attention when seen in one who is possessed of brilliant qualities than they would in any ordinary personage. Moreover, they occurred only in his dealings with Jesuits of the same official standing, and were never remarked when he had to treat with the rank and file who were entrusted to his care and guidance. They were, in any case, faults of judgment and not of perversity of will. Indeed so intent was he on acquiring the virtue of obedience that he fell into a state of almost despondency and distress when he was warned that Ignatius would disapprove of his methods and measures. Finally, he was then only on the way to sanctity; he had not yet achieved it.

It must be confessed, however, that Nadal was not at all pleased with the attitude of Borgia and the other Spanish Jesuits, when the call for the election of a new general was issued. He fancied that it was the beginning of a schism. When, as previously pointed out, Philip II allowed the Spanish delegates to go to the congregation, Borgia, remained in Spain. The fear of the red hat still haunted him. The famous *postulatum* about the prison and stocks which he sent to the congregation was, of course, promptly rejected. Borgia, however, had other reasons not to go to Rome. Several Spanish cities were up in arms against the Society; he himself was assailed openly in church by Melchior Cano; a book he had written or was accused of having written was condemned by the Inquisition, and he expected momentarily to be arrested; evil things were also said about his character. Unfortunately, Araoz took advantage of all this and began to pen a series of denunciatory letters to the General against Borgia, and, though he was rebuked for them and made public reparation for his offense, he soon relapsed into his customary antagonism. To put an end to it all Laínez summoned Borgia to Rome and conferred on him the honor of assistant. Even that lesson Araoz failed to take to heart.

Francis reached Rome only in 1561. In the following year when Laínez had to attend the re-opened Council

of Trent, he made Borgia vicar general, and, when
Laínez died at the age of fifty-three in January, 1565,
the congregation which was convened in July of that
year elected Borgia in his place. At the same time
stringent laws were enacted against the hasty multiplication of houses and the inevitable lack of formation
which ensued. This was a notice served on the new
General to control his zeal in that direction. Borgia
instituted novitiates in every province; he circulated
the book of Exercises and laid down rules for common
life, which on account of the enormous growth of the
Society had now become a matter of primary importance. Instead of showing any proneness to the
eremitical life or wishing to impose it on the Society,
he gave an example of immense and intense activity
in public matters. Thus he had much to do with the
revision of the Bible, the translation of the
" Catechism " of the Council of Trent; the foundation
of Propaganda; and, omitting other instances of his
administrative ability, when the plague broke out in
Rome in 1566, he so successfully organized the financial
and medical machinery of the city that two years
afterwards, when the plague appeared again, all the
public funds were immediately placed in his hands.

The impression that his administration was severe,
exacting, harsh and narrow has no foundation in fact.
It is sufficient to glance at the five bulky volumes
made up mainly of correspondence and documents in
the " Monumenta Borgiana " to be convinced that the
reverse was the case. There is a kindliness, a gracious-
ness, even a joyousness observable in them on every
page. He even kept a list of all the sick in the Society,
and consoled them whenever the opportunity offered.
The vastness of his correspondence is simply astounding;
his letters are addressed to all kinds of people, the
lowest as well as the highest, and deal with every

variety of topic.   Finally, there was no General who developed the missions of the Society so widely and so solidly as did St. Francis Borgia.   He reformed those of India and the Far East, created those of America, and before he died he had the consolation of knowing that sixty-six of his sons had been martyred for the Faith during his Generalate.   The discovery of him by St. Ignatius was an inspiration, for Borgia is one of the great glories of the Society.   He ended his remarkable life by a splendid act of obedience to the Pope and of devotion to the Church.

On June 27, 1571, St. Pius V, his intimate friend, requested him to accompany Cardinal Bonelli on an embassy to Spain and Portugal.   He was just then recovering from a serious illness, and felt quite sure that the journey would result in his death, but he accepted the call.   In Spain he was received with the wildest enthusiasn.   Indeed the papal legate was almost forgotten in the public ovations.   Portugal also lavished honors on him, and when in consequence of new orders from the Pope the embassy continued on to France to plead with Charles IX and Catherine de' Medici, he was received in the same manner in that country.   On February 25 he left Blois but by the time Lyons was reached he had been stricken with congestion of the lungs.   From Lyons, the route led across the snow-clad Mt. Cenis and continued by the way of Turin to Alexandria, where they arrived on April 19.

As the invalid was in too perilous a state to permit of his going any further for the moment, his relative, the Duke of Ferrara, kept him through the summer until September 3, when another start was made for Rome, where he wanted to die.   The last stage of his journey inflicted untold suffering on him, but he never complained.   On September 28, he arrived at the professed house in Rome, and throngs of cardinals and prelates hurried to see him to get his blessing, for he was already canonized in the popular mind. For two days he lingered, retaining full consciousness, conversing at times with those around him, but most of the time absorbed in prayer. When asked to name his vicar he laughed and said: " I have enough to do to give an account of my own stewardship." Towards evening he became speechless and about midnight peacefully expired, ending a career which it would be hard to equal in romance — a gorgeous grandee of Spain, a duke, a viceroy, the affectionate friend of the greatest potentate on earth, and now dying in the poor room of a Jesuit priest, atoning by his splendid sanctity for the offenses which have made the name of the family to which he belonged a synonym of every kind of iniquity.

Following close upon St. Francis Borgia came a number of men who have reflected glory upon the Church and on the Society, some of them, the most illustrious theologians of modern times, and others acting as the diplomatic agents of the great nations of Europe in the tentative but usually unsuccessful efforts to reunite Christendom. We refer to Bellarmine, Toletus, Suárez, Petavius, Possevin and Vieira.

Speaking of Bellarmine, Andrew White, in his " Conflict of Science and Religion " informs us that " there must have been a strain of Scotch in Bellarmine, because of his name, Robert,"— a typical illustration of the unreliability of Andrew White as a witness. The first Robert who appears in Scottish history is the son of William the Conqueror, and consequently a Norman. Even the name of Robert Bruce frequently occurs as Robert *de* Bruce, just as there is a John *de* Baliol; Robert *de* Pynkeny, etc. There is also a Robert of Arbrissel, associated with Urban II in preaching the Crusades; Robert of Geneva, an antipope; Robert de

Luzarches, who had to do with the building of Notre-
Dame in Paris, and scores of others might be cited.

Roberto Bellarmine was born at Montepulciano, in
1542. He was a nephew of Pope Marcellus II, and
after entering the Society was immediately admitted
to his vows. He studied philosophy for three years
at the Roman College and was then assigned to teach
humanities. In 1567 he began his theology at Padua,
but towards the end of his course, he went to Louvain
to study the prevailing heresies of the day at close
range. While there, his reputation as a preacher was
such that Protestants came from England and Germany
to hear him. In 1576 he was recalled to Rome to fill
the recently established chair of controversy, and the
lectures which he gave at that time form the ground-
work for his remarkable work " De controversiis." It
was found to be so comprehensive, conclusive and
convincing in its character that special chairs were
established in Protestant countries to refute it. It still
remains a classic. Singularly enough, though Sixtus V
had permitted the work to be dedicated to him, he
determined later to put it on the Index, because it gave
only an indirect power to the Holy See in temporal
matters. But he died before carrying out his threat,
and his successor, Gregory XIII, gave a special approbation to the book and appointed its author a member
of the commission to revise the Vulgate, which Sixtus
had inaugurated, but into which certain faults had
crept. At Bellarmine's suggestion the revision was
called the " Sixtine edition " to save the reputation
of the deceased Pontiff.

He was rector of the Roman College in 1592, and in
1595 provincial of Naples. In 1597 he was made
theologian of Pope Clement VIII, examiner of bishops,
consultor of the Holy Office, cardinal in 1599, and
assessor of the Congregation " de Auxiliis," which had

been instituted to settle the dispute between the
Thomists and Molinists on the question of the conciliation of the operation of Divine grace with man's free
will.   Bellarmine wanted the decision withheld, but
the Pope differed from him, though afterwards he
adopted the suggestion.   He had, meantime, been
consecrated Archbishop of Capua, by the Pope, and
was twice in danger of being raised to the papacy.   He
remained only three years at Capua, and passed the
rest of his life in Rome as chief theological adviser
of the Holy See.   During this period occurred the
dispute between Venice and the Holy See in which
Bellarmine and Baronius opposed the pretensions of
Paolo Sarpi and Marsiglio, the champions of the
Republic.   The English oath of allegiance also came
up for consideration at that time.   In this controversy
Bellarmine found himself in conflict with James I
of England.   He was conspicuous also in the Galileo
matter.   His life was so remarkable for its holiness that
the cause of his beatification was several times introduced, but was not then acted on, because his name
was connected with the doctrine of papal authority,
which was extremely obnoxious to the French regalis politicians.   It has, however, been recently re-introduced.

When Baius, the theological dean of Louvain, first
broached his errors on grace, he was answered by
Bellarmine; and in 1579 when he again defended them,
he was taken in hand by Toletus, who, after refuting
him, induced him to acknowledge his heresy before the
united faculties of the university.   Unlike Bellarmine,
who was of noble blood and the nephew of a Pope,
Toletus came of very humble people in Spain.   Rosa
says he was one of the " new Christians," that is, of
Jewish or Moorish blood.   He was born at Córdova
in 1532 and was, consequently, ten years older than his
friend and fellow-Jesuit, Bellarmine.   He made his

studies at Salamanca, where his master, the famous
Soto, described him as an intellectual prodigy; he
must have been such, for he occupied a chair of
philosophy when he was fifteen. He entered the
Society in 1558, and was sent to Rome as professor
of theology. He was appointed theologian and preacher
of Pius V, Gregory XIII, Sixtus V and Urban VIII,
successively. He accompanied Cardinal Commendone
in his diplomatic visit to Germany, to form a league
against the Turks, just as Bellarmine had been deputed
to go with Gaetano to France during the Huguenot
troubles. He was made a cardinal in 1593, and in
1595 he induced Pope Clement to grant Henry IV
the absolution that brought peace to France. He
warned the Pontiff that a refusal in that case would
be a grevious sin. Shortly afterwards he was named
legate to that country, but, as he had offended his
fellow-countrymen by showing himself hostile to
Philip II in the matter of the succession of Henry IV,
it was considered advisable to send someone else in his
stead. He died in the following year, and that gave
occasion to the now discredited historian, d'Etoile, to
say that the Spaniards had poisoned him.

The writings of Toletus are very numerous. Bossuet
was a great admirer of his " Instructions to Priests,"
in which, as in his " Commentaries," his enemies
discovered the " lax " principles of probabilism, ultra-
montanism, and the like, and he has been accused of
teaching even perjury, simony and regicide. He was
the preacher and theologian of four of the Popes, the
counsellor of princes, and the great defender of the
Faith in the northern countries. Cabassut, one of the
most learned of the French Oratorians in the reign of
Louis XIV, declared that we should have to wait for
several centuries before a man would appear who would
equal Cardinal Toletus. Tanner says that his life

8

could not have been more useful or better employed
for Jesus Christ if he travelled over the whole earth
preaching the Gospel. Gregory XIII indignantly
denounced what he called the lies of those who assailed
his character. " We set against those calumnies our
own testimony," he wrote, " and we affirm in all
truthfulness that he is incontestably the most learned
man living to-day; we have a greater opinion still of
his integrity and his irreproachable life. We have had
personal proofs of both. We know him perfectly and
we testify to what we know. We beg of your Highness
to give full and entire faith to the truth and to the
sincerity of our testimony, and to regard this man
henceforward as a true servant of Jesus Christ, and
marvellously useful to the whole Christian world."
These words were uttered before Toletus was clothed
with the purple. He will appear again at the election
of Aquaviva.

Very angry at the punishment he had received at
the hands of Bellarmine and Toletus, Baius turned on
Lessius, who was then teaching in the Jesuit College at Louvain, where, acting on misinformation,
the university condemned thirty-four propositions
which Baius ascribed to him. Lessius declared that
they were not his, but the university refused to accept
his word. Baius, therefore, continued his denunciation
of Lessius in particular and of the Jesuits in general
as Lutherans and heretics. Whereupon, not only the
other universities but the whole country took up the
quarrel. When the question was ultimately referred
to the Pope, he replied that he himself had taught the
same doctrine as Lessius. Besides being one of the
very great theologians of the Society, Lessius was remarkable for the holiness of his life. Pope Urban VIII,
who made such stringent laws about canonization, and
who knew Lessius personally, paid a special tribute to

his sanctity.   He is now like Bellarmine ranked among
the venerable, and the process of his beatification is
proceeding.

Another great Jesuit theologian of this period was
the Spaniard, Juan Maldonado, who was born in 1533
at Casas de Reina, about sixty-six leagues from Madrid.
He went to the University of Salmanca, where he
studied Latin under two blind professors.   He took
up Greek with El Pinciano, philosophy with Toletus,
and theology with Soto.   He was endowed with a
prodigious memory and never forgot anything he had
ever learned.   His aspirations were at first for law,
but he turned to theology; and after obtaining the
doctorate, taught theology, philosophy and Greek at
the university.   He entered the Society in 1562, and
was ordained priest in the following year.   He lectured
on Aristotle in the new College of Clermont in 1564,
and then taught theology for the four following years;
after an interruption of a year, he continued his courses
until 1576.   His lectures attracted such crowds that
at times the college courtyard was substituted for the
hall.   He was appointed a member of the commission
for revising the Septuagint; his knowledge of Latin,
Greek, Hebrew, Syriac, Chaldaic and Arabic and his
comprehensive knowledge of history, of the early
Fathers and of all the heresies, gave him the first rank
among the Scriptural exegetes of his time.   In Cornely's
opinion, his " Commentaries on the Gospels " are the
best ever published.   Above all, he was a man of
eminent sanctity, endowed with an extraordinary
instinct for orthodoxy, and an unflinching courage in
fighting for the Church as long as he had life.   " His
constant desire," says Prat, "was to make everything
the Society undertook, bear the mark of the greatness
and sanctity which St. Ignatius had stamped on the
Institute."

There was also the great Suárez, who was born at
Granada in 1548, and became a Jesuit in 1564. Pope
Paul V appointed him to answer King James of England
and wanted to retain him in the Holy City, but Philip
II claimed him for Coimbra to give prestige to the
university. When he visited Barcelona the doctors of
the university went out to meet him processionally to
pay him honor. Bossuet declared that his writings
contained the whole of Scholastic theology. In
Scholasticism he founded a school of his own, and
modified Molinism by his system of Congruism. His
book, "De defensione fidei," was burned in London
by royal command, and was prohibited as containing
doctrines against the power of sovereigns. One edition
of his works consisted of twenty-three and another of
twenty-eight volumes in folio. De Scoraille has
written an admirable biography of this great man.

Cardinal de Lugo also should be included in this
catalogue; indeed he is one of the most eminent
theologians of modern times. His precocity as a
child was almost preternatural, he was reading books
when he was three years old and was tonsured at
ten; at fourteen, he defended a public thesis in philosophy, and about the same time he was appointed to
an ecclesiastical benefice by Philip II. He studied law
at the University of Salamanca, but soon followed his
brother into the Society. After teaching philosophy
at Medina del Campo and theology at Valladolid, he
was summoned to Rome to be professor of theology.
His lectures were circulated all over Europe before they
were printed, and only when ordered by superiors did
he put them in book form. Between 1633 and 1640
he published four volumes which cover the whole field
of dogmatic theology. Their characteristic is that there
is little, if any, repetition of what other writers had
already said. St. Alphonsus Liguori rated him as only

just below St. Thomas Aquinas; and Benedict XIV styles him "a light of the Church." He was made a cardinal in 1643.

The distinguished Father Lehmkuhl appropriates four long columns in "The Catholic Encyclopedia" to express his admiration for Gregory de Valencia who was born in 1541 and died in 1603. He came from Medina in Spain and was studying philosophy and jurisprudence in Salamanca, when attracted by the preaching of Father Ramírez, he entered the novitiate and had the privilege of being trained by Baltasar Álvarez, who was one of the spiritual directors of St. Teresa. St. Francis Borgia called him to Rome, where he taught philosophy with such distinction that all North Germany and Poland petitioned for his appointment to their universities. He was assigned to Dillingen, and two years afterwards to Ingolstadt, where he taught for twenty-four years. His "Commentary" in four volumes on the "Summa theologica" of St. Thomas is one of the first comprehensive theological works of the Society. He contributed about eight polemical treatises to the war on Lutheranism, which was then at white heat; but he was not at one with his friend von Spee in the matter of witchcraft. Von Spee wanted both courts and trials abolished; Gregory thought their severity might be tempered. He had much to do with the change of view in moral theology on the subject of usury; and the two last volumes of his great work, the "Analysis fidei catholicæ" cul-minates in a proof of papal infallibility which expresses almost literally the definition of the Vatican Council.

In 1589 he was summoned to Rome to take part in the great theological battle on grace. The task assigned to him was to prove the orthodoxy of Molina, which he did so effectively and with such consummate skill that both friend and foe awarded him the palm.

But the battle was not over, for it was charged that isolated statements taken from Molina's book contradicted St. Augustine. Consequently all of St. Augustine's works had to be examined; a scrutiny which of course called for endless and crushing labor, but he set himself to the task so energetically that when the debates were resumed his health was shattered, and he was allowed to remain seated during the discussions. Thomas de Lemos was his antagonist at this stage. In the ninth session, Gregory's strength gave way and he fainted in his chair. His enemies said it was because the Pope had reproached him with tampering with St. Augustine's text, but as his holiness had decorated him with the title of " Doctor doctorum," the accusation must be put in the same category as the other which charged the Jesuits with poisoning Clement VIII so as to prevent him from condemning their doctrine.

According to the " Biographie universelle," Denis Pétau, or Petavius, was one of the most distinguished savants of his time. He was born at Orléans, August 21, 1583, and there made his early studies. Later he went to Paris, and at the end of his philosophical course defended his thesis in Greek. He took no recreation, but haunted the Royal Library, and amused himself collecting ancient manuscripts. It was while making these researches, that he met the famous Casaubon, who urged him to prepare an edition of the works of Synesius. While engaged at this work, he was chosen for the chair of philosophy at Bourges, though he was then only nineteen years old. As soon as he was ordained to the priesthood, he was made canon of the cathedral of his native city. There he met Father Fronton du Duc and entered the Society. After his novitiate, he was sent to the University of Pont-à-Mousson for a course of theology. He then taught rhetoric at La Flèche, and from there went to

Paris. His health gave way at this time, and he
occupied himself in preparing some of the works which
Casaubon had formerly advised him to publish.
In 1621, he succeeded Fronton du Duc as professor
of positive theology, and continued at the post for
twenty-two years with ever increasing distinction.

Pétau's leisure moments were given to deciphering
old manuscripts and studying history. Every year
saw some new book from his hands; meanwhile, his
vast correspondence and his replies to his critics involved an immense amount of other labor. Though
naturally of a mild disposition, his controversies
unfortunately assumed the harsh and vituperative
tone of the period. It was the accepted method.
His great work on chronology appeared in 1627 and
won universal applause; Philip IV of Spain offered him
the chair of history in Madrid, but he refused it on
the score of health. In 1637 he dedicated to Pope
Urban VIII a " Paraphrase of the Psalms in Greek
verse," for which he was invited to Rome, but he escaped
the honor on the plea of age. As a matter of fact, he
was so frightened at the prospect of being made a cardinal that he fell dangerously ill, and recovered only when
assured that his name was removed from the list.
He stopped teaching in 1644, only eight years before
his death. The complete list of his books fills twenty-
five columns in Sommervogel's catalogue of Jesuit
publications. They are concerned with chronology,
history, polemics, and the history of dogma. His
" Dogmata theologica " is incomplete, not having been
carried beyond the fifth volume.

In those days there was an extraordinary amount of
exaggerated confidence entertained by many of the
dignitaries of the Church that the Jesuits had an
especial aptitude for adjusting the politico-religious
difficulties which were disturbing the peace of Europe.

Thus, we find Father Warsewicz sent to Sweden in 1574 to strengthen the resolution of the king of that country, who, under the influence of his Catholic queen, was desirous of restoring the nation to the Faith.   Warsewicz appeared in the court of King John, not as representing the Pope, but as the ambassador of the King of Poland, who was related to Queen Catherine.   It was she who had suggested this means of approaching the king.   Accordingly, private meetings were held with the monarch during an entire week, for five and six hours consecutively, for John prided himself on his theological erudition.   He agreed to re-establish Catholicity in his realm, provided the chalice was granted to the laity and that marriage of the clergy and the substitution of Swedish for Latin in the liturgy were permitted   He had no difficulty about the doctrinal teaching of the Church.

The king's conditions were, of course, unacceptable, and in 1576 Father Nicolai was sent to see if he could induce him to modify his demand.   According to the "Realencyclopädie für protestantische Theologie und Kirche" and Böhmer–Monod, Nicolai represented himself as a Lutheran minister, and taught in Protestant seminaries.   The "Realencyclopädie" adds, "he almost succeeded in smuggling in what was virtually a Romish liturgy."   But in the first place, this "liturgy" was not "smuggled in" by the Jesuit or anyone else.   It was imposed by the king, and was in use until his death which occurred seventeen years later, (The Catholic Encyclopedia).   Secondly, Nicolai could not have been posing as a minister, for he let it be known that he had studied in Louvain, Cologne, and Douay, which were Catholic seminaries. It is true that he did not declare he was a Jesuit; but it is surely possible to be a Catholic without being a Jesuit.   It is more than likely that the school was

a sort of union seminary, which was striving to arrive
at conciliation, for, according to the king, what kept the
two sections apart was merely a matter of ecclesiastical
usage.   Finally, the Confession of Augsburg was not
admitted in Sweden as the religion of the State until
1593.   Had Nicolai advocated Luther's doctrines either
in the pulpit or the professor's chair, he would have
been instantaneously expelled from the Society.

The next Jesuit who appeared in Sweden was
Anthony Possevin, an Italian of Mantua, who was
born either in 1533 or 1534.   He began his carreer as
the secretary of Cardinal Ercole Gonzaga, and became
a Jesuit at the age of twenty-five.   He accomplished
much in France as a preacher and founder of colleges;
and in 1573 was made secretary of the Society under
Mercurian.   In 1577 he was sent as a special legate
of the Pope to John III of Sweden, and also to the
Courts of Bohemia and Bavaria to secure their support
for John in the event of certain political complications.
These political features of the mission made it very
objectionable to the Jesuits because of their possible
reaction on the whole Society.   But as the order came
from the Pope, and as the conversion of the king and
of all Sweden was the predominating idea of the
mission, the attempt was made in spite of its possible
consequence.

Like his predecessor, he did not appear in his clerical
garb, nor even as the legate of the Pope.   That would
scarcely be tolerated in a Protestant country like
Sweden, but he came as the ambassador extraordinary
of the Empress of Germany, the widow of Maximilian
II.   With him were two other Jesuits — Good, an
Englishman, and Fournier, a Frenchman.   Crétineau-
Joly makes Good an Irishman, but the English
" Menology " for July 5 says he was born at Glaston-
bury in Somersetshire, and was one of the first English-

men admitted to the Society. After his noviceship he was sent to Ireland, where he labored for four years under the Archbishop of Armagh. He then accompanied Possevin to Sweden and Poland, and after passing four years in the latter country, died at Naples in 1586.

When Possevin had finished discussing the political situation with the king, he began his work as ambassador of the Lord. He had many private interviews with his majesty, and convinced him of his errors in matters of faith; but the king insisted on points of discipline and liturgy which could not be granted. In brief, he was a Catholic, but reasons of State prevented him from making any public declaration. However, on May 16, 1578, he decided to take the step, and an altar was erected in a room of his palace. There he assisted at Mass, and in the presence of the queen, the Governor of Stockholm and his secretary, declared himself a Catholic. But he still hesitated about making it known to his people, and begged Possevin to return to Rome to see if he could not obtain the dispensation already asked for,— such as Communion under both kinds, Mass in Swedish, the marriage of priests, which Possevin knew would never be granted. However, he set out for Rome with seven young converts, and sent two Jesuits to Stockholm as preachers. He also got others ready in Austria, Poland, and Moravia, and made arrangements with the Emperor Rudolph to give his daughter in marriage to King John's son, Sigismund. He finally reached Rome, but the congregation of Cardinals, of course, rejected the king's pusillanimous petition.

In spite of this failure, Possevin was then sent as legate to Russia, Lithuania, Moravia, Hungary, and, in general, to all the countries of the North; while Philip II of Spain entrusted him with a confidential

mission to the King of Sweden. In Bavaria, he has to
see the duke; at Augsburg, he makes arrangements
for the Pope with the famous banking firm of Fugger,
the Rothschilds of those days, who had figured so
conspicuously in the question of Indulgences in Luther's
time. From there he proceeded to Prague to deliver
a message to the Emperor; and at Vilna he conferred
with Bathori, the King of Poland. A Swedish frigate
waited for him at Dantzig and, after a fourteen days'
voyage, he landed at Stockholm on July 26, 1579. He
was no longer dressed as a layman, but went to the
court in his Jesuit cassock and was received with great
ceremony by the dignitaries of the realm.

Meantime, however, the king's brother and sister-
in-law had aroused the Lutherans; the Swedish bishops
were banded against him, and finally, when the king
learned that none of his demands had been granted,
except that of keeping the confiscated ecclesiastical
property, he lost courage and reverted to Protestantism.
The assurance given him by Possevin that he could
rely on the help of Spain, of the Emperor, and of the
Catholic princes of Germany did not move him. He
saw before him the revolt of his subjects, and the
accession of his brother; and, while insisting that he
was a Catholic at heart, he refused to act, unless the
Pope granted all his demands. On February 19 he
convoked a Diet at Wadstena, at which Possevin was
present, but as the majority was clearly against returning to the old Faith, the legate had to be satisfied with
being merely an onlooker, while the king, convinced
that he was acting against his conscience, yielded to
the popular clamor. Another Diet was held with the
same result. Meantime, the legate remained in Stockholm, devoting himself to the sick and dying, in a
pestilence that was then devastating the city. He also
succeeded in so strengthening the faith of the young

Sigismund, the heir apparant, that when there was question subsequently of his renouncing Catholicity in order to ascend the throne, he had the courage to say that he would relinquish all his rights and withdraw into private life, rather than abandon the Faith.

A much more curious exercise of diplomacy came in Possevin's way in the quarrel between the King of Poland and the ruler of Muscovy. The latter had made vast conquests in the East, and then turned his attention to Livonia, which was Polish territory. Bathori, who was ruler of Poland, met and conquered the invader in a series of successful battles. Whereupon the Czar, knowing Bathori's devotion to the Holy See, asked the Sovereign Pontiff, Gregory XIII, to intervene. Possevin was again called upon, and set out as plenipotentiary to arrange peace between the two nations. Incidentally, the intention of the Pope was to obtain the toleration of Catholics in the Russian dominions, to secure a safe passage for missionaries to China through Russia, to induce the Czar to unite with the Christian princes against the Turks, and even to bring about a union of the Greek and Latin churches.

Possevin arrived at Vilna in 1581. He found Bathori elated by his victories, but in no humor to entertain proposals of peace, which he wisely judged to be merely a device of his opponent to gain time. However, he yielded to persuasion, and Possevin set out to find the Russian sovereign at Staritza. He was received with all the honors due to an ambassador, and succeeded in gaining a suspension of hostilities, the surrender of Livonia to Poland, as well as the agreement to the demands of the Pope for religious toleration, and the passage across Russia to China for Catholic missionaries. Even the proposal to join the crusade against the Turks was accepted, in the hope that it would put Constantinople in the hands of Russia. But when the question of the union of Churches was mooted, which, of course, implied the recognition of the Pope as Supreme Pastor, the savage awoke in the Czar, and, for a moment, it seemed as if the life of the ambassador was at stake. The treaty of peace was finally signed on January 15, 1582, the delegates meeting in the chapel, where the ambassador celebrated Mass; all the representatives of Poland and Russia kissing the cross as a declaration of their fidelity to their oath. Possevin and his associates then started for Rome towards the end of April. They were loaded with presents from the Czar; but to the amazement of the barbarians, they distributed them among the poor of the city.

There was, however, an appendix to this mission. Though the Polish king did all in his power to preserve the Faith in Livonia, the German Lutherans, Calvinists, Baptists, and other heretics had already invaded the country, and were inflaming the population with hatred of the Pope and the Church. Added to this was the alarm awakened in the mind of the Emperor of Germany at the growing power of the Poles. Again Possevin had to return to the scenes of his labors, but this time it was more as a priest than a diplomat. Indeed, much of his energy was expended in proving that he was neither German nor Pole, but an ambassador of Christ sent to build up the Faith of both nations against heresy. We hear of him once more in the matter of the reconciliation of Henry IV of France to the Holy See. To him and Toletus was due the credit of inducing the Pope to absolve the king, and by so doing, save France from schism. When this was done, Possevin became an ordinary Jesuit, laboring here and there, exclusively for the salvation of souls. It is a curious story, and it would be hard to find anything like it in the chronicles of the Church, except, perhaps the career of the famous Portuguese Jesuit, Antonio

Vieira, surnamed by his fellow-countrymen, " the Great."

Vieira was born in Lisbon, on February 5, 1608, and died at Bahia, in Brazil, on July 18, 1697. He was virtually a Brazilian, for he went out to the colony when still a child, and after finishing his studies in the Jesuit college there, entered the Society in 1623, when he was only fifteen years of age. At eighteen, he was teaching rhetoric and writing commentaries on the Canticle of Canticles, the tragedies of Seneca, and the " Metamorphoses " of Ovid, but it was twelve years before he was raised to the priesthood. The eloquence of his first sermon astounded everyone.

In 1640 Portugal declared its independence from Spain, to which it had been subject for sixty years. As the union had been effected by fraud and force, and as all the former Portuguese possessions in the East and a part of Brazil had been wrested from Spain by the Dutch and English; and as the taxes imposed on Portugal were excessively onerous, there was a strong feeling of hatred for the Spaniards. This hostility broke out finally in a revolution, and John IV ascended the throne of Portugal, but the change of government involved the country in a disastrous war of twenty years' duration.

Before the outbreak, the Jesuits were solemnly warned by their Superiors to observe a rigid neutrality. But in the excited state of the public mind, Father Freire forgot the injunction, and, in an Advent sermon in the year 1637, let words escape him that set the country ablaze. Crétineau-Joly says " the provincial promptly imprisoned him," which probably meant that he was kept in his room, for there are no prisons in Jesuit houses. But even that seclusion produced a popular tumult. The provincial was besieged by protests, and a delegation was even sent to Madrid to

protest that the words of the preacher had been misin-
terpreted. The Spanish king accepted the explanation,
and when the envoys returned to Lisbon, Freire had
been already liberated.

Ranke asserts in his " History of the Popes " that
as there was question of establishing a republic in
Portugal at that time, it is possible that Spain preferred
to see the innocuous John of Braganza, whose son was
a dissolute wretch, made king, than to run the risk of
a republic like those projected at that time by the
Calvinists in France and by the Lutherans in Sweden.
Later, however, an investigation was ordered, and a
Jesuit named Correa was incarcerated for having
predicted at a college reception given to John of
Braganza some years earlier that he would one day
wear the crown. Meantime the explosion took place,
and in 1640 John of Braganza was proclaimed king
of an independent Portugal.

In the following year Vieira arrived from Brazil and
was not only made tutor to the Infante, Don Pedro,
as well as court preacher, but was appointed member
of the royal council. In the last-named office he
reorganized the departments of the army and navy,
gave a new impetus to commerce, urged the foundation
of a national bank, and the organization of the Brazilian
Trading Company, readjusted the taxation, curbed the
Portuguese Inquisition, and was mainly instrumental
in gaining the national victories of Elvas, Almeixal,
Castello Rodrigo, and Montes Claros.

Between 1646 and 1650 he went on diplomatic
missions to Paris, the Hague, London, and Rome, but
refused the title of ambassador and also the offer
of a bishopric. He wanted something else, namely,
to work among his Indians, and he returned to Brazil
in 1652. There he provoked the wrath of the slave-
owners by his denunciation of their ill-treatment of

the negroes and Indians, and was soon back in Lisbon pleading the cause of the victims. He won his case, and, in 1655, we find him once more at his missionary labors in Brazil, evangelizing the cannibals, translating the catechism into their idioms, travelling over steep mountain ranges and paddling hundreds of miles on the Amazon and its numberless tributaries. Eleven times he visited every mission post on the Maranhon, which meant twenty journeys along the interminable South American rivers, on some of which he had to keep at the oar for a month at a time. It is estimated that he made 15,000 leagues on foot, and advanced 600 leagues farther into the interior of the continent than any of his predecessors. He continued this work till 1661, and then the slave-owners rose against him with greater fury than ever, and sent him a prisoner to Lisbon. He was no longer as welcome at court as previously, for the degenerate Alfonso, who had to be subsequently deposed, was on the throne. In 1665 the Inquisition forbade him to preach, and flung him into a dungeon, where he lay till 1667, when he was released by the new king Pedro II. He then went to Rome, and was welcomed by the Pope, the cardinals, and the General of the Order, Father Oliva.

While at Rome he met Christina of Sweden, who had abdicated her throne in order to become a Catholic. Ranke, in his " History of the Popes," devotes a whole chapter to this extraordinary woman, and she is referred to here merely because of her admiration for Vieira, and also to call attention to the fact that the first priest she spoke to about her conversion was the Jesuit, Antonio Macedo, who was the confessor of Pinto Pereira, the Portuguese ambassador to Sweden. The " Menology " tells us that Macedo did not wear his priestly dress in that country. He was the ambassador's secretary and interpreter, but he attracted the

attention of the queen, who remembered no doubt
that the Jesuit, Possevin, had appeared in the same
court, in the time of John III, disguised as an officer.
She finally asked Macedo about it, and he admitted
that he was a Jesuit. Then began a series of conversations in Latin, which Christina spoke perfectly, as she
did several other languages. She finally told him that
she had resolved to become a Catholic, even if she
forfeited her crown, and she commissioned him to
inform the Sovereign Pontiff of her purpose. To
reward Macedo she asked the Pope to make him a
bishop, but as he had been a missionary in Africa, the
mitre did not appeal to him, and he went back to
Lisbon, where he died after sixty-seven years passed in
the Society.

Macedo's departure from Stockholm was so sudden
that it excited comment, and possibly to persuade the
public she had nothing to do with it, the queen
pretended to despatch messengers in pursuit of him.
In fact, she had requested the General of the Society
to send some of the most trusted members of the Order
to Sweden. It may be that the old African missionary,
Macedo, was not skillful enough in elucidating some of
the metaphysical problems which she was discussing.
" In February, 1652," says Ranke, " the Jesuits who
had been asked for arrived in Stockholm. They were
two young men who represented themselves to be
Italian noblemen engaged in travel, and in this character they were admitted to her table." They were
Fathers Cavati and Molenia, who were able mathematicians as well as theologians. Descartes also was
there about that time. The queen did not recognize
the young noblemen in public, but, says Ranke: " as
they were walking before her to the dining-hall, she
said, in a low voice to one of them: ' Perhaps you have
letters for me.' Without turning his head he replied

9

that he had.   Then, with a quick word, she bade him
keep silence.   On the following morning they were
conducted secretly to the palace.   Thus," continues
Ranke, " to the royal dwelling of Gustavus Adolphus
there now came ambassadors from Rome for the
purpose of holding conferences with his daughter about
joining the Catholic Church.   The charm of this affair
for Christina was principally the conviction that no one
had the slightest suspicion about her proceedings."

The conferences seem to have been long drawn out,
although the envoys subsequently reported that " Her
Majesty apprehended with most ready penetration the
whole force of the arguments we laid before her.
Otherwise we should have consumed much time.
Suddenly she appeared to abandon every desire to
carry out her purpose, and attributed her doubts to
the assaults of Satan.   Her spiritual advisers were in
despair, when just as suddenly she exclaimed: ' There
is no use.   I must resign my crown.' "   The abdication
was made with great solemnity amid the tears and
protests of her subjects.   She left her country and
spent the rest of her life in Rome, where her unusual
intellectual abilities and great learning excited the
wonder of everyone.   Her heroism in sacrificing her
kingdom was, of course, the chief subject of the praise
that was showered upon her.

When Vieira arrived in Rome and fascinated everyone
by his extraordinary eloquence, Christina wanted him
to be her spiritual director.   But the old hero preferred
ruder work, and by 1681 he was again back in Brazil
among his Indians.   Even in his old age he was a
storm centre, and although he had done so much for
the glory of God and the good of humanity, he was
deprived of both active and passive voice in the Society,
that is to say, he could neither vote for any measures
of administration or be eligible to any office, because

he was supposed to have canvassed a provincial
congregation. It was only after he had expired, at
the age of ninety, that his innocence was established.
His knowledge of scripture, theology, history, and
literature was stupendous, and he is said to have been
familiar with the language of six of the native races.
Southey, in his " History of Brazil," calls him one of
the greatest statesmen of his country. He was a
patriot, whose one dream was to see Portugal the
standard-bearer of Christianity in the Old and New
Worlds. As an orator he was one of the world's
masters, and as a prose writer the greatest that Portugal
has every produced. His sermons alone fill fifteen
volumes, and there are many of his manuscripts to be
found in the British Museum, the National Library
of Paris, and elsewhere.

When St. Francis Borgia, the third General of the
Society, died in 1572, his most likely successor was
Polanco, who had been the secretary of St. Ignatius,
and was generally credited with having absorbed the
genuine spirit of St. Ignatius. Had he been elected,
he would have been the fourth successive Spanish
General. It would have been a misfortune at that
time, and would have fastened on the members of the
Society the name which was already given to them in
some parts of Europe: " the Spanish priests," a
designation that would have been an implicit denial
of the catholicity of the Order, even though the Spanish
monarch was " His Catholic Majesty."

Their devoted friend, Pope Gregory XIII, saw the
danger and determined to avert it. Fortunately, he
had just been asked by Philip of Spain, Sebastian of
Portugal, and the cardinal inquisitor not to allow the
election of Polanco, who was of Jewish descent. The
Pope determined to go further and to exclude any
Spaniard from the office, for the time being. At the

customary visit of the delegates, prior to the election, he intimated that as there had been three successive Spanish Generals, it might be wise, in view of the world-wide expansion of the Society, to elect someone of another nationality, and he suggested Mercurian. Doubtless his words found a ready response in the hearts of many of those to whom they were addressed, and even most of the Spaniards must have seen the wisdom of the change. A remonstrance, however, was respectfully made that His Holiness was thus withdrawing from the Society its right of freedom of election, to which the Pope made answer that such was not his intention; but in case a Spaniard was chosen he would like to be told who he was, before the public announcement was made. As the Pope's word is law, the Spaniards were excluded as candidates, and apparently, as a measure of conciliation, Everard de Mercœur, or Mercurian, was elected. As his native country, Belgium, was then subject to Spain, the blow thus given to the Spaniards was, to a certain extent, softened. But it was the beginning of trouble which at one time almost threatened the Society with destruction. Fortunately, Mercurian's successor, Aquaviva, had to deal with it when it came.

Mercurian had as yet done nothing great enough to attract public attention; but he evidently enjoyed the unqualified esteem of the Pope. In the Society itself he had filled many important posts such as vice-præpositus of the professed house in Rome, rector of the new college of Perugia, visitor and provincial of Flanders and France, and assistant of Francis Borgia. And in all of these charges he was said to have reproduced in his government the living image of St. Ignatius. A man with such a reputation was invaluable, especially for the spiritual life of the Society, and that is of infinitely greater importance than outward show. There is one thing for which the Order is especially very grateful to him namely, the " Summary of the Constitutions," and the " Common Rules " and the rules for each office, which he drew up at the beginning of his administration. This digest is read every month in the refectory of every Jesuit house and selections from it form the basis of the domestic exhortations given twice a month to the communities by the rector or spiritual father. By this means the character and purpose of the Institute is kept continually before the eyes of every Jesuit, from the youngest novice to the oldest professed, and they are made to see plainly that there is nothing cryptic or esoteric in the government of the Society. Hence, when the priest, after his ordination, goes through what is called his third year of probation, in which the study of the Institute constitutes a large part of his work, nothing really new is presented to him. It is familiar matter studied more profoundly.

There were other great men whose names might be mentioned here, but they will appear later in the course of this history.

CHAPTER V

THE ENGLISH MISSION

Conditions after Henry VIII — Allen — Persons — Campion — Entrance into England — Kingsley's Caricature — Thomas Pounde — Stephens — Capture and death of Campion — Other Martyrs — Southwell, Walpole — Jesuits in Ireland and Scotland — The English Succession — Dissensions — The Archpriest Blackwell — The Appellants — The Bye-Plot — Accession of James I — The Gunpowder Plot — Garnet, Gerard.

WHEN Dr Allen suggested to Father Mercurian to send Jesuits to the English mission, Claudius Aquaviva came forward as an enthusiastic advocate of the undertaking, and was one of the first to volunteer. He was not, however, accepted, because evidently only English-speaking priests would be of any use there. But his election as General shortly after gave new courage to Campion and his companions when they were in the thick of the fight.

Dr Allen had left England in 1561, and taken refuge in Belgium, but he returned in the following year, and went around among the persecuted Catholics, exhorting them to be steadfast in their Faith. He found that the people were not Protestants by choice, and he was convinced that all they needed was an organized body of trained men to look after their spiritual needs, to comfort them in their trials, and to keep them well-instructed in their religion. Because of the lack of such help they were not only becoming indifferent, but were almost ready to compromise with their persecutors. Henry had confiscated ninety colleges, two thousand three hundred and fourteen chantries and free chapels and ten hospitals, besides putting to death seventy-six priests and monks,

beginning with Fisher, the Bishop of Rochester, as
well as a great number of others, gentle and simple,
conspicuous among whom was the illustrious chancellor,
Thomas More. There was a partial cessation of
persecution when Edward VI, a boy, was placed
on the throne, and, of course, the conditions changed
completely when Mary Tudor came to her own. But
when the terrible Elizabeth, infuriated by her excommunication, took the reins of government in her hands,
no one was safe. Unfortunately, however, in the
interval, the people had become used to the situation,
and it began to be a common thing for them to resort
to all sorts of subterfuges, even going to Protestant
churches to conceal their Faith. Hence, there was
great danger that, in the very near future, Catholicity
would completely die out in England. Allen proposed
to Father Mercurian to employ the Society to avert
that disaster.

Some of the General's consultors balked at the
project because it implied an absolutely novel condition of missionary life. There were none of the
community helps, such as were available even in the
Indies and in Japan; for, in England, the priest would
have to go about as a peddler, or a soldier, or a sailor,
or the like, mingling with all sorts of people, in all
sorts of surroundings, and would thus be in danger of
losing his religious spirit. The obvious reply was
that if a man neglected what helps were at hand he
would no doubt be in danger of losing his vocation,
but that otherwise God would provide. Allen had
already founded a missionary house at Douai in 1568,
and its success may be estimated from the fact that
one hundred and sixty priests, most of them from
the secular clergy, who had been trained there, were
martyred for the Faith. He had succeeded also
in obtaining another establishment in Rome. In

1578, however, when the occupants of Douai were expelled, they were lodged at Rheims in the house of the Jesuits. Meantime, the Roman foundation had been entrusted to the Society; and with these two sources of supplies now at his disposal, Father Mercurian determined to begin the great work.

The most conspicuous figure in this heroic enterprise was Edmund Campion. He was born in London, and after the usual training in a grammar school was sent to Christ's Hospital. There he towered head and shoulders over everyone; and when Queen Mary made her solemn entry into London, it was he who made an address of welcome to her at St. Paul's School. With the queen on that occasion was her sister Elizabeth. Later, when Sir Thomas White founded St. John's College, Oxford, Campion was made a junior fellow there, and "for twelve years," says "The Catholic Encyclopedia," "he was the idol of Oxford, and was followed and imitated as no man ever was in an English University except himself and Newman." The "Dictionary of National Biography" goes further and informs us that "he was so greatly admired for his grace of eloquence that young men imitated not only his phrases but his gait, and revered him as a second Cicero." He was chosen to deliver the oration at the re-interment of Amy Robsart, the murdered wife of Robert Dudley, afterwards Earl of Leicester. The funeral discourse on the founder of the college was also assigned to him. In 1566 when Queen Elizabeth visited Oxford, Campion welcomed her in the name of the University, and was defender in a Latin disputation held in presence of her majesty. The queen expressed her admiration of his eloquence and commended him particularly to Dudley for advancement.

Father Persons assures us that "Campion was always a Catholic at heart, and utterly condemned all the

form and substance of the new religion. Yet the
sugared words of the great folk, especially the queen,
joined with pregnant hopes of speedy and great prefer-
ment, so enticed him that he knew not which way to
turn." While in this state of mind, he was induced by
Cheyney, the Bishop of Gloucester, who had retained
much of the ancient Faith, to accept deacon's orders and
to pronounce the oath of supremacy, but the reproaches
of a friend opened his eyes to his sin; and in anguish
of soul, he abandoned all his collegiate honors. In
August, 1569, he set out for Ireland. The reason for
going there was to participate in a movement for
resurrecting the old papal University of Dublin, the
direction of which was to be entrusted largely to him.
The scheme, however, fell through, chiefly on account
of Campion, but very much to his credit. His papistry
was too open. Meantime, he had written a " History
of Ireland " based chiefly on Giraldus Cambrensis,
which has ever since strongly prejudiced Irish people
against him, notwithstanding his sanctity. But his
good name has recently been restored by the distinguished Jesuit historian, Father Edmund Hogan, who
tells us, that when Campion fled from Dublin to escape
arrest for being a Catholic his manuscript fell into the
hands of his pursuers who garbled and mutilated it at
pleasure. He himself never published the book.

It will be of interest to students of literature to
learn that one of Shakespeare's most famous passages
was borrowed from this " History," namely, the
description of Cardinal Wolsey in Henry VIII. Whole
passages have been worked into the play. As Campion
wrote it in 1569, when Shakespeare was only four
or five years old, its authorship is beyond dispute.
Conditions finally became so unpleasant in Dublin that
he was obliged to take to flight. He left Ireland
disguised as a serving-man and reached London, in

time to witness the execution of Dr. Storey in June,
1571. That completed the work of his conversion,
and he went to Douai, where after a recantation of
his heresy, he resumed his course of scholastic theology;
a year later, he set out for Rome as a penniless pilgrim,
arriving there barefooted and in rags, much to the
amazement of one of his former Oxford admirers, who
met him on the street.

He was received into the Society by Father
Mercurian, and made his novitiate at Prague in
Bohemia, where he was ordained in 1578. He was
one of the first group of missionaries who left the
Continent for England under the guidance of Persons.
In the party were Dr. Goldwell, Bishop of Saint
Asaph, thirteen secular priests, three Jesuits: Persons,
Campion and Ralph Emerson, a lay-brother, besides
two young men not in orders. Goldwell had been
consecrated as early as 1555 and had accompanied
Cardinal Pole to England; he was England's sole
representative at the Council of Trent. He was now
on his way again to his native country, but he fell ill
at Rheims and, according to the " Dictionary of
National Biography," was recalled by the Pope.
" This," says Dr. Guilday (English Refugees, p. 125),
" was a disappointment to Persons. The presence of
a bishop in England had been a condition of the Jesuits'
taking up the burden of converting lapsed Catholics,
and despite all the rebuffs the demand for a hierarchy
met at Rome, the Jesuits themselves continually
renewed it." These words of the distinguished historian
who is the most recent witness in the matter of the
archipresbyterate are invaluable testimony on a sorely
controverted point.

The missionaries left Rome on foot, and passing
through Milan were detained for a week by St. Charles
Borromeo, who made Campion discourse every day

to the episcopal household on some theological topic.
From there they directed their steps to Geneva and
were bold enough to visit Theodore Beza in his own
house, but he refused to discuss religious matters.
At Rheims Campion spoke to the students on the
glory of martyrdom. Finally he and Persons arrived
at Calais, and made their plans to cross the Channel;
the other missionaries had meantime scattered along
the coast, as it would have been manifestly unsafe for
all to embark at the same place. Persons went aboard
the boat disguised as a naval officer, and on stepping
ashore at Dover presented himself with supreme
audacity to the port warden or governor, and asked
for a permit for his friend " Patrick," a merchant who
was waiting on the other side for leave to cross.
" Patrick " was Campion. He had used that name
when escaping from Ireland, and as it had stood him
in good stead then, he again assumed it.

Campion, however, did not play his part as well as
Persons, for the governor eyed him intently and said:
" You are Doctor Allen." " Indeed, I am not," replied
Campion. " Well, you are a suspicious character, at
all events, and your case must be looked into." A
council was accordingly held, and it was decided to
send the new-comer to London, under an armed escort.
Campion thought himself lost, but up in his heart
arose a prayer: " O Lord, let me work at least
one year for my country, and then do with me what
Thou wilt." Immediately a change came over the
Governor's face, and, to the amazement of everyone,
he said: " I was mistaken; you can go." Full of
gratitude to God, the future martyr made all haste for
London, where someone was on the look-out for him,
and he soon met Father Persons.

Such are the plain facts taken from the writings
of Campion to his superiors, describing his arrival in

England. But the public mind had to be debauched
on this as on every other point concerning the Jesuits,
even at the expense of the man whom Oxford is still
proud of as a scholar and a gentleman, who was called
by Cecil "one of the diamonds of England," and
whose grace and beauty and eloquence made him the
favorite of Dudley and Elizabeth.   In spite of all that,
however, Kingsley, in his "Westward Ho" (chap. iii),
describes Campion at this juncture of his life as "a grotesque dwarf whose sword, getting between his spindle
shanks, gave him, at times, the appearance of having
three legs, and figuring sometimes as a tail when it
stuck out behind. He was so small that he could only
scratch at the ribs of his horse which he was trying to
mount on the wrong side, but he finally succeeded in
gaining his seat by the help of a stool." He also wore
"a tonsure," we are informed, "cut by apostolic scis-
sors," and Londoner though he was, he is made to speak
of his countrymen as "Islanders." Persons also is
described as a blustering, blaspheming bully, who
gives himself absolution for his own transgressions.
All this is omitted, however, from the school edition
of "Westward Ho."

Persons and Campion set to work immediately, and
soon managed to call a meeting of the priests who were
in hiding in various places of the country.   The purpose
of the summons was to let them know that the
new-comers had received the most stringent orders
from their superiors to keep absolutely aloof from
anything savoring of politics. At Hoxton, Campion
made a written statement to that effect; and it was
there that he received a visit from one of the most
interesting, and, to some extent, the oddest of the
English missionaries — a man who was made a Jesuit
by letter — the famous Thomas Pounde.

Pounde had begun by being a very conspicuous fop
at the court of Queen Elizabeth. He was a favorite
of the queen, and had, on one occasion, prepared a
splendid pageant at which her majesty was present.
One of its features was a dance, a *pas seul* by himself.
However, as luck would have it, he stumbled and fell
right at the queen's feet. The accident was ridiculous
enough to humiliate him, but when his gracious
sovereign honored him with a brutal kick, and called
out scoffingly: " Get up, Sir Ox," Pounde arose, indeed,
but not as an ox. He was a changed man. Up to
that, though a Catholic, he had put his religion aside
altogether. Now, he openly proclaimed his Faith and
exhorted others to do the same. The result was that
he was confined in almost every dungeon of the
kingdom. He was loaded with fetters and shut up in
cells where no ray of light could penetrate; and when
liberated, either through the influence of friends, or
because he had served the appointed term, he was
incarcerated again. Everywhere and at all times he
preached the truths of the Faith, not only in a courageous, but in an extraordinarily joyous fashion to his
fellow-prisoners, or to people outside the jail, making
converts of many and inducing others to amend their
lives. Of the latter class was a certain Thomas
Cottam, an Oxford man, who, thanks to his friend
Pounde, not only became very devout, but, after he
had succeeded in getting to the Continent, became a
Jesuit and returning later was martyred at Tyburn
on May 30, 1582.

A chance reading of the Jesuit missions in India had
quite captivated Pounde, as well as a friend of his,
named Thomas Stephens, who used to go around
disguised as Pounde's servant. They determined to
make for the Continent and to ask for admission to

the Society. On the way, Pounde was captured because he had stopped too long in trying to convert a Protestant who had given him shelter; Stephens, however, reached Rome and was admitted to the Society. But instead of being sent back to England, as one would have fancied, his longing for India was satisfied, and we find him in Goa, on October 24, 1579. He was there known as Padre Estevão, or Estevan, or again as Padre Busten, Buston, or de Buston, the latter names being so many Portuguese efforts to pronounce Bulstan, in Wiltshire, England, where Stephens was born about 1549. As we see from the dates, he had then reached the age of 30. He is mentioned in Hakluyt's "Voyages" as the first Englishman who ever went to India. Hakluyt's information came from a series of letters which Stephens wrote to his father, " offering the strongest inducements to London merchants to embark on Indian speculations." These letters bore such evidence of sound commercial knowledge that they are regarded as having suggested the formation of the English East India Company.

Father Stephens spent his first five years as minister of the professed house at Goa, and was then sent to Salsette as rector, and, for a time, was socius to the visitor. After that he spent thirty-five years as a missionary among the Brahmin Catholics of Salsette, but his labors in that field did not prevent him from doing a great deal of hard literary work. Thus, he was the first to make a scientific study of Canarese. He also plunged into Hindustani, and wrote grammars and books of devotion in those languages. Most of his writings, however, were lost at the time of the Suppression of the Society. He died in Goa in 1619. (The Catholic Encyclopedia, XIV, 292.)

Pounde's Jesuit work was quite different from that
of Stephens. Not being able to present himself in
person to the General, he asked by letter to be received
into the Order. It was on December 1, 1578, while he
was imprisoned in the Tower that an answer came
from Father Mercurian granting his request. That
encouraged him to labor more strenuously than ever,
and for thirty years he kept on defying the Government.
Lingard gives one notable instance of his audacity,
though the great historian does not seem to be aware
that Pounde was a Jesuit. In the proceedings connected with the Gunpowder Plot, someone was sentenced for harboring a Jesuit. Pounde appeared in
court to protest against the ruling of the judge, with
the result that he himself was arrested. He was
condemned to have one of his ears cut off, to go to
prison for life, and to pay a fine of a thousand pounds,
if he did not tell who advised him to act as he did.
He did not lose his ear; while he was in the Tower the
queen, Anne of Denmark, interceded in his behalf.
Her loving husband, however, King James I, told her:
"never to open her mouth again in favor of a Catholic."
Finally he got off by standing a whole day in the
pillory, an experience which he probably enjoyed, for
in spite of dungeons and chains and loss of property
and his own terrible austerity — he often scourged
himself to blood — he never lost his spirit of fun. He
ended his wonderful career on March 5, 1615, at the
age of 76, at Belmont, breathing his last in the room
in which he was born.

When Campion was caught on his way to Lancashire
and brought to London, where he was stretched on
the rack and interrogated again and again while being
tortured, the story was circulated that he had, at last,
not only recanted, but had revealed secrets of the

confessional. Pounde was in a fury about it, and
wrote Campion an indignant letter, but he found out
that it was one of the usual tricks of the English
Government. The same villainy had been practised
by Elizabeth's father on More and Fisher, but like them,
Campion was too true a man to yield to suffering. On
August 31, by order of the queen, bruised as he was
and almost dismembered by the long and repeated
rackings, he was led with Sherwin to a public disputation in the royal presence. Against them were Nowell
and Day, two of the doughtiest champions of heresy
that could be found in the kingdom. The dispute
lasted for four hours in the morning and four in the
afternoon — the intention being to keep it up for days.
It was during this debate that the listeners saw with
horror, as Campion stretched out his arms to emphasize
his words by a gesture, that the nails had been torn
off the fingers of both hands. The public discussions
ended after the second session, for Nowell and Day
had been completely beaten. What happened in the
examinations held after that, behind closed doors, the
authorities never let the world know, but it leaked out
that Campion had made many converts among those
who came to hear him. One of them was Arundel,
who subsequently died for his faith on the scaffold.

On November 14 the Jesuits, Campion and Thomas
Cottam, with Ralph Sherwin, Bosgrave, Rhiston, Luke
Kirby, Robert Johnson and Orton, secular priests, were
called for trial. They all pleaded innocent of felony
and rebellion. "How could we be conspirators?"
Campion asked, "we eight men never met before;
and some of us have never seen each other." On
November 16, six others were cited. It was on this
occasion that Campion answered the question: "Do
you believe Elizabeth to be the lawful queen?" "I
told it to herself," he said, "in the castle of the Duke

of Leicester." Thither he had been called for a private interview, and Elizabeth recognized him as the Oxford man and the little lad of Christ Church, who, not then dreaming of the terrible future in store for him, had paid the homage of respectful and perhaps affectionate loyalty to her majesty. At that meeting were Leicester, the Earl of Bedford, two secretaries of state and the queen. As the prosecution was so weak and the defense made by Campion was so unassailable, everyone expected an acquittal, but to their amazement, a verdict of guilty was brought in. "The trial," says Hallam, "was as unfairly conducted and supported by as slender evidence as can be found in our books." (Constitutional History of England, I, 146.)

When the presiding judge asked the accused if they had anything to say, Campion replied: "The only thing that we have now to say is that if our religion makes us traitors we are worthy to be condemned, but otherwise we are and have been as true subjects as ever the queen had. In condemning us, you condemn all your own ancestors, all that was once the glory of England, the Island of Saints, and the most devoted child of the See of St. Peter. For what have we taught, however you may qualify it with the odious name of treason, that they did not uniformly teach? To be condemned along with those who were the glory not of England alone but of the whole world by their degenerate descendants is both glory and gladness to us. God lives; posterity will live, and their judgment is not so liable to corruption as that of those who are now going to condemn us to death." When the sentence was uttered, Campion lifting up his voice intoned the " Te Deum laudamus " in which the others joined, following with the anthem " Hæc est dies quam fecit Dominus, exultemus et lætemur in ea " (This is the day which the Lord has made; let us rejoice and exult in it.) There were conversions in the courtroom that day.

The scene at the scaffold on December 1, was characterized by the brutality of savages. The victims were placed on hurdles and dragged through the streets to Tyburn. Campion was the first to mount the fatal cart, and when the rope was put about his neck and he was addressing the crowd that thronged around, Knowles interrupted him with, "Stop your preaching and confess yourself a traitor." To which Campion replied, "If it be a crime to be a Catholic, I am a traitor." He continued to speak, but the cart was drawn from under him and he was left dangling in the air. Before he breathed his last he was cut down, his heart was torn out and the hangman holding it aloft in his bloody hand, cried out, "Behold the heart of a traitor!" and flung it into the fire. Alexander Briant and Ralph Sherwin than met the same fate. Previous to this gruesome tragedy, 4,000 people had been won back to the Faith.

Thomas Cottam and William Lacey were the next English martyrs of the Society. The latter calls for special mention. He was a Yorkshire gentleman, who for some time thought that he could, with a safe conscience, frequent Protestant places of worship, but as soon as he was made aware that it was forbidden, he desisted; and fines and vexations of all kinds failed to change his resolution. Becoming a widower, he determined in spite of his years to consecrate himself to God, and having met Dr. Allen at Rheims, he went to Rome, where, after his theological studies he was ordained a priest, and returning to England labored strenuously to revive the faith of his fellow-countrymen. He succeeded even in entering a jail in York where a number of priests were confined, and afforded them whatever help he could. As he was leaving, he

was arrested and was executed a month later, August
22, 1582. Father Possoz, S. J., the author of " Edmond
Campion," says " there is no mention of Lacy, either
in Tanner or Alegambe, but I found, in the catalogue
of Rayssius, ' Gulielmus Lacæus, sacerdos romanus
qui in carcere constitutus, in Societatem Jesu fuit
receptus.' " The same is true of Thomas Methame
who did not die on the scaffold, but after seventeen
years of captivity in various prisons, gave up the
ghost at Wisbech in 1592 at the age of sixty. He
was remarkable for his profound knowledge both
of history and theology. There also appears on the
list an O'Mahoney (John Cornelius), who was a ward
of the Countess of Arundel. He was thrown into the
Marshalsea, where Father Henry Garnet admitted
him to make his vows. He won his crown at Dorchester
on July 4, 1594. His name is not found in the " Fasti
Breviores " or the " Menology," but it is given by
Possoz.

The poet Robert Southwell was martyred on February
21, 1595. Writing about him, Thurston calls attention
to an interesting coincidence in his life. His grandfather, Sir Richard Southwell, a prominent courtier
in the reign of Henry VIII, had brought the poet
Henry Howard to the block, and yet Divine providence
made their respective grandsons, Robert Southwell
and Philip, Earl of Arundel, devoted friends and
fellow-prisoners for the Faith. The poetry, however,
had shifted to the Southwell side, for, unlike his
friend, Arundel did not cultivate the muse. Southwell
had been a pupil of the great Lessius at Louvain,
and had made the "grand act " in philosophy at the
age of seventeen. At Paris he applied for admission
to the Society, but was refused, and his grief on
that occasion elicited the first poetical effusion of
his of which we have any knowledge. Two years

later, however, he was accepted; he was ordained in
1584, and became prefect of studies in the English
College at Rome. In 1586 he was sent to England,
and passed under the name of Cotton. Two years
later he was made chaplain of the Countess of Arundel,
and thus came into relationship with her imprisoned
husband, Philip, the ancestor of the present ducal
house of Norfolk. Southwell's prose elegy, " Triumphs
Over Death," was written to console the earl. In
going his rounds he usually passed as a country gentleman, and that accounts for the " hawk " metaphors
which so often occur in his verse. He was finally
arrested at Harrow in 1592, and after three years'
imprisonment in a dungeon which was swarming with
vermin, he was hanged, drawn and quartered. Even
during his lifetime, his poetical works were highly
esteemed.

Henry Walpole was one of the spectators at the
execution of Campion, and that gave him his vocation.
He was admitted to the Society by Aquaviva, and
made his second year of noviceship at the now famous
Verdun. He was chaplain of the Spanish troops in
Flanders, and was for some time in Spain. From
there he went to Dunkirk where he embarked for
England on a Spanish ship which landed him on the
coast sixteen miles from York. There he fell into the
hands of the Earl of Huntington, a grandnephew of
Cardinal Pole, but a bitter foe of the Church. He
was shifted about from prison to prison for a year or
more, and was stretched on the rack fourteen times;
at length, he was executed at York on April 7, 1595.
Roger Filcock, who was put to death at London,
on February 22 or 27, 1601, was a secular priest who
was admitted to the Society while engaged in the work
of the missions. So also was Francis Page. He had
been a Protestant lawyer, and was engaged to a Catholic

lady who converted him, but instead of marrying her he became a priest. One day, while celebrating Mass, he was so nearly caught that the chalice on the altar was found, but he had time to get into his secular clothes and escape. He applied for admission to the Society and was received, but before he could reach the novitiate in Flanders he was seized, racked and put to death in London on April 20, 1602.

Twenty years after the visit of Salmerón and Brouet to Ireland, David Wolff was sent there as Apostolic delegate. O'Reilly in his " Memorials " says, he was one of the most remarkable men who labored in Ireland during the first years of Elizabeth's reign. About 1566, he was captured and imprisoned in Dublin Castle, from which he escaped to Spain. He returned again in 1572, and died of starvation in the Castle of Clonoan near the borders of Galway. Bishop Tanner of Cork had been a Jesuit, but was obliged to leave the Society on account of his health. He was imprisoned in Dublin, tortured in various ways and in 1678, after eighteen months' suffering, died in chains. In 1575 Father Edmund Donnelly was hanged and disembowelled in Cork and his heart thrown into the fire. In 1585 Archbishop Creagh, the Primate of Ireland, who was poisoned while in jail in Dublin made his confession, says O'Reilly " to a fellow-prisoner, Father Critonius of the Society of Jesus." In 1588 Maurice Eustace, a young novice, was hanged and quartered in Dublin. Brother Dominick Collins, who had been a soldier in France and Spain, was executed at Youghal in 1602. He was the last of Elizabeth's victims.

An interesting character appears at this juncture in the person of Father Slingsby, the eldest son of Sir Francis Slingsby, a Protestant Englishman settled in Ireland. Young Francis was converted to the Faith in 1630, when he was twenty-two years old; he made up his mind to be a Jesuit, but in obedience to his father's order he returned to Ireland. He was imprisoned in Dublin. At the request of the queen, Henrietta Maria, however, he was not executed but banished from the kingdom. Returning to Rome in 1636, he was received into the Society in the following year. It was the intention of his Superiors to send him back to Ireland but he was detained on the Continent for his studies. He was ordained a priest in 1641 and a short time afterwards died at Naples with the reputation of a saint. Meantime he had converted most of his Protestant relatives. In 1642 Father Henry Caghwell, who had taught philosophy to Father Slingsby, was dragged from his house in Dublin, paralytic though he was, scourged in the public square, and left lying on the ground in the sight of his friends, none of whom dared to lift him up. He was then thrown into prison and after a while flung with twenty other priests into a ship. He reached France in a dying condition, but unexpectedly recovered and made his way back to Ireland, in spite of a storm that lasted twenty-one days. A few days after landing, he fell a victim to his charity in attending the sick.

Scotland had been visited in 1562 by Father Gouda who was sent to Mary Queen of Scots to invite her to have her bishops go to the Council of Trent. He brought back with him six young Scots who were to be the founders of the future mission. Prominent among them was Edmund Hay, who became rector of Clermont. In 1584 Crichton and Gordon attempted to enter their country, but Crichton was captured, while Gordon succeeded in finding his way in, and was afterwards joined by Hay and Drury. The Earl of Huntley, who was Gordon's nephew, and for a time the leader of the Catholic party, joined the Kirk in 1597, and that put an end to the mission. Prior to

that, Father Abercrombie made a Catholic of the
queen, Anne of Denmark, but she was not much to
boast of. Meantime, the Scots College had been
founded by Mary Stuart in Paris, and later other
colleges were begun in Rome and Madrid. In 1614
Father John Ogilvie was martyred at Glasgow, while
his associates were banished.

Coming back to England, where more tragedies were
to be enacted, we find that before Campion was excuted,
Persons had succeeded in reaching France. He had
intended to return after he had secured a printing-
press to replace the one that had been seized, but, as
a matter of fact, England never saw him again. Dr.
Allen would not allow him to return; he, therefore,
remained on the Continent and was conspicuous as a
staunch supporter of the French League in its early
days, and an advocate of the invasion of England by
Philip II, primarily in the interest of Mary Queen of
Scots, but also, to secure a successor to Queen Elizabeth.
We find him frequently in Spain on various missions:
in 1588 to reconcile Philip with Father Aquaviva;
at other times, to obtain from the king the foundations
of the seminaries of Valladolid, Seville and Madrid,
as well as of two residences which afterwards developed
into collegiate establishments. Allen had left England
in 1565, sixteen years before Persons, and it is worth
noting that during the three years which he spent in
going around from place to place to sustain the courage
of the persecuted Catholics he was not yet a priest.
He was ordained only when he crossed over to Mechlin,
sometime in 1565; it was not until 1587, twenty-two
years afterwards that he was made a cardinal; he
was never raised to the episcopal dignity. He was
mentioned, it is true, for the See of Mechlin by Philip
II, but, for some reason which has never been thoroughly explained, the nomination, although publicly

allowed to stand several years, was never confirmed.
He continued to reside at the English College in Rome
until his death on October 16, 1594.

For some time previously the burning question
of the English succession was being discussed by
English Catholics and it did more harm to the Church
in England than the persecutions of Henry and Elizabeth. Elizabeth had left no issue, and had not designated her heir. Some were in favor of a certain
princess of Spain, who could trace her lineage back to
John of Gaunt, and both Allen and Persons espoused
her cause. Others held out for James VI of Scotland;
a rabid partisan on this side was the Scotch Jesuit,
Crichton, who was supported by a very large contingent
of the secular clergy. A similar divergence of sentiment
showed itself in Rome. Thus, for example, the cardinal-
protector of the English mission, Gaetano, was
pro-Spanish; the vice-protector, Cardinal Borghese,
was pro-French, and with him was the Jesuit Cardinal
Toletus, who, though a Spaniard, was against his
countrymen in this matter. The Pope was not pro-
Spanish. The result was that the English College in
Rome was torn asunder by dissensions or " stirs "
and some of the students gave public scandal in the
city. Order was not restored till Persons was recalled
from Spain to be rector of the college, but even he
was told to his face by some of his boisterous pupils
that they would never change their opinion, and they
contended that if they died for it they would be martyrs
of the Faith. Conditions were much worse in England
itself. Even among the priests who were confined at
Wisbeach, bitter disputes were kept up year after year
in a way that was the reverse of edifying. Finally,
when cognizance of this deplorable state of affairs
was taken at Rome, Father Persons was requested to
suggest a remedy, after Dr. Stapleton, who was a

pro-Spaniard, had been summoned to Rome, but had failed to arrive on account of ill-health. In 1597 Persons, now no longer rector of the college, presented to the Pope a memorial drawn up in England asking for the appointment of two bishops, one for England proper, and the other for the English in Flanders. This proposition was sent to a commission of the Holy Office, but they gave an adverse decision, namely that the new hierarchy should not be episcopal, but sacerdotal, with an archpriest at its head.

Persons, who had been from the outset insisting on the necessity of sending a bishop to England, did not easily give up his plan, and he persuaded Cardinal Gaetano to take him around to all the members of the commission in order to press his views upon them, but without avail. Out of caution, the Pope resolved not to set up the hierarchy by Papal brief, and he gave orders to the cardinal-protector, Gaetano, to issue " constitutive letters " to that effect. The draft for these letters was prepared in the Papal *Archivi dei Brevi*, where it is still extant (Pollen, Institution of the Archpriest Blackwell, p. 25; see also Meyer, England and the Church under Elizabeth, p. 409. Meyer is a German Protestant). Hence, it is clear that the Jesuits are not responsible for the establishment of an archipresbyterate instead of an episcopate to rule England. It was the explicit act of the Holy Office and of the Pope. Moreover, the trouble that subsequently arose was due, not from the function itself, but from the person to whom it was entrusted; for, though Blackwell was the man most in evidence at that time, and one for whom everyone would have voted, he had too exalted an idea of his new dignity, and resorted to such high-handed and autocratic methods that his rule became intolerable. As a result, two Appellants made their way to Rome, as representatives of the clergy, though, as a matter of fact, no such commission had been given them. On their arrival, they were promptly put in seclusion in one of the colleges, and were forbidden to return to England.

Then began a bitter war of pamphlets between the adherents and the adversaries of the archpriest. Persons, and the Jesuits, in general, were especially assailed. One of the malcontents, Bluet, actually put himself in communication with the Protestant Bishop Bancroft, who expressed the opinion that " it was clearer than light that Persons had no other object except the conquest of England by the Spaniards." Bluet assented, and added that " the charge against the Jesuit would be proved best by our appeal to the Pope, in which we should make all our grievances manifest." Bancroft revealed this to the queen, and the government then did all in its power to foment the dissensions and facilitate the appeal to the Pope. In 1602 another party of Appellants set out for Rome with no authorization whatever, except that of their own faction. On their way they were joined by a Dr. Cecil, who was, though they were unaware of it, in the employ of the English Government as a spy — a degradation to which he had descended, not precisely to ruin his co-religionists, but because he was under the delusion that he could so reconstruct the Church in England that it would be acceptable to the queen.

Cecil and his companions were admitted to Rome only because the French Ambassador, de Béthune, took them under his protection. He had constituted himself their patron, not, however, for religious reasons, but merely to score a point against the influence of the King of Spain with the Pope. Their reception by his Holiness was extremely cold, and when they reported back to de Béthune, he appeared before the Pope on

the next day, and said: " Hitherto the Catholic policy
has been grossly wrong (*turpiter erratum est*). Nothing
has been tried except arms, poisons, and plots. If
only these were laid aside Elizabeth would be tolerant.
Therefore, (1) Your Holiness must withdraw your
censures from the queen; (2) you must threaten the
Catholics with censure if they attempt political
measures against her directly or indirectly; (3)
Father Persons and his like must be chastised and
expelled from your seminaries; (4) the Archpriest,
who seems to have been constituted solely to help the
Spanish faction by false informations, should be
removed or much restrained; (5) if perhaps all this
cannot be done at once, a beginning should be made
by giving satisfaction to the Appellant priests; (6)
then, by degrees, Henri will intervene and Elizabeth's
anger will cool down." As Pollen remarks: " The
Frenchman's boldness was almost sublime. To throw
over St. Pius V, Cardinal Allen, Gregory, Sixtus,
Campion and all the seminaries, with one sweeping
remark: *turpiter erratum est* — was worthy of *la furie
francaise*. De Béthune scoffed at a past already
acknowledged to be one of the glories of the Church,
as a period of murder plots, diversified by armed
invasions."

On October 12 the Pope gave a Brief to the contending parties to settle their quarrel. Both sides
shouted victory, and the paper was at once sent to
England, where it was intercepted by Elizabeth's
spies. The government responded by a proclamation
against the Catholic clergy, banishing them from the
realm lest it might be thought that Elizabeth had ever
meant to grant toleration. " God doth know our
innocency," it said, " of any such imagining." The
royal proclamation was cunningly devised. It declared
that all Jesuits were unqualified traitors and must

leave the country within thirty days. For other
Catholics, a commission was to be appointed which,
after three months, was to begin an individual examination of all suspects and deal with them at discretion.

By the Scottish party this was regarded as the beginning of a new era, and they, consequently, drafted an
instrument stating: (1) that they owed the same civil
obedience to the queen as that which bound Catholic
priests to Catholic sovereigns; (2) that they would
inform her of any plots or attempts at evasion, even
when made to place a Catholic sovereign on the
throne; (3) that were any excommunication issued
against them on account of their performance of this
duty, they would regard it as not binding. This statement was issued on January 31, 1693. It never reached
Elizabeth, for she died in the following March. But
as it stood, it was in direct contravention of the Pope's
instructions to the clergy to do all in their power,
short of rebellion, to restore the Catholic succession.

Before the death of Elizabeth, two clergymen,
Watson and Clarke had gone to Scotland to sound
James on his possible attitude to English Catholics
in case he obtained the throne. Of course, he was
extremely affable, to them, as he was to the English
Puritans, who were just then arrayed in opposition
to the Established Church. But he was no sooner
king than he began to treat both Puritans and Catholics
with such rigor that a plot was formed by both of the
aggrieved parties to seize his person and compel him
to modify his policy. Among the Protestant conspirators were such men as Cobham, Markham, Grey
and Walter Raleigh. The whole history of this singular
combination, however, is so confused that it is hard to
pronounce with certainty as to what really was done
or intended. But it appears that the purpose of the
Catholic conspirators was to allow the king to be taken

prisoner by the Puritans and then to rescue him from
their hands. It was called the Bye Plot, and was
based on the hope that James would be so grateful
for this act of devotion to his interest that he would
grant all their requests. On the other hand, such
childish simplicity seems almost incredible. It was
worthy of the visionary, Watson, who planned it.

The farce ended in a tragedy. The two priests were
hanged without more ado. Of the Puritans, Cobham
was sent to the scaffold, and Grey, Markham and
Raleigh, after being condemned, were pardoned.
King James received a letter from the Pope regretting
the action of Watson and Clarke, and assuring him
of the abhorrence with which he regarded all acts of
disloyalty. He also expressed his willingness to recall
any missionary who might be an object of suspicion,
and both Jesuits and seculars were ordered to confine
themselves to their spiritual duties and to discourage
by every means in their power any attempt to disturb
the tranquillity of the realm (Lingard, History of
England, IX, 21).

In 1604 James drew up for Catholics an oath of
allegiance which not only denied the power of the Pope
to depose kings, but declared that such a claim was
heretical, impious and damnable. It was condemned
by Paul V, but the Archpriest Blackwell publicly
announced that notwithstanding the condemnation,
the oath might be conscientiously taken by any English
Catholic, and he accepted it himself before the Commissioners of Lambeth. Bellarmine and Persons
wrote long expostulations to him, but without avail,
He was finally deposed from office, and Birkhead
took his place as archpriest. " This measure," says
Lingard, " was productive of a deep and long-continued
schism in the Catholic body. The greater number,
swayed by the authority of the new Archpriest and

of the Jesuit missionaries, looked upon the oath as a denial of their religion; but, on the other hand, many preferring to be satisfied with the arguments of Blackwell and his advocates, cheerfully took it, when it was offered, and thus freed themselves from the severe penalties to which they would have been subject by the refusal " (op. cit, IX, 77).

Now came the disaster. Irritated beyond measure by the treachery and the tyranny of King James I, a number of Catholic gentlemen, some of them recent converts, formed a plot to blow up the House of Parliament and so get rid of king, lords and commons by one blow.

While the plans were being laid, some of the conspirators began to doubt about their right to involve so many innocent people in the wholesale ruin that must result from this terrible crime. To settle their scruples, Catesby, the chief plotter, proposed a supposititious case to Father Garnet, the Jesuit provincial. " I am going to join the army of the Archduke on the Continent," he said, "and I may be ordered, for example, to blow up a mine in order to destroy the enemy. Can I do so, even if a number of innocent persons are killed?" The answer of course was in the affirmative, and then Catesby made haste to assure his friends that they could proceed in their work with a safe conscience. But as time wore on, he was noticed by his friends to be habitually excited, very often absent from home, and apparently not preparing to go abroad, as he had said he intended to do. Hence, suspicion was aroused, and Garnet, having received some vague hints of the conspiracy, took occasion at Catesby's own table, to inculcate on his host the necessity of submitting meekly to the persecution then going on. Whereupon Catesby burst out in a rage: " It is to you and such as you," he exclaimed,

" that we owe our present calamities. This doctrine of non-resistance makes us slaves. No priest or pontiff can deprive a man of the right to repel injustice." Garnet, alarmed at this utterance, immediately wrote to his superior in Rome, and in due time received two letters, one from the General, the other from the Pope, putting him under strict orders to do all in his power to prevent any attempt against the State. These letters were shown to Catesby, but he protested that they were written on wrong information, and he volunteered to send a special messenger to Rome to put before the authorities there the true state of things. This promise satisfied Garnet, and he felt sure the matter was disposed of, at least, for a time.

This was on May 8, 1605. On October 26, Catesby went to confession to Father Greenwell, or Greenway, or Texmunde, or Tessimond, a Yorkshire man, and revealed the whole plot. Greenwell showed his horror at the proposition and forbade him to entertain it, but Catesby refused to be convinced, and asked him to state the case to Garnet, under seal of confession, with leave to speak of it to others, after the matter, had become public. This will explain how the fact of the confession came out in the trial. Unfortunately, Greenwell was foolish enough to communicate it to Garnet under seal of confession. He was bitterly reproved for doing so, but it was too late; had he kept it to himself, Garnet would not have died on the scaffold. On November 5 after midnight, the plot was discovered, and Guy Fawkes, who was guarding the powder in the cellar of the building where Parliament was to meet, was seized, and acknowledged that the thirty-five barrels of powder which had been placed there were " to blow the Scottish beggars back to their native mountains "— an utterance that won from the king the expression: " Fawkes is the English Scævola."

The other conspirators had time to flee, but were
caught on November 8, at Holbeach House. They
made a brief stand, but in the fight four were killed,
among them Catesby. The others, with the exception
of Littleton, who, it would seem, had betrayed them,
purposely or otherwise, were taken prisoners and
lodged in the Tower.

" More than two months intervened," says Lingard,
"between the apprehension and the trial of the conspirators. The ministers had persuaded themselves,
or wished to persuade others, that the Jesuit missionaries were deeply implicated in the plot. On this
account the prisoners were subjected to repeated
examinations; every artifice which ingenuity could
devise, both promises and threats, the sight of the
rack, and occasionally the infliction of torture were
employed to draw from them some avowal which
might furnish a ground for the charge; and in a proclamation issued for the apprehension of Gerard,
Garnet, and Greenway, it was said to be plain and
evident from the examinations that all three had been
peculiarly practisers in the plot, and therefore no
less pernicious than the actors and counsellors of the
treason."

The mention of Gerard in the warrant arose from
the fact that two years previously, namely on May 1,
1604, the first five conspirators, Catesby, Percy,
Wright, Fawkes, and Winter, met " at a house in the
fields beyond St. Clement's Inn, where," according to
Fawkes' confession, " they did confer and agree on the
plot; and they took a solemn oath and vowed by all
their force to execute the same, and of secrecy not
to reveal it to any of their fellows, but to such as
should be thought fit persons to enter into the action,
and in the same house they did receive the sacrament
of Gerard, the Jesuit, to perform their vow and oath

of secrecy aforesaid, but that Gerard was not acquainted with their purpose." This document is in the handwriting of Sir Edward Coke, but there appear in the original paper, just before the phrase exculpating Gerard, the words *huc usque* (i. e. up to this). Coke read the passage to the judges, " up to this " but the words that would have freed Gerard from suspicion he witheld. " At length," continues Lingard, " the eight prisoners were arraigned. They all pleaded not guilty, not, they wished it to be observed, because they denied their participation in the conspiracy, but because the indictment contained much to which till that day they had been strangers. It was false that the three Jesuits had been the authors of the conspiracy, or had ever held consultations with them on the subject: as far as had come to their knowledge, all three were innocent." They maintained their own right to do as they had done, because " no means of liberation was left but the one they had adopted."

Gerard and Greenwell escaped to the Continent, whereas Garnet, after sending a protestation of his innocence to the Council, secreted himself in the house of Thomas Abingdon, who had married a sister of Lord Mounteagle, the nobleman who had first put the authorities on the scent. According to Jardine (Criminal Trials, 67-70) much ingenuity was employed at the trial to prevent Mounteagle's name from being called in question. With Garnet were Father Oldcorne and Owen, a lay-brother, and also a servant named Chambers. Oldcorne was the chaplain of the house, but Hallam in his " Constitutional History (I-554) says: " the damning circumstance against Garnet is that he was taken at Hendlip in concealment, along with the other conspirators." As Oldcorne and the two others had nothing whatever to do with the affair and as all the conspirators had been already shot or hanged, "the damning evidence" of perverting the facts of the case is against Hallam.

On February 1, the Bill of Attainder was read, and day after day, till March 28, the commissioners visited the Tower to elicit evidence. Oldcorne was repeatedly put on the rack, but nothing was extorted from him. So also with Owen, Chambers and Johnson, the chief steward of the house where the priests were found. On March 1, after Owen had been tortured, he was told he would be stretched on the rack the two following days. The third experiment killed him, and it was given out that "he had ripped his belly open with a blunt knife." Garnet, when threatened with the rack, replied that "the threat did not frighten him — he was not a child."

The trial was finally called for March 28. The most distinguished lawyer in the realm at that time was Attorney-General Coke. He began his charge by recalling the history of all the plots that had been hatched since Elizabeth's time; he declaimed against Jesuitical equivocation and the temporal power of the Pope, and insisted that all missionaries, and the Jesuits in particular, were leagued in conspiracy against the king and his Protestant councillors. But when he got down to the real merits of the indictment, he soon betrayed the groundlessness of his charge. Not a word did he say of the confessions or the witnesses or their dying declarations, although he had boasted he would prove that Garnet had been the original framer of the plot and the confidential adviser of the conspirators. His whole charge rested on his own assertions, and was supported only by a few unimportant facts, susceptible of a very different interpretation (Lingard, op. cit. IX, 63).

Garnet answered that he had been debarred from making known his information of the plot for the reason that it had been imparted to him under the seal of confession, and could not be revealed until it had become public property. His concealment of it, nevertheless, was considered by the judges as misprision of treason, and on that ground, and not by anything adduced by the attorney-general, was he condemned. Indeed, Coke had so utterly failed to prove his case that even Cecil confessed that nothing had been produced against Garnet, except that he had been overheard to say in conversation with Oldcorne in the Tower, that "only one person knew of his acquaintance with the conspiracy." It is this particular feature of the trial that has evoked ever since a great deal of hypocritical denunciation of Garnet's lack of veracity. When asked if he had spoken to Oldcorne or written to Greenway, he replied in the negative; but it was proved that he had done both. As it is Coke who alleges this inveracity of Father Garnet, we may reject it as a calumny for that same distinguished personage declared in his official report that Garnet, when on the scaffold, admitted his complicity in the crime, whereas this was flatly denied by those who were present at the execution. If Coke could lie about one thing, he could lie about another. But in any case a criminal court is not a confessional, and the worst offender can plead "not guilty" without violating the truth. Garnet was executed on March 3, 1606, but his body was not quartered until life had left it.

Gerard, who had been proscribed, but who was perfectly innocent of any knowledge of the conspiracy, had made haste to leave the country. It was a difficult thing to do but he finally succeeded, and at the very time that Garnet was standing on the scaffold, Gerard was leaving London as a footman in the train of the Spanish ambassador. A lay-brother was with him in some other capacity. Such was his farewell to his native country. He had been sent there as a missionary in 1588, and had stepped ashore on the Norfolk coast just after the defeat of the Armada — a time when everyone was hunting for Papists. The story of the adventure of this handsome, courtly gentleman, who had three or four languages at his disposal, who was a keen sportsman, a skilful horseman, and a polished man of the world, and was at ease in the highest society, yet who was always preaching the Gospel wherever he went, in prisons and even on the rack, forms one of the most attractive pages in the records of the English mission. He died in Rome at the age of seventy-three.

During the trial of Father Garnet, Oldcorne had been removed from the Tower and executed at Worcester on April 7 or 17. Littleton, who had saved himself at the time of the conspiracy by informing on the others, begged the father's pardon on the scaffold and died with him. Two years afterwards, on June 23, 1608, Father Garnet's nephew, Thomas was martyred in London. He was then thirty-four years old, and had been only three years a Jesuit.

After the execution of Garnet a much more drastic penal code was enacted. Henry IV of France, through his ambassador and the Prince de Joinville, tried hard to restrain the anger of King James, but without avail, except that two missionaries, under sentence of death for refusing to take the oath, were saved by the French king's intercession. He could not obtain the reprieve of Drury, however, who was condemned to death because a copy of a letter from Persons denouncing the oath of allegiance was found in his possession. Whether this Drury was a Jesuit or not cannot be ascertained, for the "Fasti Breviores" and the "Menology" speak only of a Drury who was killed with another Jesuit in the collapse of a church

at old Blackfriars in 1623. James would not listen to
the remonstrances of Henry; he assured the ambassador
that he was, by nature, an enemy of harsh and cruel
measures, and that he had repeatedly held his ministers
in check, but that the Catholics were so infected with
the doctrine of the Jesuits that he had to leave the
matter to parliament. When the ambassador remarked
that there was apparently no difference of treatment
whether Catholics took the oath or not, the king did
not reply.

CHAPTER VI

JAPAN

1555–1645

WHEN Francis Xavier bade farewell to Japan in 1551, he left behind him Fathers Torres and Fernandes. They could not possibly have sufficed for the vast work before them, and hence, in August of the following year, Father Gago was sent with two companions, neither of whom was yet in Holy Orders. They were provided with royal letters and well supplied with presents to King Civandono, who was a devoted friend to Francis Xavier.

The newcomers were amazed at the piety of the 3,000 Christians, who were awaiting further instruction. They found them kind and charitable, very much given to corporal austerities, and extremely scrupulous in matters of conscience and there was no difficulty in getting enthusiastic catechists among them to address the people and teach them the new religion. As the belief of the Japanese, was then, as it is today, Shintoism, which has no dogma, no moral law, and no books, and is tinctured with Buddhism, the main doctrine of which is the transmigration of souls, it was easy to arouse interest in a religion which presented to their consideration spiritual doctrines, a moral law and sacred books. In 1554 there were 1500 baptisms in the kingdom of Arima alone, though no priest had as yet entered that part of the country. The feudal system of government then prevailing made conversions easy. Thus, when the Governor of Amaguchi became a Christian, more than three hundred of his vassals and friends immediately followed his example. This influence was still more in evidence whenever a distinguished bonze accepted the Faith, an example of which occurred when the two most celebrated personages of that class came down from Kioto to Amaguchi for a public disputation. After the conference they fell at the feet of Torres, and not only asked for baptism, but became zealous instructors of the people. Naturally all the bonzeries of the Empire were alarmed and they rose in revolt against the Government for not checking these conversions. But Civandono called his troops together to quell what soon assumed the proportions of organized warfare. Indeed at one time, the insurgents seemed to be getting the upper hand: but just as the king was on the point of being entrapped, Fernandes at the risk of his life slipped through the ranks of the enemy and gave Civandono information which won the victory. After that the friendship of the monarch never failed his Christian subjects. He had ample opportunity to show his devotion to them, for uprisings were as common as the earthquakes in Japan, which were said to average three a day.

Father Nunhes, the provincial, had been induced by the Viceroy of the Indies to pay a visit to Japan at this juncture, and he arrived with Father Vilela and a number of young scholastics. With them was a

rich Portuguese named Pinto, who had resolved to
employ most of his money in building a school in
Civandono's dominions. In order to help the scheme,
the viceroy had made Pinto his ambassador. They
arrived in April, 1556, after a perilous journey, only to
find a letter there from St. Ignatius, reminding Father
Nunhes that provincials had no business to undertake
such journeys and leave their official work to others.
However, such a pressing invitation had come meantime
from the King of Firando or Hirando, as it is now
called, and the chance seemed so promising for the
king's conversion, that Father Nunhes presumed
permission to delay his return to India. He was
received by Civandono, whom he had to visit on his
way to Hirando, with the same splendid ceremonies
that had been accorded to St. Francis Xavier; and,
during a long conference which was held with the help
of Fernandes, he urged the king to become a Christian,
but Civandono insisted that reasons of State prevented
him from doing so for the moment. Nunhes then set
out for Hirando, but fell ill before he reached it, and,
in consequence, was compelled to return to Goa. As
he had not converted a single idolater, and as Pinto's
grand plans for the education of the Japanese were a
failure, the provincial concluded that it would have
been wiser to have remained in Hindostan, where he
was accomplishing great things, than to engage in
apostolic work to which obedience had not assigned
him. Pinto's failure, however, was compensated for by
the devotion of another rich man, Louis Almeida,
who had come with Father Nunhes to Japan. Almeida
being a physician, immediately set to work to build
two establishments — a hospital for lepers and a refuge
for abandoned childern, which the immorality of the
Japanese women made extremely necessary. This was
another expression of gratitude to Civandono, which

the king appreciated. By this time Almeida had become a Jesuit.

Meantime the King of Hirando, who had asked for Nunhes, was propitiated by having Father Gago sent to him. The missionary's success was marvellous. Numberless conversions followed his visit, beginning with that of the king himself. Helpers were sent, among them being the illustrious bonze, Paul of Kioto, whose conversion had caused a great stir some few years before. In a month or so 1400 baptisms were recorded; but Paul had reached the end of his apostolic career and he returned to die in the arms of Father Torres.

The usual uprising occurred, and the king who had made so much ado about calling Father Nunhes turned out to be a very weak-kneed Christian. Churches were destroyed, crosses desecrated, and other outrages committed, but he did nothing to quell the disturbance. Political reasons, he alleged, prevented him. It was in this outbreak that the first martyrdom occurred, that of a poor slave-woman who had been accustomed to pray before a cross erected outside the city. She had been warned that it was as much as her life was worth to declare her Christianity so openly; she persisted, nevertheless, and was killed as she knelt down in the roadway to receive the blow of the executioner's sword. Even Father Gago himself came near falling a victim to the popular fury. In view of subsequent events, if they were as reported, it is to be regretted that he missed the opportunity of winning the crown.

The first Jesuit who reached Kioto and remained there was Vilela. He had travelled a long distance to visit a famous bonzery to which he had been invited; and then, finding himself not far away from the imperial city, he determined to present himself to the emperor, or Mikado as he was called. His method of approaching that great potentate amazed the onlookers by its novelty. Holding his cross high in the air, he proclaimed his purpose in coming to Japan. To the surprise of every one, the Mikado seemed extremely pleased; but that alarmed the bonzes, and they accused Vilela of all sorts of crimes, not excluding cannibalism. Indeed, they had seen great pieces of human flesh at Vilela's house, they said. To stop their clamors, the Mikado finally consented to a public debate, doing so with great apprehension, however, for Vilela's success. The discussion took place, but, if the metempsychosis set forth by their spokesman on that occasion, represented the popular creed, one is forced to say that the Japanese mentality of that period was not of a very superior character. Vilela's easy victory gave him the right to preach everywhere in the Empire; and the number of converts was so great that many missionaries were needed to help him.

Father Gago, who had missed the chance of martyrdom a short time before, was looked upon as the man for the emergency. Francis Xavier had chosen him expressly for Japan; his facility in learning the language was marvellous; his piety was admitted by all; his zeal knew no bounds, and his success corresponded with his efforts. Indeed, he was almost adored wherever he went; but suddenly, just as he was needed he appeared to be a changed man. His energy, his zeal, his enthusiasm had all evaporated. There was, absolutely, nothing amiss in his conduct — not even a suspicion suggested itself. But he wanted to give up his work; and to the dismay of his associates he returned to Goa. He was nearly shipwrecked on his way, but that resulted only in a temporary revival of his fervor. He was sent to Salsette and was taken prisoner but was subsequently released. He was never again, however, the man that he had been in the beginning of his career. " I have enlarged on this," says Charlevoix, " for I am writing a history and not a panegyric." The " Menology " of Portugal, however, assails both Charlevoix and Bartoli for this charge, but the defence lacks explicitness.

From Kioto, Vilela went to Sacai, which was an independent city — republican in its administration, but in its rule as tyrannical as Venice was about that time. Over and above that, it was grossly immoral, and only one family in it would have anything to do with the missionary. So he shook its dust from his feet and went elsewhere.

Almeida, the physician, distinguished himself in his missionary journeys at this time, and he tells how he came across a whole community of people in a secluded district who had seen a priest only once in passing, yet had remembered all that had been told them, and were keeping the commandments as well as they knew how. He baptized them all, and leaving them capable catechists, one of whom had written a book about Christianity, he continued on his way, hunting for more souls to save. It was largely due to him that some of the reigning princes were gained over. One of them, Sumitanda by name, had distinguished himself by throwing down a famous idol, called the God of War, just at the moment the army was going into battle. As the fight was won, most of the soldiers not only became Christians, but, later on, when Sumitanda found himself attacked by two kings who resented his conversion, a great number of his men fastened crosses on their armor and swept the enemy from the field.

Meantime a revolution had broken out at Kioto against the Mikado; he was besieged in his citadel, but finally succeeded in beating back the foe. When peace was restored in 1562 Vilela returned to the capital; and multitudes, not only of the people, but many princes of the blood and distinguished nobles, made a public profession of Christianity. This again brought the bonzes to the fore, and as a prelude to a decree of expulsion of the missionaries, they succeeded in having two of the most influential men of the kingdom, both bitter pagans, constituted as a commission to examine into the new teachings. So convinced was everyone that it was only the beginning of a process of extermination that Vilela was advised to withdraw from the capital. He acquiesced, much against his will; but it happened that two of his Christians of the humbler class so astounded the inquisitors by their answers that both of the great men asked for baptism. A discourse of Vilela gained another convert in the person of the father of a man who became famous in those days of Japanese history — Justus Ucondono.

In 1565 the missionaries were treated with special consideration by the Mikado, on the occasion of the splendid court ceremonies which marked the opening of the new year. The whole nation was astounded at the unprecedented favor, but as usual it was only the prelude of a storm. In the following year the Mikado was murdered; and all his adherents were either put to the sword or expelled from the capital. This was the first act of a tragedy that would make a theme for a Shakespeare. It is as follows: The successful rebels had placed the younger brother of the emperor on the throne, but fearing a similar fate, he had fled to the castle of the distinguished soldier, Vatadono, who, finding himself not strong enough to maintain the claim of the fugitive monarch, induced the ablest military man of Japan, Nobunaga, the King of Boari, to take up the cause of their sovereign. The offer was accepted; two bloody battles followed; the insurgents were cut to pieces, and the young emperor,

under the name of Cubosama, was enthroned at Kioto.
The palace, which had been wrecked in the war, was
replaced by a new one, built of the stones of the
bonzeries and the statues of the national idols. The
two conquerors then made haste to show their esteem
for the missionaries and assured them of protection;
Nobunaga withdrew to his kingdom when the work
was completed, and Vatadono, his lieutenant, remained
as viceroy at Kioto. All these events occurred in the
single year of 1568.

Just then the illustrious Alexander Valignani, the
greatest man of the missions in the East after Francis
Xavier, came on the scene. For thirty-two years all
his efforts were directed to shaping and guiding the
various posts of the vast field of apostolic work in
this new part of the world, his success being marvellous.
He was born at Chieti. The close friendship of his
father with Pope Paul IV made the highest offices
of the Church attainable if he chose to aspire to them;
but he left the papal court, and was received into the
Society by Francis Borgia, beginning his life as a
Jesuit by the practice of terrible bodily mortifications,
which he continued until the end of his career. He
was chosen by Mercurian to be visitor to the Indies;
thirty-two companions were given him, and he was
authorized to select eight more, wherever he might
find them.

At that time Japan had only twenty missionaries,
while there were none at all in China. When Valignani
died, there were in the empire of Japan one hundred
and fifty Jesuits and six hundred catechists, who in spite
of wars and persecutions had three hundred churches
and thirty-one places for the missionaries to assemble.
There were a novitiate, a house of theological and
philosophical studies, two colleges where the Japanese
nobles sent their sons, besides a printing establishment,

two schools of music and painting, multitudes of sodalities, schools, and finally, hospitals for every kind of human suffering, and when the persecutions began, he had resources enough at his disposal to provide for nine hundred exiled Japanese. Finally, it was his guidance and help that enabled Matteo Ricci to plant the cross in the two capitals of China. He wielded such an influence over the terrible Taicosama that it was a common saying in the empire that if Father Alexander had survived, the Church of Japan would never have succumbed. There was great rejoicing when his arrival was announced. The ship which brought him to port had not dropped anchor, before it was surrounded by hundreds of boats filled with Christians, all of them carrying flags on which a cross was painted. When he approached the city, throngs of people came out to meet him, some kissing his robe, others his hands, others his feet, and a long procession led him in triumph to the Church, where a Te Deum was sung to thank God for his coming.

In that year, Nagasaki, which was afterwards to furnish so many matryrs to the faith, suddenly developed from an inconspicuous village to a great city, because of the number of Christians who had settled there. A great sorrow, however, just then fell on the Church; Fernandes, one of the missionaries whom Xavier had left behind him in Japan, had died. Torres still remained, indeed, but he also was to end his glorious career in a year or two. However, they had built up a splendid Church; and under such conditions the work of evangelization could not fail to proceed rapidly. Indeed, the records of that period teem with accounts of conversions of princes and entire populations; and when Cabral arrived as superior in place of Torres, the emperor gave the missionaries his protection, in spite of the unrelenting opposition of

the bonzes, who still exercised a preponderating
influence at Court. In one of the provinces, Cabral,
in his official visitations, found a very remarkable
evidence of solidity in the faith. No priest had been
there for ten years; yet a beautiful church had been
erected and a fervent congregation filled it continually.
In another place where the constant wars in which
the ruler was engaged and the carnage which he had
committed in conquering the territory had kept out the
missionaries for at least twenty years, thanks to an
old blind man named Tobias whom St. Francis Xavier
had baptized and named, all the people who were left
in the vicinity were thoroughly instructed in their
Faith.

Meantime a new historical drama was being enacted,
which was more marvellous than the first. The weak
character of Cubosama had made him the victim of the
bonzes, whom he heartily detested. They had also
succeeded in disrupting the friendship of Vatadono and
Nobunaga. Fortunately, the two friends were reconciled in time, but that gave rise to a counter movement
to destroy them. War was declared on some pretext
or other, and in one of the first engagements Vatadono
was killed. It was a sad blow for the missionaries,
for the hero was a catechumen and was waiting to be
baptized. Left alone now and supposed to be unable
to defend himself, Nobunaga was more fiercely assailed
than ever by the bonzes. Wearied of it all, he called
his troops together and set out for Kioto. His enemies
fled before him. He took the city and set it on fire,
and then, not because he was actuated by motives of
personal ambition, but because he saw that if Cubosama
was allowed to rule the state of warfare would continue,
he locked up the feeble monarch in a fortress, and
constituted himself supreme military commander or
Shogun. It was then that Civandono, King of Bungo,

the original friend of Francis Xavier, became a Christian and took the name of Francis; furthermore he built a city in which only Christians were allowed to live. There he passed the rest of his days an example of piety to all.

Meantime, Nobunaga continued to shower favors on the missionaries. He built a new and splendid city, and in the best part of it founded a college and a seminary. Christianity made great strides under his administration, as he was the deadly enemy of the bonzes who for years had endeavored to compass his ruin. Nevertheless, though he listened with interest and pleasure to explanations of the creed, and asked the missionaries, half roguishly, if they really believed all they said, and if they were not as bad as the bonzes, he went no further.

In the first years of Nobunaga's rule, Valignani conceived the idea of having a solemn embassy sent by the various Christian kings of the country, to pay their homage to the Sovereign Pontiff in the Eternal City. It was not an imperial delegation, but was restricted to the three devout rulers of Bungo, Arima and Omura. Nobunaga willingly gave his consent, and the ambassadors left Nagasaki on February 22, 1582, and repaired to Kioto. From there they went by the way of Malacca to Goa. On this part of the journey they were frequently in imminent danger of shipwreck, but they arrived safely in Goa at the beginning of 1583. There they were received with great ceremony by the Viceroy, Mascaregnas, who entertained them for several months. Valignani, who had conducted them thus far, returned to Japan after putting them in the hands of Fathers Mesquita and Rodrigues, who remained with them till they reached Rome.

They set sail at the end of February, and on August 10 dropped anchor in the Tagus. Charlevoix

remarks that " this part of the journey was not long,"
though it was nearly six months in duration. The
prince cardinal who was at that time Viceroy of Portugal
showered honors upon them, and made them his guests
in the royal palace for an entire month. They then
visited the principal cities of Portugal. Nothing was
too much for them in the way of honor and even in
the way of money. Finally they were conducted to
Madrid and had a public audience with Philip II, to
whom they presented their credentials and offered the
presents of the Christians of Japan and their expression
of gratitude for all that his majesty had done for the
infant Church of their country. Philip is said to have
embraced them affectionately, assuring them of the
great regard he had for the kings whom they represented. The Queen Maria put her carriages at their
disposal, and on the following day they were conducted
to the Escorial where they received the congratulations
of the princes and grandees of Spain. The French
ambassador also paid them a ceremonious visit. Even
the king himself called upon them and had a vessel
equipped at Alicante to conduct them to Italy. They
left Madrid on November 26, and were received with
almost royal honors in every city on their way. It was
already January, 1585, when they left Spain. The
Mediterranean treated them badly; and it was only in
the month of March that they stepped ashore at
Leghorn, amid the salvos of artillery from the fort.
The carriages of the grand duke carried them on their
journey to Pisa. There the prince and all his court
were waiting to receive them, and led them to the
palace, where a splendid banquet was prepared, after
which Pietro de' Medici and the grand duke came to
pay them their respects.

They saw the carnival at Pisa, and then journeyed
on to Florence, where the papal nuncio and the cardinal

12

archbishop, who was afterwards Pope Leo XI, bade
them welcome. From there they passed to Siena,
where, as guests of the Pope, they were met at the
frontier by two hundred arquebusiers sent by the
vice-legate of Viterbo to show them special honor.
Gregory XIII was then on the Pontifical throne; and
feeling that his end was approaching, he sent a company
of light horse to hasten their coming. It was Friday,
March 20, 1585, when they entered Rome, and their
first visit was to Father Aquaviva, who was then
General of the Society. He led them to the church,
where a Te Deum was sung; and on the following day
the Pope held a consistory which ordered that the
envoys should be regarded as royal ambassadors; that
their reception should be as splendid as possible; and
that their first audience should be at the full consistory
in the papal palace.

On the day appointed for the solemn entry, March 23,
the Spanish ambassador sent his carriages to convey
the visitors to the villa of the Pope; and then with the
papal light horse at the head, followed by the Swiss
guards, the cardinalitial officials and the ambassadors
of Spain and Venice, with their pages and officers and
trumpeters and all the papal household in their purple
robes, the delegates proceeded to the City. The
Japanese were on horseback and wore the costume of
their country; princes and archbishops rode on either
side, and followed by Father Diego, who acted as
interpreter. A throng of mounted cavaliers in gorgeous
apparel closed the pageant. The whole city turned out
to receive them. The streets were crowded with
people, as were the roofs of the houses, all observing a
reverential silence, interrupted only by the blast of the
trumpets or the occasional but enthusiastic acclama-
tions of the multitude. When the bridge of Castle
Sant' Angelo was reached, the cannon boomed out a

welcome which was repeated by the guns of the papal palace and taken up by strains of musical instruments that resounded from every quarter as the envoys approached the palace.

So great was the throng of cardinals and prelates in the hall that the Swiss guards had to force their way through it, to conduct the Pontiff to his throne. When he was seated the ambassadors approached, holding their credentials in their hands; and then, kneeling at the feet of the Pope, they announced in a clear and loud voice that they had come from the ends of the earth to see the Vicar of Jesus Christ and to offer him the homage of the princes whose envoys they were. Tears flowed down the cheeks of the Pontiff as he lifted the envoys up and embraced them tenderly, again and again, with an affection they never forgot. They were then conducted to a raised platform; and the secretary of the Pope read aloud the letters, which they had brought. When that was concluded, Father Gonzales explained at length the purpose of their mission, and a bishop replied in the name of His Holiness. The second kissing of the feet was next in order, and the cardinals crowded around the wondering Japanese to ask them numberless questions about their country and the events of their voyage, to all of which replies were given with a refinement and courtesy that charmed all who heard them. The session was now ended, and rising from his throne, the Pope withdrew, giving to the visitors the honor, conferred only on the imperial ambassadors, of bearing the papal train. They were then entertained at a sumptuous banquet.

Private interviews with the Pope followed; and after receptions by various dignitaries, at some of which the Japanese wore their national dress, at others appearing in the Italian apparel, the Pope gave them expensive robes, which they wore with an ease and grace that was amazing for men so unaccustomed to such surroundings and ceremonies. When they went to offer their prayers at the seven churches they were received processionally at each of them, the bells ringing and organs playing. Meantime physicians were sending hourly bulletins to His Holiness, who was deeply concerned about one of the envoys who had been debarred from all these ceremonies by an attack of sickness. The invalid, however, did not die, but, later on, in his native country, gave his life for the Faith.

Indeed it was the Pope himself who died a few days after these pageants. He was ill only a few days, but in his very last moments he was making inquiries about the sick man from the Far East. He departed this life on April 10, and on the 25th Sixtus V mounted the throne. Before his election he had been most effusive in his attention to the Japanese, and was more so after his election, even giving them precedence over cardinals, when there was question of an audience. They assisted at his coronation, served as acolytes at his Mass, and were guests at a banquet in his villa. He even decorated them as knights, and when they had been belted and spurred by the ambassadors of France and Venice, he hung rich gold chains and medals on their necks, lifted them up and kissed them and gave them communion at his private Mass. He sent letters and presents to the kings they represented, and the ambassadors themselves were recipients of rich rewards from the generous Pontiff.

Finally, they were made patricians by the Senate, which assembled at the Capitol for that purpose; and were given letters patent with a massive gold seal attached. They then bade farewell to the Pope, who defrayed all the expenses of their journey to Lisbon. Invitations were extended to them from other sovereigns of Europe, but it was impossible to accept them, and they left Rome on June 3, 1585, conducted a considerable distance by the light horse and numbers of the nobility. At Spoleto, Assisi, Montefalcono, Perugia, Bologna, Ferrara and elsewhere, every honor was given them. As they approached Venice, for instance, forty red-robed senators received them and accompanied them up the Grand Canal in a vessel that was usually kept for the use of kings. Every gondola of the city followed in their wake; the patriarch and all the nobility visited them; and they were then conducted to the palace of the Doge, where the attendant senators accorded them the first places in the assembly. Tintoretto painted their portraits, and they were shown tapestries on which their reception by the Pope had been already represented. A hundred pieces of artillery welcomed them to Mantua; the city was illuminated and the people knelt in the street to show their veneration for these new children of the Faith from the Far East. They even stood sponsors at the baptism of a Jewish rabbi. It was the same story at Milan and Cremona. They approached Genoa by sea, and galleys were sent out to convoy them to the city. Leaving there on August 8 they reached Barcelona on the 17th. At Moncon they again saw Philip II who had a vessel specially equipped for them at Lisbon; he lavished money and presents on them, and gave orders to the Viceroy of India to provide them with everything they wished till they reached Japan. They finally left Lisbon on April 30, 1586. During their stay in Europe they had the happiness of meeting St. Aloysius Gonzaga, who was then a novice in the Society.

The splendor of these European courts must have dazzled the eyes of the dark-skinned sons of the East as they journeyed through Portugal, Italy and Spain; but they were probably not aware of the tragedies that

were enacted near-by in the dominions of the Most
Christian King, where Catholics and Huguenots were
at each other's throats; nor did they know of the
fratricidal struggles in Germany that were leading up
to the Thirty Years War, which was to make Christian
Europe a desert; nor of the fury of Elizabeth who was
at that very time putting to death the brothers of the
Jesuits whom they so deeply revered.   The revolutions,
assassinations and sacrileges committed all through
those countries would have been startling revelations
of the depths to which Christian nations could descend.
However, they may have been informed of it all, and
could thus understand more easily the remorseless
cruelty of their own pagan rulers whose victims they
were so soon to be.

Cubosama, as we have seen, had been kind to the
Christians, and Nobunaga had welcomed the priests
to his palace and found pleasure in their conversations.
He had given them a place in the beautiful city he
built; but in reality he doubted the sincerity of their
belief just as he disbelieved the teaching of the bonzes.
In default of another deity, he had begun to worship
himself, and, like, Nabuchodonosor of old, he finally
exacted divine honors from his subjects.   Such an
attitude of mind naturally led to cruelty, and in 1586
he was murdered by one of his trusted officials who, in
turn, perished in battle when Ucondono, the Christian
commander of the imperial armies, overthrew him.
Unwisely, perhaps, Ucondono did not assume the office
of protector of the young son of Nobunaga, but left
it to a man of base extraction, the terrible Taicosama,
who quickly became the Shogun.   At first he protected
the Christians, made the provincial, Coelho, his friend
and permitted the Faith to be preached throughout
the empire.   The chief officers of his army and navy
were avowed believers.

Three years passed and the number of neophytes had doubled. There were now 300,000 Christians in Japan — among them kings and princes, and the three principal ministers of the empire. But it happened that, in the year 1589 two Christian women had refused to become inmates of Taicosama's harem, and that turned him into a terrible persecutor. Ucondono was deprived of his office and sent into exile; Father Coelho was forbidden to preach in public, and the other Jesuits were to withdraw from the country within twenty days, while every convert was ordered to abjure Christianity. The two hundred and forty churches were to be burned. The recreant son of the famous old king of Bungo gave the first notable example of apostasy, but, as often happens in such circumstances, the persecution itself won thousands of converts who, up to that, had hesitated about renouncing their idols. At this juncture, Father Valignani appeared as ambassador of the Viceroy of the Indies, and in that capacity was received with royal magnificence by Taicosama. But the bonzes, who had now regained their influence over the emperor, assured him that the embassy was only a device to evade the law, and, hence, though he accepted the presents, he did not relent in his opposition; yet in his futile expedition against China two Jesuits accompanied the troops.

Blood was first shed in the kingdom of Hirando. Fathers Carrioni and Martel were poisoned, and Carvalho and Furnaletto, who took their places, met the same fate. A fifth, whose name is lost, was killed in a similar fashion. Unfortunately, the Spanish merchants in the Philippines just at that time induced the Franciscan missionaries of those islands to go over to Japan, for the rumor had got abroad that the Jesuits in Japan had been wholly exterminated, although there were still, in reality, twenty-six of them in the country. It is true they were not in evidence as formerly, for with the exception of the two army chaplains, they were exercising their ministry secretly. Of that, however, the Spaniards were not aware and probably spoke in good faith. The Franciscans, on arriving, discovered that they had been duped in believing that the persecution was prompted by dislike of the Jesuits' personality, some of whom no doubt they met. Nevertheless, they determined to remain, and Taicosama permitted them to do so, because of the letters they carried from the Governor of the Philippines, who expressed a desire of becoming Taicosama's vassal. Meantime, a Spanish captain whose vessel had been wrecked on the coast had foolishly said that the sending of missionaries to Japan was only a device to prepare for a Portuguese and Spanish invasion. Possibly he spoke in jest, but his words were reported to Taicosama, with the result that on February 5, 1597, six Franciscans and three Jesuits were hanging on crosses at Nagasaki. The Jesuits were Paul Miki, James Kisai, and John de Goto, all three Japanese. On the same day a general decree of banishment was issued.

Just then Valignani, who had withdrawn, returned to Japan with nine more Jesuits and the coadjutor of the first bishop of Japan — the bishop having died on the way out. Valignani, who was personally very acceptable to Taicosama, was cordially received and the storm ceased momentarily; but unfortunately, Taicosama died a year afterwards and, strange to say, two Jesuit priests, Rodrigues and Organtini, who had won his affection, were with him when he breathed his last, but they failed to make any impression on his mind or heart. He left a son, and Daifusama became regent or Shogun. Fortunately, Valignani had some success in convincing him that to establish himself

firmly on his throne it would be wise to extend his
protection to his Christian subjects. Moreover, the
King of Hirando, though at first bent on continuing
the persecution, was constrained by the threatening
attitude of his Christian subjects, who were very
numerous and very powerful in his kingdom, to desist
from his purpose, at least for a while. Probably he
was assisted in this resolution by the fact that in the
first year after the outburst, namely in 1599, seventy
thousand more Japanese had asked for baptism.
In 1603 there were 10,000 conversions in the single
principality of Fingo.

Father Organtini succeeded in getting quite close
to Daifusama who, to strengthen himself politically,
allowed the churches to be rebuilt in the empire and
even in Kioto. Unfortunately, however, in 1605 he
heard that Spain was sending out a number of war
vessels to subjugate the Moluccas, and fancying that
its objective was really Japan, he gave orders to the
Governor of Nagasaki to allow no Spanish ships to
enter the harbor. To make matters worse, it happened
that Valignani, who exercised an extraordinary influence
on Daifusama, was not at hand to disabuse him of his
error. He was then dying, and expired the next year
at the age of sixty-nine. For the moment Daifusama
was so much affected by the loss of his friend that he
forgot his suspicions and gave full liberty to the missionaries to exercise their ministry everywhere. In fact,
he summoned to his palace the famous Charles Spinola,
who appears now for the first time in the country for
which he was soon to shed his blood. With Spinola
was Sequiera, the first bishop who had succeeded
in reaching Japan. The imperial summons was eagerly
obeyed by Spinola and the bishop, for such progress
had already been made in the formation of a native
clergy that five parishes which they had established

in Nagasaki were at that time in the hands of Japanese priests, and an academy had been begun in which, besides theology, elementary physics and astronomy were taught. Organtini, who had labored in Japan for forty-nine years, had even built a foundling asylum, to continue the work which Almeida had inaugurated elsewhere. A hospital for lepers had also been started.

Nothing happened for the moment, but though outwardly favoring the missionaries, Daifusama was in his heart worried about this amazingly rapid expansion of Christianity, and when in 1612 two merchants, one from Holland and one from England, which were plotting to oust the Spanish and Portuguese from the control of the commerce of Japan, aroused his old suspicions by assuring him that the priests were in reality only the forerunners of invading armies, the old hostility flamed out anew. The opportunity to work on Daifusama's fears presented itself in a curious way. A Spanish ship had been sent from Mexico by the viceroy to see what could be done to establish trade relations with Japan, and on coming into port it was seen to be taking the usual soundings — a mysterious proceeding in the eyes of the Japanese. The fact was reported to Daifusama, who asked an English sea-captain what it meant. "Why," was the reply, " in Europe that is considered a hostile act. The captain is charting the harbor so as to allow a fleet to enter and invade Japan. These Jesuits are well known to be Spanish priests who have been hunted out of every nation in Europe as plotters and spies, and the religion they teach is only a cloak to conceal their ulterior designs."

Whether Daifusama believed this or not is hard to say, but greater men than this rude barbarian have been deceived by more ridiculous falsehoods. There was no delay. Fourteen of the most distinguished families of the empire were banished, and others awaited a like proscription. Then the persecution became general; the churches were destroyed and all the missionaries were ordered out of the empire. Daifusama died in 1616, but his son and successor outdid him in ferocity though there was a short lull on account of internal political troubles.

It was during this period that thirty-three Jesuits slipped back into the country under various disguises. Their purpose was to work secretly, so that the government would not remark their presence. Unfortunately, twenty-four Franciscans, deceived by a rumor that a commercial treaty had been made with Spain and under the impression that the root of the trouble was personal dislike for Jesuits, landed at Nagasaki at the end of the year 1616, and insisted on going out in the open and proclaiming the Gospel publicly. They reckoned without their host. A decree was issued making it a capital offense to harbor missionaries of any garb. Not only that, but it was officially announced that death would be inflicted on the occupants of the ten houses nearest the one where a missionary was discovered. The Jesuits took to the mountains and marshes to save their people, but the Franciscans defied the edict. The result was that immediate orders were issued to take every priest that could be found. Nagasaki was first ransacked. The Jesuits had all vanished except Machado; he and a Franciscan were captured, and on May 21, 1617, were decapitated. In spite of this warning, however, a Dominican and an Augustinian publicly celebrated Mass, under the very eyes of Sancho, an apostate prince who was an agent of the Shogun. The result was immediate death for both. The same useless bravado was repeated elsewhere. Different tactics, as we have said, were adopted by the Jesuits. Thus, de Angelis covered the mountains of Voxuan; Navarro and Porro lived in a cave in Bungo, and crept out when they could, to visit their scattered flocks. There was a group also on the rich island of Nippon — among them Torres, Barretto, Fernandes and a Japanese named Yukui. From this place of concealment they spread out in all directions, usually disguised as native peddlers; all of them, even in those terrible surroundings, winning many converts to the Faith.

A phenomenon not unusual in the Church, but carried to extraordinary lengths in this instance, now presented itself. Instead of striking terror into the hearts of the Christians, the very opposite result ensued. A widespread eagerness, a special devotion for martyrdom, as it were, manifested itself. Crowds gathered in every city to accompany the victims to the place of execution; the women and children put on their richest attire; songs of joy were sung and prayers aflame with enthusiasm were recited by the spectators, who kept reminding the sufferers that the scaffold was the stairway to heaven. At Kioto there was no trouble in filling out the lists of those who were to be executed. People came of themselves to give their names. Those who did not were rated as idolaters. The number ran up to several thousands and the emperor was so alarmed that he cut them down to 1700. There were fifteen Jesuits in the city. Six of them were banished, but the other nine went from place to place, keeping up the courage of their flocks. Gomes and the bishop had died in the midst of these horrors; and the duties of both devolved on Carvalho.

Unfortunately, at this juncture, a paper was found signed in blood by a number of Christians pledging themselves to fight to death against the banishment of the missionaries. That was enough for the Shogun.

The Jesuits, to the number of one hundred and seventeen, with twenty-seven members of other religious orders, Augustinians, Franciscans and Dominicans, were dragged down to Nagasaki and shipped to Macao and the Philippines. With them was Ucondono, the erstwhile commander of the forces of Taicosama, On the vessels also were several families of distinguished people. Some died on the journey; and others, Ucondono among the number, gave up the ghost shortly after arriving at the Philippines. Twenty-six Jesuits and some other religious succeeded in remaining in Japan. As the provinicial Carvalho, was among the exiles, he named Rodrigues as his successor, and appointed Charles Spinola to look after Nagasaki and the surrounding territory. The work had now become particularly difficult. Thus, one of these concealed apostles tells how most of his labor had to be performed at night. Often he found himself groping along unknown roads through forests and on the edges of precipices, over which he not infrequently rolled to the bottom of the abyss. Another says: " I am hiding in a hut, and a little rice is handed in to me from time to time. The place is so wet that I have got sciatica, and cannot stand or sit; most of my work is done at night, visiting my flock, while my protectors are asleep." So it was for all the rest.

The Protestant historian Kampfer is often quoted in this matter. In his " History of Japan " he says that " the persecution was the worst in all history, but did not produce the effect that the government expected. For, although, according to the Jesuit accounts, 20,570 people suffered death for the Christian religion in 1590, yet in the following years, when all the churches were closed, there were 12,000 proselytes. Japanese writers do not deny that Hideyori,

Taicosama's son and intended successor, was suspected of being a Catholic, and that the greater part of the court officials and officers of the army professed that religion. The joy that made the new converts suffer the most unimaginable tortures excited the public curiosity to such an extent that many wanted to know the religion that produced such happiness in the agonies of death; and when told about it, they also enthusiastically professed it."

Spinola, who was seized at Nagasaki, was called upon to explain why he had remained in Japan, in spite of the edict. He replied: " There is a Ruler above all kings — and His word must be obeyed." The answer settled his fate, and he and two Dominicans were condemned to a frightful imprisonment. It is recorded that as the three victims approached the jail, they intoned the Te Deum, and that the refrain was taken up by a Dominican and a Franciscan who had already passed a year in that horrible dungeon. When the martyrs met inside the walls they kissed each other affectionately and fell on their knees to thank God. Leonard Kimura, a Japanese, was arrested at Nagasaki on suspicion of having concealed the son of the Shogun, and also of having killed a man while defending the prince. He was acquitted, but when withdrawing he was asked if he could give the court information about any Jesuit who might be hiding in the vicinity. " Yes, I know one," he said, " I am a Jesuit." After three years in a dungeon he was burned at the stake.

In 1619 the Jesuits, Spinola and Fernandes, with fourteen others, Dominicans and Franciscans, were brought out of prison and kept in a pen with no protection from cold or heat and so narrow that it was impossible to assume any but a crouching posture. It was hoped that by exposing them publicly, emaciated, hungry, filthy, and diseased, that the heroic element

which the executions seemed to develop in the victims
would be eliminated, and their converts alienated from
the Faith. The contrary happened, and from that
enclosure Spinola not only preached to the people, but
actually admitted novices to the Society. As he stood
at the stake where he was to be burned, a little boy
whom he had baptized was put in his arms; Spinola
blessed him, and the child and his mother were executed
at the same time as their father in God. Five Jesuits
died in 1619; and in 1620 six others came from Macao
to replace them. Next year brought down an edict
on all shipmasters, forbidding them to land such
undesirable immigrants as missionaries. Nevertheless,
two months after the edict was published, Borges,
Costanza, de Suza, Carvalho and Tzugi, a Japanese,
appeared in the disguise of merchants and soldiers.
The Dutch and English traders volunteered after that
to search all incoming vessels, and report the suspicious
passengers. An attempt at a prison delivery precipitated the condemnation of Spinola and his companions
in the pens. They were burned alive on September 10,
1622; on the 19th of the same month three more met
the same fate, and in November two others went to
heaven through the flames.

In 1623 de Angelis and Simon Jempo, with a number
of their followers, were burned to death, after having
their feet cut off. Carvalho and Buzomo were caught
in a forest in mid-winter, and on February 21, 1624,
were plunged naked into a pond, and left there to
freeze for the space of three hours. Four days afterwards the experiment was repeated for six consecutive
hours. But the night was so cold that they were both
found dead in the morning, wrapped in a shroud of ice.
Another Carvalho perished in the same year. Petitions
were sent from the Philippines and elsewhere, imploring
a cessation of these horrors, but the appeals made the

Shogun more cruel. As the persecutions had produced only a few apostacies, the executioners were told to scourge the victims down to the bone, to tear out their nails, to drive rods into their flesh or ears or nose, to fling them into pits filled with venomous snakes, to cut them up piece by piece, to roast them on gridirons, to put red-hot vessels in their hands, and, what was the most diabolical of all, the consider the slightest movement or cry as sign of apostacy. Another favorite punishment was to hang the sufferer head down over a pit from which sulphurous or other fumes were rising, or to stretch them on their backs and by means of a funnel fill them full of water till the stomach almost burst, and then by jumping on the body to force the fluid out again.

It is unnecessary here to enter into all the details of these martyrdoms; but it will be enough to state that in a very few years, twenty-eight native Japanese Jesuits, besides multitudes of people who were living in the world, men, women and children, gave up their lives for the Faith, side by side with those who had come from other parts of the world to teach them how to die. In 1634 only a handful of Jesuits remained. Chief among them was Vieira. He had been sent to report conditions to Urban VIII, and in 1632 he returned to die. He re-entered Japan as a Chinese sailor, and for nearly two years hurried all over the blood-stained territory, facing death at every step, until finally he and five other Jesuits stood before the tribunal and were told to apostatize or die. Vieira, the spokesman, said: " I am 63 years old, and all my life I have received innumerable favors from Almighty God; from the emperor — nothing, and I am not going now to bow down to idols of sticks and stones to obey a mortal man like myself. So say the others." They were put to death.

Japan 193

In that year, however, it is painful and humiliating to be obliged to say there was a Jesuit in Japan who apostatized: Father Ferara. It was the only scandal during those terrible trials. He had even been provincial, at one time, but when the test came, he fell, and the glorious young Church was thrilled with horror at seeing a man who had once taught them the way to heaven now throwing away his soul. The shame was too much for the Society, and it resolved to wipe it out. Marcellus Mastrilli, a Neapolitan, made the first attempt to atone for the crime. No one could enter Nagasaki without trampling on the cross — a device suggested by the Dutch and English merchants. However, Mastrilli made up his mind to enter without committing the sacrilege. He succeeded, but was arrested and led through the streets of Nagasaki, with the proclamation on his back: " This madman has come to preach a foreign religion, in spite of the emperor's edict. Come and look at him. He is to die in the pit." For sixty hours he hung over the horrible opening through which the poisonous fumes continually poured. Finally he was drawn up and his head struck off. It was October 17, 1637, and Ferara was looking on. Three years afterwards a similar execution took place. There were four victims this time, and the apostate stood there again.

In 1643 the final attempt was made to win back the lost one. Father Rubini and four other Jesuits landed on a desolate coast. They were captured and dragged to Nagasaki. To their horror the judge seated at the tribunal was none other than Ferara. " Who are you, and what do you come here for?" he asked. " We are Jesuits," they answered, " and we come to preach Jesus Christ, who died for us all." " Abjure your faith," cried Ferara, " and you shall be rich and honored." " Tell that to cowards whom you want to

13

dishonor," answered Rubini. " We trust that we shall
have courage to die like Christians and like priests."
Ferara fled, and the missionaries died, but the shaft
had struck home, though it took nine years for Divine
grace to achieve its ultimate triumph. The victory
was won in 1652, when an old man of eighty was
dragged before the judge at Nagasaki. " Who are
you?" he was asked. " I am one," he replied, " who
has sinned against the King of Heaven and earth. I
betrayed Him out of fear of death. I am a Christian;
I am a Jesuit." His youthful courage had returned,
and for sixty hours he remained unmoved in the pit,
in spite of the most excruciating torture. It was
Ferara; and thus Christianity died in Japan in his
blood and in that of 200,000 other martyrs. Eighty
Jesuits had given their life for Christ in this battle.

This disaster in Japan has been frequently laid at
the door of the Society, because of its unwillingness to
form a native clergy. Those who make the cruel charge
forget a very important fact. It is this: precisely at
that time a native clergy was not saving England
or Germany or any of the Northern nations. Not only
that, but the clergy themselves first gave the example
of apostasy in those countries. Secondly, it had been
absolutely impossible, up to that time, to obtain a
bishop in Japan to ordain any of the natives. Sixteen
years had not elapsed from the moment the first
Jesuits began their work in Japan, namely in 1566,
when Father Oviedo, the Patriarch of Ethiopia, was
appointed Bishop of Japan. But he entreated the
Pope to let him die in the hardships and dangers by
which he was surrounded in Africa. Father Carnero
was then sent in his place, but he died when he reached
Macao. In 1579 a petition was again dispatched to
Rome asking for a bishop, but no answer was given.
When the Japanese embassy knelt at the feet of the

Pope, they repeated the request. Morales was then named, but he died on the way out. In 1596 Martines arrived with a coadjutor, Sequiera, and immediately a number of young Japanese who had been long in preparation for the priesthood were ordained; in 1605 a parish was established in Nagasaki and put in the hands of a native priest. In 1607 four more parishes were organized. Then Martines died, and in 1614 Sequiera followed him to the grave. Finally, Valente was appointed, but he never reached Japan.

Rohrbacher, the historian, was especially prominent in fastening this calumny on the Society, and when Bertrand, the author of " Mémoires sur les missions," put him in possession of these facts, not only was the charge not withdrawn, but no acknowledgment was made of the receipt of the information. As a matter of fact, it would be difficult to find in the history of the Church an example of greater solicitude to provide a native priesthood than was given by the Jesuits of Japan. The crushing out in blood of the marvellous Church which Xavier and his successors had created in that part of the world cannot be considered a failure — at least in the minds of Catholics who understand that " the blood of martyrs is the seed of the Church." Nor can such a conclusion be arrived at by any one who is aware of what occurred in the city of Nagasaki as late as the year 1865.

The ports of Japan had been opened to the commerce of the world in 1859. But even then all attempts to penetrate into the interior had been hopelessly frustrated. On March 17, 1865 Father Petitjean, of the Foreign Missions, was praying, disconsolate and despondent, in a little chapel he had built in Nagasaki. No native had ever entered it. One morning he became aware of the presence of three women kneeling at his side. " Have you a Pope?" they asked. " Yes,"

was the answer. " Do you pray to the Blessed Virgin?"
" Yes." " Are you married?" " No." " Do you
take the discipline?" To the last interrogatory he
replied by holding up that instrument of penance.
" Then you are a Christian like ourselves." To his
amazement he found that in Nagasaki and its immediate
surroundings, which had been the principal theatre of
the terrible martyrdoms of former times — there were
no less than 2,500 native Japanese Catholics. In a
second place there was a settlement of at least a
thousand families, and, later on, five other groups were
found in various sections of the country; and it was
certain that there was a great number of others in
various localities. As many as 50,000 Christians were
ultimately discovered. Pius IX was so much moved
by this wonderful event, that he made the 17th of
March the great religious festival of the Church of
Japan, and decreed that it was to be celebrated under
the title of " The Finding of the Christians."

A Church that could preserve its spiritual life for
over two hundred years in the midst of pagan hatred
and pagan corruption, without any sacramental help
but that of baptism, and without priests, without
preaching, without the Holy Sacrifice, and could
present itself to the world at the end of that long
period of trial and privation with 50,000 Christians,
the remnants of those other hundreds and hundreds
of thousands who, through the centuries, had never
faltered in their allegiance to Christ, was not a failure.
It may be noted, moreover, that this survival of the
Faith after long years of privation of the sacraments
of the Church is not the exclusive glory of Japan.
Other instances will be noted when the Society resumed
its work after the Suppression.

CHAPTER VII

THE GREAT STORMS

1580–1597

Manares suspected of ambition — Election of Aquaviva — Beginning of Spanish discontent — Denis Vásquez — The " Ratio Studiorum " — Society's action against Confessors of Kings and Political Embassies — Trouble with the Spanish Inquisition and Philip II — Attempts at a Spanish Schism — The Ormanetto papers — Ribadeneira suspected — Imprisonment of Jesuits by the Spanish Inquisition — Action of Toletus — Extraordinary Congregation called — Exculpation of Aquaviva — The dispute " de Auxiliis "— Antoine Arnauld's attack — Henry IV and Jean Chastel — Reconciliation of Henry IV to the Church — Royal protection — Saint Charles Borromeo — Troubles in Venice — Sarpi — Palafox.

WHEN Mercurian died, on August 1, 1580, Oliver Manares, who, like the deceased General, was a Belgian, called the general congregation for February 7, 1581. Two of the old companions of St. Ignatius, Salmerón and Bobadilla, were there, as were also the able coadjutor of Canisius, Hoffæus, and Claude Matthieu, the latter of whom was beginning to be conspicuous in the League against the King of Navarre. Maldonatus, also, occupied a seat in the distinguished assembly. Before the congregation met, rumors began to be heard that Manares was seeking the generalship for himself. The grounds of the suspicions seem almost too frivolous for an outsider, but in an order which had pronounced so positively against ambition in the Church, it was proper that it should be scrupulously sensitive about any act in the body itself that might resemble it. The grounds of the accusation were that he had sent a present to Father Toletus who was very close to the Pope, and had also once said to a lay-brother: " If I were General, I would do so and so." A committee was appointed

to examine the case, and Manares was declared in-
eligible. The Pope found the action of the congre-
gregation excessively rigid, but, possibly, as in the
preceding congregation it had been decided that the
succession of three Spanish Generals contained in it
an element of danger, so it was feared that as the dead
General who had appointed one of his own race to be
vicar, there might be reason for apprehension in that
also. As a matter of fact, the power given to the
General to appoint his vicar was by some looked upon
as quite unwise, as it afforded at least a remote opportunity for self-perpetuation.

On February 19, 1581, Claudius Aquaviva was
elected General of the Society by thirty-two votes
out of fifty-one. He was not yet thirty-eight years of
age. The Pope was astounded at the choice, but the
sequel proved that it was providential. " No one,"
says Bartoli, " was raised to that dignity who had
given more evident or more numerous signs that his
election came from God, and perhaps, no one, with
the exception of St. Ignatius, has a greater claim to
the gratitude of the Society or has helped it more
efficaciously to achieve the object for which it was
founded." He was the youngest son of the Duke of
Atri, and was born at Naples in 1543. As his youth
was passed in his father's palace, he could at most
only have heard the names of some of the companions
of St. Ignatius, but when he was about twenty years
of age he was sent to Rome to defend some family
interest, and he attracted so much attention that he
was retained at court, first by Paul IV, and afterwards
by Pius V, both of whom were struck by his superior
qualities of mind and heart. There for the first time
he came in contact with the Jesuits. It happened
that Christopher Rodriguez, John Polanco, and Francis
Borgia were frequently admitted to an audience with

the Holy Father, and young Aquaviva was so drawn
to them when he heard them speaking of Divine
things, that he began to make inquiries about their
manner of life and the rule they followed. He felt
called to join them but he hesitated a while, for the
Roman purple was an honor that was assured him;
finally, however, he made up his mind, and after the
Pontifical Mass on St. Peter's day he fell at Borgia's
feet and asked for admission to the Society. When
Ormanetto, the papal legate, heard of it, he exclaimed:
" The Apostolic College has lost its finest ornament."

Nine years later, Aquaviva was made rector of the
Roman Seminary, and then, by a strange coincidence,
became rector of the College of Naples, as successor
of Dionisio Vásquez, who later on was to be very conspicuous in an attempt by the Spanish members
to disrupt the Society, and thus occasion the bitterest
trial of Aquaviva's administration as General. After
rapidly repairing the ruin that Vásquez had caused in
Naples, Aquaviva was made provincial, and was then
entrusted with the care of the Roman province. He
had served in that capacity only a year when he was
elected General. Some years before that, Nadal must
have foreseen the promotion when he advised Aquaviva
to make the Constitutions of Saint Ignatius his only
reading. " You will stand very much in need of it,"
he said. The congregation formulated sixty-nine
decrees, one of which gave the General power to appoint
his vicar, and another to interpret the Constitutions.
Such interpretations, however, were not to have the
force of law, but were to be considered merely as
practical directions for government. Another decree
regulated the method to be followed in the dissolution
of houses and colleges.

Aquaviva's first letter to the Society was concerned
chiefly with the qualities which superiors should possess

— especially those of vigilance, sweetness and strength. His second was more universal, and dealt with the necessity of a constant renewal of the spiritual life. To him the Society is indebted for the " Directorium," or guide of the Spiritual Exercises.

Under his administration the "Ratio Studiorum," or scheme of studies, was produced. It was the result of fifteen years of collaboration (1584–99) by a number of the most competent scholars that could be found in the Society. It covers the whole educational field from theology down to the grammar of the lower classes, exclusive, however, of the elements. Of course, this "Ratio" has not escaped criticism, for scarcely anything the Society ever attempted has had that good fortune. Thus, to take one out of many, Michelet bemoans the fact that " the Ratio has been in operation for 300 years and has not yet produced a man." Such a charge, of course, does not call for discussion.

The greatest service that Aquaviva rendered the Society, and for which it will ever bless his memory is that he saved it from destruction in a fight that ran through the thirty years of his Generalate, and in which he found opposed to him Popes, kings, and princes, along with the terrible authority of the Spanish Inquisition and, worst of all, a number of discontented members of the Order, banded together and resorting to the most reprehensible tactics to alter completely the character of the Institute and to rob it of that Catholicity which constitutes its glory and its power.

He began his work by making it impossible, as far as it lay in his power, for a Jesuit to be used as the tool of any prince or potentate, no matter how dazzling might be the dignity with which one so employed was invested, or the glory which his work reflected on the Society. Thus, he put his ban on the office of

royal confessor, which some of the members of the
Society in those days were compelled to accept. He
could not prevent it absolutely just then, but he laid
down such stringent laws regarding it, that all ambition
or desire of that very unapostolic work was eliminated.
Its inconveniences were manifest. It is inconceivable,
for instance, that a sovereign like Henry IV, who was
a devoted friend of the Society, ever consulted Father
Coton about scruples of conscience; for his majesty
was never subject to spiritual worry of that description;
and on the other hand, the unfortunate confessor was
often suspected or accused of influencing or advising
political measures with which he could have had
nothing whatever to do. Jealousy also, of those
who were appointed to the office was inevitable, and
dislike and hatred not only of the individual who
occupied the post, but of the order to which he belonged
was aroused. Even the confessor's own relatives and
friends were alienated, because he was forbidden to
make use of his spiritual influence for their worldly
advantage. Finally, apart from the loss of time,
daily contact with the vice of the court, which he
could not openly reprehend, necessarily reacted on the
spiritual tone of the religious himself.

The same objections obtained for the flamboyant
embassies which had been so much in vogue up to
that time, and which are still quoted as evidencing
the wonderful influence wielded by the Society in those
days. They, too, were stopped, for the reason that
although they were nearly always connected with the
interests of the Faith, yet they were very largely
controlled by worldly politics. Hence Possevin, who
had made such a stir by his embassies to Muscovy,
Sweden, Poland and elsewhere, was relegated to a
class-room in Padua. Matthieu, who figured conspicuously in the politico-religious troubles of France

as the " Courier de la Ligue," was told to desist from
his activities, although Pope Sixtus V judged otherwise;
and finally, the most famous orator of his day in France,
Father Auger, who was loud in his denunciation of
the Holy League, received peremptory orders to
desist from discussing the subject at all. His quick
obedience to the command was the best sermon he
ever preached.

Aquaviva had also a very protracted struggle with
Philip II in relation to the Spanish Inquisition. The
king had frequently expressed a desire to have a Jesuit
in one or other of the conspicuous offices of that
tribunal, but Aquaviva stubbornly refused, first,
because of the odium attached to the Inquisition itself,
and also because he suspected that Philip designed, by
that means, to lay hold of the machinery of the 'Society
and control it. His most glorious battle, however,
was one that was fought in the Society itself, against
an organized movement which was making straight for
the destruction of the great work of St. Ignatius. It
is somewhat of a stain on the splendid history of the
Order, but it should not be concealed or palliated or
explained away, for it not only reveals the masterful
generalship of Aquaviva, but it also brings out, in
splendid relief, the magnificent resisting power of the
organization itself.

The Spanish Jesuits were profoundly shocked when
the Pope prevented the perpetuation of Spanish rule
in the Society. The psychological reason of their
surprise was that the average Spaniard at that time
was convinced that Spain alone was immune from
heresy. As a matter of fact, all the other nations of
Europe, Ireland excepted, had been infected, and
possibly it was a mistaken loyalty to the Church that
prompted a certain number of them to organize a plot
to make the Society exclusively Spanish or destroy it.

It will come as a painful discovery for many that the
originator of this nefarious scheme was Father Araoz,
the nephew of St. Ignatius. Astrain (II, 101) regrets
to admit it, but the documents in his hands make it
imperative. He quotes letters which show that even
in the time of St. Ignatius, Araoz complained of the
Roman administration, putting the blame, however,
on Polanco. His discontent was more manifest under
Laínez, when he maintained that the General should
not be elected for life; that provincials and rectors
should be voted for, as in other Orders; that there
should be a general chapter in Spain to manage its own
affairs, and not only that no foreigner should be
admitted to a Spanish province, but that there should
not even be any communication with non-Spaniards
in other sections of the Society. One would not expect
such Knownothingism in a Jesuit, but the documents
setting forth these facts which were found among the
papers of Araoz after his death make it only too
manifest. They contain among other things accounts
of the opposition of Araoz to Laínez, to Francis Borgia,
and to Nadal, none of which is very pleasant reading.

In a letter unearthed by Antonio Ibáñez, the visitor
of the province of Toledo, Araoz goes on to say:
" (1) We must petition the Pope and ask that all
religious orders in Spain shall have a Spanish general,
independent of the one in Rome, so as to avoid the
danger of heresy. (2) No Spaniard living outside of
Spain should be elected general, commissary or visitor
in Spain. (3) As there is such a diversity of customs
and usages in each nation, they should not mix with
one another. (4) General congregations expose the
delegates to act as spies for the enemy. (5) The king
should write to the cardinal protector of the religious
orders not to oppose this plan." Other papers by
Spanish Jesuits were found among those of Ormanetto,

nuncio at Madrid, who died on June 17, 1577. They call for drastic changes, in the difference of grades, the manner of electing superiors, dismissals from the Society, and such matters. The authorship of the Ormanetto papers could not be determined with certainty, but suspicion fell upon Father Solier, and for a time, even upon Ribadeneira who, at that time, was in Madrid for his health, and was in the habit of calling frequently at the nunciature with Solier. In the following year, it was admitted that the suspicion about him was unfounded. As a matter of fact, he subsequently wrote a denunciation of the conspiracy and a splendid defense of the Institute. That King Philip knew what was going on was revealed by certain remarks he let drop, such as: " Your General does not know how to govern; we need a Spanish superior independent of the General; we have able men here like Ribadeneira and others, etc."

At the end of 1577 it was discovered that Father Dionisio Vásquez, who was of Jewish extraction, was disseminating these ideas by letter and by word of mouth. The friendship that existed between him and Ribadeneira from childhood again threw a cloud over the latter, but finally the provincial learned from Vásquez himself that Ribadeneira knew nothing at all about the whole affair. By that time the names of the chief plotters were revealed, and it was also discovered that Vásquez had given one copy of his memorial to the king and another to the Inquisition. Two more had been shown to various other people. Vásquez alleged eight reasons for this attempt to change the character of the Society: (1) Because the General had to treat with so many depraved and heretical nations, that there was a danger of contaminating the whole Society. (2) Money and subjects were being taken from Spain to benefit other provinces. (3) If any one was in

danger of being punished by the Inquisition it was
easy to send the culprit elsewhere. (4) Rome was
governing by means of information which was frequently false. (5) There were delays in correspondence.
(6) As the General never left Rome, he could not visit
his subjects. (7) When the king asks for missionaries,
Rome often answers that there are none to send.
(8) There should be a commissary in Spain, because
Spaniards are badly treated in Rome. Astrain notes
that these pretences of the danger of heresy, respect
for the Inquisition, and the needs of satisfying the
king's demands for missionaries were devised merely to
win the favor of Philip. Another conspirator whose
name appears is Estrada. He is described by the
provincial as a " *novus homo* whose conversation is
pestilential."

There was no public manifestation of this spirit
of schism in the first years of Aquaviva's Generalship,
though in Spain a great deal of underhand plotting
was going on between some of the discontented ones
and the Inquisition. Four persons, however, had
caused grave anxiety to their Superiors, namely:
Dionisio Vásquez, Francisco de Abreo, Gonzalo
González and Enrique Enríquez. Following in their
wake, came Alonso Polanco, nephew of the famous
Polanco, José de San Julian, Diego de Santa Cruz, and
a certain number of inconspicuous persons whose
names it is not necessary to give. In the background,
however, there were two men of considerable importance: Mariana, whose writings have given so much
trouble to the Society, and José de Acosta. To these
Jouvancy in his "Epitome" and Prat in his
"Ribadeneira" add the name of Jerome de Acosta,
but according to Astrain, the two historians are in error
both as to the character of Jerome and his participation
in the plot. He was, indeed, suspected of being mixed

up in it, but the suspicion was soon dispelled, as in the case of Ribandeneira. Manuel López was at most a suspect, because he was a friend and admirer of Araoz and because, although the oldest man in the province, he gave no aid to the defenders of the Institute. When the fight was ended, however, he pronounced for those who had won.

Meantime Enríquez, by means of false accusations, had induced the Inquisition to put in prison on various charges Fathers Marcen, Lavata, López and the famous Ripalda. That tribunal also expelled others from Valladolid and Castile, and called for the Bulls, the privileges, and the "Ratio studiorum" of the Society. The findings of the judges were put before the king, and the Inquisition then demanded all the copies of the aforesaid documents that the Fathers had (Astrain, III, 376). So far the inquisitors were safe, but they took one step more which ruined the plot in which they were conscious or unconscious participators. Under pain of excommunication they forbade a band of thirty Jesuit missionaries who were on their way to Transylvania to leave Spain, the reason being that they endangered their faith in embarking on such an enterprise. It was the plotter, Enrique Enríquez who suggested this piece of idiocy. When Sixtus V, who was then Pope, heard of the order, he sent such a vigorous reprimand to the Inquisition that all the confiscated papers were immediately restored and the imprisoned theologians were liberated from jail after two years' confinement.

But the enemy was not yet beaten. Anonymous petitions kept pouring in upon the Inquisition, "all of them," says Astrain, "bearing the stamp of the atrabilious Vásquez, the rigorist González, the underhanded Enríquez, and the sombre Abreo." Besides the old demands, a new one was made, namely, the investigation of the Society by an official of the Inquisition. Finally, in the provincial congregation of 1587, the hand of Vásquez was visible when a general congregation was asked for unanimously and a request made for a procurator for the Spanish provinces. Meantime, Philip had been wrought upon and he supported the petition for the visit of an inquisitor, who was none other than D. Jerónimo Manrique, the Bishop of Cartagena, a choice which shows that these Jesuit insurrectos were not gifted with the shrewdness usually attributed to their brethren. For apart from the odiousness of having an unfriendly outsider investigate, it so happened that Manrique had a very unsavory past, and when that was called to the attention of Sixtus, the whole foolish project collapsed of itself, and King Philip confessed his defeat.

All this finally convinced Sixtus V that there was something radically wrong with the Society, and he ordered the Congregation of the Holy Office (the Roman Inquisition) to examine the Constitutions. Aquaviva protested that it was unjust to judge the Order from anonymous writings, many of them forgeries by a single individual; and that the faults were alleged not with a view to correction, but to alter the Institute radically. With regard to the proposal of a capitular government, several objectionable consequences, he said, must follow, such as ambition, simony, laxity of discipline, and the like, and he emphasized the fact that Sixtus himself, only a short time before, had urged the appointment of Italian superiors in France. He convinced the Pope, also, that the exclusiveness advocated by the Spaniards, in refusing subjects from other parts of the world would soon shrivel up the Spanish provinces themselves. Finally, a capitular government in missionary countries was a physical impossibility, and would disrupt the whole Order.

Indeed, when Cardinal Colonna mentioned the word
" capitular " to the Pope, His Holiness interjected:
" I don't want chapters in the Society. You would
have one in every city and every family; and that does
not suit the system of the Jesuits."

While this was going on, letters were received from
the Emperor Rodolf, King Sigismond, the Duke of
Bavaria, and other princes and distinguished personages, entreating the Pope to make no change in the
Institute. The protest of the Duke of Bavaria especially startled the Pontiff, and he surmised that it was
a Jesuit fabrication, or that it had been asked for or
suggested. Such was really the case. The points had
been drawn up by Alber, the provincial of Germany,
and the Duke had heartily approved of them. At
that, the Pope relented and declared that he never had
any intention of changing the Institute. What he
chiefly desired was to prevent certain Jesuits from
interfering in politics more than was proper — an
allusion, in Sacchini's opinion, to Possevin and Auger,
who had already been retired by the General. Sixtus
had apparently changed his mind about these semi-
political occupations.

Thus ended the year 1589, but the year 1590 had
new troubles in store. Up to that time, the Sacred
Congregation, whose members, especially Caraffa, were
friendly to the Society, had purposely delayed sending
in a report to the Pope. He was indignant at this,
and handed the case over to four theologians. Their
verdict was in conformity with the views of Sixtus.
They were more timid than the cardinals. By de-
duction from Aquaviva's argument against the findings,
the first complaint was about the name: " The
Society of Jesus." Then follow the various matters
of stipends, penances, the profession, the examinations
for grade, doctrines, the eighth rule of the Summary

forbidding assistance to relatives, obedience, the
acoount of conscience, delay of profession, fraternal
correction, censors, and simple vows. Astrain gives
Aquaviva's answer to all these charges in detail
(III, 465). The cardinals, without exception, admitted
Aquaviva's rebuttal, and when they gave the Pope
their verdict, he said: " All of you, even those who
are of my own creation, favor these Fathers." One
thing, however, he insisted on, and that was the
change of name, and he therefore ordered Aquaviva
to send in a formal request to that effect. There was
nothing to do but to submit, and the Pope signed
the Brief, but as the bell of San Andrea summoned the
novices to litanies that night, Sixtus died, and ever
since the tradition runs in Rome that if the litany
bell rings when the Pope is sick, his last hour has
come. As was to be expected, the Society was accused
of having had something to do with the Pope's
opportune demise. The successor of Sixtus tore up
the Brief, and the Society kept its name.

In spite of all this, the battle continued. Clement
VIII succeeded Sixtus V on January 29, 1592, and his
election was welcomed by the Spanish rebels, for he
was credited with a personal antipathy to Aquaviva.
Hence they revived Philip's interest in the matter.
His ambassador at Rome was more than friendly
to the project, and it was confidently hoped that the
great Spanish Jesuit, Toletus, the friend of the Pope,
could be won over. The fact that, at the suggestion of
Aquaviva, the Pope had rendered a decision about
the sacrament of Penance which the Inquisition
regarded as an infringement of its rights, again brought
that tribunal into the fray. The new plan of the
conspirators was, first, to re-assert the claims advanced
by Vásquez the year before, and failing that, to demand, at least, a commissary general for Spain. They

14

wrote to Philip asking for his authorization and support.
When Aquaviva was apprised of all this, he requested
the king to name anyone he chose to pass on the
proposal for a commissary. Philip picked out Loyasa,
the instructor of the heir apparent; but he, after
examining the question, bluntly told the insurgents:
" I do not at all share your opinion, and I am positive
that Ignatius, like St. Dominic and St. Francis, was
inspired by God in the foundation of his Order. One
Pope is enough to govern the Church, and one General
ought to be enough for the Society." Foiled in this,
they induced the Pope and the king to compel the
General to call a general congregation; and in order
to make it easier to carry out their plot, they persuaded the Pope to send Aquaviva to settle a dispute
between the Dukes of Parma and Mantua, thus
keeping him out of Rome for three whole months.
Toletus is accused of having been a party to this
removal of Aquaviva, but the proof adduced is not
convincing. At Naples, Aquaviva fell seriously ill, and
the Fathers demanded his recall. It was only on his
return that he began to appreciate the full extent
and bearing of the movement as well as the peril in
which the Society was involved. For although all the
cardinals were on his side, yet arrayed against him
were the king, the Pope and a number of the professed. The case seemed hopeless. Finally, Toletus
informed him that the Pope insisted on a general
congregation and it was summoned for November 4,
1593.

To make matters worse, Toletus was then made
cardinal; whereupon the insurgents asked the Pope to
authorize José Acosta and some of his associates to
enter the congregation — a privilege they had no
claim to — and also to have Toletus preside. The
congregation began its sessions on the day appointed.

There were sixty-three professed present among them
Acosta, but Aquaviva, not Toletus, was in the chair.
The usual committee was appointed for the business
of the congregation, and Aquaviva insisted that they
should begin by investigating the complaints against
his administration. They did so, and were amazed to
find that all the charges were based on false impressions,
personal prejudices, and imaginary acts. They were
naturally indignant and when they reported to the
Pope, he said: " They wanted to find a culprit and
they have discovered a saint." The demands of the
Spaniards were then examined. According to
Jouvancy, the province of Castile fathered them.
They were in the main: a modification of the time
and manner of profession; the abolition of grades;
the introduction of a new mode of dismissal; and
the full use of the " Bulla Cruciata."

The business of the congregation was conducted as
usual up to the twenty-first decree. Philip II of Spain
had asked that the members of the Society should
not avail themselves of the privileges accorded them
— first of reading prohibited books; secondly, of
absolving from heresy; thirdly, of exemption from
honors and dignities outside the Society. The twenty-
first decree states that the first two royal requests
had already been acted upon. With regard to the
third, it was decreed that his majesty should be entreated to use his authority against the acceptance of
ecclesiastical and civic honors by members of the
Society. It was only in the fifty-second decree that
the Society expressed its mind on the race question,
by ruling that applicants of Hebrew and Saracenic
origin were not to be admitted to the Society. It
even declared that those who were admitted through
error should be expelled if the error were discovered
prior to their profession. It had been found that out

of the twenty-seven conspirators, twenty-five were of
Jewish or Moorish extraction.

The twenty-seven guilty men were denounced as
" false sons, disturbers of the common peace, and
revolutionists (*architecti rerum novarum*) whose punishment had been asked for by many provinces. The
congregation, therefore, while grievously bewailing the
loss of its spiritual sons, was nevertheless compelled
in the interests of domestic union, religious obedience,
and the perpetuation of the Society, to employ a severe
remedy in the premises." After recounting their
charges against the Society, and their claim to be
" the whole Society," although they were only a few
" degenerate sons " the decree denounces them and
their accomplices as having incurred the censures and
penalties contained in the Apostolic Bulls, and orders
them to be expelled from the Society. " If for one
reason or another, they cannot be immediately dismissed they were declared incapable of any office or
dignity and denied all active or passive voice." It
also orders that " those suspected of being parties to
such machinations shall make a solemn oath to
support the Constitution as approved by the Popes,
and to do nothing against it. If they refuse to take
the oath, or having taken it, fail to keep it, they are
to be expelled, even if old and professed."

Aquaviva had thus triumphed all along the line.
He had not only saved the Institute, but had received
the power of expelling every one of the insurgents
if they refused the oath of submission. Acosta, the
leading rebel, was one of the chief sufferers; although
he was the representative of Philip II, he was struck,
like his associates, by the condemnation. The one
who was punished, most, however, was Toletus, who
like Acosta had a Jewish strain, which may explain
the moroseness which the delegates remarked when-

ever they met him, and also his complaints that
" the proceedings of the Congregation could not have
been worse...........that it had treated Philip like
a valet."

Toletus, however, continued to fight. On January
12 he advised Aquaviva to propose the discussion of
a change of assistants and a sexennial congregation.
A commission was immediately formed to wait on the
Pope, but it failed to see him; whereupon Toletus
appeared on January 14 and informed the General that
the two points should be regarded as settled without discussion. Accordingly, four days later, new
assistants were elected, but the law of the six-year
convocations became a dead letter. On January 8
Toletus had presented a document to the Pontiff
urging nine different changes in the Constitutions,
adding that Philip II had asked for them, though in
reality the king had only asked that they should be
discussed. Doubtless Toletus had misunderstood.
Fortunately, the Pope would not admit all of the changes,
but suggested to the congregation four harmless ones
— first, that except for the master of novices,
the term of office should be three years; second, that
at the end of their term the provincials should give an
account of their administration; third that the papal
reservations should be observed; and fourth, that the
assistants should have a deciding vote. The three
first were readily accepted, and the fourth respectfully
rejected. The remaining business was then expedited,
and the congregation adjourned on January 19, 1594.

The conspirators, however, had not yet been beaten.
They proposed to the Pope to appoint Aquaviva
Archbishop of Capua. Of course, Aquaviva refused,
and then it was cunningly suggested that it would be
an excellent thing if the General, in the interests of
unity and peace, should visit the Spanish provinces.

Philip III, who was now on the throne, had been approached, and he wrote to the Pope to that effect. Clement rather favored the proposition, but Henry IV of France, Sigismund of Poland the Archdukes Ferdinand and Matthias and other German princes protested. Then the Pope took the matter under consideration, but before he reached any conclusion he died, and the plot was thus thwarted.

The one who planned this visit to Spain was the plotter Mendoza. His purpose was simply to humiliate the General by confronting him with the king, the greatest nobles of the realm and the Inquisition, and then to force from him all sorts of permissions which were in direct violation of the methods of Jesuit life. The story, as it appears in Astrain, is simply amazing. Mendoza had actually procured from the Pope, through the magnates of Spain, permission to receive and spend money as he wished, to be free from all superiors, and to go and live wherever he chose. When Aquaviva protested to the Pope that such permissions were subversive of all religious discipline, His Holiness suggested a way out of the difficulty, which took every one by surprise — Mendoza was made Bishop of Cuzco in Peru. This interference of rich and powerful outsiders in the family life of the Society, as well as the shameful way in which some of the members sought the favor of men of great influence in the State may explain how, after the angry fulminations of the congregation against the Spanish plotters, it took several years to get even a few of them out of the Society.

The dispute, known as the " De Auxiliis," which raged with great theological fury for many years, had for its object the reconciliation of Divine grace with human freedom. " The Dominicans maintained that the difficulty was solved by their theory of physical pre-

motion and predetermination, whereas the Jesuits
found the explanation of it in the *Scientia media* whereby
God knows in the objective reality of things what a man
would do in any circumstances in which he might be
placed. The Dominicans declared that this was con-
ceding too much to free will, and that it tended towards
Pelagianism, while the Jesuits complained that the
Dominicans did not sufficiently safeguard human
liberty and hence seemed to lean towards the doctrines
of Calvin " (Astrain). It was not until 1588, that Luis
de Molina, whose name is chiefly connected with the
doctrine of the *Scientia media*, got into the fight. Domingo Ibánez, the Dominican professor at Salamanca,
was his chief antagonist. The debates continued for
five years, and by that time there were public disturbances in several Spanish cities. Clement VIII then
took the matter in his own hands, and forbade any
further discussion till the Holy See had decided one
way or the other. The opinions of universities and
theologians were asked for, but by 1602 no conclusion
had been arrived at, and between that year and 1605,
sixty-eight sessions had been held with no result. Thus
it went on till 1607, when the Pope decided that both
parties might hold their own opinions, but that each
should refrain from censuring the other. In 1611, by
order of the Pope, the Inquisition issued a decree
forbidding the publication of any book concerning
efficacious grace until further action by the Holy See.
The prohibition remained in force during the greater
part of the seventeenth century. The principal theologians who appeared on the Jesuit side of this controversy were Toletus, Bellarmine, Lessius, Molina,
Padilla, Valencia, Arubal, Bastida and Salas.

While these constitutional and theological wars were
at their height a discussion of quite another kind was
going on in the immediate surroundings of the General.

It was to determine what amount of prayer and penitential exercises should be the normal practice of the Society. Maggio and Alarcón, two of the assistants, were for long contemplations and great austerities, while Hoffæus and Emmanuel Rodrigues advocated more sobriety in those two matters. Aquaviva decided for a middle course, declaring that the Society was not established especially for prayer and mortification, but, on the other hand, that it could not endure without a moderate use of these two means of Christian perfection. As this was coincident with the Spanish troubles, these five holy men were like the old Roman senators who were speculating on the improvement of the land which was still occupied by the Carthaginian armies. Meantime, another storm was sweeping over the Society in France.

When Henry IV entered Paris in triumph, his former enemies, the Sorbonne and the parliament, hastened to pay him homage; but something had to be done to make the public forget their previous attitude in his regard. The usual device was resorted to of denouncing the Jesuits. A complaint was manufactured against the College of Clermont, about the infringement of someone's property rights, and the rector was haled to court to answer the charge. The orator for the plaintiffs was Antoine Arnauld, the father of the famous Antoine and Angélique, who were to be, later on, conspicuous figures in the Jansenist heresy. Absolutely disregarding the point at issue, Arnauld launched out in a fierce diatribe against the Jesuits in general; "those trumpets of war," he called them, "those torches of sedition; those roaring tempests that are perpetually disturbing the calm heavens of France. They are Spaniards, enemies of the state, the authors of all the excesses of the League, whose Bacchanalian and Catalinian orgies were held in the Jesuit college

and church. The Society is the workshop of Satan,
and is filled with traitors and scoundrels, assassins
of kings and public parricides. Who slew Henry III?
The Jesuits. Ah, my King!" he cried, "when I
contemplate thy *bloody shirt*, tears flow from my eyes
and choke my utterance." And yet every one knew
that it was his own clients, the Sorbonne and the
parliament, who were the centre of all "the orgies
of the League"; that it was they who had glorified
the assassin of Henry III as a hero, and made the
anniversary of his murder a public holiday; that it
was they who had heaped abuse on Henry IV, and had
sworn that he never should ascend the throne of
France, even if he were absolved from heresy by the
Pope, and had returned to the Faith. The travesty
of truth in this discourse is so glaring that Frenchmen
often refer to it as "the second original sin of the
Arnauld family," the source, namely, of its ineradicable
habit of misrepresentation.

A short time after this, Jean Chastel struck Henry IV
with a knife and cut him slightly on the lip. Immediately everyone recalled Arnauld's furious denunciation
of the Jesuits, and a descent was made on the college.
A scrap of paper was conveniently found in the library,
incriminating the custodian, but the volumes upon
volumes of denunciations which had been uttered in
the university and in parliament, and which were piled
upon the library shelves, were not discovered. The
scrap of paper sufficed. The college was immediately
confiscated, the inmates expelled from France, and
after Jean Chastel had been torn asunder by four
horses, Father Guéret was stretched on the rack and
Father Guignard was hanged. This occurred at the
end of December, 1594.

Up to this Henry IV had not yet been reconciled to
the Church, for the Pope doubted his sincerity and

refused to withdraw the excommunication which the king had incurred at the time of his relapse. At last, however, owing to the persistency of Father Possevin and of Cardinal Toletus, he was absolved from his heresy, and could be acknowledged, with a safe conscience by all Catholics, as the legitimate King of France. The action of Toletus in this matter is all the more remarkable from the fact that he was a Spaniard, and in espousing the cause of Henry he was turning his back on his own sovereign, who was using all his power to prevent the reconciliation. This service was publicly recognized by Henry who thanked the Cardinal for his courageous act, and when Toletus died elaborate obsequies were held by the king's orders in the cathedrals of Paris and Rheims. Of course, the appeal of the banished Jesuits was then readily listened to by the king. He restored Clermont to them; gave them other colleges, including the royal establishment of La Flèche, and was forever after their devoted helper and friend. It must have been a great consolation for Father Aquaviva, during the battle he was waging and from which he was to emerge triumphant, to be told of this support of Henry; and also to hear of the welcome the Society had received in loyal Belgium in spite of the persistent animosity of Louvain. Almost every city had been asking for a college.

About this time, the Jesuits lost a devoted friend in the person of St. Charles Borromeo, who died in 1584. It is a calumny to say that he had turned against them and had taken the seminary of Milan from their direction. It was they themselves who had asked to be relieved of the responsibility, for he had so multiplied their colleges in his diocese, that it was impossible to give the seminary the attention it required. It is true that he was greviously offended by one individual Jesuit who injected himself into a controversy that

was going on between the governor and the archbishop,
and assailed the great prelate in the pulpit of the very
church which had been given to the Society by
Borromeo; but Aquaviva quickly brought him to the
cardinal's feet to ask forgiveness, and then suspended
him for two years from preaching.   That incident, however, in no way diminished the affection of the saint for
the Society.   His last Mass was said in the Jesuit novitiate which he had founded, and he died in the arms of his
Jesuit confessor, Father Adorno, two days afterwards.

Seven years later, on June 21, 1591, another saint
died, the young Aloysius Gonzaga.   Borromeo knew
him well, and had given him his first Communion.
This boy saint was not only an angel of purity, but
also a martyr of charity, for he died of a fever he had
caught from the victims of a plague whom he was
attending during a pestilence that devastated Italy.
The venerable Bellarmine was his confessor and
spiritual father, and, later, when he was about to
expire, he said to those around him: " Bury me at the
feet of Aloysius Gonzaga."

There was still another trouble before Aquaviva, for
while the disturbances were going on in France and
Spain, a storm arose in Venice.   The Society had been
expelled from the republic; but it is to its credit to
have been hated by the government that ruled Venice
at that time.   The republic had become embroiled
with the Holy See, and war was imminent.   The Pope
put the city under interdict, and as the Jesuits who
were established there submitted to the injunction,
they were all exiled; their property was confiscated,
and they were forbidden ever to return.   This treatment was in keeping with the traditions of the government of " a republic," as some one had said, " which
in reality was a monarchy tempered by assassination."
Hallam (Hist. of Europe during the Middle Ages, iii,

144) insists that " it had all the pomp of a monarchy; and its commerce with the Mohammedans had deadened its sense of religious antipathy." Its action in this instance is ascribed to the influence of the Servite friar, Paolo Sarpi, whom the apostate Bishop de Dominis and Duplessis-Mornay, the chief of the French Huguenots at that time, describe as " another Calvin." He was in league with the Dutch and English to create a schism by defying the Pope, and to convert Venice into a Protestant republic. He is also the author of the virulent and calumnious " History of the Council of Trent."

Henry IV of France interested himself in this quarrel, and finally succeeded in having the papal and Venetian representatives meet to discuss their grievances. After protracted negotiations, the republic finally came to terms, but on one condition, namely that the Jesuits should not be allowed to return. As both the Pope and Henry absolutely refused to admit that clause, a deadlock ensued, until Aquaviva declared himself unwilling to allow any such difficulty to stand in the way of reconciliation: and as a consequence, the Society did not return to Venice until after fifty years of exile. Henry, however, had his revenge on Sarpi. He intercepted a letter written by a minister of Geneva to a Calvinist in Paris which revealed the fact that the Doge and several senators had already made arrangements to introduce the Reformation into Venice; and that Sarpi and his associate, Fulgenzio, had formed a secret society of more than a thousand persons, among whom were three hundred patricians, who were merely awaiting the signal to abandon the Church (Daru, Hist. de la république de Venise). The letter was read in the Senate, and many a guilty face grew pale. That was the end of Sarpi's influence. It was, probably also Henry IV ·who prevented him from going to England when the friar wrote to Casaubon to provide him a home there in case he had to leave Venice. In view of all that Henry IV had done for the Society, the sixth general congregation voted unanimously and enthusiastically to establish a French assistancy in the Society as an expression of gratitude to the monarch.

In Mexico the storm evoked by Palafox did not, it is true, result in expulsions, confiscations and executions as elsewhere, nevertheless it was deadly in its effects; and a century later it furnished the Jansenists of Europe with an exhaustless supply of calumnies against the Society. Its arraignment by Palafox was particularly efficacious because it expressed the mind of a distinguished functionary of the Church who was held by some to be a saint and whose canonization was insisted on by the politicians and nobility of Spain.

The character of this extraordinary personage has always been a mystery, and perhaps it would have been better or, at least, more comfortable to have left it in its shroud instead of revealing the truth about his life. He tells us himself in his " Vida interior " that his university days were wild; but though the text is explicit enough, it may be a pious exaggeration. In 1628 occurred what he calls his conversion. He made a general confession and determined to embrace an ecclesiastical career. His preparation for it was amazingly brief, and we find him soon occupying the post of grand almoner of the Princess Mary, whom he accompanied to Germany. On his return to Spain, he resumed his occupation as fiscal, and in 1639 was consecrated Bishop of Puebla in Mexico and, in the following year, was sent to America with the most extravagant plenipotentiary powers. Besides being Bishop of Puebla, he was simultaneously administrator of the vacant see of the city of Mexico and visitor of the *audiencia* of the colony, with the absolute right to depose any civil official whom he judged unsuitable.

He did not wait long to exercise his power, and in 1641, to the consternation of everyone, he flung out of office no less a personage than the viceroy himself who was universally esteemed for his upright and virtuous life. By this extraordinary act, Palafox became practically viceroy and captain general, while retaining his ecclesiastical dignities. In a few months, however, the new viceroy, Salvatierra, arrived. Palafox was soon to clash with him also, by blocking all the official work of the audiencia; holding up despatches, delaying decisions, absenting himself from the city, etc. For five years complaints against him poured into Spain but without effecting any change. Salvatierra even accused him of malversation in office, particularly in its finances and added that his whole occupation seemed to consist in writing the Life of St. Peter. His ecclesiastical government was no less disorderly. To gain the favor of those around him he transformed the Indian missions into parishes and put them in charge of priests who were absolutely ignorant both of the habits and language of the natives. The motive back of this change was that as mere mission posts the Indian settlements paid no tithes.

During all this time he continued to proclaim himself a friend of the Jesuits, but in 1641 when a canon of the cathedral wanted to make over a farm to the College of Vera Cruz, he was forbidden to do so under pain of excommunication unless the property was made subject to tithes. When the canon submitted the case to the audiencia he of course, lost it, because Palafox was the visitor of that tribunal. A further appeal was then made to the council of the Indies, but after two years of litigation the case was dropped without a decision. In the course of this contest, Palafox

wrote in his plea that the Jesuits were enormously
wealthy, while the cathedral of Puebla was destitute
of resources. When Father Calderón refuted these
assertions, the bishop was wrought up to fury and
laid down as a diocesan rule that, under pain of excommunication, no property transfers could be made to
religious orders unless this tithe clause was inserted,
and he enjoined that the sick and dying should be
admonished of that censure. He followed this up by
sending an order to all the Jesuits to deliver up their
faculties for inspection within twenty-four hours,
under penalty of excommunication. Their reply was
that they would have to refer the matter to the provincial. This was, according to Astrain, a grave act
of imprudence on the part of the Fathers, and such,
later on, was the ruling of the Roman Congregation
and of the Pope himself.

Of course, in the rigor of the law the bishop had an
absolute right to demand the faculties of all the priests
of his diocese, but in the concrete it is hard to blame
the action of the Fathers in this instance. They did
not refuse, but merely wanted time to lay the case
before their superior. Moreover, the action of the
bishop was altogether out of the ordinary. Up to
that time, his own confessor was a Jesuit, and faculties
had been issued by the bishop to several others of the
Society; during his incumbency he had employed
them in various missions of the diocese, he had invited
them to preach in his cathedral; and, indeed, they
had been using their faculties to confess and preach
ever since 1572. It is true that some of their original
privileges had been modified or curtailed, but in these
two principal functions no radical change had been
made. Might they not then have thought that, in
view of what the bishop had already done both in
civil and ecclesiastical matters, he was mentally

deranged? The average man of the world would have arrived at that conclusion.

At all events, the faculties were not forthcoming within the twenty-four hours, and all the Jesuit priests of Puebla not only found themselves dishonored and disgraced by being held up to the people as excommunicated, but by this act of the bishop doubt was thrown upon the validity of all the absolutions they had given in the administration of the sacrament of Penance. Astrain tells us that Father Legaspi attempted to preach in the Jesuit church, and when forbidden to do so by a messenger from the bishop's palace, refused to obey, but apart from the fact that this would be in absolute contradiction with the traditional instincts and training of any Jesuit, Astrain himself relates in the following chapter that the Roman Congregation which examined the whole miserable quarrel decided that Legaspi's sermon was delivered before and not after the prohibition. Recourse was then had to a privilege accorded to the Spanish colonies of constituting a commission of judges to consider and decide the case. This also was subsequently condemned by the Roman Congregation and by Innocent X, but on the other hand, communication with Rome was difficult in those days, and the course entered upon was taken with the approval of the heads of other religious orders, of the viceroy and of the *cabildo* or mayor. It is true that efforts should have been made to placate the angry prelate, but the documents show that the most humble supplications had been made to him only to be repulsed with abuse.

It would have been futile to refer the case to the *audiencia*, for Palafox controlled it absolutely. Moreover, it was urged that the plea presented to the commission did not regard merely the wholesale suspension and excommunication, but other grievances as well.

There were twenty-nine in all. The commission brought in a verdict against the bishop, but he refused to recognize the authority and even excommunicated the members of the court who, with what Father General Caraffa described as an "exorbitancia grande," had excommunicated the prelate. Then the whole city was in an uproar and Palafox rode through the throngs of the excited populace conjuring them to keep the peace, but at the same time preventing it by proceeding to the cathedral, and, amid the most lugubrious ceremonies and in full pontificals, excommunicating all his opponents. The Mexican Inquisition now intervened and enjoined silence on all parties. Salvatierra, the viceroy, also helped to quell the disturbance. Nevertheless, on June 6, Palafox issued another proclamation declaring that his enemies had been assembling arms in their houses, and were bent on getting control of the country. He again made a public appearance in the streets of Mexico, but two days afterwards he submitted the whole matter to the viceroy.

Salvatierra then implored him with the greatest respect and kindness to restore tranquillity and peace to the distracted colony, but on June 15, Palafox disappeared from the city; and no one knew whither he had gone. It was officially reported later on, that he had betaken himself first to the *hacienda* of Juan de Vergus, but after two days had disappeared again. For two months his whereabouts could not be ascertained, but in a letter to the Pope, he described himself as wandering for ten days in the forest and mountains without shelter or food, and exposed to death from serpents and wild beasts. He called himself another Athanasius. Finally he returned to the original *hacienda* and remained there until November. Before his departure, he had empowered the *cabildo* to have

15

the diocese administered by three ecclesiastics whom he designated; but one of them was imprisoned by the viceroy, and the two others refused to serve. Whereupon, the *cabildo* called a meeting at the city hall. Alonzo Salazar de Baraona presided and the Jesuits were ordered to display their faculties, which they did; they were then declared rightful ministers of the sacraments.

During his retirement Palafox had received two letters from Spain, one deposing him from his office of visitor, and another announcing the transfer of Salvatierra to Peru. The first was the reverse of pleasant, but the second was a source of great satisfaction for, if we are to believe Salvatierra, Palafox had aspirations for the viceregal office. Possibly with that in view, he willingly assented to the conditions on which he was to be allowed to re-enter his diocese, namely to regard as binding all that had been done in his absence. It was fully nine months before Salvatierra left Mexico, and during all that time there was peace in Puebla; but hostilities were resumed immediately afterwards. Palafox refused to be bound by his contract with Salvatierra; he declared the acts of the commission to be null and void, reasserted the invalidity of the Jesuit faculties, and put three of his own canons in jail. In September, he received a brief from the Pope which he regarded as a justification of all that had been done. In the main, the document asserted the fundamental right of the bishop to examine the faculties of the priests and condemned the proceedings of the commission. Whereupon twelve of the Fathers submitted their faculties to the bishop. But that did not satisfy him. He insisted on the Jesuits appearing in public in a penitential garb, as at an auto-da-fé, and receiving from him a solemn absolution from their excommunication. He also made it a matter of con-

fession for the faithful to have been absolved by Jesuits
or to have listened to their sermons.

From this odious ruling an appeal was taken to the
royal council; whereupon Palafox despatched three
letters to the Pope. The first was about the parochial
rights of the other religious orders; the second complaining of the silver mines, vast *haciendas* and wealth
of the Jesuits, and the third consisting of fifty-eight
pages of the most atrocious calumnies ever written by
a Catholic, and asking finally that they should be made
like other religious orders with choir, cloister, etc.
Ten years later, the General of the Discalced Carmelites
inquired of Palafox why he wrote these letters. " I
did so," he says, " because I was incensed against the
Jesuits for not treating me with proper respect, but
I am surprised that I have lost their affection and was
not aware of it till now ." At last, wearied of it all,
Philip IV ordered him to return to Spain immediately,
but he obeyed in a very leisurely fashion. In Rome,
the case dragged on for four more years and finally
a verdict was rendered affirming among other things
that the Fathers had been properly provided with
faculties, and had ceased to preach and hear confessions
when ordered to do so. The only censure they received
was for having convoked the commission to judge the
case in the absence of the bishop. The trouble had
lasted for sixteen years, but it created a deep prejudice
against the Society a century later.

CHAPTER VIII

THE ASIATIC CONTINENT

The Great Mogul — Rudolph Aquaviva — Jerome Xavier — de Nobili — de Britto — Beschi — The Pariahs — Entering Thibet — From Peking to Europe — Mingrelia, Paphlagonia and Chaldea — The Maronites — Alexander de Rhodes — Ricci enters China — From Agra to Peking — Adam Schall — Arrival of the Tatars — Persecutions — Schall condemned to Death — Verbiest — de Tournon's Visit — The French Royal Mathematicians — Avril's Journey.

AT the very time that Queen Elizabeth was putting Jesuits to death in England, there was a remarkable pagan monarch reigning in what is now part of English India, who was inviting Jesuits to his court and making them his friends. His name was Akbar, and he is known in history as the Great Mogul. He was born in 1542, and ruled four years longer than the forceful Eliza. She was queen from 1558 to 1603; he was king from 1556 to 1605. Akbar appears first as the ruler of the Punjab and the country around Delhi and Agra; but in 1572 he drove the Afghans out of Bengal, and reunited the lower valley of the Ganges to Hindostan. Later, he annexed Cabul, Kashmir, Sind and Kandahar. He was a mighty warrior, but remarkable likewise as a civil ruler, the proof in this case being that he levied more money in taxes than England extracts at the present day from the same territory. He was very much interested in religious matters, and Christianity appealed to him, because one of his numerous wives had been a Christian; but he fancied that it was part of a general system which could be incorporated in a new cult which he had devised to conciliate the conflicting creeds of his realm. His own personal devotion was sun-worship, and he appeared

every morning in public, devoutly offering up his
orisons to the god of day. He fancied it was the world-
soul that animates all things, a concrete form of one
of the illusions of the present time.

At the invitation of Akbar, Rudolph Aquaviva,
accompanied by Anthony Montserrat and Francisco
Henriques, left Goa in 1579, to present himself
at his court for the purpose of explaining to
him the doctrines of the Christian Faith. He
listened with pleasure and intelligence, but his
interest was purely academic. As with other Oriental
despots, nothing practical could be hoped for, on
account of the harem. Seeing that it was lost time to
remain there, Aquaviva returned to Goa, and was
then sent down to the peninsula of Salsette, as superior
of the mission established at that place. His stay
there was not a long one, for on July 15, 1583, he and
Alfonso Pacheco were attacked by the natives and
cut to pieces. Fathers Pietro Berno, Antonio Francisco
and Francisco Aranha, a lay-brother, together with
twenty of their neophytes were included in the massacre.

Hearing of the tragedy, the Great Mogul despatched
an embassy to the viceroy and to the superior of the
Jesuits to express his sympathy, and also to urge that
other missionaries might be sent to instruct his people.
In compliance with the request, Jerónimo Xavier, a
nephew of St. Francis Xavier, was sent there in 1595
and succeeded in winning the favor of Akbar. The
" Encyclopedia Britannica " informs us that Jerónimo,
at the suggestion of the monarch, translated the four
Gospels into Persian. Ranke adds in his " History of
the Popes " that " while the Jesuit was there the
insurrections of the Mahometans contributed to dispose
the emperor towards the Christians, for in the year
1599 Christmas was celebrated at Lahore with the
utmost solemnity. The manger and the leading facts

of the Nativity were represented for twenty days
consecutively, and numerous catechumens proceeded
to the Church with palms in their hands to receive
baptism. The emperor read, with great pleasure, a
' Life of Christ ' composed in Persian, and a picture
of the Virgin, copied from the Madonna del Popolo
in Rome, was by his orders taken to the palace that
he might show it to the women of his household. It
is true that the Christians drew more favourable
conclusions from these things than the facts justified;
still, great progress was really made. Indeed, after
the death of Akbar, three princes of the blood royal
were solemnly baptized. They rode to the church on
white elephants, and were received with the sound
of trumpets, kettle-drums and martial music. This
took place in 1610, so that Christianity seemed gradually to acquire a position of a fixed character, although
suffering from certain vicissitudes and the prevalence
of fickleness in the matter of religious opinion. Political
considerations, also, largely affected the public mind.
In 1621 a college was founded in Agra, and a station
established at Patna. In 1624 hopes were entertained
that the Emperor Jehanguire would himself become a
Christian.''

Shortly after Jerónimo Xavier had settled down in
the court of the Great Mogul, Father Robert de Nobili,
a nephew of Cardinal Bellarmine, broke through the
caste barrier in India in a way that, for a time, gave
considerable scandal. He had gone to the mission of
Madura, a territory somewhat in the interior towards
the northeast of the Fisheries, and found there that
Father Fernandes, a very pious and energetic missioner
who had been living for fourteen years among his
pagans, had never made a convert, as he could not
get in touch with the influential people of the country.
Two difficulties stood in the way: first, he was a Portu-

guese or a Prangui, and the Prangui were held in
abhorrence, because they ate meat and drank wine;
secondly, he mingled with the most degraded castes
of India.

De Nobili determined to get rid of these obstacles.
First, he insisted, that he was not a Prangui but a
Roman nobleman in name and in fact; secondly, with
regard to wine and meat, he would abstain from them
and live on rice; thirdly, he would become a Brahmin,
as far as their manner of life and dress was concerned,
and, morever, he would outdo them in the knowledge
of their own language, literature and religion. Indeed,
within a year, he was master of Tamil, Telugu and
Sanskrit. He was now equipped for his work, and in
1606 he bade good-bye to Fernandes, and shut himself
up in a hut which, for a long time, no one was allowed
to enter. He wanted the news to spread among the
natives that a great European Brahmin had made
his appearance. Curiosity, he said, would do the rest,
for his rigid seclusion would make them all the more
intent on seeing him. The scheme succeeded, and
when, at last, visitors were admitted to speak to him,
they found him to be even holier in appearance than
they had imagined him to be, and were amazed to
hear him converse in Tamil, and show a perfect
acquaintance with the literature of the language. He
made it a point, also, to recite and even to sing the
songs of their poets, for he was an able musician and
had a good voice.

When his reputation was established he began to
discuss some of the truths of fundamental theology,
not as coming from himself, but which, as he showed
them, were actually set down in their own Vedas.
His knowledge of Sanskrit — perhaps he was the first
European to venture into that field — had given him
a more thorough knowledge of the sacred books than

was possessed by any of the Brahmins themselves, and hence it happened that, before a year had passed, he had baptized several persons who were conspicuous both for their nobility and learning. He permitted his converts to continue to besmear their foreheads with sandal-wood paste, to cultivate the tuft of hair on the top of their heads, and to wear a string on the left shoulder. He did this after he had thoroughly convinced himself that there was no superstition in such practices. Meantime he was living on milk, rice, herbs and water, which were handed to him once a day by the servant of a Brahmin. It was a precaution to forestall any suspicion that other food was supplied surreptitiously.

In the second year, his flock was so numerous that the hut he lived in was insufficient to contain them all, and he had to build a church. That, of course, caused some alarm among the Brahmins, but it was nothing in comparison to the storm that de Nobili's life excited in Europe. Cardinal Bellarmine, his uncle, thought he had apostatized, and wrote him an indignant letter, and the General of the Society added to it a very severe reprehension. His brother Jesuit, Fernandes, had denounced him as a traitor, because of his rejection of the name " Prangui," or Portuguese, and also of his connivance at idolatry in allowing his neophytes to retain their heathenish customs. This was the origin of the famous question of the " Malabar Rites " which created such a stir in the Church, one hundred years later. These charges gave de Nobili a great deal of trouble for some time, but at last everything was satisfactorily explained, and the cardinal, the General and the Pope told the innovating missionary to continue as he had begun. Hence in order to obviate the apparent neglect and even contempt of the lower castes, other priests were assigned to that work, and

de Nobili restricted himself to his peculiar vocation
for forty-two years. He then lost his sight and was
sent to Jafanapatam in Ceylon, and afterwards to
Mylapore, where he died on January 16, 1656.

The mission had prospered. About the time de Nobili
ended his labours, it had an average of 5000 converts
a year, and it never dropped below 3000, even in the
times of persecution. At the end of the seventeenth
century its territory had extended beyond Madura to
Mysore, Marava, Tanjore and Gingi, and the Christians
of the entire Madura Mission, as it was called, amounted
to 150,000 souls. Besides being a field for apostolic
zeal, the mission also produced eminent scholars in
Tamil and Sanskrit, like Beschi, Cœurdoux, and others.
In 1700 it reached into the Carnatic and probably took
in what Christians had been left there by the missionaries among the Moguls. This mission glories in its
great martyr, John de Britto, who arrived there
twelve years after the death of de Nobili. He, too,
adopted the manners of a Saniassi, and labored as
such for twenty-one years. It was a life of continual
and horrible martyrdom. He was finally put to death
as a magician, because of the multitudes of people
attracted to the Faith by his holiness and teaching.
Like his predecessor de Nobili, he did not worry his
converts about their tufts of hair or the cotton cords
on their shoulders, and it is noteworthy that long
after his death, and just while the process of his beatification was going on, the theologians were hotly
discussing the liceity of the Malabar Rites. If they
were condemned, how would the decision affect de
Britto's canonization? Pope Benedict XIV decided
that it would not stand in the way, and so de Britto
was placed among the Blessed.

The companions of de Nobili and de Britto went
everywhere in Hindostan, they even reconciled to the

Church the community of natives who called themselves the Christians of St. Thomas the Apostle, but who were in reality commonplace Nestorians. They built the first Church of Bengal, and penetrated into the kingdoms of Arracan, Pegu, Cambogia, and Siam, all the time busy avoiding the Dutch pirates who were prowling along the coast.

The most dazzling of these picturesque missionaries was undoubtedly the Italian, Constant Beschi, who arrived in Madura in 1700, one hundred years after de Nobili, and twenty-eight after de Britto. He determined to surpass all the other Saniassis or Brahmins in the austerity of his life. He remained in his house most of the time, and would never touch anything that had life in it. On his forehead was the pottu of Sandanam, and on his head the coulla, a sort of cylindrical head dress made of velvet. He was girt with the somen, was shod with the ceremonious wooden footgear, and pearls hung from his ears. He never went out except in a palanquin, in which tiger skins had to be placed for him to sit on, while a servant stood on either side, fanning him with peacock feathers, and a third held above his head a silken parasol surmounted by a globe of gold. He was called " the Great Viramamvuni ", and like Bonaparte, he sat " wrapped in the solitude of his own originality." Not even a Jesuit could come near him or speak to him. A word of Italian never crossed his lips, but he plunged into Sanskrit, Telugu, and Tamil, studied the poets of Hindostan, and wrote poems that conveyed to the Hindoos a knowledge of Christianity. For forty years he was publicly honored as the Ismat Saniassi, that is, the penitent without stain. The Nabob of Trichinopoli was so enthusiastic about him that Beschi had to accept the post of prime minister, and thenceforth he never went abroad unless accompanied by thirty horsemen, twelve banner-bearers, and a band of military music, while a long train of camels followed in the rear. If, on his way, any Jesuit who was looking after the Pariahs came across his path, there was no recognition on either side, but both must have been amused as the Jesuit in rags prostrated himself in the dust before the silk-robed Jesuit in the cavalcade, the outcast not daring even to look at the great official, though, perhaps, they were intimate friends.

Numbers of Jesuits were, meantime, besieging the General with petitions to be made missionaries among the Pariahs, for few could act the part that Beschi was playing. To be a Pariah was easy, and attempts to evangelize that class continued to be made in Madura up to the time of the Suppression. Conversions were numerous, and Bouchet, a contemporary of Beschi, heard as many as 100,000 confessions in a single year. It is said that the particularly fervent converts among the Brahmins used to cut off their hair as a sacrifice, when they were baptized, and a great number of locks, some of which were four and five feet long, adorned Beschi's church in Tiroucavalor.

But these conversions connoted persecution. Bouchet, who was Beschi's successor among the high-class Brahmins, was several times arrested and condemned to death. On one occasion, when he was sentenced to be burned alive and was being covered with oil to make the flames more active, the executioners were so startled by his apparent unconcern that they dropped the work and set him free. Bouchet thought that the Church of Madura was specially blessed by being persecuted, and that explained for him how he was able to baptize 20,000 Hindoos. He had the care of thirty churches, which meant untold labor. About the trifles of never eating meat, fresh eggs or fish, living in straw-covered cabins without beds, seats or furniture, and never having the luxury of a table or spoon or knife or fork at meal times,— that never gave the missionaries a thought. The consolation for these privations was that at times they would hear the confessions of entire villages and never have to deal with a mortal sin. Probably Simon Carvalho,— Marshall calls him Laynez — who had received 10,000 people into the Church, and was at one time almost torn to pieces by a mob, and at another hunted for five months to be put to death, would have preferred this work, in which he had been employed for thirty years, to that of administering the diocese of Mylapore, of which Clement XI made him bishop later.

" They were giants," wrote the Abbé Dubois who was a missionary in India in modern times, " and they triumphed in their day, because neither the world nor the devil could resist the might that was in them. Possessing for the most part the rarest mental endowments, so that if they had aimed only at human honors they would have encountered scarcely a rival in their path, versed in all the learning of their age, and conspicuous even in that great Society, which attracted to itself for more than a century the noblest minds of every country in Europe, they had acquired in addition to their natural gifts such a measure of Divine grace and wisdom, such perfection of evangelical virtue, that the powers of darkness fled away from before their face, and the Cross of Christ wherever they lifted it up, broke in pieces the idols of the Gentiles." And Perrin in his " Voyage dans l'Indoustan," II, 166, writes: " I confess that I have criticized the Jesuits of Hindostan with critical, perhaps with malignant temper. I have changed my mind now, and if I spoke ill of them, all India would tax me with imposture."

The hermit kingdom of Thibet was first entered by Father Antonio de Andrada. He was one of the missionaries in the kingdom of the Great Mogul, and started from Agra in 1624 to cross the Himalayas and enter, if possible, the Grand Lama's mysterious domain. He joined a troop of idolaters who were going to present their offerings at the celebrated pagoda of Barrinath, whither thousands flocked from all the kingdoms of India and even from the island of Ceylon. " That part of the trip, " he says in his narrative, " was the easiest, although in ascending the valley of the Ganges I had often to creep along a narrow path cut in the face of the rock, sometimes scarcely a palm in breadth, while far below me were roaring torrents into which, from time to time, some unfortunate traveller would be hurled. Here and there we had to pass rivers with the help of ropes strung across the stream, or perhaps on heaps of snow which the avalanches had piled up in the valley, but which were especially perilous, for the mountain torrents were all the while eating through them at the base. If there was a cave-in the whole party would disappear in the depths. It was dreadful work, but when I saw my companions, many of them old men, keeping up their courage by repeating the name of Barrinath, I was ashamed not to do more for Jesus Christ than these poor pagans for their idols and pagodas."

After the shrine was reached, the valiant missionary continued his journey, and arrived at the town of Manah, the last habitation of the mountaineers on the India slope. " Before us was a desert of snow, inaccessible for any living creature for ten months of the year, and which called for a twenty days' march, without shelter and without a bit of wood to make a fire. With me were two natives and a guide. However, I had put my trust in God, for whom alone I was attempting this dangerous task. Each step costs incredible struggles, for every morning there was a new layer of snow, knee-deep or up to the waist or even to the shoulders. In some places, to get across the drifts, we had to go through the motions of a swimmer; and to avoid being smothered at night, we were compelled to remove the snow, at least every hour." He finally arrived at his destination and was well received by the Lama. He was given leave to establish a mission in the country, he then made haste to return to Agra and in the following year he established a base at Chaparang. But he himself was not to remain in the country which he had so gloriously opened to the world. He was named provincial of the Indies, and had to set out for Goa immediately. Nine years later, on March 19, 1634, he was poisoned by the Jews. Meantime the Thibet mission tottered and fell.

In 1661 Father Johann Gruber, one of Schall's assistants in Pekin, reached Thibet on his way to Europe. He could not go by sea, for the Dutch were blockading Macao, so he made up his mind to go overland by way of India and Thibet. With him was Father d'Orville, a Belgian. After reaching Sunning-fu, on the confines of Kuantsu, they crossed Kukonor and Kalmuk Tatary to the Holy City of Lhasa in Thibet, but did not remain there. They then climbed the Himalayas and from Nepal journeyed over the Ganges plateau to Patna and Agra. At the latter city d'Orville died, he was replaced by Father Roth, and the two missionaries tramped across Asia to Europe. Gruber had been two hundred and fourteen days on the road. In 1664 he attempted to return to China by way of Russia, but for some reason or other failed to get through that country. He then made for Asia but fell ill at Constantinople, finally he died either in Italy at Florence or at Patak in Hung-

ary. Fortunately he had left his " Journal " and charts
in the hands of the great Athanasius Kircher, who
published them in his famous " China Illustrata."

Other missionaries entered Mingrelia, Paphlagonia,
and Chaldea; in the latter place they brought the
Nestorians back to the Church. Besides laboring in
nearby Greece and Thessaly, at Constantinople, they
were in Armenia and at Ephesus, Smyrna, Damascus,
Aleppo, at the ruins of Babylon, and on the shores of
the Euphrates and the Jordan, and they founded the
missions of Antourah for the Maronites of Libanus,
whom Henry IV of France took under his protection.

The origin of these Maronite missions reads like a
romance. It is found in the French " Menology "
of October 12 which tells us that one day, at a meeting
of his sodalists in Marseilles, Father Amien was talking
about the propagation of the Faith and incidentally
mentioned Persia, which only one missionary had as
yet entered. Among his hearers was a rich merchant
named François Lambert, who, excited by the sermon,
determined to go and put himself at the disposal of
that solitary Persian apostle. He crossed the Arabian
desert, reached Bagdad, embarked on the Euphrates,
with the intention of getting to Ispahan in Persia and
when he failed in this, he turned towards Ormuz on the
straits connecting the Persian Gulf with the Arabian
Sea. That place, however, could not keep him; it was
too luxurious and too licentious; so he went over to
upper Hindostan, where the Great Mogul was
enthroned. He passed through Surate and Golconda,
but from Mylapore, which holds the tomb of St.
Thomas, he could not tear himself away for several
weeks. Finally, he boarded a ship which was wrecked
on the shores of Bengal, and twice he came within an
inch of disappearing in the deep. After two days and
two nights on the desolate sands, he and five other

castaways sang the Te Deum to make them forget
their sorrow.   They must have struck inland after that
for we are told that later they built a raft and floated
down one of the great rivers of India.   It was a journey
of thirty-five days, and several of the poor wanderers
died of hunger on the way.   At last they reached a
native settlement and were led to the nearest Portuguese post.   Unfortunately, the geography at this part
of Lambert's narrative is too vague for us to be sure
of the places he saw on his journey.

From India he made his way to Rome, where he
entered the Jesuit novitiate of San Andrea, and from
there, after his ordination, he was sent to Syria.   Again
he was shipwrecked, and when picked up on the beach
he was taken for a pirate and brought in chains to the
chief of the mountaineer clan.   Happily they were the
Maronites of Libanus, and there Lambert remained
till the end of his days, helping the persecuted people to
keep their faith against their furious Mussulman
neighbours.   These Maronites had been represented,
by postulatory letters at the Lateran Council as early
as 1516, and later Pope Gregory XIII built for them
in Rome a hospital and a college which produced some
very eminent scholars.   In 1616 Clement VIII sent
the Jesuit, Girolamo Dandini, to preside at the Maronite
council, for the purpose of introducing certain liturgical
reforms; but it was the wanderer Lambert who was
the first to remain permanently among this heroic
people.   He lived only three years after his arrival;
it was long enough, however, to prepare the way for the
five mission centres which were were subsequently
established there.

Alexandre de Rhodes, who appears at this juncture,
is another of the picturesque figures in the history of
the Society.   According to Fénelon, it is he who
inspired the formation of the great association of the

Missions Etrangères, which has sent so many thousands
of glorious apostles, many of whom were martyrs, to
evangelize the countries from which he had come in
a most unexpected and extraordinary fashion. He
was born in Avignon, the old French City of the Popes,
and was called by his contemporaries the " Francis
Xavier of Cochin-China and Tonkin." He left Rome
for the Indies when he was only twenty-six years of
age, and began his missionary work in the East by
looking after the slaves and jailbirds of Goa. On his
way from that city to Tuticorin he baptized fifty
pagans on shipboard, his eloquence being helped by
the furious tempest that threatened to send the frail
bark to the bottom. While waiting at Malacca for the
ship to get ready, he and his companion captured
another two thousand souls for the Lord, and when
he arrived at his destination, other thousands came
into the fold, among them the king and eighteen members of the royal household, and two hundred of the
priests of the pagan temples. Nor did this rapidity denote instability, for twenty-five years later the Church
of Tuticorin which he founded could count at its altars
no less than 300,000 Christians.

It is said that he had even the power of making
thaumaturgists out of his catechumens. By the use
of holy water or the relic of the cross, they restored
people to health, and as many as two hundred and
seventy sufferers from various maladies were the
recipients of such favors. When he was thrown into
prison and loaded with fetters, as he often was, he
converted his jailers and others besides. When carried
off in a ship to be ejected from the country, he baptized
the captain and crew and got them to put him ashore
in a desolate place where he began a new apostolate.
Fifteen times, in his journeys to Tonkin and Cochin-
China, he crossed the Gulf of Tonkin, which had a

16

terrible record of tempests and shipwrecks, and finally he started on his famous overland tramp to Europe in search of evangelical laborers. He achieved his purpose, though it took him three years and a half to do it.

On that memorable journey he risked his life at every step, for he had to travel through countries whose language he did not understand, and where he could expect nothing but suspicion, ill-treatment and, if he escaped death, privations and sufferings of every description. On his way to Rome the Dutch in Java threw him in jail, but he converted his keepers, and was segregated in consequence and put in solitary confinement; he regarded that seclusion only as a splendid chance to make his annual retreat, and when he was let out he resumed his pilgrimage through India and Asia. As he said himself, he was carried on the wings of Divine Providence, through storms and shipwrecks, and cities and deserts, and barbarians and pagans, and heretics and Turks. He finally reached Rome in 1648, and told the Father General and the Pope what was needed in the far-away Orient. The purpose of this voyage, so replete with adventure, was of very great importance.

It was chiefly by the help of Portugal, which was then at the most brilliant epoch of its history, that missions had been extended for thousands of miles in the East, beginning at Goa and Malabar, and stretching round the Peninsula of Hindostan to Cochin-China, Corea, and Japan, in many of which splendid ecclesiastical establishments had been founded. They were all begun, supported and protected by Portugal. But unfortunately, Christianity and Portugal were so inextricably entangled, mixed and confused with one another that the religion taught by the missionaries came to be considered by the people not so much the religion of Christ as the religion of the Portuguese.

Another consequence was that a quarrel between any
little Portuguese official or merchant with an Oriental
potentate meant a persecution of the Church.   Furthermore, as Portugal's possession of the country was so
exclusive that not even the most humble missionary
could leave Europe unless he was acceptable to the
Government, it amounted to an actual enslavement of
the Church. Finally, as every other nation was
debarred from commercial rights in the East, it became
the practice of rivals to represent to the natives that
the missionaries were merely Portuguese spies or
advance agents who were preparing for invasion and
conquest.

Unfortunately, in return for all that Portugal had
done and was to do for the advancement of Christianity
in those newly discovered lands, an arrangement had
been made with the Pope that no bishop in all that
vast territory could take his see unless Portugal
accepted him; no new diocese could be created unless
Portugal were consulted; no papal bull was valid
unless passed upon by the Portuguese kings.   To put
an end to all that, was the reason why de Rhodes
went to Europe.   But he did not dare to appear
before the Pope as a Jesuit, for if it were known what
his mission was every Jesuit house in the Portuguese
possessions would have been immediately closed, as
happened later.   Hence it was that he had to wait in
Rome for three whole years until 1651 before he could
even get his petition considered, and this explains also
why he made the extravagant demand for " a patriarch,
three archbishops, and twelve bishops." By asking
much he thought he might at least get something.

The Pope wanted de Rhodes himself to be a bishop;
he refused the honor, and then was told to go and find
some available candidates.   For that purpose he
addressed himself to a group of ecclesiastics at Paris

whom the Jesuit Father Bagot was directing in the ways of the higher spiritual life, and who were often spoken of as the Bagotists. Among them were Montmorency de Laval, the future Bishop of Quebec, and M. Olier, who was, later on, to found the Society of St. Sulpice. His appeal had no immediate result, and he then prepared to return to Tonkin, but he received an order to go elsewhere. Probably no Portuguese vessel would take him back, for the purpose of his visit to Europe must have by that time got abroad. He was, therefore, sent to Persia, although he was then over sixty years old; so to Persia he went, and we find him studying the language on his way thither, and, when travelling through the streets of Ispahan, making a fool of himself in trying to stammer out the few words he had learned, but always making light of the laughter and sometimes of the kicks and cuffs and even threats of death that he received. He was planning new missionary posts in Georgia and Tatary when death called him to his reward. But he had already won the admiration of Ispahan, and the city never saw a costlier funeral than the one which, on November 7, 1660, conveyed to the grave the mortal remains of the glorious Alexandre de Rhodes.

This journey of the great missionary is a classic in its emphasis of the earnestness the Society has always shown to have the episcopacy established in its missions. It is idle to pretend that this project of de Rhodes was due to his own initiative, and was not sanctioned by his superiors. He may, indeed, have suggested it, but no one in the Society undertakes a work from which he may be withdrawn at any moment, except he is assigned to it. Now de Rhodes continued at his task for several years, and evidently with the approval of his superiors.

Apparently unsuccessful though his effort was, it brought about some results. Mme. d'Aiguillon, the niece of Cardinal Richelieu, took the matter up, but even she, with her great influence, could induce the ecclesiastical authorities to do no more than create one little vicariate Apostolic. It was a far cry from the great hierarchical scheme of de Rhodes. One of the Bagotists, Pallu, was appointed, though, for a time there was a question of sending Laval also to the East; but the necessity of having a bishop in Quebec was so urgent that Pallu was sent alone to Tonkin.

Portugal, however, refused to carry him thither, although Louis XIV asked it as a special favor. In 1658 when Pallu attempted to go out at his own risk he reached not Cochin-China but Siam. He was back again in France in 1665, begging protection against the Portuguese, who were arresting his priests and putting them in jail at Goa and Macao. In 1674 he was shipwrecked in the Philippines and carried off a prisoner to Spain, and was liberated only by the united efforts of the Pope and Louis XIV. He set sail again, but was driven ashore on the Island of Formosa and never reached Tonkin.

Meantime the Jesuits had not forgotten Francis Xavier's dream about China. The Dominican Gaspar de la Cruz had found his way through its closed gates, four years after Xavier expired on the island opposite Canton, but he was promptly expelled. It was only in 1581, fully thirty-six years subsequent to the attempt of de la Cruz, that the Jesuits finally succeeded. All that time they had been waiting at Macao,— a settlement granted to the Portuguese in return for the assistance given to China in beating off a fleet of plundering sea-rovers. They had long since seen the folly of attempting to enter a new country under the

shadow of some pretentious embassy, for inevitably
a suspicion was left lurking in the minds of both the
governments and the people that there was an ulterior
political motive back of the preaching of the priests.
Hence it was that Valignani, though in general believing
in embassies to kings and rulers, after the new religion
was well understood and accepted in a country, had
become convinced that it was unwise to begin the
work in that ostentatious fashion. He, therefore,
took three clever young Italians, Michele Ruggieri,
Francesco Pasio and Matteo Ricci, and after training
them thoroughly in mathematics and in all the branches
of the natural sciences, ordered them not only to
master the Chinese language, but also to familiarize
themselves with the literature and the history of the
country. Ricci was available especially as a mathematician, having been the favorite pupil of Father
Clavius, who was one of the chief constructors of the
Gregorian Calendar.

According to Huc (p. 40) they gained access to the
forbidden land by taking part in a comedy. A viceroy,
he tells us, who lived near Canton, summoned to his
tribunal on some charge or other both the bishop
and the governor of Macao. This was a grievous
insult to those dignitaries, but on the other hand if
they refused to appear, the result might be disastrous
for the whole Portuguese colony. To extricate themselves from the dilemma a trick was resorted to — one
which was quite in keeping with Chinese methods.
Instead of going themselves, they sent two persons
who pretended to be the bishop and governor. For
the former Father Ruggieri was chosen, for the latter,
a layman. On the face of it, the story is absurd.
It would be impossible to impersonate two such well-
known functionaries as a bishop and a governor, and
the discovery of such a fraud would inevitably entail

condign punishment. Most probably Ruggieri and his companion went simply as representatives of the two functionaries. They were well provided with presents, which had the desired effect of making the viceroy forget his grievances, if he had any. He accepted everything very graciously and suggested a second visit. Then Ruggieri apprised him of the longing he had always entertained of passing his whole life in the wonderful land of China, with its marvellously intellectual people, and was assured that his wish might possibly be gratified later on. But when a hint was thrown out about a wonderful clock which the missionary possessed and was extremely anxious to show such an important personage as the viceroy, every difficulty about a permanent residence immediately disappeared.

The party was conducted back to the boat with great ceremony; and when Ruggieri's return was delayed by an attack of sickness, the viceregal junk was sent to the Island to convey him to Tchao-King; and also to deliver into his hands a formal authorization to establish a house in the town. Valignani, who was then at Macao, hesitated for a time about accepting the offer, but finally consented. On December 18 Ruggieri embarked, taking with him Father Pasio and a scholastic, along with several Chinese. This addition to the party somewhat surprised the viceroy, but Ruggieri told him that being a priest, it was in keeping with his dignity to have an attendant. The others were only servants, but the clock did the work, and the audacious apostles received a Buddhist temple outside the town as their place of residence, and were the recipients of frequent favors in the way of food from the delighted viceroy. He even granted permission to Ruggieri to call Ricci from Macao. Their temple-residence soon became famous, and every one in Tchao-King, from the highest civil and military functionaries down to what we now call coolies, came out to see the occupants.

Unfortunately, the viceroy was deposed and his successor, objecting to the presence of the foreigners, ordered the whole party to return to Macao. They did not obey, but made an attempt to reach Canton, which the former official had given them authority to enter. They succeeded by purposely getting themselves arrested in Hong-Kong. But in Canton no attention was paid to the document they had with them, and so they made their way back to Macao, convinced that there was no hope of remaining in China under the new incumbent. Yet to their great surprise, the very man they feared sent an envoy over to Macao to bring the three missionaries back to Tchao-King. He welcomed them effusively and gave them a beautiful site for their residence, quite close to a famous porcelain tower, which had just been erected and was considered a monument of Chinese architecture. This was the cradle of Christianity in China.

In 1589, however, there arrrived a new viceroy who took a fancy to their residence, and without any ceremony dispossessed them. But as they had already won such favor by their maps and globes and astronomical instruments, when they came to Tchao-Tcheou looking for a house, they were received with the wildest demonstrations of joy. They grew more popular every day, and soon the mandarins of Canton invited Ricci to speak in their assemblies. He availed himself of all these opportunities afforded him to inject into his scientific discourses something about religion, and he noted that they showed greater attention when he broached such topics than when he restricted himself to purely human science. Troubles occurred from time to time, but the number of neophytes increased daily, and Ricci, who up to that time had worn the dress of a bonze now discarded it and assumed the garb of a Chinese man of letters.

In 1595 the news came that the Japanese emperor, Taicosama was preparing an expedition against Corea, whereupon, the general-in-chief of the Chinese troops came down to Tchao-Tcheou to consult Ricci. But it was not so much to discuss the military situation as to get him to restore a favorite child to health. Ricci promised to pray for the boy, and in return asked to accompany the general back to Pekin for he was convinced that if he could once convert the educated classes of the capital the rest of his work would be easy. The request was granted, and Ricci was thus, very probably, the first white man to travel through the interior of China and to see the people of the cities and country at close range. At Nankin, however, he noted the deep suspicion entertained for foreigners, and although he went as far as Pekin itself, he thought it wiser not to enter the city, and consequently he returned by the Yellow River to Tchao-Tcheou.

Taicosama's expedition from Japan proved a failure, and the public anxiety about foreigners ceased to be acute. This lull enabled Ricci to establish himself at Nankin, which seemed to have struck his fancy as he passed through it on his way to Pekin. The city was in a fever about the the study of astronomy and astrology, and he found a hearty welcome among its learned men. He taught them in his daily intercourse many of the doctrines of the Faith, and got in return from them the real meaning of their ancestor-worship and ceremonies. Hence, he had no scruples at all about taking part in the honors paid to Confucius, who was the great legislator and teacher of China, and he never suspected that there would be later a hue and cry in the Church about the alleged idolatry of these very ceremonies.

Meantime he forwarded information about the observatory of Nankin that quite astounded scientific Europe. Nankin, however, did not satisfy him, and he made constant but unavailing efforts to reach the imperial city of Pekin. Finally, in 1600, after seventeen years of patient waiting, he succeeded. His coming produced a great sensation. He was even admitted to the palace, but really never saw the emperor, though the people at large fancied he had been accorded that privilege. However, it amounted almost to the same thing, for the effect produced and his real missionary success dated from that moment. The greatest mandarin of the court became a Christian and almost a saint, though his name was Sin. Later, Sin went about preaching Christianity. His conversion itself was a sermon, and was the beginning of many others. Meantime the five Jesuits at Canton drew multitudes around them. The upper classes flocked to hear their discourses, and began to take pride in being considered Christians, but it was hard for them to understand why the Gospel was not exclusively restricted to their set. They could not yet grasp the fact, even after baptism, that the lower classes had the same privilege of salvation as themselves. To the Chinese mind it was a social revolution, and they were right, but they were wrong in objecting to it.

Here an interesting episode occurs. Associated with Father Geronimo Aquaviva in the court of the Grand Mogul at Agra was a Portuguese lay-brother named Benedict Goes. Although engaged only in domestic service, he was in great favor with the barbarian monarch, and if the Viceroy of India was saved from disaster, it was due to Goes, who not only persuaded the Grand Mogul to desist from war with the Portuguese, but succeeded in having himself sent down to Goa with all the children who had been captured in the various raids of Akbar's armies into Portuguese territory. While he was at Agra, reports had been coming in that the Fathers had at last entered China — the Cathay of the old Franciscans of the thirteenth century, and it was deemed advisable to try to establish communications with them. Goes was chosen to carry out the project, and, in 1602, he started from Agra, which lies in the northern part of Hindostan, about south of Delhi and west of Lucknow. It meant a journey from the centre of Hindostan, across the whole of Thibet and China, among absolutely unknown nations, savage and semi-civilized, Mohammedans and idolaters, through trackless forests and over snow-clad mountains, facing the dangers of starvation and sickness and wild beasts at every step. But all that was not thought to be beyond the powers of the courageous brother. Disguised as an Armenian, he had a hard time of it from robber chiefs and barbarian princes. He was ill-treated by most of them, for he openly professed that he was a Christian. When he refused to pay respect to Mohammed, he was sentenced to be trampled to death by elephants, but he was finally pardoned and allowed to resume his journey. On he plodded for five years, and just as he was nearing the goal his strength gave out. Fortunately Father Ricci, at Pekin, had heard of his coming, and sent Father Fernandes to meet him. When Fernandes arrived, Goes was breathing his last in the frontier town of Su-Chou. It was then 1607, and the dying man told his brother Jesuit: " For five years I have been without the sacraments, but I do not remember any serious sin since I set out from Agra." He died on April 7, 1607.

In 1606 there was worry in China about certain reports originating in Macao, where the Portuguese were stationed, The Jesuits were accused of aspiring to nothing else than the imperial throne; to prove it, attention was called to the fact that all their houses were built on hills, and could be easily transformed into citadels in time of war. It was said, too, that a Dutch fleet in the offing was at their service, and that arrangements had been made with the Japanese for an invasion. The result was a general panic throughout the empire and not a few apostacies. Threats to kill the missionaries also began to be heard. Coincident with this, came an unwise act on the part of the Vicar-General of Macao, who, because of a decision against him in a dispute he had with the Franciscans, put the whole island under interdict. The result was that the political situation became still more threatening, and Father Martines was arrested at Canton, tortured in the most horrible fashion, and finally executed. This death, however, marked as it was by the heroic courage of the victim, his affirmations in the midst of his sufferings of his own innocence and that of his brethren, quelled the storm. Ricci's influence, also, contributed to calm the excited people, and he became greater than ever in their estimation. He was called another Confucius, and was even empowered by the authorities to establish a novitiate at Pekin. Ricci was well on in years by that time, but continued valiantly at his work, making saints as well as great littérateurs and mathematicians out of his Jesuit associates; he wrote treatises in Chinese on Christian ethics, while continuing his mathematical works, and all day long he was busy with the great mandarins who came to consult him. In 1610 he succumbed under these accumulated labors, and his obsequies were such as had never been accorded to any other foreigner. The funeral procession, preceded by the cross, traversed the entire city, and by order of the emperor his remains were laid in a temple, which was thenceforth transformed into a Christian church.

Mr. Gutzlaff, a Protestant missionary in China of modern times, says that " Ricci had spent only twenty-seven years in China but when he died there were more than three hundred churches in the different provinces." Gutzlaff's testimony is all the more precious, because, according to Marshall, his own associates describe him as "more occupied in amassing wealth than in making Christians." Referring to the scientific labors of Ricci and his successors, Thornton (History of China, Preface, p. 13) says: " The geographical labors performed in China by the Jesuits and other missionaries of the Roman Catholic Faith will always command the gratitude and excite the wonder of all geographers. Portable chronometers and aneroid barometers, sextants and theodolites, sympiesometers and micrometers, compasses and artificial horizons are, notwithstanding all possible care, frequently found to fail, yet one hundred and fifty years ago a few wandering European priests traversed the enormous state of China Proper, and laid down on their maps the positions of cities, the direction of rivers and the height of mountains with a correctness of detail and a general accuracy of outline that are absolutely marvellous. To this day all our maps are based on their observations." " Whatever is valuable in Chinese astronomical science," adds Mr. Gutzlaff, " has been borrowed from the treatises of Roman Catholic missionaries."

Ricci's death was a calamity to the Church, for in the following year a mandarin who was in charge at

Nankin started a genuine persecution. The missionaries were summoned to his tribunal, publicly scourged and sent back to Macao — and all this with the authorization of the emperor. Matters grew worse, but at the emperor's death in 1620, there was a lull, for the Tatars were invading China and the help of the Portuguese had to be invoked; as that, however, could not be done unless the Europeans were placated by recalling the missionaries, the exiles returned to their posts. The emperor overcame the Tatars, and the tranquillity and good feeling that followed allowed the Fathers, who were scattered all over the empire, some of them 800 leagues from Pekin, to get together and decide on uniformity of methods in treating with their converts. In that congregation the doubts which met them at every step as to what they were to tolerate and what to forbid were settled. They knew the people thoroughly by this time, their ideas, their customs; and their scrupulous love of the Faith guided them in their decisions.

About this time the great Adam Schall arrived. He was a worthy successor of Ricci. His reputation had preceded him as a mathematician, and he was immediately employed by the emperor to reform the Chinese calendar. His influence, in consequence of this distinction, was unbounded in extending the field of missionary work. The pagans themselves built a church at his request in Sin-gan-fou, and he obtained an edict from the emperor which empowered the Jesuits to preach throughout the empire. The extraordinary success of Schall was the talk of Europe; and applications poured in on the General from all sides to be sent out to share the labors and the triumphs of the mission. Great numbers of Jesuits were sent there, but many perished on the way out, for shipwrecks were very common in those unknown seas, and the crowded and unhealthy ships as well as the long and difficult journey claimed throngs of victims.

The work soon became too great for the laborers and then there came a reinforcement from the Philippines, largely from the other religious orders who had been long waiting to enter China, and who now devoted themselves to the work. Not knowing the country, however, they were horrified to see that many of the practices of Confucianism were still retained by the Chinese Christians, and they denounced as idolatry what the old Jesuits had decided, after years of close scrutiny, to be nothing but a ceremonial which had been thoroughly and scrupulously purified from all taint of superstition. But the newcomers would not look at it in that light. They immediately wrote to the Archbishop of Manila and to the Bishop of Cebú that the Jesuits not only concealed from their converts the mysteries of the Cross, but permitted them to prostrate themselves before the idol of Chin-Hoam, to honor their ancestors with superstitious rites, and to offer sacrifices to Confucius. Rome was then informed of it, but some years later, namely in 1637, both the archbishop and the bishop wrote to Urban VIII that on examining the matter more carefully, they had arrived at the conclusion that the Jesuits were right. It was then too late. A series of bloody persecutions had already begun. The first explosion of wrath occurred when one of the new preachers, speaking through an interpreter, told his congregation that Confucius and all their pagan ancestors were in hell, and that the Jesuits had not taught the Chinese the truth. Public indignation followed on this unwise utterance and expulsions began.

Fortunately, the persecutions were checked for a while by fresh attempts of the Tatar element in China to seize the imperial crown. The Jesuits kept out of the strife by pronouncing for neither party. Happily, the Tatar element took a fancy to Schall, while Father Coeffler baptized the Chinese empress, giving her the Christian name of Helen and calling her infant son Constantine. The Tatars finally prevailed, and Schall was made a mandarin and president of the board of mathematics of the empire. He was given access to the emperor at all times, and might have made him a Christian had not the empress induced him to resume the pagan practices from which Schall had weaned him. Nor did the death of the troublesome lady mend matters; on the contrary, her disconsolate husband lapsed into melancholia, and in 1661 died, leaving a child of eight as his successor. In pursuance of the emperor's command, Schall was appointed instructor of the prince, but, as was to be expected, that arrangement aroused the fury of the people and especially of the bonzes. They maintained, rightfully from their point of view, that if Schall were left in position during the long minority of the prince, he would be absolute master of the future emperor — a result that must be prevented by crushing out Christianity. Forthwith all the missionaries were summoned to Pekin and thrown into prison. There was now no longer any discussion about the worship of Confucius, for the disputants were all in the dungeons of Pekin or elsewhere waiting for death.

The Christians were without pastors, but Father Gresson, who was in China at that time, tells us in his "History of China under the Tatars" that, during the persecution, the catechists baptized 2000 converts. It is not surprising, for before the outbreak of the persecution, the Jesuits had one hundred and fifty-one churches and thirty-eight residences in China; the Dominicans twenty-one churches and two residences, and the Franciscans one establishment. The total

Christian population amounted to 250,000. Up to that time the Fathers of the Society had written one hundred and thirty-one works on religious subjects, one hundred and three on mathematics, and fifty-five on physics.

While the missionaries lay in chains expecting death at every moment, a Dominican named Navarrete succeeded in making his escape. It was lucky for him in one respect, but in all probability it would mean as soon as it was discovered the massacre of all the other prisoners; to avert this calamity, the illustrious Jesuit, Grimaldi, took his place in the prison. Unfortunately, Navarrete had no sooner reached Europe than he began an attack on the methods of the Jesuits in dealing with the Chinese rites. It caused great grief to his fellow Dominicans, and when the news of the publication of his " Tratados históricos " reached China in 1668, the Dominican Father Sarpetri sent a solemn denunciation of it to Rome, declaring that the practice of the Jesuits in permitting such rites was not only irreproachable under every point of view, but most necessary in propagating the Gospel. He denied under oath that the Jesuits refused to explain the mysteries of the Passion to the Chinese, and affirmed that his protest against the charge was not in answer to an appeal, but was prompted by the pure love of truth. Another Dominican, Gregorio López, who was Bishop of Basilea and Vicar-Apostolic of Nan-King, sent the Sacred Congregation a " memoir" in favor of the Jesuits. Navarrete atoned for his act of mistaken judgment later; for when he was Archbishop of Santo Domingo he asked leave of the king and viceroy to establish a Jesuit college in his residential city, and he paid a glowing tribute to the Society.

When Schall was brought up for trial there was, at his side, another Jesuit named Ferdinand Verbiest, a native of Pilthem near Courtrai in Belgium. He had come out to China when he was thirty-six years old, and was first engaged in missionary work in Shen-si. In 1660 he was summoned to Pekin to assist Father Schall, and in 1664 was thrown into prison with him. In the court-room, Verbiest was the chief spokesman, for Schall, being then seventy-four years of age and paralyzed, was unable to utter a word. The charges against the old missionary had been trumped up by a Mohammedan who claimed to be an astronomer. They were: first, that Schall had shown pictures of the Passion of Jesus Christ to the deceased emperor; secondly, that he had secured the presidency of the board of mathematics for himself in order to promote Christianity; thirdly, that he had incorrectly determined the day on which the funeral of one of the princes was to take place. It was an "unlucky" day. Verbiest had no difficulty in proving that the accused had been ordered by the emperor to be president of the board of ma hematics, and furthermore, that he never had anything to do with "lucky" or "unlucky" days. The charge about the pictures of the Passion was admitted, and that may have been the reason why, in spite of the eloquence of Verbiest, who was loaded with chains while he was pleading, Father Schall was condemned to be hacked to pieces. In this trouble, however, the Lord came to the rescue: a meteor of an extraordinary kind appeared in the heavens, and a fire reduced to ashes that part of the imperial palace where the condemnation was pronounced. The sentence was revoked, and the missionaries were set free. Father Schall lingered a year after recovering his freedom. When Kang-hi came to the throne in 1669, an official declaration was made denouncing both the trial and the sentence as iniquitous, and although Schall had

then been three years dead, unusually solemn funeral
services were ordered in his honor. His remains were
laid beside those of Father Ricci. The emperor himself
composed the eulogistic epitaph which was inscribed
on the tomb.

.Schall had given forty-four years of his life to China,
when at the age of seventy-five, he breathed his
last in the arms of Father Rho, who, like him,
was to hold a distinguished position as mathematician in the imperial court. Rho had preluded
his advent to China by organizing the defense of the
Island of Macao against a Dutch fleet. He had new
ramparts constructed around the city; he planted
four pieces of artillery on the walls, and when the
Dutchmen landed for an assault he led the troops in
a sortie and drove the enemy back to their ships.
In his "Promenade autour du Monde" (II, 266), Baron
de Hübner gives an enthusiastic description of the
Jesuit Observatory at Pekin.

"Man's inhumanity to man" is cruelly exemplified
in a foul accusation urged against the venerable Schall,
a century after he was buried with imperial honors
in Pekin. In 1758 a certain Marcello Angelita, secretary
of Mgr. de Tournon, the prelate who was commissioned
to pass on the question of the Malabar Rites, published
a story, which was repeated in many other books,
that Schall had spent his last years "separated from
the other missionaries, removed from obedience to
his superiors, in a house which had been given him by
the emperor, and with a woman whom he treated as his
wife, and who bore him two children. After having
led a pleasant life with his family for some years, he
ended his days in obscurity." If there was even the
shadow of truth in these accusations the Dominican
Navarrete, who knew Schall personally, and who
wrote against him and his brethren so fiercely in 1667,

would not have failed to mention this fact to confirm his charges about the Chinese Rites. But he does not breathe a word about any misconduct on the part of the great missionary. Moreover, it is inconceivable that the vigorous Father General Oliva, who governed the Society at that time, would have tolerated that state of things for a single instant.

The foundation upon which the charge was built appears to be that the old missionary used to call a Chinese mandarin his " adopted grandson " and had helped to advance him to lucrative positions in the empire. The libel was written forty years after Schall's death, and was largely inspired by the infamous ex-Capuchin Norbert.

Possibly the mental attitude of Angelita's master, de Tournon, may also account in part for the publication of this calumny. De Tournon was known to be a bitter enemy of the Society, and he took no pains to conceal it when sent to the East to decide the vexed question of the Rites. Although on his arrival at Pondicherry in 1703, the Fathers met him on the shore and conducted him processionally to the city, he interpreted these marks of respect and the lavish generosity with which they looked after all his needs as nothing but policy. Not only did he refuse to give them a hearing on their side of the controversy, but he hurried off elsewhere as soon as he had formulated his decree. When he arrived in Canton, the first words he uttered were: " I come to China to purify its Catholicity," and before taking any information whatever, he ordered the removal of all the symbols which he considered superstitious. The act created an uproar, as it was only through the influence of the Fathers that de Tournon was permitted to go to Pekin; and although they managed to make his entrance into the imperial city unusually splendid,

he immediately informed the emperor of a plan he
had made to reconstruct the missions but, expressed
himself in such an offensive fashion that the emperor
immediately dismissed him. He then repaired to
Canton, and on January 28, 1707, issued the famous
order forbidding the cult of the ancestors, with the
result that the emperor sent down officials to conduct
him to Macao, where he was reported to have died
in prison, on June 8, 1710.

The Mohammedan mandarin, Yang, who had
trumped up the astronomical accusations against
Schall, had meantime succeeded to the post as head of
the mathematical board, but the young emperor was
not satisfied with the results obtained, and he ordered
a public dispute on the relative merits of Chinese and
European astronomy. Verbiest was on one side, and
Yang on the other. The test was to be first, the
determination, in advance, of the shadow given at
noon of a fixed day by a gnomon of a given height;
second, the absolute and relative position of the sun
and the planets on a date assigned; third, the time of
a lunar eclipse. The result was a triumph for Verbiest.
He was immediately installed as president, and his
brethren were allowed to return to their missions.
Verbiest's career, at Pekin, was more brilliant than
that of either Ricci or Schall. There is no end of the
things he did. The famous bronze astronomical
instruments which figured so conspicuously in the
Boxer Uprising of 1900 were of his manufacture; he
built an aqueduct also, and cast as many as one hundred
and thirty-two cannon for the Chinese army. The
emperor followed his astronomical classes, appointed
him to the highest grade in the mandarinate, and
gave him leave to preach Christianity anywhere in the
empire. Innocent XI, to whom he dedicated his
Chinese Missal, sent him a brief in 1681, which con-

tained the greatest praise for "using the profane sciences to promote Christianity," a commendation which was more than welcome at that time, when the book of Navarrete was doing its evil work against the Society.

In 1677 when Verbiest was appointed vice-provincial, he appealed for new laborers from Europe. He even advocated the use of the native language in the liturgy in order to facilitate the ordination of Chinese priests. It was a bold petition to make when the memory of Luther and his German liturgy was still so fresh in the mind of Europe. The reason for the petition was that otherwise the conversion of China was impossible. Brucker in his history of the Society tells us that for one hundred years no native had been ordained a priest in China. He gives as a reason for this, the disgust of the Portuguese government at the failure met with in Hindostan, where the formation of a native clergy was attempted. That alone would be sufficient to acquit the Society of any guilt in this matter; but he gives facts to his readers which go to show very plainly that this failure to create a native Chinese priesthood clearly evidences the Society's desire to have one at any cost. It is paradoxical, but it is true.

The great lapse of time that passed without any ordinations need cause no alarm. There are instances of greater delay with less excuse very near home. For instance, there were secular priests and religious in Canada as early as 1603, but there was no seminary there till 1663, although the colony had all the power of Catholic France back of it. There were Catholics in Maryland in 1634, yet there was no theological seminary until 1794, that is for a space of 160 years. After a few years' struggle with only five pupils, and in some of these years none, it was closed and was not

re-opened until 1810, which is a far cry from 1634.
New York did not attempt to found a seminary until
the time of its fourth bishop. The house at Nyack was
burned down before it was occupied; the Lafargeville
project also proved a failure and it was not until 1841
that the diocesan seminary was opened at Fordham.

Morever, in none of these seminaries was there the
remotest thought of forming a *native* clergy in the
sense of the word employed in the anti-Jesuit indictment. The seminarians were all foreigners or sons of
foreigners. There were no native Indians in these
establishments, as that, apart from intellectual and
moral reasons, would have been a physiological impossibility. Nature rebels against the transplanting of a
creature of the woods and mountains to the confinement of a lecture hall. The old martyr of Colonial
times, Father Daniel, brought a number of Indian
boys from Huronia to Quebec to educate them, but
they fled to the forests, while the Indian girls, who were
lodged with the Ursulines, died of consumption. Even
in our own times, Archbishop Gillow of Oaxaca,
Mexico, brought a number of pure-blooded Indians to
Rome, in the hope of making them priests, but they
all died before he attained any results. In brief, we
in America have never formed a *native* clergy.

Morever, this century-stretch of failure in China is
cut down considerably when we recall the fact that
for a considerable time there were only two or, at most,
three Jesuits in that vast empire, and that they contrived to remain there only because they interested
the learned part of the populace by their knowledge
of mathematics and astronomy, never daring to
broach the subject of religion, though they succeeded
under the pretence of science in circulating everywhere
a catechism which enraptured the *literati*. It was only
in the year 1601 that permission was given to them

to preach. Hence, the figure 100 has to be cut down
to 83. In two years time, namely in 1617, there were
13,000 Christians in China. How were the rest to be
reached? No help could be expected from Europe,
which was being devastated by the Thirty Years War
(1618-1648). Independently of that, the caste system
prevailed in China, and the learned, even those who
were converted, found it difficult to understand why
the wonderful truths of Christianity should be communicated to the common people, yet it is from the
people that ecclesiastical vocations usually come.
Thirdly, the Chinaman has an instinctive horror of
anything foreign. Yet here was a foreign creed which,
moreover, could be thoroughly learned only by a
language which was itself foreign even to the priests
who taught it.

The audacious project was then formed to petition
the Pope to have the liturgy, even the Mass, in Chinese.
No other modern mission ever dared to make such a
request. As early as 1617, the petition was presented,
and although Pope Paul V favored the scheme, yet
the undertaking was so stupendous and the project
so unusual that he withheld any direct or official
recognition. Whereupon the missionaries began the
work of translating into Chinese not only the Missal
and Ritual, but an entire course of moral theology
with the cases of conscience. In addition a large part
of the " Summa " of St. Thomas along with many
other books which might be useful to the future priest
were rendered into the vernacular. The work was
begun by Father Trigault in 1615 and was continued
by others up to 1682, when the Pope while accepting
the dedication of a Chinese Missal by Verbiest, finally
concluded that it would be impolitic to grant permission for a liturgy in Chinese. This gigantic undertaking ought of itself to be a sufficient answer to the

charge that the Jesuits were averse to the formation
of a native clergy. The scheme failed, it is true, but
the attempt is a sufficient answer to the hackneyed
charge against the Society.

It might be asked, however, why did they not
foresee the possible failure of their request and provide
otherwise for priests? In the first place, there were
Dominicans and Franciscans in China, and it might
be proper to ask them why they excluded the Chinese
from the ministry? Secondly, the Jesuits had all they
could do to defend themselves from the charge of
idolatry for sanctioning the Chinese Rites. Thirdly
when Schall arrived in 1622 there were no missionaries
to be met anywhere — they were in prison or in exile.
Fourthly, in 1637 there was a bloody persecution.
Fifthly, in 1644 the Tatar invasion occurred with the
usual havoc, and the Manchu dynasty was inaugurated.
Sixthly, in 1664 Schall hitherto such a great man in
the empire was imprisoned and condemned to be hacked
to pieces and Verbiest was lying in chains. It is quite
comprehensible, therefore, that in such a condition of
things, quiet seminary life was impossible, and as the
Jesuits were suspected of leaning to Confucianism it
would have been quite improper to entrust to them the
formation of a secular clergy.

When Verbiest wrote home for help, numbers of
volunteers left Europe for China. Louis XIV was
especially enthusiastic in furthering the movement,
and, among other favors he conferred the title of
" Fellows of the Academy of Science and Royal
Mathematicians " on six Jesuits of Paris, and sent
them off to Pekin. But when they arrived, Verbiest
was dead. They were in time, however, for his funeral,
which took place on March 11, 1688, with the same
honors that had been accorded to Ricci and Schall.
He was laid to rest at their side. His successors began

their work by establishing what was called the French Mission of China, which lasted until the suppression of the Society. The great difficulty in sending missionaries thither by sea had long exercised the minds of the superiors of the Society, especially after a startling announcement was made by Father Couplet, who, after passing many years in China, had returned home, shattered in health and altogether unable to continue his work. He said that, after a very careful count, he had found that of the six hundred Jesuits who had attempted to enter China from the time that Ruggieri and Ricci had succeeded in gaining an entrance there, as many as four hundred had either died of sickness on the way or had been lost at sea. De Rhodes had shown that an overland route was possible from India to Europe; the lay-brother Goes had succeeded in getting to China from the land of the Great Mogul, Gruber had reversed the process, and in 1685 an attempt was made by Father Avril, to reach it by the way of Russia, but he failed.

Avril's account of his journey has been shockingly " done out of French " by a translator who prudently withheld his name. It was " published in London, at Maidenhead, over against St. Dunstan's Church, in Fleet Street." Its date is 1693. From it we learn that Father Avril started from Marseilles and made for Civita Vecchia, after paying his respects in Rome to Father General de Noyelle, he went to Leghorn, where he took ship on a vessel that was convoyed by a man-of-war called the " Thundering Jupiter." Passing by Capraia, Elba, Sardinia, and nearly wrecked off the " Coast of Candy," his ship dropped anchor in the Lerneca roadstead after three days' voyage, but without the " Thundering Jupiter." It was still at sea. He touched at Cyprus and Alexandretta, then proceeded to Aleppo, crossing the plain of Antioch in a caravan. He was fleeced by an Armenian who professed to be a friend of the Jesuits, then he crossed the Tigris or Tiger, and arrived at Erzerum in time for an earthquake. Continuing his journey through the intervening territory to what he calls the " Caspian Lake ", he finally reached Moscow, after being almost burned to death on the Volga, when his ship took fire. At Moscow he was welcomed by the German Jesuits who had a house there, for Prince Gallichin (Galitzin) was then prime minister. He was soon bidden to depart, and crossed a part of Muscovy, Lithuania and White Russia, reaching Warsaw on March 12, 1686. It was eighteen months since he had left Leghorn. He made effort after effort to get back to Muscovy, but in vain. Ambassadors and princes and even Louis XIV found the Czar obdurate, and so, after two years of unsuccessful endeavor, Avril arrived at Constantinople, after being imprisoned by the Turks on his way thither. Finally, he reached Marseilles, having proved, at least, that the road through Russia would have to be abandoned; hence, it was determined to make those overland journeys in the future through the territory of the Shah of Persia.

CHAPTER IX

BATTLE OF THE BOOKS

Aquaviva and the Spanish Opposition — Vitelleschi — The " Monita Secreta "; Morlin — Roding —" Historia Jesuitici Ordinis "— " Jesuiticum Jejunium "—" Speculum Jesuiticum "— Pasquier — Mariana —" Mysteries of the Jesuits "—" The Jesuit Cabinet "— " Jesuit Wolves "—" Teatro Jesuítico "—" Morale Pratique des Jésuites " — " Conjuratio Sulphurea " — " Lettres Provinciales " — " Causeries de Lundi " and Bourdaloue — Prohibition of publication by Louis XIV — Pastoral of the Bishops of Sens — Santarelli — Escobar — Anti-Coton —" Les Descouvertes "— Norbert.

FATHER CLAUDIUS AQUAVIVA died on January 31, 1615, after a generalship of thirty-four years. To him are to be ascribed not only all of the great enterprises inaugurated since 1580, but, to a very considerable extent, the spirit by which the Society has been actuated up to the present time and which, it is to be hoped, it will always retain. The marvellous skill and the serene equanimity with which he guided the Society through the perils which it encountered from kings and princes, from heretics and heathens, from great ecclesiastical tribunals and powerful religious organizations, and most of all from the machinations of disloyal members of the Institute, entitle him to the enthusiastic love and admiration of every Jesuit and the unchallenged right to the title which he bears of the " Saviour of the Society." Far from being rigid and severe, as he is sometimes accused of being, he was amazingly meek and magnanimously merciful. The story about forty professed fathers having been dismissed in consequence of their connection with the sedition of Vásquez is a myth. The entire number of plotters on this occasion did not exceed twenty-eight,

and only a few of those were expelled. In any case,
whatever penalty was meted out to them was the act
of the congregation and not of Aquaviva. Indeed,
Aquaviva's methods are in violent contrast with those
of Francis Xavier, who gave the power of expulsion
to even local Superiors, and we almost regret that
Xavier had not to deal with his fellow-countrymen at
this juncture. It must also be borne in mind that the
great exodus from the Society which occurred in
Portugal antedated Aquaviva's time, and was due
to the mistaken methods of government by Simon
Rodriguez.

The congregation convened after his death met on
November 5, 1615, and the majority of its members
must have been astounded to find the Spanish claim
to the generalship still advocated. Mutio Vitelleschi
an Italian, however, was most in evidence at that time;
he was forty-five years old, and had been already
rector of the English College, provincial both of Naples
and Rome, and later assistant for Italy. As in all
of those positions of trust he had displayed a marvellous
combination of sweetness and strength which had
endeared him to his subjects, the possibility of his
election, at this juncture, afforded a well-grounded
hope of a glorious future for the Society. Nevertheless
some of the Spanish delegates determined to defeat
him, and with that in view they addressed themselves
to the ambassadors of France and Spain, to enlist
their aid; but the shrewd politicians took the measure
of the plotters, and, while piously commending them
for their religious zeal and patriotism, politely refused
their co-operation. That should have sufficed as a
rebuke, but prompted by their unwise zeal they
approached the Pope himself and assured him that
Vitelleschi was altogether unfit for the position. The
Pontiff listened to them graciously and bade them be

of good heart, for, if Vitelleschi were half what they said he was, there could be no possibility of his election. The balloting took place on November 15, and Mutio was chosen by thirty-nine out of seventy-five votes. The margin was not a large one, and shows how nearly the conspirators had succeeded. To-day an appeal to laymen in such a matter would entail immediate expulsion.

Vitelleschi's vocation to the Society was a marked one. When only a boy of eleven, he was dreaming of being associated with it, and before he had finished his studies he bound himself by a vow to ask for admittance, and, if accepted, to distribute his inheritance to the poor. But as the Vitelleschi formed an important section of the Roman nobility, such aspirations did not fit in with the father's ambition for his son, and the boy was bidden to dismiss all thought of it. He was a gentle and docile lad, but he possessed also a decided strength of character, and like the Little Flower of Jesus in our own times, he betook himself to the Pope to lay the matter before him. The father finally yielded, and on August 15, 1583, young Mutio, after going to Communion with his mother at the Gesù, hurried off to lay his request before Father Aquaviva. His great desire was to go to England, which was just then waging its bloody war against the Faith, but, as with Aquaviva himself, his ignorance of the English language deprived him of the crown of martyrdom.

Crétineau-Joly is of the opinion that the generalate of Vitelleschi was *monotone de bonheur*. Whether that be so or not, it certainly had its share in the monotony of calumny which has been meted out to the Society from its birth. Thus, the beginning of Vitelleschi's term of office coincided with the publication of the famous " Monita secreta " which, with the exception of the " Lettres provinciales " is perhaps the cleverest piece of literary work ever levelled against the Society. The compliment is not a very great one, for nearly all the other books obtained their vogue by being extravagant distortions of the truth. But good or bad they never failed to appear.

The first in order was the diatribe of Morlin in 1568. This was a little before Vitelleschi's time. It was directed against the schools, and denounces the professors for having intercourse with the devil, practising sorcery, initiating their pupils in the black art, anointing them with some mysterious and diabolical compound which gave the masters control of their scholars after long years of separation. "God's gospel," they said, "was powerless before those creatures of the devil whom hell had vomited forth to poison the whole German empire and especially to do away with the Evangelicals who were the especial object of Jesuitical hatred." The immediate expulsion of the "sorcerers" was demanded, and even their burning at the stake, for "they not only deal in witchcraft themselves, but teach it to others, and impart to their pupils the methods of getting rid of their foes by poisons, incantations and the like." It was asserted that "those who send their boys to be educated by them are throwing their offspring into the jaws of wolves; or like the Hebrews of old immolating them to Moloch."

In 1575 Roding, a professor of Heidelberg dedicated a book to the elector, in which he denounces the Jesuit schools as impious and abominable, and warns parents "not to give aid to the Kingdom of Satan by trusting those who were enemies of Christianity and of God." "They are wild beasts," he said, "who ought to be chased out of our cities. Though outwardly modest, simple, mortified and urbane, they are in reality furies and atheists — far worse indeed than atheists and idolaters. The children confided to them are constrained to join with their swinish instructors in grunting at the Divine Majesty" (Janssen, VIII, 339). "They are not only poisoners but conspirators and assassins. Their purpose is to slay all those who have accepted the Confession of Augsburg. They have been seen in processions of armed men, disguised as courtiers, dressed in silks, with gold chains around their necks, going from one end of Germany to the other. They caused the St. Bartholomew massacre; they killed King Sebastian; in Peru, they plunged red hot irons into the bodies of the Indians to make them reveal where they hid their treasures. In thirty years the Popes killed 900,000 people, the Jesuits 2,000,000; the cellars of all the colleges in Germany are packed with soldiers; and Canisius married an abbess." This latter story went around Germany a hundred times and was widely believed.

The chief storehouse of all these inventions in Germany was the "Historia jesuitici ordinis," which was published in 1593, and was attributed by the editor, Polycarp Leiser, to an ex-novice, named Elias Hasenmüller, who was then six years dead — a circumstance which ought to have invalidated the testimony for ordinary people, but which did not prevent the "Historia" from being an immense success. Its publication was said to be miraculous, for it was given out as certain that any member of the Order who would reveal its secrets was to be tortured, poisoned or roasted alive. It was only by a special intervention of the Lord that Hasenmüller escaped. The readers of the "Historia" were informed that the Order was founded by the devil, who was the spiritual father of St. Ignatius. Omitting the immoralities detailed in the volume, "the Jesuits were professional assassins, wild boars, robbers, traitors, snakes, vipers,

etc. In their private lives they were lecherous goats,
filthy pigs." Even Carlyle says this of St. Ignatius —
" The Pope had given them full power to commit
every excess. If we knew them better we would spit
in their faces, instead of sending them boys to be
educated. Indeed it would not be well to trust them
with hogs." There were other productions of the
same nature, such as the " Jesuiticum jejunium " and
" Speculum jesuiticum." Some of these " histories "
denounced Father Gretser as " a vile scribbler, an open
heretic and an adulterer who carried the devil around
in a bottle." Bellarmine was " an Epicurean of the
worst type, who had already killed 1642 victims; 562
of whom were married women. He used magic and
poison, and pitched the corpses of his victims into the
Tiber. He died the death of the damned, and his
ghost was seen in the air in broad daylight flying
away on a winged horse," and so on.

Etienne Pasquier was the leader of the French
pamphleteers. It was he who had acted as advocate
against the Jesuits of the College of Clermont. The
plaidoyer presented to the court on that occasion was
embodied in his " Recherches," and, in 1602, when
he was seventy-three years of age, he published " Le
Catéchisme des jésuites, ou examen de leur doctrine."
He finds that the Order, besides being Calvinistic, is
also spotted with Judaism. Ignatius was worse than
Luther or Julian the Apostate; he was a sort of Don
Quixote, who laughed at the vows he made at Montmartre; he was a trickster, a glutton, a demon incarnate,
an ass. The first chapter in book II is entitled
" Anabaptism of the Jesuits in their vow of blind
obedience." Chapter 2 is on the execution of the
Jesuit, Crichton, for attempting to kill the Scotch
chancellor, of which he had been accused by " Robert
de Bruce." In chapter 3, a Mr. Parry is sent by the

18

Jesuits to assassinate Queen Elizabeth. In chapter 4, another attempt is made by the same person, in 1597, etc. Father Garasse wrote an answer to the book, and though he found no difficulty in showing its absurdities, yet his language was rough and abusive and quite out of keeping with the dignity of his state; besides, it centred public attention on him to such extent that later when, three pamphlets with which he had had nothing to do were written against Cardinal Richelieu, he was accused of being the author of them and had to swear in the most solemn manner that he knew nothing whatever about them. This charge against Garasse came near alienating Louis XIII from the Society.

Much harm had also been done by Mariana's alleged doctrine on regicide. On the face of it, the book could not have been seditious, for it was written as an instruction for the heir of Philip II, and it is inconceivable that an autocrat, such as he was, should not only have put a book teaching regicide in the hands of his son, but should have paid for its publication. As a matter of fact, the king conjured up by Mariana as a possible victim of assassination is a monster who could have scarcely existed. In other circumstances the book would have passed unnoticed, but it served as a pretext to attack the Society by ascribing Mariana's doctrine to the whole Society.

Now, Mariana never was and never could be a representative of the Society, for: first sixteen years before the objectionable book attracted notice in France, namely in 1584, Mariana had been solemnly condemned by the greatest assembly of the Society, the general congregation, as an unworthy son; a pestilential member who should be cut off from the body, and his expulsion was ordered. He was one of the leaders of the band of Spanish conspirators who did all in their power to destroy the Society. Secondly, his expulsion did not take place, possibly because of outside political influence like that of Philip II and the Inquisition. Nevertheless in 1605, that is five years before the French flurry, he wrote another book entitled, " De defectibus Societatis " (i. e. the Weak Points of the Society), which was condemned as involving the censure of the papal bull " Ascendente Domino." Instead of destroying the MS., as he should have done, if he had a spark of loyalty in him, he kept it, and when in 1609, he was arrested and imprisoned by the Spanish authorities for his book on Finance which seemed to reflect on the government, that MS. was seized, and subsequently served as a strong weapon against the Society. Why should such a man be cited as the representative of a body from which he was ordered to be expelled and which he had attempted to destroy?

Another harmful publication was the " Monita secreta," which represented the Jesuit as a sweet-voiced intriguer; a pious grabber of inheritances for the greater glory of God; enjoying a vast influence with conspicuous personages; working underhand in politics, and revealing himself in every clime, invariably the same, and always monstrously rich. The " Monita " appeared in Poland in the year 1612. It was printed in a place not to be found on any map: namely Notobirga, which suggests " Notaburgh," or " Not a City." It purported to be based on a Spanish manuscript, discovered in the secret archives of the Society at Padua. It was translated into Latin, and was then sent to Vienna, and afterwards to Cracow, where it was given to the public. It consists of sixteen short chapters, of which we give a few sample titles: " I. How the Society should act to get a new foundation. II. How to win and keep the friendship of princes and important personages. III. How to act with people who wield political influence or those who, even if not rich, may be serviceable. VI. How to win over wealthy widows. VII. How to induce them to dispose of their property. VIII. How to induce them to enter religious communities, or at least to make them devout."

To achieve all this the Jesuits were to wear outwardly an appearance of poverty in their houses; the sources of revenue were to be concealed; purchases of property were always to be made by dummies; rich widows were to be provided with adroit confessors; their family physicians were to be the friends of the Fathers; their daughters were to be sent to convents, their sons to the Society, etc. The vices of prominent personages were to be indulged; quarrels were to be entered into, so as to get the credit of reconciliation; the servants of the rich were to be bribed; confessors were to be very sweet; distinguished personages were never to be publicly reprehended, etc., etc. As the phraseology of these " Monita secreta " was a clever imitation of the official document of the Society known as the " Monita generalia," the forgery scored a perfect success in being accepted as genuine. It was such a cleverly devised instrument of warfare in a country like Poland, for instance, with its mixed Protestant and Catholic population, that it would be sure to strengthen the Protestants, and, at the same time, shame the Catholics, by discrediting the Jesuits, who were then in great favor. It was anonymous, but was finally traced to Jerome Zahorowski, who had been dismissed from the Society. When charged by the Inquisition with being the author, he denied it, and said he had no complaint against his former associates. The book was put on the Index, and Zahorowski's declaration that he was not the author was believed. Later, however, it was publicly declared

by those who had the means of knowing the facts that
he was really the guilty man.   Indeed, just before he
died, he confessed the authorship and bitterly regretted
the crime he had committed.   He recanted all that
he had said in the book, but it was too late; the mis-
chief had been done and the evil work has continued.
There were twenty-two editions of it, issued during
the seventeenth century, and it was translated into
many languages.   Its title was changed from time to
time and it was called: " The Mysteries of the Jesuits;"
" Arcana of the Society;" " Jesuit Machiavelism;"
" The Jesuit Cabinet;" " Jesuit Wolves;" " Jesuit
Intrigues," and so on.   There appeared also a huge
publication of six or seven bulky volumes entitled
" Annales des soi-disants Jésuites," which is an encyclo-
pedia of all the accusations ever made against the
Society.

Another ex-Jesuit named Jarrige perpetrated the
libel known as " The Jesuits on the Scaffold, for their
Crimes in the Province of Guyenne."   He, too, like
Zahorowski, when he came to his senses, repented
and tried ineffectually to make amends.   The " Teatro
jesuítico " was also a source from which the assailants
of the Society drew their ammunition.   It was condemned by the Inquisition on January 28, 1655, and
the Archbishop of Seville burned it publicly.   Arnauld
borrowed from it most of his material for the " Morale
pratique des Jésuites," and to give it importance, he
ascribed its authorship to the Bishop of Malaga,
Ildephonse of St. Thomas.   Whereupon the bishop
wrote to the Pope complaining that " an infamous
libel, unworthy of the light of day, and composed
in the midst of the darkness of hell and bearing the
title: ' Morale pratique des Jésuites ' has fallen into
my hands, and I am said to be the author of it,—
a feat which would have been impossible, for it was

published in 1654, when I was yet a student, and in
ill-health." Although this solemn denial was published
all through Europe, Pascal and his friends continued
to impute it to the bishop, according to Crétineau-
Joly; but Brou says that the mistake or the deceit
was admitted. The book, however, was not withdrawn,
and continued to do its evil work.

It was the Gunpowder Plot that inflicted on the
English language a great number of absurdities about
Jesuits. King James I of England led the way by
writing a book with the curious title: " Conjuratio
sulphurea, quibus ea rationibus et authoribus cœperit,
maturuerit, apparuerit; una cum reorum examine,"
that is " The sulphureous or hellish conjuration, for
what reasons and by what authors it was begun,
matured and brought to light; together with the
examination of the culprits." He also published a
" Defence of the Oath of Allegiance " which he had
exacted of Catholics. This elucubration was called:
" Triplici nodo triplex cuneus," which probably means
" A triple pry for the triple knot." In it he charges
the Pope with sending aid to the conspirators " his
henchmen the Jesuits who confessed that they were
its authors and designers. Their leader died con-
fessing the crime, and his accomplices admitted their
guilt by taking flight."

Such a charge formulated by a king against the
Sovereign Pontiff aroused all Europe, and Bellarmine
under the name of " Matthæus Tortus " descended
into the arena. Dr. Andrews replied with clumsy
humor by another book entitled, " Tortura Torti;"
that is " The Tortures of Tortus," for which he was
made a bishop. Then Bellarmine retorted in turn
and revealed the fact that his majesty had written
a personal letter to two cardinals, himself and Aldo-
brandini, asking them to forward a request to the

Pope to have a certain Scotchman, who was Bishop of Vaison in France, made a cardinal, "so as to expedite the transaction of business with the Holy See." The letter was signed: "Beatitudinis vestræ obsequentissimus filius J. R." (Your Holiness' most obsequious son, James the King.) This sent James to cover and now quite out of humor with himself, because of the storm aroused in England by the disclosure of his duplicity, he handed over new victims to the pursuivants, "so that," as he said, "his subjects might make profit of them," that is by the confiscation of estates. He then got one of his secretaries to take upon himself the odium of the letter to Bellarmine, by saying that he had signed the king's name to it. Every one, of course, saw through the falsehood.

A most unexpected and interesting defender of Father Garnet, who had been put to death by James, appeared at this juncture. He was no less a personage than Antoine Arnauld, the famous Jansenist, who was at that very moment tearing Garnet's brethren to pieces in France. "No Catholic," he said, "no matter how antagonistic he might be to Jesuits in general, would ever accuse Garnet of such a crime, and no Protestant would do so unless blinded by religious hate" (Crétineau-Joly, III, 98). James I and Bellarmine came into collision again on another point not, however, in such a personal fashion.

A Scotch lawyer named Barclay had written a book on the authority of kings, in which he claimed that their power had no limitations whatever; at least, he went to the very limit of absolutism. Strange to say, Barclay, who was a Catholic, had Jesuit affiliations. He was professor of law in the Jesuit college of Pont-à-Mousson, in France, where his uncle, Father Hay, was rector. For some reason or another he went over to England shortly after the accession of James I,

whom he greatly admired, possibly because he was
a Scot. There is no other reason visible to the naked
eye. He was received with extraordinary honor at
court and offered very lucrative offices if he would
declare himself an Anglican. He spurned the bribe
and returned to France where he resumed his office
of teaching. Cardinal Bellarmine ·then appeared, refuting Barclay's ideas of kingship. The peculiarity of
Bellarmine's work was that it had nothing new in it.
It was merely a collation of old authorities, chiefly
French jurists who cut down the royal power considerably. This threw the Paris parliament into a
frenzy, for they had all along been persuading their
fellow countrymen that the autocracy they claimed
for their monarchs was the immemorial tradition of
France. To hide their confusion, they ascribed to the
illustrious cardinal all sorts of doctrines, such as
regicide and the right of seizure of private property
by the ·Pope, and they demanded not only the condemnation but the public burning of the book.

The matter now assumed an international importance. Bellarmine was a conspicuous figure in the
Church, and his work had been approved by the
Pope, whose intimate friend he was. To condemn him
meant to condemn the Sovereign Pontiff, and would
thus necessarily be a declaration of a schism from
Rome. Probably that is what these premature
Gallicans were aiming at. Ubaldini, the papal nuncio,
immediately warned the queen regent, Mary de'Medici,
that if such an outrage were committed, he would hand
in his papers and leave Paris. Parliament fought
fiercely to have its way, and the battle raged with
fury for a long time until, finally, Mary saw the peril
of the situation and quashed the parliamentary decree
which had already been printed and was being circulated.

In the midst of it all, the theory of Suárez on the
" Origin of Power " came into the hands of the parlia-
mentarians, and that added fuel to the flame; Ubaldini
wrote to Rome on June 17, 1614, that " the lawyer
Servin, who was like a demon in his hatred of Rome,
made a motion in parliament, first, that the work of
Suárez should be burned before the door of the three
Jesuit houses in Paris, in presence of two fathers of
each house; secondly, that an official condemnation
of it should be entered on the records; thirdly, that the
provincial, the superior of the Paris residence and four
other fathers should be cited before the parliament
and made to anathematize the doctrine of Suárez, and
fourthly, if they refused, that all the members of the
Society should be expelled from France." The
measure was not passed.

The book which did most harm to the Society in the
public mind was the " Lettres provinciales " by Pascal,
though the " Lettres " were not intended primarily
or exclusively as an attack on the Jesuits. Their
purpose was to make the people forget or condone the
dishonesty of the Jansenists in denying that the five
propositions, censured by the Holy See, were really
contained in the " Augustinus " of Jansenius. At the
suggestion of Arnauld, Pascal undertook to show that
other supposedly orthodox writers, including the
Jesuits, had advanced doctrines which merited but had
escaped censure. The letters appeared serially and
were entitled: " Les Provinciales, ou Lettres écrites
par Louis de Montalte à un Provincial de ses amis,
et aux RR. PP. Jésuites, sur la morale et la politique
de ces Pères." They took the world by storm, first
because they revealed a literary genius of the first
order in the youthful Pascal, who until then had been
engrossed in the study of mathematics, and who was
also, at the time of writing, in a shattered state of

health. Secondly, because they blasted the reputation
of a great religious order, and reproduced in exquisite
language the atrocious calumnies that had been
poured out on the world by the " Monita secreta,"
the " Historia jesuitici ordinis," Pasquier's " Catechism " and the rest. The doctrinal portion of the
letters was evidently not Pascal's; that was supplied
to him by Arnauld and Quinet, for Pascal had neither
the time nor the training necessary even to read the
deep theological treatises which he quotes and professes
to have read.

To be accused of teaching lax morality by those
who were intimately associated with and supported
by such an indescribable prelate as the Cardinal
Archbishop of Paris, Gondi, was particularly galling
to the French Jesuits, and unfortunately it had the
effect of provoking them to answer the charges. " In
doing so," says Crétineau-Joly, " the Jesuits killed
themselves;" and Brou, in " Les Jésuites et la légende,"
is of the opinion that " more harm was done to the
Society by these injudicious and incompetent defenders
than by Pascal himself. It would have been better
to have said nothing." On the other hand, Petit de
Julleville, in his " Histoire de la langue et de la
littérature française," tells us that one of these Jesuit
champions induced Pascal to discontinue his attacks,
just at the moment that the world was rubbing its
hands with glee and expecting the fiercest kind of an
onslaught. " I wish," said Morel, addressing
himself to Pascal, " that after a sincere reconciliation
with the Jesuits, you would turn your pen against the
heretics, the unbelievers, the libertines, and the
corruptors of morals." The fact is that although
Pascal did not seek a reconciliation with the Jesuits,
he suddenly and unaccountably stopped writing against
them; and in 1657 he actually turned his pen against

the libertines of France, as he had been asked (IV, 604).
Mère Angélique, Arnauld's sister, is also credited
with having had something to do with this cessation
of hostilities, when she wrote: "Silence would be
better and more agreeable to God who would be more
quickly appeased by tears and by penance than by
eloquence which amuses more people than it converts."

Perhaps the entrance of the great Bourdaloue on
the scene contributed something to this change of
attitude on the part of the Jansenist. As court preacher,
he had it in his power to refute the calumnies of Arnauld
and Pascal, and he availed himself of the opportunity
with marvellous power and effect. In the "Causeries
du Lundi" Sainte-Beuve, who favored the Jansenists,
writes: "In saying that the Jesuits made no direct
and categorical denial to the *Provinciales*, until forty
years later, when Daniel took up his pen, we forget
that long and continual refutation by Bourdaloue
in his public sermons in which there is nothing lacking
except the proper names; but his hearers and his
contemporaries in general, who were familiar with the
controversies and were partisans of either side, easily
supplied these. Thus in his Sermon on 'Lying' he
paints that vice with most exquisite skill, adding
touch after touch, till it stands out in all its hideousness.
As he speaks, you see it before you with its subtle
sinuosities from the moment it begins the attack,
under the pretence of an amicable censorship, up to
the moment when the complete calumny is reiterated
under the guise of friendship and religion." The
following extract is an example of this method.

"One of the abuses of the age," says Bourdaloue,
" is the consecration of falsehood and its transformation
into virtue; yea, even into one of the greatest of
virtues: zeal for the glory of God. 'We must humiliate
those people;' they say, ' it will be helpful to the Church

to blast their reputation and diminish their credit.'
On this principle they form their conscience, and there
is nothing they will not allow themselves when actuated
by such a charming motive. So, they exaggerate;
they poison; they distort; they relate things by halves;
they utter a thousand untruths; they confound the
general with the particular; what one has said badly,
they ascribe to all; and what all have said well they
attribute to none. And they do all this — for the
glory of God. This forming of their intention justifies
everything; and though it would not suffice to excuse an
equivocation, it is more than sufficient in their eyes
to justify a calumny when they are persuaded that
it is all for the service of God."

" If Bourdaloue," continues Sainte-Beuve, "while
detailing, in this exquisite fashion, the vice of lying,
had not before his mind Pascal and his *Provinciales*,
and if he was not painting, feature by feature, certain
personalities whom his hearers recognized; and if
while he was doing it, they were not shocked, even
though they could not help admiring the artist, then
there are no portraits in Saint-Simon and La Bruyère
......It would not be hard to prove that the preaching
of Bourdaloue for thirty years was a long and powerful
refutation of the *Provinciales*, an eloquent and daily
drive at Pascal."

It must have been an immense consolation for the
Jesuits of those days, wounded as they were to the quick
by the misrepresentation and calumnies of writers like
Arnauld, Pascal, Nicole and others, to have the
saintly Bourdaloue, the ideal Jesuit, occupying the
the first place in the public eye, thus defending them.
Bourdaloue had entered the Society at fifteen, and
hence was absolutely its product. He was a man of
prayer and study, and when not in the pulpit he was
in the confessional or at the bedside of the sick and

dying poor. He was naturally quick and impulsive, but he had been trained to absolute self-control; he was even gay and merry in conversation, and his eyes sparkled with pleasure as he spoke. The story that he closed them while preaching is, of course, nonsense, and the picture that represents him thus was taken from a death masque. He labored uninterruptedly till he was seventy-two and died on May 13, 1704. Very fittingly his last Mass was on Pentecost Sunday.

An excellent modern discussion of the Letters appeared in the Irish quarterly "Studies" of September, 1920. The writer, the noted author Hilaire Belloc, reminds his readers of certain important facts. First, casuistry is not chicanery nor is it restricted to ecclesiastics; it is employed by lawyers, physicians, scientific, and even business men, in considering conditions which are without a precedent and have not yet reached the ultimate tribunal which is to settle the matter. Secondly, as in the discussion of ecclesiastical "cases," the terms employed are technical, just as are those of law, medicine, science; and as the language is Latin, no one is competent to interpret the verdict arrived at, unless he is conversant both with theology and the Latin language. " I doubt," he says, " if there is any man living in England to-day — of all those glibly quoting the name of Pascal against the Church — who could tell you what the *Mohatra* Contract was " — one of the subjects dragged into these " Lettres." Thirdly, the " Lettres " are not so much an assault on the Society of Jesus, as on the whole system of moral theology of the Catholic Church. There are eighteen letters in all, and it is not until the fifth that the Jesuits are assailed. The attack is kept up until the tenth and then dropped. From the thousands of decisions advanced by a vast number of professors 'regular and secular' Pascal brings forward

only those of the Jesuits; and of the many thousands
of " cases " discussed he selects only one hundred and
thirty-two, which, if the repetitions be eliminated,
must be reduced to eighty-nine.

Of these eighty-nine cases three are clearly misquo-
tations — for Pascal was badly briefed. Many others
are put so as to suggest what the casuist never said,
that is a special case is made a general rule of morals.
Many more are frivolous, and others are purely
domestic controversy upon points of Catholic practice
which cannot concern the opponents of the Jesuits,
and in which they cannot pretend an active interest
on Pascal's or the Society's side. When the whole list
has been gone through there remain fourteen cases of
importance.   In eight of these, relating to duelling
and the risk of homicide, the opinions of some casuists
were subsequently, at one time or another, condemned
by the Church (seven of the decisions had declared
the liceity of duelling under very exceptional circumstances, when no other means were available to
protect one's honor or fortune). Pascal was right in
condemning the opinions, but was quite wrong in
presenting them as normal decisions, given under
ordinary circumstances by Jesuits generally.   Three
of the remaining six decisions have never been censured;
but Pascal by his tricky method of presenting them
out of their context has caused the solutions to be
confused with certain condemned propositions.

A just analysis leaves of the one hundred and
thirty-two decisions exactly three —one on simony,
one on the action of a judge in receiving presents,
and the third on usury — all three of which are doubtful
and matters for discussion. There is besides these,
the doctrine of equivocation, which is a favorite shaft
against the Society. Of this Belloc says: " This
specifically condemned form of equivocation (that is,

equivocation involving a private reservation of meaning), moreover, was not particularly Jesuit. It had been debated at length, and favorably, long before the Jesuit Order came into existence, and within the great casuist authorities of that Order there were wide differences of opinion upon it. Azor, for instance, condemns instances which Sánchez allows. Of all this conflict Pascal allows you to hear nothing." Finally, it may be noted that the " Provincial Letters " were not a plea for truth, but a device to distract the public mind from the chicanery of the Jansenists, who, when the famous " five propositions " were condemned, pretended that they were not in the " Augustinus " written by Jansenius.

Perhaps the commonest libel formulated against the Society is the accusation that it is the teacher, if not the author, of the immoral maxim: " the end justifies the means ", which signifies that an action, bad in itself, becomes good if performed for a good purpose. If the Society ever taught this doctrine, at least it cannot be charged with having the monopoly of it. Thus, for instance, the great Protestant empire which is the legitimate progeny of Martin Luther's teaching, proclaimed to the world that the diabolical " frightfulness " which it employed in the late war was prompted solely by its desire for peace. On the other side of the Channel, an Anglican prelate informed his contemporaries that " the British Empire could not be carried on for a week, on the principles of the ' Sermon on the Mount ' " (The Month, Vol. 106, p. 255). The same might be predicated of numberless other powers and principalities past and present. The ruthless measures resorted to in business and politics for the suppression of rivalry are a matter of common knowledge. Finally, every unbiased mind will concede that the persistent use of poisonous gas by the foes of the Society is nothing else than a carrying out of the maxim of " the end justifies the means."

It has been proved times innumerable that this odious doctrine was never taught by the Society, and the average Jesuit regards each recrudescence of the charge as an insufferable annoyance, and usually takes no notice of it; but, in our own times, the bogey has presented itself in such an unusual guise, that the event has to be set down as one more item of domestic history. It obtruded itself on the public in Germany in 1903, when a secular priest, Canon Dasbach, an ardent friend of the Society, offered a prize of 2000 florins to any one who would find a defense of the doctrine in any Jesuit publication. The challenge was accepted by Count von Hoensbroech, who after failing in his controversy with the canon, availed himself of a side issue to bring the question before the civil courts of Trèves and Cologne.

Apparently von Hoensbroech was well qualified for his task. He was an ex-Jesuit and had lived for years in closest intimacy with some of the most distinguished moralists and theologians of the Order: Lehmkuhl, Cathrein, Pesch and others, in the house of studies, at Exaeten in Holland; so that the world rubbed its hands in glee, and waited for revelations. He was, however, seriously hampered by some of his own earlier utterances. Thus, when he left the Society in 1893, he wrote in " Mein Austritt aus dem Jesuit-enorden," as follows: " The moral teachings, under which members of the Society are trained, are beyond reproach, and the charges so constantly brought against Jesuit moralists are devoid of any foundation." Over and above this, he was somewhat disqualified as a witness, inasmuch as he not only had left the Society but had apostatized from the Faith, and, though a priest, had married a wife; he was, moreover, notorious

as a rancorous Lutheran (Civiltà Cattolica, an. 56,
p. 8.) But the lure of the florins led him on, only to
have the case thrown out by one court, as beyond its
jurisdiction, and decided against him in the other;
the verdict was also heartily endorsed by conspicuous
Protestants and Freethinkers. Hoensbroech is dead,
but the spectre of " the end justifying the means "
still stalks the earth, and may be heard from at any
moment.

Pascal's " Provincial Letters " were not the only
source of worry for the Jesuits in the seventeenth
and eighteenth centuries. Many other calumnious
publications appeared, such as " La morale des jésuits,"
" Disquisitions," " Nullités " etc., all of which had
the single purpose of poisoning the public mind. The
battle continued until an enforced peace was obtained
by a joint order of the Pope and king prohibiting any
further issues of that character from the press. That,
however, did not check the determination of the Jansenists to crush the Society in other ways. Thus, as
early as 1650, the Archbishop of Sens, who was strongly
Jansenistic, forbade the Jesuits to hear confessions
in his diocese at Easter-time, and three years later,
he declared from the pulpit that the theology of the
Jesuits was taken from the Koran rather than from
the Gospels, and that their philosophy was more
pagan than Christian. He called for their expulsion as schismatics, heretics and worse, and declared that all confessions made to them were invalid
and sacrilegious. Finally, he proceeded to excommuni-
cate them with bell, book and candle. They withdrew
from his diocese but were brought back by the next
bishop a quarter of a century later.

Another enemy of the Society was Cardinal Le
Camus of Grenoble, who forbade them to teach or
preach; and when Saint-Just, who had been fifteen years

rector of the college, complained of it to some friends, he was suspended and accused of a grievous crime of which he was absolutely innocent. When he brought the matter to court, Father General Oliva censured him for doing so and removed him from office. Santarelli, an Italian Jesuit, launched a book on the public which produced a great excitement. He proposed to prove that the Pope had the power of deposing kings who were guilty of certain crimes, and of absolving subjects from their allegiance. In Paris it was interpreted as advocating regicide, and was immediately ascribed to the whole Society; and it was condemned by the Sorbonne. Richelieu was especially wrought up about it. Poor Father Coton, the king's confessor, who was grievously ill at the time, almost collapsed at the news of its publication. The author had not perceived that the politics of the world were no longer those of the Middle Ages.

The " Manual of Cases of Conscience " of Antonio Escobar y Mendoza, the Spanish theologian, furnished infinite material for the Jansenists of France to blacken the name of the Society. Necessarily, every enormity that human nature can be guilty of is discussed in such treatises, but it would be just as absurd to charge their authors with writing them for the purpose of inculcating vice, as it would be to accuse medical practitioners of propagating disease by their clinics and dissecting rooms. The purpose of both is to heal and prevent, not to communicate disease, whether it be of the soul or body. In both cases, the books that treat of such matters are absolutely restricted to the use of the profession, and as an additional precaution, in the matter of moral theology, the treatises are written in Latin, so that they cannot be understood by people who have nothing to do with such disagreeable and sometimes disgusting topics. To accuse the men who condemned themselves to the study of such subjects solely that they might lift depraved humanity out of the depths into which it descends, is an outrage.

This literary war crossed the ocean to the French possessions of Canada, and much of the religious trouble that disturbed the colony from the beginning may be traced to the editorial activity of the Jansenists of France. Thus, when Brébeuf, Charles Lalemant and Massé came up the St. Lawerence, after a terrible voyage across the Atlantic, they were actually forbidden to land. The pamphlet known as "Anti-Coton" had been distributed and read by the few colonists who were then on the Rock of Quebec, and they would have nothing to do with the associates of a man who like Coton, was represented as rejoicing in the assassination of Henry IV. It did not matter that Father Coton and the king were not only intimate but most affectionate friends, and that assassination in such circumstances would be inconceivable; that it was asserted in print was enough to cause these three glorious men, who were coming to die for the Catholic Faith and for France, to be forbidden to land at Quebec. This anti-Coton manifestation in the early days of the colony was only a prelude to the antagonism that runs all through early Canadian history. It was kept up by a clique of writers in France, chief of whom were the Jansenist Abbés Bernou and Renaudot. Their contributions may be found in the voluminous collection known as Margry's "Découvertes," which Parkman induced the United States government to print in the language in which they were written. They teem with the worst kind of libels against the Society. Some of them pretend to have been written in America, but are so grotesque that the forgery is palpable. Indeed, among them is a letter from Bernou to Renaudot which says: " Get La Salle to give me some points and I will write the Relation."

The missionary labors of de Nobili, de Britto, Beschi and others in Madura, a dependency of the ecclesiastical province of Malabar, had been so successful that they evoked considerable literary fury, both inside and outside the Church, chiefly with regard to the liceity of certain rites or customs which the natives had been allowed to retain after baptism. In 1623 Gregory XV had decided that they could be permitted provisionally, and the practice was, therefore, continued by Beschi, Bouchet and others who had extended their apostolic work into Pondicherry and the Carnatic. But about the year 1700 the question was again mooted, in consequence of the transfer of the Pondicherry territory to the exclusive care of the Jesuits. The Capuchins who were affected by the arrangement appealed to Rome, adding also a protest against the Rites. The first part of the charge was not admitted, but the latter was handed over for examination to de Tournon, who was titular Patriarch of Antioch.

As soon as he arrived at Pondicherry, without going into the interior of the country, he took the testimony of the Capuchins, questioned the Jesuits only cursorily, and also a few natives through interpreters. He then condemned the Rites and forbade the missionaries under heavy penalties to allow them. His decree was made known to the Jesuit superior only three days before he left the place, and hence there was no possibility of enlightening him. The Pope then ordered de Tournon's verdict to be carried out, qualifying it, however, by adding " in so far as the Divine glory and the salvation of souls would permit." The missionaries protested without avail, and the question was discussed by two successive pontiffs. Finally, Innocent XIII insisted on de Tournon's decree being obeyed in all its details, but it is doubtful if the document ever reached the missions. Benedict XIII reopened the question later, and ruled upon each article of de Tournon's decision, and a Brief was issued to that effect in 1734.

Into this question the Jansenists of France injected themselves so vigorously that even the bibliography for and against the Rites is bewildering in its extent. One contribution consists of eight volumes in French and seven in Italian. In his history of Jansenism in " The Catholic Encyclopedia " Dr. Forget of the University of Louvain says: " The sectaries [in the middle of the eighteenth century] began to detach themselves from the primitive heresy, but they retained unabated the spirit of insurbordination and schism, the spirit of opposition to Rome, and above all a mortal hatred of the Jesuits. They had vowed the ruin of that order, which they always found blocking their way, and in order to attain their end they successively induced Catholic princes and ministers in Portugal, France, Spain, Naples, the Kingdom of the Two Sicilies, the Duchy of Parma, and elsewhere to join hands with the worst leaders of impiety and philosophism." Besides the Jansenists, " every Protestant writer of distinction with two or three exceptions," says Marshall (Christian Missions, I, 226), "has ascribed the success of the mission of Madura and its wonderful results to a guilty connivance with pagan superstition. La Croze, Geddes, Hough and other writers of their class in a long succession luxuriate in language of which we need not offer a specimen, and direct against de Nobili and his successors charges of forgery, imposture, superstition, idolatry, and various other crimes."

" There is one name," continues the same writer, "which invariably occurs in the writings referred to; one witness whom they all quote and to whom the

whole history is to be traced. That witness is Father
Norbert, ex-Capuchin and ex-missionary of India."
In a work published by this person in 1744, all the
fables which have since been repeated as grave historical
facts are found. He is quoted, apparently without
suspicion, by Dr. Grant in his "Bampton Lectures,"
yet a very little inquiry and even a reference to so
common a book, as the "Biographie universelle"
would have revealed to him the real character of the
witness by whose help he has not feared to defame
some of the most heroic and evangelical men who
ever devoted their lives to the service of God, and the
salvation of their fellow creatures.

"Norbert," says Marshall, "was one of those
ordinary missionaries who had utterly failed to convert
the Hindoo by the usual methods, and who was as
incapable of imitating the terrible austerities by which
the Jesuits prepared their success, as he was of rejoicing in triumphs of which he had no share. Stung
with mortal jealousy and yielding to the suggestions
of a malice which amounted almost to frenzy, he
attacked the Jesuits with fury even from the pulpit.
The civil power was forced to interfere, and Dupleix,
the Governor of Pondicherry, though he had been his
friend, put him on board ship and sent him to America.
There he spent two years less occupied in the work of
the missions than in planning schemes to revenge
himself on the Jesuits. The publication of the
mendacious work in which he treated the Society of
Jesus as a band of malefactors was prohibited by the
authorities; but he quitted Rome and printed it secretly.

"Condemned by his Order, though he affected to
vindicate it from the injuries of the Jesuits, he fled
to Holland and thence to England, in both of which
countries he found congenial spirits. In the latter, he
established first a candle and afterwards a carpet

factory, under the patronage of the Duke of Cumberland. Thence he wandered into Germany, and subsequently, having obtained his secularization and put off the religious habit which he had defiled, he went to Portugal. Here remorse seems to have overtaken him and he was permitted by an excess of charity to assume once more the habit of a Capuchin, which he a second time laid aside. Finally, after having attempted to deceive the Sovereign Pontiff, he died in a wretched condition in an obscure village of France." The " Biographie universelle " gives some more details which are useful as a matter of history. After Benedict XIV had forbidden Norbert to print his book, he brought it out either at Lucca or Avignon; in England he assumed his old name of Peter Parisot; when he landed in Germany he was known as Curel, and when in France his pen-name was Abbé Platel. According to the " Biographie," " Norbert was dull and heavy, without talent or style and would have been incapable of writing a single page if he were not actuated by hate. All of his works have passed into oblivion."

Americans have not been troubled to any extent by such publications, except, perhaps in one instance, when a certain R.W. Thompson, who had been Secretary of the Navy, though he lived 1000 miles from the sea, warned his fellow-countrymen in 1894 that the one danger for the Constitution of the United States was the teaching of the Jesuits. Even the Church is in peril, because " their system of moral theology is irreconcilable with the Roman Catholic religion." " I refrain from discussing it," he says, " because that has been sufficiently done by Pascal and Paul Bert." No one was excessively alarmed by the " Footprints of the Jesuits."

CHAPTER X

THE TWO AMERICAS

1567-1673

Chile and Peru — Valdivia — Peruvian Bark — Paraguay Reductions — Father Fields — Emigration from Brazil —Social and religious prosperity of the Reductions — Martyrdom of twenty-nine missionaries — Reductions in Colombia — Peter Claver — French West Indies — St. Kitts — Irish Exiles — Father Bath or Destriches — Montserrat — Emigration to Guadeloupe — Other Islands — Guiana — Mexico — Lower California — The Pious Fund — The Philippines — Canada Missions — Brébeuf, Jogues, Le Moyne, Marquette — Maryland — White — Lewger.

IN 1567 Philip II asked for twenty Jesuits to evangelize Peru. The request was granted, and in the Lent of 1568 the first band arrived at Callao and made its way to Lima. They were so cordially welcomed, says Astrain, that the provincial found it necessary to warn his men that much would have to be done to live up to the public expectation. Means were immediately put at their disposal, and they set to work at the erection of a college. While the college was being built they heard confessions, visited the jails and hospitals, gave lectures on canon law to the priests of the cathedral, and started their great training school on Lake Titicaca, to which we have already referred. There the novices were set to learn the native languages to prepare them for their future work. For the moment the population of the city also gave them plenty to do. It was made up of three classes of people: negroes, half-breeds, and wealthy Spaniards. Father López looked after the negroes, and by degrees succeeded in putting a stop to their orgies and indecent dances. Others were, meantime, taking care of the whites and

mestizos. The usual Jesuit sodalities were put in
working order, and soon it was a common thing to see
the young fashionables of the city laying aside their
cloaks and swords, and helping the sick in the hospitals,
going around to the huts of the poor or visiting criminals
in the jails.

A new detachment of missionaries arrived in the
following year with the Viceroy Toledo, who evidently
took to them too kindly on the way over, for besides
their normal duties, he wanted them to assume the
office of parish priests, and he immediately wrote to
Philip II to that effect. They refused, of course,
with the consequence of an unpleasant state of feeling
in their regard on the part of the authorities. Indeed,
the pressure became so great that the superior finally
yielded to a certain extent, and even assigned some
of his professed to the work, but he was promptly
summoned to Europe for his weakness. Meantime
novices came swarming in, among them Bernardin
d'Acosta, whose virtues merited for him, later on,
a place in the " Menology." There was also little
Oviando, called the Stanislaus of Peru. He was an
abandoned child whose parents had come out to America
and had lost him or had died, and he was begging his
bread in the streets of Lima when the Fathers picked
him up. They sent him to the college and helped him
to become a saint.

The great man of Peru and, subsequently, of
Chile, was Father Luis de Valdivia, who was hailed
by both Indians and whites as " the apostle, pacificator
and liberator of Peru." The Indians had fascinated him,
and he learned their language in a month or so. When
he saw that the only difficulty in making them
Christians was the slavery to which they were subjected, coupled with the immorality of their Spanish
masters, he got himself named as the representative

of the colonial authorities, and started to Spain to
lay before Philip III the degraded condition of his
overseas possessions.   The king received him cordially,
enacted the most stringent laws against the abuses,
and appointed him royal visitor and administrator of
Chile, where similar disorders were complained of.
He also wanted to make him a bishop, but Valdivia
refused.   Returning to Peru from Spain, he gave
10,000 Indians their freedom.   When that got abroad
among the savages, all the tribes that were then in
rebellion immediately came to terms, and on December
8, 1612, the grand chief Utablame, with sixty caciques
and a half-a-score of pagan priests, all of them wearing
wreaths of sea-weed on their heads, and holding green
branches in their hands, descended from their fast-
nesses and the grand chief, their spokesman, addressed
Valdivia as follows: "It is not fear that makes me
accept the peace. Since my boyhood I have not
ceased to defy the Spaniards, and I have withstood
sixteen governors one after another.   I yield now only
to you, good and great Father, and to the King of Spain,
because of the benefits you have bestowed upon me
and my people."

In spite of the difficulties and dangers of the work,
as well as the calumnies of the slave-hunters and even
the wrong impressions of some of his brethren,
Valdivia succeeded in establishing four great central
Indian missions, which evoked the commendation of
successive kings of Spain.   Before Valdivia went to
Chile, Viga, who had been there since 1593, had already
compiled a dictionary and grammar in Araucanian,
and Valdivia followed his example by writing other
books to facilitate the work of the missionaries.   The
colleges founded at Arauco and also at Valdivia —
a town named not after the missionary, but to honor
his namesake, the governor of the province — furnished

a base of operations among the Araucanian savages, a fierce and, for a long time, indomitable people, who were united against the Spaniards in a league composed of forty different tribes. The work among them was slow and hard, and three of the priests were killed by them in the wilderness. Their success also aroused the colonists to fury, and a war of extermination of the Indians was resolved upon, but Valdivia opposed it, and not only succeeded in getting the Araucanians to agree to terms of peace, but brought in the Guagas, and persuaded them to lay down their arms. The great missionary was eighty-two years of age when called to his reward.

The famous Peruvian bark was brought to Europe about this time, but it was regarded with extreme suspicion because of its sponsors, and the wildest stories were told of it. Medical treatises teemed with discussions about its properties, some condemning, others commending it. Von Humboldt says: " It almost goes without saying that, among Protestant physicians, hatred of the Jesuits and religious intolerance were at the bottom of the long conflict over the good or evil effected by the drug." The illustrious physician, Bado, gave as his opinion that " it was more precious than all the gold and silver which the Spaniards obtained in South America."

It was in 1586, eighteen years after their arrival in Peru, that the work of the Jesuits in Paraguay was inaugurated. Francisco de Victoria, Dominican Bishop of Tucumán had invited them to his diocese, which lay east of the Andes, and his brother in religion, Alonso Guerra, Bishop of Asunción, which was on the Rio de la Plata or Paraná River, also summoned them to his aid, both for the whites and Indians of his flock. They obeyed, and without delay colleges, residences, and retreats for the Spiritual Exercises were instituted in Santiago del Estero, Asunción, Córdoba, Buenos Aires, Corrientes, Tarija, Salta, Tucumán, Santa Fe and elsewhere. These were for the civilized portion of the community, while a new system was devised to save the Indians from their white oppressors. These poor wretches knew the colonists only as slave-dealers and butchers; hence, every attempt to teach them a religion which the whites were alleged to follow was futile.

On the other hand, when it was represented to the authorities that Indian slavery had to cease before the natives could be pacified, angry protests were heard on all sides, even from some of the resident priests who maintained that the proper thing for a savage was to be a Spaniard's slave. The missionaries took the matter in their own hands, as they had done in Peru. They went to Spain and applied for royal protection. They obtained what they wanted, so without waiting for the edict to arrive, began their work by plunging into the woods, where cougars, pumas, serpents and savages met them at every step. But this vigorous act only enraged the colonists the more, and the inhuman method of cutting off the missionaries' food-supplies was resorted to in order to force them into submission.

In this group of heroic apostles there was, curiously enough, an Irish Jesuit whom Crétineau-Joly calls Tom Filds, which is probably a Spanish or French attempt at phonetics for Tom Fields, or O'Fihily, or O'Fealy, a Limerick exile. Paraguay was the second field of his missionary labors, for he had previously been associated with the Venerable José Anchieta in the forests of Brazil. He had left Ireland when very young, and after studying at Paris, Douay and Louvain, had gone to Rome to begin his novitiate. Six months of trial were sufficient to prove the solidity of his virtue, and he then walked all the way from Rome to Lisbon, to take ship for America. He reached the Bay of All Saints in 1577, and spent ten years in the wilderness, with sufferings, privations and danger of death at every step. From thence he was sent to Paraguay, but was captured by pirates at the mouth of the Rio Plata, and then, loaded with chains, he and his companion, Manuel de Ortega were cast adrift in a battered hulk which drifted ashore at Buenos Aires, where their help as missionaries was gladly welcomed. He was at Asunción when the plague broke out, and the way in which he faced his duty won "Father Tom" as great a reputation among the white men as he had already acquired among his copper-colored brethren. When the plague was over, he again became a forest ranger, and in 1602 found himself all alone among the Indians, his companion, Father de Ortega, having been cited before the Inquisition on some ridiculous charge or other. O'Fealy finally died at Asunción on May 8, 1624, at the good old age of seventy-eight, after fifty hard years as a South American missionary — ten in Brazil and forty in Paraguay.

These journeys among the wandering tribes in the wilderness gave occasion, it is true, for extraordinary heroism, and saved many a soul, but the results were far from being in proportion to the energy expended. Hence, at the suggestion of Father Aquaviva, the missionaries all met at Saca, far out under the Andes, and determined to gather the Indians together in separate colonies which no white man, except the government officials, would be allowed to enter. Such was the origin of the "Paraguay Reductions," which have won such enthusiastic admiration from writers like Chateaubriand, Buffon, de Maistre, Haller, Montesquieu, Robertson, Mackintosh, Howitt, Marshall, Muratori, Charlevoix, Schirmbeck, Grasset, Kobler, du Graty, Gothain, and even Voltaire. The most recent eulogist of all is Cunninghame-Graham in his " Vanished Arcadia." The villages in which these converted Indians lived were called " reductions," because the natives had been brought back (*re, ducir*) from the wilds and forests by the preaching of the missionaries to live there in organized communities under Christian laws.

The first reduction was begun in 1609, in the province of Guayará, approximately the present Brazilian territory of Paraná. In 1610 another was inaugurated on the Rio Paranapanema; in 1611 the Reduction of San Ignacio-miní, and, between that year and 1630, eleven others with a total population of about 10,000 Indians. The savages flocked to them from all quarters, for these reservations afforded the only protection from the organized bands of man-hunters who scoured the country — the Mamelukes, as they were called because of their relentless ferocity. They were also described as " Paulistas," probably because they generally foregathered in the district of lower Brazil, known as St. Paul. These wretches, half-breeds or the offscourings of every race, made light of royal decrees or the angry fulminations of helpless governors, and when they could find no victims in the forests, did not hesitate to attack the Reductions themselves. These raids began in 1618. In 1630 alone, according to Huonder (in the Catholic Encyclopedia) no less than 30,000 Indians were either murdered or carried off into slavery in what is now the Brazilian state of Rio Grande do Sul.

This led to the great exodus. Father Simon Maceta abandoned the northern or Guayará mission altogether, and taking the survivors of the massacres, along with the Indians who were every day hurrying in from the forests, led them to the stations on the Paraná and Uruguay. It was a difficult journey, and only 12,000 reached their destination, but they served to reinforce the population already there, and in 1648 the Governor of Buenos Aires reported that in nineteen Reductions there was a population of 30,548; by 1677 it had risen to 58,118. He found also that they had determined to live no longer as sheep, waiting to be devoured by the first human wolves that might descend on them, but were fully armed and disciplined by their Jesuit preceptors. Indeed, in 1640 ten years after the Guaraní massacre, they could put a well-trained army in the field, not only against the Mamelukes, but against the Portuguese, who, from time to time, attempted an invasion of Spanish territory from Brazil. This military formation was not only permitted but encouraged by the king. He repeatedly sent the Indians muskets and ammunition, and later they built an armory themselves, and made their own powder. They had their regular drills and sham battles, with both infantry and cavalry, which did splendid service year after year in repelling invasions and suppressing rebellions. Nor did they ever cost the crown a penny for such services. Loyalty to the king was inculcated, and Philip V declared in a famous decree that he had no more faithful subjects than the Indians of Paraguay.

The Indians of the Reductions were taught all the trades, and became carpenters, joiners, painters, sculptors, masons, goldsmiths, tailors, weavers, dyers, bakers, butchers, tanners etc., and their artistic ability is still seen in the ruins of the missions. They were also cultivators and herdsmen, and some of the stations could count as many as 30,000 sheep and 100,000 head of cattle. They built fine roads leading to the other Reductions, and, on the great waterways of the Paraná alone, as many as 2000 boats were employed transporting the merchandise of the various centres. They were, above all, taught their religion, and their

morals were so pure that the Bishop of Buenos Aires
wrote to the king that he thought no mortal sin was
ever committed in the Reductions. The churches
occupied the central place in the villages, and their
ruins show what architectural works these men of the
forest were capable of accomplishing. The streets were
laid out in parallel lines, and the principal ones were
paved. In course of time the primitive huts were
replaced by solid stone houses with tiled roofs, and
were so constructed that connecting verandas enabled
the people to walk from house to house, under shelter,
from one end to the other of the settlement.

The Reductions extended as far as Bolivia on one
side, and to northern Patagonia on the other, and from
the Atlantic to the Andes. Altogether there were
about a hundred of them, and as their formation
required the subduing and transforming of the wildest
type of savage into a civilized man, it is not surprising
that in effecting this stupendous result as many as
twenty-nine Jesuits suffered death by martyrdom.

In 1598 the Jesuits Medrano and Figuero were in
Nueva Granada or what is now called The United
States of Colombia. They also buried themselves in
the forests, after having done their best to reform the
morals of the colonists at Bogotá. Not that they had
abandoned the city; on the contrary, they established
a college there in 1604, and others later in Pamplona,
Mérida and Honda. At first the natives fled from them
in terror, but little by little, the presents which these
strange white men pressed on them won their confidence, and helped to persuade them to settle in
Reductions. Three of the Fathers lost their lives in
that work, devoured by cougars or stung by venomous
serpents. Unfortunately, the bishop was persuaded
that the Indian settlements were merely mercantile
establishments gotten up by the Jesuits for money-

making, and all the fruit of many years of dangers and hardships was taken out of their hands and given to others.

There was no one, however, to covet the place of Peter Claver, who was devoting himself to the care of the filthy, diseased, and brutalized negroes who were being literally dumped by tens of thousands in Cartagena, to be sold into slavery to the colonists. He had come out from Spain in 1610, after the old lay-brother, Alfonso Rodriguez, had led him to the heights of sanctity and determined his vocation in the New World. His work was revolting, but Claver loved it, and as soon as a vessel arrived he was on hand with his interpreters. They hurried down into the fetid holds with food, clothing and cordials, which had been begged from the people in the town. It did not worry Claver that the poor wretches were sick with small pox or malignant fevers; he would carry them out on his back, nurse them into health, and even bury them with his own hands when they died. The unfortunate blacks had never seen anything like that before, and they eagerly listened to all he had to say about God, and made no difficulty about being baptized, striving as well as they could to shape their lives along the lines of conduct he traced out for them.

He was on his feet night and day, going from bed to bed in the rude hospitals, with supplies of fruit and wine for the sick. He even brought bands of music to play for them, and showed them pictures of holy scenes in the life of Christ to help their dull intellects to grasp the meaning of his words. No wonder that often when he was among the lepers, who were his especial pets, people saw a bright light shine round him. His biographers tell us that he did not find these ordinary sufferings enough for him, and though he wore a hair-shirt and an iron cross with

20

sharp points all day long, he was scourging himself to blood at night and praying for hours for his negroes. He died on September 8, 1654, and is now ranked among the saints, like his old master, Brother Alfonso.

To the long line of islands, alternately French and English, which form, as it were, the eastern wall of the Caribbean Sea, and are known as the Lesser Antilles, the French Jesuits were sent in 1638. They are respectively Trinidad, Grenada, Saint-Vincent, Martinique, Guadeloupe, and near the northern extremity of the line, one that is of peculiarly pathetic interest, Saint Christopher, or, as it is sometimes popularly called, Saint Kitts. When the French expedition under d'Esnambuc landed at Saint Kitts in 1625, they found the English already in possession, but like sensible men, instead of cutting each other's throats, the two nationalities divided the island between them and settled down quietly, each one attending to 'its own affairs. In 1635 'the French annexed Guadeloupe and Martinique, and, later still, Saint-Croix, Saint-Martin and a few others.

The population of these islands consisted of white settlers and their negro and Indian slaves. They were cared for spiritually by two Dominicans, one of whom, Tertre, has written a history of the islands. But these priests had no intercourse with the savages, whose languages they did not understand, and hence to fill the gap, three Jesuits, one of them a lay-brother, were sent to Martinique, arriving there on Good Friday, 1638. They began in the usual way, namely by martyrdom. Two of them were promptly killed by the savages. Others hurried to carry on their work but many succumbed to the climate, and others to the hardships inseparable from that kind of apostolate. An interesting arrival, though as late as 1674, was that of Father Joseph-Antoine Poncet, one of the apostles of Canada, who is remembered for having brought the great Ursuline, Marie de l'Incarnation, to Quebec, and also for having been tortured by New York Mohawks at the very place where Isaac Jogues had suffered martyrdom a few years before. Poncet was old when he went to Martinique and he died there the following year. The names of de la Barre, Martinière, de Tracy and Iberville, all of them familiar to students of Canadian history, occur in the chronicles of the Antilles.

For people of Irish blood these islands, especially Saint Kitts and Montserrat, are of a thrilling interest. On both of them were found numbers of exiled Irish Catholics held as slaves. As early as 1632 Father White on his way to Maryland saw them at Saint Kitts. He tells us in his " Narrative " that he " stopped there ten days, being invited to do so in a friendly way by the English Governor and two Catholic captains. The Governor of the French colony on the same island treated me with the most marked kindness." He does not inform us whether or not he did any ministerial work with them but in all likelihood he did. He is equally reticent about Montserrat, and contents himself with saying that " it is inhabited by Irishmen who were expelled from Virginia, on account of their Catholic Faith." He remained at Saint Kitts only a day, and on this point his " Relation " is very disappointing. In 1638 the Bishop of Tuam sent out a priest to the island, but he died soon after. He was probably a secular priest, for in the following year the bishop was authorized by Propaganda to send out some religious. But there is no information available about what was done until 1652, when an Irish Jesuit was secured for them. In the " Documents inédits " of Carayon he is called Destriches, which may have been Stritch, but there is no mention of either name in any

of the menologies; Hughes, in his " History of the
Society of Jesus in North America " (I, 470), calls
him Christopher Bathe. He was not, however, the
first choice. A Father Henry Malajon had been
proposed, but the General did not allow him to go.
A Welshman named Buckley was then suggested, but
though his application was ratified he never left Europe.
Next a Father Maloney offered himself, but was kept
in Belgium; finally, however, Father Christopher
Bathe or Stritch arrived.

The missionary found there a very great multitude
of enslaved Irish exiles, for on April 1, 1653, the London
Council gave " license to Sir John Clotworthie to
transport to America 500 *natural* Irishmen." On
September 6, 1653, he asked leave to transport 400
Irish children. Ten days later liberty was granted to
Richard Netherway of Bristol to transport from
Ireland one hundred *Irish 'tories.* When Jamaica was
captured by the English in 1655, one thousand Irish
girls and a like number of Irish boys were sent there.
The earlier throngs had been sent first to Virginia, but
had been driven over to the islands, as we learn from
White's " Narrative." The English authorities in
Ireland wrote to Lord Thurlow: " Although we must
use force in taking them up, yet it being so much for
their own good and likely to be of great advantage to
the public, it is not the least doubted but that you may
have as many as you wish." He offers to send 1500
or 2000 boys. " They will thus," he said, " be made
good Christians." The first of these " good
Christians " were found by Father Bathe when he
arrived in Saint Kitts in 1652 and they eagerly came
to the little chapel which he built on the dividing line
between the English and French settlements. For
three months he was busy from dawn till nightfall
saying Mass, hearing confessions, baptizing babies and

preaching. After that he started for Montserrat which was entirely under English control and hence he was compelled to go there disguised as a lumber merchant who was looking for timber. As soon as he landed he passed the word to the first Irishman he met and the news spread like wildfire. A place of meeting was chosen in the woods where every day Mass was said and the people went to confession and communion. That took up the whole morning, and in the afternoon they began chopping down the trees so as to carry out the deception. Unfortunately, the Caribs found them one day, and killed some of them, but we have no more details of the extent of the disaster.

By the time Father Bathe got back to Saint Kitts, the English had taken alarm and had forbidden their Irish slaves ever to set foot on the French territory. But there must have been disobedience to the order, for one night, after they had returned home, a descent was made upon their houses, and one hundred and twenty-five of the most notable among them were flung into a ship and cast on Crab Island, two hundred leagues away, where they were left to starve, while those who remained behind at Saint Kitts were treated with the most frightful inhumanity. One instance is cited of a young girl who, for having refused to go to the Protestant church, was dragged by the hair of her head along the road, and treated with such brutality that some of the more timid of the victims were terrified and obeyed the order about keeping away from the chapel. The greater number, however, came to Mass secretly, walking all night through dense forests and at the edge of precipices, so as to escape the sentries posted along the ordinary road. Two very old men were conspicuous in this display of faith.

The castaways on Crab Island kept life in their bodies for a few days by eating what grass or roots

they could find or by gathering the shell-fish on the
beach. At last to their great delight a ship was
sighted in the distance and when they hailed it, came to
take them off. Unfortunately, however, it was too
small for such a crowd, and only as many as it was
safe to receive were allowed on board. The rest had
to be abandoned to their fate. What became of them
nobody ever knew. It is supposed that they made
a raft and were lost somewhere out on the ocean.
Even those who sailed away came to grief. When they
reached Santo Domingo, they were not permitted to
land, because they came from Saint Christopher, which
made the Spaniards in the fort suspect a trick. Then
they were caught by a tornado and carried four hundred
leagues away. At one time hunger had brought them
so low that they were on the point of casting lots to
see who should be killed and eaten, but fortunately
they caught some fish and that sustained them till
they reached the land. What land it was we do not
know.

A characteristic example of Irish feminine virtue
is recorded in this very interesting account, which is
worth repeating here. A young girl, for her better
protection, had been disguised as a boy by her father
when both were exiled. After he died, she obtained
work in the household of a respectable family where her
efficiency so charmed the mistress of the household
that the husband grew jealous of the friendship of his
wife for this estimable man-servant. To avert a
domestic disaster, the good girl had to make known
her identity and she was then more esteemed than
ever. What became of her ultimately is not recorded.
Meantime, Father Bathe had gathered what was left
of his poor people and carried them off to Guadeloupe,
where there were no English. God spared him for five
years more, and he went from island to island under

all sorts of disguises, if there was danger of meeting the English. He even succeeded in converting not a few of the persecutors.

Hughes informs us further that in 1667 an Irish priest named John Grace returned to Europe from the islands, and reported on the deplorable condition of his compatriots in the Caribbean. Passing through Martinique, Guadeloupe and Antigua he heard the confessions of more than three hundred of them. He related, also, that fifty of the three hundred had died while he was there. In Barbadoes there were many thousands who had no priests and were conforming to Protestantism. In St. Bartholomew, there were four hundred Irish Catholics who had never seen a priest. At Montserrat, however, Governor Stapleton was an Irishman and a Catholic, and consequently there was no difficulty in having a priest go there. There were as many as four hundred Catholics at that place and they formed six to one of the population. These islands of the Caribbean were the favorite hiding places of the "filibusteros," a set of abandoned men of various nationalities, French, Dutch and English, who were lying in wait for the rich galleons of Spain, on their way from the silver mines of Peru to the palaces of Madrid. Their life was a continued series of daring adventures, robberies, massacres and wild debauchery. They were ready for any expedition and against any foe. With them nothing could be done, but with the great numbers of negro slaves who were sold at Martinique and elsewhere there was ample opportunity for apostolic work. It was a most revolting task; the whites, regarded them as devils, but the Fathers took care of them and sent many of them to heaven.

It was from the Antilles that the French Jesuits went to Guiana. Its conversion had been attempted

in 1560 by two Dominicans, but they were both
martyred almost on their arrival. No other effort
was made until late in the following century, when in
1643 two Capuchins essayed it, only to be killed.
Four years before that, however, the Jesuits Meland
and Pelliprat entered the country at another point
and succeeded in subduing the savage Galibis, who
were particularly noted for ferocity. In 1653 Pelliprat
published a grammar and a dictionary of their language;
in the following year Aubergeon and Gueimu were
killed; then the Dutch took possession of the country,
expelled the Jesuits and obliterated every vestige of
Catholicity. Nevertheless, the missionaries returned
later and renewed their work with the intractable
natives. In 1674 Grillet and Béchamel started for the
interior, and were followed later by Lombard, who,
after fifteen years of heroic toil, erected a church at
the mouth of the River Kourou to the northwest of
Cayenne. There he labored for twenty-three years,
and in 1733 was able to report to his fellow missionary,
de la Neuville: " Acquainted as you are with the
fickleness of our Indians, you will no doubt be surprised
to hear that their inconstancy has been overcome.
The horror with which they now regard their former
superstitions, their regularity in frequently approaching the sacraments, their assiduity in assisting at the
Divine service, the profound sentiments of piety which
they manifest at the hour of death, are effectual proofs
of a sincere and lasting conversion."

Father Grillet's story of the capture of the French
fort in Guiana makes interesting reading. He went
out with the garrison to meet the English who were
landing from their ships, but the French commander
was killed and his men fled. Grillet, with some others,
made his way to the forests and swamps of the interior,
but was finally captured at the point of the pistol.

He was ordered to hand over his money, but as he had
none, he would probably have been killed had not
a party of English officers recognized him as the priest
who had rendered them some service over in the
Antilles some time before. They led him to Lord
Willoughby the governor, who showed him every
attention. It will be of interest to know that these
gentlemen carried on their conversation with the priest,
in French and Latin. When the ship arrived at
Barbadoes, Grillet was lodged with a Scotch gentleman
whose son-in-law was a Protestant minister; " a clever
man, a good philosopher and well up in his theology,"
says Grillet. They discussed religious questions
amicably, and on Sunday the priest had the satisfaction
to hear that the parson told his congregation how he
" wished they had the same sorrow for their sins as
Catholics have when they go to confession."

Grillet remained a month with his Protestant
friends, Lord Willoughby coming occasionally to visit
him. From Barbadoes he was conducted to Montserrat, where " Milord, after celebrating Christmas ten
days later than we do," notes Grillet, " for the English
did not accept the Gregorian Calendar," then handed
him over to a Catholic colonel of a Yorkshire regiment,
who finally delivered him safe and sound to the French
Governor de la Barre. This was the de la Barre who
was afterwards to figure in Canadian history. Grillet
then returned to his old mission work at Cayenne,
for the English had abandoned it, and with Father
Béchamel set out to explore the interior, with a view to
future missionary establishments. With no other
provision than a little cassava bread, and no other
escort than a negro and a few Indians, they began
a journey of 1920 miles, through forests and swamps
and across mountains and down rivers which were
continually broken by cataracts merely to find where

the Indians were living, so as to send them missionaries later. They had started from Cayenne on January 25, 1674, and returned there on June 27. Both died shortly after.

Along both banks of the Oyapoch, throughout its whole course, missions were established by other valiant apostles who, as a French historian relates, had formed the gigantic project of uniting by a chain of stations both extremities of Guiana. Indeed, the church on the Kourou was only an incident in this work. Eleven years before that, Arnaud d'Ayma had fought his way to the Pirioux, the remotest of all the known tribes. There he lived like the savages in a miserable hut, spending every moment among them in studying their language and teaching them in turn the truths of salvation. He then founded a mission on the Oyapoch where he collected the entire tribe of the Caranes. Meantime, D'Ausillac looked after the Toeoyenes, the Maowrioux, and the Maraxones on the Ouanari. Up to the time when de Choiseul, minister of Louis XV, drove the Jesuits out of Guiana, one hundred and eleven of them had devoted their lives to the evangelization of that country.

Bandelier, writing in " The Catholic Encyclopedia " (IV-123), tells us that in the district in which Cartagena was situated, " the religious of the Society of Jesus were the first during the Colonial period to found colleges for secondary instruction; eight or ten colleges were opened in which the youth of the country and the sons of Spaniards were educated, In the Jesuit College of Bogotá the first instruction in physics and mathematics was given. In the expulsion of the Jesuits by Charles III the Church in New Granada lost her principal and most efficacious aid to the civilization of the country.......To this day the traveller may see the effects of this arbitrary act, in the immense plains of the regions of Casanare, converted in the space of one century into pasture lands for cattle, but which were once a source of great wealth, and which would have been even more so. It is only within the last ten years that the Catholic Church, owing to the peace and liberty which she now enjoys, has turned her eyes once more to Casanare; a vicariate Apostolic has been erected there, governed by a bishop of the Order of St. Augustine, who with the members of his order labours among the savages and semi-savages of these plains."

The first Jesuits, as we have already said, arrived in Mexico in September, 1572. They were sent out at the expense of the king, but as he did nothing more, a wealthy benefactor immediately put his money at their disposal and gave them a site for a college and church. The latter was erected with amazing expedition at a trifling expense, for three thousand Indians who had heard that the Fathers were going to take care of their spiritual welfare worked at it for three months. The structure was declared to be *muy hermoso por dentro*, but as much could not be said of the exterior. It was simply a thatched structure and was long known by the name of Japalteopan. Their college, which took more time, was called St. Ildefonso. Guadalajara, Zacatecas and Oaxaca also became Jesuit centres, while Chihuahua, Sinaloa, Sonora, and, later Lower California were their fields of labor among the savages. It may be noted here that Father Sánchez was one of the presiding engineers in the work of the Nochistongo tunnel on which 471,154 men were employed. The purpose of the work was to drain the valley of Mexico.

Among the very early missionaries of Mexico was an Irish Jesuit named Michael Wadding, though he was known among the Spaniards as Miguel Godinez.

He was born at Waterford in 1591, but his mother was a Frenchwoman, named Marie Valois. He made his studies in Salamanca and entering the Society April 15, 1609 was sent to Mexico in the following year. He labored for a long time in the rude missions of Sinaloa and won to the Faith the whole tribe of the Basirvas, and then taught for several years in the colleges. He was famous as a director of souls, and wrote a " Teologia mística " which, was not published until forty years after his death; however, it made up for the delay by going through ten editions. His editor, Manuel La Reguera, S. J., says that he also wrote a " Life of Sister Mary of Jesus," a holy religious whom he was directing in the way of perfection.

The Jesuit mission work in Mexico which has attracted most attention is that of Fathers Kino, Salvatierra, Ugarte and their associates. They were engaged mostly in the evangelization of the Peninsula of Lower California and the vast northern district of Mexico, known as the Pimería, or land of the Pima Indians, which extended into what is now the State of Arizona. The success achieved there and the resources of the " Pious Fund " which Salvatierra had gathered made the work of Junípero Serra and the Franciscans in Upper California possible in later days.

Gilmary Shea (Colonial Days, p. 527) maintains that Eusebio Kino is one of the greatest of American missionaries. Many historians claim that he was a German and say that his name " Kino " was an adaptation of Kühn. That such is not the case is shown by Alegre in his history of the Jesuits in Mexico; by Sommervogel in his " Bibliothèque des écrivains " and by Bolton, who has just published Kino's long lost " Autobiography." Hubert Bancroft pronounces for Kühn, but he publishes an autograph map which is signed " carta autoptica a Patre Eusebio Chino;"

Huonder, in " The Catholic Encyclopedia," declares
him to be a German of Welch Tyrol, but the " Welch "
Tyrol is precisely that part of the country where there
are no Germans. The Chino family still exists, near
Trent and has never spoken anything but Italian.
The change from *Ch* to *K* had to be made to prevent
the Spaniards from thinking he was a Chinaman;
furthermore the *ch* in Spanish being always soft would
not represent the Italian letters when they are pronounced *k*.

Kino was born on August 10, 1644, and entered the
Society of Jesus in Bavaria on November 20, 1665.
He subsequently taught mathematics at Ingolstadt,
and while occupying that post applied for the foreign
missions. He left the university in 1678, but did not
reach Mexico until late in 1681. The reason of the
delay was his assignment as an observer of the famous
comet of 1680 and 1681. During that time, he lived in
Cadiz, but he did not publish the result of his observations until after his arrival in Mexico. The book
has a very portentous title and is listed in Sommervogel
as: " Exposicion Astronomica de el Cometa, que el
año de 1680, por los meses de Noviembre y Diziembre,
y este año de 1681 por los meses de Enero y Febrero,
se ha visto en todo el mondo, y le ha observado en
Ciudad de Cadiz el P. Eusebio Francisco Kino, de la
Compañi de Jesus, con licencia en Mexico por Francisco Rodriguez Lupercio, 1681." Possibly this pomp-
ous announcement was intended as an apology for
Kino's audacity in questioning the findings of a famous
astronomer of the period who rejoiced in the name
and title Don Carlos de Sigüenza y Gongora, Cos-
mógrafo y Mathemático Regio en la Academia
Mexicana.

The settlement of Lower California had been
attempted as early as 1535 by a Franciscan who

landed with Cortes at Santa Cruz Bay near the present La Paz. "After a year of privations", says Engelhardt, "which had cost the famous conqueror $300,-000, the project had to be abandoned. Another effort was made in 1596, but the mission did not last a single year. Almost a century later, namely in 1683, the Jesuit Fathers Kino and Goni, along with Fray José Guijosa of the Order of St. John of God, accompanied Admiral Otondo on an expedition to that unhappy country." They embarked on the "Limpia Concepción" and the "San José y San Francisco Javier" and set sail on January 18. A sloop with provisions was to accompany them, but it never left port. The voyage lasted until March 30, and on that day they entered the harbor of La Paz, but not until April 5 did the admiral set foot on shore to take solemn possession of the land. The mission, however, lasted only a short time; and thus Spain failed for the third time to establish a post in desolate Lower Calfornia. Kino then applied for work among the Pima Indians. His offer was welcomed by the provincial, who would have sent him thither immediately, if a government permission as well as a royal assignment of funds had not been prerequisites. Neither difficulty dismayed Kino; he immediately interviewed the viceroy and was so eloquent in his plea that he received not only permission and financial aid to work in the new field, but authorization for whatever post he might choose among the Seris of Sonora. When that much was accomplished, he set off for Guadalajara, where the royal audiencia was in session, to address it on another matter which was very close to his heart, namely the abrogation of the stupid policy of imposing labor on the convert Indians in the mines and haciendas, while the others who refused to be Christians were allowed to go scot free. It was putting a premium on paganism. All

that he could get, however, from the audiencia was
a five-year exemption, in spite of the fact that as far
back as 1607 Philip III had ruled that for ten years after
baptism every convert should be exempt from compulsory labor. The same royal order had been renewed
in 1618, and was most faithfully observed where there
were no mines or haciendas to put the converts at work.

In 1764 the Pimería was the northern limit of Spain's
possessions, about 400 leagues from the city of Mexico
and about 130 from Sinaloa. On the east a mountain
range separated it from Taurumara, and on the west
the Gulf of California bathed its shores from the Yaqui
River to the Colorado. Its northern boundary was
the Hila, Gila, or Xila River, and its southern, the
Yaqui. According to Alegre " the soil is rich, there is
no end of game, such as lions, tigers, bears, deer, boars,
rabbits and squirrels. The woods are full of serpents,
poisonous or otherwise, but there are herbs and plants
innumerable," which possessed most wonderful healing
powers. The birds were numerous and " two-headed
eagles," the reader is assured, " were not rare." Kino,
as far as we can find, makes no mention of " two
headed eagles."

The people were robust and lived to an extreme old
age, except where the fogs of the lowland prevailed.
There all sorts of ailments occur. The Pimas were
composed of a number of tribes such as the Opas,
Cocomaricopas, Hudcoacanes, and the Yumas. They
lived on both sides of the Gila River in rancherias,
which the missionaries united into pueblos. They
numbered in all about 30,000. The Seris who were
found along the Gulf coast were mostly identified with
the Giuamas. To the north were the savage Apaches.

None of these people had any means of recording the
doings of the past, such as the hieroglyphics of the
Mexicans, but they made much of certain traditions

which they refused to impart to strangers. As far as
could be ascertained, they had no sacrifice or idols,
no kind of worship and no priests except the wizards,
whom they regarded with abject terror. Tatooing
around the eyes was universal, even for children. At
birth a sort of sponsor for the child was summoned,
and he was given more authority than the parent. At
death all the trappings and household belongings of
the departed were buried with him. They believed in
divinations like the ancient Greeks and Romans,
with the difference that the creature inspected was
not a bird but a lobster. Statues and emblems were
placed on the roadsides, before which every passer-by
had to leave an offering. Alegre gives a long list of
their superstitions, some of which Bancroft denounces
as hideously obscene. The initiation of the warrior
resembled the horrible ritual common among the
northern Mandans, and the torture of captives, even
of little children, by old squaws, was as fiendish as
similar practices among the Iroquois.

The Jesuit missions among these people were
inaugurated as early as 1637 or 1638, by Father
Castano, who had been trained in the Sonora district
by Méndez, but the Pima section to which Kino
betook himself was a new field. He called his first
post Nuestra Señora de los Dolores, and it may be
found on the map just north of Cucurpé at the source
of the river called Horcasitas or San Miguel. From
there he developed dependent stations, and before
1691, he had three at San Ignacio, Remedios, and
San José, in each of which he built a fine church.

" The work which Father Kino did as a ranchman
or stockman," says Bolton, "would alone stamp him as
an unusual business man and make him worthy of
remembrance. He was easily the cattle king of his
day and region. The stock raising industry of nearly

20 places on the modern map owes its beginnings to this indefatigable man. And it must not be supposed that he did this for private gain for he did not own a single animal. It was to furnish a food supply for the Indians of the missions established and to be established and to give these missions a basis of economic prosperity and independence. Thus we find Saeta thanking him for the gift of 115 head of cattle, and as many sheep to begin a ranch at Caborca. In 1700 when San Xavier was founded, Kino rounded up 1400 head of cattle on the ranch of his own mission at Dolores, and dividing them into droves, sent one of them under his Indian overseer to San Xavier. In the same year he took 700 cattle from his own ranch, and sent them to Salvatierra, across the Gulf at Loreto — a transaction which was several times repeated."

Kino had often spoken to Salvatierra about the failure of the attempt to evangelize Lower California, to which his heart still clung, and he suggested to his companion that in his capacity of official visitor he might make another effort to redeem the unfortunate people who lived there. It was true, he admitted, that the country was so barren that it could not be self-sustaining, but he was convinced that it would be an easy matter to convey provisions from fertile Pimería to the starving Californians if a ship could be constructed to transport to the other side of the Gulf whatever the future missionaries and people might need. Salvatierra took fire at the idea, and, before they parted, ordered Kino to build the barque at any point he might select along the west coast of Mexico and assured him that he himself would further the project with all the power at his disposal.

It was not until 1694 that Kino attempted to build the ship. He was then among the Sobas on the Gulf, and with him were Father Campo and Captain Manje, the latter of whom has left a diary of that journey. He began to cut his timber on March 16, 1694, but he was informed that Lower California was not an island, but a peninsula, and he then inaugurated a series of amazing overland journeys to reach the head of the Gulf. His companion Captain Manje had told him of the wonderful structures on the Gila River and thither he directed his steps. He is said to have celebrated Mass in the largest of those ruined buildings, the famous Casa Grande. It was quadrilateral in form and four stories high. The rafters were of cedar and the walls of solid cement and masonry. It was divided into various compartments, some of them spacious enough for a considerable assembly. The tradition among the people was that Montezuma's predecessors built it on the way from the north to the southern countries where they ultimately settled.

At a distance of three leagues from this Casa and on the other side of the river are the ruins of another edifice, which appears to have been still more sumptuous. Indeed the ruins at that place would indicate that at one time there had been not merely a palace but a whole city, and the natives assured the missionaries that there were other buildings further north which were marvelous for their symmetry and arrangements. Among them was a labyrinth which appears to have been a pleasure house of some great king. Excavators have discovered in various places, sometimes leagues away from these great buildings, shapely and variously colored slabs, and two leagues from the Casa Grande there was found the basin of a reservoir large enough to supply a populous city and to irrigate the fertile plains around for great distances; while to the west was a lagoon which was emptied by a narrow sluice. The regularity of the circular form of this lagoon and its rather contracted dimensions would suggest that it was the work of men were it not for its extraordinary depth. Holes had been cut into the solid rock which subsequently were found large enough to be used as storehouses for provisions for troops.

These ruins, however, do not appear to have interested Kino to any great extent. There were other ruins that worried him about that time. His own missions seemed to be facing universal destruction. He himself was being denounced in Mexico as conveying false information to the government about his Indians; they were accused of being in secret alliance with the Apaches, who were destroying the country and defying the Spaniards. Kino again and again had denied the truth of these charges, but he was not only not believed but was held up as a deliberate liar.

On March 29, 1695, the Pimas of Tubutama burned the priest's house and church, profaned the sacred vessels and then, starting down the river to Caborca, had, after murdering Father Saeta and desecrating the church, killed four servants of the mission. An armed force was quickly sent after them and succeeded in killing a certain number in the battle that ensued. Fifty of them then gave themselves up on a promise of immunity, but on arriving in camp they were brutally murdered. The troops then hastened to Cocospera, fancying that they had restored peace, but they were no sooner out of sight than the Pimas laid waste the whole Tubutama Valley and destroyed every town on the San Ignacio River. Where was Kino all this time? Quietly waiting to be killed at Dolores. He had concealed the sacred vessels in a cave and was kneeling in prayer, expecting the tomahawk or a poisoned arrow. But no one came. He was too much beloved by all the Indians to be injured in the least, even in their wildest excess of fury.

Of course the Spaniards ultimately won. They ravaged the whole country and slaughtered the savages until the entire tribe was terror-stricken and forced by hunger or fear of annihilation to sue for peace. Through the influence of the missionaries, a general pardon was granted, and then the work of reconciling the red men to the terrible whites had to be begun all over again. When Kino returned to Dolores, he was received with the utmost enthusiasm by his people. Not only the Pimas, but the Sobas and Sobaipuris came out to welcome him. They loaded him with gifts and made all sorts of promises of future good behavior, and he then set himself to the task of re-building the devastated rancherias. Notwithstanding this return, however, to normal conditions and the great increase of his influence over the Indians, Kino still longed to devote himself to the regeneration of the degraded Californians, and he asked to be associated with Salvatierra, who had gone thither in 1697, but owing to the protest of the Pimas, the Mexican government positively refused to permit him to leave the district where his presence was so essential for peace.

After endless journeys up and down the country, providing for the material and spiritual wants of his own flock, but ever keeping in his mind the great project of reaching Lower California by land, Kino at last climbed the mountain of Santa Brigida and saw quite near to him the Gulf of California with a port or bay which, because it was in latitude about 31° 36′ must have been what the old cosmographers called the Santa Clara range. "From its summit," says Kino himself, " I clearly descried the beach at the mouth of the Colorado, but as there was a fog on the sea I could not make out the California coast." On another occasion, however, namely in 1694, he and Juan Mates had seen the other side from Mt. Nazarene de Caborca,

lower down the coast.   A point of identification left
by Kino was that the mountain on which he stood in
1698, had been once a volcano.   The marks of it were
all around him.

Kino could not then pursue his exploration to the
mouth of the river.   His guides and companions refused
to go any farther, so he had to turn homeward.   On
the way back, however, he was consoled by discovering
more than " 4,000 souls," to use Alegre's expression,
" in rancherias which were until then unknown to
him.   He baptized about four hundred babies and sent
little presents to his Indian friends along the Colorado
and Gila," or, as Kino spells it, Hila.   After making
arrangements for future explorations he set out for
Dolores, which he reached on October 18 after a
journey of three hundred leagues.   In 1699 he was
joined by his friend Captain Manje, and they resolved
to reach the Colorado itself and go down the stream
to the mouth.   But they failed to find guides, for it
was an unfriendly country, and so the disappointed
men again returned to Dolores.   Kino was seriously
ill on his arrival, but was on his feet again in October
when the visitor, Father Leal, wanted to inspect the
country.   The official got no farther than Bac, while
Kino and Manje started west, but they did not succeed
in going far, and were at the mission again in November.

On September 24, 1700, Kino attempted a new
route.   Striking the Gila east of the bend, he followed
its course down to the Yuma country.   After settling
a quarrel between the Yumas and their neighbors,
he climbed a high hill to explore, but saw only land.
He then crossed to the north bank of the Gila with
some Yumas and journeyed on to their principal ran-
cheria, which he called San Dionisio, because he
arrived there on the feast of that saint, October 9.
There he ascended another mountain and this time

he was rewarded. The sun was setting as he reached
the summit, but he clearly saw the river running ten
leagues west of San Dionisio and, after a course of
twenty leagues south, emptying into the Gulf. From
another hill to the south he saw before his eyes the
sandy stretches of Lower California. The wonderful
old man, however, was not yet satisfied. He would
make one more attempt and with Father Gonzales,
a new arrival in the missions, he set his face to the west,
reaching San Dionisio by the way of Sonoito and
from there went down to Santa Isabel. "From this
point," says Bancroft (XV, p. 500), "they were in
new territory. Going down the river they reached
tide-water on March 5, 1702, and on the 7th, the very
mouth of the river. Nothing but land could be seen
on the south, west and north. Surely, they thought
there can be no estrecho, and California is a part of
America."

According to Clavigero these journeys totalled about
twenty thousand miles. It is almost incredible, but
Bolton tells us that "Kino's endurance in the saddle
was worthy of a seasoned cowboy." Thus when he
went to the City of Mexico in 1695, he travelled on
that single journey no less than 1500 miles; and he
accomplished it in fifty-three days. Two years later,
when he reached the Gila on the north, he did seven
or eight hundred miles in thirty days. In 1699, on
his trip to and from the Gila he made seven hundred
and twenty miles in thirty nine days; in 1700, a thousand miles in twenty-six days; and in 1701, eleven
hundred miles in thirty-five days. He was then
nearly sixty years of age.

Meantime, Salvatierra had been painfully establishing missions all along the barren peninsula, but was so
woefully discouraged that he was on the point of returning to Mexico. At this juncture Father Juan Ugarte

arrived on the scene. He had been Salvatierra's
agent in Mexico for collecting funds, but when he
heard of the threatening condition of things in California
he had himself relieved of his rectorship in San Gregorio
and became a missionary. It was really he who saved
the whole enterprise from destruction. He was born
in Honduras about the year 1660, and entered the
Society at Tapozotclan. As soon as he set foot on the
Peninsula, he began a reorganization of the whole
economic system of the missions. With St. Paul,
he believed that a man who did not work should not
eat, and consequently that Salvatierra's benignant
method of feeding every savage who would come to
the "doctrina," or catechism, was psychologically,
religiously and economically wrong. Hence, when he
found himself fixed at San Javier, he taught the
natives how to cultivate the land, to dig ditches for
irrigation, to plant trees, to trim vines and to raise
live stock.

Of course, the savages were surprised at the new
system, but although Ugarte was very kind, he was
very positive and his bodily strength astounded and
appalled his neophytes. The result was that while
other missions were starving, San Javier had fields of
corn, rich pastures and great herds of cattle. It
took a long time to make this system acceptable
everywhere on the Peninsula; when it was adopted it
was difficult to make it a success — even Ugarte's
own fields were devastated and his cattle stolen. Indeed,
conditions grew so desperate in 1701, that Salvatierra
at last determined to abandon California and go back
to Mexico. Ugarte stood out against it and protested
that he would never give up until his superiors called
him back. To show that he meant what he said, he
went to the church and laid a vow to that effect on the
altar.

Just when the sky was darkest, information came
that Philip V had ordered 6000 pesos a year to be
allotted to the missions. The first payment however,
was made with extreme reluctance by the viceroy.
But the royal example stimulated the piety of others,
with the result that the Marquis of Villapuente gave
an estate of 30,000 pesos for three missions; Ortega
and his wife came forward with 10,000; and other
friends hastened with their contributions. In 1704
Salvatierra went over to Mexico to collect the usual
subsidy. He was rejoiced at being told on his arrival
that not only would he receive the stipend, but that
his majesty had ordered that the churches should be
supplied with whatever was necessary for Divine
services, that a seminary was to be founded in California, that a presidial force of thirty men was to be
stationed on the coast to protect a galleon, a sort of
mission ship for provisions and exploration, and
that 7000 pesos a year were to be added to the former
allowance. It was a splendid example of royal
munificence; however, not only were none of these
royal orders carried out, but even the original grant of
6000 pesos could not be collected. "It may be fairly
stated," says Bancroft (XV, 432) "that the missions of
California were from the first to the last founded and
supported by private persons whose combined gifts
formed what is known as the Pious Fund."

Salvatierra was absent from California for a little
over two years while filling the office of provincial,
"a flattering honor," says Bancroft, "that would be
gladly accepted by most Jesuits." Before the end of
his term, however, he hastened back to labor in the
land of desolation to which he had consecrated his
life. He lasted only a short time, and died in 1717 in
Guadalajara. "His memory," says Bancroft, "needs
no panegyric; his deeds speak for themselves, and in

the light of these, the bitterest enemies of his religion or
of his Order cannot deny the beauty of his character
and the disinterestedness of his devotion to California.
The whole city assembled at his funeral and his remains
were deposited amidst ceremonies rarely seen at the
burial of a Jesuit."

Meantime, Ugarte's methods were being followed
elsewhere than in San Javier, and a new impetus was
given to them when he succeeded Salvatierra as
general superior. It must have been hard to keep
the pace that he set; thus, for instance, he used 40,000
loads to make a road from San Javier to one of the
out-lying missions; he built a reservoir there and
carted to it 160,000 loads of earth to make a garden
and executed many similar works. He was also very
eager to carry out Salvatierra's purpose of exploring
the coast, but he was not satisfied with the antiquated
ships which had been in use up to that time — " worn
out and rotten old hulks," he said, " only fit to drown
Jesuits in." He determined to have a ship of his
own built in California and after his own ideas. For
that purpose he hired shipwrights from the other
side of the Gulf, where also he proposed to get his
timber. But hearing of some large trees thirty leagues
above Mulege he went thither in 1718 to look them
over. He found the trees, but they were in such
inaccessible ravines that the shipbuilder declared it
was impossible to get them.

Ugarte was not swayed from his purpose by this
difficulty; he went down to Loretto and returned
with three mechanics and all the Indians he could
induce to follow him. After four months of hard work
he not only had all the trees felled and shaped, but
he had opened a road for thirty leagues over the
mountains and with oxen and mules hauled his material
to the coast. He built his " Triumph of the Cross,"

as he called it, in four months. The provincial was
told meanwhile, that it was going to be used for pearl
fishing, and sent the supposed culprit a very sharp
letter in consequence. No doubt he made amends for
this when he was disabused. The " Triumph of the
Cross " was not to carry a cargo of pearls but was
intended to explore the upper Gulf, so as to realize
the dream of Kino and Salvatierra.

The good ship left Loretto on May 15, 1721, with
twenty men, six of whom were Europeans, the
captain being a William Stafford. It was followed by
the " Santa Barbara," a large open boat carrying
five Californians, two Chinese and a Yaqui. They
made their first landing at Concepción Bay, and then,
after creeping along the shore northward, crossed the
Gulf to Santa Sabina and San Juan Bautista on the
Seri coast. The sight of the cross on the bow-sprit
delighted the natives and assured the travellers of a
hearty welcome. Tiburon was the next stop, and
while there Ugarte felt his strength giving out; but
despite his sixty-one years he continued his voyage, and
headed the " Triumph "for the mouth of the Colorado,
while the " Santa Barbara " hugged the shore. Meantime, a few men were landed and made for the nearest
mission. They found the trail to Caborca and soon
the Jesuits of that place and of San Ignacio hurried
down with provisions for the travellers.

While the " Santa Barbara " was being loaded, the
" Triumph " was nearly stranded at the mouth of the
river, so it was decided to cross to the other side, which
they reached only after a hard three days' sail. There
the " Santa Barbara " met them and both ships pointed
north, crossing and recrossing the gulf until finally
they anchored at the mouth of the river on the Pimería
side. There was some talk of going up the stream,
but the ship's position in the strong current was danger-

ous, the weather was threatening, and besides, Ugarte
had achieved his purpose; he had seen the river from
the Gulf and had added a convincing proof to Kino's
assertion that California was a peninsula. On July
16 they started south; the storm they had feared
broke over them and the sloop nearly went to the
bottom. The sailors, who were nearly all sick of the
scurvy, got confused in the Salsipuedes channel, and
it was only on August 18 that they cleared that passage
so aptly called "Get out if you can." But a triple
rainbow in the sky that day comforted them, just as
they had been cheered when the St. Elmo's fire played
around the mast head during the gale. But they were
not free yet. Another storm overtook them and they
had great difficulty in dodging a waterspout, but they
finally reached Loretto in the month of September.

Besides its orginal purpose, this voyage resulted in
furnishing much valuable information about the shores,
ports, islands and currents of the Upper Gulf. The
original account of the journey with maps and a
journal kept by Stafford was sent to the viceroy for
the king, but Bancroft says they have not been traced.
Ugarte lived only eight years after this eventful
journey. Picolo, Salvatierra's first companion had
preceded him to the grave, dying on February 22,
1729, at the age of 79, whereas Ugarte's life-work
did not cease till the following December 29. Perhaps
Lower California owes more to him than to the great
Salvatierra.

A classic example of the influence of ignorance in
the creation of many of the false statements of history
is furnished by a publication about these missions in
the " Montreal Gazette " of 1847, under the title of
" Memories of Mgr. Blanchet." " The failure of the
Jesuits in Lower California," he says," must be attributed to their unwillingness to establish a hierarchy

in that country. Had they been so disposed, they
might have had a metropolitan and several suffragans
on the Peninsula. They failed to do so, until at last,
in 1767, word came from generous Spain to hand over
their work to some one else." In the first place,
" generous Spain " had not the slightest desire to
establish a hierarchy on that barren neck of land
when it expelled the Jesuits in 1767. Again as " generous Spain " appointed even the sacristans in its
remotest colonies, the Society must be acquitted of all
blame in not giving an entire hierarchy to Lower
California. Finally, one hundred and fifty-one years
have elapsed since the last Jesuits left both Mexico
and Lower California and there is nothing there yet,
but the little Vicariate Apostolic of La Paz down at
the lower end of the Peninsula.

In describing the work of the Jesuits in Mexico,
Bancroft (XI, 436) writes as follows: " Without
discussing the merits of the charges preferred against
them, it must be confessed that the service of God in
their churches was reverent and dignified. They
spread education among all classes, their libraries
were open to all, and they incessantly taught the
natives religion in its true spirit, as well as the mode
of earning an honest living. Among the most notable
in the support of this last assertion are those of Nayarit,
Sonora, Sinaloa, Chihuahua and lower California,
where their efforts in the conversion of the natives
were marked by perserverance and disinterestedness,
united with love for humanity and prayer. Had the
Jesuits been left alone, it is doubtful whether the Spanish-American province would have revolted so soon, for
they were devoted servants of the crown and had great
influence with all classes — too great to suit royalty,
but such as after all might have saved royalty in these
parts." Indeed, when the Society was re-established

in 1814, Spain had already lost nearly all of its American colonies. The punishment had rapidly followed the crime.

Although Mexico and the Philippines are geographically far apart, yet ecclesiastically one depended on the other. Legaspi, who took possession of the islands in 1571, built his fleet in Mexico, and also drafted his sailors there. Andrés de Urdaneta, the first apostle of the Philippines, was an Augustinian friar in Mexico who accompanied Legaspi as his chaplain. Twenty years after that expedition, the Jesuits built their first house in Manila, and Father Sánchez, who was, as we have said, one of the supervisors of the great tunnel, was sent as superior from Mexico to Manila. One of his companions, Sedeño, had been a missionary in Florida, and it was he who opened the first school in the Philippines and founded colleges at Manila and Cebú. He taught the Filipinos to cut stone and mix mortar, to weave cloth and make garments. He brought artists from China to teach them to draw and paint, and he erected the first stone building in the Philippines, namely the cathedral, dedicated in honor of the Immaculate Conception of the Blessed Virgin. His religious superior, Father Sánchez had meanwhile acquired such influence in Manila as to be chosen in 1585, by a unanimous vote of all the colonists, to go to arrange the affairs of the colony with Philip II and the Pope. He brought with him to Europe a Filipino boy who, on his return to his native land, entered the Society, and became thus the first Filipino Jesuit.

The college and seminary of San José was established in Manila in 1595. It still exists, though it is no longer in the hands of the Society; being the oldest of the colleges of the Archipelago, it was given by royal decree precedence over all other educational institutions. During the first hundred years of its educational life, it counted among its alumni, eight bishops and thirty-nine Jesuits, of whom four became provincials. There were also on the benches eleven future Augustinians, eighteen Franciscans, three Dominicans, and thirty-nine of the secular clergy. The University of St. Ignatius, which opened its first classes in 1587, was confirmed as a pontifical university in 1621 and as a royal university in 1653. Besides these institutions, the Society had a residence at Mecato and a college at Cavite, and also the famous sanctuary of Antipole. They likewise established the parishes of Santa Cruz and San Miguel in Manila.

France began its colonization in North America by the settlement of Acadia in 1603. De Monts, who was in charge of it, was a Huguenot and, strange to say, had been commissioned to advance the interests of Catholicity in the colony. Half of the settlers were Calvinists, and the other half Catholics more or less infected with heresy. A priest named Josué Flesché was assigned to them; he baptized the Indians indiscriminately, letting them remain as fervent polygamists as they were before. The two Jesuit missionaries, Pierre Biard and Enemond Massé, who were finally forced on the colonists, had to withdraw, and they then betook themselves, in 1613, to what is now known as Mount Desert, in the state of Maine, but that settlement was almost immediately destroyed by an English pirate from Virginia. Two of the Jesuits were sentenced to be hanged in the English colony there, but thanks to a storm which drove them across the Atlantic, they were able, after a series of romantic adventures, to reach France, where they were accused of having prompted the English to destroy the French settlement of Acadia.

Meantime, Champlain, who had established himself at Quebec in 1608, brought over some Recollect Friars in 1615. It was not until 1625 that Father

Massé, who had been in Acadia, came to Canada proper
with Fathers de Brébeuf, Charles Lalemant, and two
lay-brothers. With the exception of Brébeuf, they
all remained in Quebec, while he with the Recollect
La Roche d'Aillon went to the Huron country, in the
region bordering on what is now Georgian Bay, north
of the present city of Toronto. The Recollect returned home after a short stay, and Brébeuf remained
there alone until the fall of Quebec in 1629. As the
English were now in possession, all hope of pursuing
their missionary work was abandoned, and the priests
and brother returned to France. Canada, however,
was restored to its original owners in 1632, and Le
Jeune and Daniel, soon to be followed by Brébeuf
and many others, made their way to the Huron country
to evangelize the savages. The Hurons were chosen
because they lived in villages and could be more
easily evangelized, whereas the nomad Algonquins
would be almost hopeless for the time being.

The Huron missions lasted for sixteen years. In
1649 the tribe was completely annihilated by their
implacable foes, the Iroquois, a disaster which would
have inevitably occurred, even if no missionary had
ever visited them. The coming of the Jesuits at that
particular time seemed to be for nothing else than to
assist at the death agonies of the tribe. The terrible
sufferings of those early missionaries have often been
told by Protestant as well as Catholic writers. At
one time, when expecting a general massacre, they sat
in their cabin at night and wrote a farewell letter to
their brethren; but, for some reason or other, the
savages changed their minds, and the work of evangelization continued for a little space. Meantime, Brébeuf
and Chaumonot had gone down as far as Lake Erie in
mid-winter and, travelling all the distance from Niagara
Falls to the Detroit River, had mapped out sites for

future missions. Jogues and Raymbault, setting out in the other direction, had gone to Lake Superior to meet some thousands of Ojibways who had assembled there to hear about "the prayer."

The first great disaster occurred on August 3, 1642. Jogues was captured near Three Rivers, when on his way up from Quebec with supplies for the starving missionaries. He was horribly mutilated, and carried down to the Iroquois country, where he remained a prisoner for thirteen months, undergoing at every moment the most terrible spiritual and bodily suffering. His companion, Goupil was murdered, but Jogues finally made his escape by the help of the Dutch at Albany, and on reaching New York was sent across the ocean in mid-winter, and finally made his way to France. He returned, however, to Canada, and in 1644 was sent back as a commissioner of peace to his old place of captivity. It was on this journey that he gave the name of Lake of the Blessed Sacrament to what is called Lake George. In 1646 he returned again to the same place as a missionary, but he and his companion Lalande were slain; the reason of the murder being that Jogues was a manitou who brought disaster on the Mohawks. Two other Jesuits, Bressani and Poncet, were cruelly tortured at the very place where Jogues had been slain, but were released.

In 1649 the Iroquois came in great numbers to Georgian Bay to make an end of the Hurons. Daniel, Garnier and Chabanel were slain, and Brébeuf and Lalemant were led to the stake and slowly burned to death. During the torture, the Indians cut slices of flesh from the bodies of their victims, poured scalding water on their heads in mockery of baptism, cut the sign of the cross on their flesh, thrust red-hot rods into their throats, placed live coals in their eyes, tore out their hearts, and ate them, and then danced in glee

around the charred remains. This double tragedy of
Brébeuf and Lalemant occurred on the 16th and 17th
of March, 1649. After that the Hurons were scattered
everywhere through the country, and disappeared
from history as a distinct tribe.

As early as 1650 there was question of a bishop for
Quebec. The queen regent, · Anne of Austria, the
council of ecclesiastical affairs, and the Company of
New France all wrote to the Vicar-General of the
Society asking for the appointment of a Jesuit. The
three Fathers most in evidence were Ragueneau,
Charles Lalemant and Le Jeune. All three had
refused the honor and Father Nickel wrote to the
petitioners that it was contrary to the rules of the
Order to accept such ecclesiastical dignities. The
hackneyed accusation of the supposed Jesuit opposition
to the establishment of an episcopacy was to the fore
even then in America. The refutation is handled in a
masterly fashion by Rochemonteix (Les Jésuites et
la Nouvelle France, I, 191). Incidentally the prevailing suspicion that Jesuits are continually extolling
each other will be dispelled by reading the author's
text and notes upon the characteristics of the three
nominees which unfitted them for the post. "Le Jeune,"
he says, " would be unfit because he was a converted
Protestant who had never rid himself of the defects of
his early education." It was not until 1658 that
Laval was named.

Meantime in 1654, through the efforts of Father
Le Moyne to whom a monument has been erected in
the city of Syracuse, a line of missions was established
in the very country of the Iroquois. It extended all
along the Mohawk from the Hudson to Lake Erie.
Many of the Iroquois were converted such as Gara-
gontia, Hot Ashes and others, the most notable of
whom was the Indian girl, Tegakwitha, who fled from

22

the Mohawk to Caughnawaga, a settlement on the
St. Lawrence opposite Lachine which the Fathers had
established for the Iroquois converts. The record of
her life gives evidence that she was the recipient of
wonderful supernatural graces. These New York
missions were finally ruined by the stupidity and
treachery of two governors of Quebec, de la Barre
and de Denonville, and also by the Protestant English
who disputed the ownership of that territory with the
French. By the year 1710 there were no longer any
missionaries in New York, except an occasional one
who stole in, disguised as an Indian, to visit his scattered
flock. There were three Jesuits with Dongan, the
English governor of New York during his short tenure
of office, but they never left Manhattan Island in
search of the Indians.

Attention was then turned to the Algonquins, and
there are wonderful records of heroic missionary endeavor all along the St. Lawrence from the Gulf to Montreal, and up into the regions of the North. Albanel
reached Hudson Bay, and Buteux was murdered at the
head-waters of the St. Maurice above Three Rivers.
The Ottawas in the West were also looked after, and
Garreau was shot to death back of Montreal on his
way to their country, which lay along the Ottawa and
around Mackinac Island and in the region of Green
Bay. The heroic old Ménard perished in the distant
swamps of Wisconsin; Allouez and Dablon travelled
everywhere along the shores of Lake Superior; a great
mission station was established at Sault Ste. Marie,
and Marquette with his companion Joliet went down
the Mississippi to the Arkansas, and assured the
world that the Great River emptied its waters in the
Gulf of Mexico. A statue in the Capitol of Washington commemorates this achievement and has been
duplicated elsewhere.

The beatification of Jogues, Brébeuf, Lalemant,
Daniel, Garnier, Chabanel and the two *donnés*, Goupil
and Lalande, is now under consideration at Rome.
Their heroic lives as well as those of their associates
have given rise to an extensive literature, even among
Protestant writers, but the most elaborate tribute to
them is furnished by the monumental work consisting
of the letters sent by these apostles of the Faith to
their superior at Quebec and known the world over
as " The Jesuit Relations." It comprises seventy-
three octavo volumes, the publication of which was
undertaken by a Protestant company in Cleveland.
(See Campbell, Pioneer Priests of North America.)

On March 25, 1634, the Jesuit Fathers White and
Altham landed with Leonard Calvert, the brother of
Lord Baltimore, on St. Clement's Island in Maryland.
With them were twenty " gentlemen adventurers," all
of whom, with possibly one exception, were Catholics.
They brought with them two hundred and fifty
mechanics, artisans and laborers who were in great
part Protestants. It took them four months to
come from Southampton and, on the way over, all
religious discussions were prohibited. They were
kindly received by the Indians, and the wigwam of
the chief was assigned to the priests. A catechism
in Patuxent was immediately begun by Father White,
and many of the tribe were converted to the Faith
in course of time, as were a number of the Protestant
colonists. Beyond that, very little missionary work
was accomplished, as all efforts in that direction were
nullified by a certain Lewger, a former Protestant
minister who was Calvert's chief adviser. The adjoining colony of Virginia, which was intensely bitter
in its Protestantism, immediately began to cause
trouble. In 1644 Ingle and Claiborne made a descent
on the colony in a vessel, appropriately called the

" Reformation." They captured and burned St. Mary's, plundered and destroyed the houses and chapels of the missionaries, and sent Father White in chains to England, where he was to be put to death, on the charge of being " a returned priest." As he was able to show that he had " returned " in spite of himself, he was discharged.

Calvert recovered his possessions later, and then dissensions began between him and the missionaries because of some land given to them by the Indians. In 1645 it was estimated that the colonists numbered between four and five thousand, three-fourths of whom were Catholics. They were cared for by four Jesuits. In 1649 the famous General Toleration Act was passed, ordaining that " no one believing in Jesus Christ should be molested in his or her religion." As the reverse of this obtained in Virginia, at that time, a number of Puritan recalcitrants from that colony availed themselves of the hospitality of Maryland, and almost immediately, namely in 1650, they repealed the Act and ordered that " no one who professed and exercised the Papistic, commonly known as the Roman Catholic religion, could be protected in the Province." Three of the Jesuits were, in consequence, compelled to flee to Virginia, where they kept in hiding for two or three years. In 1658 Lord Baltimore was again in control, and the Toleration Act was re-enacted. In 1671 the population had increased to 20,000, but in 1676 there was another Protestant uprising and the English penal laws were enforced against the Catholic population. In 1715 Charles, Lord Baltimore, died. Previous to that, his son Benedict had apostatized and was disinherited. He died a few months after his father. Benedict's son Charles, who was also a turncoat, was named lord proprietor by Queen Ann, and made the situation so intolerable for Catholics that they were seriously considering the advisability of abandoning Maryland and migrating in a body to the French colony of Louisiana. As a matter of fact many went West and established themselves in Kentucky.

Of the Jesuits and their flock in Maryland, Bancroft writes: "A convention of the associates for the defence of the Protestant religion assumed the government, and in an address to King William denounced the influence of the Jesuits, the prevalence of papist idolatry, the connivances of the previous government at murders of Protestants and the danger from plots with the French and Indians. The Roman Catholics in the land which they had chosen with Catholic liberality, not as their own asylum only, but as the asylum of every persecuted sect, long before Locke had pleaded for toleration, or Penn for religious freedom, were the sole victims of Protestant intolerance. Mass might not be said publicly. No Catholic priest or bishop might utter his faith in a voice of persuasion. No Catholic might teach the young. If the wayward child of a Catholic would become an apostate the law wrested for him from his parents a share of their property. The disfranchisement of the Proprietary related to his creed, not to his family. Such were the methods adopted to prevent the growth of Popery. Who shall say that the faith of the cultivated individual is firmer than the faith of the common people? Who shall say that the many are fickle; that the chief is firm? To recover the inheritance of authority Benedict, the son of the Proprietary, renounced the Catholic Church for that of England, but the persecution never crushed the faith of the humble colonists."

The extent of the Jesuit missions in what is now Canada and the United States may be appreciated by a glance at the remarkable map recently published by Frank F. Seaman of Cleveland, Ohio. On it is indicated every mission site beginning with the Spanish posts in Florida, Georgia and Virginia, as far back as 1566. The missions of the French Fathers are more numerous, and extend from the Gulf of Mexico to Hudson Bay, and west to the Great Lakes and the Mississippi. Not only are the mission sites indicated, but the habitats of the various tribes, the portages and the farthest advances of the tomahawk are there also. Lines starting from Quebec show the source of all this stupendous labor.

CHAPTER XI

CULTURE

Colleges — Their Popularity — Revenues — Character of education: Classics; Science; Philosophy; Art — Distinguished Pupils — Poets: Southwell; Balde; Sarbievius; Strada; Von Spee; Gresset; Beschi. — Orators: Vieira; Segneri; Bourdaloue.— Writers: Isla; Ribadeneira; Skarga; Bouhours etc.— Historians — Publications — Scientists and Explorers — Philosophers — Theologians — Saints.

To obviate the suspicion of any desire of self-glorification in the account of what the Society has achieved in several fields of endeavor especially in that of science, literature and education it will be safer to quote from outside and especially from unfriendly sources. Fortunately plenty of material is at hand for that purpose. Böhmer-Monod, for instance, in " Les Jésuites " are surprisingly generous in enumerating the educational establishments possessed by the Society at one time all over Europe, though their explanation of the phenomenon leaves much to be desired. In 1540, they tell us, " the Order counted only ten regular members, and had no fixed residence. In 1556 it had already twelve provinces, 79 houses, and about 1,000 members. In 1574 the figures went up to seventeen provinces, 125 colleges, 11 novitiates, 35 other establishments of various kinds, and 4,000 members. In 1608 there were thirty-one provinces, 306 colleges, 40 novitiates, 21 professed houses, 65 residences and missions, and 10,640 members. Eight years afterwards, that is a year after the death of its illustrious General Aquaviva, the Society had thirty-two provinces, 372 colleges, 41 novitiates, 123 residences, 13,112 members. Ten years later, namely in 1626,

there were thirty-six provinces, 2 vice-provinces, 446
colleges, 37 seminaries, 40 novitiates, 24 professed
houses, about 230 missions, and 16,060 members.
Finally in 1640 the statistics showed thirty-five
provinces, 3 vice-provinces, 521 colleges, 49 seminaries, 54 novitiates, 24 professed houses, about 280
residences and missions and more than 16,000 members."

Before giving these "cold statistics," as they are
described, the authors had conducted their readers
through the various countries of Europe, where this
educational influence was at work.   "Italy," we are
informed, "was the place in which the Society received
its programme and its constitution, and from which it
extended its influence abroad. Its success in that
country was striking, and if the educated Italians
returned to the practices and the Faith of the Church,
if it was inspired with zeal for asceticism and the
missions, if it set itself to compose devotional poetry
and hymns of the Church, and to consecrate to the
religious ideal, as if to repair the past, the brushes
of its painters and the chisels of its sculptors, is it not
the fruit of the education which the cultivated classes
received from the Jesuits in the schools and the con-
fessionals?   Portugal was the second fatherland of
the Society.   There it was rapidly acclimated.   Indeed,
the country fell, at one stroke, into the hands of the
Order; whereas Spain had to be won step by step.
It met with the opposition of Spanish royalty, the
higher clergy, the Dominicans.   Charles V distrusted
them; Philip II tried to make them a political machine,
and some of the principal bishops were dangerous
foes, but in the seventeenth century the Society had
won over the upper classes and the court, and soon
Spain had ninety-eight colleges and seminaries richly
endowed, three professed houses, five novitiates, and

four residences, although the population of the country at that time was scarcely 5,000,000.

"In France a few Jesuit scholars presented themselves at the university in the year 1540. They were frowned upon by the courts, the clergy, the parliament, and nearly all the learned societies. It was only in 1561, after the famous Colloque de Poissy, that the Society obtained legal recognition and was allowed to teach, and in 1564 it had already ten establishments, among them several colleges. One of the colleges, that of Clermont, became the rival of the University of Paris, and Maldonatus, who taught there, had a thousand pupils following his lectures. In 1610 there were five French provinces with a total of thirty-six colleges, five novitiates, one professed house, one mission, and 1400 members. La Flèche, founded by Henry IV, had 1,200 pupils. In 1640 the Society in France had sixty-five colleges, two academies, two seminaries, nine boarding-schools, seven novitiates, four professed houses, sixteen residences and 2050 members.

"In Germany Canisius founded a boarding school in Vienna, with free board for poor scholars, as early as 1554. In 1555 he opened a great college in Prague; in 1556, two others at Ingolstadt and Cologne respectively, and another at Munich in 1559. They were all founded by laymen, for, with the exception of Cardinal Truchsess of Augsburg, the whole episcopacy was at first antagonistic to the Order. In 1560 they found the Jesuits their best stand-by, and in 1567 the Fathers had thirteen richly endowed schools, seven of which were in university cities. The German College founded by Ignatius in Rome was meantime filling Germany with devoted and learned priests and bishops, and between 1580 and 1590 Protestantism disappeared from Treves, Mayence, Augsburg, Cologne, Pader-

born, Münster and Hildesheim. Switzerland gave
them Fribourg in 1580, while Louvain had its college
twenty years earlier.

" In 1556 eight Fathers and twelve scholastics made
their appearance at Ingolstadt in Bavaria. The
poison of heresy was immediately ejected, and the
old Church took on a new life. The transformation was
so prodigious that it would seem rash to attribute it
to these few strangers; but their strength was in inverse
proportion to their number. They captured the heart
and the head of the country, from the court and the
local university down to the people; and for centuries
they held that position. After Ingolstadt came Dillingen and Würzburg. Munich was founded in 1559,
and in 1602 it had 900 pupils. The Jesuits succeeded
in converting the court into a convent, and Munich
into a German Rome. In 1597 they were entrusted
with the superintendence of all the primary schools
of the country, and they established new colleges at
Altoetting and Mindelheim. In 1621 fifty of them
went into the Upper Palatinate, which was entirely
Protestant, and in ten years they had established four
new colleges.

" In Styria, Carinthia, and Carniola there was
scarcely a vestige of the old Church in 1571. In 1573
the Jesuits established a college at Grätz, and the
number of communicants in that city rose immediately
from 20 to 500. The college was transformed into a
university twelve years later, and in 1602 and 1613
new colleges were opened at Klagenfurth and Leoben.
In Bohemia and Moravia they had not all the secondary
schools, but the twenty colleges and eleven seminaries
which they controlled in 1679 proved that at least the
higher education and the formation of ecclesiastics was
altogether in their hands, and the seven establishments
and colleges on the northern frontier overlooking

Lutheran Saxony made it evident that they were determined to guard Bohemia against the poison of heresy." The writer complains that they even dared to dislodge " Saint John Huss " from his niche and put in his place St. John Nepomucene, " who was at most a poor victim, and by no means a saint." Böhmer's translator, Monod, adds a note here to inform his readers that the Jesuits invented the legend about St. John Nepomucene, and induced Benedict XIII to canonize him.

Finally, we reach Poland where, we are informed that " the Jesuits enjoyed an incredible popularity. In 1600 the college of Polotsk had 400 students, all of whom were nobles; Vilna had 800, mostly belonging to the Lithuanian nobility, and Kalisch had 500. Fifty years later, all the higher education was in the hands of the Order, and Ignatius became, literally, the *preceptor Poloniæ*, and Poland the classic land of the royal scholarship of the north, as Portugal was in the south.

"In India, there were nineteen colleges and two seminaries; in Mexico, fourteen colleges and two seminaries; in Brazil, thirteen colleges and two seminaries; in Paraguay, seven colleges," and the authors might have added, there was a college in Quebec, which antedated the famous Puritan establishment of Harvard in New England, and which was erected not " out of the profits of the fur trade," as Renaudot says in the Margry Collection, but out of the inheritance of a Jesuit scholastic.

After furnishing their readers with this splendid list of houses of education, the question is asked: " How can we explain this incredible success of the Order as a teaching body? If we are to believe the sworn enemies of the Jesuits, it is because they taught gratuitously, and thus starved out the legitimate successors of the Humanists. That might explain it somewhat, they say, especially in southern Italy, where the nobleman is always next door to the lazzarone, but it will by no means explain how so many princes and municipalities made such enormous outlays to support those schools; for there were other orders in Catholic countries as rigidly orthodox as the Jesuits. No; the great reason of their success must be attributed to the superiority of their methods. Read the pedagogical directions of Ignatius, the great scholastic ordinances of Aquaviva, and the testimony of contemporaries, and you will recognize the glory of Loyola as an educator. The expansion is truly amazing; from a modest association of students to a world-wide power which ended by becoming as universal as the Church for which it fought; but superior to it in cohesion and rapidity of action — a world power whose influence made itself felt not only throughout Europe, but in the New World, in India, China, Japan; a world power on whose service one sees at work, actuated by the same spirit, representatives of all races and all nations: Italians, Spaniards, Portuguese, French, Germans, English, Poles and Greeks, Arabians, Chinamen and Japanese and even red Indians; a world power which is something such as the world has never seen."

Another explanation is found in the vast wealth which " from the beginning was the most important means employed by the Order." We are assured that the Jesuits have observed on this point such an absolute reserve that it is still impossible to write a history or draw up an inventory of their possessions. But, perhaps it might be answered that if an attempt were also made to penetrate " the absolute reserve " of those who have robbed the Jesuits of all their splendid colleges and libraries and churches and residences

which may be seen in every city of Europe and Spanish
America, with the I.H.S. of the Society still on their
portals, some progress might be made in at least
drawing up an inventory of their possessions.

As a matter of fact the Jesuits have laid before the
public the inventories of their possessions and those
plain and undisguised statements could easily be found
if there was any sincere desire to get at the truth.
Thus Foley has published in his "Records of the
English Province" (Introd., 139) an exact statement
of the annual revenues of the various houses for one
hundred and twenty years. Dühr in the "Jesuiten-fabeln" (606 sqq.) gives many figures of the same
kind for Germany. Indeed the Society has been
busy from the beginning trying to lay this financial
ghost. Thus a demand for the books was made as
early as 1594 by Antoine Arnauld who maintained that
the French Jesuits enjoyed an annual revenue of
1,200,000 livres, which in our day would amount to
$1,800,000. Possibly some of the reverend Fathers
nourished the hope that he might be half right, but an
official scrutiny of the accounts revealed the sad fact
that their twenty-five colleges and churches with a
staff of from 400 to 500 persons could only draw on
60,000 livres; which meant at our values $90,000 a
year — a lamentably inadequate capital for the gigantic work which had been undertaken. Arnaulds under
different names have been appearing ever since.

How this "vast wealth" is accumulated, might also
possibly be learned by a visit to the dwelling-quarters
of any Jesuit establishment, so as to see at close range
the method of its domestic economy. Every member
of the Society, no matter how distinguished he is or
may have been, occupies a very small, uncarpeted
room whose only furniture is a desk, a bed, a wash-
stand, a clothes-press, a prie-dieu, and a couple of

chairs. On the whitewashed wall there is probably a cheap print of a pious picture which suggests rather than inspires devotion. This room has to be swept and cared for by the occupant, even when he is advanced in age or has been conspicuous in the Society, " unless for health's sake or for reasons of greater moment he may need help." The clothing each one wears is cheap and sometimes does service for years; there is a common table; no one has any money of his own, and he has to ask even for carfare if he needs it. If he falls sick he is generally sent to an hospital where, according to present arrangements, the sisters nurse him for charity, and he is buried in the cheapest of coffins, and an inexpensive slab is placed over his remains.

Now it happens that this method of living admits of an enormous saving, and it explains how the 17,000 Jesuits who are at present in the Society are able not only to build splendid establishments for outside students, but to support a vast number of young men of the Order who are pursuing their studies of literature, science, philosophy, and theology, and who are consequently bringing in nothing whatever to the Society for a period of eleven years, during which time they are clothed, fed, cared for when sick, given the use of magnificent libraries, scientific apparatus, the help of distinguished professors, travel, and even the luxuries of villas in the mountains or by the sea during the heats of summer. It will, perhaps, be a cause of astonishment to many people to hear that this particular section of the Order, thanks to common life and economic arrangements, could be maintained year after year when conditions were normal at the amazingly small outlay of $300 or $400 a man. Of course, some of the Jesuit houses have been founded, and devoted friends have frequently come to their rescue by gen-

erous donations, but it is on record that in the famous
royal foundation of La Flèche, established by Henry IV,
where one would have expected to find plenty of money,
the Fathers who were making a reputation in France
by their ability as professors and preachers and scientific men were often compelled to borrow each other's
coats to go out in public. Such is the source of Jesuit
wealth. " They coin their blood for drachmas."

Failing to explain the Jesuits' pedagogical success
by their wealth, it has been suggested that their popularity in the seventeenth and eighteenth centuries
arose from the fact that it was considered to be " good
form " to send one's boys to schools which were frequented by princes and nobles; but that would not
explain how they were, relatively, just as much favored
in India and Peru as in Germany or France. Indeed
there was an intense opposition to them in France,
particularly on the part of the great educational
centres of the country, the universities: first, because
the Jesuits gave their services for nothing, and secondly
because the teaching was better, but chiefly, according
to Boissier, who cites the authority of three distinguished German pedagogues of the sixteenth century
— Baduel, Sturm, and Cordier — " because to the disorder of the university they opposed the discipline
of their colleges, and at the end of three or four years
of higher studies, regularly graduated classes of upright, well-trained men." (Revue des Deux Mondes,
Dec., 1882, pp. 596, 610).

Compayré, who once figured extensively in the
field of pedagogical literature, finds this moral control an objection. He says it was making education
subsidiary to a " religious propaganda." If this
implies that the Society considers that the supreme
object of education is to make good Christian men out
of their pupils, it accepts the reproach with pleasure;

and, there is not a Jesuit in the world who would not walk out of his class to-morrow, if he were told that he had nothing to do with the spiritual formation of those committed to his charge. Assuredly, to ask a young man in all the ardor of his youth to sacrifice every worldly ambition and happiness to devote himself to teaching boys grammar and mathematics, to be with them in their sports, to watch over them in their sleep, to be annoyed by their thoughtlessness and unwillingness to learn; to be, in a word, their servant at every hour of the day and night, for years, is not calculated to inflame the heart with enthusiasm. The Society knows human nature better, and from the beginning, its only object has been to develop a strong Christian spirit in its pupils and to fit them for their various positions in life. It is precisely because of this motive that it has incurred so much hatred, and there can be no doubt that if it relinquished this object in its schools, it would immediately enjoy a perfect peace in every part of the world.

Nor can their educational method be charged with being an insinuating despotism, as Compayré insists, which robs the student of the most precious thing in life, personal liberty; nor, as Herr describes it, " a sweet enthrallment and a deformation of character by an unfelt and continuous pressure " (Revue universitaire, I, 312). " The Jesuit," he says, " teaches his pupils only one thing, namely to obey," which we are told, " is, as M. Aulard profoundly remarks, the same thing as to please " (Enquête sur l'enseignement secondaire, I, 460). In the hands of the Jesuit, Gabriel Hanotaux tells us, the child soon becomes a mechanism, an automaton, apt for many things, well-informed, polite, self-restrained, brilliant, a doctor at fifteen, and a fool ever after. They become excellent children, delightful children, who think well, obey well, recite well, and dance well, but they remain children all their lives. Two centuries of scholars were taught by the Jesuits, and learned the lessons of Jesuits, the morality of the Jesuits, and that explains the decadence of character after the great sixteenth century. If there had not been something in our human nature, a singular resource and things that can not be killed, it was all up with France, where the Order was especially prosperous.

As an offset to this ridiculous charge, the names of a few of "this army of incompetents," these men marked by "decadence of character," might be cited. On the registers of Jesuit schools are the names of Popes, Cardinals, bishops, soldiers, magistrates, statesmen, jurists, philosophers, theologians, poets and saints. Thus we have Popes Gregory XIII, Benedict XIV, Pius VII, Leo XIII, St. Francis of Sales, Cardinal de Bérulle, Bossuet, Belzunce, Cardinal de Fleury, Cardinal Frederico Borromeo, Fléchier, Cassini, Séquier, Montesquieu, Malesherbes, Tasso, Galileo, Corneille, Descartes, Molière, J. B. Rousseau, Goldoni, Tournefort, Fontenelle, Muratori, Buffon, Gresset, Canova, Tilly, Wallenstein, Condé, the Emperors Ferdinand and Maximilian, and many of the princes of Savoy, Nemours and Bavaria. Even the American Revolutionary hero, Baron Steuben, was a pupil of theirs in Prussia, and omitting many others, nearly all the great men of the golden age of French literature received their early training in the schools of the Jesuits.

It is usual when these illustrious names are referred to, for someone to say: " Yes, but you educated Voltaire." The implied reproach is quite unwarranted, for although François Arouet, later known as Voltaire, was a pupil at Louis-le-Grand, his teachers were not at all responsible for the attitude of mind which afterwards made him so famous or infamous. That

23

was the result of his home training from his earliest
infancy. In the first place, his mother was the intimate friend of the shameless and scoffing courtesan of
the period, Ninon de l'Enclos, and his god-father was
Chateauneuf, one of the dissolute abbés of those days,
whose only claim to their ecclesiastical title was that,
thanks to their family connections, they were able to
live on the revenues of some ecclesiastical establishment. This disreputable god-father had the additional distinction of being one of Ninoñ's numerous
lovers. It was he who had his *fileul* named in her will,
and he deliberately and systematically taught him to
scoff at religion, long before the unfortunate child
entered the portals of Louis-le-Grand. Indeed, Voltaire's mockery of the miracles of the Bible was nothing
but a reminiscence of the poem known as the "Moïsade"
which had been put in his hands by Chateauneuf and
which he knew by heart. The wonder is that the
Jesuits kept the poor boy decent at all while he was
under their tutelage. Immorality and unbelief were
in his home training and blood.

Another objection frequently urged is that the
Jesuits were really incapable of teaching Latin, Greek,
mathematics or philosophy, and that in the last
mentioned study they remorselessly crushed all
originality.

To prove the charge about Latin, Gazier, a doctor of
the Sorbonne, exhibited a " Conversation latine, par
Mathurin Codier, Jésuite." Unfortunately for the
accuser, however, it was found out that Codier not
only was not a Jesuit, but was one of the first Calvinists
of France. Greek was taught in the lowest classes;
and in the earliest days the Society had eminent
Hellenists who attracted the attention of the learned
world, such as: Gretser, Viger, Jouvancy, Rapin,
Brumoy, Grou, Fronton du Duc, Pétau, Sirmond,

Garnier and Labbe. The last mentioned was the author of eighty works and his "Tirocinium linguæ græcæ" went through thirteen or fourteen editions. At Louis-le-Grand there were verses and discourses in Greek at the closing of the academic year. Bernis says he used to dream in Greek. There were thirty-two editions of Gretser's "Rudimenta linguæ græcæ," and seventy-five of his "Institutiones." Huot, when very young, began a work on Origen, and Bossuet, when still at college, became an excellent Greek scholar. They were both Jesuit students.

"The Jesuits were also responsible for the collapse of scientific studies," says Compayré (193, 197). The answer to this calumny is easily found in the "Monumenta pedagogica Societatis Jesu" (71–78), which insists that "First of all, teachers of mathematics should be chosen who are beyond the ordinary, and who are known for their erudition and authority." This whole passage in the "Monumenta," was written by the celebrated Clavius. Surely it would be difficult to get a man who knew more about mathematics than Clavius. It will be sufficient to quote the words of Lalande, one of the greatest astronomers of France, who, it may be noted incidentally, was a pupil of the Jesuits. In 1800 he wrote as follows: "Among the most absurd calumnies which the rage of Protestants and Jansenists exhale against the Jesuits, I found that of La Chalotais, who carried his ignorance and blindness to such a point as to say that the Jesuits had never produced any mathematicians. I happened to be just then writing my book on 'Astronomy,' and I had concluded my article on 'Jesuit Astronomers,' whose numbers astonished me. I took occasion to see La Chalotais, at Saintes, on July 20, 1773, and reproached him with his injustice, and he admitted it."

" As for history," says Compayré, " it was expressly enjoined by the ' Ratio ' that its teaching should be superficial." And his assertion, because of his assumed authority, is generally accepted as true, especially as he adduces the very text of the injunction which says: " Historicus celerius excurrendus," namely " let historians be run through more rapidly." Unfortunately, however, the direction did not apply to the study of history at all, but to the study of Latin, and meant that authors like Livy, Tacitus, and Cæsar were to be gone through more expeditiously than the works of Cicero, for example, who was to be studied chiefly for his exquisite style. In brief, the charge has no other basis than a misreading, intentional or otherwise, of a school regulation.

The same kind of tactics are employed to prove that no philosophy was taught in those colleges, in spite of the fact that it was a common thing for princes and nobles and statesmen to come not only to listen to philosophical disputations in the colleges, in which they themselves had been trained, but to take part in them. That was one of Condé's pleasures; and the Intendant of Canada, the illustrious Talon, was fond of urging his syllogisms against the defenders in the philosophical tournaments of the little college of Quebec. Nor were those pupils merely made to commit to memory the farrago of nonsense which every foolish philosopher of every age and country had uttered, as is now the method followed in non-Catholic colleges. The Jesuit student is compelled not only to state but to prove his thesis, to refute objections against it, to retort on his opponents, to uncover sophisms and so on. In brief, philosophy for him is not a matter of memory but of intelligence. As for independence of thought, a glance at their history will show that perhaps no religious teachers have been so frequently cited before the Inquisition on that score, and none to whom so many theological and philosophical errors have been imputed by their enemies, but whose orthodoxy is their glory and consolation.

Their failure to produce anything in the way of painting or sculpture has also afforded infinite amusement to the critics, although it is like a charge against an Academy of Medicine for not having produced any eminent lawyers, or vice versa. It is true that Brother Seghers had something to do with his friend Rubens, and that a Spanish coadjutor was a sculptor of distinction, and that a third knew something about decorating churches, and that two were painters in ordinary for the Emperor of China, but whose masterpieces however have happily not been preserved. Hüber, an unfriendly author, writing about the Jesuits, names Courtois, known as Borgognone, by the Italians, who was a friend of Guido Reni; Dandini, Latri, Valeriani d'Aquila and Castiglione, none of whom, however, has ever been heard of by the average Jesuit. An eminent scholar once suggested that possibly the elaborate churches of the Compañía, which are found everywhere in the Spanish-American possessions, may have been the work of the lay-brothers of the Society. But a careful search in the menologies of the Spanish assistancy has failed to reveal that such was the case. That, however, may be a piece of good fortune, for otherwise the Society might have to bear the responsibility of those overwrought constructions, in addition to the burden which is on it already of having perpetrated what is known as the " Jesuit Style " of architecture. From the latter accusation, however, a distinguished curator of the great New York Metropolitan Museum of Art, Sir Caspar Purdon Clarke, in an address to an assembly of artists and architects, completely exonerated the Society. " The Jesuit Style," he said, " was in existence before their time, and," he was good enough to add, " being gentlemen, they did not debase it, but on the contrary elevated and ennobled it and made it worthy of artistic consideration."

So, too, the Order has not been conspicuous for its poets. One of them, however, Robert Southwell, was a martyr, and wore a crown that was prized far more by his brethren than the laurels of a bard. He was born at Norfolk on February 21, 1561, and entered the Society at Rome in 1578. Singularly enough, the first verses that bubbled up from his heart, at least of those that are known, were evoked by his grief at not being admitted to the novitiate. He was too young to be received, for he was only seventeen, and conditions in England did not allow it; but his merit as a poet may be inferred from an expression of Ben Jonson that he would have given many of his works to have written Southwell's " Burning Babe," and, according to the " Cambridge History of Literature " (IV, 129), " though Southwell may never have read Shakespeare, it is certain that Shakespeare read Southwell." Of course, his poems are not numerous, for though he may have meditated on the Muse while he was hiding in out of the way places during the persecutions, he was scarcely in a mood to do so when he was flung into a filthy dungeon, or when he was stretched on the rack thirteen different times as a prelude to being hanged, drawn and quartered at Tyburn.

Eleven years after that tragedy, Jacob Balde was born in the imperial free town of Ensisheim in Alsace. He studied the classics and rhetoric in the Jesuit college of that place, and philosophy and law at Ingolstadt, where he became a Jesuit on July 1, 1624. To amuse himself, when professor of rhetoric, he wrote his mock-heroic of the battle of the frogs and mice,

" Batrachomyomachia." His mastery of classical
Latin and the consummate ease with which he handled
the ancient verse made him the wonder of the day.
" His patriotic accents," says Herder, " made him
a German poet for all time." The tragedies of the
Thirty Years War urged him to strive to awaken the
old national spirit in the hearts of the people. He was
chiefly a lyrist, and was hailed as the German Horace,
but he was at home in epic, drama, elegy, pastoral
poetry and satire. Of course, he wrote in Latin, which
was the language of the cultured classes, for German
was then too crude and unwieldy to be employed
as a vehicle for poetry. His works fill eight volumes.

No less a personage than Isaac Watts, the English
hymnologist, makes Mathias Sarbiewski (Sarbievius),
the Pole, another Horace, though his poetry was mostly
Pindaric. Grotius puts him above Horace (Brucker,
505). He was a court preacher, a companion of the
king in his travels, a musician and an artist. He
wrote four books of lyrics, a volume of epodes, another
of epigrams, and there is a posthumous work of his
called " Silviludia." His muse was both religious and
patriotic, and because of the former, he was called
by the Pope to help in the revision of the hymns of
the Breviary; and for that work he was crowned by
King Wladislaw. His prose works run into eight
volumes. There are twenty-two translations of his
poems in Polish, and there are others in German,
Italian, Flemish, Bohemian, English and French.

Gosse in his " Seventeenth Century Studies " says
that Famian Strada who wrote " The Nightingale "
was not professedly a poet but a lecturer on rhetoric.
" The Nightingale " was first published in Rome in
1617 in a volume of " Prolusiones " on rhetoric and
poetry, and occurs in the sixth lecture of the second
course. " This Jesuit Rhetorician," Gosse informs us,

" had been trying to familiarize his pupils with the
style of the great Classic poets, by reciting to them
passages in imitation of Ovid, Lucretius, Lucian and
others. 'This,' he told them 'is an imitation of
the style of Claudian,' and so he gives us the lines
which have become so famous. That a single fragment
in a schoolbook should so suddenly take root and
blossom in European literature, when all else that its
voluminous author wrote and said was promptly
forgotten, is very curious but not unprecedented."
In England, the first to adopt the poem was John
Ford in his play of " The Lover's Melancholy " in
1629; Crashaw came next with his " Music's Duel,"
Ambrose Philips essayed it a century later; and in our
own days, François Coppée introduced it with charming
effect in his " Luthier de Cremone."

The French Jesuit Santeul was a contemporary of
Strada and Balde. He was considered the Ovid of
his time, and was as remarkable for the holiness of his
life as for his unusual poetical ability.

About this time, there was a German Jesuit, named
Jacob Masen or Masenius, who was a professor of
rhetoric in Cologne, and died in 1681. Among his
manuscripts found after his death were three volumes,
the first of which was a treatise on general literature,
the second a collection of lyrics, epics, elegies etc.,
and the third a number of dramas. In the second
manuscript was an epic entitled " Sarcotis." The
world would never have known anything about
" Sarcotis " had not a Scotchman, named Lauder,
succeeded in finding it, somewhere, about 1753, i. e.
seventy-two years after Masen's death. He ran it
through the press immediately, to prove that Milton
had copied it in his " Paradise Lost." Whereupon
all England rose in its wrath to defend its idol.
Lauder was convicted of having intercalated in the

" Sarcotis," a Latin translation of some of the lines
of " Paradise Lost," and had to hide himself in some
foreign land to expiate his crime against the national
infatuation. Four years later (1757), Abbé Denouart
published a translation of the genuine text of " Sarcotis."
The poem was found to be an excellent piece of work,
and like " Paradise Lost," its theme was the disobedience of Adam and Eve, their expulsion from
Paradise, the disasters consequent upon this sin of
pride. Whether Milton ever read " Sarcotis " is not
stated.

Frederick von Spee is another Jesuit poet. He
was born at Kaiserwerth on the Rhine on February
25, 1591, entered the Society in 1610, and studied,
taught and preached for many years like the rest of
his brethren. An attempt to assassinate him was made
in 1629. He was in Treves, when it was stormed by
the imperial forces in 1635, witnessed all its horrors,
and died from an infection which he caught while
nursing the sick and wounded soldiers in the hospital.
It was only in the stormy period of his life that he
wrote in verse. Two of his works, the " Goldenes
Teigendbuck," and the " Trutznachtigal " were published after his death. The former was highly prized
by Leibniz as a book of devotion. The latter, which
has in recent times been repeatedly reprinted and
revised, occupies a conspicuous place among the lyrical
collection of the seventeenth century. His principal
work, however, the one, in fact, which gave him a world-
wide reputation, (a result he was not aiming at, for the
book was probably published without his consent), is
the " Cautio Criminalis," which virtually ended the
witchcraft trials. It is written in exquisite Latin,
and describes with thrilling vividness and cutting
sarcasm the horrible abuses in the prevailing legal
proceedings, particularly the use of the rack. The

moral impression produced by the work soon put a
stop to the atrocities in many places, though many
a generation had to pass before witch-burning ceased
in Germany.

Perhaps it may be worth while to mention the wonderful Beschi, a missionary in Madura, whose Tamil
poetry ordinary mortals will never have the pleasure
of enjoying. Besides writing Tamil grammars and
dictionaries, as well as doctrinal works for his converts,
not to speak of his books of controversy against the
Danish Lutherans who attempted to invade the
missions, he wrote a poem of eleven hundred stanzas in
honor of St. Quiteria, and another known as the
" Unfading Garland," which is said to be a Tamil
classic. It is divided into thirty-six cantos, containing
in all 3615 stanzas. Baumgartner calls it an epic
which for richness and beauty of language, for easy
elegance of metre, true poetical conception and execution, is the peer of the native classics, while in nobility
of thought and subject matter it is superior to them
as the harmonious civilization of Christianity is above
the confused philosophical dreams and ridiculous fables
of idolatry. It is in honor of St. Joseph. His satire
known as " The Adventures of Guru Paramarta " is
the most entertaining book of Tamil literature.
Beschi himself translated it into Latin; it has also
appeared in English, French, German and Italian.

These are about the only poets of very great prominence the Socity can boast of; but though she rejoices in
the honor they won, she regards their song only as an
accidental attraction in the lives of those distinguished
children of hers. What she cherishes most is the
piety of Sarbiewski and Balde, the martyrdom of
charity gladly accepted by von Spee, the missionary
ardor of Beschi, and the blood offering made by Southwell to restore the Faith to his unhappy country.

Apart from these, Gresset also may be claimed as a
Jesuit poet, but unfortunately it was his poetry that
blasted his career as an apostle, for the epicureanism
of one of his effusions compelled his dismissal from
the Society. His brilliant talents counted for nothing
in such a juncture. He left the Order with bitter
regret on his part, but never lost his affection for it,
and never failed to defend it against its calumniators.
His "Adieux aux Jésuites" is a classic. In vain
Voltaire and Frederick the Great invited him to Potsdam. He loathed them both, and withdrew to Amiens,
where he spent the last eighteen years of his life in
seclusion, prayer and penance, never leaving the
place except twice in all that time. On both occasions
it.was to go to the French Academy, of which his
great literary ability had made him a member. In
1750 he founded at Amiens the Academy of Sciences,
Arts and Letters which still exists. It is said that
before he died he burned all his manuscripts, and one
cannot help regretting that instead of publishing he
had not committed to the flames the poem that caused
his withdrawal from the Society. For Gresset the
Jesuits have always had a great tenderness, and
it might be added here that he is a fair sample
of most of those who, for one reason or another,
have severed their connection with the Society.
There have been only a few instances to the contrary, and even they repented before they died.

In the matter of oratory, the Society has had some
respectable representatives as for example, that
extraordinary genius, Vieira, the man whose stormy
eloquence put an end to the slavery of the Indians in
Brazil, and whose "Discourse for the success of the
Portuguese arms," pronounced when the Dutch were
besieging Bahia in 1640, was described by the sceptical
Raynal to be "the most extraordinary outburst of

Christian eloquence." He is considered to have been
one of the world's masters of oratory of his time,
and to have been equally great in the cathedrals of
Europe and the rude shrines of the Maranhão. He was
popular, practical, profoundly original and frequently
sublime. He has left fifteen volumes of sermons alone.
Though brought up in Brazil he is regarded as a
Portuguese classic.

Paolo Segneri, who died in 1694, is credited with
being, after St. Bernardine of Siena and Savonarola,
Italy's greatest orator. For twenty-seven years he
preached all through the Peninsula. His eloquence was
surpassed only by his holiness, and to the ardor of an
apostle he added the austerities of a penitent. He has
been translated into many languages, even into Arabic.

Omitting many others, for we are mentioning only
the supereminently great, there is a Bourdaloue, who is
entitled by even the enemies of the Society the
prédicateur des rois et le roi des prédicateurs
(the preacher of kings and the king of preachers.)
For thirty-four years he preached to the most exacting
audience in the world, the brilliant throngs that gathered
around Louis XIV, and till the end, it was almost
impossible to approach the church when he was to
occupy the pulpit. Lackeys were on guard days
before the sermon. The "Edinburgh Review" of
December, 1826, says of him: "Between Massillon
and Bossuet, at a great distance certainly above the
latter, stands Bourdaloue, and in the vigor and energy
of his reasoning he was undeniably, after the ancients,
Massillon's model. If he is more harsh, and addressed
himself less to the feelings and passions, it is certain
that he displays a fertility of resources and an exuber-
ance of topics, either for observation or argument,
which are not equalled by any orator, sacred or profane.
It is this fertility, this birthmark of genius, that makes

us certain of finding in every subject handled by
him, something new, something which neither his
predecessors have anticipated nor his followers have
imitated."

To this Protestant testimony may be added that of
the Jansenist Sainte-Beuve in his " Causeries du Lundi."
His estimate of Bourdaloue is as follows: " I know
all that can be said and that is said about Bossuet.
But let us not exaggerate. Bossuet was sublime in
his ' Funeral Orations ', but he had not the same excellence in his sermons. He was uneven and unfinished.
In that respect, even while Bossuet was still living,
Bourdaloue was his master. That was the opinion of
their contemporaries, and doubtless of Bossuet himself.
Unlike Bossuet, Bourdaloue did not hold the thunders
in his hand, nor did the lightnings flash around his
pulpit, nor, like Massillon, did he pour out perfumes
from his urn. But he was the orator, such as he
alone could have been, who for thirty-four years in
succession could preach and be useful. He did not
spend himself all at once, did not gain lustre by a
few achievements, nor startle by some of those splendid
utterances which carry men away and evoke their
plaudits; but he lasted; he built up with perfect
surety; he kept on incessantly, and his power was like
an army whose work is not merely to gain one or two
battles, but to establish itself in the heart of the
enemy's country and stay there. That is the wonderful achievement of the man whom his contemporaries
called ' The Great Bourdaloue ', and whom people
obstinately persist in describing as ' the judicious and
estimable Bourdaloue.'

" He had what was called the *imperatoria virtus*,
that sovereign quality of a general who rules every
alignment and every step of his soldiers, so that nothing
moves them but his command. Such is the impres-

sion conveyed by the structure of his discourses; by their dialectical form, by their solid demonstrations, which move forward from the start, first by pushing ahead the advance corps, then dividing his battalions into two or three groups, and finally establishing a line of battle facing the consciences of his hearers. On one occasion, when he was about to preach at St. Sulpice there was a noise in the church because of the crowd, when above the tumult the voice of Condé was heard, shouting, as Bourdaloue entered the pulpit: ' Silence! Behold the enemy!' "

We may subjoin to these two appreciations the judgment of the Abbé Maury, himself a great orator. He is cited by Sainte-Beuve: " Bourdaloue is more equal and restrained than Bossuet in the beauty and incomparable richness of his designs and plans, which seem like unique conceptions in the art and control of a discourse wherein he is without a rival; in his dialectic power, in his didactic and steady progress, in his ever increasing strength, in his exact and serried logic, and in the sustained eloquence of his ratiocination, in the solidity and opulence of his doctrinal preaching he is inexhaustible and unapproachable." Sainte-Beuve adds to this eulogy: " Bourdaloue's life and example proclaim with a still louder emphasis, that to be eloquent to the end, to be so, both far and near, to wield authority and to compel attention, whether on great or startling, simple or useful themes, you must have what is the principle and source of it all, the virtue of Bourdaloue."

With the exception of Padre Isla, the satirist, and Baltasar Gracián, the author of "Wordly Wisdom" and of "El Criticón," which seems to have suggested Robinson Crusoe to Defoe, the Society has not produced any very remarkable prose writer in the lighter kind of literature, and perhaps even their style in other kinds

of writing may have suffered because of the intensity
and rapidity with which they were compelled to work.
Nevertheless some of them are said to be classics in
their respective languages as, for instance, Vieira in
Portuguese, Ribadeneira in Spanish, and Skarga in
Polish. The Frenchman, Dominique Bouhours, is perhaps the one who is most remarkable in this respect.
Petit de Julleville in his " Histoire de la langue et
de la littérature française " says that " Bouhours was
incontestably the master of correct writing in his
generation. The statutes of the Jesuits prevented
him from being an Academician, but he ' was something
better,' as someone said when the Father was striving
to evade him: ' Academiam tu mihi solus facis —
For me you constitute the Academy.' Not only in
his Order was he considered the official censor, under
whose eyes all sorts of writings had to pass, even those
of Maimbourg and Bourdaloue, but people came
from all parts of the literary world to consult him.
Saint-Evremond and Bossuet were only too glad
to be guided by him. The President Lamoigno submitted to him his official pronouncements, and Racine
sent his poems with the request to ' mark the faults
that might have been made in the language of which
you are one of the most excellent judges.' In the
history of the French language Bouhours left no date —
he made an epoch."

The Jesuits were also literary arbiters in countries
and surroundings where there was no Bouhours.
Thus the Society had four or five hundred grammarians
and lexicographers of the languages of almost every
race under the sun. Wherever the missionaries went,
their first care was to compile a dictionary and make
a grammar of the speech of the natives among whom
they were laboring, and if the learned world at present
knows anything at all of the language of vast numbers

of aboriginal tribes who have now vanished from the earth, it is due to the labors of the Jesuit missionaries.

But this was only an infinitesimal part of their literary output. In his " Bibliothèque des écrivains de la compagnie de Jésus," which is itself a stupendous literary achievement, Sommervogel has already drawn up a list of 120,000 Jesuit authors and he has restricted himself to those who have ceased from their labors on earth and are now only busy in reading the book of life. Nor do these 120,000 authors merely connote 120,000 books; for some of these writers were most prolific in their publications. The illustrious Gretser, for instance, " the Hammer of Heretics," as he was called, is credited with two hundred and twenty-nine titles of printed works and thirty-nine MSS. which range over the whole field of erudition open to his times: archæology, numismatics, theology, philology, polemics, liturgy, and so on. Kircher, who died in 1680, wrote about everything. During the time he sojourned in Rome, he issued forty-four folio volumes on subjects that are bewildering in their diversity and originality: hieroglyphics, astronomy, astrology, medico-physics, linguistics, ethnology, horoscopy, and what not else besides. We owe to him the earliest counting-machine, and it was he who perfected the Aeolian harp, the speaking tube, and the microscope.

We have chosen these great men merely as examples of the literary activity of the Society during the seventeenth and eighteenth centuries. Indeed, this inundation of books grew so alarming in its proportions that the enemies of the Church complained that it was a plot of the Jesuits who, being unable to suppress other books, had determined to deluge the world with their own publications.

In the domain of church history they have, it is true, nothing to compare, in size, with the thirty volumes

of the Dominican Natalis Alexander; the thirty-six
of Fleury; or the twenty-eight of the "España Sagrada"
of the Augustinian Flórez, which, under his continuator, Risco, reached forty volumes. Bérault-
Bercastel, indeed, wrote twenty-eight, but it was after
the Society was suppressed. Perhaps they refrained
from entering that field because they regarded it to be
sufficiently covered, or because, in order to devote
one's self to historical work, one needs leisure, great
libraries, and security of possession. Their absorbing
pedagogical and missionary work left leisure to but
a few Jesuits in those stirring times, and they were
besides being continually despoiled of the great libraries
they had gathered, and never sure of having a roof
over their heads the day after a work might be begun.
Seizures and expulsions form a continual series in the
Society's history. On the other hand, they were
making history by their explorations, and the letters
they sent from all parts of the world which according
to rule they were compelled to write, furnish to-day
and for all time, the most invaluable historical data
for every part of the globe. As a matter of fact, they
had not even time to write an account of their own
Order. Cordara, Orlandini, Jouvancy, and Sacchini
cover only limited periods, and as has been remarked
above, it was not until Father Martín ordered a complete series of histories of the various sections of the
Society that the work was undertaken. This is
planned on a much vaster scale than the older writers
ever dreamt of, and some of the volumes have already
been published.

In profane history, however, the versatile Famian
Strada distinguished himself in 1632 by his " Wars of
Flanders," and the work was continued by two of his
religious brethren, Dondini and Gallucio. Clavigero's
" Ancient History of Mexico," in three quarto volumes,

24

published after the Suppression, is a notable work,
as are also his " History of California," and a third
on the " Spanish Conquest." Alegre's three volumes,
" History of the Society of Jesus in New Spain" is of
great value. Mariana's complete " History of Spain,"
in twenty-five books, is still recognized as an authority,
and it will be of interest to know that as late as
1888 a statue was erected at Talavera, in honor of
the same tumultuous writer, who was incarcerated for
his book on " Finance." Charlevoix's voluminous
histories of New France, of Japan, of Paraguay, and
of Santo Domingo are also worthy of consideration.
Bancroft frequently refers to him as a valuable historian, and John Gilmary Shea insists that he is too
generally esteemed to need commendation.

There is, however, an historical work of the Society
which has no peer in literature: the great hagiological
collection known as the " Acta Sanctorum " of the
Bollandists, which was begun in the first years of
the seventeenth century, and is still being elaborated.
It consists at present of sixty-four folio volumes.
This vast enterprise was conceived by the Belgian
Father Rosweyde, but is known as the work of the
Bollandists, from the name of Rosweyde's immediate
successor, Bollandus. When the first volume, which
was very diminutive when compared with the present
massive tomes, was sent to Cardinal Bellarmine, he
exclaimed: " this man wants to live three hundred
years." He regarded the plan as chimerical, but it has
been realized by a self-perpetuating association of
Jesuits living at Brussels. When one member is worn
out or dies, someone else is appointed to fill the gap,
and so the work goes on uninterruptedly. The two
first volumes, containing pages, which appeared in
1643, aroused the enthusiasm of the scientific world,
and Pope Alexander VII publicly testified that " there

had never been undertaken a work more glorious or more useful to the Church."

In other fields of work the Society has not been idle. Even the acrid " Realencyclopädie fur protestantische Theologie und Kirche " says (VIII, 758), " the Order has not lacked scholars. It can point to a long series of brilliant names among its members, but they have only given real aid to the advancement of science in those spheres which have close connection with the doctrines of the Church, such as mathematics, the natural sciences, chronology, explanation of classical writers and inscriptions. The service of Jesuit astronomers like Christopher Schlüssel (Clavius), the corrector of the calendar; Christopher Schreiner, the discoverer of the sun spots; Francesco Da Vico, the discoverer of a comet and observer of the transit of Venus; Angelo Secchi, the investigator of the sun, and a meteorologist, are universally acknowledged. And no less credit is given to the services of the Order afforded by the optician Grimaldi; and that much praised all-round scholar and universal genius (Doctor centum artium) Athanasius Kircher. Among the classical writers is Angelo Mai."

This is certainly not a bad list from an unfriendly source, and possibly might be helped out by a few suggestions. Thus Otto Hartig, the Assistant Librarian of the Royal Library of Munich, tells us in " The Catholic Encyclopedia " that Ritter very justly traces the source and beginning of modern geography to the " Acta Sanctorum " of the Jesuit Bollandists, who gathered up the crude notes of the journeys of the early missionaries with their valuable information about the customs, language and religion of the inhabitants on the frontiers of the Roman Empire, along the Rhine and Danube, of the British Isles, Russia, Poland, the Faröe Islands, Iceland and the

Far East. Another signal contribution to geography
was the " Historia naturaly moral de las Indias " of
José d'Acosta, one of the most brilliant writers on the
natural history of the New World and the customs
of the Indians. The first thorough exploration of
Brazil was made by Jesuit missionaries led by Father
Ferre (1599-1632). The Portuguese priests, Alvares
and Bermuder, who went to Abyssinia on an embassy
to the king of that country, were followed by the Jesuits.
Fernandes crossed southern Abyssinia in 1613, and set
foot in regions which until recently were closed to
Europeans. Páez and Lobo were the first to reach the
sources of the Blue Nile, and as early as the middle
of the seventeenth century they with Almeida,
Menendes and Teles drew up a map of Abyssinia which
is considered the best produced before the time of
Abbadie (1810-97). The Jesuit missionaries, Machado,
Affonso and Paiva, in 1630 endeavored to establish
communications between Abyssinia and the Congo;
Ricci and Schall, both of whom were learned
astronomers, made a cartographic survey of China.
Ricci is commonly known as the Geographer of China,
and is compared to Marco Polo. Andrada was the first
to enter Tibet, a feat which was not repeated until
our own times. The Jesuits of Canada, among whom
was Marquette, were the first to furnish the learned
world with information about upper North America;
Mexico and California as far as the Rio Grande, were
travelled by Kino (1644-1711), Sedlmayer (1703-79)
and Baegert (1717-77); and the Jesuit, Wolfgang
Beyer, reached Lake Titicaca between 1752 and 1766 —
eighty years before the celebrated globe-navigator
Meyer arrived there. Ramion sailed up the Cassi-
quiare, from the Río Negro to the Orinoco in 1744,
and thus anticipated La Condamine, Humboldt, and
Bonpland. Samuel Fritz in 1684 established the

importance of the Maranhão as the main tributary of the Amazon, and drew the first map of the country. Techo (1673), Harques (1687), and Durán (1638) told the world all about Paraguay, and d'Ovaglia (1646) about Chile. Gruber and d'Orville reached Lhasa from Pekin, and went down into India through the Himalaya passes.

Possibly it is worth while here to give more than a passing notice to the ascent of the Nile in the seventeenth century, made by the noted Pedro Páez, a Spanish Jesuit. He left an account of it which Kircher published in his " Œdipus Ægyptiacus " but which James Bruce angrily described as an invention. Bruce claims that he himself was the first to explore the river. But Bruce followed Páez by at least 150 years. The question is discussed at length by two writers in the " Biographie universelle," under the titles " Bruce " and " Paez."

Páez was born at Olmeda in 1564. He entered the Society when he was eighteen years of age and was sent to Goa in 1588. He was assigned to attempt an entry of Abyssinia; to facilitate his work, he assumed the dress of an Armenian. He had to wait a year for a ship at Ormuz, and when, at last, he embarked he was captured by an Arab pirate, ill-treated and thrown into prison. As he was unable to procure a ransom, he spent seven years chained to the oar as a galley slave, but was finally set free and reached Goa in 1596. He was then employed in several missions of Hindostan, but again set out for Abyssinia which he reached in 1603. To acquaint himself with the language of the people he buried himself in a monastery of Monophysite monks, and then began to give public lessons in the city. His success as a teacher attracted attention, and he was finally called before the emperor, where his eloquence and correctness of speech capti-

vated and ultimately helped to convert the monarch.
A grant of land was given him at Gorgora where he
built a church. The question of the sources of the
Nile was frequently discussed, and in 1618 Páez
ascended the river. He was thus the first modern
European to make the attempt. He told the story in
the two large octavos, which at the time of the Suppression could be found in most of the libraries of the
Society. Bruce asserts, however, that nothing is said
in these volumes about the discovery, and he accuses
Kircher of imposture. But, says the writer in the
" Biographie universelle," the fact is that between
the account of Páez and that of Bruce there is scarcely
any difference except in a few insignificant details; so
that if Bruce is right, so also are Páez and Kircher.
Páez explored the river as early as 1618, whereas Bruce
arrived there only in 1772, that is 154 years later,
" Bruce," says another writer " makes it clear that
someone had preceded him and displays his temper in
every line."

The great English work, " The Dictionary of National Biography," handles Bruce more severely.
" He was in error," it says, " in regarding himself
as the first European who had reached these fountains.
Pedro Páez, the Jesuit, had undoubtedly done so in
1615, and Bruce's unhandsome attempt to throw
doubt on the fact only proves that love of fame is not
literally the last infirmity of noble minds, but may
bring much more unlovely symptoms in its train.
He was endowed with excellent abilities, but was
swayed to an undue degree by self-esteem and thirst
for fame. He was uncandid to those he regarded as
rivals, and vanity and the passion for the picturesque
led him to embellish minor particulars and perhaps in
some instances to invent them. He delayed for
twelve years the composition of his narrative and then

dictated it to an amanuensis, indolently omitting to refer to the original journals and hence frequently making a lamentable confusion of facts and dates. His report is highly idealised and he will always be the poet of African travel." The book did not appear till 1790. The missionary success of Páez consisted in uniting schismatical Abyssinia to Rome in 1624. He died shortly afterwards, and, when the depraved Emperor Basilides mounted the throne in 1634, the Jesuit missionaries were handed over to the axe of the executioner. Páez, it may be remarked, was not the only one whom Bruce vilified. After Páez came the Portuguese Jesuit Jeronimo Lobo, a very interesting and lengthy account of whose daring missionary work may be found in the "Biographie universelle." The writer tells us that Lobo published his narrative in 1659, and that it was again edited by the Royal Society of London in 1688. Legrand translated it into French in 1728, and Dr. Samuel Johnson gave a compendious translation of it in 1734. The complete book was reprinted in 1798, and in the preface the editors take Bruce to task for his treatment of both Páez and Lobo. It is worthy of remark that the notice of "Bruce" in the "Encyclopedia Britannica" (ninth edition) does not say a single word either of Páez or Lobo, although both had attracted so much notice in the modern literary world.

It was due to the Jesuits that France established subventions for geographical research. In 1651 Martino Martini, kinsman of the celebrated Eusebio Kino, published his "Atlas Sinensis", which Richtoven described as "the fullest geographical description of China that we have." Kircher published his famous "China illustrata" in 1667. Verbiest was the imperial astronomer in China, and so aroused the interest of Louis XIV that he sent out six Jesuit astronomers at his own expense and equipped them with the finest instruments. One of these envoys, Gerbillon, explored the unknown regions north of China, and he, with Buvet, Régis and Jarton and others, made a survey of the Great Wall, and then mapped out the whole Chinese empire (1718). Manchuria and Mongolia as far as the Russian frontier and Tibet to the sources of the Ganges were included. The map ranks as a masterpiece even to-day. It consists of 120 sheets, and it has formed the basis of all the native maps made since then. De Halde edited all the reports sent to him by his brethren, and published them in his " Description géographique, historique, politique, physique et chronologique de l'empire de Chine et de la Tartarie chinoise." The material for the maps in this work was prepared by d'Anville, the greatest geographer of the time, but he was not a Jesuit. In addition to these works, were written fifteen volumes by the missionaries of Pekin about the history and customs of the Chinese, and published in Paris.

These Jesuit astronomers and geographers were associate members of all the learned societies of Europe, and were especially serviceable to those bodies in being able to determine the longitude and latitude of the places they described. Between 1684 and 1686 they fixed the exact position of the Cape of Good Hope and of Louveau in Siam. As early as 1645 Riccioli attempted to determine the length of a degree of longitude. Similar work was done by Thoma in China, Boscovitch and Maire in the Papal States, Leisganig in Austria; Mayer in the Palatinate, and Beccaria and Canonica in northwestern Italy. Veda published the first map of the Philippines about 1734. Mezburg and Guessman made maps of Galicia and Poland, Andrian of Carinthia, and Christian Meyer of the Rhine from Basle to Mainz. Riccioli, a distin-

guished reformer of cartography, published his " Almagestum novum ", and his " Geographia et hydro-
graphia reformata " as early as 1661. Kircher gave
the world his " Arsmagnetica " and "Mundus subter-
raneus " about the same time, and made the ascent
of Etna and Stromboli at the risk of his life, to measure
their craters. His theory of the interior of the earth
was accepted by Leibniz and by the entire Neptunist
school of geology. He was the first to attempt to
chart the ocean currents. Heinrich Scherer of Dillingen (1620–1740) devoted his whole life to geography,
and made the first orographical and hydrographical
synoptic charts. Johann Jacob Hemmer was the
founder of the first meteorological society, which had
contributors from all over the world. This list is
sufficiently glorious.

Perhaps it might be noted here that these eminent
men were not primarily seeking distinction or aiming
at success in the sciences to which they devoted themselves. That consideration occupied only a secondary
place in their thoughts and the glory they achieved
was sought exclusively to enable them the more easily
to reach the souls of men. But on the other hand,
that motive inspired them with greater zeal in the
prosecution of their work than a merely human purpose would have done. Assuredly, it would have been
much more comfortable for Ricci and Schall and Verbiest
and Grimaldi to be looking through telescopes in the
observatories of Europe than at Canton or Pekin,
where every moment they were in danger of having their
heads cut off. As a matter of fact, after more than
forty years of service for China's education in mathematics and astronomy, the only reward that Father
Schall reaped was, as we have seen, to be dragged to
court, though he was paralyzed and speechless, and
to be condemned to be hacked to pieces.

It is quite true that the philosophers of the Society have never evolved any independent philosophical or theological thought, in the modern acceptation of that term.   That is, they have never acted like the captain of a ship who would throw his charts and compass overboard, and insist that North is South because he thinks it so.   The aim of philosophy is intellectual truth and not the extravagances of a disordered imagination.   Contrary to the modern superstition, Catholic philosophers are not hampered in their speculations by authority, nor are they compelled in their study of logic, metaphysics and ethics to draw proofs from revelation.   Philosophy is a human not a divine science, but on the other hand, Catholic philosophy is prevented from going over the abyss by the possession of a higher knowledge than unassisted human reason could ever attain.   Thus protected, it speculates with an audacity, of which those who are not so provided can have no conception.   For them philosophy runs through the whole theological course, and when Holy Scripture, the pronouncements of the Church, and the utterances of the Fathers have established the truth of the particular doctrine which is under consideration, then reason enters, and elevated, ennobled, fortified and illumined, it walks secure in the highest realms of thought.   Three entire years are given to the explicit study of it, in the formation of the Jesuit scholastic, and it continues to be employed throughout his four or five years of theology.   Both sciences are fundamental in the Society's studies, and it has not lacked honor in either.   But as philosophy is subsidiary and ancillary, it will be sufficient to set forth what is said about the Society's theologians.

Dr. Joseph Pohle writing in " The Catholic Encyclopedia " tells us that controversial theology was carried to the highest perfection by Cardinal Bellarmine.

Indeed, there is no theologian who has defended almost the whole of Catholic theology against the attacks of the Reformers with such clearness and convincing force. Other theologians who were remarkable for their masterly defence of the Catholic Faith were the Spanish Jesuit Gregory of Valencia (d. 1603) and his pupils Adam Tanner (d. 1635) and Jacob Gretser (d. 1625). Nor can there be any question that Scholastic theology owes most of its classical works to the Society of Jesus. Molina was the first Jesuit to write a commentary on the theological " Summa " of St. Thomas, and was followed by Cardinal Toletus and those other brilliant Spaniards, Gregory of Valencia, Suárez, Vásquez, and Didacus Rúiz. Suárez, the most prominent among them, is also the foremost theologian the Society of Jesus has produced. His renown is due not only to the fertility and wealth of his literary productions, but also to his clearness, moderation, depth and circumspection. He had a critic, both subtle and severe, in his colleague, Gabriel Vásquez. Didacus Rúiz wrote masterly treatises on God and the Trinity, as did Christopher Gilles; and they were followed by Harruabal, Ferdinand Bastida, Valentine Herice, and others whose names will be forever linked with the history of Molinism. During the succeeding period, John Præpositus, Caspar Hurtado, and Antonio Pérez won fame by their commentaries on St. Thomas. Ripalda wrote the best treatise on the supernatural order. To Leonard Lessius we owe some beautiful treatises on God and his attributes. Coninck made the Trinity, the Incarnation, and the Sacraments his special study. Cardinal John de Lugo, noted for his mental acumen and highly esteemed as a moralist, wrote on the virtue of Faith and the Sacraments of Penance and the Eucharist. Claude Tiphanus is the author of a classical monograph on the notions of personality and hypostasis, and Cardinal Pallavicini, known as the historiographer of the Council of Trent, won repute as a dogmatic theologian by several of his writings (XIV, 593-94).

With regard to moral theology, Lehmkhul tells us that in the middle of the eighteenth century there arose a man who was, so to say, a blessing of Divine Providence. Owing to the eminent sanctity which he combined with solid learning, he definitely established the system of moral theology which now prevails in the Church. That man was St. Alphonsus Maria Liguori, who was canonized in 1839, and declared a Doctor of the Church in 1871. In his youth he was imbued with the stricter principles of moral theology, but as he himself confesses, the experience of fifteen years of missionary life and careful study brought him to realize the falseness and the evil consequences of the system in which he had been educated, and the necessity of a change. He, therefore, took the " Medulla " of the Jesuit, Hermann Busembaum, subjected it to a thorough examination, confirmed it by internal reasons and external authority, and then published a work which was received with universal applause, and whose doctrine is entirely on Probabilistic principles. This approval and appropriation of Busembaum's teaching by one who has been made a Doctor of the Church is a sufficient vindication of the doctrine of Probabilism, for which the Society suffered so much, and is at the same time a magnificent tribute to the greatness of Busembaum, " whose book," Lemkuhl contents himself with saying, " was widely used," whereas forty editions of it had been issued during the author's own life, which happened to be an entire century before the publication of Liguori's great work. Busembaum's " Medulla " was printed in 1645, and Liguori's " Moral Theology " in 1748.

Up to 1845, there were 200 editions of Busembaum; that is, one edition for every year of its existence. In the history of moral theology Sánchez, Layman, Azor, Castro Palao, Torres, Escobar also may be cited as leading lights.

In Scripture there are the illustrious names of Maldonado, Ribera, Prado, Pereira, Sancio and Pineda. Of the saintly Cornelius a Lapide (Vanden Steen) a Protestant critic, Goetzius, said in 1699: ". He is the most important of Catholic Scriptural writers." His " Commentary of the Apocalypse " has been translated into Arabic. In ascetical theology, St. Ignatius is a leader in modern times; and his " Spiritual Exercises " form a complete system of asceticism. With him are a great number of his sons, whose names are familiar in every religious house, such as Bellarmine, Rodríguez, Alvarez de Paz, Gaudier, da Ponte, Lessius, Lancicius, Surin, Saint-Jure, Neumayr, Dirckink, Scaramelli, Nieremberg and many others. Finally, it can not be denied that the Society has hearkened to the second rule of the Summary of its Constitutions, which is read publicly and with an unfailing regularity every month of the year, in every one of its houses throughout the world, namely: that " the End of this Society is not only to attend to the salvation and perfection of our own souls, with the divine grace, but with the same, seriously to employ ourselves in procuring the salvation and perfection of our neighbor."

The canonization of saints proceeds very slowly in the modern Church. Years and years are spent in preliminary investigations of the life, the holiness, the doctrines, and the miracles of the one who is to be presented to the public recognition of the Church. Theologians and canonists have to pass on all those points and those who testify speak only under the

most solemn oaths and the threat of dire censure
if they witness to what they know to be false. Infinite
labor has been expended before the question is presented to the Holy See. Very many of these causes
never reach even that stage, for everywhere, in its
progress, stands an official called the Promoter of the
Faith, but popularly known as the " Devil's Advocate,"
whose work consists in doing his utmost to throw
obstacles in the way of the canonization. Nevertheless,
the Society has a sufficient number on its roll of fame,
in spite of its comparatively brief and perpetually
perturbed existence, to convince the world that it is
not the maleficent organization that it is credited with
being.

At the head of the list come the two friends, Ignatius
and Xavier, dying within four years of each other:
the latter in 1552, the former in 1556. The third is
Borgia, who died in 1572. He had set aside all the
honors of the world, except that of actual royalty, in
order to take the lowest place in the Society, but he
became its chief. In charming contrast with these
three great men, are the three boy saints: Stanislaus,
Aloysius, and Berchmans, dying respectively in 1568,
1591 and 1621. Stanislaus, the little Polish noble,
travelled all the way from Vienna to Rome on foot,
a distance of 1500 miles, to enter the novitiate. He
had no money, or guide, or friends, but he arrived
safely, for the angels gave him Communion on his
journey, and he has ever since been the darling of the
beginners in religious life. Aloysius was of princely
blood, but died nursing the sick in the hospital. He is
the patron of youthful purity, and was never a priest,
though an unwise writer makes a missionary of him.
The third, John Berchmans, was neither prince nor
noble. On the contrary, it used to be the delight of
foreigners, when rambling through the little Flemish

town of Diest, to see the name of " Berchmans " on the
humble shops of hucksters and grocers, and to fancy
that some of the little lads who clattered about in their
sabots, on their way to school, were relatives of his.
His sanctity has made his family name famous in the
world. His beatification was especially welcome, because, as Berchmans was the very incarnation of the
Jesuit rule, the Order cannot have been the iniquitous
organization it is frequently said to be.

Then there are three Japanese Jesuits who were
crucified at Nagasaki in 1597 ; and in 1616 came Alfonso
Rodríguez, who had prepared Peter Claver to be the
Apostle of the negro slaves in America, and who went
quietly from his post at the gates of the College of
Minorca to the gates of heaven. Peter Claver had
to wait for thirty-eight years before going to join his
venerable friend. Besides the two St. Francises of the
early days, there are two more of that name in the
Society: the Frenchman, John Francis Regis, who died
in 1640, and the Italian, Francis Hieronymo, whose
work ended in 1716. They were both preachers to
the most abandoned classes. Hieronymo could gather
as many as 15,000 men to a regular monthly Communion, and when he entered the royal convict ships,
he converted those sinks of iniquity into abodes of
peace and resignation.

It may be noted here that St. Francis Regis had
a distinction peculiarly his own. Long after his
canonization as a saint, he was proclaimed to have
been actually expelled from the Society, and that the
public disgrace was prevented only by his death,
which occurred before the official papers arrived from
Rome. This accusation is trident-like in its wounding
power or purpose. It transfixes Regis, and kills his
reputation for virtue; then it inflicts a gash on the
Society by making it present to the Church, as worthy

of being raised to the altars, a man whom it was unwilling to keep in its own houses; finally, it assails the Church and attempts to show that no respect should be had for its decrees of canonization. It was almost unnecessary for the learned Bollandist, Van Ortroy, to show that there is no foundation whatever for this story of the dismissal of St. John Francis Regis from the Society of Jesus.

Such are the canonized Jesuits. The Blessed are more numerous. There are ninety-one of them. First in time are the forty Portuguese martyrs under Ignatius de Azevedo, who were slain by the French Huguenots in a harbor of the Azores in the year 1570. Then follow the English witnesses to the Truth. The first to die was Thomas Woodhouse, who was executed in 1573. Between that date and 1582 four others were put to death; among them the illustrious Edmund Campion. Of those who died in the persecutions of Japan, between 1617 and 1627, there are thirty-one Japanese as well as European Jesuits. Rudolf Aquaviva was put to death in Madura in 1583, and John de Britto in 1693. Two Hungarians, Melchior Grodecz and Stephen Pongracz were slain in Hungary in 1619, and Andrew Bobola was butchered by the Cossacks in 1657. There are others among the Society's Blessed who were not martyred, but would have been willing to win their crown in that way, if God so wanted. They are Peter Faber, the first priest of the Society; Peter Canisius, the Apostle of Germany; and the Italian Antonio Baldinucci, a great missionary who used to whip himself to blood, to move the hearts of the hardened sinners around him, and who lighted bonfires of bad books and pictures and playing cards in the public squares to impress his excitable fellow-countrymen. His missionary methods were somewhat like those of Savonarola.

Those who are ranked as Venerable are fifty in number, including Claude de la Colombiére, the Apostle of the devotion to the Sacred Heart; Cardinal Bellarmine; Nicholas Lancicius, the well-known ascetical writer; Julien Maunoir, the apostle of his native Brittany; and José Anchieta, the thaumaturgus of Brazil. There are, however, a great many others under consideration, among them being the heroes of North America—Jogues, Goupil, Lalande, Brébeuf, Lalemant, Garnier, Daniel, Chabanel—who were slain by the Iroquois. In the conclaves of 1605, which elected Clement VIII and Leo XI, Bellarmine was very seriously considered as a possible pope, but the fact that he was a Jesuit was an obstacle in the eyes of many. When he died in 1621, there was a general expectation that he would be canonized for his extraordinarily holy life. In fact, Urban VIII who was so rigid in such matters placed him among the " Venerable " six years after his death. His case was re-introduced for beatification in 1675, 1714, 1752 and 1832, but nothing was done chiefly because it would have angered the French regalist politicians, as his name was associated with a doctrine most obnoxious to them. In 1920 the case was again taken up.

We omit the countless thousands of Jesuits who ever since the Society was established have striven in every possible way to realize its ideals; the heroes who have hurried with delight to the most disgusting and dangerous missions they could find in the farthermost parts of the world; who have died by thousands of disease and exhaustion in the pest-laden ships that carried them to their destination or flung them dead on some desolate coast; or those who have been slain by savages or devoured by wild beasts; or who died of starvation in the forests and deserts where they were hunting for souls; or have given their lives with

25

joy for the privilege of ministering to the plague-stricken. Nor do we mention here the great phalanxes of the unknown who, without a single regret for what they might have been in the world, have endeavored to obey, to some extent, at least, that startling admonition that they hear so often: *Ama nesciri et pro nihilo reputari:* "Love to be unknown and to be reputed as nothing,"—the men who have truly lived up to that ideal in the repulsiveness of hospitals and jails and asylums, or in the ceaseless drudgery and obscurity of the class-room and the unchanging routing of household occupations.

These men have seen themselves time and time again robbed of all their possessions, hounded out of their own countries and cities as if they were criminals, their names branded with infamy and a by-word for all that is vile, and they understood better and better, as time went on, what is meant by that page which stares at them from their rule book and which is entitled: "The Sum and Scope of Our Constitutions," and which tells them: "We are men crucified to the world, and to whom the world is crucified; new men who have put off their own affections to put on Christ, dead to themselves to live to justice; who, with St. Paul, in labors, in watching, in fastings, in chastity, in knowledge, in long-suffering, in sweetness, in the Holy Ghost, in charity unfeigned, in the word of truth, shew themselves ministers of God; and, by the armor of justice, on the right hand and on the left, by honor and dishonor, by evil report and good report, by good success and ill success, press forward with great strides to their heavenly country, and by all means possible, and with all zeal, urge on others also, ever looking to God's greatest glory."

CHAPTER XII

PROM VITELLESCHI TO RICCI

1615-1773

Pupils in the Thirty Years War — Caraffa; Piccolomini; Gottifredi — Mary Ward — Alleged decline of the Society — John Paul Oliva — Jesuits in the Courts of Kings — John Casimir — English Persecutions. Luzancy and Titus Oates — Jesuit Cardinals — Gallicanism in France — Maimbourg — Dez — Troubles in Holland. De Noyelle and Innocent XI — Attempted Schism in France — Gonzáles and Probabilism — Don Pedro of Portugal — New assaults of Jansenists — Administration of Retz — Election of Ricci — The Coming Storm.

As Mutius Vitelleschi's term of office extended from 1615 to 1645, it coincided almost exactly with the Thirty Years War. Of course, the colleges, which had been established in almost every country in Europe, felt the effects of this protracted and devastating struggle, but, on the other hand, comfort was found in the fact that many of the great statesmen and soldiers of that epoch had been trained in those schools. There was, for instance, the Emperor Ferdinand, of whom Gustavus Adolphus used to say, "I fear only his virtues," and associated with him was Maximilian, the Great, who was so ardent in the practice of his religion that Macaulay describes him as, "a fervent missionary wielding the powers of a prince." He appointed the Jesuit poet, Balde, as his court preacher, and called to Ingolstadt the Jesuit astronomer, Scheiner, who disputed with Galileo the discovery of the sun-spots — as a matter of fact, the discoveries of both synchronized with each other, but Fabricius is asserted to have anticipated both. Scheiner suggested and planned the optical experiment which bears his name, and also invented the pantograph.

Tilly, one of the greatest warriors of his time, had first thought of entering the Society, but, on the advice of his spiritual guides, took up the profession of arms. According to Spahn " he displayed genuine piety, remarkable self-control and disinterestedness and seemed like a monk in the garb of a soldier " (The Catholic Encyclopedia, XIV, 724). As he was in command of the league of the Catholic states, and was ordered to restore the lands which had been wrested from their Catholic owners, of course, he gained the reputation of being a bitter foe of Protestantism — an attitude of mind which was attributed to his education at Cologne and Chatelet. Wallenstein, his successor, was educated at the Jesuit college of Olmütz and was a liberal benefactor of his old masters in the work of education. The fact that in 1633 they saved from the fury of a Vienna mob their rancorous enemy, the famous Count de Thurn, when he was taken prisoner by Wallenstein in the Bohemian uprising, ought to count for something in dissipating the delusion that Jesuits are essentially persecutors. When the Emperor Mathias sent them back to Bohemia and founded a college for them at Tirnau and affiliated it to the University of Prague, they showed their gratitude by sacrificing a number of their men in the pestilence which was then raging.

Richelieu, who was prominent in what was called the French period of the war, was particularly solicitous in protecting the interests of his former teachers. Although politically supporting the Protestant cause, he invariably stipulated in his treaties that the Jesuits should be protected in the territories handed over to Protestant control, even when they opposed him, as for instance, in the Siege of Prague, where Father George Plachy, a professor of sacred history in the university, led out his students in a sortie and drove

back the foe — an exploit which merited for him a
mural crown from the city while Emperor Ferdinand
III sent an autograph letter to the General of the
Society to thank him for the patriotism displayed by
Plachy. Indeed, when the Protestant ministers of
Charenton wanted Richelieu to suppress the Jesuits,
he answered that " it was the glory of the Society to
be condemned by those who attack the Church, cal-
umniate the saints, and blaspheme Christ and God.
For many reasons, the Jesuits ought to be esteemed by
everyone; indeed there are not a few who love them
precisely because men like you hate them."

There is one of their pupils who, at this time, though
a man of unusual ability, brought sorrow not only on
the Society but also on the universal Church: Marc
Antonio de Dominis. He was a Dalmatian, whose
family had given a Pope and many illustrious prelates
to the Church. He followed the course of the Jesuit
college in Illyria, and amazed his masters by the
brilliancy of his talents. He entered the novitiate,
and contrary to the practice of the Society was immediately made a professor of sacred eloquence, philosophy
and mathematics. Crowds flocked to hear him;
meantime he distinguished himself in the pulpit.
Apparently he was a priest when he became a novice.
The fame he acquired, however, turned his head and
he left the Society to become a bishop, and later an
archbishop, in Dalmatia. But his utterances soon
showed that he was at odds with the Church. He was
with Venice in its quarrel with the Pope, and then
relinquishing his archbishopric, he fled to England,
where he was received with enthusiasm by James I,
who kept him at court, showered rich benefices on
him and made him Dean of Windsor. There he wrote
a book entitled " De republica christiana " (1620),
which denied the primacy of the Pope. Pursued by

remorse he went to Rome and at the feet of Gregory XV implored forgiveness for his apostasy. But his repentance was feigned. His letters to certain individuals showed that he was still a heretic, and he was imprisoned in Sant' Angelo, where he died in 1624, giving signs at the last moment of genuine repentance.

The long Generalate of Vitelleschi was clouded by one disaster: the expulsion of the Jesuits from the Duchy of Lorraine. They had opposed the bigamous marriage of the duke, but his confessor, Father Cheminot, claimed that there were sufficient grounds for invalidating the first marriage, and took the opposite side. He was expelled from the Society or left it.

During Vitelleschi's time, the famous English nun, Mary Ward, appeared in Rome. She had been a Poor Clare, but found that it was not her vocation to be a contemplative, and she, therefore, proposed to establish a religious congregation which would do for women in their own sphere what the Jesuits were doing for men. For that end she asked for dispensation from enclosure, choir duty, the religious habit and also freedom from diocesan control. As all this was an imitation of the Society's methods, she and her companions began to be called by their enemies " Jesuitesses." Their demands, of course, evoked a storm, but Father Vitelleschi encouraged them, and Suárez and Lessius were deputed to study the constitutions of the new congregation. Nevertheless, although the women were the recipients of very great consideration from three Popes, Paul V, Gregory XV, and Urban VIII, the committee of cardinals to whom the matter was referred, refused in 1630 to approve of their rules. In 1639 the little group returned to England where, under the protection of Queen Henrietta Maria, they began their work, and were approved by the Holy See. At first, they were known in Rome as "The English Ladies." In Ireland and America they are "The Loretto Nuns" (A masterly review of this incident may be found in Guilday's "English Refugees," I, c. vi).

Vitelleschi died in February, 1645, and was followed in rapid succession by Fathers Caraffa, Piccolomini, Gottifredi and Nickel, whose collective terms amounted only to seventeen years. Caraffa governed the Society for three years; Piccolomini for two; and Gottifredi died before the congregation which elected him had terminated its work. Nickel was chosen in 1652. He was old and infirm and after nine years, felt compelled to ask for a Vicar-General to assist him in his work. The one chosen for this office was John Paul Oliva. He served three years in that capacity, but as he had been made Vicar with the right of succession, he became General automatically when Father Nickel died on July 31, 1664. This departure from usage had been allowed with the approval of Pope Alexander VII. Oliva was a Venetian and two of his family, his grandfather and uncle, had been Doges of the Republic. Before his election to the office of General he had been ten years master of novices and had also been named rector of the Collegium Germanicum. He was on terms of intimacy with Condé and Turenne; and Innocent X died in his arms. His election evidently gave great satisfaction. Princes and cardinals began to multiply the colleges of the Society throughout Italy, where they already abounded. Milan, Naples, Cuneo, Monbasileo, Volturna, Genoa, Turin, Savigliano, Brera and other cities all wanted them.

It is this period from 1615 to 1664, which, for some undiscoverable reason, is described both by Ranke and Böhmer-Monod as marking the deterioration and decay of the Society. An examination of this indictment is, of course, imperative; and though it must necessarily be somewhat polemical, it may be helpful to a better understanding of the situation and give a more complete knowledge of facts. Ranke begins his attack by throwing discredit on Vitelleschi, describing him as a man of " little learning," adducing as his authority for this assertion a phrase in some Italian writer who says that Vitelleschi was a man *di poche lettre ma di santità di vita non ordinaria.*" Now the obvious meaning of this is, not that he was a man of " little learning," but that " he wrote very few letters." As he belonged to an unusally illustrious family of princes, cardinals, and popes; and as he had not only made the full course of studies in the Society, but had taught philosophy and theology for several years and was subsequently appointed to be the Rector of the Collegium Maximum of Naples, which was the Society's house of advanced studies, and as he was, besides, the author of several learned works, it is manifestly ridiculous to class him with the illiterates. As a matter of fact, Mutius Vitelleschi was a far better educated man than Leopold von Ranke.

Father Nickel, in turn, is set down as " rude, discourteous, and repulsive; to such an extent that he was deposed from his office by the general congregation, which explicitly declared that he had forfeited all authority."

It would be hard to crowd into a whole chapter as many false statements as this much and perhaps over-praised historian contrives to condense in a single sentence. For apart from the inherent impossibility of anyone who was " rude, repulsive and discourteous " arriving at the dignity of General of the Society, it is absolutely false that Father Nickel " was deposed from his office and was explicitly told that he had forfeited his authority." Far from this being the case, it was he who had summoned the congregation in

order to lay before it the urgent necessity of his being
relieved from the heavy burden of his office. On its
assembling, the first thing he did was to ask for a
Vicar because his infirmities and his age — he was
then seventy-nine years old — made it impossible for
him to fulfill the duties of his office, or even to take part
in the proceedings of the congregation. Moreover,
it is absolutely calumnious to say that the congregation
explicitly declared that he had forfeited all his authority.
Even Ranke, who makes the charge, declares that he
was guilty of no trangression; nor was the action of
the congregation in defining the Vicar's position as
" not being in conjunction with that of the retiring
General," anything else than a desire to avoid having
the Society governed by two heads. Nor did this
denote " a change in the Society's methods;" for there
had been a provision in the constitution from the very
beginning for even the deposition of a general. Again,
far from being repulsive in his manners, the congregation proclaimed him to have been the very opposite.
Indeed, all his brethren sympathized with him, especially
at that moment, because, besides the usual burden of
his office and his age, he was afflicted by the sad news
which had just reached him that three of the Fathers
who were delegates to the congregation — the Vice-
Provincial of Sardinia and his two associates — had
been shipwrecked at the mouth of the Tiber. The
words of the congregation's acceptance of his withdrawal denote nothing but the deepest reverence and
affection. They are: *Congregatio obsequendum duxit
voluntati charissimi optimeque meriti Parentis*, that is,
" The congregation deemed it proper to comply with the
desire of the most beloved and most deserving Father."

Böhmer-Monod, likewise, in spite of their joint
claim to sincerity and lack of bias, are especially
denunciatory of the character of the Society at this

juncture. " It is no longer," they say, " an autocracy, but a many-headed oligarchy, which defends its rights against the General as jealously as did the Venetian nobles against the doges. The military and monastic spirit has relaxed and a spirit of luxurious idleness and greed of worldly possessions has taken its place. Not only the writings of the enemies of the Jesuits, but the letters of their own Generals go to prove it. Thus, Vitelleschi wrote, in 1617, that the reproach of money-seeking was a universal one against the Society. Nickel also sent a grand circular letter to recall the Order to the observance of Apostolic poverty. Indeed, John Sobieski, a devoted friend of the Order, could not refrain from writing to Oliva: ' I remark with great grief that the good name of the Society has much to suffer from your eagerness to increase its fortune without troubling yourselves about the rights of others. I feel bound, therefore, to warn the Jesuits here against their passion for wealth and domination, which are only too evident in the Jesuits of other countries. Rectors seek to enrich their colleges in every way. It is their only thought.' But these reproaches made no impression on Oliva who was a sybarite leading an indolent life at the Gesù or in his beautiful villa of Albano. Even if he were the proper kind of man, he would have been powerless, for, in 1661 Goswin Nickel was deposed solely because of his rigidity towards the most influential members of the Order. The Constitution of the Order was changed, for Oliva was made General because he had humored the nepotism of the Pope."

The answer to this formidable arraignment is: — First, the General of the Society cannot be an auto-crat. He must rule according to the Constitutions; failing in this, he may be deposed by the general congregation. Secondly, the society can never be ruled by an oligarchy, especially by " an oligarchy with many heads " which is a contradiction in terms. The only oligarchy possible would be the little group around the General known as the assistants, representing the different national or racial sections of the Society. But they are invested with no authority whatever. They are merely counsellors, are elected by the Congregation, and *ipso facto* lose their office at the death of the General, though of course they hold over until the election of his successor. The metaphor of the Venetian nobles and the doges has no application in the Society of Jesus.

Nor is it true that after Vitelleschi's death, " it lost its monastic spirit " for the simple reason that it never had that spirit. The Jesuits are not monks and their official designation in ecclesiastical documents is *Clerici Regulares Societatis Jesu* (Clerks, or Clerics, Regular of the Society of Jesus). It is precisely because they broke away from old monastic traditions and methods that they were so long regarded with suspicion by the secular and regular or monastic clergy, especially as the innovation was made at the very time that Martin Luther was furiously assailing monastic orders. If, however, by " the monastic spirit " is meant the religious spirit, and that is possibly the meaning of the writers, it will not be difficult to show that piety and holiness of life had not departed from the Society. For instance, some of the greatest modern ascetic writers appeared just at that time in the Society. Thus, Suárez died in 1617, and Lessius in 1623, both of whom may some day be canonized saints. To the latter, St. Francis de Sales wrote to acknowledge his spiritual indebtedness to the Society. Living at that time also were Bellarmine, Petavius, Nieremberg, Layman, Castro Palao, Surin, Nouet, de la Colombiére, and others equally spiritual. Álvarez de Paz died in 1620, Le Gaudier in 1622, Drexellius in 1630, Louis Lallemant in 1635, Lancisius in 1636, de Ponte in 1644, Saint-Jure in 1657. Meantime, the famous work on "Christian Perfection" by Rodríguez, who died in 1616, had been making its way to every religious house in Christendom. There was also a great number of holy men in the Society at that moment. Had that not been the case, Cardinal Orsini, who died in 1627, would not have asked for admission; nor Charles de Lorraine, Prince Bishop and Count of Verdun, who had entered a few years before; nor would the Pope have made the great Hungarian Pazmany a cardinal in 1616, and Pallavicini in 1659. Blessed Bernardino Realini was not yet dead; St. John Berchmans was living in 1621; and St. Peter Claver died in 1654, before his adviser St. Alphonsus Rodríguez; St. John Francis Regis made his first vows in 1633, and Vitelleschi himself is admitted to have been a man of extraordinary sanctity. A religious order with such members is the reverse of decadent.

The "military spirit" which the Society was reproached with having lost was no doubt the daring "missionary spirit" which won her so much glory in the early days. But it was by no means lost. Andrada made his famous journey to Tibet in 1624; de Rhodes started about 1630 on his famous overland trip from India to Paris, and then set off for Persia where he died; the missionaries of North America were exploring Hudson Bay and the Great Lakes and searching for the Mississippi; those of South America were following the wonderful Vieira through thousands of miles of forests and along endless rivers in Brazil; others were searching the Congo or Gold Coast or Abyssinia for souls; Jerónimo Xavier and de Nobili were in India; others again in Persia and the Isles of Greece; and Ricci and Schall and their companions were converting China.

There were martyrdoms all over the world, like those of Brébeuf and his companions in Canada; Jesuits were laying down their lives in Mexico, Paraguay, the Caribbean Islands, the Philippines, Russia, England, Hungary, and above all in Japan, where every member of the Society was either butchered or exiled; while thousands of their brethren in Europe were clamoring to take their places in the pit or at the stake. That condition of things would not seem to connote degeneracy or decadence.

As for the "grand circular letter," which Father Nickel sent out to the whole Society, that document was nothing but an academic disquisition on the relative importance of poverty as against the two other vows. It was not a censure of the Society for its non-observance of poverty. With regard to Sobieski, it is impossible to imagine that he ever uttered such a calumny against his most devoted friends. They had trained him intellectually and spiritually; just before the great battle with the Tatars, he spent the whole night in prayer with his Jesuit confessor, Przeborowski, and in the morning he and all his soldiers knelt to receive the priest's blessing. Finally, when the bloody battle was won, they knelt before the altar, at the feet of the same priest, and intoned a hymn of thanksgiving to God for the glorious victory. When Przeborowski died, Father Vota took his place, and it was he who induced the hero to join the League of Augsburg, thus helping him to win the glory of being regarded as the saviour of Europe, when on September 12, 1683, he drove back the Turks from the gates of Vienna. As Sobieski died in Vota's arms, it is not very likely that he ever regarded his affectionate friends as " greedy and rapacious."

What Böhmer-Monod says regarding Vitelleschi's encyclical to the Society on the occasion of his election is equally unjustifiable. Not only does the General not denounce the Society for its degeneracy, but he explicitly says, "Although I am fully aware that there is still in the body of the Society the same spirit that animated it at the beginning, and moreover, that this spirit not only actually persists, but is conspicuously robust and full of life and vigor; nevertheless, as each one desires to see what he loves absolutely and in every respect perfect, we should all, from the highest to the lowest, strive to the utmost to have it free from the slightest stain or wrinkle. To urge this is the sole purpose of this epistle." Later on he says, "There are three things which help us to conserve this spirit: prayer, persecution and obedience." The second, at least, has never failed the Society.

That there was no such decadence or degeneracy later is placed beyond all possibility of doubt by a man whose integrity cannot for a single moment be questioned: Father John Roothaan, General of the Society, who wrote to all his brethren throughout the world concerning the third century in the life of the Order. Had he made any misstatement, he would have been immediately contradicted. As for his competency in the premises it goes without saying that no one had better means than he for becoming acquainted with the condition of the Society at that period. He testifies as follows:

"When the Society began its third centenary, it was flourishing and vigorous as it always has been in literature, theology, and eloquence; it engaged in the education of youth with distinguished success, in some countries without rivals; in others it was second almost to no other religious order; its zeal for souls was exercised in behalf of men of every condition of life not only in the countries of Europe, Catholic and Protestant alike, but among the savages of the remotest part of the world, nor was the commendation awarded them less than the fruit they had gathered; and what is most important, amid the applause they won and the favors they were granted, their pursuit of genuine piety and holiness was such, that although in the vast number of more than twenty thousand then in the Society there may have been a few, a very few, who in their life and conduct were not altogether what they should have been, and who in consequence brought sorrow on that best of mothers, the Society, nevertheless there were very many in every province who were conspicuous for sanctity and who diffused far and wide the good odor of Jesus Christ. It waged a bitter war against error and vice; it fought strenuously in defence of Holy Church and the authority of the See of Peter; it displayed a ceaseless vigilance in detecting the new errors which then began to show themselves, and whose object was to overturn the thrones of kings and princes and to revolutionize the world; and it bent every one of its energies of voice, pen, counsel and teaching to refute and as far as possible to destroy those pernicious doctrines. Hence it was sustained and favored by the Sovereign Pontiffs and by the hierarchy of the Church and its authority was held in the highest esteem by princes and people alike. It seemed like a splendid abiding-place of science and piety and virtue; an august temple extending over the earth, consecrated to the glory of God and the salvation of souls."

The characterization of Oliva, by Böhmer-Monod as " a sybarite leading an indolent life at the Gesù or in his beautiful villa at Albano," is nothing else than an outrage. Sybarites do not live till the age of eighty-one; nor are they summoned to fill the office of " Apostolic Preacher " by four successive Popes — Innocent X, Alexander VI, Clement IX, and Clement X; nor

do they write huge folios of profound theology; nor
do they act as advisers to popes, kings, and princes;
nor could they govern fifteen or twenty thousand men
scattered all over the world, all of whom looked up
to them as saints. Such in fact was this really great
man, and falsehood could scarcely go further, than to
pillory him in history as a degraded voluptuary. As
for his luxurious villa, it will suffice to say that the
individual who conceived that idea of a Jesuit country-
house, never saw one. It is never luxurious; but
always shabby, bare and poor.

The whole available income of the English province
at this period (1625-1743) may be found in Foley's
" Records " (VII, pt. I, xviii), and is quoted in Guilday's " English Refugees " (I, 156). " The entire
revenue in 1645 for colleges, residences, seminaries
under their charge, as well as fourteen centres in
England and Wales is recorded at something like
£3915. This sum maintained 335 persons, which
at the present rate of money would be at £34.10
per head. In 1679 after the Orange Rebellion this
sum was reduced." What was true of the English
province, may also in great measure be predicated of
the rest, especially of the one in which the General
resided.

Another curious instance of this systematic calumniation is found in the preface of a volume of poems of
Urban VIII, edited in 1727 by a professor of Oxford,
who was prompted to publish them, we are informed,
" because the poems would be an excellent corrective
of the obscenity and unbridled licentiousness of the
day." But while thus extolling the Pope, this heretical
admirer of His Holiness, goes on to say that the Pontiff
was particularly beloved by Henry IV, and when that
monarch was attacked by an assassin, " the Jesuits,
the authors of the execrable deed, were expelled from

the kingdom, and a great pillar was erected to perpetuate their infamy. Whereupon Urban, who was then Cardinal Barberini, was sent to France, and induced Henry to destroy the pillar, and recall the Jesuits without inflicting any punishment on them."

For a person of ordinary intelligence, the conclusion would be that Barberini recognized that the Society had been grossly calumniated; if not, he had a curious way of showing his affection for the King by bringing back his deadly enemies and destroying the pillar. The author of this effusion also fails to inform his readers that Pope Urban VIII was a pupil of the Jesuits; that during all his life he was particularly attached to the Order; that one of the first acts of his pontificate was to canonize Ignatius Loyola and Francis Xavier, and beatify Francis Borgia; that the Jesuit, Cardinal de Lugo, was his particular adviser, and that in the reform of the hymnody of the Breviary, he entrusted the work exclusively to the Jesuits. With regard to the expulsion of the Society from France, Henry IV had no hand in it whatever. That injustice is to be laid to the score of the parliament of Paris over which Henry had no control. Far from being an enemy he was the devoted and affectionate friend of the Society, as well he might be, for it was the influence of the Spanish Jesuit, Cardinal Toletus, that made it possible for him to ascend the throne of France.

Long before his election as General Oliva had achieved considerable reputation as an orator; and, as his correspondence shows, he was held in the highest esteem by many of the sovereigns of Europe for his wisdom as a counsellor. Unfortunately, however, nearly all the trouble that occurred in his time originated in the courts of kings. Thus in France, Louis XIV made his confessor, Father François Annat, a member of his council on religious affairs, with the result that

26

when the king fell out with the Pope, Annat's position
became extremely uncomfortable; but it is to his
credit that he effected a reconciliation between the
king and the Pontiff.   After Annat, François de Lachaise
was entrusted with the distribution of the royal
patronage, and, of course, stirred up enmity on all
sides.   In Portugal, Don Pedro insisted upon Father
Fernandes being a member of the Cortes; but Oliva
peremptorily ordered him to refuse the office.   In
Spain, the queen made Father Nithard, her confessor,
regent of the kingdom, and, German though he was,
grand inquisitor and councillor of state.   When he
resisted, she appealed to the Pope, and the poor man
was obliged to accept both appointments.   Of course
he aroused the opposition of the politicians and resigned.
The queen then sent him as ambassador to Rome,
and on his arrival there, the Pope made him a cardinal.
He wore the purple for eight years and died in 1681.
The saintly Father Claude de la Colombière, the
spiritual director of the Blessed Margaret Mary, also
enters into the category of "courtier Jesuits."   He
was sent to England as confessor of the young Duchess
of York, Mary Beatrice of Este, and though he led
a very austere and secluded life in the palace, he was
accused of participation in the famous Titus Oates
plot, about which all England went mad; and although
there was absolutely no evidence against him, he was
kept in jail for a month, and in 1678 was sent back to
France.

It was Father Petre's association with James II
of England that gave Oliva most trouble.   He was
not the confessor, but the friend of the king, who
had taken him out of the prison to which Titus Oates
had consigned him.   James wanted to make him
grand almoner, and when Oliva protested, Castlemain,
the English ambassador at Rome, was ordered to

ask the Pope to make him a bishop and a cardinal. When that was prevented an attempt was made to give him a seat in the privy councils. Crétineau-Joly not only questions Petre's sincerity in these various moves, but accused the English provincial of collusion. Pollen, however, who is a later and a better authority, insists that, if we cannot aquit Petre of all blame, it is chiefly because first-hand evidence is deficient. Petre made no effort to defend himself but the king completely exonerated him. The king's evidence, however, counted for nothing in England with his Protestant subjects. The feeling against Petre was intense and William of Orange fomented it for political reasons, and the most extravagant stories were accepted as true; such, for instance, as that the Jesuits were going to take possession of England; or that the heir-apparent was a suppositious infant. Finally, when James fled to France, Petre followed him and remained by his side till the end. " He was not a plotter," says Pollen, " but an easy-going English priest who was almost callous to public opinion." It is perfectly clear that he had nothing to do with the foolish policies of James. On the contrary, he had done everything in his power to thwart them. " Had I followed his advice," James admitted to Louis XIV, " I would have escaped disaster."

A romantic figure appears at this time in the person of John Casimir, who after many adventures ascended the throne of Poland. In spite of the remonstrances of his mother he not only refused to dispute the claim of his elder brother, but espoused his cause, fought loyally for his election and was the first to congratulate him when chosen. He then withdrew from Poland and we find him, first, as an officer in the imperial army, and at the head of a league against France. Afterwards, while in command of a fleet in the Medi-

terranean, he was driven ashore near Marseilles by
a storm; he was recognized and kept in prison for two
years, but was finally released at the request of his
brother. In passing by Loreto, on his way home, the
fancy of becoming a Jesuit seized him. He applied
for admission and was received, but left three or four
years afterwards, and, though not in orders, was made
a cardinal. When the news of his brother's death
arrived, he returned the red hat to the Pope and set
out for Poland to claim the crown, and simultaneously
that of Sweden. The latter pretence, of course, meant
war with Gustavus Adolphus, who forthwith invaded
Poland, but Casimir drove him out and also expelled
the Prussians from Lithuania. Probably on acount of
the dissensions in his own country which gave him
occupation enough, he ceased to urge his rights to the
throne of Sweden, and after some futile struggles
relinquished that of Poland likewise.

In the Convocation of Warsaw where he pronounced
his abdication, he is said to have made the following
utterance which sounds like a prophecy but which
may have been merely a clever bit of political foresight. " Would to God," he exclaimed " that I were
a false prophet, but I foresee great disasters for Poland.
The Cossack and the Muscovite will unite with the
people who speak their language and will seize the
greater part of Lithuania. The frontiers of Greater
Poland will be possessed by the House of Brandenburg; and Prussia, either by treaty or force of arms,
will invade our territory. In the dismemberment
of our country, Austria will not let slip the chance of
laying hands on Cracow." John was the last representative of the House of Vasa. He was succeeded
by Michael, who reigned only three years (1669–72)
and then the great Sobieski was elected after he and
his 20,000 Poles had routed an army of 100,000 Tatars

— an exploit which made him the country's idol as well as its king.

In becoming General, Oliva inherited the suffering inflicted on the Society by the English persecutions which had been inaugurated by Elizabeth and continued by James I. A lull had occurred during the reign of Charles I, probably because the queen, Henrietta Maria, was a Catholic; and in 1634 there were as many as one hundred and sixty Jesuits in the British dominions; but Cromwell was true to his instincts, and, between the time of the Long Parliament and the Restoration of the Stuarts, twenty-four Catholics died for the Faith. Naturally, the Jesuits came in for their share. Thus Father James Latin was put in jail on August 3, 1643, and was never heard of afterwards. "From which," says O'Reilly, "it is easy to conjecture his fate." William Boyton was one of the victims in a general massacre that took place in 1647, in the Cashel Cathedral; and two years afterwards, John Bathe and Robert Netterville were put to death by the Cromwellians in Drogheda. Bathe was tied to a stake and shot, while Netterville, who was an invalid, was dragged from his bed, beaten with clubs and flung out on the highway. He died four days afterwards.

The Stuarts were restored in 1660, but the easygoing Charles II made no serious effort to erase the laws against Catholics from the statute-book, and from time to time proclamations were issued ordering all priests and Jesuits out of the realm. Two occasions especially furnished pretexts for these expulsions. One was the " Great Plague," and the other was the " Great Fire," for both of which the Jesuits were held responsible. No one knew what was going to happen next, when there appeared in England an individual to whom Crétineau-Joly devotes considerable space, but who receives scant notice from English writers. He announced himself as Hippolyte du Chatelet de Luzancy. He was the son of a French actress, and was under indictment for forgery in his native country; added to these attractions, founded or not, he claimed to be an ex-Jesuit. Of course, he was received with great enthusiasm by the prelates of the Established Church, for he let it be known he was quite willing to accept any religious creed they might present to him. The Government officials also welcomed him. His first exploit was to accuse Father Saint-Germain, the Duchess of York's confessor, of entering his apartment with a drawn dagger and threatening to kill him. Whereupon all England was startled and the House of Lords passed a bill consigning all priests and Jesuits to jail. Saint-Germain was the first victim. Luzancy was then called before the privy council and told a blood curdling story of a great conspiracy that was being hatched on the Continent. It implicated the king and the Duke of York. The story was false on the face of it, but Luzancy was taken under the protection of the Bishop of London; he was given the degree of Master of Arts by Oxford and was installed as the Vicar of Dover Court, Essex. A most unexpected defender of the Society appeared at this juncture in the person of Antoine Arnauld, the fiercest foe of the Jesuits in France. He denounced Luzancy as an imposter, and berated the whole English people for accepting the conspiracy myth. His indignation, however, was not prompted by any love of the Society, but because Luzancy claimed to have lived for a considerable time with the Jansenists and with Arnauld, in particular, at Port-Royal.

It was probably the success achieved by Luzancy that suggested the greater extravagances of Titus Oates. Titus Oates was a minister of the Anglican

Establishment, and first signalized himself in association with his father, Samuel, who also wore the cloth, by trumping up an abominable charge against a certain Protestant schoolmaster, for which the father lost his living, and the son was sent to prison for trial. Escaping from jail, Titus became a chaplain on a man-of-war, but was expelled from the navy in a twelve-month. He then succeeded in being appointed Protestant chaplain in the household of the Duke of Norfolk and was thus brought into contact with Catholics. He promptly professed to be converted and was baptized on Ash-Wednesday 1677. The Jesuit provincial was induced to send him to the English College at Valladolid, but the infamous creature was expelled before half a year had passed. Nevertheless, he was granted another trial and was admitted to the Seminary of St. Omers, which soon turned him out of doors.

Coming to London, he took up with Israel Tonge who is described as a " city divine and a man of letters," and together they devised the famous " Popish Plot," each claiming the credit of being its inventor. It proposed: first, to kill " the Black Bastard," a designation of Charles II which they said was in vogue among Catholics. His majesty was to be shot " with silver bullets from jointed carbines. " Secondly, two Benedictines were to poison and stab the queen's physician, "with the help," as Titus declared, "of four Irish ruffians who were to be hired by Doctor Fogarthy." The Prince of Orange, the Lord Bishop of Hertford and several minor celebrities were also to be put out of the way. Thirdly, England, Ireland and all the British possessions were to be conquered by the sword and subjected to the Romish obedience. To achieve all this, the Pope, the Society of Jesus and their confederates were to send an Italian bishop to England

to proclaim the papal programme. Subsequently,
Cardinal Howard was to be papal legate. Father
White, the Jesuit provincial, or Oliva, Father General
of the Order, would issue commissions to generals,
lieutenant generals, naval officers. When the king
was duly assassinated, the crown was to be offered to
the Duke of York, after he had approved of the
murder of his royal brother as well as the massacre
of all his Protestant subjects. Whereupon the duke
himself was to be killed and the French were to be
called in. The Jesuit provincial was to be made
Archbishop of Canterbury, and so on.

No more extravagant nonsense could have been
conceived by the inhabitants of a madhouse. Nevertheless, "all England," says Macaulay, " was worked
up into a frenzy by it. London was placed in a state
of siege. Train bands were under arms all night. Prep-
arations were made to barricade the main thorough-
fares. Patrols marched up and down the streets,
cannon were planted in Whitehall. Every citizen
carried a flail, loaded with lead, to brain the popish
assassins, and all the jails were filled with papists.
Meantime Oates was received in the palaces of the
great and hailed everywhere as the saviour of the
nation." The result of it all was that sixteen innocent
men were sent to the gallows, among them seven
Jesuits: William Ireland, John Gavan, William Har-
court, Anthony Turner, Thomas Whitebread, John
Fenwick and David Lewis, besides their illustrious
pupil, Oliver Plunket, Archbishop of Armagh. As
the saintly prelate has been beatified by the Church
as a martyr for thus shedding his blood, inferentially
one might claim a similar distinction for all his companions. On the list are one Benedictine, one Franciscan and six secular priests. The Earl of Stafford
who was sentenced like the rest to be hanged, drawn

and quartered was graciously permitted by his majesty to be merely beheaded. For these murders Oates was pensioned for life, but in 1682 Judge Jeffries fined him one hundred thousand pounds for *scandalum magnatum* and condemned him to be whipped, pilloried, degraded and imprisoned for life. " He has deserved more punishment," said the judge, " than the law can inflict." But when William of Orange came to the throne he pardoned the miscreant and gave him a pension of three hundred pounds.

In his " Popish Plot," Pollock continually insists, by insinuation rather than by direct assertion, that Oates was a novice of the Society. Thus, we are told that he was sent to the " Collegio de los Ingleses at Valladolid to nurse into a Jesuit;" and subsequently " the expelled novice was sent to complete his education at St. Omers." But, in the first place, a " Collegio " at Valladolid or anywhere else can never be a novitiate, for novices are forbidden all collegiate study; secondly, St. Omers in France was a boys' school and nothing else; thirdly, the description of Oates by the Jesuit Father Warner absolutely precludes any possibility of his ever having been admitted as a novice or even as a remotely prospective candidate.

Warner's pen picture merits reproduction. Its general lines are: " Mentis in eo summa stupiditas; lingua balbutiens; sermo e trivio; vox stridula, et cantillans, plorantis quam loquentis similior. Memoria fallax, prius dicta numquam fideliter reddens; frons contracta; oculi parvi et in occiput retracti; facies plana, in medio lancis sive disci instar compressa; prominentibus hic inde genis rubicundus nasus; os in ipso vultus centro, mentum reliquam faciem prope totam æquans; caput vix corporis trunco extans, in pectus declive; reliqua corporis hisce respondentia; monstro quam homini similiora." In English this

means that the lovely Oates "was possessed of a
mind in which stupidity was supremely conspicuous, a
tongue that stuttered in vulgar speech; a voice that
was shrill, whining, and more of a moan than an
articulate utterance; a faulty memory that could not
recall what had been said; a narrow forehead, small
eyes, sunk deep in his head; a flat face depressed in the
middle like a plate or a dish; a red nose set between
puffy cheeks; a mouth so much in the centre of his
countenance that the chin was almost as large as the
rest of the features; his head bent forward on his
chest; and the rest of his body after the same build,
making him more of a monster than a man." If the
English provincial could for a moment have ever
dreamed of admitting such an abortion into the
Society, he would have verified his name of Father
Strange. On the other hand it was natural for the
fanatics of that time to adopt Oates.

During Oliva's administration, and in spite of his
protests, Father Giovanni Salerno and Francisco
Cienfuegos were made cardinals; under Peter the Great
a few Jesuits were admitted to Russia, but the terrible
Czar was fickle and drove out his guests soon after.
There was also some missionary success in Persia,
where 400,000 Nestorians were converted between the
years 1656 and 1681, the date of Oliva's death.

Charles de Noyelle, a Belgian, was now appointed
Vicar; and at the congregation which assembled in
1682 he was elected General, receiving every vote
except his own. He was then sixty-seven years old.
His first task was to adjust the difficulty between
Innocent XI and Louis XIV on the question of the
régale, or the royal right to administer the revenues of
a certain number of vacant abbeys and episcopal sees
claimed by the kings of France. Such invasions of
the Church-rights by the State were common extending

as far back as the times of St. Bernard. By 1608 the French parliament had extended this prerogative to the whole of France; but the upright Henry IV, half Protestant though he was, refused to accept it; whereas later on the Catholic Louis XIV had no scruples about the matter, and issued an edict to that effect. The Pope protested and refused to send the Bulls to the royal nominees for the vacant dioceses, with the result that at one time there were thirty sees in France without a bishop. Only two prelates stood out against the king and, strange to say, one of them was Caulet, the Jansenist Bishop of Pamiers; who, stranger still, lived on intimate terms with the Jesuits.

So far the Jesuits had kept out of the controversy, but, unfortunately, Father Louis Maimbourg published a book in support of the king, and, eminently distinguished though he was in the field of letters, especially in history, he was promptly expelled from the Society. The king angrily protested and ordered Maimbourg not to obey, but the General stood firm and Maimbourg severed his connection with his former brethren. As substantially all the bishops were arrayed against the Pope, copies of the Bull against Louis were sent to the Jesuit provincials for distribution. The situation was most embarrassing, but before the copies were delivered, they were seized by the authorities. In retaliation for the Bull, the king took the principality of Benevento, which was part of the patrimony of the Church, and thus drew upon himself a sentence of excommunication. As this document would also have been refused by the bishops, it was entrusted to a Jesuit Father named Dez, who was on his way from Rome to France.

For a Frenchman to be the bearer of a Bull excommunicating his king, especially such a king as Louis XIV, was not without danger; but Dez was equal to

the task. He directed his steps in such a leisurely
fashion towards Paris that his brethren in Italy had
time to appeal to the Pope to withdraw the decree.
Fortunately the Pope yielded, and the excommunication was never pronounced; much to the relief of
both sides. It would probably have ended in a schism;
as a matter of fact it provoked the famous Assembly
of the Clergy of 1682 which formulated the Four
Articles of the Gallican Church. These Articles were
then approved by the king and ordered to be taught
in all theological schools of France — a proceeding
which again angered the Sovereign Pontiff, who refused
to confirm any of the royal nominees for the vacant
bishoprics. The contest now became bitter, and it
is said that Father Lachaise, whether prompted by
the king or not, wrote to the General asking him to
plead with the Pope to transmit the Bulls. That
brought down the Papal displeasure not only on
Lachaise personally but on all the Jesuits of France.

In 1689 the Pope died, and the king, who was by this
time alarmed at the lengths to which he had gone,
suggested that each of the bishops whom he had named
should write a personal letter to the new Pontiff,
Alexander VIII, disclaiming the acts of the Assembly
of the Clergy of 1682. Subsequently, the king himself
sent an expression of regret for having made the
Four Articles obligatory on the whole kingdom; he
thus absolutely annulled the proceedings of the famous
gathering. The régale, however, was and is still
maintained as a right in France whether it happens
to be monarchical or republican. At present, it holds
all church property but has nothing to say about
episcopal appointments.

In 1685 the Revocation of the Edict of Nantes was
issued. It cancelled all the privileges granted to the
Huguenots by Henry IV, and Protestants were given

the choice either of renouncing their creed or leaving
the country. The result was disastrous industrially,
as France was thus deprived of a great number of
skilled workmen and well-to-do merchants; in addition
fictitious conversions were encouraged. As usual, the
Jesuits were blamed for this measure by the Calvinists
and Jansenists, and in retaliation the states general of
Holland imposed the most outrageous taxes on the
forty-five establishments which the Society possessed
in that little country, hoping thereby to compass their
ruin. But the sturdy Netherlanders drew up a formal
protest and demanded from the government an explanation of why men of any religious views, even
foreigners, should find protection in Holland while
native Dutchmen were so unfairly treated. The claim
was allowed, but the antagonism of the government,
inspired as it was by William of Orange, who recognized
that hostility to the Order was a good recommendation
to his English subjects, was not laid aside. It was
vigorous twenty years later.

The Vicar-Apostolic of Holland, who was titular
Archbishop of Sebaste, had long been scandalizing the
faithful by his heretical teachings. He was finally
removed by the Holy See; but against this act the
government of the states general protested, and ordered
the Jesuits to write to Rome and ask for the rehabilitation of the vicar. The plea was that by doing so,
they would restore peace to the country which was
alleged to have been very much disturbed by the
Papal document. The refusal to do so, they were
warned, would be regarded as evidence of hostility to
the government. De Bruyn, the superior, wrote to
the Pope in effect, but instead of asking for the vicar's
rehabilitation, he thanked the Holy Father for removing him. The consequence was that on June 20,
1705, three months after they had been told to write,

the forty-five Jesuit houses in Holland were closed,
and the seventy-four Fathers took the road of exile,
branded as disturbers of the public peace.

It was during the Generalate of Father de Noyelle,
that Innocent XI is said to have determined to suppress
the Society by closing the novitiates. This is admitted,
even by Pollen, and is flourished in the face of the
Jesuits by their enemies as a mark of the disfavor in
which they are held by that illustrious Pontiff. The
assertion is based on a Roman document, the con-
demnatory clause of which runs as follows: " The
Father General and the whole Society should be forbidden in the future to receive any novices, or to
admit anyone to simple or solemn vows, under pain
of nullity or other punishment, according to the wish
of His Holiness, until they effectually submit and
prove that they have submitted to the decree issued
with regard to the aforesaid missions." Crétineau-
Joly or his editor points out in a note that this is not
a papal document at all. The Pope would never
address himself as " His Holiness," nor tell himself
what he should do. It was simply an utterance of
the Propaganda, in which body the Society did not
lack enemies. It was dated 1684, and in the very next
year its application was restricted by the Propaganda
itself to the provinces of Italy. It was never approved
by the Holy See, and when it was presented to Innocent
XI under still another form, namely to prevent the
reception of novices in Eastern Asia, he flatly rejected it.

Louis XIV had lost the Netherlands to Spain and
in a fit of childish petulance he insisted that the Jesuit
province there on account of being half Walloon
should be annexed to the French assistancy. When
this demand was disregarded he ordered the French
Jesuits who were in Rome to return to France, as

he proposed to make the French part of the Society independent of the General. He was finally placated by a promise that men who had been superiors in France proper, should be chosen to fill similar positions in the Walloon district. It was a very silly performance.

Tirso González, a Spaniard, was chosen as the successor of de Noyelle in 1687. He had taught theology at Salamanca for ten years, and had been a missionary for eleven. He is famous for his antagonism to the doctrine known as Probabilism, as he advocated Probabiliorism. Probabilism is that system of morals according to which, in every doubt that concerns merely the lawfulness or unlawfulness of an action, it is permissible to follow a solidly probable opinion, in favor of liberty, even though the opposing view is more probable. This freedom to act, however, does not hold when the validity of the sacraments, the attainment of an obligatory end, or the established rights of another are concerned. González maintained with considerable bitterness that, even apart from the three exceptions, it was permitted to follow only the more probable opinion — a doctrine which is now almost universally rejected.

During the Generalate of Oliva, González had written a book on the subject, which was twice turned down by all the censors; whereupon, he appealed to Pope Innocent XI in 1680 asking him to forbid the teaching of Probabilism. The Pope did not go so far, but he permitted it to be attacked. Of course, González strictly speaking had a right to appeal to the Sovereign Pontiff, but it was a most unusual performance for a Jesuit, especially as the doctrine in question was only a matter of opinion, with all the great authorities of the Society against him. It must have been with dismay that his brethren heard of his election as General by the thirteenth general congregation. It appears certain, says Brucker in his history of the Society (p. 529), that on the eve of the election the Pope expressed his opinion that González was the most available candidate. That evidently determined the suffrage, though González seems to have had no experience as an administrator.

One of the first things the general did was to start a campaign against the doctrines of Gallicanism, as formulated in the famous Assembly of 1682, which every one thought was already dead and buried. His friend, Pope Innocent XI, died in August, 1689, and his successor Alexander VIII ordered González to call in all the copies that had been printed. In 1691 González began to print his book which Oliva had formerly forbidden. It was run through the press in Germany without the knowledge of his assistants; copies appeared in 1694, and threw the Society into an uproar, especially as González's appeared on the title page as " Former Professor of Salamanca and actual General of the Society of Jesus." Nevertheless, at the general congregation which met in 1697 Father González was treated with the profoundest consideration. Not a word was uttered about his doctrine and assistants who were most acceptable to him were elected. Although a few more probabiliorists subsequently appeared, the Society, nevertheless, remained true to the teaching of Suárez, Lugo, Laymann, and their school.

A quarrel then arose between Don Pedro II of Portugal and Cardinal Conti, the papal nuncio, about the revenues of certain estates. The question was referred to González, who decided in favor of the Pope, whereupon Pedro's successor, John V, closed all the Jesuit novitiates in Portugal and banished some of the Fathers from the country. González died before this affair was settled. He passed away on October

27, 1705, in the eighty-fourth year of his age. He had been a Jesuit for sixty-three years, and during nineteen years occupied the post of General.

Father Michael Angelo Tamburini was the fourteenth General; his tenure of office extended from January 30, 1706, till his death on February 28, 1730. He was a native of Modena, and had filled several important offices with credit, before he was chosen to undertake the great responsibility of governing the entire Order, at the age of fifty-eight. The troubles in France were increasing. For although the implacable leaders of the Jansenist party, Arnauld and Nicole, had disappeared from the scene — Arnauld dying at Malines, a bitter old man of eighty-three, and Nicole soon following him to the grave — yet the antagonism created by them against the Society still persisted and was being reinforced by the atheists, who now began to dominate France.

Quesnel, who succeeded Arnauld and Nicole, wrote a book entitled " Moral Reflections on the New Testament ", the style of which quite captivated de Noailles, Bishop of Châlons-sur-Marne, and without adverting to its Jansenism he gave it his hearty approval. Later however, when he became Archbishop of Paris, he condemned another Jansenist publication whose doctrine was identical with the one he had previously recommended; whereupon an anonymous pamphlet calling attention to the 'contradiction was published; in it the cardinal was made to appear in the very unpleasant attitude of stultifying himself in the eyes of the learned. He accused the Jesuits of the pamphlet, whereas, it was the work of their enemies, and was written precisely to turn him against the Society. The situation became worse when other members of the hierarchy began to comment on his approval of the Jansenistic publication, and he was exasperated

27

to such an extent that he suspended every Jesuit in the diocese. The Jansenists were naturally jubilant over their success, and began to look forward hopefully to the approaching death of Louis XIV, who had never wavered in his defense of the Society. His successor, the dissolute Philip of Orléans, could be reckoned on as their aid, they imagined, but they were disappointed. He began by refusing their petition to revoke the university rights of the Jesuits and although he dissolved all the sodalities in the army, he lodged a number of Jansenists in jail for an alleged conspiracy against the government, a measure which they, of course, attributed to the machinations of the Society.

It was during this Generalate that the Paraguay missions reached their highest degree of efficiency. In a single year no fewer than seventy-seven missionaries left Europe to co-operate in the great work. Meantime, Francis Hieronymo and Anthony Baldinucci were astonishing Italy by their apostolic work, as was Manuel Padial in Spain — all three of whom were inscribed later on the Church's roll of honor. Finally, the canonization of Aloysius and Stanislaus Kostka along with the beatification of John Francis Régis put the stamp of the Church's most solemn approval on the Institute of Ignatius Loyola. Father Tamburini died at the age of eighty-two. He had lived sixty-five years as a Jesuit; and at his death, the Society had thirty-seven provinces with twenty-four houses of professed, 612 colleges, 340 residences, 59 novitiates, 200 mission stations, and 157 seminaries. Assuredly, it was doing something for the Church of God.

Francis Retz, a Bohemian, was the next General. His election, which took place on March 7, 1730, was unanimous; and his administration of twenty years gave the Society a condition of tranquillity such as it had never enjoyed in its entire history. Perhaps, however, there would have been a shade of sorrow if the future of one of the Jesuits of those days could have been foreseen. Father Raynal left the Society in 1747 and joined the Sulpicians. Subsequently he apostatized from the Faith, became the intimate associate of Rousseau, Diderot and other atheists and died at an advanced age apparently impenitent. Before Father Retz expired, two more provinces had been added to the thirty-seven already existing; the colleges had increased to 669; the seminaries to 176 and there were on the registers 22,589 members of whom 11,293 were already priests. During this period several great personages, who were to have much to do with the fortunes of the Society, began to assume prominence in the political world. They were Frederick the Great of Prussia, Maria Theresa of Austria, the Duc de Choiseul in France, and Carvalho, Marquis de Pombal in Portugal.

Eight months after the death of Father Retz which occurred on November 19, 1750, the Society chose for its General Ignatius Visconti, a Milanese. He was at that time sixty-nine years of age and survived only two years. He was succeeded by Father Louis Centurione, who, besides the burden of his seventy years of life, had to endure the pain of constant physical ailments. In two years time, on October 2, 1757, he breathed his last, and on the 21st of May following, Lorenzo Ricci was elected. According to Huonder, the choice was unanimous, but the digest of the nineteenth congregation states that he was elected by a very large majority.

Who was Ricci? He was a Florentine of noble blood, and was born on August 3, 1703. He was, therefore, fifty-three years of age when placed at the head of the Society, whose destruction he was to witness fifteen years later. From his earliest youth, he had attracted attention by his unusual intellectual ability as well as by his fervent piety. He had been professor of Rhetoric at the colleges of Siena and Rome to which only brilliant men were assigned, and at the end of his studies he was designated for what is called the " Public Act," that is to say an all-day defense of a series of theses covering the entire range of philosophy and theology. He subsequently taught theology for eleven years and was spiritual father at the Roman College. The latter office brought him in contact with the most distinguished prelates of the Church, who chose him as the guide of their consciences. In 1755 Father Centurione called him to the secretaryship of the Society, and he was occupying that post when elected General. The regret is very often expressed that a General of the stamp of Aquaviva was not chosen at that time; one who might have been equal to the shock that was to be met. Hence, the choice of a man who had never been a superior in any minor position is sometimes denounced as fatuous. One distinguished enemy is said to have exclaimed when he heard the result of the balloting: " Ricci! Ricci! Now we have them."

It must not, however, be forgotten that the battle which brought out Aquaviva's powers bears no comparison with that which confronted Father Ricci. Against Aquaviva were ranged only the Spanish Inquisition, a small number of recalcitrant Spanish Jesuits, and to a certain extent, Philip II. But in the first place, the Spanish Inquisition had no standing in Rome; in the second, the Jesuits who were in opposition had all of them a strain in their blood, which their fellow countrymen disliked; and, finally, though Philip II would have liked to have had his hand on the machinery of the Society he was at all times a staunch Catholic. Against this coalition,

Aquaviva had with him as enthusiastic supporters all the Catholic princes of Germany and they contributed largely to his triumph.   Father Ricci, on the contrary, found arrayed against the Society the so-called Catholic kings: Joseph I of Portugal; Charles III of Spain and Joseph II of Austria, all of them absolutely in the power of Voltairean ministers like Pombal, de Choiseul, Aranda, Tanucci and Kaunitz, who were in league, not only to destroy the Jesuits, but to wreck the Church. The suppression of the Society was only an incident in the fight; it had to be swept out of the way at any cost.   A thousand Aquavivas would not have been able to avert it.   Two Popes succumbed in the struggle.

Carayon, in his " Documents inédits," describes Father Ricci as " timid, shy, and lacking in initiative " Among the instances of his timidity, there is quoted his reprehension of Father Pinto, who had of his own accord asked Frederick II to pronounce himself as a defender of the Society.   Of course, he was sternly reproved by Father Ricci and properly so, for one cannot imagine a more incongruous situation than that of the Society of Jesus on its knees to the half-infidel friend of Voltaire, entreating him to vouch for the virtue and orthodoxy of the Order.   Frederick himself was very much amused by the proposition.

In any case, the fight was too far advanced to afford any hope of its being checked.   Eight years before that time, Pombal had made arrangements with Spain to drive the Jesuits out of Paraguay, and had extorted from the dying Benedict XIV the appointment of Saldanha to investigate the Jesuits of Portugal. Indeed, it was soon discovered that Pombal's performances were only a part of the general plot to destroy the Society and the Church.

As soon as Benedict's successor ascended the papal throne, Father Ricci laid a petition before him repre-

senting the distress and injury inflicted on the Society
by what was going on in Portugal. Crimes which had
no foundation were attributed to it, and all of the
Fathers, whether guilty or not, had been suspended
from their priestly functions. The petition could
not have been more humble or more just, but it brought
down a storm on the head of Father Ricci. The sad
feature of it was that, although it was intended to be an
absolutely secret communication, it was immediately
circulated with notes throughout Europe, and a fierce
votum, or protest, was issued against it by Cardinal
Passionei, who denounced it as an absolutely untruth-
ful and subtle plea to induce the Holy Father to hand
over the rest of his flock to the ferocious wolves (the
Jesuits). The cardinal stated that the King of Portugal had complained of the Jesuits, and that Cardinal
Saldanha was a person capable of obtaining the best
information about the case, and was absolutely without bias or animosity for any party, besides being
known for his ecclesiastical zeal and his submission
to the head of the Church.

Far from being influenced by this utterance of
Passionei, Pope Clement XIII appointed a congregation to examine the question; the report was favorable to
the Society, so that Pombal was momentarily checked.
On the other hand, it was very clear that the battle
was not won. A false report of the proceedings of
the congregation was published, and although the
Pope ordered it to be burned by the public executioner,
it was, nevertheless, an open proclamation that the
enemies of the Society were willing to go to any lengths
to gain their point. Portuguese gold flowed into
Rome and Mgr. Bottari was employed to revive all
the ancient calumnies against the Society. In a
short time, he produced a work called "Reflections of a
Portuguese on the Memorial presented to His Holiness

Clement XIII by the Jesuits." When there was question of putting the book on the Index, Almada, the Portuguese ambassador declared that if such a proceeding were resorted to Portugal would secede from the Church. Furthermore, when the Papal Secretary of State, Achito, wrote a very mild and prudent letter to the nuncio in Lisbon, instructing him to let the king know that the petition of the Jesuits was very humble and submissive, he was denounced as issuing a declaration of war against Portugal. Meantime, the author of the " Reflections " continued to pour out other libellous publications in Rome itself, and Papal prohibitions were powerless to prevent him.

CHAPTER XIII

CONDITIONS BEFORE THE CRASH

State of the Society — The Seven Years War — Political Changes — Rulers of Spain, Portugal, Naples, France and Austria — Febronius — Sentiments of the Hierarchy — Popes Benedict XIV; Clement XIII; Clement XIV.

JUST before its suppression, the Society had about 23,000 members. It was divided into forty-two provinces in which there were 24 houses of professed fathers, 669 colleges, 61 novitiates, 335 residences and 273 mission stations. Taking this grand total in detail, there were in Italy 3,622 Jesuits, about one-half of whom were priests. They possessed 178 houses. The provinces of Spain had 2,943 members (1,342 priests) and 158 houses; Portugal, 861 members (384 priests), 49 houses; France, 3,350 members (1,763 priests), 158 houses; Germany, 5,340 members (2,558 priests), 307 houses; Poland, 2,359 members; Flemish Belgium, 542 members (232 priests), 30 houses; French Belgian, 471 members (266 priests), 25 houses; England, 274 members; and Ireland, 28. Their missions were in all parts of the world. In Hindostan, de Nobili, and de Britto's work was being carried on; in Madura, there were forty-seven missionaries. The establishments in Persia extended to Ispahan and counted 400,000 Catholics. Syria, the Levant and the Maronites were also being looked after. Although Christianity had been crushed as early as 1644, the name of the province of Japan was preserved, and in 1760 it counted fifty-seven members. There were fifty-four Portuguese Fathers attached to China at the time of the Suppression, and an independent French

mission had been organized at Pekin with twenty-three
members mostly priests. In South America, the
whole territory had been divided into missions, and
there were 445 Jesuits in Brazil, with 146 in the vice-
province of Maranhão. The Paraguay province contained 564 members of whom 385 were priests; they
had 113,716 Indians in their care. In Mexico, which
included Lower California, there were 572 Jesuits,
who were devoting themselves to 122,000 Indians.
New Granada had 193 missionaries; Chili had 242;
Peru, 526; and Ecuador, 209.

In the United States, they were necessarily very
few, on account of political conditions. At the time
of the Suppression, they numbered only nine, two of
whom Robert Molyneux and John Bolton survived
until the complete restoration of the Society. The
French had missions in Guiana, Hayti and Martinique;
and in Canada, the work inaugurated by Brébeuf
among the Hurons, was kept up among the Iroquois,
Algonquins, Abenakis, Crees, Ottawas, Miamis and
other tribes in Illinois, Alabama and Lower Mississippi.
At the time of the Suppression there were fifty-five
Jesuits in Canada and Louisiana.

This world-wide activity synchronized with the
Seven Years War, which was to change the face of
the earth politically and religiously. The unscrupulous
energy of Lord Clive had, previous to the outbreak of
hostilities, given Bombay, Madras, Calcutta and the
Carnatic to England. Before war had been proclaimed, Boscawen, who was sent to Canada, had
captured two French warships and the feeble protest of
France was answered by the seizure of three hundred
other vessels, manned by 10,000 seamen and carrying
cargoes estimated to be worth 30,000,000 francs. In
1757 Frederick the Great won the battle of Rosbach
against the French; and in the same year triumphed

over the imperial forces. In 1759 he defeated the
Russians, only to meet similar reverses in turn; but
in 1760 when all seemed lost, Russia withdrew from
the fight and became Frederick's friend. In 1758
France scored some victories in Germany, but in 1762
was completely crushed and consented to what a
French historian describes as " a shameful peace."
Quebec fell in 1759, and Vaudreuil capitulated at
Montreal in 1760.

Peace was finally made by the treaties of Paris and
Hubertsburg in 1763, in virtue of which, France
surrendered all her conquests of German territory as
well as the Island of Minorca. In North America,
she gave up Canada with its 60,000 French inhabitants.
She also lost the River and Gulf of St. Lawrence, the
valley of the Ohio, the left bank of the Mississippi,
four islands in the West Indies, and her African trading-
post of Senegal. In return, she received the Islands
of Guadeloupe, Martinique, Marie-Galande, Désirade
and St. Lucia. In Asia, she was granted Pondicherry,
Chandernagor and other places, but was prohibited
from fortifying them. Spain yielded Florida and
Pensacola Bay to England, in order to recover Cuba
and the Philippines; and after a while, France made
her a present of Louisiana. Thus, New France was
completely effaced from the map of America; and
France proper, while losing almost all her other colonial
possessions, saw her maritime power, her military
prestige and her political importance disappear. She
was now only in the second grade among the nations.
On the same level stood Spain, while Portugal had
long since ceased to count. Austria had declined and
Protestant England and Prussia ruled, while schis-
matic Russia was looming up in the North.

In Spain, Charles III had succeeded to the throne
in 1759. He had previously been King of Naples,

where he had reigned not without honor. It is true he made the mistake of accepting Choiseul's " Family Compact " which united the fortunes of Spain with those of the degenerate Bourbons, but he is nevertheless credited with being paternal in his administrations and virtuous in his private life. Unfortunately while in Naples, he had chosen as his minister of finance, the Marquis de Tanucci, a Tuscan who had at an early stage inaugurated a contest with the Holy See on the right of asylum. " But one seeks in vain anything on which to build the exalted reputation which Tanucci enjoyed during life and which clung to him even after death. His financial system was false; for instead of encouraging the arts, perfecting agriculture, building roads, opening canals, establishing manufactures in the fertile country over which he ruled, he did nothing but make it bristle with custom-houses. Men of science, jurists, archæologists, literary and other distinguished men, he left in prison or allowed to starve " (Biographie universelle).

Tanucci's moral character may be inferred from the fact that when entrusted with the regency at Naples, he purposely neglected the education of the crown prince, keeping him aloof from political life, and giving him every opportunity to indulge his passions. He declared war against the Holy See; he restricted the ancient rights of the nuncios; diminished the number of bishoprics; suppressed seventy-eight monasteries; named one of his henchmen Archbishop of Naples, and forbade a ceremonial homage to be paid to the Pope which had been in use ever since the time of Charles of Anjou. He governed the Two Sicilies for fifty years and took with him to the grave the execration of the nobles and the hatred of the people of the Two Kingdoms. Duclos said of him " he was of all the men I ever knew the least fitted to govern."

The Spanish ministers were very numerous and very bad. There was Wall, whom Schoell described as Irish, whereas Ranke deprives him of that distinction by classing him among the political atheists of that time. Of Squillace, little is said except that he was a Neapolitan and probably belonged to one of the branches of the Borgia family. He is the individual whose legislation caused a burlesque disturbance in Madrid about cloaks and sombreros. The Jesuits were falsely accused of being the instigators of the riot and suffered for it in consequence. Finally, after many changes, there came the saturnine and self-sufficient Aranda, "who, "says Schoell, "sniffed with pleasure the incense which the French Encyclopedists burned on his altar, and whose greatest glory was to be rated as one of the enemies of the altar and the throne." A former minister of Ferdinand V with the ominous title of the Duke of Alva was his intimate and shared his many schemes in fomenting anti-Jesuitism. Aranda is described as follows, by the Marquis de Langle in his "Voyage en Espagne" (I, 27): "He is the only Spaniard of our time whose name posterity can inscribe on its tablets. He is the man who wanted to cut in the façade of every temple and unite on the same shield the names of Luther, Calvin, Mahomet, William Penn and Jesus Christ; and to proclaim from the frontiers of Navarre to the straits of Cadiz, that Torquemada, Ferdinand and Isabella were blasphemers. He sold altar-furniture, crucifixes and candelabra for bridges, wine-shops and public roads."

In France, conditions were still worse. During a reign of fifty-six years, Louis XV trampled on all the decencies of public and private life. He was the degraded slave of Pompadour, a woman who dictated his policies, named his ministers, appointed his ambassadors, made at least one of his cardinals, and even

directed his armies. Her power was so great that the
Empress of Austria felt compelled to address her as
" *ma bonne amie.*" She was succeeded by du Barry
who was taken from a house of debauch. The coarse-
ness of this creature deprived her of much of the power
possessed by her predecessor, except that Louis was
her slave. It was Pompadour who brought Choiseul
out of obscurity to reward him for revealing a plot
to make one of his own cousins supplant her in her
relations to the king. For that, he was made ambassador to Rome in 1754, where during the last illness of
Benedict XIV, he was planning with other ambassadors
to interpose the royal vetos in the election of Benedict's
successor. Before that event, however, he was sent
to Vienna, from which post, he rose successively until
he had France completely in his grasp. The " Family
Compact " or union of all the Bourbon princes, which
was a potent instrument in the war against the Jesuits,
was his conception. He was a friend of La Chalotais,
one of the arch-enemies of the Society, and was an
intimate of Voltaire, whose property at Ferney he
exempted from taxation. The spirit of his religious
policy consisted in what was then called " an enlightened despotism," or a systematic hatred of everything
Christian.

Crétineau-Joly describes him as follows: " He was
the ideal gentleman of the eighteenth century. He
was controlled by its unbelief, its airs, its vanity, its
nobility, its dissoluteness, insolence, courage, and by a
levity which would have sacrificed the peace of Europe
for an epigram. He was all for show; settling questions
which he had merely skimmed over and sniffing the
incense offered to him by the Encyclopedists, but
shuddering at the thought that they might fancy
themselves his teachers. He would admit no master
either on the throne or below it. His life's ambition

was to govern France and to apply to that sick nation the remedies he had dreamed would restore her to health.   He could not do so except by winning public opinion, and for that purpose, he flattered the philosophers, captured the parliament, cringed to Madame de Pompadour and made things pleasant for the king. When he had gathered everyone on his side, he set himself to hunting the Jesuits."

On the throne of Portugal sat Joseph I, of whom, Father Weld in his " Suppression of the Society of Jesus " (p. 91) writes: " Joseph I united all those points of character which were calculated to make him a tool in the hands of a man who had the audacity to assume the command and astuteness to represent himself as a most humble and faithful servant.   Timid and weak, like Louis XV, he was easily filled with fear for the safety of his own person, and, to a degree never reached by the French king, was incapable of exerting his own will when advised by any one who had succeeded in gaining his confidence.   To this mental weakness, he also added the lamentable failing of being a slave to his own voluptuous passions.   It required but little insight into human nature to see that a terrible scourge was in store for Portugal. To the evils of misrule, it pleased God to add other terrible calamities which overwhelmed the country in misery that cannot be described.   The licentious habits of his father, John V had already impaired the national standard of morals.   The nobility had ceased to visit their estates and had degenerated into a race of mere courtiers.   The interests of the common people were neglected by the Government, and almost their only friends were the religious orders." (The Catholic Encyclopedia, XII, 304).

The real master of Portugal in those days was Don Sebastioa José Carvalho, better known as Pombal —

the gigantic ex-soldier who, despite his herculean
strength and reckless daring, was ignored when there
was question of promotion. He left the army in
disgust, and by the influence of the queen, Maria
of Austria, and that of his uncle, the court chaplain,
was sent as ambassador to London and then to Vienna.
In both places he was a disastrous failure, probably
on account of his brutal manners. Returning to
Lisbon, he paid the most obsequious attention to
churchmen, especially to the king's confessor, the Jesuit
Carbone, who kept continually recommending him
until John V bade him never to mention Carvalho's
name. To the Marquis of Valenza, who also urged
Carvalho's promotion, John said: " that man has hairs
in his heart and he comes from a cruel and vindictive
family." At the death of John and the retirement of
the aged Motta, the former prime minister, the queen
regent, who was fond of Carvalho's Austrian wife
made Pombal prime minister: and Moreira, another
Jesuit confessor, was insistent in proclaiming his
wonderful ability. Never was departure from the
principles and rules of the religious state by meddling
with things outside the sphere of duty so terribly
punished. Father Weld, however, when speaking of
Moreira, who was a prisoner in Jonquiera, has a note
which says that " Moreira protested to the end that
he had never uttered a word in favor of Carvalho."

No sooner was Carvalho in power than the violence
of his character began to display itself in the sanguinary
measures he employed to suppress the brigandage that
was rife in the country and even in the capital
itself. The nobility, especially, were marked out for
punishment; and when public criticism began to be
heard, he issued furious edicts against the calumniators
of the administration. He suppressed with terrible
severity a rising at Porto against a wine-company

which he had established there, and began a series of attacks on the most eminent personages of the kingdom. He dismissed in disgrace the minister of the navy, Diego de Mendoza; and de la Cerda, the ambassador to France; as well as John de Braganza, the Marquis of Marialva and many others. He gave the highest positions, ecclesiastical and political, to his relatives; forced the king to sign edicts without reading them, some of which made criticism of the government high treason, and he extended their application even to the ordinances of his minister; he silenced the preachers who spoke of public disasters as punishment of God; and forbade them to publish anything without his approbation. Though he reorganized the navy, he left the army a wreck, lest the nobles might control it. There was no public press in Portugal during his administration, and the mails were distributed only once a week. He encouraged commerce and organized public works, but always to enrich himself and his family. He flung thousands into prison without even the pretence of a trial, and at his downfall in 1782 says the "Encyclopédie catholique," "out of the subterraneous dungeons there issued eight hundred of his victims, the remnants of the nine thousand who had survived their entombment; and a government order was issued declaring that none of the victims living or dead had been guilty of the crimes imputed to them." This was the man who was declared by the Philosophers of the eighteenth century to be " the illuminator of his nation."

Nor was there much comfort to be hoped for in Austria. Maria Theresa was undoubtedly pious, kind hearted and devoted to her people, but as ruler is very much overrated. Her advisers were commonly the men who were plotting the ruin of all existing govern- ments — Jansenists and Freethinkers. Even her court

physicians were close allies of the schismatical Jansenist
Archbishop of Utrecht, and they made liberal and
constant use of the great esteem they enjoyed at
Vienna to foment hostility to the Holy See. They
even succeeded in persuading the empress, though they
were only laymen, to appoint a commission for the
reform of theological teaching in the seminaries; and
one of their friends, de Stock, was appointed to direct
the work. The Jesuits were removed from the pro-
fessorships of divinity and canon law; lay professors
were appointed in their stead by the politicians, in
spite of the protests of the bishops; and books were
published in direct opposition to orthodox teaching.
At this time appeared the famous treatise known as
" Febronius " by Hontheim, a suffragan bishop of
Treves, who thus prepared for the coming of Joseph II.
The universities were quickly infected with his doctrines;
and new schools were established at Bonn and Münster
out of the money of suppressed convents in order to
accelerate the spread of the poison. When the University of Cologne protested, it was punished for its
temerity.

It goes without saying that if Maria Theresa, with
her strong Catholic instincts, was so easy to control,
it was not difficult for the statesmen who governed
France, Spain, Portugal and Italy to carry out their
nefarious schemes against the Church. The Free-
masons were hard at work, and immoral and atheistic
literature was spread broadcast. It had already made
ravages among the aristocracy and the middle classes,
and now the grades below were being deeply gangrened.
Cardinal Pacca writing about a period immediately
subsequent to this, says: " In the time of my two
nunciatures at Cologne and Lisbon, I had occasion to
become acquainted with the greater part of the French
émigrés, and I regret to say that, with the exception
28

of a few gentlemen from the Provinces, they all made
open profession of the philosophical maxims which
had brought about the catastrophe of which they were
the first victims. They admitted, at times, in their
lucid moments, that the overturning of the altar had
dragged down the throne; and that it was the pretended
intellectuality of the Freethinkers that had introduced
into the minds of the people the new ideas of liberty
and equality, which had such fatal consequence for
them. Nevertheless, they persisted in their errors and
even endeavored to spread them both orally and by the
most abominable publications. God grant that these
seeds of impiety, flung broadcast on a still virgin soil,
may not produce more bitter and more poisonous
fruit for the Church and the Portuguese monarchy."
The editor of the " Memoirs " adds in a note: " They
have only too well succeeded in producing the fruit."

" I remember," continues Pacca, " that during my
nunciature at Cologne, some of these distinguished
" *emigrés* " determined to have a funeral service for
Marie Antoinette, not out of any religious sentiment,
but merely to conform to the fashion followed in the
courts of Europe. I was invited and was present.
The priest who sang the Mass preached the eulogy
of the dead queen. In his discourse which did not
lack either eloquence or solidity, he enumerated the
causes of the French Revolution, and instanced chiefly
the irreligious doctrines taught by the philosophy of
the period. This undeniable proposition evoked loud
murmurs of discontent in the congregation, which was
almost exclusively composed of Frenchmen; and when
the orator said that Marie Antoinette was one of the
first victims of modern philosophy, a voice was heard
far down in the church crying out in the most insulting
fashion: ' That's not true.' " When laymen who
professed to be Catholics were so blind to patent facts

and would dare to conduct themselves so disgracefully in a church at a funeral service for their murdered queen, there was no hope of appealing to them to stand up for truth and justice in the political world.

The hierarchy throughout the Church was devoted to the Society, but it could only protest. And hence as soon as the first signs appeared of the determination to destroy the Order, letters and appeals, full of tender affection and of unstinted praise for the victims, poured into Rome from bishops all over the world. There were at least two hundred sent to Clement XIII, but many of them were either lost or purposely destroyed, as soon as the great Pontiff breathed his last. Father Lagomarsni found many of them which he intended to publish but, for one reason or another, did not do so.

Some of these papers, however have been reproduced by de Ravignan, in his " Clément XIII et Clément XIV." They fill more than a hundred pages of his second volume, and he chose only those that came from the most important sees in the Church, such as the three German Archbishoprics of Treves, Cologne and Mayence, whose prelates were prince electors of the empire. There are also appeals from Cardinal Lamberg the Prince-Bishop of Passau, from the Primate of Germany, the Archbishop of Salzburg, the Primates of Bohemia, of Hungary, and of Ireland. The Archbishop of Armagh says " he lived with the Jesuits from childhood, and loved and admired them." There are letters from the Cardinal Archbishop of Turin; the Archbishops of Messina, Monreale, Sorrento, Seville, Compostella, Tarragona, and even from the far north,— from Norway and Denmark, where the vicar-Apostolic begs the Pope to save those distant countries from the ruin which will certainly fall on them if the Jesuits are withdrawn. They are all

dated between the years 1758 and 1760. The Polish
Bishop of Kiew begs the Pope to stand " like a wall
of brass" against the enemies of the Society, which
he calls a *religiosissimus cœtus*. For the Bishops of
Lombez, it is the *dilectissima Societas Jesu, quæ
concussa, confugit in sinum nostrum* — "the most
beloved Society of Jesus which, when struck, rushed
to our arms." The Bishop of Narbonne declares:
" It is known and admitted through all the world
that the Society of Jesus, which is worthy of all respect,
has never ceased to render services to the Church
in every part of the world. There never was an order
whose sons have fulfilled the duties of the sacred
ministry with more burning, pure and intelligent zeal.
Nothing could check their zeal; and the most furious
storm only displayed the constancy and solidity of
their virtue." Du Guesclin denounces the persecution
as "atrocious; the like of which was never heard of
before." "I omit," says the Archbishop of Auch,
" an infinite number of things which redound to their
praise." The Bishop of Malaga recalls how Clement
VIII described them as " the right arm of the Holy See."
The Archbishop of Salzburg bitterly resents "the
calumnious and defamatory charges against them."
And, so, in each one of these communications to the
Holy Father, there is nothing but praise for the victims
and indignant denunciations of their executioners.

The three Pontiffs who occupied the Chair of St.
Peter at that period were Benedict XIV, Clement XIII
and Clement XIV. Benedict died on May 3, 1758,
eighteen days before Father Ricci was elected General.
Clement XIII was the ardent defender of the Society
during the ten stormy years of his pontificate; and
finally Clement XIV yielded to the enemy and put his
name to the Brief which legislated the Order out of
existence.

Perhaps there never was a Pope who enjoyed such universal popularity as the brilliant Benedict XIV. His attractive personality, his great ability as a writer, his readiness to go to all lengths in the way of concession, elicited praise even from heretics, Turks and unbelievers. As regards his attitude to the Society, there can be no possible doubt that he entertained for it not only admiration, but great affection. He had been a pupil in its schools, and had always shown its members the greatest honor. He defended it against its enemies, and lavished praise again and again on the Institute. It is true that he re-affirmed the Bulls of his predecessor condemning the Malabar and Chinese Rites, but he denied indignantly that he was thereby explicitly condemning the Jesuits. It is also true that he appointed Saldanha, at the request of Pombal, to investigate the Jesuit houses in Portugal; but in the first place, that permission was wrung from him when he was a dying man; and there is no doubt whatever that in doing so, he was convinced that the concession would propitiate Pombal and not injure the Jesuits, whose conduct he knew to be without reproach. Moreover, he had put as a proviso in the Brief that Saldanha who, though the Pope was unaware of it, was an agent of Pombal, should not publish any grievous charge if any such were to be formulated, but should refer it to Rome for judgment. Finally, as the Brief was signed on April 1, 1758, and as the Pope died on May 3, Saldanha's powers ceased. That however, did not trouble him and he did everything that Pombal bade him to do, to defame and destroy the Society. He was not Benedict's agent.

Far from being prejudiced against the Society, Benedict XIV did nothing but bestow praise on it during all his long pontificate. In 1746 in the Bull

"Devotam," he says that "it has rendered the greatest services to the Church and has ever been governed with as much success as prudence." In 1748 the " *Præclairs* " declared that " these Religious are everywhere regarded as the good odor of Jesus Christ, and are so in effect," and, in the same year, the Bull " *Constantem* " affirmed that " they give to the world examples of religious virtue and profound science." Benedict died in the arms of the Jesuit, Father Pepe, his confessor and friend.

Clement XIII, whose name was Carlo della Torre Rezzonico, was born at Venice, March 7, 1693; after studying with the Jesuits at Bologna, he was appointed referendary of the tribunal known as the Segnatura di Giustizia, and later became Governor of Rieti, cardinal-deacon and in 1743 Bishop of Padua. He was called a saint by his people; in spite of the vast revenues of his diocese, he was always in want for he gave everything to the poor, even the shirt on his back. On July 5, 1758, he was elected Pope to succeed Benedict XIV. The first shock he received as head of the Church was in 1758 from Pombal, who insulted him by sending back an extremely courteous letter which the Pontiff had written in answer to a demand for leave to punish three Jesuits who happened to know a nobleman against whom a charge had been lodged of attempting to assassinate the king. Pombal followed up the outrage by flinging all the exiled Jesuits on the Papal States; and then, in 1760, by dismissing the Papal ambassador from Lisbon. In 1761 Pope Clement wrote to Louis XV of France, imploring him to stop the proceedings against the Jesuits: in 1762 he protested against the proposed suppression of the Society in France; and in 1764 he denounced the government programme which he declared was an assault upon the Church itself.

Spain was guilty of the next outrage when, in 1767, Charles III imitated Pombal by expelling the Jesuits and deporting them to Civita Vecchia: and then refusing to answer a letter of the Pope who asked for an explanation of the proceeding.   Naples and Parma insulted him in a similar fashion.   And to add injury to outrage, the Bourbon coalition seized the Papal possessions of Avignon and Venaissin in France, and Benevento and Montecorvo in Italy. Finally, when Spain, France and Naples sent him a joint note demanding the universal suppression of the Society, he died of grief on February 3, 1769. He was then seventy-five years old, and had governed the Church for ten years, six months and twenty-six days. Canova, one of the last of the Jesuit pupils, built his monument, putting at the feet of the Pontiff two lions — one asleep, the other erect and ready for the combat. It was a representation in the mind of the sculptor portraying the meekness of Clement, combined with an indomitable courage which defied the kings of Europe who were attacking the Church.

De Ravignan says of him: " Not because I am a Jesuit, but independently of that affiliation, I regard Clement XIII as endowed with the most genuine traits of grandeur and glory that ever shone in the most illustrious popes. He brings back to me the lineaments of Innocent III, of Gregory VII, of Pius V, of Clement XI. Like them he had to fight; like them he had to face the powers of earth in league against the Church; like them he knew how to unite the most inflexible firmness with the most patient moderation. Alone, as it were, in the midst of a Christendom that was conspiring against the Chair of Peter, he suffered and moaned, but he fought. He was not a politician; he was a Pope. As a worthy successor of St. Peter, he stood solidly on the indestructible rock. Always in the presence of God and his duty, when every earthly interest and when the most appealing entreaties seemed to suggest to him to be silent and to yield basely, he heard within his soul the strong voice of the Church, which can never relinquish the rights with which heaven has invested it; and neither threats, nor outrages, nor spoliations nor sacrilegious assaults availed to bend his resolution to resist, or induced him to display any suspicion of feebleness for a single instant. Until he died, Clement fulfilled the august mission of a Supreme Pontiff. He fought for the Church though it cost him his life. His death was really that of a martyr."

The successor of Clement XIII was not so heroic. He was Lorenzo or Giovanni Antonio Ganganelli. He was born at Sant' Archangelo near Rimini on October 31, 1705; and received his education from the Jesuits at Rimini and from the Piarists at Urbano. At the age of nineteen, he entered the order of the Minor Conventuals, and changed his baptismal name of Giovanni to Lorenzo. His talents and virtue raised him to the dignity of definitor generalis of his order in 1741. Benedict XIV made him consultor of the Holy Office, and Clement XIII gave him the cardinal's hat at the instance, it is said, of Father Ricci, the General of the Jesuits. On May 18, 1769, he was elected Pope by 46 out of 47 votes. By eliminating a great number of possible cardinals, the veto power of the Catholic kings had restricted the choice of a Pope to four out of the forty-seven in the Sacred College. In the beginning of his career, Ganganelli was extremely favorable to the Jesuits: but when he was made a cardinal, a change of disposition manifested itself, although in giving him the honor, Clement XIII had said that he was "a Jesuit in the disguise of a Franciscan." Once on the Papal throne, he refused even

Father Ricci an audience, possibly through fear of
the Great Powers; for, before Clement's accession the
work of the destruction had already begun, and the
new Pope found himself in the centre of a whirlwind.
It was now clear that the Society could never weather
the storm.

CHAPTER XIV

POMBAL

Early life — Ambitions — Portuguese Missions — Seizure of the Spanish Reductions. Expulsion of the Missionaries — End of the Missions in Brazil — War against the Society in Portugal — The Jesuit Republic — Cardinal Saldanha — Seizure of Churches and Colleges — The Assassination Plot — The Prisons — Exiles — Execution of Malagrida.

THE first conspirator who set to work to carry out the plot to destroy the Society, which had long been planned by the powers, was, as might be expected, the ruthless Pombal He was more shameless and savage than his associates and would adopt any method to accomplish his purpose. The insensate fury which possessed his whole being against the Society is explained by Cardinal Pacca, who was Papal nuncio in Lisbon shortly after Pombal's fall (Notizie sul Portogallo, 10). He writes: " Pombal began his diplomatic career in Germany where he probably drank in those principles of aversion to the Holy See and the religious orders, which, when afterwards put in practice, merited for him from the irreligious philosophers the title of a great minister, and an illuminator of his nation; from good people, however, that of a vile instrument of the sects at war with the Church. Having obtained the office of prime minister, he made himself master of the mind of the king, Don Joseph; and for a quarter of a century governed the kingdom as a despot.

" To wage war against the Holy See, and to oppress the clergy, he adopted the measures and employed the arms which, in the hands of the irreligious men of

our time, have done and are still doing harm and
inflicting grievous wounds on the Church. He corrupted and perverted public education in the schools
and universities, especially in Coimbra which soon
became a centre of moral pestilence. He took from
the hands of the youth of the kingdom the sound
doctrinal works which they had so far been made to
study; and substituted schismatical and heretical publications such as Dupin's 'De antiqua ecclesia' which
had been condemned by Innocent XII; and Hontheim's
'Febronius' condemned by Clement XIII. He also
brought into Portugal the works of the régalists, and
excluded those writers who maintained the rights
and authority of the Holy See, in defence of which he
would not allow a word to be uttered. And to the
horror of all decent people, he imprisoned in a loath-
some dungeon a holy and venerable bishop who had
warned his flock against those pernicious publications.
Meantime the notorious Oratorian Pereira, who was
condemned by the Index, and others who flattered him
were remunerated for their writings and could print
whatever they liked. He was a Jansenist who, in
the perfidious fashion of the sect, exalted the authority
of the bishops in order to diminish that of the Pope;
and enlarged the authority of kings in church matters
to such an extent that the system differed very little
from that of the Protestant Anglican Church. Queen
Marìa, who succeeded Joseph on the throne, did much
to improve conditions; but did not undo all the harm
that Pombal had already inflicted on the nation.
Disguised Anglicanism continued to exist in Portugal."

Father Weld adds his own judgment to that of the
cardinal, and tells us that "the bias in Pombal's
nature may be traced to his English associations when
he was ambassador in London." He advances this
view, probably because of a note of Pacca's, who says

that he could venture no opinion about the influence of England on Pombal, merely for want of documents on that point. The author of the " Memoires pour servir à l'histoire ecclésiastique du xviiie siècle " assures us that Pombal's purpose was to extend his reforms even into the bosom of the Church; to change, to destroy; to subject the bishops to his will; to declare himself an enemy of the Holy See; to protect authors hostile to the Holy See; to encourage publications savoring of novelty; to favor in Portugal a theological instruction quite different from what had been adopted previous to his time; and finally to open the way to a pernicious teaching in a country which until then had enjoyed religious peace.

This scheme did not restrict itself to a religious propaganda but got into the domain of politics; for the author of the " Vita di Pombal " (I, 145) notes the report, which is confirmed by the " Memoria Catholica secunda " that " Pombal had formed the design of marrying the Princess Marìa to the Duke of Cumberland, the butcher of Culloden — but that this was thwarted by the Jesuit confessor of the king." On this point the Maréchal de Belle Isle writes (Testament politique, 108): " It is known that the Duke of Cumberland looked forward to becoming King of Portugal, and I doubt not he would have succeeded, if the Jesuit confessors of the royal family had not been opposed to it. This crime was never forgiven the Portuguese Jesuits."

Whatever the truth may be about these royal schemes, Pombal soon found his chance to wreak his vengeance on the Society for balking his plans of making Portugal a Protestant country. A scatter-brained individual, named Pereira, who lived at Rio Janerio, raised the cry which may have been suggested to him, that the Jesuits of the Reductions excluded white intercourse with the natives because of the valuable gold mines they possessed; and that it would be a proper and, indeed, a most commendable thing in the interests of religion for the government to seize this source of wealth, and thus compel the Jesuits who controlled that territory to live up to the holiness of their profession. It was also added that the missions were little else than a great commercial speculation; and finally that the ultimate design of the Society was to make a Republic of Paraguay, independent of the mother country.

These three charges had been reiterated over and over again ever since the foundation of the Reductions, and had been just as often refuted and officially denied after the most vigorous investigation. But there was a man now in control of Portugal who would not be biased by any religious sentiment or regard for truth, if he could injure the Society. The first step was to transfer the aforesaid missions to Portuguese control. They all lay on the east shore of the Uruguay, and belonged to Spain. Hence, in 1750, a treaty was made between Spain and Portugal, to concede to Spain the undisputed control of the rich colony of San Sacramento, at the mouth of the River La Plata, in exchange for the territory, in which lay the seven Reductions of St. Michael, St. Lawrence, St. Aloysius, St. John, St. Francis Borgia, Holy Angels and St. Nicholas. According to the treaty, it was stipulated that the Portuguese should take immediate possession and fling out into the world, they did not care where, the 30,000 Indians who had built villages in the country, and were peacefully cultivating their farms, and who by the uprightness and purity of their lives were giving to the world and to all times an example of what Muratori calls a *Cristianesimo felice*.

To add to the brutality of the act, the Fathers themselves were ordered to announce to the Indians the order to vacate. Representations were made by the Spanish Viceroy of Peru, the Royal Audiencia of Charcas and various civil and ecclesiastical authorities of Spain that not only was this seizure a most atrocious violation of justice which could not be carried out except by bloodshed, no one could say to what extent, but that it was giving up the property of the Indians to their bitterest enemies, the Portuguese. For it was precisely to avoid the Mamelukes of Brazil that the Reductions had been originally created. Moreover, it would almost compel the Indians to conclude that the Fathers had betrayed them, and that they were not only parties to, but instigators of, the whole scheme of spoliation. Southey, in his " History of Brazil," denounces it as " one of the most tyrannical commands that were ever issued, in the recklessness of unfeeling power," and says that " the weak Ferdinand VI had no idea of the importance of the treaty."

The Jesuits appealed; but they were, of course, unheeded; and the Father General Visconti ordered them to submit without a murmur. Unfortunately, the commissioner Father Altamirano, whom he sent out was a bad choice. He was hot-headed and imperious; and according to Father Huonder (The Catholic Encyclopedia) actually treated his fellow Jesuits as rebels, when they advised him to proceed with moderation. Perhaps the fact that he was the representative of the king, as well as of the General, affected him; at all events the Indians would have killed him if he had not fled. Ten years would not have sufficed for a transfer of such a vast multitude with their women and children, and the old and infirm, not to speak of the herds and flocks and farming implements and household furniture, yet they were ordered to decamp within thirty days. Pombal would soon treat his Jesuit fellow countrymen as he had treated the Indians.

When, at last, the cruel edict was published, all the savage instincts of the Indians awoke, and it seemed for a time as if the missionaries would be massacred. It speaks well for the solid Christian training that had been given to these children of the forest that they at last consented to consider the matter at all. Some of the caciques were actually won over to the advisability of the measure, and started out with several hundred exiles to find a new home in the wilderness. A number of the children and the sick succumbed on the way. When, at last they found a place in the mountains of Quanai, they were attacked by hostile tribes. They resisted for a while, but finally returned in despair to their former abode. To make matters worse, the Bishop of Paraguay notified the Fathers that if they did not obey, they would be *ipso facto* suspended. " Whereas," says Weld, " if the Fathers really wished to oppose the government, a single sign from them would have sent an army of fifty thousand men to resist the Europeans; but owing to their fidelity and incredible exertions, there were never as many as seven hundred men in the field against the united armies of Spain and Portugal when hostilities at last broke out."

During the year 1754, the Indians harassed the enemy by the skirmishes and won many a victory; and they would have ultimately triumphed if they had had a leader. At last in 1755, the combined forces of the enemy with thirty pieces of artillery attacked them with the result that might have been expected. The natives rushed frantically on their foes; but the musketry and cannon stretched four hundred of them in their blood; and the rest either fled to the mountains

or relapsed into savage life; or made their submission
to the government, many becoming as bad as their
kindred in the forests because of the corruption they
saw around them. The Portuguese entered into
possession of the seven Reductions, but failed to find
any gold. So great was their chagrin that, in 1761,
Carvalho wanted the rich territory which he had given
to Spain returned to Portugal; and when Spain naturally
demurred, he prepared to go to war for it. He finally
gained his point, and on February 12, 1761, the
territories were restored to their original owners,
but nothing was stipulated, about restitution to the
unfortunate natives and Jesuits who had been the
victims of this shameful political deal.

Some of the Indians who fled to the forests kept up
a guerilla warfare against the invaders; but the greater
number followed the advice of the Fathers and settled
on the Paraná and on the right bank of the Uruguay.
In 1762 there were 2,497 families scattered through
seventeen Reductions or *doctrinas*, as they had begun
to be called, a term that is equivalent to "parish."
But the expulsion of the Fathers which followed soon
after completed the ruin of this glorious work. The
Indians died or became savage again; and today only
beautiful ruins mark the place where this great commonwealth once stood. At the time of the Suppression,
or rather when Pombal drove the Jesuits out of every
Portuguese post into the dungeons of Portugal or
flung them into the Papal States, the Paraguay province
had five hundred and sixty-four members, twelve
colleges, one university, three houses for spiritual
retreats, two residences, fifty-seven Reductions and
113,716 Christian Indians. The leave-taking of the
Fathers and Indians was heart-rending on both sides.

It is a long distance from the River La Plata to the
Amazon; for there are about thirty-five degrees of

latitude between the two places. But they were not too far apart to check Carvalho in his work of destruction. After having done all he could for the moment at one end of Brazil, he addressed himself to the Jesuit missions at the other. A glance at the past history of these establishments will reveal the frightful injustice of the brutal acts of 1754.

One hundred years before that time, Vieira had made his memorable fight against his Portuguese fellow-countrymen for the liberation of the Indians from slavery. By so doing, he had, of course, aroused the fury of the whites, and they determined to crush him. They put him in prison; and in 1660 sent him and his companions to Portugal, in a crazy ship to be tried for disturbing the peace of the colony. Nevertheless, he won the fight, although meantime three Jesuits had been killed by the Indians, and their companions expelled from the colony, in spite of the king's protection. In this act, however, the Portuguese had gone too far. His majesty saw the truth and sent the missionaries back. That was as early as 1680. In 1725 new complaints were sent to Portugal, but the supreme governor of the Maranhão district wrote, as follows, to the king: "The Fathers of the Society in this State of Maranhão are objects of enmity and have always been hated, for no other reason than for their strenuous defence of the liberty of the unfortunate Indians, and also because they used all their power to oppose the tyrannical oppression of those who would reduce to a degraded and unjust slavery men whom nature had made free. The Fathers take every possible care that the laws of your majesty on this point shall be most exactly observed. They devote themselves entirely to the promotion of the salvation of souls and the increase of the possessions of your majesty; and have added

29

many sons to the Church and subjects to the crown
from among these barbarous nations."

With regard to their alleged commerce, the governor
says: "Whatever has been charged against the
Fathers by wicked calumniators who, through hatred
and envy, manufacture ridiculous lies about the wealth
they derive from those missions, I solemnly declare to
your majesty, and I speak of a matter with which
I am thoroughly acquainted, that the Fathers of the
Society are the only true missionaries of these regions.
Whatever they receive from their labors among the
Indians is applied to the good of the Indians themselves and to the decency and ornamentation of the
churches, which, in these missions, are always very
neat and very beautiful. Nothing whatever that is
required in the missions is kept for themselves. As
they have nothing of their own, whatever each
missionary sends is delivered to the procurator of the
mission, and every penny of it reverts to the use
of the particular mission from whence it came.
Missioners of other orders send quite as much produce,
but each one keeps his own portion separate, to be used
as he likes, so that the quantity however great being
thus divided, does not make much impression on
those who see it. But as the missionaries of the
Society send everything together to the procurator,
the quantity, when seen in bulk, excites the cupidity
of the malevolent and envious."

About 1739, Eduardo dos Santos was sent by John V
as a special commissioner to Maranhão. After spending
twenty months in visiting every mission and examining
every detail he wrote as follows: "The execrable
barbarity with which the Indians are reduced to slavery
has become such a matter of custom that it is rather
looked on as a virtue. All that is adduced against
this inhuman custom is received with such repugnance

and so quickly forgotten that the Fathers of the
Society in whose charity these unfortunate creatures
often find refuge and protection, and who take compassion on their miserable lot, become, for this very
reason, objects of hatred to these avaricious men."

Such were the official verdicts of the conduct of
the Jesuits on the Amazon a few years before Pombal
came into power. But in 1753 regardless of all this
he sent out his brother Francis Xavier Mendoza, a
particularly worthless individual, and made him
Governor of Gran Para and Maranhão, giving him a
great squadron of ships and a considerable body of
troops with orders to humble the Jesuits and send
back to Portugal any of them who opposed his will.
Everything was done to create opposition. They
were forbidden to speak or to preach to the Indians
except in Portuguese; the soldiers were quartered in
the Jesuit settlements, and were instructed to treat
the natives with especial violence and brutality.

In 1754 a council was held in Lisbon to settle the
question about expelling the Society from the missions
of Maranhão. The order was held up temporarily by
the queen; but when she died, a despatch was sent in
June 1755 ordering their immediate withdrawal from
all "temporal and civil government of the missions."
The instructions stated that it was "in order that
God might be better served." Unfortunately the
bishop of the place co-operated with Carvalho in
everything that was proposed. He suppressed one of
the colleges, restricted the number of Fathers in the
others, to twelve, and sent the rest back to Portugal;
and in order to excite the settlers against the Society,
he had the Bull of Benedict XIV which condemned
Indian slavery read from the pulpits, proclaiming that
it had been inspired by the Jesuits. Meantime, in
the reports home, the insignificant Indian villages where

they labored were magnified into splendid cities and towns all owned by the Society; two pieces of cannon which had never fired a ball were described as a whole park of artillery, and a riot among the troops was set down as a rebellion excited by the Jesuits.

The first three Fathers to be banished from Brazil were José, Hundertpfund and da Cruz. José was a royal appointee sent out to determine the boundary line between the Spanish and Portuguese American possessions. But that did not trouble Pombal; nor did the German nationality of Hundertpfund, nor did he deign to state the precise nature of their offenses. A fourth victim named Ballister had had the bad taste to preach on the text: " Make for yourself friends of the Mammon of iniquity." He was forthwith accused of attacking one of Carvalho's commercial enterprises, and promptly ordered out of the country. Again, when some mercantile rivals sent a petition to the king against Carvalho's monopolies, Father Fonseca was charged with prompting it, and he was outlawed though absolutely innocent. And so it went on. Carvalho's brother was instructed to invent any kind of an excuse to increase the number of these expatriations.

While these outrages were being perpetrated in the colonies, Lisbon's historic earthquake of 1755 occurred. The city was literally laid in ruins. Thousands of people were instantly killed; and while other thousands lay struggling in the ruins, the rising flood of the Tagus and a deluge of rain completed the disaster. Singularly enough, Carvalho's house escaped the general wreck; and the foolish king considered that exception to be a Divine intervention in behalf of his great minister, and possibly, on that account, left him unchecked in the fury which even the awful calamity which had fallen on his country did not at

all moderate. The Jesuits were praised by both
king and patriarch for their heroic devotion both
during and after the great disaster, but those commendations only infuriated Pombal the more. When
one of the Fathers, the holy Malagrida, had dared
to say in the pulpit that the earthquake was a punishment for the vice that was rampant in the capital,
Pombal regarded it as a reflection on his administration; and the offender, though seventy years old and
universally regarded as a saint, was banished from
the city as inciting the people to rebellion.

However, the furious minister meted out similar
treatment to others, even to his political friends.
Thus, although the British parliament had voted
£40,000 for the relief of the sufferers, besides giving a
personal gift to the king and sending ships with cargoes of food for the people, Pombal immediately
ran up the tax on foreign imports, for he was financially
interested in domestic productions. Even in doling
out provisions to the famishing populace, he was so
parsimonious that riots occurred, whereupon he hanged
those who complained. The author of the " Vita "
(I, 106) vouches for the fact that at one time there
were three hundred gibbets erected in various parts of
Lisbon. The Jesuit confessors at the court were
especially obnoxious to him and he dismissed them all
with an injunction never to set foot in the royal
precincts again. The anger of their royal penitents
did not restrain him, so absolute was his power both
then and afterwards. The plea was that the priests
were plotters against the king. To increase that
impression he pointed out to his majesty the number
of offenders against him; all members of the detested
Order who were coming back in every ship from
Brazil. The General of the Society, Father Centurioni,
wrote to the king pleading the innocence of the

victims; but the letter never got further than the minister. The king did not even know it had been sent.

The next step in this persecution was to publish the famous pamphlet entitled: " A Brief Account of the Republic which the Jesuits have established in the Spanish and Portuguese dominions of the New World, and of the War which they have carried on against the armies of the two Crowns; all extracted from the Register of the Commissaries and Plenipotentiaries, and from other documents." A copy was sent to every bishop of the country; to the cardinals in Rome, and to all the courts of Europe. Pombal actually spent 70,000 crowns to print and spread the work of which he himself was generally credited with being the author. In South America it was received with derision; in Europe mostly with disgust. Sad to say, Acciajuoli, the Apostolic nuncio at Lisbon, believed the Brazilian stories; but he changed his mind, when on the morning of June 15, 1760, just as he was about to say Mass, he received a note ordering him in the name of the king to leave the city at once, and the kingdom within four days; adding that to preserve him from insult a military escort would conduct him to the frontier. Other publications of the same tenor followed the " Brief Account." One especially became notorious. It was: " Letters of the Portuguese Minister to the Minister of Spain on the Jesuitical Empire, the Republic of Maranhao; the history of Nicholas I." The Nicholas in question was a Father named Plantico. To carry out the story of his having been crowned king or Emperor of Paraguay, coins with his effigy were actually struck and circulated throughout Europe. Unfortunately for the fraud, none of the coins were ever seen in Paraguay where they ought to have been current. Moreover, as Plantico was transported with the other Jesuits of Brazil, he would have been hanged on his arrival in Portugal, if he had tried to set up a kingdom of his own in Paraguay. On the contrary, he went off to his native country of Croatia, and was Rector of the College of Grosswardein when the general suppression of the Society took place. Frederick II and d'Alembert used to joke with each other about " King Nicholas I "; and in Spain, that and the other libels were officially denounced and their circulation prohibited.

As for Carvalho, these hideous imaginings of his brain became realities; and the list of Jesuitical horrors which his ambassador at Rome repeated to the Pope, all, as he alleged, for the sake of the Church, almost suggest that Pombal was a madman. Long extracts of the document may be found in de Ravignan and Weld, but it will be sufficient here to mention a few of the charges. They are, for instance, " seditious machinations against every government of Europe; scandals in their missions so horrible that they cannot be related without extreme indecency; rebellion against the Sovereign Pontiff; the accumulation of vast wealth and the use of immense political power; gross moral corruption of individual members of the Order; abandonment of even the externals of religion; the daily and public commission of enormous crimes; opposing the king with great armies; inculcating in the Indian mind an implacable hatred of all white men who are not Jesuits; starting insurrections in Uruguay so as to prevent the execution of the treaty of limits; atrociously calumniating the king; embroiling the courts of Spain and Portugal; creating sedition by preaching in the capital against the commercial companies of the minister; taking advantage of the earthquake to attain their detestable ends; surpassing Machiavelli in their diabolical plots; inventing prophecies of new disasters, such as warnings of subterranean fires and invasions of the sea; calumniating the venerable Palafox; committing crimes worse than those of the Knights Templars, etc."

Unfortunately, Cardinal Passionei who was unfriendly to the Society, exercised great power at Rome at that time. He was so antagonistic that he would not allow a Jesuit book in the library, which made d'Alembert say: "I am sorry for his library." He also refused to condemn the work of the scandalous ex-monk Norbert, who was in the pay of Carvalho. To make matters worse, Benedict XIV was then at the point of death. And a short time previously, yielding to Carvalho's importunities, he had appointed Cardinal Saldanha, who was Carvalho's tool, to investigate the complaints and to report back to Rome, without however taking any action on the premises. The dying Pontiff was unaware of the intimacy of Saldanha with the man in Portugal or he would not have ordered him in the Brief of appointment to " follow the paths of gentleness and mildness, in dealing with an Order which has always been of the greatest edification to the whole world; lest by doing otherwise he would diminish the esteem which, up to that time, they have justly acquired as a reward of their diligence. Their holy Institute had given many illustrious men to the Church whose teachings they have not hesitated to confirm with their blood." As the Pope died in the following month, Saldanha made light of the instructions. His usual boast was that " the will of the king was the rule of his actions; and he was under such obligations to his majesty, that he would not hesitate to throw himself from the window if such were the royal pleasure."

It was currently reported in Lisbon, says Weld (130), that the office of visitor had been first offered to Francis of the Annunciation, an Augustinian who had reformed the University of Coimbra; and on his refusal he was sent to prison where he ended his days. But the obliging Saldanha saw in it an opportunity for still further advancement; he accepted the work and performed it in accordance with the wishes of Pombal. Meantime, new dungeons were being made in the fortress of Jonquiera in which the offending Jesuits were to be buried. Saldanha began his work as Inquisitor on May 31, by going with great pomp to the Jesuit Church of St. Roch. Seated on the throne in the sanctuary, he gave his hand to be kissed by all the religious. When the provincial knelt before him, the cardinal told him to have confidence — he would act with clemency. When the ceremony was over, he departed abruptly without asking any questions or making any examination. But a few days afterward, the provincial received a letter bearing the date May 15, that is sixteen days before this visit to the Church, declaring that the Fathers in Portugal and in its dominions to the ends of the earth were, on the fullest information, found to be guilty of a worldly traffic which was a disgrace to the ecclesiastical state; and they were commanded under pain of excommunication to desist from such business transactions at the very hour the notification was made. The language employed in the letter which was immediately spread throughout the country was insulting and defamatory to the highest degree.

All the procurators were then compelled to hand over their books to the government. And when the horrified people, who knew there was nothing back of it all but Carvalho's hatred, manifested their discontent, it was ascribed to the Jesuits. Hence on June 6, the cardinal patriarch, at the instigation of the prime minister, suspended them all from the function of preaching and hearing confessions throughout the patriarchate. The cardinal had, at first, demurred, for he knew the Jesuits in Lisbon to be the very reverse of Saldanha's description of them, and he therefore demanded a regular trial. Whereupon Carvalho flew into such a rage that out of sheer terror, and after a few hours' struggle, he issued the cruel order. The poor cardinal, who was an ardent friend and admirer of the Society, was so horrified at what he had done that he fell into a fever, and died within a month. Before he received the last sacraments, he made a public declaration that the Society was innocent, and he drew up a paper to that effect; but Carvalho never let it see the light. When the Archbishop of Evora heard that the dying man had shed tears over his weakness, he said: " Tears are not enough. He should have shed the last drop of his blood."

Saldanha was made patriarch in the deceased prelate's place; and though his office of visitor had ceased *ipso facto* on the death of the Pope, he continued to exercise its functions nevertheless. He appointed Bulhoens, the Bishop of Para, a notorious adherent of Carvalho, to be his delegate in Brazil. Bulhoens first examined the Jesuits of Para, but could find nothing against them. He then proceeded to Maranhão; but the bishop of that place left in disgust; and the governor warned Bulhoens that if he persisted, the city would be in an uproar. Not being able to effect anything, he asked the Bishop of Bahia to undertake the work of investigation. The invitation was promptly accepted; and all the superiors were ordered to show their books under pain of excommunication. They readily complied, and no fault was found with the accounts. He then instituted a regular tribunal; received the depositions of seventy-five witnesses, among them Saldanha's own brother who had lived twenty-five years in Maranhão. Next he examined the tax commissioner, through whose hands all contracts

and bills of exchange had to pass; and that official
affirmed under oath that he had never known or
heard of any business transactions having been carried
on by Jesuits. The result was that the courageous
bishop declared " it would be an offence against God
and his conscience and against the king's majesty to
condemn the Fathers." When his report was forwarded to Portugal, Carvalho ordered the confiscation
of his property; expelled him from his palace, and
declared his see vacant. The valiant prelate passed
the rest of his days in seclusion, supported by the
alms of the faithful.

In September 1758, a charge was trumped up in
Lisbon in a most tortuous fashion, based on the alleged
discovery of a plot to assassinate the king. Those
chiefly involved were the Duke de Averio and the
Marquis de Tavora, with his wife, his two sons, his
two brothers and his two sons-in-law, all of whom
were seized at midnight on December 12. The
marchioness and her daughter-in-law were carried off
to a convent in their night-dresses; the men of the
family, to dens formerly occupied by the wild beasts
of the city menagerie. De Aveiro, who was supposed
to be the assassin-in-chief, was not taken until next
day. Several others were included in this general
round-up, some of them for having asserted that the
whole conspiracy was a manufactured affair. At the
same time, some of the domestic servants of the
marquis, probably for having offered resistance at the
time of the arrest, were put to death so that they could
tell no tales. Not being able to have the accused
parties tried before any regularly constituted tribunal,
because of the lack of evidence, Carvalho drew up a
sentence of condemnation himself, and presented it to
a new court which he had just established, called the
inconfidenza, and demanded the signatures of the judges

who were all his creatures. After being stormed at
for a while, all, with one exception, put their names
to the paper. Then, as by the law of the land no
nobleman could be condemned to death except by his
peers, he constituted himself as a tribunal, along with
his secretary of the Navy and the secretary of Foreign
Affairs, neither of whom had any difficulty in complying with the wish of their master.

On January 11, 1759, three of the noblemen involved,
Aveiro, Tavora and Antongia, were led out to execution
before the king's palace. Vast multitudes had
assembled in the public square; and to ensure order,
fresh regiments had been summoned from other parts
of the kingdom. A riot was feared, for the Tavoras
were among the noblest families of the realm. The
accused had not even been defended and had been
interrogated on the rack. The execution was most
expeditious, and the heads of the three victims quickly
rolled in the dust. That night, the marchioness was
taken from the convent to the new dungeons in the
fort; and on January 12, she heard the sentence of
death passed on her by Carvalho himself who was
both judge and accuser. The scaffold was erected in
the square of Belem; and long before daylight of
January 13 an immense multitude had gathered to
witness the hideous spectacle. The marchioness advanced and took her seat in the chair. The axe
quickly descended on her neck — and all was over.
She was despatched in this hurried fashion because
the interference of the king was feared. Indeed, the
messenger arrived just when the head had been severed
from the body. The two sons of the marchioness and
her son-in-law were then stretched on the rack and
strangled. The father of the family, the old marquis
followed next in order. As a mark of clemency, his
torture was brief but effective. Four others were then

executed; fire was set to the gibbet; and its blood-stained timbers along with the bodies of the victims were reduced to ashes and thrown into the Tagus. This was not a scene in a village of savages, but in a great European capital which had just passed through a terrible visitation of God but apparently had not understood its meaning. Carvalho was thirsting for more blood, but the king held him back; so he contented himself with destroying the palaces of the Aveiras and Tavoras; sprinkling the sites with salt; forbidding anyone to bear the names hitherto so illustrious, and even effacing them from the monuments and the public archives. He was not allowed to commit any more official murders for the moment; but at least he had thousands who were dying in his underground dungeons.

What had the Jesuits to do with all this? Nothing whatever. They were accused of being the spiritual advisers of the Tavora family which it was impossible to disprove, because though the persons implicated by the accusation were all arrested on the 11th, sentence of death had been already passed on the 9th. There were twenty-nine paragraphs in the indictment. The twenty-second said that "even if the exuberant and conclusive proofs already adduced did not exist, the presumption of the law would suffice to condemn such monsters." Of course, no lawyer in the world could plead against such a charge, and it is noteworthy that in the Brief of Suppression of the whole Society by Clement XIV which brings together all the accusations against it, there is no mention whatsoever, even inferentially, of any conspiracy of the Jesuits against the life of the King of Portugal. Moreover, the Inquisition and all the Bishops of Spain judged this Portuguese horror at its proper value, when on May 3, 1759 they put their official stamp of condemnation on the pamphlets with which the whole of Europe was flooded immediately after Pombal's infamous act. They denounced the charges one by one as " designed to foment discord, to disturb the peace and tranquillity of souls and consciences, and especially to discredit the holy Society of Jesus and religious who laudably labor in it to the benefit of the Church; as is known throughout the world." Over and over again as each book is specifically anathematised, the " holy Society of Jesus " is spoken of with commendation and praise. The condemned publications were then burnt in the market place. That exculpation ought to have been sufficient, coming as it did not only from all the Spanish bishops but from the Inquisition, which from the very beginning had been uniformly suspicious of everything Jesuitical. Against this utterance Pombal was powerless for it was the voice of another nation.

When the year 1759 began, three of the most conspicuous and most venerable Fathers of Portugal were in jail under sentence of death. But neither the king nor Carvalho dared to carry out the sentence of execution. Something however had to be done; and therefore a royal edict, which had been written long before, was issued. After reciting all that had been previously said about Brazil, etc. it declared that " these religious being corrupt and deplorably fallen away from their holy institute, and rendered manifestly incapable by such abominable and inveterate vices to return to its observances, must be properly and effectually banished, denaturalized, proscribed and expelled from all his majesty's dominions, as notorious rebels, traitors, adversaries and aggressors of his royal person and realm; as well as for the public peace and the common good of his subjects; and it is ordered under the irremissible pain of death, that

no person, of whatever state or condition, is to admit
them into any of his possessions or hold any communication with them by word or writing, even though they
should return into these states in a different garb or
should have entered another order, unless with the
King's permission." It is sad to have to record that
the Patriarch of Lisbon endorsed the invitation to the
Jesuits to avail themselves of this royal clemency.

The procurators of the missions who occupied a
temporary house in Lisbon had been already carried
off to jail; and their money, chalices, sacred vessels,
all of which were intended for Asia and Brazil, were
confiscated. The Exodus proper began at the College
of Elvas on September 1. At night-fall a squadron
of cavalry arrived; and taking the inmates prisoners,
marched them off without any intimation of whither
they were going. On the following day, Sunday,
they were lodged in a miserable shed, exhausted
though they were by the journey, with nothing but a
few crusts to eat, after having suffered intensely from
the heat all day long. They were not even allowed to
go to Mass. During the next night and the following
day, they continued their weary tramp and at last
arrived at Evora. There the young men were left
at the college, and the sixty-nine Professed were
compelled to walk for six consecutive days till they
reached the Tagus. Many were old and decrepit and
one of them lost his mind on the journey. When they
reached the river, they were put in open boats and exposed all day long to the burning sun, with nothing to
eat or drink. They were then transferred to a ship
which had been waiting for them since the month of
April. It was then late in September.

Other exiles soon joined them, after going through
similar experiences, until there were one hundred and
thirty-three in the same vessel. They were all kept

in the hold till they were out of sight of land. There
was no accommodation for them: the food was insufficient; the water was foul; there were no dishes, so that
six or seven had to sit around a tin can, and take out
what they could with a wooden spoon, and the same
vessel had to serve for the water they drank. The
orders were to stop at no port until they reached
Civita Vecchia. However, after passing the Straits
of Gibraltar, it became evident that unless the captain
wanted to carry a cargo of corpses to Italy, he must
take in supplies somewhere: for many of the victims
were sixty or seventy years of age. There were even
some octogenarians among them. Hence, on reaching
Alicante, in Spain, one of the Fathers went ashore.
There was a college of the Society in that city; and as
soon as the news spread of the arrival of the prisoners,
the people rushed to the shore to supply their wants,
but the messenger was the only one allowed to be seen.
They then sailed away from Alicante. Off Corsica, a
storm caught them and so delayed their progress that
a stop had to be made at Spezia for more food. At
last, on October 24, more than a month after they had
left Lisbon, they were flung haggard, emaciated and
exhausted on the shores of the Papal States at Civita
Vecchia. Of course, they were received by the people
there with unbounded affection; and as Father Weld
relates "none exceeded the Dominican Fathers in
their tender solicitude for the sufferers. A marble
slab in their church records their admiration for these
confessors of the Faith with whom the sons of St.
Dominic declared they were *devinctissimi* — "closely
bound to them in affection."

On September 29, troops surrounded the College of
Coimbra. The astonished populace was informed
that it was because the Fathers had been fighting;
that some were already killed and others wounded;

and the soldiers had been summoned to prevent
further disorders. That night amid pouring rain, the
tramp of horses' hoofs was heard; and as the people
crowded to the windows, they saw the venerable men
of the college led away between squads of cavalry as
if they were brigands or prisoners of war. They
arrived at the Tagus on October 7, where others were
already waiting. They numbered in all 121, and
were crowded into two small ships which were to
carry them into exile. They had scarcely room to
move. Yet, when they arrived at Genoa, they were
all packed into one of the boats. At Leghorn, they
were kept for a whole month in close confinement on
board the ship. When they started out, they were
buffeted by storms, and not until January 4, 1760 did
they reach the papal territory. They were in a more
wretched state of filth and emaciation than their
predecessors.

These prisoners were the special criminals of the
Society, namely — the professed Fathers. The other
Jesuits were officially admitted to be without reproach
and were exhorted, both by the civil and ecclesiastical
authorities, to abandon the Order and be dispensed
from their vows. As these non-Professed numbered
at least three-fourths of the whole body, the difficult
problem presents itself of explaining how the Professed
who are looked up to by the rest of the Society for
precept and example should be monsters of iniquity and
yet could train the remaining three-fourths of the
members in such a way as to make them models of
every virtue.

Pombal was convinced that he could separate the
youth of the Society from their elders; and he was
extremely anxious to do so, because of the family
connections of many of them, and because of the loss
to the nation at one stroke of so much ability and

30

talent. But he failed egregiously. They were all gathered in the colleges of Coimbra and Evora. No seclusion was observed. Everybody was free to visit them from the world outside; and inducements of every kind were held out to them to abandon the Society: family affection, worldly ambition, etc.— but without avail. They had no regular superior, so they elected a fourth-year theologian who had just been ordained a priest. Another was made minister; and a third, master of novices. The house was kept in excellent order; the religious discipline was perfect and the exercises of the community went on with as much regularity as if nothing were happening. Pombal sent commissioner after commissioner to shake the constancy of the young men, but only two of the tempted ones weakened. "Who is their superior?" he asked one day in a rage. The answer was: "Joseph Carvalho — your namesake and relative." On October 20, a letter from the cardinal was read in both houses. He expressed his astonishment that these young Jesuits did not avail themselves of the royal favor to desert; and he warned them that they were not suffering for their faith, and that "their refusal of His Majesty's offer to release them from their vows was not virtuous constancy but seditious obstinacy."

Finally, October 24 was fixed for their departure, and notice was given that they could not expect to go to any civilized land, but would probably be dropped on some desolate island off the African coast. That shook the resolution of two of the band, but the rest stood firm. In the morning, all went to Holy Communion and at an hour before sunset, the word was given to start. They sang a Te Deum and then set out — 130 in all. They were preceded by a troop of cavalry; a line of foot soldiers marched on either side;

while here and there torches threw their glare over this grim nocturnal procession. It took them four days to reach Oporto, where they met their brethren from Braganza and Braza. There were only ten from the former place, but sixty soldiers had been detailed to guard them. Indeed, the troopers from Braza had to keep the crowds back with drawn swords, so eager were the people along the road to express their sympathy. At Oporto the young heroes had to witness the desertion of four Professed Fathers; but that did not weaken their resolution. They were all crammed into three small craft, but the weather was too stormy to leave the port; and there they remained a whole week, packed so close together that there was scarcely room to lie side by side. The air became so foul that it was doubtful if they could survive. Even their guards took sick, and, at last, a number of the prisoners were transferred to a fort in the harbor.

At last to the number of 223 they sailed down the Tagus. One of them died, and his companions sang the Office of the Dead over him and buried him in the sea. When the ship did not roll too much, Mass was said and they went to Communion. All the exercises that are customary in religious houses were scrupulously performed, and the Church festivals were observed as if they were a community at home. They were quarantined two weeks at Genoa without being permitted to go ashore. Then another scholastic died, and they found that his earthly goods consisted of nothing but a few bits of linen, that must have been foul by this time, besides a discipline and a hair shirt. They cast anchor at Civita Vecchia on February 7, having left inhospitable Portugal in October.

The band from Evora to the number of ninety-eight, of whom only three were priests, had not such a rude experience except in the distress of seeing some deserters, among them two Professed Fathers. The officer in charge of the ship, unlike most of the government employees, was tender and kind to them. How could he have been otherwise? His name was de Britto — the same as that of the Portuguese martyr in India. It meant the loss of his position, perhaps, but what did he care? When they reached Lisbon, the nineteen who had been separated from the first detachment to be kept in jail came aboard, and the little band numbered 115 all told, when the ship hoisted anchor and made for the sea. They reached Civita Vecchia where the two happy troops of valiant young Jesuits met in each others arms. Their number was then 336. They were distributed among the various establishments of Italy, the novices being sent to Sant' Andrea in Rome. Two cardinals and a papal nuncio who were making their retreat in the house at the time insisted on serving them at table, while the Pope sent a message to the General to say: " These young men have reflected great honor on the Society and have shown how well they have been trained."

The fury of Pombal was not yet sated. Not an island of the Atlantic, not a station in Africa or India, not a mission in the depths of the forests of America that was not searched and looted by his commissioners, who ruthlessly expelled the devoted missionaries who were found there. Men venerable for age and acquirements were given over to brutal soldiers who were ordered to shoot them if any attempt at escape was made. They were dragged hundreds of miles through the wildest of regions, over mountains, through raging torrents, amid driving storms; they were starved and had nothing but the bare ground on which to rest; they were searched again and again as if their rags held treasures; were made to answer the roll call twice

a day like convicts in jail; and then tossed in the holds
of crazy ill-provisioned ships with no place to rest
their weary heads, except on a coil of rope or in the
the filth of the cattle; and when dead, they were to
be flung to the sharks.   When at last they reached
Lisbon they were forbidden to show themselves on
deck, lest their fellow-countrymen and their families
might be shocked by their degradation.   They were
then spirited away to the dungeons of St. Julian and
Jonquiera to rot, until death relieved them of their
sufferings.   Those who were not placed in the crowded
jails were sent in their rags to find a refuge somewhere outside of their native land.

As has been said, there were two provinces in Portuguese South America — Brazil and Maranhão.   In the
former, besides the Seminary of Belem, the Society
had six colleges and sixty-two residences with a total
of 445 members.   Orders were given to the whole
445 to assemble at Bahia, Pernambuco and San
Sebastian.   Everything was seized.   At Bahia, the
novices were stripped of their habits and sent adrift,
though the families of some of them lived in far away
Portugal.   The rest were confined in a house surrounded
by armed troops while the bishop of the city proclaimed
that any one who would encourage the victims to
persevere in their vocation would be excommunicated.
Then, one day, without a moment's notice, all were
ordered out of the house and sent to jail in different
places.   There they remained for the space of three
months waiting for the missionaries from the interior
to arrive.   They came in slowly, for some of them
lived eight hundred miles away, and had to tramp all
that distance through the forests and over mountain
ranges.   Before all had made their appearance, however,
the first batches were sent across to the mother country
to make space.   They started on March 16 and reached

the Tagus on June 6. Those from Bahia had taken from April to June, and it was fully three months before the convict ship from Pernambuco arrived in port.

All this time the deported religious were kept between decks, and soldiers stood at the gangway with drawn swords to prevent any attempt to go up to get a breath of fresh air. Their food was nothing but vegetables cooked in sea-water, for there was not enough of drinking water even to slake their thirst. The result was that the ship had a cargo of half-dead men when it anchored off Lisbon; but the unfortunate wretches were kept imprisoned there for fifteen days with the port-holes closed. They were then transferred to a Genoese ship and sent to Civita Vecchia. It appears that the Provincial of these Brazilian Jesuits was named Lynch; but strange to say, there is no mention of him in any of the Menologies. The deportation from Pernambuco and San Sebastian were repetitions of this organized brutality; and the same methods were employed at Goa in India, and the other dependencies, such as Macao and China. In the transportations from these posts in the Orient, the ships had to stop at Bahia which had been witness of the first exportations; but the victims in the China ships could learn nothing of what had happened. Twenty-three of them died on one of the journeys from India. It is noted that a Turk at Algiers and a Danish Lutheran sea-captain, had shown the greatest humanity to the victims whose fellow country-men seemed transformed into savage beasts. The prisoners had been kept in confinement twenty months before they left Goa; and when they arrived at Lisbon on October 18, 1764, they were taken off in long boats at the dead of night, and lodged in the foulest dungeons of the fortress of St. Julian.

But these were not the only victims of Carvalho.
There were prisoners from every grade of society;
and their number reached the appalling figure of
nine thousand. Among them were eminent ecclesiastics, bishops and canons and some of the most distinguished laymen of the kingdom. A description
of the prisons in which they were confined for years
or till they died has been given to posterity by some
of the victims. Father Weld in his " Suppression of
the Society in Portugal " quotes extensively from
their letters. The jails were six in number: Belem,
Almeida, Azeitano, St. George, Jonquiera and St.
Julian. They had annexes, also, along the African
coasts or on the remote islands of the Atlantic. Belem,
the Portuguese name for Bethlehem, so called because
it had once been an abbey, was about four miles from
Lisbon towards the ocean. It had the distinction of
keeping its prisoners behind iron bars, but exposed
to the public like wild beasts in a menagerie; so that
the public could come and look at them and feed them
if so disposed. The Portuguese criminals were given a
pittance by the government, to purchase food, but the
foreigners had to beg from the spectators for the means
to support life. It was admirably contrived to induce
insanity.

Jonquiera lay between Belem and Lisbon. The
cells were numerous in this place. Moreira, the king's
former confessor, and Malagrida were among the
inmates. The Marquis de Lorna who was also confined there says " there were nineteen cells, each about
seven paces square, and so tightly closed that a light
had to be kept burning continually; otherwise they
would have been in absolute darkness. When the
prisoners were first put in them, the plaster was
still wet and yielded to the slightest pressure. The
cold was intense. Worst of all for a Catholic country,

the sacraments were allowed the prisoners only once a
year." The Marquis says that during the sixteen
years he spent there " he never heard Mass." In
these dungeons there were 221 Jesuits, 88 of whom
died in their chains. The Castle of St. Julian stood
on the banks of the Tagus and the walls were washed
by the tide. In this place, there were 125 Jesuits of
all nations; men of high birth, of great virtue and
intellectual ability. The cells were situated below the
sea-level; and were damp, unventilated, choked with
filth and swarming with vermin. Some of the Fathers
passed nineteen years in those tombs. The drinking
water was putrid; the prisoners' clothes were in rags;
often not sufficient for decency; many had no under
garments and no shoes; their hair and beards were
never cut; the food was scant and of the worst quality,
and was often carried off before there was time to eat it.
The oil of the single lamp in the cells was so limited that
to save it, the wick was reduced to two or three threads.
The same conditions prevailed in the other prisons.
Meantime the jailers were making money on the supplies supposed to be served to the prisoners. Such
was prison life in Portugal during the twenty years
of Pombal's administration.

One of the particularly outrageous features of these
imprisonments was that Pombal preferred to hold
foreigners rather than native Portuguese. The
foreigners, having no friends in the country, would
not, in all probability, be claimed by their relatives;
and as the ministers of nearly all the nations of Europe
were of the same mind as himself, he had no fear of
political intervention. Thus we find in a letter of
Father Kaulen, a German Jesuit, which was published
by Christopher de Murr, that in one section of St.
Julian, besides fifty-four Portuguese Jesuits, there were
thirteen Germans, one Italian, three Frenchmen,

two Spaniards, and three Chinese. These Chinese
Jesuits must have made curious reflections on the meaning of the term "Christian nations." "There are
others in the towers," adds Father Kaulen, "but I
cannot find out who they are, or how many, or to
what country they belong."

The three Frenchmen, Fathers du Gad and de
Ranceau along with Brother Delsart were set free
at the demand of Marie Leczinska, the wife of Louis XV;
it was through them that Father Kaulen was able to
send his letter to the provincial of the Lower Rhine.
He himself was probably liberated later by the intervention of Maria Theresa, but there is no record of
it. His letter is of great value as he had personal
experience of what he writes. His experience was a
long one, for he entered the prison in 1759; and this
communication to his provincial is dated October 12,
1766. In it he writes:—

"I was taken prisoner by a soldier with a drawn
sword and brought to Fort Olreida on the frontier of
Portugal. There I was put in a frightful cell filled
with rats which got into my bed and ate my food.
I could not chase them away, it was so dark. We
were twenty Jesuits, each one in a separate cell.
During the first four months we were treated with some
consideration. After that, they gave us only enough
food to keep us from dying of hunger. They took
away our breviaries, medals, etc. One of the
Fathers resisted so vigorously when they tried to
deprive him of his crucifix that they desisted. The
sick got no help or medicine.

"After three years they transferred nineteen of us
to another place because of a war that had broken out.
We travelled across Portugal surrounded by a troop
of cavalry, and were brought to Lisbon; and after
passing the night in a jail with the worst kind of

criminals, we were sent to St. Julian, which is on the seashore. It is a horrible hole, underground, dark and foul. The food is bad, the water swarming with worms. We have half a pound of bread a day. We receive the sacraments only when we are dying. The doctor lives outside but if we fall sick during the night, he is not called. The prison is filled with worms and insects and little animals such as I never saw before. The walls are dripping wet, so that our clothes soon rot. One of the Fathers died and his face was so brilliant that one of the soldiers exclaimed: ' That's the face of a saint.' We are not unhappy, and the three French Fathers who left us envied our lot.

" Very few of us have even the shreds of our soutanes left. Indeed we have scarcely enough clothes for decency. At night a rough covering full of sharp points serves as a blanket; and the straw on which we sleep as well as the blanket that covers us soon become foul, and it is very hard to get them renewed. We are not allowed to speak to any one. The jailor is extremely brutal and seems to make a point of adding to our sufferings; only with the greatest reluctance does he give us what we need. Yet we could be set free in a moment if we abandoned the Society. Some of the Fathers who were at Macao and had undergone all sorts of sufferings at the hands of the pagans, such as prison chains and torture say to us that perhaps God found it better to have them suffer in their own country for nothing, than among idolaters for the Faith.

" We ask the prayers of the Fathers of the province, but not because we lament our condition. On the contrary, we are happy. As for myself, though I would like to see my companions set free, I would not change places with you outside. We wish all our Fathers good health so that they may work courage-

ously for God in Germany to make up for the little
glory he receives here in Portugal.

> Your Reverence's most humble servant
> Lawrence Kaulen,
>> Captive of Jesus Christ."

Pombal was determined now to make a master-
stroke to discredit the Portuguese Jesuits. He would
disgrace and put to death as a criminal their most
distinguished representative, Father Malagrida, now
over seventy years of age, who had already passed
two years in the dungeons of Jonquiera. Malagrida
was regarded by the people as a saint. He had labored
for many years in the missions of Brazil and was
marvelously successful in the work of converting the
savages. Unfortunately he had been recalled to
Portugal in 1749 by the queen mother to prepare her
for the end of her earthly career. As Malagrida knew
how Carvalho's brother was acting in Brazil, he was
evidently a dangerous man to have so near the Court.
Hence when the earthquake occurred and the holy old
missionary dared to tell the people that possibly it was
a punishment of God for the sins of the people, Carvalho banished him to Setubal and kept him there
for two years. When the supposed plot against the
king's life occurred, Malagrida was sent to prison as
being concerned in it, though he had never been in
Lisbon since his banishment. He was condemned to
death with the other supposed conspirators; but his
character as a priest, and his acknowledged sanctity
made the king forbid the execution of the sentence.
Pombal, however, found a way out of the difficulty.
A book was produced which was said to have been
written by Malagrida during his imprisonment. It
was crammed with utterances that only a madman
could have written: In any case it could not have

been produced by the occupant of a dark cell, where there was no ink and no paper. When it was presented to the Inquisition whose death sentences the king himself could not revoke, the judges refused to consider the case at all; whereupon they were promptly removed by Pombal who made his own brother chief inquisitor; and from him and two other tools, promptly drew a condemnation of Malagrida for heresy, schism, blasphemy and gross immorality.

The sentence of death was passed on September 20, 1761, and on the same day the venerable priest was brought to hear the formal proclamation of it in the hall of supplication. There he was told that he was degraded from his priestly functions, and was condemned to·be led through the public streets of the city, with a rope around his neck, to the square called do Rocco, where he was to be strangled by the executioner, and after he was dead, his body was to be burned to ashes, so that no memory of him or his sepulchre might remain. He heard the sentence without emotion and quietly protested his innocence. On the very next day, September 21, the execution took place. Platforms were .erected around the square. Cavalry and infantry were massed here and there in large bodies; each soldier had eight rounds of ammunition. Pombal presided. The nobility, the members of the courts, and officers of the State were compelled to be present, and great throngs of people crowded the square and filled the abutting avenues and streets.

When everything was ready, a gruesome procession started from the prison. Malagrida appeared with the *carocha*, or high cap of the criminal, on his head, and a gag in his mouth. With him were fifty-two others who had been condemned for various crimes; but only he was to die. They were called from their cells merely to accentuate his disgrace. Having

arrived at the place of execution, the sentence was
again read to him; and when he was relieved of the
gag, he calmly protested his innocence and gave himself up to the executioners, uttering the words of
Our Lord on the Cross: " Father, into Thy hands, I
commend my spirit." He was quickly strangled;
then fire was set to his lifeless body and the ashes were
scattered to the winds. He was seventy-two years of
age, and had spent forty-one of them working for the
salvation of his fellowmen.

All this happened in Portugal which once gloried
in having the great Francis Xavier represent it before
the world; which exulted in a son like de Britto, the
splendid apostle of the Brahmans, who waived aside
a mitre in Europe but bent his neck with delight to
receive the stroke of an Oriental scimitar. The same
Portugal which inscribed on its roll of honor the forty
Jesuits who suffered death while on their way to
evangelize Portugal's possessions in Brazil, now made
a holiday to witness the hideous torture of the venerable
and saintly Malagrida. The Jesuits of Portugal had
done much for their country. They had borne an
honorable part in the struggle that threw off the Spanish
yoke: the magnificent Vieira was a greater emancipator
of the native races than was Las Casas; and he and his
brethren had won more territories for Portugal than
da Gama and Cabral had ever discovered. But all
that was forgotten, and they were driven out of their
country, or kept chained in fetid dungeons till they
died or were burned at the stake in the market-place,
in the preseence of the king and the people. No wonder
that Portugal has descended to the place she now
occupies among the nations.

CHAPTER XV

CHOISEUL

THE result of Pombal's work in Portugal was applauded by his friends in France, but his methods were condemned. " He was a butcher with an axe." Their own procedure was to be along different lines. They would first poison the public mind, would enjoy the pleasure of seeing the heretical Jansenist condemning the Jesuit for heterodoxy, and the professional debauchee assailing his morality, and then they would put the Society to death by process of law for the good of the commonwealth and of the Church. There would be no imprisonments, no burnings at the stake, no exiles, but simply an authorized confiscation of property which would leave the Jesuits without a home, replenish the public purse and ensure the peace of the nation. It was much easier and more refined. Meantime, the Portuguese exhibition was a valuable object lesson to their followers, who saw a king lately honored with the title of His Most Faithful Majesty putting to death the most ardent champions of the Faith. Later on, The Christian King, The Catholic King, and The Apostolic Emperor would unite to show that " Faith " and " Christianity " and Apostolicity " were only names.

With all their refinement, however, the French were more radical and more malignant than the Portuguese. Pombal had no other idea beyond that of a state Church such as he had seen in England, forming a part of the government machinery, and when his effort to bring that about by marrying the Protestant Duke of Cumberland to the Infanta of Portugal was thwarted by the Jesuits, he simply treated them as he did his other political enemies; he put them in jail or the grave. In France, the scheme was more comprehensive. With men like Voltaire and his associates in the literary world, and Choiseul and others of his set controlling the politics of the country, the plan was not merely to do away with the Church, but with all revealed religion. As the Jesuits were conspicuous adversaries of the scheme, it was natural that they should be disposed of first.

Such is the opinion of St. Liguori, who says: " The whole thing is a plot of the Jansenists and unbelievers to strike the Pope and the Church." The Protestant historian Maximilian Schoell is of like mind (Cours d'histoire, xliv.): " The Church had to be isolated; and to be isolated, it had to be deprived of the help of that sacred phalanx which had avowed itself to the defence of the Pontifical throne...... Such was the real cause of the hatred meted out to that Society." Dutilleul, in his " Histoire des corporations religieuses en France " (p. 279) expresses himself as follows: " The Jesuit is a missionary, a traveller, a mystic, a man of learning, an elegant civilizer of savages, a confessor of queens, a professor, a legislator, a financier, and, if need be, a warrior. His was not a narrow and personal ambition, as people erroneously suppose and assert. He was something more. He was a reactionist, a Catholic and a Roman revolutionist. Far from being attached, as is supposed, to his own interests, the Society has been in the most daring efforts of its indefatigable ambition only the protagonists of the spiritual authority of Rome."

Indeed, we have it from Voltaire himself, who wrote to Helvetius in 1761: "Once we have destroyed the Jesuits, we shall have easy work with the Pope." Rorbacher (Histoire de l'église, tom. XXVII, p. 28) holds the same view, "They are attacking the Society only to strike with greater certainty at the Church and the State." But the real, the ultimate purpose of Voltaire was expressed by his famous phrase *Ecrasons l'infâme* — "Let us crush the detestable thing," the detestable thing meaning God or Christ, and such has ever been the aim of his disciples. That it still persists was proclaimed officially from the French tribune by Viviani, "Our war is not against the Church, nor against Christianity, but against God." This open and defiant profession of atheism, however, would not have been possible in 1761. Hence, to conceal their purpose, they allied themselves with the most pretentious professors of the religion of the time; the only ones, according to themselves, who knew the Church's dogma and observed her moral law; the orthodox and austere Jansenists, who probably flattered themselves they were tricking *les impies*, whereas, d'Alembert wrote to one of his friends "Let the Pandours destroy the Jesuits; then we shall destroy the Pandours."

The programme was to compel the parliament to terrorize the king, which was very easy, because of the gross licentiousness of Louis XV. He was simply a tool in the hands of his mistresses, and Guizot in his "Histoire de France" has a picture in which Madame du Barry stands over the king and points to the picture of Charles I of England, who was beheaded for resisting parliament.

The Jansenist section of the coalition began the fight by the time-worn accusation of the " lax morality " of the Jesuits — a method of assault that was by no means acceptable to Voltaire who as early as 1746 had written to his friend d'Alembert, as follows: " What did I see during the seven years that I lived in the Jesuit's College? The most laborious and frugal manner of life; every hour of which was spent in the care of us boys and in the exercises of their austere profession. For that I call to witness thousands of men who were brought up as I was. Hence, it is that I can never help being astounded at their being accused of teaching lax morality. They have had like other religious in the dark ages casuists who have treated the *pro* and *con* of questions that are evident today or have been relegated to oblivion. But, *ma foi* are we going to judge their morality by the satire of the *Lettres Provinciales*. It is assuredly by Father Bourdaloue and Father Cheminais and their other preachers and by their missionaries that we should measure them. Put in parallel columns the sermons of Bourdaloue and the *Lettres Provinciales*, and you'll find in the latter the art of raillery pressed into service to make indifferent things appear criminal and to clothe insults in elegant language; but you will learn from Bourdaloue how to be severe to yourself and indulgent to others. I ask then, which is true morality and which of the two books is more useful to mankind? I make bold to say that there is nothing more contradictory; nothing more iniquitous; nothing more shameful in human nature than to accuse of lax morality, the men who lead the austerest kind of life in Europe, and who go to face death at the ends of Asia and America."

The romances about the immense wealth of the Society best appealed to the public imagination,

31

especially as the news of an impending financial disaster was in the air. One instance of this style of propaganda may suffice. The others all resemble it. A Spaniard, it was said, had arrived at Brest with, 2,000,000 *livres* in his wallet and was promptly killed by the Jesuits. Soon the 2,000,000 had grown to 8,000,000. Then there was a distinguished conversion; that of a Jesuit named Chamillard who had turned Gallican and Jansenist on his death-bed; and although Chamillard a few days afterwards appeared in the flesh and protested that he was neither dead nor a Gallican nor a Jansenist, his testimony was set aside. It had appeared in print and that was enough. Such absurdities of course could do no serious harm, but at last, a splendid fact presented itself which could not be disproved; especially as a vast number of people, in France and elsewhere, were financial sufferers in consequence of it. It was the bankruptcy of Father de la Valette. In the public mind it proved everything that had ever been written about the Order. Briefly it is as follows:

At the very beginning of the Seven Years War, the British fleet had destroyed 300 French ships, captured 10,000 sailors and confiscated 300,000,000 *livres* worth of merchandise. Among the sufferers was Father La Valette, the superior of Martinique, who was engaged in cultivating extensive plantations on the island, and selling the products in Europe, for the support of the missions. Very unwisely he borrowed extensively after the first disaster, going deeper and deeper into debt, until at last he was unable to meet his obligations which by this time had run up to the alarming sum of 2,000,000 *livres*, or about $400,000. Suit was therefore brought by some of the creditors, but instead of submitting the case to a commission established long before by Louis XIV for adjusting the affairs of the missions, they laid it before the usual parliamentary tribunal in spite of the fact of its inveterate and well-known hatred of the Society. Guizot says that they did it with a certain pride, so convinced were they of the justice of their plea. Hundreds of others had suffered like themselves at the hands of the enemy in the Seven Years War, and they had no desire to avail themselves of any special legislation in their behalf. They underrated the honesty of the judges.

A verdict was, of course, rendered against them, and the whole Society was made responsible for the debt, though by the law of the land there was no solidarity between the various houses of religious orders. Nevertheless, they set to work to cancel their indebtedness. They had made satisfactory arrangements with their principal creditors, and although Martinique, where much of the property was located, had been seized by the English; yet one-third of their liabilities had been paid off when the government took alarm. If this continued, the public treasury would reap no profit from the transaction. Hence, an order was issued to seize every Jesuit establishment in France. A stop was put to the reimbursement of private individuals and the government seized all that was left. But although the Society was not to blame it incurred the hatred of all those who were thus deprived of their money. That, indeed, was the purpose of the government seizure.

Long before the crash, the superiors had done all in their power to stop La Valette, but in those days Martinique was far from Rome. Although attempt after attempt was made to reach him, it was all in vain. One messenger was crippled when embarking at Marseilles; another died at sea; another was captured by pirates, until in 1762 Father de la Marche arrived on the island. After a thorough investigation de la

Marche declared (1) that La Valette had given himself up to trading in defiance of canon law and of the special laws of the Society; (2) that he had concealed his proceedings from the higher superiors of the Society and even from the Fathers of Martinique; (3) that his acts had been denounced by his superiors, not only as soon as they were made known, but as soon as they were suspected. The visitor then asked the General of the Society (1) to suspend La Valette from all administration both spiritual and temporal: and (2) to recall him immediately to Europe.

La Valette's submission was appended to the verdict of the visitor; in it, he acknowledges the justice of the sentence, although as soon as he knew what harm he was doing he had stopped. He attests under oath that not one of his superiors had given him any authorization or counsel or approval; and no one had shared in or connived at his enterprises. He takes God to witness that he did not make his avowals under compulsion or threat, or out of complaisance, or for any inducement held out to him, but absolutely of his own accord, and for truth's sake; and in order to dispel and refute, as far as in him lay, the calumnies against the Society consequent upon his acts. The document bore the date of April 25, 1762. He was expelled from the Society and passed the rest of his life in England. He never retracted or modified any of the statements he had made in Martinique.

Following close on the decision in the La Valette case, parliament ordered the immediate production of a copy of the Constitutions of the Society. On the following morning, it was in their hands and was submitted to several committees made up of Jansenists, Gallicans and Atheists. These committees were charged with the examination of the Institute and also of various publications of the Society. Extracts were to be made and presented for the consideration of the court. The most famous of these reports was the one made by La Chalotais, a prominent magistrate of Brittany. He discovered that the Society was in conflict with the authority of the Church, the general Councils, the Apostolic See, and all ecclesiastical and civil governments; moreover that, in their approved theological works, they taught every form of heresy, idolatry and superstition, and inculcated suicide, regicide, sacrilege, robbery, impurity of every kind, usury, magic, murder, cruelty, hatred, vengeance, sedition, treachery — in brief, whatever iniquity mankind could commit was to be found in their writings. As soon as the report was laid before the judges, a decree was issued on May 8, 1761 declaring that the one hundred and fifty-eight colleges, churches and residences with the foreign missions of the Order were to be seized by the government; all the physical laboratories, the libraries, moneys, inheritances of its members, the bequests of friends for charitable, educational or missionary purposes — all was to go into the Government coffers.

Crétineau-Joly estimated that the total value of the property seized amounted to about 58,000,000 francs or $11,600,000. The amount of the booty explains the zeal of the prosecution. To soften the blow a concession of a pension of thirty cents a day was made by the Paris parliament to those who would take an oath that they had left the Society. The Languedoc legislators, however, cut it down to twelve. Moreover this pension was restricted to the Professed. The Scholastics got nothing; and as they were considered legally dead, because of the vows they had taken in the Society, they were declared incapable of inheriting even from their own parents. The decree also forbade all subjects of the king to enter the Society;

to attend any lecture given by Jesuits; to visit their houses previous to their expulsion; or to hold any communication with them. The Jesuits themselves were enjoined not to write to each other, not even to the General. It is noteworthy that the lawmakers who issued these regulations profess to be shocked by the Jesuit doctrine of " blind obedience."

By a second decree it was ordered that the works of twenty-seven Jesuits which had been examined should be burned by the public executioner. Among them were such authors as Bellarmine, Lessius, Suárez, Valentia, Salmerón, Gretser, Vásquez, Jouvancy, — all of whom were and yet are considered to be among the greatest of Catholic theologians, but the lay doctors of the parliament held them to be dangerous to public morals; and to the peace of the nation and in order to express their horror emphatically, they called for this *auto da fé.* It should be noted that all of these works were written in Latin, and that their technical character as well as the terminology employed would make it absolutely impossible for even these solons of the French parliament to grasp the meaning of the text. In order to sway the public mind, a summary of the Chalotais report, commonly known as " Extraits des assertions" was scattered broadcast throughout the country. The desired effect was produced and even to-day if an attempt is made to answer any of its charges the answer is always ready, " We have the authority of La Chalotais; he was an eminent magistrate; he examined the books; the highest court in France accorded him the verdict, and any attempt to explain away the charges is superfluous!"

Yet there was in Paris at that time a higher tribunal than the one which gave La Chalotais his claim to notoriety. It was the General Assembly of the Clergy which had been convoked by the King to pass upon the character of the Jesuits as a body, before he affixed his signature to the decree of expulsion. It consisted of fifty-one prelates, some of them cardinals. They met on June 27 and with the exception of the Bishop of Angers, Allais, and especially of Fitzjames, the Bishop of Soissons, who was the head of the Jansenist party and whose pastoral utterances were condemned by the Pope as heretical, addressed a " Letter " to the king conjuring him " to preserve an institution which was so useful to the State," and declaring that " they could not see without alarm the destruction of a society of religious who were so praiseworthy for the integrity of their morals, the austerity of their discipline, the vastness of their labors and their erudition and for the countless services they had rendered to the Church.

" Charged as they are with the most precious trust of the education of youth, participating as they do under the authority of the bishops, in the most delicate functions of the holy ministry, honored as they are by the confidence of kings in the most redoubtable of tribunals, loved and sought after by a great number of our subjects and esteemed even by those who fear them, they have won for themselves a consideration which is too general to be disregarded."

" Everything, Sire, pleads with you in favor of the Jesuits: religion claims them as its defenders; the Church as her ministers; Christians as the guardians of their conscience; a great number of your subjects who have been their pupils intercede with you for their old masters; and all the youth of the kingdom pray for those who are to form their minds and their hearts. Do not, Sire, turn a deaf ear to our united supplication; do not permit in your kingdom, that in violation of the laws of justice, and of the Church and of the State an entire and blameless society should be destroyed."

The Archbishop of Paris, the famous Christophe de Beaumont was not satisfied with this general appeal. He was the chief figure in France at that time; and every word he uttered was feared by the enemies of the Church. He was great enough to be in correspondence with all the crowned heads of Europe, and Frederick the Great said of him: " If he would consent to come to Prussia, I would go half way to meet him." Louis XV had forced him to accept the See of Paris, but had not the courage to support him when assailed by his foes. He was a saint as well as a hero; he lent money to men who were libelling him, and would give the clothes on his back to the poor. When a hospital took fire in the city, he filled his palace and his cathedral with the patients. Hence, he did not hesitate, after parliament had condemned the Society, to issue a pastoral which he foresaw would drive him from his see. " What shall I say, Brethren," he asks, " to let you know what I think of the religious society which is now so fiercely assailed? We repeat with the Council of Trent that it is ' a pious Institute;' that it is ' venerable,' as the illustrious Bossuet declared it to be. We spurn far from us the ' Extraits des assertions ' as a resumé of Jesuit teaching; and we renew our declaration that in the condition of suffering and humiliation to which they have been brought that their lot is a most happy one, because in the eyes of religious men, it is an infinitely precious thing to have no reproach on one's soul when overwhelmed by misfortune." As he foresaw he was expelled from his see for this utterance, not by parliament but by Louis XV whose cause he was defending.

Perhaps this treatment of the great Archbishop of Paris explains the silence maintained through all the uproar by the Jesuits themselves. One would expect some splendid outburst of eloquence in behalf of the

Society from one of its outraged members; but not a
word was uttered by any of them. Their protests
would not have been printed or published. Even
Theiner who wrote against the Society says: " All
France was inundated with libellous pamphlets against
the Jesuits. The most notable of all was the one
entitled ' Extracts of the dangerous and pernicious
doctrines of all kinds which the so-called Jesuits have
at all times, uninterruptedly maintained, taught and
published.' Calumny and malice fill the book from
cover to cover. There is no crime which the Jesuits
did not teach or of which they are not accused. Never
was bad faith carried to such extremes. And yet
there is no book that is so often cited as an authority
against the Society and its spirit."

Meantime, the government had approached the
Pope for the purpose of obtaining for the French
Jesuits a special vicar who should be quasi-independent
of the General. It was harking back to the old scheme
of Philip II and Louis XIV. His Holiness replied
in the memorable words: " Sint ut sunt aut non sint "
(Let them be as they are or not at all.) We find in
a letter of the procurator of Aquitaine that in case a
vicar was appointed every member of the province
of Paris would leave the Order, which under such an
arrangement would be no longer the Society of Jesus.
Again in his letter to the king, after declaring that the
appointment of a French Vicar would be a substantial
alteration of the Institute which he could not authorize,
the Pope says: " For two hundred years the Society has
been so useful to the Church, that, though it has never
disturbed the public tranquillity either in your kingdom
or in any one else's, yet because it has inflicted such
damage on the enemies of religion by its science and
its piety, it is assailed on all sides by calumny and
imposture when fair fighting was found insufficient to

destroy them." Finally, on January 9, 1765, after the final knell had sounded, Clement XIII issued his famous Bull "Apostolicum." It is given at length in de Ravignan's "Clément XIII et Clément XIV," but a few extracts will suffice.

After enumerating the glories of the Society in the past, and calling attention to the fact that it had been approved by nineteen Popes, who had most minutely examined their Institute, Clement XIII continues: " It has, nevertheless, in our days been falsely and malignantly described both by word and printed book as irreligious and impious, and has been covered with opprobrium and ignominy until even the Church has been denounced for sustaining it. In order, therefore, to repel these calumnies and to put a stop to the impious discourses which are uttered in defiance of both reason and equity; and to comfort the Regular Clerks of the Society of Jesus who appeal to us for justice; and to give greater emphasis to our words by the weight of our authority and to lend some solace in the sufferings they are undergoing; and finally to defer to the just desires of our venerable brothers, the bishops of the whole Catholic world, whose letters to us are filled with eulogies of this Society from whose labors the greatest services are rendered in their dioceses; and also of our own accord and from certain knowledge, and making use of the plenitude of our Apostolic authority, and following in the footsteps of our predecessors, we, by this present Constitution, which is to remain in force forever, say and declare in the same form and in the same manner as has been heretofore said and declared, that the Institute of the Society of Jesus breathes in the very highest degree, piety and holiness both in the principal object which it has continually in view, which is none other than the defence and propagation of the Catholic Faith, and also in the means it

employs for that end. Such is our experience of it
up to the present day. It is this experience which
has taught us how greatly the rule of the Society has
formed up to our day defenders of the orthodox Faith
and zealous missionaries who animated by an invincible
courage dare a thousand dangers on land and sea,
to carry the light of the Gospel to savage and barbarous
nations......Let no one dare be rash enough to set
himself against this my present approbative and con-
firmative Constitution lest he incur the wrath of God."

These splendid approvals of their labors did much
to keep up the courage of the harassed Jesuits, but if
what Father de Ravignan and Crétineau-Joly relate
be true, they had ample reason to keep themselves in
a salutary humility or rather bow their heads in shame.
On December 19, 1761, we are told, the provincial of
Paris, Father de La Croix and one hundred and fifteen
Fathers addressed a declaration to the clergy assembled
in Paris, by order of the king, which ran as follows:
" We the undersigned, provincial of the Jesuits of the
province of Paris, the superior of the professed house,
the rector of the College of Louis Le Grand, the
superior of the novitiate and other Jesuits professed,
even of the first vows, residing in the said houses, and
renewing as far as needs be the declarations already
made by the Jesuits of France in 1626, 1713 and 1757,
declare before their Lordships the cardinals, archbishops and bishops now assembled in Paris, by order
of the king, to give their opinion on several points of
the Institute: (1) That it is impossible to be more
submissive than we are, or more inviolably attached
to the laws, maxims and usages of this kingdom with
regard to the royal power, which in temporal matters
depends neither directly nor indirectly from any power
on earth, and has God alone above it. Recognizing
that the bonds by which subjects are attached to their

rulers are indissoluble, we condemn as pernicious and
worthy of execration at all times every doctrine contrary to the safety of the king, not only in the works of
some theologians of our Society who have adopted
such doctrines but also those of every other theologian
whosoever he may be. (2) We shall teach in our
public and private lessons of theology the doctrine
established by the Clergy of France in the Four Articles
of the Assembly of 1682, and shall teach nothing
contrary to it. (3) We recognize that the bishops of
France have the right to exercise in our regard what,
according to the canons of the Gallican Church,
belongs to them in their dealings with regulars;
and we renounce all the privileges to the contrary
that may have been accorded to our Society or may
be accorded in the future. (4) If, which may God
forbid, it happens that we are ordered by our General
to do anything contrary to the present declaration,
persuaded as we are that we cannot obey without sin,
we shall regard such orders as unlawful, and absolutely
null and void; which we could not and should not obey
in virtue of the rules of obedience to the General such
as is prescribed in the Constitutions. We, therefore,
beg that the present declaration may be placed on the
official register of Paris, and addressed to the other
provinces of the kingdom, so that this same declaration
signed by us, being deposited in the official registers of
each diocese may serve as a perpetual memorial of
our fidelity.

Etienne de la Croix, Provincial."

Quoting this document and admitting its genuineness
Father de Ravignan exclaims: " In my eyes nothing
can excuse this act of weakness. I deplore it; I condemn
it; I shall merely relate how it came to pass " (Clément
XIII et Clément XIV, I 135). He goes on to say:-

"In a personal letter the original of which is in the archives of the Gesù at Rome, Father La Croix, provincial of Paris explains to the General the circumstances and occasion of this unfortunate affair. He tells how the royal commissioners came to him with the aforesaid declaration already drawn up and accompanied by a formal order of the king to sign it immediately. It was a most unforeseen demand, for although the Jesuits of France had already suffered considerable trouble about the question of the Four Articles in 1713, and also in 1757, when Damiens attempted to assassinate Louis XV, they had been compelled on both occasions to sign only the first article which dealt with the temporal independence of the king. Shortly afterwards, a new royal decree had been brought to their attention. It consisted of eighteen articles, the fourth of which was as follows: 'Our will is that in every theological course followed by the students of the Society, the propositions set forth by the Clergy of France in 1682, should be defended, at least in one public discussion, to which the principal personages of the place shall be invited, and over and above that, the arrangements laid down by the edict of March 1682 shall be observed.'

"While these matters were being debated by the king and his ministers on one side and by parliament on the other, a royal order was despatched to the Jesuits of Paris to affix their signatures to the disgraceful capitulation given above. It is said that Louis XV imagined that he could mollify the recalcitrant parliament by this new concession: and, hence, La Croix and his associates were foolish enough to imagine that such a result could ensue."

Continuing his indictment of La Croix and his one hundred and fifteen associates, de Ravignan informs his readers that "an unpublished document

which no writer has so far made mention of, furnishes
important details about the matter.   It is entitled
' An exact relation of all that took place with regard
to the interpretation of the decree of Aquaviva in
1610, which was sent to Rome in 1761 and rejected
by the General; and also the declaration which the
General refused to approve.' The author is M. de
Flesselles, who was charged by the commission to
report to Choiseul whose agent he was.

" With regard to the declaration about Gallicanism "
says de Flesselles " the Jesuits, after some difficulties
regarding its form, determined to sign it, and even
when urged by the royal commissioners they undertook
to send it to their General for approbation.   Soon
after, when the Jesuits received the reply of their
General, the provincial came to tell me that when the
Pope was made aware of the declaration which the
French Jesuits had made and of the one they proposed
to make, His Holiness angrily reprimanded the General
for permitting the members of the Society in France
to maintain doctrines which are in conflict with the
teachings of the Holy See."

Now it is unpleasant to contest the authority of such
an eminent man as de Ravignan, but, on the other
hand, his conclusions that this letter was a Jesuit
production or received a Jesuit endorsement are by no
means convincing. In the first place, no Jesuit would
ever sign a paper which began with the words: " We
the Professed, even of the first vows." There is no
such category in the Society. Secondly, no Jesuit or
indeed any one in his senses would ever ask a superior
for a permission to teach error, and say, in the
same breath, that it was a matter of indifference
whether the permission was granted or not. Thirdly,
as all the Jesuits of the province had announced their
intention of leaving the Society if Louis XV imposed

on them a commissary General independent of their
superior at Rome — as we recited above from an
extant letter from the procurator of the province of
Aquitaine — it is inconceivable that those same men,
at that very same time should solemnly declare themselves rebels against the Father General at Rome.
Fourthly, as no association rewards a man who
attempts to destroy it, one finds difficulty in understanding how, after this revolt, the 'leader in the rebellion, La Croix, was not only not expelled from the
Society but was retained in his responsible post of
provincial and later was made assistant general of the
Society.

Moreover, it is difficult to understand why, when
de Flesselles says that " the Fathers determined to sign
the document," de Ravignan should go one step further
and say that " they signed it." Nor does it help matters
to say that this was " *un acte de faiblesse*," when, it
was a wholesale, corporate and deliberate crime of
cowardice and treason; nor will it avail to suggest that
the Pope and General must have been intensely, grieved
—" Ils durent être amèrement affligés." History does
not deal with conjectures but with facts. The question
is not whether they must have been, but whether they
were really grieved over an act which had really occurred
and which reflected such discredit on the Society?
Again, as one of the greatest glories of the French
Jesuits was their long and successful battle against
Gallicanism, it is inconceivable that they should
suddenly reverse and stultify themselves at the very
moment when all the bishops of France, save one,
had abandoned Gallicanism and had united in eulogizing the Society; and to do it at a time when the greatest
friend they ever had, Pope Clement XIII, glorified
them for their orthodoxy and pronounce dthe famous
words: " Let them be as they are or not at all! "

To have declared for Gallicanism would have stripped them of their priestly functions, it would have aroused the intense disgust and contempt of the hierarchy of France and of the world and would have called down on them the anathema of the Pope. Indeed, is it likely that Pope Clement XIV would have omitted to note the defection in his Brief of Suppression, if they had been guilty? Fortunately, we may refer to the explicit declaration of the Protestant historian, Schoell (Cours d'histoire, xl, 53), who says: " These men who are accused of playing with religion, refused to take the oath to sustain the principles of the Gallican Church. Of 4000 Fathers who were in France, hardly five submitted." If there were " hardly five " Gallicans in all the provinces of France, it is a justifiable conclusion that 116 Jesuits of the provinces of Paris did not sign the famous " Statement " of de Flesselles.

Louis XV made a feeble attempt to save the situation by withdrawing the decree of expulsion from the jurisdiction of parliament, but Mme. de Pompadour and Choiseul so effectively worked on his fears that he ignominiously rescinded his order. The Pope had meantime delivered an allocution in a consistory on September 3, 1762; and had sent a letter to Cardinal Choiseul, the brother of the minister, on September 8 of the same year, in both of which he declared that " by a solemn decree, he had quashed and nullified the proceedings of the various parliaments against the Jesuits." He enjoined upon the cardinal " to use all his episcopal power against the impious act which was directed against the Church and against religion." He wrote to other bishops in the same tone of indignation and anger. It was not, however, until the November of 1764 that Choiseul succeeded in extorting the royal signature which made the decree irrevocable. Of course, Mme. de Pompadour was to the fore in

securing this shameful surrender of the royal prerogative. The poor king cuts a sorry figure in signing the
document. After making some feeble scrawls on the
paper, he complained that the preamble was too long
and that it would have sufficed to state that " the
Jesuits had produced a great tumult in his kingdom."
He added he did not think the word " punish " should
be used; it was too strong; " he never cordially liked
the Jesuits, yet they had the glory of being hated by
all heretics......I send them out of my kingdom
against my will; at least, I don't want people to think
that I agree with everything the parliament said or
did against them." He ended by saying: " If
you do not make these changes, I will not sign, but
I must stop talking. I would say too much and I
do not want anyone in France to discuss it." One
could hardly say of Louis that " he was every inch a
king."

The desire to close the mouths of every one of his
subjects on a matter that concerned them all as
intelligent beings and as citizens was carried out with
extreme rigor. Thus, when two secular priests had
the temerity to condemn the decree, they were promptly
hanged. The audacity of the ministers and parliament
went still further; and on December 3 the Duke de
Praslin sent a note to Aubeterre, the French ambassador
at Rome to advise him that " under the circumstances,
it would be very futile and still more dangerous for the
Pope to take any measures either directly or indirectly
in contravention of the wishes and intention of his
majesty; and hence His Holiness must, out of zeal for
religion and out of regard for the Jesuits, observe the
same silence which His Majesty had ordered to be
observed in his states." The Pope replied to the insult
by the Bull "Apostolicum," which was a splendid
proclamation of the absolute innocence of the pro-

32

scribed Order. It aroused the fury of the Governments of France, Portugal, Naples and other countries. In France it was burned in the streets of several cities by the public executioner. In Portugal, any one who circulated it or had it in his possession was adjudged guilty of high treason; but on the other hand, from the bishops of the entire Catholic world came enthusiastic letters of approval and praise for the fearless Pope who dared to stand forth as the enemy of tyranny and injustice.

Böhmer-Monod, in their " Jésuites," are of the opinion that the Pope was " injudicious, and that out of the hundreds of Catholic bishops, only twenty-three assured him of their approbation." De Ravignan, who is better informed, tells us that " almost the whole episcopacy of the world were a unit in this manifestation of loyalty to the supreme Pastor. Before the event, two hundred bishops had sent their appeals to the Pope, in favor of the Society; and the Pope himself says in the Bull: " Ex omni regione sub cœlo est una vox omnium episcoporum " (From every region under the canopy of heaven, there is but one voice from the episcopal body). After the Bull appeared, other bishops hastened to send him their adhesions and felicitations. Even in France itself, in spite of the terrorism exercised by parliament, the assembly of the clergy of 1765, by a unanimous vote, protested against the condemnation of the Jesuits, extolled " the integrity of their morals, the austerity of their lives, the greatness of their labors and science"; and declared that their expulsion left a frightful void in the ministry, in education, and in the sublime and laborious work of the missions. Not only that, but they wanted it put on record that " the clergy would never cease to pray for the re-establishment of the Order and would lay that plea at the feet of the king."

The exiles lingered for a while in various parts of
France; for some of the divisional parliaments were
not at one with Paris in their opposition to the Society.
Indeed, in many of them, the proscription was voted
only by a small majority. Thus at Rennes, there was
a majority of three; at Toulouse two; at Perpignan
one; at Bordeaux five; at Aix two; while Besançon,
Alsace, Flanders and Artois and Lorraine pronounced
in their favor and proclaimed " the sons of St. Ignatius
as the most faithful subjects of the King of France
and the surest guarantees of the morality of the people."
On the other hand, Brittany, the country of Chalotais,
author of the " Extraits," was especially rancorous in
its hate. Thus, it voted to deprive of all civil and
municipal functions those parents who would send
their children abroad to Jésuit schools; and the children
on their return home were to be punished in a similar
fashion. The Fathers lingered for a few years here
and there in their native country employed in various
occupations; but in 1767 a decree was issued expelling
them all from the territory of France.

An interesting manifestation of affection by the
pupils of St. Omers for their persecuted masters occurred
when the parliament of Paris issued its order of expulsion in 1767. St. Omers was founded by Father
Persons in 1592 or 1593. It was not for ecclesiastics
as were the colleges of Douai, Rome and Valladolid,
but to give English boys an education which they could
not get in their own country. It was twenty-four
miles from Calais and in territory which at that time
belonged to the King of Spain. Shortly after its
transfer from Eu in Normandy where an attempt
had been made to start it, there were one hundred
boys on its register and, thirty years later, the number
had doubled. For years it was a favorite school for
English Catholics and it rejoices in having had twenty

of its students die for the Faith. It continued its work for a century and a half. When the expulsion of the Jesuits left the college without teachers it was handed over to the secular clergy, but when they arrived there were no boys. They had all decamped for Bruges in Belgium, and there the classes continued until the general suppression of the Society in 1773. Even after that, the English ex-Jesuits kept the college going until 1794, when the French Revolution put an end to it. By that time, however, one of the former students, Mr. Thomas Weld, had established the Fathers on his property at Stonyhurst in England, so that St. Omers and Stonyhurst are mother and daughter.

The buildings and land at St. Omers were handed over by the French government to the English secular priests, who were at Douai. Alban Butler, the author of .the " Lives of the Saints," was its president from 1766 to 1773. At present a military hospital occupies the site.

In Louisiana, which still owed allegiance to France, the dismissal of the Fathers was particularly disgraceful. For no sooner had the news of Choiseul's exploit in the mother-country arrived than the superior council of Louisiana set to work. " This insignificant body of provincial officers " as Shea calls them (I, 587), " issued a decree declaring the Society to be dangerous to the royal authority, to the rights of bishops, to the public peace of society " and pronounced their vows to be null and void. These judges in matters ecclesiastical, it should be noted, were all laymen. They ordered all the property to be seized and sold at auction, though personal books and clothes were exempted. The name and habit of the Society were forbidden; the vestments and plate of the chapel at New Orleans were given by the authorities to the Capuchins; but all the Jesuit churches in Louisiana and Illinois were ordered to be levelled to the ground. Every Jesuit was to embark on the first ship that set sail for France; and arriving there, he was to report to Choiseul. Each one was given about $420 — to pay for his passage and six month's subsistence.

There was a deviation in some cases about going to France, for Father Carette was sent to San Domingo; and Father Le Roy made his way to Mexico. A difficulty arose about Father Beaudoin, who was a Canadian. Why should he be sent to France where he had no friends? Besides, his health was shattered by his privations on the missions, and he was at that time seventy-two years old. He was to go to France, however, but just as he was about to be dragged to the ship a wealthy friend interceded for him and gave him a home. Another Father in Alabama did not hear of the order for several months; and when at last he made his appearance in New Orleans, he was arrested like a criminal and packed off to France.

On September 22, a courier reached Fort Chartres, which was on English territory; and in spite of the danger of embroiling the government, Father Watron who was then sixty-seven years old was expelled, and with him his two fellow missionaries. The official from Louisiana gave the vestments to negro wenches and the altar-plate and candelabra were soon found in houses of ill-fame. The chapel was then sold on condition that the purchaser should demolish it. At Vincennes, the same outrages were perpetrated and Father Duvernay, who had been for six months confined to his bed, was carried off with the others to New Orleans and despatched to France. Two only were allowed to remain, owing to the entreaties and protests of friends. One of the exiles was Father Viel, who was a Louisianian by birth. The most conspicuous

personage enforcing this expulsion was a certain
Lafrenière, but he soon met his punishment. In 1766
Louis XV made a gift of the entire province to his
cousin of Spain, and when Count Alexander O'Reilly
was sent out with three thousand soldiers to quell the
disturbance that ensued, Lafrenière and three associates
were taken into the back yard of the barracks and shot
to death. Others were sent in chains to Havana.

Thus the Suppression of the Society in France was
not carried out with the same brutality as in Portugal.
There were no prisons, or chains, or deportation, and
they had not the glory of suffering martyrdom. They
were merely stripped of all they had and told to go where
they wished. Whether they lived or died was a matter
of unconcern to the government. It was merely a
difference of methods; but both were equally effective.
The Portuguese Jesuits were scourged; their French
brethren were sneered at. Perhaps the latter was
harder to bear.

There is a curious sequel to all this. Choiseul,
proud of his achievement in expelling the Jesuits from
France and its colonies, now conceived the magnificent
project of colonizing Guyana on lines quite different
from those followed by the detested Order. He induced
14,000 deluded French people to go and take possession
of the rich and fertile lands of Guyana. They found
one poor old Jesuit there, who because he was not
a subject of France, had refused to obey the decree
of expulsion. His name was O'Reilly, but what could
he do with 14,000 people He simply disappeared
from the scene. Very likely, he joined the Indians,
who fled into the forests at the sight of this immense
army of Frenchmen, who now had the country to
themselves without striking a blow. But two years
later, Chevalier de Balzac had to report back to France,
that of the 14,000 colonists only 918 were alive. Thus,

expelling 6,000 Jesuits from France, Choiseul had murdered 13,000 of his fellow-countrymen (Christian Missions, II, 168).

In 1766, M. de Piedmont, the governor wrote to the Duc de Praslin, that he had already informed the Duc de Choiseul how necessary it was to send priests to this colony. He then described the destruction of the mission posts, the flight of the Indians, the growth of crime amongst the negroes and the rapid ruin of the colony, and added that religion was dying out among the whites as well as among the colored races. For ten years, he kept on repeating this complaint, but no heed was paid to him. At length, Louis XVI, who was so soon to be himself a victim of Choiseul's iniquity sent there, three Jesuits, not Frenchmen, perhaps he had not the heart to ask any of them, but three Jesuits, who had been expelled from Portugal by Pombal, Choiseul's accomplice. They were Padilla, Mathos, and Ferreira. They accepted the mission and the " Journal " of Christopher de Murr says: " The poor savages beholding once again men clothed in the habit which they had learned to venerate, and hearing them speak their own language, fell at their feet, bathing them with tears, and promised to become once more good Christians, since the Fathers, who had begotten them in Jesus Christ, had come back to them." No doubt, these three holy men remained till they died with their poor abandoned Indians.

France's folly in this governmental act was summed up in a letter of d'Alembert to Choiseul, just before the expulsion. In it he says: " France will resort to this rigorous measure against its own subjects at the very moment she is doing nothing in her foreign policy, and in the chronological epitomes of the future we shall read the words for the year 1762: ' This year France lost all her colonies and threw out the Jesuits.' "

CHAPTER XVI

CHARLES III

The Bourbon Kings of Spain — Character of Charles III — Spanish Ministries — O'Reilly — The Hat and Cloak Riot — Cowardice of Charles — Tricking the monarch — The Decree of Suppression — Grief of the Pope — His death — Disapproval in France by the Encyclopedists — The Royal Secret — Simultaneousness of the Suppression — Wanderings of the Exiles — Pignatelli — Expulsion by Tanucci.

SPAIN had begun to deteriorate in the seventeenth century; it lost all of its European dependencies in the eighteenth, and in the beginning of the nineteenth was stripped of almost every one of its rich and powerful colonies in America. During two-thirds of that period, it was governed by foreigners, none of whom had any claim to consideration, much less respect. Until 1700 it owed allegiance to the house of Austria; after that, the French Bourbons hurried it to its ruin.

Its first Bourbon king, Philip V, had already, in 1713, succeeded in losing Sicily, Milan, Sardinia, the Netherlands, Gibraltar, and the Island of Minorca; that is one-half of its European possessions. Meantime, Catalonia was in rebellion. But little else could be expected from such a ruler. He was not only constitutionally indolent, but apparently mentally defective. His queen kept him in seclusion, and he did nothing but at her dictation; he was professedly devout, but was racked by ridiculous scruples; " outwardly pious," says Schoell, quoting Saint-Simon, " but heedless of the fundamental principles of religion; he was timid and hence sporadically stubborn; and when not in temper, he was easily led. He was without imagination, except that he was continually dreaming of conquering Europe, although he never left Madrid; he

was satisfied with the gloomiest existence, and his
only amusement was shooting at game, which his
servants drove into the brush for him to kill." His
conscience often smote him for the sin he said he had
committed when he renounced his claim to the throne
of France; and, in consequence, he made a vow to lay
aside the Spanish crown until what time he should be
summoned by England to be King of France. To help
him keep his vow, he built the palace of San Ildefonso,
which cost the nation 45,000,000 pesos. He appointed
his son Louis, a lad of 17, to reign in his stead, and the
boy, of course, did nothing but enjoy himself, and
died of small-pox in six months' time, having first gone
through the ridiculous farce of making his father his
heir. Philip then began to doubt whether he could
resume his duties as king after having vowed to
relinquish them. Besides being thus troubled with
scruples, he was in constant dread of catching the
disease which carried off his son; he died of apoplexy,
July 9, 1764 at the age of 53.

Ferdinand VI, who succeeded him, was as indolent
as his father, and with less talent and strength of will;
he was afflicted with melancholia, and like his father
was haunted by the fear of death. He took no part
in the government of the kingdom, but spent most of
his time listening to the warblings of the male-soprano,
Farinelli, who was so adored by the king that he was
sometimes consulted on state affairs. The queen was
another of his idols, and when she died, he shut himself
in, saw no one, would eat next to nothing; never
changed his linen; let his hair and beard grow, and
never went to bed. An hour or two in a chair was
all he allowed himself for rest. He died at the end
of the year, leaving a private fortune of 72,000,000
francs. He was only forty-seven years old. Like the
king, the queen was dominated by fear, not however

of death, but of poverty. To guard against that contingency she hoarded all the money she could get; accepted whatever presents were offered; and let it be known that the easiest way to win her favor was to have something to give. It is gravely said that though she was very corpulent she was extravagantly fond of dancing.

Ferdinand VI was succeeded by his brother Charles III, who had been King of Naples for twenty-four years. He had six sons, the eldest of whom, Philip Anthony was then twelve years of age, but a hopeless imbecile. The right of succession, therefore, devolved on his second son. The third, who was then eight years old, was to succeed to the crown of Naples, and was left in the hands of Tanucci to be trained for his future office. As Tanucci was a bitter enemy of Christianity, this act of Charles, who had a Jesuit confessor and was regarded as a pious man, would imply that he also was mentally deficient. Like his forebears, he was haunted by a fear of death, a weakness that revealed itself in all his political acts, notably in the suppression of the Society. That was one of the reasons why, long after France and Portugal would have willingly ended the fight with the expulsion of the Jesuits, the supposedly pious Charles persisted until he had wrung the Brief of Suppression from the unwilling hands of Clement XIV.

The ministers of state who controlled the destinies of Spain at this period are of a species whose like cannot be found in the history of any other nation. They begin with the Italian Alberoni who started life as a farm laborer; then became an ecclesiastic, and ultimately a cardinal. "He was destined to trouble the tranquillity of the world for years," says Schoell. According to Saint-Simon, he prevented the restitution of Gibraltar to Spain which England was willing to grant; he was banned by the Pope; and was subsequently turned out of office, chiefly by the intrigues of two Italian ecclesiastics. The queen's nurse, old Laura Piscatori, also figures in the amazing diplomacy of those days, and is charged with an ambition to be as important as Cardinal Alberoni, who came from her native village. The next prime minister was the Biscayan Grimaldi, whose physical appearance Saint-Simon describes, but which we omit. It will suffice to say that "he was base and supple when it suited his convenience, and he never made a false step in that direction." Following him, came Ripperda, who was born in the Netherlands and educated by the Jesuits at Cologne, but became a Protestant in Holland, and a Catholic in Spain, where he lasted only four months, as minister. He turned Protestant a second time, on his return to Holland, and subsequently led an army of Moors against Spain. It is not known whether he died a Christian or a Mohammedan.

Patino and de la Quadra followed each other in quick succession, one good, the other timid and weak. Enseñada, though skilful, was greedy of money, and was considered the head of the French faction in court. Carvajal is next on the list, and displays the English propensities which were natural to him, for he belonged to the house of Lancaster. Indeed, his policy was entirely pro-English and he was in collusion with Keene, the British ambassador. Wall, an Irishman, then flits across the scene, and has with him two associates: Losada and Squillace, both Italians. When Wall quarrelled with the Pope and the Inquisition, he fell, and then another Grimaldi came to the fore; not a Biscayan, like his namesake, but a Genoese. Squillace, apparently from the Italian branch of the Borgias, was next in order, and then in rapid procession came the Spaniards: Roda, de Alva, Aranda,

Roda, Moniño, Campomáñez, either as prime ministers or prominent in the government, and nearly all of them under French influence. Finally, the generalissimo of the army and the most popular man in Spain was an Irishman, Alexander O'Reilly. The native Spaniards counted for little; even the king's bodyguard was made up of Walloons.

O'Reilly was probably not in sympathy with the free-thinking politicians who then ruled the nation, for the reason that he was born in Ireland and had all his life been a soldier. Moreover, he was hated by the Aranda faction and retained his post, at the head of the army, only because the king thought that no one could shield the royal life as well as O'Reilly. He was born in 1735, and when still a youth was sub-lieutenant in the Irish Regiment serving in Spain. In 1757 he fought under his countryman de Lacy in Austria, and then followed the *fleur-de-lys* in France. He so distinguished himself, that the Maréchal de Broglie recommended him to the King of Spain. There he soon became brigadier and restored the ancient prestige of the Spanish army. He was made a commandant at Havana, and rebuilt its fortifications, and from there went to Louisiana to secure it to the Spanish crown. His only military failure was in Algiers, but that was not due to any lack of wisdom in his plans, but because his fleet did not arrive at the time appointed. Even then, there was no one so highly esteemed as O'Reilly, and when he died at an advanced age in 1794, the people all declared that the disasters which fell on the nation would have been averted if he had lived. He is credited with possessing besides his military ardor a sweet and insinuating disposition which may explain how he could easily win over the mob which so terrified King Charles at Madrid.

Meantime, the sinister Choiseul in France had all the ministers of Spain in his grip, and he then determined to capture the king. He first made him a present of what up to that time, had been the special pride of France; the precedence of its ambassadors in public functions over those of all other countries, the German Empire excepted. Charles naturally took the gift, but apparently failed to fathom its significance. The next move was to get rid of the court confessor; and his majesty was given a confidential letter from Pombal of Portugal accusing Father Ravago of having fomented the insurrection of the Indians of Paraguay, against the Spanish troops at the time of the transfer of that territory. The plot failed, however, for Charles knew Ravago too well, and then something more drastic was resorted to. Squillace was at that time in power and under him occurred the historic riot which, in the course of time, assumed such dimensions in the king's imagination, that it was one of the three or four things, besides his " royal secret," which he urged on the Pope as a reason for suppressing the Society.

The story of the riot is as follows: Squillace was very energetic in developing the material resources of the kingdom, but always with an eye to his personal and pecuniary profit. He promoted public works; established monopolies even in food stuffs; loaded the people with taxes; and being intensely anti-clerical, was very active in curtailing ecclesiastical privileges. The people and clergy meekly submitted, but something happened which brought Squillace's career to an end; though it had much more serious consequences than that. It scarcely seems credible, but the incident became one of the serious events of the time. Though none suspected it, the whole thing had been deliberately planned, and was the initial step in the plot to expel the Jesuits from Spain. Squillace objected or pretended to object to the kind of dress especially affected by the people of Madrid: a slouched sombrero and an all-enveloping cloak; and he gave orders to change it. Naturally, this exasperated the people, for although they had patiently submitted to the imposition of taxes; the creation of oppressive monopolies; the curtailment of ancient rights and privileges, etc., the audacity of a foreigner interfering with the cut of their garments brought about a popular upheaval. On March 26, 1766, the mob stormed the residence of Squillace, and he ignominiously took to flight. All night long, the excited crowds swarmed through the streets shouting, " Down with Squillace." On the following morning, they surrounded the palace of the king himself and he, in alarm, called for O'Reilly to quell the disturbance. When it was represented to his majesty that it might entail bloodshed, he deprecated that and hurriedly left Madrid. Had he shown himself to the people, they would have done him no harm, for reverence for royalty was still deep in the popular heart, and the age of royal assassinations had not yet come. But the king was not a hero, and he thrust his subaltern into what he fancied was a post of danger. Thereupon, unarmed and unattended, O'Reilly faced the excited mob.

Delighted by his trust in them, they greeted him with cheers, but demanded a redress of their grievances. Unfortunately, while he was keeping them in good humor, the Walloons, who were guarding another gate of the palace, got into an altercation with some of the rioters. Hot words were exchanged, shots were fired and several persons were killed. The whole scene changed instantly, and the capital would have been drenched in blood, and perhaps Charles would

have been dethroned, had not a number of Jesuits
headed by the saintly Pignatelli, hurried through the
crowd and held the rioters in check. Finally, when a
placard was affixed to the palace walls, granting all
their demands, the mob dispersed, cheering for the
Jesuits — a fatal cry for those whom it was meant to
honor. They were accused of provoking the riot; and,
from that moment, the king's hatred for the Society
began. It was made more acute by the consciousness of
his own cowardice. Thus, a farce was to introduce a
tragedy. Ten years afterwards, the Duke of Alva, a
descendant of the old tyrant of the Netherlands,
confessed that it was he, who had planned the sombrero and cloak riot to discredit the Jesuits (de Murr,
" Journal," ix, 222).

Towards the end of January 1767, another episode
in this curious history presents itself. Like the
affair of the riot it seems to be taken from a novel,
but unfortunately it is not so. Its setting is the principal Jesuit residence at Madrid. The provincial and
the community are at dinner, when a lay-brother
enters with a package of letters, which he places
before the provincial. It is not the usual way of
delivering such communications in the Society, but the
story is told by de Ravignan in " Clément XIII et
Clément XIV " (I, 186), and he is quoting from Father
Casseda, who is described as " a Jesuit Father of
eminence and worthy of belief." The package was
handed back to the brother, along with the keys of
the provincial's room, where it was left. Immediately
afterwards, an officer of the court arrived, searched the
room and extracted one of the letters, said to be from
Father Ricci, the General of the Jesuits, who among
other things, declared that the king was an illegitimate
son and was to be superseded by his brother, Don
Luis. That such a letter was really written, is vouched

for by several historians: Coxe, Ranke, Schoell, Adam, Sismondi, Darras, and others; and it is generally admitted to have been the work of Choiseul in France though he covered up his tracks so adroitly that no documentary evidence can be adduced to prove it against him. His intermediary was a certain Abbé Beliardy an attaché of the French embassy in Madrid.

According to Carayon (XV Opp., 16–23) and Boero (" Pignatelli " Appendix) there is a second scene in this melodrama. Two Fathers are leaving Madrid for Rome. A sealed package is entrusted to them, purporting to be from the papal ambassador in Spain. On the road they are held up and searched; the package is opened, and a letter is found in it reflecting on the king's legitimacy. Precisely at the same moment, the trick of the refectory letter was being played in the Jesuit residence at Madrid, and thus a connection was established. With this scrap of paper and the " cloak and sombrero riot " at their disposal, the plotters concluded that they had ample material to carry out their scheme, and the next chapter shows Aranda, the prime minister, Roda, Moniño and Campomáñez meeting frequently in an old abandoned mansion in the country. With them was a number of boys, probably pages about the court, who were employed in copying a pile of documents whose import they were too unsophisticated to understand. Older amanuenses might have betrayed the secret.

The chain of evidence was finally completed, and these grave statesmen then presented themselves before his majesty and, with evidence in hand, proved to him the undoubted iniquity of the religious order which up to that moment he had so implicitly trusted. He fell into the trap, and a series of cabinet meetings ensued in which information previously gathered or invented about every Jesuit in France was discussed.

The result was that on January 29, 1767 a proposal was drawn up by Campománez and laid before his majesty to expel the Society from Spain, and advising him, first, to impose absolute silence on all his subjects with regard to the affair, to such an extent that no one should say or publish anything either for or against the measure, without a special permission of the government; secondly, to withhold all knowledge of the affair, even from the controller of the press and his subordinates; and finally to arrange that whatever action was taken, should proceed directly from the president and ministers of the extraordinary council.

The advice was assented to by the king, and a decree was issued in virtue of which silence was passed on 6,000 Spanish subjects who not only had no trial but who were absolutely unaware that there was any charge against them. They had been as a body irreproachable for two hundred years, had reflected more glory, and won more territory for Spain than had ever been gained by its armies. They were men of holy lives, often of great distinction in every branch of learning; some of them belonged to the noblest families of the realm; and yet they were all to be thrown out in the world at a moment's notice, though not a judge on the bench, not a priest or a bishop, not even the Pope had been apprised of the cause of it, and, as we have seen, it was forbidden even to speak of the act. A more outrageous abuse of authority could not possibly be conceived.

It was arranged that on the coming second of April, 1767, a statement should be made throughout Europe by which the world would be informed: first, that for the necessary preservation of peace, and for other equally just and necessary reasons (though the world is not to be told what they are), the Jesuits are expelled from the king's dominions, and all their goods confis-

cated; secondly, that the motive will forever remain
buried in the royal heart; thirdly, that all the other
religious congregations in Spain are most estimable and
are not to be molested. The decree was signed by
Charles and countersigned by Aranda and then sent
out. The ambassador at Rome was ordered to hand
it to the Pope and withdraw without saying a word.
The despatches to the civil and military authorities
in both worlds were enclosed in double envelopes and
sealed with three seals. On the inner cover appeared
the ominous words, as from a pirate addressing his
crew: " Under pain of death this package is not to be
opened until April 2, 1767, at the setting sun." The
letter read as follows: " I invest you with all my
authority and all my royal power to descend immediately with arms on the Jesuit establishments in your
district; to seize the occupants and to lead them as
prisoners to the port indicated inside of 24 hours. At
the moment of seizure, you will seal the archives of the
house and all private papers and permit no one to carry
anything but his prayer-book and the linen strictly
necessary for the voyage. If after your embarcation
there is left behind a single Jesuit either sick or dying
in your department, you shall be punished with death."

" I, the King."

The motive that prompted Charles to keep the secret
of this amazing proceeding " shut-up in his royal
heart " has been usually ascribed to his intense resentment at the suspicion cast on his legitimacy, and his
fear that even the mention of it would lead people to
conclude that there was some foundation for the charge.
Davila, quoted by Pollen in " The Month " (August,
1902), finds another explanation.

" Charles III," he says, " had become an extravagant
regalist, and was convinced by his Voltairean ministers,

mostly by Tanucci, whom he had left in charge of his son at Naples, that in all things the Church should be subject to the State. It was on that account that he kept the reasons for the expulsion of the Jesuits 'buried in his royal heart.' The sole cause of this act was his change of policy; a true reason of state such as, on some occasions, covers grave acts of injustice — for it must be always a grave injustice to charge a religious society with having conspired against the fundamental institutions of a country, and yet not be able to point out in any way the object and plan of so dark a conspiracy. If such be the case," continues Davila, "it is easy to understand why his majesty could not reveal this 'secret of his royal heart' even to the Pope, or perhaps least of all to him, for it would be a painful avowal that his Catholic Majesty was a yoke-fellow with the Voltaireans of Europe whose avowed purpose was to destroy the Church."

Clement XIII was overwhelmed with grief when he read the king's decree and wrote to him as follows: "Of all the blows I have received during the nine unhappy years of my pontificate the worst is that of which your majesty informs me in your last letter, telling me of your resolution to expel from all your vast dominions the religious of the Society of Jesus. So you too, do this, my son, *Tu quoque fili mi.* Our beloved Charles III, the Catholic King, is the one who is to fill up the chalice of our woe and to bring down to the grave our old age bathed in tears and overwhelmed with grief. The very religious, the very pious King of Spain, Charles III, is going to give the support of his arm, that powerful arm which God has given him to increase his own honor and that of God and the Church, to destroy to its very foundation, an order so useful and so dear to the Church, an order which owes its origin and its splendor to those saintly heroes whom

God has deigned to choose in the Spanish nation to extend His greater glory throughout the world. It is you who are going to deprive your kingdom and your people of all the help and all the spiritual blessings which the religious of that Society have heaped on it by their preaching, their missions, their catechisms, their spiritual exercises, the administration of the sacraments, the education of youth in letters and piety, the worship of God, and the honor of the Church.

"Ah! Sire! our soul cannot bear the thought of that awful ruin. And what cuts us to the heart still deeper perhaps is to see the wise, just King Charles III, that prince whose conscience was so delicate and whose intentions were so right; who lest he might compromise his eternal salvation, would never consent to have the meanest of his subjects suffer the slightest injury in their private concerns without having their case previously and legitimately tried and every condition of the law complied with, is now vowing to total destruction, by depriving of its honor, its country, its property, which was legitimately acquired, and its establishments, which were rightfully owned, that whole body of religious who were dedicated to the service of God and the neighbor, and all that without examining them, without hearing them, without permitting them to defend themselves. Sire! this act of yours is grave; and if perchance it is not sufficiently justified in the eyes of Almighty God, the Sovereign Judge of all creatures, the approval of those who have advised you in this matter will avail nothing, nor will the plaudits of those whose principles have prompted you to do this. As for us, plunged as we are in inexpressible grief, we avow to your majesty that we fear and tremble for the salvation of your soul which is so dear to us.

"Your Majesty tells us that you have been compelled to adopt these measures by the duty of main-

taining peace in your states,— implying we presume
that this trouble has been provoked by some individual
belonging to the Society of Jesus. But, even if it
were true, Sire, why not punish the guilty without
making the innocent suffer? The body, the Institute,
the spirit of the Society of Jesus, we declare it in
the presence of God and of man, is absolutely innocent
of all crime, and not only innocent, but pious, useful,
holy in its object, in its laws, in its maxims. It matters
not that its enemies have endeavored to prove the
contrary; all calm and impartial minds will abhor
such accusers as discredited liars who contradict
themselves in whatever they say. You may tell
me that it is now an accomplished fact; that the
royal edict has been promulgated and you may ask
what will the world say if I retract? Should you not
rather ask, Sire, what will God say? Let me tell you
what the world will say. It will say what it said of
Assuerus when he revoked his edict to butcher the
Hebrews. It accorded him the eternal praise of being
a just king who knew how to conquer himself. Ah!
Sire, what a chance to win a like glory for yourself.
We offer to your majesty the supplications not only
of your royal spouse, who from heaven recalls to you
the love she had for the Society of Jesus, but much
more so, to the Sacred Spouse of Jesus Christ, the
Holy Church, which cannot contemplate, without
weeping, the total and imminent extinction of the
Society of Jesus, which until this very hour has rendered
to her such great assistance and such signal services.
Permit, then, that this matter be regularly discussed;
let justice and truth be allowed to act, and they will
scatter the clouds that have arisen from prejudice and
suspicion. Listen to the counsels of those who are
doctors in Israel; the bishops, the religious, in a cause
that involves the interests of the State, the honor of

the Church, the salvation of souls, your own conscience and your eternal salvation." "

How Charles could resist this appeal, which is among the most admirable and eloquent state papers ever given to the world, is incomprehensible. But he did. He merely replied to the Pope: "To spare the world a great scandal, I shall ever preserve as a secret in my heart the abominable plot which has necessitated this rigor. Your Holiness ought to believe my word, the safety of my life exacts of me a profound silence."

Not satisfied with writing to the king himself, the Pope also pleaded with the greatest prelate in the realm, the Archbishop of Tarragona as follows: "What has come over you? How does it happen that, in an instant, the Society of Jesus has departed so far from the rules of its pious Institute, that our dear Son in Jesus Christ, Charles III, the Catholic King, can consider himself authorized to expel from his realm all the Regular Clerks of the Society? This is a mystery we cannot explain; only a year ago, the numberless letters addressed to us by the Spanish episcopacy afforded us some consolation in the deep grief that affected us when these same religious were expelled from France. Those letters informed us that the Fathers in your country gave an example of every virtue, and that the bishops and their dioceses received the most powerful support by their pious and useful labours. And now, behold, in an instant, there come dreadful charges against them and we are asked to believe that all these Fathers or almost all have committed some terrible crime; nay the king himself, so well known for his equity, is so convinced of it, that he feels obliged to treat the members of that Institute with a rigor hitherto unheard of."

Addressing himself personally to the king's confessor he says: "We write to you, my dear son, that you

may lay this before the prince who has taken you
for his guide, and we charge you to speak in our name
and in virtue of the obligations which the duty of your
office imposes, and the authority it bestows on you.
As for us, we do not refuse to employ measures of the
severest and most rigorous justice against those
members of the Society of Jesus who have incurred
the just anger of the king, and to employ all our power
to destroy and to root out the thorns and briars which
may have sprung up in a soil hitherto so pure and fertile.
As for you, it is part of your sacred ministry to consider
with fear and trembling as you kneel at the feet of the
image of Jesus Christ, to compel the king to consider
the incalculable ruin that religion will suffer, especially
in pagan lands, if the numberless Christian missions
which are now so flourishing, are abandoned and left
without pastors." Evidently the confessor could do
nothing with his royal penitent.

This mad act of Charles did not please some of his
friends in France. Thus, on May 4, 1767, D'Alembert
wrote to Voltaire: " What do you think of the edict
of Charles III, who expels the Jesuits so abruptly?
Persuaded as I am that he had good and sufficient
reason, do you not think he ought to have made them
known and not to ' shut them up in his royal heart?'
Do you not think he ought to have allowed the Jesuits
to justify themselves, especially as every one is sure
they could not? Do you not think, moreover, that it
would be very unjust to make them all die of starvation,
if a single lay-brother who perhaps is cutting cabbage
in the kitchen should say a word, one way or the other
in their favor? And what do you think of the com-
pliments which the King of Spain addresses to the
other monks and priests, and curés and sacristants of
his realm, who are not in my opinion less dangerous
than the Jesuits, except that they are more stupid and

vile? Finally, does it not seem to you that he could act with more common sense in carrying out what after all, is a reasonable measure?"

In spite of the royal order enjoining silence on his subjects high and low, there was a great deal of feeling manifested at the outrage. Roda, an agent of the ministry at Madrid, tried to conceal it and wrote to the Spanish Embassy at Rome on April 15, 1767: "There is not much agitation here. Some rich people, some women and other simpletons are very much excited about it, and are writing a great deal of their affection for the Jesuits, but that is due to their blindness. You would be astounded to find how numerous they are. But papers discovered in the archives and libraries, garrets and cellars, furnish sufficient matter to justify the act. They reveal more than people here suspect." And yet not one of these incriminating documents "found in archives and libraries and garrets and cellars" was ever produced.

Among "the simpletons" who denounced the act was the Bishop of Cuenca, Isidore de Carvajal, who told the king to his face, what he thought of the whole business. The Archbishop of Tarragona did the same, but they both incurred the royal displeasure. The Bishop of Terruel published a pamphlet "The Truth unveiled to the King our Master" and he was immediately confined in a Franciscan convent, while his Vicar-general and chancellor were thrown into jail. The Archbishop of Toledo, Cardinal de Córdova, wrote to the Pope and the contents of his letters were known in Spain, for Roda, the individual above referred to, hastened to tell the Spanish ambassador on May 12, 1767: "In spite of all their tricks, the Archbishop of Toledo and his vicar-general have written a thousand stupid things to the Pope about this affair. We would not be a bit surprised if the Bishop of Cuenca,

Coria, Cuidad Rodrigo, Terruel and some others have
done the same thing, but we are not sure." A year
and a half after the blow was struck something happened
which again threw the timid Charles into a panic
about his royal life. According to custom, he presented himself on November 4, 1768, on the balcony
of his palace to receive the homage of his people,
and to grant them some public favor out of his munificence. To the stupefaction of both king and court,
one universal cry arose from the vast multitude.
" Send us back the Jesuits! " Charles withdrew in
alarm and immediately investigations began with the
result that he drove out of the kingdom the Cardinal
Archbishop of Toledo and his vicar on the charge
that they had prompted the demand of the people
(Coxe, " Spain under the Bourbons," v, 25).

With regard to the supposed letter of Father Ricci
which brought on this disaster, it may be of use to
refer here to what was told thirty years after these
events, in a work called "Du rétablissement des Jésuites
et de l' éducation publique " (Emmerick, Lambert,
Rouen). The author says: " It is proper to add an
interesting item to the story of the means employed
to destroy the Society of Jesus in the mind of Charles
III. Besides the pretended letter of Father Ricci,
there were other suppositious documents, and among
these lying papers was a letter in the handwriting of
an Italian Jesuit which had been perfectly imitated.
It contained outrageous denunciations of the Spanish
government. When Clement XIII insisted on having
some proof to throw light on the allegations, this letter
was sent to him. Among those who were commissioned
to examine it, was a simple prelate, who afterwards
became Pius VI. Glancing at the missive he remarked that the paper was of Spanish manufacture,
and he wondered why an Italian should send to Spain

for writing material. Looking at it closer and holding it up to the light he saw that the water-mark gave not only the name of a Spanish paper-factory, but also the date on which it was turned out. Now it happened that this date was two years after the letter was supposed to have been written. The imposture was manifest, but the blow had already been struck. Charles III was living at the time, yet he was not man enough to acknowledge and repair the wrong he had done." (Crétineau -Joly, v, 241).

On the day appointed by the king, April 2, 1767, every ship selected to carry out the edict was in the harbor assigned to it, in every part of the Spanish world, where there happened to be a Jesuit establishment. The night before at sundown the captain had opened the letter which had the threat on its envelope: " Your life is forfeited if you anticipate the day or the hour." He obeyed his instructions; and early in the morning the Fathers in the college of Salamanca, Saragossa, Madrid, Barcelona and all the great cities, as well as in every town where the Jesuits had any kind of an establishment, heard the tramp of armed men entering the halls. The members of the household were ejected from their rooms, seals were put on the doors, and the community marched down like convicts going to jail. Old men and young, the sick and even the dying, all had to go to the nearest point of embarcation. Not a syllable were they allowed to utter as they tramped along, and no one could speak in their defence without being guilty of high treason. When they reached the ships, they were herded on board like cattle and despatched to Civita Vecchia, to be flung on the shores of the States of the Pope, whose permission had not even been asked; nor had any notice been given him. It was a magnificent stroke of organized work, and incidentally very profitable to the government, for at one and the same moment it came into possession of 158 Jesuit houses, all of considerable value as real estate and some of them magnificent in their equipment. How much was added to the Spanish treasury on that eventful morning, we have no means of computing.

There was one difficulty in the proceedings, however. The supply of ships was insufficient, for 2,643 men had to be simultaneously cared for; but their comfort did not interfere with the progress of the movement. " They were piled on top of each other on the decks or in the fetid holds," says Sismondi, " as if they were criminals." It was worse than the African slave-trade. Saint-Priest thinks " it was a trifle barbarous, but the precipitation was unavoidable." It was indeed a trifle barbarous and the precipitation was not unavoidable.

In rounding up the victims, the king and the ministers were naturally anxious about the effect it might have upon many of the best Spanish families who had sons in the Order; notably the two Pignatellis, who were of princely lineage. Inducements were held out to both of them to abandon the Society, but the offer was spurned with contempt. Indeed very few even of the novices failed in this sore trial. As for the Pignatellis they were the angels of this exodus, particularly Joseph, whose exalted virtue is now being considered in Rome in view of his beatification. He was at Saragossa when the royal order arrived, and though suffering with hemorrhages, he started out afoot on the weary journey to Tarragona, and from there to Salu, nine miles further on, where nineteen brigantines were assembled to receive this first batch of 600 outcasts. He was so feeble that he had to be carried on board the ship.

From there, they set sail for Civita Vecchia, where they arrived on May 7, but were not allowed to land.

Even the generally fair Schoell describes the Pope's action in this instance as " characterized by the greatest inhumanity." On the contrary, it would have been an act of the greatest inhumanity to receive them. There were some thousands of Portuguese Jesuits there already, who had been flung on the shore unannounced, and in that impoverished region there was no means of providing them with food or medicine or even clothes and beds. To have admitted this new detachment of 600 who were merely the forerunners of 4,500 more, and who, in turn were to be followed by all the Jesuits whom Tanucci would drive out of the Neapolitan Kingdom, and those whom Choiseul would hasten to gather up in France, the result would have been that ten or fifteen thousand Jesuits without money or food or clothing, some of them old and decrepit and ill, would have to be cared for and the native population in consequence would be subjected to a burden that would have been impossible to bear. It was " inhuman " no doubt, but the inhumanity must be ascribed to Charles III who had plundered these victims, and not to Clement XIII who would have died for them. His first duty was to his own people and his next was to proclaim to the world and to all posterity, the grossness of the insult as well as the injustice inflicted on the Vicar of Christ by the Most Catholic King, Charles III. Nor were the " unhappy wretches," as Böhmer-Monod call them, " received by cannon shot, at the demand of their own General, who had trouble enough with the Portuguese already on his hands;" (p. 274) nor did the Jesuits, as Saint-Priest adds: " vent their rage against Ricci and blame his harsh administration, as the cause of all their woes." Ricci was begging for bread to feed his Portuguese sons at that time, and he certainly would not have received those from Spain with a cannon shot;

nor would the Jesuits have vented their rage against
him and blamed his harsh administration, especially
as his administration was the very reverse of harsh;
and, finally, Jesuits were not accustomed to vent their
rage against their superior.

Sismondi (Hist. des Français, xxix, 372) says that
"many of them perished on board ship, and Schoell
describes them as lying on top of one another on deck
for weeks, under the scorching rays of the sun or down
in the fetid hold." The filthy ships finally turned their
prows towards Corsica where arrangements had been
made for them to discharge their human cargo. It
took four days to reach that island, but Paoli was
just then fighting for the independence of his country,
and French ships which were aiding Genoa occupied
the principal ports. At first the exiles remained in
their ships, but, later, they were allowed to go ashore
during the day. Meantime, a vessel had been despatched to Spain for instructions and when it returned
on July 8, the " criminals " were ordered to go to
Ajaccio, Algoila or Calvi. They reached Ajaccio on
July 24, and as they were then in a state of semi-
starvation, Father Pignatelli went straight to the
insurgent camp, though at every step he risked being
shot or seized and hanged, but he did not care, he
would appeal to Paoli's humanity. He was well
received, help was sent to the sufferers, and they were
given liberty to go where they chose on the island.

They remained there a month and were then sent
to the town of Saint-Boniface, where they bivouacked
or lived in sheds until the 8th of December, when they
were ordered to Genoa. This time the number of
brigantines in which they embarked had been reduced
from thirteen to five, though the number of the victims
had considerably increased; but that mattered little;
they finally reached the mainland but were not per-

mitted to go ashore. Meantime, other Jesuits had arrived and they now numbered 2,000 or 2,400. After a short delay in the harbor, they made their way separately or in groups to different cities in the Papal States, chiefly to Bologna and Ferrara.

Their ejection from the Two Sicilies was a foregone conclusion, for it was ruled by the terrible Bernardo Tanucci, whom Charles III on his accession to the throne of Spain had left as regent during the minority of Ferdinand IV. Tanucci was a lawyer who began his career in a most illegal fashion by exciting riots in Pisa against his rival Grandi. They had quarrelled about the discovery of the Pandects of Justinian. He next drew the attention of Charles by assailing the right of asylum for criminals, which he maintained was in contravention of all law human and divine. " He attacked the prerogatives of the Court of Rome and of the nobles of Naples, with more fury than prudence," says de Angelis (Biographie universelle). Subsequently he showed himself the enemy of the Church in every possible way, and, meantime, so neglected to provide for the security of the State that during the war of the Pragmatic Sanction, King Charles had to sign an act of neutrality at the mouth of the cannons of a British man-of-war. His political incapacity continued to injure the country during the reign of Ferdinand until it was no longer reckoned among the military powers of Europe. Meantime, he kept the young king in ignorance of everything so as to maintain himself in power. He robbed the courts of justice of their power; drew up the Caroline Code which was never published; ruined the finances of the country, as well as its industry and agriculture, and allowed men of the greatest ability and learning to die in penury. In brief, says his biographer, "Tanucci's reputation both before and after his death is a mystery.

It is probably due to his prominence as a bitter enemy of the Holy See. He seized Beneventum and Pontecorvo which belonged to the Patrimony of Peter; he suppressed a great number of convents, distributed abbeys to his followers, fomented dissensions against the bishops and, of course, persecuted the Jesuits."

When Charles III of Spain expelled the Society from Spain everyone knew what was going to happen in Sicily, and news was eagerly expected from the peninsula. While they were waiting, an eruption of Vesuvius took place, which the excitable Italians regarded as a sign of God's wrath. Penitential pilgrimages were organized to avert the danger and angry murmurs were heard against the government. To quell the tumult, Tanucci sent out word that the Jesuits would be undisturbed, though ships were at that time on their way to carry off the victims. The young king's signature to the decree had, however, to be procured, but he angrily refused to give it until the official confessor, Latelle, the retired Bishop of Avellino entreated him to yield, saying that he himself would answer for it on the Day of Judgment. The prelate did not know that he himself was to die at the end of the month. The expulsion took place in the usual dramatic fashion. At midnight of November 3, 1767, squads of soldiers descended on every Jesuit establishment in the land. The doors were smashed in; the furniture shattered; all the papers seized, both official and personal, and then surrounded by platoons of soldiers, the Fathers were led like criminals through the streets to the nearest beach with nothing but the clothes on their backs. The whole affair was managed with such lightning-like rapidity, that though the prisoners had been taken from their houses at midnight, they were out at sea before dawn and were heading for Ferrara.

At Parma another Spanish prince ruled. He was still a child, however, but his minister was du Fillot, a statesman of the school of Tanucci and Choiseul. The expulsion took place simultaneously on the night of February 7, 1768 at Piacenza, Parma, San Domino and Busseto. In the first city, all the available vehicles of the place had been requisitioned. At seven o'clock at night a dozen soldiers entered the house. Later, an officer, two adjutants and a magistrate appeared, read the decree, the fourth article of which declared that any one not a priest or professor who would take off the habit of the society would be received among the faithful subjects of his royal highness. The fifth announced that the innate clemency of his highness accorded an annual pension of sixty *scudj* to the professed and forty to the brothers who were his subjects. The scholastics were to get nothing. In a quarter of an hour they were hurried to the citadel where carriages and carts were waiting and were driven all night at top speed to Parma, where they arrived at day break. Passing through the city they caught up with those who had been expelled from the other places. Half an hour's rest and a bite to eat were allowed and then the journey was continued on to Reggio and Bologna. Not to be outdone in zeal for the king, the Knights of Malta drove them from the island on April 22, 1768. The expulsion at Parma was disastrous not only to the Jesuits but to the Pope. Parma was his fief, and he protested against the action of the duke. It was precisely what the plotters were waiting for. France immediately seized the Comtat Venaissin, and Naples took possession of Beneventum, both of which belonged to the Patrimony of St. Peter. Of course, the Jesuits were immediately expelled and their property confiscated.

The expulsion in Spanish America meant the seizure
of at least 158 establishments belonging to the Jesuits
in Mexico, New Granada, Ecuador, Peru and Chili.
It involved the flinging out into the world of 2,943
Jesuits, some of them old and infirm and absolutely
unable to earn their living. Of those who embarked
at Valparaiso sixty were drowned in the wreck of the
ship "Our Lady of the Hermitage." Carayon gives
some interesting diaries of the journeys of these exiles
(Doc. inédits, xvi), while Hubert Bancroft in his
monumental work of thirty-nine volumes about the
Pacific Coast furnishes abundant and valuable information about the exodus from the missions of Mexico.
The victims underwent the same sufferings as their
Portuguese brethren in the long journeys over mountains
and through the primeval forests and in the long,
horrible crossing of the ocean to their native land,
which they were thought unworthy to enter.

CHAPTER XVII

THE FINAL BLOW

Ganganelli — Political plotting at the Election — Bernis, Aranda
Aubeterre — The Zelanti — Election of Clement XIV — Renewal of
Jesuit Privileges by the new Pope — Demand of the Bourbons for a
universal Suppression — The Three Years Struggle — Fanaticism of
Charles III — Menaces of Schism — Moñino — Maria Theresa —
Spoliations in Italy — Signing the Brief — Imprisonment of Father
Ricci and the Assistants — Silence and Submission of the Jesuits to
the Pope's Decree.

As early as 1768, the Bourbon courts let it be known
that they would make a formal demand for the suppression of the Society throughout Christendom. On
January 14 of that year, Cardinal Torregiani wrote
to the papal nuncio at Madrid as follows: " His
Holiness is horrified at the attitude of the king, and
indignant that the demand should be accompanied
by threats to force his hand, so as to wring from him
a concession which is in violation of divine, natural
and ecclesiastical law. If any mention of it is made
to you again, dismiss immediately the person who
dares to suggest it." That stinging rebuke, however,
did not halt the stubborn Charles, and in the January
of 1769 the coalition began its attack. First came the
Spanish representative who presented himself for an
audience on the eighteenth. The Pope received him
with dignified reserve; gave expression to the intense
pain caused by the request, and then, bursting into
tears, withdrew. On the twentieth and twenty-second
respectively, Orsini, representing Naples, made his
appearance and after him Aubeterre, on behalf of
France. They were both abruptly dismissed. The
French document was especially insulting. It advised

the Pope to admit the demand on the ground that it
was based on a sincere and well-informed zeal for the
progress of religion, the interest of the Roman Church,
and the peace of Christendom. The use of the expression " Roman " Church was an evident hint at
schism.

On January 25, a formal reply was sent to the three
courts, informing them that " the Pope could not
explain the deplorable audacity they had displayed in
adding to the sorrows that already overwhelmed the
Church, a new anguish the only purpose of which
was to torture the conscience and distress the soul
of His Holiness. An impartial posterity would judge
if such acts could be regarded as a new proof of that
filial love which these sovereigns boast of having for
His Holiness personally, and an assurance of that
attachment which they pretend to show for the Holy
See." On January 28, Cardinal Negroni told the
ambassadors: " You are digging the grave of the
Holy Father." The prophecy was almost immediately
fulfilled, for on February 2 Clement XIII died of a
stroke of apoplexy. He had officiated at the ceremonies
of that day, and had shown no sign of illness. The
blow was a sudden one, and there is no doubt that
this joint act of the Bourbon kings had caused his
death. De Ravignan does not hesitate to describe him
as a martyr who died in defence of the rights of the
Church. He is blamed by some for " his lack of
foresight in not yielding to the exigencies of the times."
But there were other " exigencies of the times " besides
those formulated by the men " who knew not the secrets
of God, nor hoped for the wages of justice, nor esteemed
the honor of holy souls," and the Pope's foresight
was not limited by the horizons of Pombal, Choiseul
and Charles III. " His pontificate," as has been well
said, " affords the spectacle of a saint clad in moral

strength, contending alone against the powers of
the world. Such a spectacle is an acquisition forever."
For it should not be forgotten that those arrayed against
him in this fight were not aiming merely at the annihilation of the Society of Jesus. That was only a
secondary consideration. Their purpose was to destroy
the Church, and in its defence Pope Clement XIII
died.

A new Pope was now to be elected and the alarming
influence wielded by the statesmen of Europe in
ecclesiastical affairs now assumed proportions which
seemed to menace the destruction of the Church
itself. In his " Clément XIII et Clément XIV "
(p. 552) de Ravignan gives an extract from Theiner
which is startling. In 1769, that is before the election,
we find all the cardinals tabulated as " good;" " bad;"
" indifferent;" " doubtful;" " worst;" " null." Their
ages are given; their characters, their political tendencies.
Among those marked " good " is Ganganelli; Rezzonico,
the nephew of Clement XIII is in the category of the
" worst;" the Cardinal of York is " null." There are
eleven who are labelled " *papabili*," ten to be excluded
and fourteen to be avoided. It is even settled who
is to be secretary of State. Weekly instructions in
this matter were sent from the court of Spain to its
agents at Rome, whose motto was: " nec turpe est
quod dominus jubet — nothing is base if the king orders
it." They were at that time precisely the kind of
men that the implacable Charles III needed to sustain
him in his iniquitous measure: unprincipled clerics like
Sales, or savages like Moniño, or Aspuru, who could
write: " What matter that the charges are not
proved? The accused has been condemned. We have
not to establish his guilt." As for the flippant Bernis
and the infidel Aubeterre, they were good enough for
the royal debauchee, Louis XV. Aubeterre had been

a soldier, was now a diplomat and had lost his faith
by contact with the revolting indecencies of the
regency, while Bernis, says Carayon, was "a distinguished type of French vanity who talked much,
schemed continually and fancied he controlled the
conclave though he was only a fly on the wheel. He
was not ashamed to admit that he owed his red hat to
la Pompadour."

Bernis' correspondence with his government is
valuable not only in showing how unscrupulous were
the methods of coercion employed but in revealing
the ultimate purpose of the conspirators, viz. the
establishment of state churches in their several kingdoms. He and de Luynes were instructed to insist
that the new Pope should: first, annul the Brief of
Clement XIII against Parma; secondly, recognize the
independent sovereignty of the Prince; thirdly, relinquish Avignon and the Comtat Venaissin to France,
and Beneventum to Sicily; fourthly, exile Cardinal
Torregiani, the prime minister of Clement XIII;
fifthly, completely abolish the Society of Jesus;
secularize its members, and expel Father Ricci, the
the General, from Rome. They let it be known that
there would be no backing down on these five points.

It was chiefly to secure the suppression of the
Society that the fight was to be made. The other
matters could be left, if necessary, for future adjust-
ment. If every other means failed, intimidation was
to be resorted to. Indeed, as a preparation, veiled
threats began to be heard from several quarters.
Thus, for instance, Louis XV put his name to the
following insulting letter: "My sincere and constant
wish is," he said, "that the Barque of Peter should
be entrusted to a pilot who is enlightened enough to
appreciate the necessity of having the Head of the
Church remain in the most perfect harmony with all

the sovereigns of the Roman Faith; and of being wise
enough to avoid every inconsiderate measure prompted
by indiscreet and extravagant zeal; in brief, one who
will shape his policy by the rules of moderation,
prudence and sweetness in keeping with divine wisdom
and human politics." Such language from the " Most
Christian King " was an outrage on the memory of
Clement XIII; and the words " Roman Faith "
contained, as on a previous occasion, a threat of schism.
Schoell, the Protestant historian, says that " the
formation of State Churches in the three kingdoms
was clearly the avowed purpose of these plotters."

The " Zelanti " were in the majority, but that
difficulty was soon disposed of by the veto power
which had been granted to the Catholic sovereigns.
Making full use of it, they shamelessly forbade the
consideration of any candidate who was suspected of
being unfriendly to them, with the result that the
number of eligible candidates was speedily reduced
to eleven; and as most of these latter were old or
infirm they could not be even considered by the electors.
At this point, Bernis protested against being excessive
in the eliminations. Finally there were only two
cardinals who could be considered *papabili*: Ganganelli
and Stoppani.

On March 7, 1769, instructions arrived from Madrid
emphatically insisting that the election of no Pope
would be recognized who would not first bind himself
to grant the five points insisted upon by the Bourbon
kings, but when the two Spanish cardinals at Rome
represented to Charles III that such a proposal to the
electors would involve serious risks, the obstinate
king insisted, nevertheless, that he would yield on
three of the points, but that he would have to exact
absolutely as a condition of election that the new Pope
would promise to cancel the previous Pontiff's action

with regard to the Duke of Parma, and also suppress
the whole Society of Jesus. He wanted the conclave
to pass a decree to that effect. Even in the Parma
affair, he was willing to relent, because as Clement
XIII was dead, his ruling might be considered as
having lapsed, but as for the Society of Jesus, nothing
would satisfy him except its absolute extinction. That
much was due, he said, to the three powerful monarchs
on whom the Church depended for support. On the
other hand, as it would not be proper to compromise
the reputation of these kings by letting it be known
that such a deal was being made, for it might happen
to fail; it was thought better not to give any precise
orders, but to leave to the discretion of those who were
on the spot to determine what means should be employed for bringing about the desired results.

The project of getting a distinct decree from the
conclave in the sense of the King of Spain was
abandoned, but while the political cardinals would
not hear of exacting a written promise, the ambassadors
who were working on the outside, openly avowed that
they had no scruples about it. Indeed, Aubeterre, the
French ambassador, wrote to Choiseul in France
complaining that he and his fellow-diplomats felt hurt
that their proposal should be rejected for moral reasons,
especially as they had secretly consulted an excellent
canonist, who ruled that there would be no harm
in imposing on the new Pontiff the obligation of
fulfilling the contract inside of a year, dating from the
day of his election. Not only was it permissible, he
said, but, in the circumstances, it was imperatively
urgent for the good of the Church. " The excellent
canonist " here referred to was Azpuru, the Spanish
ambassador, but as Cardinals Orsini, Bernis and de
Luynes insisted that such a contract would be
simoniacal, they were informed that if an unacceptable

Pope was elected there would be an immediate rupture
of relations with the Holy See and the representatives
of the three Powers would withdraw from Rome.
They were further told that it was hoped that the
fanatics, or Zelanti, would not drive them to such
an extremity. D'Aubeterre who voiced the opinion
of his associates went so far as to say, that any election
which had not been arranged beforehand with the
court would not be recognized.

Finally, after the conclave had been in session from
February 13 to May 19, Cardinal Ganganelli was
elected Pope and took the name of Clement XIV. He
was considered "acceptable," especially by Spain.
According to Cordara, however, his elevation to the
pontifical throne was not due to the influence or the
manipulations of the Spanish cardinals but was brought
about as follows:— " From the beginning of the conclave two or three votes were deposited in his favor, but
he was never seriously thought of as Pope. Indeed,
Cardinal Castelli, whose learning and piety gave
him great influence in the Sacred College, was strongly
opposed to him. Suddenly, however, he changed his
opinion and declared that, having considered the matter
more thoroughly, he was convinced that in the actual
circumstances, no one was better fitted for the post
than Ganganelli. From that moment, those who had
been opposed to him regarded him favorably. Even
Rezzonico, the nephew of Clement XIII, who had
many reasons to vote against him said he would take
the opinion of the majority of the cardinals. Hence the
only one against him was Orsini who said that " the
Franciscan was a Jesuit in disguise." He was, therefore, after the fight had raged for 100 days, elected by
forty-six out of forty-seven votes. The forty-seventh
was his own, which he cast in favor of Rezzonico.
It is not true that he had made a promise to suppress

the Society in case of election. Azpuru, the Spanish
agent, wrote on May 8: " No one has gone so far as
to propose to anyone to give a written or verbal
promise "; and after May 13, he added: " Ganganelli
neither made a promise nor refused it." Unfortunately some of his written words were interpreted as
implying it.

Ganganelli was born in the town of Sant' Arcangelo,
near Rimini, on October 31, 1705, and was baptised
Giovanni Vincenzo Antonio, but took the name of
Lorenzo when he became a Conventual of St. Francis.
His life as a friar was characterized by piety and
intense application to study. He was noted for his
admiration of everything pertaining to the Society of
Jesus, and, indeed, Pope Clement XIII when making
him a cardinal said, " there is now a Jesuit in the
Sacred College in the habit of a Franciscan." But
" the purple seemed to change him," says Cordara,
" and from that out he was more reserved in his
manifestations of friendship." As Pope he was as
simple in his way of life as when living with his community; he was gentle, affable, kind, rarely ruffled, never
precipitate and never carried away by inconsiderate zeal.
He would have made an admirable Pope in better
times. But when he was given control of the Barque
of Peter a wild storm was sweeping over the world.
Venice, Parma, Naples, France, Spain and Portugal
were arrayed against him — some of them threatening
separation from the Church. Austria, the only Catholic government that remained, observed neutrality at
first, but finally went to the wrong side. In brief,
a fierce and united anti-religious element dominated all
Catholic Europe, and the rest was Protestant.

Of course, immediately after his election, felicitations rained upon him, but as de Ravignan expresses
it, " they were like flowers on the head of the victim

that was to be immolated." Indeed, even in the
congratulations harsh notes were heard, as when France
expressed its hope that the Holy See would show more
condescension to the powers than usual, and when
Spain "urgently called the attention of His Holiness to certain petitions which had been presented
to him." The Spanish ambassador, Azpuru, reminded
him in the very first audience that application had
already been made to his predecessor for the suppression of the Jesuits. The representatives of France,
Portugal and Naples chanted the same dirge. Before
three months had elapsed, there was an explosion that
shook Christendom. Following an accepted custom,
the Pope issued the septennial Brief of indulgences in
favor of the missionaries " to bestow the treasures of
heavenly blessings on those who, to our knowledge,
are laboring with indefatigable zeal for the salvation
of souls. We include among these fervent apostles,
the Religious of the Society of Jesus, and especially
those whom our beloved son, Lorenzo Ricci, is to assign
this year and afterwards, in various provinces of the
Society, to that work; and we most certainly desire to
promote and increase by these spiritual favors the piety
and the active and enterprising zeal of those Religious."

It was a thunderbolt. Fierce protests were made in
Spain, Naples, Parma and France. Choiseul, who, up
to that time, had been suave in his malice, lost his
temper completely and ordered the Ambassador Bernis
not only to make a public demand for the suppression
of the Society but to order the Pope to begin it inside of
two months. "This Pope is trifling with us," he
said; "and if he does not come to terms he can consider all relations with France at an end." He became
grossly insulting and declared that " he had enough of
this monkery;" he would upset the plans of the *Fratacci*;
and annihilate his Roman finesse. "A monk was

always a monk," he said "and it was very hard for an Italian monk to be honest and frank in business matters." Choiseul's varnish of courtesy had been all rubbed off by the incident, and he wanted to know " who were going to win in the fight? the kings or the Jesuits? If I were amabssador at Rome," he wrote to Bernis, " I would be ashamed to see Father Ricci the antagonist of my master."

Bernis, Cardinal though he was, meekly replied: " Of course the kings must win, but only the Pope can make them win. However, he has to do it according to the prescriptions of canon law, and must save his own reputation as well as that of the clergy. Moreover, as he is a temporal sovereign, he has to consider the courts of Vienna, Turin and Poland, and all that takes time. Personally, he means to keep the promise already given to the three crowns to suppress the Society, and has shown his mind on that point by public acts against the Fathers. He will renew the promise explicitly and immediately, in a letter written in his own hand to the King of Spain. He is not feeble or false as you seem to think. Time will show that such is his purpose. But, first, the way to lose the battle with the Jesuit General is to begin now. The Pope cannot and will not do it without preparation. Secondly, France and Spain must agree on the time and manner of arriving at the extinction of the Jesuits. Thirdly, it would be wiser to restrict the suppression to the Papal States, and not attempt it in countries that are favorable to the Society. Fourthly, a good preliminary would be to forbid the reception of novices, as the Pope has already done in his own dominions. Marefoschi and I put that into his head. Fifthly, I also proposed the seizure of the archives, the appointment of a Vicar General, to whom Father Ricci will render an account of his administration."

Bernis' temporising, however, only exasperated the foes of the Society, especially Charles III. Nevertheless, he succeeded in inducing the Pope to write to Louis XV on September 30, and in this communication a promise was made to do all the king wanted. But that was not enough for Charles. To force the issue, he ordered all the Jesuit property in Spain to be put up at auction, and a copy of the decree was sent to the Pope. That was on November 8, and on November 13, a joint letter was sent by the three powers requesting Clement to publish a Brief *motu proprio*, that is on his own initiative, as if they had had nothing to do with it, approving all that the Bourbon princes had done against the Society; and also to send to their majesties the plan he proposed to follow in carrying out its complete suppression. Clement humbly submitted to the outrage, and seven days later, Bernis was able to write to Choiseul: " His Holiness has renewed in the strongest manner the two promises he had made to the Bourbon kings with regard to the Brief approving the missionaries, and the plan to suppress the Jesuit Order. He has commissioned me to positively assure the ministers of the powers on that point."

Spain wanted even more than that; and on November, 22d, Azpuru told the Pope that if he did not send a manuscript letter to the king promising the suppression, extreme measures would be resorted to, and the rupture of relations which had been begun in 1767 and which was so disastrous to the Church in Spain would be carried to its limit. He was not exaggerating, and the nuncio at Madrid wrote that the king was so set on his purpose, that they did not know what mad thing he might do to gain his point. The general impression was that Charles was on the verge of insanity.

To quiet him, the Pope wrote, on November 30, to say positively that he would carry out the will of the courts. "We have gathered all the documents," he said, "that are needed for writing the *motu proprio* agreed upon; so as to justify to the whole world, the wise conduct of your majesty in expelling the Jesuits, as troublesome and turbulent subjects. As we are carrying on our government, unaided, although crushed by the weight and multiplicity of questions that have to be settled, you will understand that it is not forgetfulness but merely the unavoidable delay required to bring this important matter to a successful issue." Indeed at that time Clement had secluded himself from everyone. He was in constant fear of being poisoned, and had his food prepared by a Cordelier lay-brother. "We beg Your Majesty," he continued, "to put your entire confidence in us, for we have fully resolved to act, and we are preparing to give to the public incontestable proofs of our sincerity. We shall submit to the wisdom and intelligence of Your Majesty a plan for the total extinction of this Society; and Your Majesty will receive it shortly. We shall not cease to give genuine proofs of our attachment and our veneration for Your Majesty to whom in the plenitude of our paternal affection we give our apostolic benediction " (De Ravignan, " Clément XIII et Clément XIV," I, 295).

Bernis gave himself the credit of having got the Pope to write this letter, and said that now: " His Holiness could not escape carrying out his promise. He will be forced to do it, in spite of his unwillingness, for he knows that the king is too intelligent not to publish the letter, and the Pope will be disgraced if he does not keep his word " (Saint-Priest, p. 131). Thus six months after his election, he was bound by a written

and absolute promise to suppress the Society; though he
was continually saying " *questa supressione mi darà
la morte*" (this suppression will kill me). At this
stage of the proceedings little Naples was becoming
obstreperous. Tanucci had seized the Greek College
and expelled the Jesuits. He then claimed the property
of all religious communities, and when remonstrated
with, he replied that " he was going to keep on thwart-
ing every order that came from Rome, until the Society
of Jesus was abolished." In 1770 the Pope cancelled
the excommunication of the Duke of Parma to gratify
the sovereigns, but the satisfaction that ensued did not
last long. Cardinal Pacca, who was quasi-nuncio at
Lisbon just then, notes the disorders prevalent in
the country especially in the University of Coimbra,
where the worst kind of teaching was permitted.

On July 3, 1770, Bernis wrote to Choiseul: " I
heard that the Founder of the Passionists, Paul of
the Cross, has warned the Pope to watch over his
kitchen, and hence Brother Francisco who looks after
the Pope's household has redoubled his vigilance.
I do not know if it is on account of this warning, but
in any case the Pope has gone to some mineral springs
for treatment and is to be there for the next fortnight."
Ten days afterwards, Choiseul replied: " I cannot
imagine the Pope is so credulous or so cowardly as to
be so easily frightened by reports about attempts on
his life. The Society of Jesus has been looked upon
as dangerous because of its doctrines, its Institute
and its intrigues in the countries from which they
have been expelled; but they have not been accused
of being poisoners. It is only the base jealousy and
fanatical hatred of some monks that could suspect
such a thing. The General of the Passionists might
have dispensed himself from giving such indiscreet
advice to the Pope, which seems to have aggravated

the illness of which he was already complaining."
As this General of the Passionists was no other than
the saintly Paul of the Cross, who has been since
raised to the honors of the altar, one may form some
idea of the infamous devices resorted to in all this business.
Far from being unfriendly, Paul of the Cross writes:
" I am extremly pained by the sufferings of the
illustrious Company of Jesus. The very thought of
all those innocent religious being persecuted, in so many
ways, makes me weep and groan. The devil is triumph-
ing; God's glory is diminished, and multitudes of
souls are deprived of all spiritual help. I pray, night
and day that, after the storm is passed, God who gives
both life and death may resuscitate the Society with
greater glory than before. Such have been always, and
such still are, my feelings towards the Jesuits."

The fact is, however, that the Pope was really
frightened. His cheerfulness had vanished, his health
had failed, and his features wore an anxious and haunted
look. He kept in seclusion, and, as has been said,
would let no one prepare his meals but his fellow-friar,
Brother Francisco, who remained with him till the end.
He was evidently fighting for time; hoping, no doubt,
that something might occur to absolve him from his
promise. But his enemies were relentless. Charles
III was more than fanatical in his insistency, and
finally Clement appointed Marefoschi, an open enemy
of the Jesuits, to prepare the Brief. The task was
joyfully accepted, but the Pope discovered that it
was not written in the usual pontifical style. That
excuse, however, was regarded by his assailants, as
a trick, and they complained of it bitterly. Then
it was alleged that the Empress Maria Theresa, who
was not averse to the Jesuits, had to be consulted.
Indeed, she had given out that as long as she lived
they had nothing to fear in her dominions, but she

failed to keep her word. Subsequently, a promise
was given not to allow Father Ricci to have a successor
or to admit novices into the Order; then a general
council was proposed to decide the question, but all
was of no avail.

At this point, December 25, 1770, Choiseul fell from
power, and the world began to breathe for a short
spell, hoping that this might affect the situation, but
d'Aiguillon, his successor, was just as bad. Moreover,
Saint-Priest, in his " Chûte des Jésuites " (p. 127)
uses the incident for a nasty insult. He attributes
Choiseul's fall to the regard that Madame du Barry
had for the Society. " Thank God! " exclaims de
Ravignan, " the Society has never had such a protectress." She was admired by Voltaire, who hailed
her as another Egeria, but no Jesuit ever sought her
protection. Their only advocate at the court at
that sad period was the saintly daughter of the king,
who became a Carmelite nun to expiate her father's
sins. The real cause of Choiseul's downfall was that
Maupeou showed to Louis XV some of Choiseul's
letters urging parliament " not to yield in the fight,
for the king would sustain the Society with all his
power." " It was not hard," says Foisset in " Le
Président des Brosses " (p. 302), " for du Barry to
persuade the king that those letters were meant to
incite the parliament to rebellion against him." She
hated Choiseul who, though willing to pay court to
Pompadour, had no respect for the low and coarse
du Barry.

At this point, the Pope offered another inducement
to the King of Spain : the canonization of Palafox,
whom Charles III worshipped, but that failed, though
a little respite was gained by the help of the king's
confessor; and certain discussions with regard to the
restitution of the papal territories also contributed

to delay the disaster. The year 1771 had now been
reached, and to afford some satisfaction to the foe,
the Pope established a commission or congregation of
cardinals to examine the financial conditions of the
Society. At its head was the fierce Marefoschi, who
began by seizing the Roman Seminary. Thus matters
dragged on till 1772. Up to that time very little
progress had been made, and people were beginning
to talk about the impossibility of abolishing the whole
Order, or even a part of it without "proper juridical
investigation." Even Bernis told his government that
"there was too much heat in this Jesuit affair to
permit the Pope to explain his real thoughts about
the suppression;" but, though Aranda was out of
office and Cholseul likewise, the implacable Charles III
was determined to put an end to the delay and instead
of Azpuru, he sent the fierce José Moñino, otherwise
known as Florida Blanca to be his ambassador in Rome.

Under an affable and polished exterior Moñino was
in reality very brutal. He simply terrorized the Pope,
who put off receiving him for a week after his arrival
and invented all sorts of excuses not to see him. When
at last they met, the Pope was pale and excited but
Moñino had resolved to end the siege. He dismissed
absolutely all question of a reform of the Order. What
he wanted was suppression, or else there would be a
rupture with Spain. In vain the Pope entreated him
to wait for Ricci's death; but the angry minister rejected the offer with scorn, and the Pope after being
humiliated, insulted and outraged, withdrew to his
apartments, exclaiming with sobs in his voice: "God
forgive the Catholic King." "It was Moñino," said a
diplomat then at Rome, "who got the Brief of 1773;
but he did not obtain it; he tore it from the Pope's
hand." Under instructions from Charles III, Moñino
told the Pope, "I will disgrace you by publishing the

35

letter you wrote to the king," and he laid before the
Pontiff a plan drawn up by himself and the other
ministers of Charles III to carry out the suppression.
De Ravignan condemns Crétineau-Joly for having
published this paper. "It would have been better to
have left it in the secret archives."

In Moñino's plan of action he declares that "it was
not advisable to enter into details; so as not to allow
any ground for discussion, as it would do harm to
religion and uselessly defame the character of the
Jesuits." The king's reasons had already been made
known to the Holy See. They were three in number.
The first was "they had caused the Sombrero Riot
in Madrid;" the second: "their moral and doctrinal
teaching was bad;" the third, and this was the most
extraordinary of all: "they had always persecuted
the holiest bishops and persons in the Kingdom of
Spain." The last item probably referred to Palafox.
His Majesty had not yet revealed the important
secret which he kept "locked in his royal heart." All
the terrible statements of the documents alleged to
have been seized by Marefoschi were to be of no use,
when compared with the Riot of the Sombreros.

Meantime conditions were every day growing worse
in Europe. The publications of Voltaire and his
friends were destroying both religion and morality.
The fulminations of the Pope against these books
availed little, and meantime he was about to crush the
men who were best able to face the enemy. Finally,
poor Poland was being cut up by Prussia, Russia and
Austria and the Pope was powerless to prevent it. On
the other hand, there were some consolations. Thus
in 1771 the Armenian patriarch and all his people
renounced Nestorianism and returned to the unity of
the Church. Between 1771 and 1772 seven thousand
families and their ministers in the country of Sickelva

abandoned Socinianism, and became Catholics. Again, wonderful conversions were made in Transylvania and Hungary, not only among Protestants but among the schismatical Greeks. Similar triumphs had been achieved in Armenia and Syria among the subjects of the Grand Turk, and the whole peninsula of Italy under the eyes of the Pope was in a transport of religious zeal. The peculiarly interesting feature about all this was that it was the work of the members of the Society of Jesus. But that did not check the progress of the anti-Christian plot of the Catholic kings of Europe to obliterate from the face of the earth the organization which even in its crippled condition and in the very last moments of its existence was capable of such achievements. Cardinal Migazzi, the Archbishop of Vienna, called the Pope's attention to this fact, but without avail.

Up to this time, Maria Theresa had been the devoted friend of the Society. She had even said she would never cease to be so, but yielding to the influence of her son, Joseph II, and of her daughter, the Queen of Naples, she consented to their supression, on condition that she could dispose arbitrarily of their property (Clément XIII et Clément XIV, I, 362.) The illustrious queen displayed great worldly prudence in withdrawing her affections. This desertion destroyed the last hope that the Pope had cherished of putting off the Suppression. Moñino returned to the attack again and received an assurance from Clement that the document of suppression would be ready in eight days, and copies would be sent to the Kings of Spain, France and Naples. Meantime, as a guarantee, he began the work in his own States. Under all sorts of pretexts, individuals and college corporations were haled to court; and official visits were made of the various establishments. On March 10, 1773, Malvezzi,

the Archbishop of Bologna, applied to the Pope for
" permission to dissolve the novitiate, if it would
seem proper to do so." If you think well of it, I
shall carry that measure into effect, as soon as I arrive.
I also judge it advisable to shut up St. Lucia, by
dismissing the Jesuit theologians and philosophers.
In doing so, Your Holiness will be dispensed from the
trouble of investigating and will thus avoid the publicity
of any notable offence which an examination might
reveal."

There were two difficulties in the way, however.
The people objected to the expulsion, and the Jesuits
refused to be released from their vows. The latter
obstacle was thought to be overcome by tearing off
the cassocks of the young men and sending them
adrift as laymen, and when the rector, Father Belgrado,
who besides being a theologian was one of the foremost
physicists and mathematicians of the day, and had
been the confessor of the Duke and Duchess of Parma,
informed the archbishop that dispensation from substantial vows must come from the Pope and from no
one else, that did not stop Malvezzi. He had the
rector arrested and exiled; and with the help of a band
of soldiers expelled the scholastics from the house.
He then wrote to the Pope regretting that he had
not proceeded more rapidly. Besides this, Frascati
was taken from the Jesuits and given to the Cardinal
of York, who asked for it, though his royal pension
had made him already immensely wealthy. Similar
visitations were made in Ferrara and Montalto, and
the looting became general.

In Poland, as we learn from " Les Jésuites de la
Russie blanche," the spoliation had started even before
the promulgation of the edict. Libraries were broken
up and the books were often used to kindle bonfires;
the silver of the churches was melted down and sold,

and medals and chains from statues were seen on the
necks of abandoned women. Even the cattle on the
farms were seized. The Jews were especially conspicuous in these depredations.

All this was the prelude of the fatal Brief, which was
signed on July 21, 1773, but was not promulgated
until August 16 of that year. Theiner is the only
author who gives August 17 as the date. As a matter
of fact it was held up by Austria so as to gain time to
prevent the secular clergy from seizing the property.
The preparation of the Brief was conducted with the
profoundest secrecy. Even on July 28, the French
Ambassador wrote to D'Aiguillon: "the Pope is
doing nothing in the Jesuit matter." He was unaware
that not only was the Brief already signed but that a
Congregatio de rebus extinctæ Societatis (a Committee
on the affairs of the Extinct Society) had been appointed,
and that its members had been bound under pain of
excommunication not to reveal the fact to any one.
However, Bernis found it out on the 11th, and complained that he had not been consulted. He wrote as
follows: " Last Friday, the Pope summoned Cardinals
Marefoschi, Casali, Zelada, Corsini and Caraffa, and
after having made them take an oath, he put a Brief
in their hands, which constituted them members of a
congregation which was to meet every Monday and
Thursday to discuss whatever concerned the Jesuit
establishments, their benefices, colleges, seminaries,
foundations, and such matters. It held its first meeting
last Monday. Macedonio, the Pope's nephew, was
the secretary; Alfani, a prelate, was the assessor; and
Fathers Mamachi, a Dominican, and de Casal, a
Recollect, were consulting theologians. The last two
mentioned are men of repute."

" The 16th day of August 1773, the day of sad
memories," writes de Ravignan, " arrived. Towards

nine at night, Macedonio went to the Gesù and officially notified the General of the Brief that suppressed the Society throughout the world. He was accompanied by soldiers and officers of the police to keep order, though no one dreamed of creating any trouble. At the same hour, also by command of the Pope, other distinguished prelates and ecclesiastics gave notice of the Brief to the various Jesuit rectors in Rome. They also were accompanied by soldiers and notaries. Seals were put on the archives, the accounts, the offices of the treasurers and the doors of the sacristies. The Jesuits were suspended from all ecclesiastical functions such as confessions and preaching, and they were forbidden, for the time being, to leave their houses. The Father General and his assistants were carried off to jail." "Such," said Schoell (xliv, 84), "was the end of one of the most remarkable institutions that perhaps ever existed. The Order of the Jesuits was divided into five nations, Italian, Portuguese, Spanish, French and German, each one of which had a representative living with the General. In 1750 the organization comprised 39 provinces, had 84 professed houses, which were residences where the most experienced members worked unceasingly for the Order without being distracted by public instruction. There were 679 colleges, 61 novitiates, 176 seminaries, 335 residences, and 273 missions. There were 22,589 members of whom 11,293 were priests."

This official act of the Pope really added very little to the temporal injury already done to the Order in Spain, France and Portugal where they had already been robbed of everything. But to be regarded as reprobates by the Pope and branded as disturbers of the peace of the Church was a suffering with which all they had hitherto undergone bore no comparison.

Nevertheless, they uttered no protest. They submitted absolutely and died without a murmur, and in this silence they were true to their lifelong training, for loyalty to the See of Peter had always been the distinctive mark of the Society of Jesus from the moment that Ignatius Loyola knelt at the feet of the Sovereign Pontiff, for his approval and blessing. When the blow fell, the Society was found to be faithful. If it had during its lifetime achieved something for the glory of God and the salvation of souls; if it had been constantly appealed to for the most dangerous missions and had accepted them with enthusiasm; if it had poured out its blood lavishly for the Faith; if it had given many glorious saints to the Church, now, in the last terrible crisis which preceded the French Revolution and perhaps precipitated it, when the ruler of the Militant Church judged that by sacrificing one of his legions he could hold back the foe, the Society of Jesus on being chosen did not hesitate; it obeyed, and it was cut to pieces. Not a word came from the heroic band to discuss the wisdom or the unwisdom of the act. Others protested but not they. Those who condemned Clement XIV were not Jesuits, though their enemies said they were. On the contrary, the Jesuits defended and eulogized him and some of them even maintained that in the terrible circumstances in which he found himself, he could not have done otherwise. The Suppression gave them the chance, which they did not miss, to prove to the world the solidity of virtue that reigned throughout the Order, and to show that their doctrine of " blind obedience " was not a matter of mere words, but an achievable and an achieved virtue. They would have stultified themselves had they halted when the supreme test was asked for, and so they died to uphold the judgment of the Vicar of Christ, and in similar circumstances would do it again. They had preached sermons in every part of the world, but never one like this. Nor was it a sublime act such as some individual saints might have performed. It was the act of the whole Society of Jesus.

Silent themselves, they did their best to persuade others to refrain from all criticism. One example will suffice. It was after the Pope's death when the ex-Jesuits at Fribourg held a funeral service in their collegiate Church of St. Nicholas. The whole city was present, and the preacher, Father Matzel, amid the sobs of the congregation uttered these words: " Friends! beloved Friends of our former Society! whoever and wherever you may be! If ever we have had the happiness to be of help and comfort to you by our labor in city or country; if ever we have contributed anything to the cause of Christianity in preaching the word of God or catechising or instructing youth, or laboring in hospitals or prisons, or writing edifying books now, on this occasion, although in our present distress we have many favors to ask of you, there is one we ask above all and we entreat and implore you to grant it. It is never to speak a word that would be harsh or bitter or disrespectful to the memory of Clement XIV, the Supreme Head of the Church of Christ."

The famous Brief is designated by its first words, *Dominus ac Redemptor.* Its general tenor is as follows: It begins by enumerating the various religious orders which, in course of time, had been suppressed by successive Popes, and it then gives a list of the privileges accorded to the Society by the Holy See, but it notes that " from its very cradle " there were internal and external disagreements and dissensions and jealousies, as well as opposition to both secular and ecclesiastical authority, chiefly because of the excessive privileges that had been granted to it by the different Sovereign Pontiffs. Its moral and dogmatic theology also gave rise to considerable discussion, and it has frequently been accused of too great avidity in the acquisition of earthly goods. The Pontiff merely declares that such " charges " were made against the Society; he, in no place, admits that the " charges " were based on truth. These accusations, he continues, caused much chagrin to the Holy See, and afforded a motive for several sovereigns of Europe to range themselves in opposition to the Society; while, on the other hand, a new confirmation of the Institute was obtained from Pope Paul IV of happy memory. That, however, did not succeed in putting an end to the disputes with the ordinaries or with other religious orders on many points, and notably with regard to certain ceremonies which the Holy See proscribed as scandalous in doctrine, and subversive of morality; nor did it avail to quell the tumult which ultimately led to the expulsion of the Society from Portugal, France, Spain and the Two Sicilies, and induced the kings of those countries to ask Clement XIII for its complete suppression. " Hence, finding that the Society of Jesus can no longer produce the abundant fruits for which it was instituted, and for which it was approved by so many Popes, and rewarded by so many privileges, we now abolish and suppress it. But as the purpose which we have set for ourselves and are eager to achieve is the general good of the Church and the tranquillity of the people, and, at the same time, to give help and consolation to each of the members of this Society, all of whom we tenderly cherish in the Lord, we ordain as follows with regard to them." He then explains the various ways in which each section of the Society is to be dealt with.

Such in general is the substance of this very long Brief. In it, however, there is not one word about the decadence of the Society in its morality or its theology. The Pontiff merely says that many have " charged " them with such offenses. He even goes so far as to say that " he tenderly loved all of the individuals who composed the Society." The real purpose of it was to bring peace to the Church. Cahours in his " Des Jésuites par un Jésuite," (II, p. 278) says, " Every judge who passes a sentence affirms two things: the existence of a crime and the fitness of the penalty. Clement XIV pronounces on the second, but says nothing of the first. Hence the sentence is not something exacted by justice, but is merely an administrative measure called for by the embarrassment of the moment."

Was it legitimate? Yes; for the Holy See has a right to suppress what it has created.

CHAPTER XVIII

THE INSTRUMENT

Summary of the Brief of Suppression and its Supplementary Document.

THE Brief of Clement XIV which suppressed the Society begins by enumerating the various religious orders which have been treated in a similar manner at different periods in the history of the Church, but it omits to note that their extinction occurred only after a juridical examination. Thus, for instance, when Clement V suppressed the Knights Templars in 1321, he first ordered all the bishops of the world to summon the Knights who had chapters in their dioceses; to subject them to a regular trial and then to forward a report of their proceedings to Rome. When this was done a general council was convened at Vienne in Dauphiné to go over the whole matter and then submit its decision to the Pope. The council brought in a favorable verdict by a majority vote, although the Knights were very poorly defended, but the Pope, terrorized by Philip the Fair, ordered the dissolution of the Order. In the case of the Society there was a dissolution but no trial.

After recounting these facts, the Pontiff says: " Having before my eyes these and other examples of Orders suppressed by the Church and being most eager to proceed with perfect confidence in carrying out the purpose which shall be referred to later, we have left nothing undone to make ourselves acquainted with the origin, progress and actual condition of the religious order commonly known as the Society of Jesus. We have seen that it was established by its Holy Founder for the salvation of souls, the conversion of heretics and especially of the heathen, and also for the increase of piety and religion. To accomplish these purposes its members were bound by a very strict vow of evangelical poverty both in common and individually, with the exception of its houses of study or colleges which are allowed to possess certain revenues, but in such wise that they could not be diverted or applied to the use of this Society.

" In consequence of these statutes and of others equally wise, our predecessor Paul III approved of the Society of Jesus, by his Bull of September 27, 1540, and allowed it to draw up rules and statutes to ensure its peace, its existence and its government; and although he had restricted this Society to sixty members, yet by another Bull dated February 28, 1543, he permitted the superiors to receive all who appeared to possess the proper qualifications for the work proposed. Subsequently, the same Pontiff by a Brief of November 15, 1549, accorded very great privileges to this Society and gave its Generals the power of accepting twenty priests as spiritual coadjutors and of conferring on them the same privileges, the same favor and the same authority as the Professed. His wish was and he so ordained that there should be no limit or restriction put on the number of those whom the General should judge worthy of being so received. Furthermore, the Society itself, all its members and their possessions were entirely withdrawn from all superiorship, control and correction of bishops and taken under the protection of the Holy See.

" Others of our predecessors have exhibited the same munificent liberality to this order. In effect Julius III, Paul IV, Paul V, Gregory XIII, Sixtus V, Gregory XIV, Clement VIII and other Popes have either confirmed or augmented, or more distinctly defined and determined the privileges already conferred on these religious. Nevertheless, the tenor and even the terms of these Apostolic Constitutions show that even at its inception the Society saw spring up within it various germs of discord and jealousies, which not only divided the members, but prompted them to exalt themselves above other religious orders, the secular clergy, the universities, colleges, public schools and even the sovereigns who had admitted and welcomed them in their realms. These troubles and dissensions were sometimes caused by the character of the Society's vows, by its power to admit novices to the vows, to dismiss from the Society, to present its subjects for ordination without any ecclesiastical title and without having made solemn vows. Moreover, it was in conflict with the decisions of the Council of Trent and of Pius V, our predecessor, both with regard to the absolute power arrogated by the General, as well as in other articles which not only relate to the government of the Society, but also on different points of doctrine, and in the exemptions and privileges which the ordinaries and other dignitaries both ecclesiastical and secular claim to be an invasion of their jurisdiction and their rights. In brief, there is scarcely any kind of a grave accusation that has not been brought against this Society, and in consequence, the peace and tranquillity of Christendom has been for a long time disturbed.

" Numberless complaints backed by the authority of kings and rulers have been urged against these religious at the tribunals of Paul IV, Pius V and Sixtus V. Thus, Philip II, King of Spain, laid before Sixtus V not only the urgent and grave personal reasons which prompted his action in this matter, but also the protest of the Spanish Inquisition against the excessive privileges of the Society. His majesty also complained of the Society's form of government, and of points in the Institution which were disputed by some of the members of the Society who were conspicuous for their knowledge and piety, and he asked the Sovereign Pontiff to name a commission for an Apostolic visitation of the Society.

" As the zealous demands of Philip seemed to be based on justice and equity, Sixtus V appointed as visitor Apostolic a bishop generally recognized for his prudence, virtue and intellectual gifts. A congregation of cardinals was also instituted to dispose of the matter, but the premature death of Sixtus prevented any action. On the other hand, the first act of Gregory XIV on his accession to the Chair of Peter was to give by his Bull of June 28, 1591, the most extensive approval of the Institute. He confirmed and ratified all the privileges accorded by his predecessors, and especially that of dismissal from the Order without juridical procedure, that is to say without having taken any previous information, without drawing up any indictment, without observing any legal process, or allowing any delay, even the most essential, but solely on the inspection of the truth of the fact and without regard to the fault or whether it or the attendant circumstances sufficiently justified the expulsion of the person involved.

" Moreover, Pope Gregory absolutely forbade under pain of excommunication *ipso facto*, any direct or indirect attack on the institute, the constitutions, or the decrees of the Society, or any attempt to change them, although he permitted an appeal to himself or his successors, either directly or through the legates and nuncios of the Holy See, and also the right to represent whatever one might think should be added, modified or retrenched.

" However, all these precautions did not avail to silence the clamorous complaints against the Society.

On the contrary, strife arose everywhere about the doctrines of the Order, which many maintained were totally opposed to the orthodox faith and sound morality. The Society itself was torn by internal dissensions while this external warfare was going on. It was also everywhere reproached with too much avidity and eagerness for earthly goods and this complaint caused the Holy See much pain and exasperated many rulers of nations against the Society. Hence, to strengthen themselves on that point these religious, wishing to obtain from Paul V of happy memory a new confirmation of their Institute and their privileges, were compelled to ask for a ratification of some decrees published in the fifth general congregation and inserted word for word in his Bull of September 14, 1606. These decrees expressly declared that the Society assembled in general congregation had been compelled both by the troubles and enmities among the members, and by the charges from without, to formulate the following statute:—

"'Our Society which has been raised up by God for the propagation of the Faith and the salvation of souls, is enabled by the proper functions of its Institute which are the arms of the spirit to attain under the standard of the Cross the end it proposes, with edification to the neighbor and usefulness to the Church. On the other hand, it would do harm and expose itself to the greatest danger if it meddled in affairs of the world and especially with what concerns the politics and government of States. But, as in these unfortunate times our Order, perhaps because of the ambition or indiscreet zeal of some of its members, is attacked in different parts of the world and is complained of to certain sovereigns whose consideration and affection we have been bidden by St. Ignatius to preserve so that we may be more acceptable to God, and as, besides, the good odor of Jesus Christ is necessary to produce fruits of salvation, this congregation is of the opinion that it is incumbent upon all to avoid as far as possible even the appearance of evil, and thus to obviate the accusations that are based on unjust suspicions. Hence, the present decree forbids all under the most rigorous penalties to concern themselves in any way with public affairs, even when invited to do so or when for some reason they may seem to be indispensable. They are not to depart from the Institute of the Society no matter how entreated or solicited, and the definitors are to lay down rules and to prescribe the means best calculated to remedy abuses in cases which may present themselves.'

" We have observed with bitter grief that these remedies and many others subsequently employed failed to put an end to the troubles, complaints and accusations against the Society, and that Urban VIII, Clement IX, Clement X, Clement XI, Clement XII, Alexander VII, Alexander VIII, Innocent X, Innocent XI, Innocent XII, Innocent XIII, and Benedict XIV were unable to give the Church peace. The constitutions which were drawn up with regard to secular affairs with which the Society should not concern itself, whether outside of these missions or on account of them, failed to have any result. Nor did they put an end to the serious quarrels and dissensions caused by members of the Society with the ordinaries and religious orders, or about places consecrated to piety, and also with communities of every kind in Europe, Asia and America; all of which caused great scandal and loss of souls. The same was true with regard to the practice and interpretation of certain pagan ceremonies which were tolerated and permitted in many places while those approved of by the Universal Church were put aside. Then, too, there was the use and interpretation of maxims which the Holy See deemed to be scandalous and evidently harmful to morality. Finally, there were other things of great moment and of absolute necessity for the preservation of the dogmas of the Christian religion in its purity and integrity which in our own and preceding centuries led to abuses and great evils such as the troubles and seditions in Catholic states, and even persecutions of the Church in some provinces of Asia and Europe.

" All of our predecessors have been sorely afflicted by these things, among others Innocent XI of pious memory, who forbade the habit to be given to novices; Innocent XIII, who was obliged to utter the same threat; and, finally, Benedict XIV, who ordered a visitation of the houses and colleges of our dear son in Christ, the most faithful King of Portugal and the Algarves. But the Holy See derived no consolation from all this; nor was the Society helped; nor did Christianity secure any advantage from the last letter, which had been rather extorted than obtained from our immediate predecessor Clement XIII (to borrow the expression employed by Gregory X in the Ecumenical Council of Lyons.)

" After so many terrible shocks, storms and tempests, the truly faithful hope to see the day dawn which will bring peace and calm. But under the pontificate of our predecessor Clement XIII, the times grew more stormy. Indeed, the clamors against the Society augmented daily and in some places there were troubles, dissensions, dangerous strifes and even scandals which, after completely shattering Christian charity, lighted in the hearts of the faithful, party spirit, hatred and enmity. The danger increased to such a degree that even those whose piety and well-known hereditary devotion to the Society, namely our very dear sons in Jesus Christ, the Kings of France, Spain, Portugal and

36

the Two Sicilies, were forced to banish from their kingdoms, states and provinces all the religious of this Order; being persuaded that this extreme measure was the only means of remedying so many evils and putting an end to the contentions and strife that were tearing the bosom of Mother Church.

"But these same kings, our very dear sons in Jesus Christ, thought that this remedy could not be lasting in its effects or could avail to tranquillize Christendom unless the Society was altogether abolished and suppressed. Hence, they made known to Clement XIII their desire in this matter and asked him with one accord and with all the authority they possessed, adding also their prayers and entreaties to bring about in that way the perpetual tranquillity of their subjects and the general good of the Church. But the sudden death of that Pontiff checked all progress in the matter. Hardly, however, had we, by the mercy of God, been elevated to the Chair of St. Peter, than the same prayers were addressed to us, the same insistent demands were made and a great number of bishops and other personages illustrious by their learning, dignity and virtue united their supplications to this request.

"Wishing, however, to take the surest course in such a grave and important matter, we believed we needed a much longer time to consider it, not only for the purpose of making the most exact examination possible and then to deliberate upon the most prudent methods to be adopted and also to obtain from the Father of Light His especial help and assistance, we offered our most earnest prayers, mourning and grieving over what was before us, and we entreated the faithful to come to our aid by their prayers and good works. We have especially thought it advisable to find out upon what basis this widespread feeling rested with regard to the Society, which had been confirmed and approved in the most solemn manner by the Council of Trent. We discovered that the council mentions the Order only to exempt it from the general decree passed for other Orders. The Jesuit novices were to be admitted to profession if judged worthy, or they were to be dismissed from the Society. Hence the council (Session 25, c. xvi, de reg.) declared that it wished to make no innovation nor to prevent these religious from serving God and the Church in accordance with their pious Institute which had been approved by the Church.

" Wherefore, after having made use of so many necessary means, and aided as we think by the presence and inspiration of the Holy Ghost, and, moreover, compelled by the duty of our office which essentially obliges us to procure, maintain and strengthen with all our power, the repose and tranquillity of Christendom, and to root out entirely what could cause the slightest harm; and, moreover, having recognized that the Society of Jesus could no longer produce the abundant fruit and the great good for which it was instituted and approved by so many Popes, our predecessors, who adorned it with so many most admirable privileges, and seeing that it was almost and, indeed, absolutely impossible for the Church to enjoy a true and solid peace while this Order existed, being bound as we are by so many powerful considerations and compelled by other motives which the laws of prudence and the wise administration of the Church suggest but which we keep in the depths of our heart: Following in the footsteps of our predecessors and especially of Gregory X at the Council of Lyons, since the cases are identical, we do, hereby, after a mature examination, and of our certain knowledge, and by the plenitude of our Apostolic power, suppress and abolish the Society of Jesus. We nullify and abrogate all and each of its offices, functions, administrations, houses, schools, colleges, retreats, refuges and other establishments which belong to it in any manner whatever, and in every province, kingdom or state in which it may be found. We do the same for its statutes, customs, usages, decrees, constitutions, even those confirmed by the oath and by the approbation of the Holy See or otherwise, as well as all and each of its indults, both general and particular whose tenor we wish to be regarded as fully and sufficiently set forth by these present letters, as if they were here inserted word for word; notwithstanding any clause or formula to the contrary, no matter upon what decrees or obligations they may be based. Hence, we declare as forever broken and entirely extinct all authority, spiritual or temporal, of the General, provincials, visitors and other superiors of this Society, and we transfer absolutely and without restriction this same authority and this same jurisdiction to the ordinaries of the places where the aforesaid are, according to the case or persons, in the form and under the conditions which we shall explain hereafter; forbidding, as we do by these presents forbid, that any one should be received into this Society or admitted to the novitiate or invested with the habit. We also forbid any of those who have already been received to pronounce the simple or solemn vows, under pain of nullity either of their admission or profession and under other penalties as we may see fit. Moreover, we wish, ordain and enjoin that those who are at present novices, should be immediately, instantly and effectually dismissed, and we forbid those who have not made solemn vows and who have not yet been admitted to the priesthood to be promoted to either under the title or pretext of their profession or in virtue of any privileges accorded to the Society and in contravention of the decrees of the Council of Trent.

" But as the object we have in view and which we are most eager to attain is to watch over the general good of the Church and the peace of the nations, and at the same time to help and console each one of the members of this Society whom we tenderly cherish in the Lord, so that, freed at last from all the quarrels and disputes and annoyances in which they have until now been engaged, they may cultivate with more fruit the vineyard of the Lord and labor with more success for the salvation of souls, we decree and ordain that the members of this Society who have made only simple vows and who are not yet in Holy Orders shall depart from their houses and colleges freed from their vows, and that they are free to embrace whatever state they judge most conformable to their vocation, their strength and their conscience. The ordinary of the place will fix the time which may be deemed sufficient to procure an employment or an occupation, without, however, extending it beyond a year, just as in the Society they would be dismissed without any other reason than because the prudence of the superior so judges, and that without any previous citation or juridical proof.

" We allow those in Holy Orders either to leave their houses and colleges and enter some religious order approved by the Holy See, in which case they must pass the probation prescribed by the Council of Trent, if they have only taken simple vows, if they have taken solemn vows, the time of their probation will be six months in virtue of a dispensation which we give to that effect; or they may remain in the world as secular priests or clerics, and in that case they shall be entirely subject to the authority and jurisdiction of the ordinary of the place in which they reside. We ordain, also, that a suitable pension shall be assigned to those who remain in the world, until such time as they shall be otherwise provided for. This pension shall be derived from the funds of the house where they formerly lived, due consideration, however, being had to the revenues and the indebtedness of such houses.

" The professed who are already in Holy Orders and who fear they may not be able to live respectably on account of the smallness of their pension, either because they can find no other refuge or are very old and infirm, may live in their former houses on condition that they shall have no share in its administration, that they dress like secular priests and be entirely subject to the bishop of the place. We expressly forbid them to supply anyone's place or to acquire any house or place in the future, or, as the Council of Lyons decrees, to alienate the houses, goods or places which they actually possess. They may, nevertheless, meet in one or more houses, in such a manner that such houses may be available if needed for pious purposes, as may appear most in conformity, in time and place, with the Holy Canons and the will of the founders, and also more conducive to the growth of religion, the salvation of souls and public utility. Moreover, some one of the secular clergy, commendable for his prudence and virtuous life, must appear in the administration of such houses, as the name of the Society is now totally suppressed and abolished.

" We declare, also, that those who have been already expelled from any country whatever are included in the general suppression of the Order, and we consequently decree that those banished Jesuits, even if they are in Holy Orders and have not entered a religious order, shall from this moment belong to the secular clergy and be entirely subject to the ordinary of the place.

" If the ordinaries recognize in those who in virtue of the present Brief have passed from the Society to the state of secular priests necessary knowledge and correctness of life, they may grant or refuse them, as they choose, the permission to confess and preach, and without such authorization none of them can exercise such functions. However, the bishops or ordinaries will never grant such powers as are conceded to those not of the diocese, if the applicants live in houses or colleges formerly belonging to the Society; and therefore we forbid such persons to preach or administer the sacraments, as Gregory X, our predecessor prescribed in the general council already referred to. We lay it on the conscience of the bishops to watch over the execution of all this and we command them to reflect on the rigorous account they will have one day to render to God of the sheep committed to their care and of the terrible judgment with which the Sovereign Judge of the living and the dead menaces those who govern others.

" Moreover, if among those who were members of the Society there are any who were charged with the instruction of youth or who have exercised the functions of professors in colleges and schools, we warn them that they are absolutely deposed from any such direction, administration or authority and that they are not permitted to be employed in any such work, except as long as there is a reason to hope for some good from their labors and as long as they appear to keep aloof from all discussions and points of doctrine whose laxity and futility only occasion and engender trouble and disastrous contentions. We furthermore ordain that they shall be forever forbidden to exercise the functions aforesaid, if they do not endeavor to keep peace in their schools and with others; and that

they shall be discharged from the schools if they happen
to be employed in them.

" As regards the missions, we include them in
everything that has been ordered in this suppression,
and we reserve to ourselves to take measures calculated
to procure more easily and with greater certainty of
results the conversion of the heathens and the cessation
of disputes.

" Therefore, we have entirely abolished and abrogated all the privileges and statutes of this Order and
we declare that all of its members shall as soon as they
have left their houses and colleges and have embraced
the state of secular clerics, be considered proper
and fit to obtain, in conformity with the Holy Canons
and the Apostolic Constitutions, all sorts of benefices
either simple or with the care of souls annexed; and
also to accept offices, dignities and pensions, from
which in accordance with the Brief of Gregory XIII of
September 10, 1584, which begins with the words:
' Satis superque,' they were absolutely excluded as
long as they belonged to the Society. We allow them
also to accept compensations for celebrating Mass,
which they were not allowed to receive as Jesuits, and
to enjoy all the graces and favors of which they would
have always been deprived as long as they were Clerks
Regular of the Society. We abrogate likewise all
permissions they may have obtained from the General
and other superiors, in virtue of the privileges accorded
by the Sovereign Pontiff, such as leave to read heretical
books and others prohibited and condemned by the
Holy See, or not to fast or abstain, or to anticipate
the Divine Office or anything, in fact, of that nature.
Under the severest penalties we forbid them to use
such privileges in the future, as our intention is to
make them live in conformity with the requirements
of the common law, like secular priests.

" After the publication of the Brief, we forbid anyone, no matter who he may be, to dare to suspend its execution even under color, title or pretext of some demand, appeal or declaration or discussion of doubt that may arise or under any other pretext, foreseen or unforeseen; for we wish that the suppression and cessation of the whole Society as well as of all of its officers should have their full and entire effect, at the moment, and instanteously, and in the form and manner in which we have described above, under pain of major excommunication incurred *ipso facto* by a single act, and reserved to us and to the Popes, our successors. This is directed against anyone who will dare to place the least obstacle, impediment or delay in the execution of this Brief. We order, likewise, and we forbid under holy obedience all and every ecclesiastic secular and regular, whatever be their grade, dignity, quality or condition, and notably those who are at present attached to the Society or were in the past, to oppose or attack this suppression, to write against it, even to speak of it, or of its causes or motives, or of the extinct Institute itself, its rules, constitutions or discipline or of anything else, relative to this affair, without the express permission of the Sovereign Pontiff. We likewise forbid all and everyone under pain of excommunication reserved to us and our successors to dare to assail either in secret or in public, verbally or in writing, by disputes, injuries and affronts or by any other kind of contempt, anyone, no matter who he may be and least of all those who were members of the said Order.

" We exhort all Christian princes whose attachment and respect for the Holy See we know, to employ all the zeal, care, strength, authority and power which they have received from God for the execution of this Brief, in order to protect and defend the Holy Roman

Church, to adhere to all the articles it contains; to issue and publish similar decrees by which they may more carefully watch over the execution of this our present will and so forestall quarrelling, strife and dissensions among the faithful.

" Finally, we exhort all Christians and we implore them by the bowels of Jesus Christ Our Lord to remember that they have the same Master, Who is in heaven; the same Savior, Who redeemed them at the price of His blood; that they have all been regenerated by the grace of Baptism; that they have been all made sons of God and co-heirs of Christ; and are nourished by the same bread of the Divine word, the doctrine of the Church; that they are one body in Jesus Christ, and are members of each other; and consequently, it is necessary that being united by the bonds of charity they should live in peace with all men, as their only duty is to love each other, for he who loves his neighbor fulfills the law. Hence, also, they should regard with horror injuries, hatred, quarrels, deceits and other evils which the enemy of the human race has invented, devised and provoked to trouble the Church of God and to hinder the salvation of souls; nor are they to allege the false pretext of scholastic opinions or that of greater Christian perfection. Finally, let all endeavor to acquire that true wisdom of which St. James speaks (iii,13): ' Who is a wise man and indued with knowledge among you? Let him show, by a good conversation, his work in the meekness of wisdom. But if you have a bitter zeal, and there be contentions in your heart; glory not, and be not liars against the truth. For this is not wisdom, descending from above; but earthly, sensual, devilish. For, where envying and contention is, there is inconstancy, and every evil work. For the wisdom, that is from above, first indeed is chaste, then peaceable, modest, easy to be persuaded, consenting to the good, full of mercy and good fruits, without judging, without dissimulation. And the fruit of justice is sown in peace, to them that make peace.'

" Even if the superiors and the other religious of this Order, as well as all those who are interested or pretend to be, in any way whatever, in what has been herein ordered, give no assent to the present Brief and were not summoned or heard, we wish, nevertheless, that it should never be attacked, weakened or invalidated on the plea of subreption, obreption, nullity, invalidity or defect of intention on our part or for any other motive, no matter how great or unforeseen or essential it may be, or because formalities and other things have been omitted which should have been observed in the preceding enactments or in any one of them, or for any other capital point deriving from the law or any custom, or indeed contained in the body of the law; nor can there be any pretext of an enormous or a very enormous and extreme injury inflicted; nor, finally, can there be any reasons or causes however just or reasonable they may be, even one that should have necessarily been expressed, needed to give validity to the rules above given. We forbid that it should be ever retracted, discussed or brought to court or that it be provided against by way of restitution, discussion, review according to law or in any other way to obtain by legal procedure, fact, favor or justice, in any manner in which it might be accorded, to be made use of either in court or out of it.

"Moreover, we wish expressly that the present Constitution should be from this moment valid, stable and efficacious forever, that it should have its full and entire effect; that it should be inviolably observed by all and each of those to whom it belongs or will belong in the future in any manner whatever."

Such was the famous Brief which condemned the Society to death. Distressing as it is, it attributes no wrong doing to the Order. It narrates a few of the accusations against the Jesuits, but does not accept them as ever having been proved. The sole reason given for the suppression — and it is repeated again and again — is that the Society was the occasion of much trouble in the Church. It is thus, on the whole, a vindication and not a condemnation. It was not a Bull but a Brief, and on that account could be much more easily revoked than the more solemn document to which the papal *bulla* is affixed.

Father Cordara's view of this act of the Pope is generally considered to reflect that of the Society at large. It is of special value for he was one of the suppressed Jesuits and happened to be living in Rome at the time. He maintained that " the Pope could, without injustice, suppress the Society, even if innocent, just as a king can deliver over an innocent man to be put to death by an enemy who otherwise would sack a city. Clement XIV thought to save the Church whose existence was menaced."

Two years later however, Cardinal Antonelli when interrogated by Clement's successor, Pius VI, and,. consequently, when he was compelled to speak, did not hesitate to condemn the Brief absolutely. His statement is quoted here, not as a view that is adopted, but merely as a matter of history. The document is of considerable importance, for Antonelli was prefect of the Propaganda and with Consalvi was the confidant of Pius VII and was his fellow-prisoner in 1804. We sum it up briefly, omitting its harsher phrases.

" Your Holiness knows as well as the cardinals that Clement XIV would never consent to give the Brief of Suppression the canonical forms which were indispensable to make it definitive. Moreover this Brief

of Clement XIV is addressed to no one, although
such letters usually are. In its form and execution all
law is set aside, it is based on false accusations and
shameful calumnies; it is self-contradictory, in speaking
of vows both solemn and simple. Clement XIV claims
powers such as none of his predecessors claimed, and,
on the other hand, leaves doubts on points that should
have been more clearly determined. The motives
alleged by the Brief could be applied to any other
Order, and seem to have been prepared for the destruction of all of them, without specifying reasons it
annuls many Bulls and Constitutions received and
recognized by the Church; all of which goes to show
that the Brief is null and void."

A copy of the Brief was sent to every bishop in
Christendom, even to the remotest missions. Accompanying it was another document called an " Encyclical from the Congregation styled ' For the abolition
of the Society of Jesus,' with which is sent an exemplar
to every bishop of the Brief of Extinction: Dominus
ac Redemptor, with the command of His Holiness
that all the bishops should publish and promulgate
the Brief." The Latin text may be found in de Ravignan's " Clément XIII et Clément XIV " (p. 560).
We give here the translation:

" Most Illustrious and Most Reverend Lord and
Brother.

"From the printed copy herein contained of the
Apostolic Letters in the form of a Brief, under the date
of the 21st of the preceding month of July, your
lordship will learn of the suppression and extinction
for just causes of the Regular Clerics hitherto called
" of the Society of Jesus " by the most holy Lord
Clement XIV; you will also learn by what legal process
His Holiness has decreed that the suppression should
be carried out in every part of the world. For the

complete destruction of the same, he has established a special congregation of their eminences, the Cardinals Corsini, Marefoschi, Caraffa, Zelada, and Casali, together with the Reverend Macedonio and Alfani, who possess the most ample faculties for what is necessary and proper. The Brief establishing this congregation, under date of the 18th of the current month of August, is herein enclosed.

"By command of His Holiness the same congregation transmits the present letters to your lordship, in order that in each house and college and place where the individuals of the aforesaid suppressed Society may be found, your lordship shall assemble them in any house whatever (*in qualibet domo*) and you shall regularly (*rite*) announce, publish and intimate, as they say, and force and compel them to execute these letters; and your lordship shall take and retain possession for the use afterwards to be designated by His Holiness, of all and each of the houses, colleges and places of the same, with the lawful rights to their goods and appurtenances, after having removed the aforesaid individuals of the suppressed Society; and in their execution, your lordship will do whatever else is decreed in the letters of suppression and will advise the special congregation that such execution has been carried out. Your lordship will see to it. Meantime we entreat the Lord that all things may prosper with you.

"Yours with brotherly devotedness.
"Rome, Aug. 18, 1773."

Carayon gives us the personnel of this congregation (Doc. inédits, xvii). Cardinal Marefoschi, who had been for sixteen years secretary of the Propaganda, had made a digest of all the complaints uttered by missionaries in various parts of the world against the Jesuits, omitting, however, all that had been said in their favor. The Pope had named him visitor of the Irish College, which had been entrusted to the Society by Cardinal Ludovisi, and he immediately removed the Jesuits. Among other professors he put in a certain Tamburini, who had been expelled from Brescia for Jansenism. In Marefoschi's report to the Pope, the former professors (the Jesuits) were accused of neglect of the studies, alienation of ecclesiastical property and swindling, with a consequent diminution of the revenues. He was then sent to visit the College of Tuccioli and similar disastrous results ensued. In June, 1772, he and the Cardinal of York expelled the Jesuits from the Roman Seminary and in the same year from Frascati. The entire city addressed a petition to the cardinal begging him not to drive out the Fathers, but his royal highness was so wrought up by the audacity of the request that he was on the point of putting some of the chief petitioners in jail, magistrates though they were.

With Marefoschi were three other cardinals, Casali, Caraffa, and Zelada, all three of whom had been raised to the purple in the month of May at the suggestion of Mgr. Bottari, who had been filling Rome with defamatory books against the Jesuits. In spite of the entreaties of his family, young Cardinal Corsini accepted the presidency. Macedonio was made secretary, and Alfani, assessor; both of these clergymen were subsequently charged with pillage of the sequestrated property. Finally, to give an appearance of acting in conformity with canon law, two theologians were added to the commission; Mamachi, a Dominican, and de Casal, a Minor Reformed; both were avowed enemies of Probabilism and Molinism, and, singularly enough, were bitterly opposed to the Apostolic Constitution " Unigenitus " in which Clement XI condemned the Jansenistic errors of Pasquier Quesnel.

The Protestant historian Schoell (xliv, 83) speaking of the brief of suppression says: " This Brief does not condemn the doctrine nor the morals, nor the rules of the Jesuits. The complaints of the courts are the sole motives alleged for the suppression of the Order, and the Pope justifies himself by the precedents of other Orders which were suppressed to satisfy the demands of public opinion." As he was about to sign it, he heard the bells of the Gesù ringing. "What is that for?" he asked. "The Jesuits are about to recite the Litany of the Saints," he was told; " Not the Litany of the Saints," he said, "but the Litany of the Dead." It was July 21, 1773.

CHAPTER XIX

THE EXECUTION

Seizure of the Gesù in Rome — Suspension of the Priests — Juridical Trial of Father Ricci continued during Two Years — The Victim's Death-bed Statement — Admission of his Innocence by the Inquisitors — Obsequies — Reason of his Protracted Imprisonment — Liberation of the Assistants by Pius VI — Receipt of the Brief outside of Rome — Refused by Switzerland, Poland, Russia and Prussia — Read to the Prisoners in Portugal by Pombal — Denunciation of it by the Archbishop of Paris — Suppression of the Document by the Bishop of Quebec — Acceptance by Austria — Its Enforcement in Belgium — Carroll at Bruges — Defective Promulgation in Maryland.

Two days before the subsidiary Brief was signed, namely on August 16, 1773, the commissioner began operations. Led by Alfani and Macedonio, a squad of soldiers invaded the Gesù, where the General and his assistants were notified of the suppression of the Society. Apparently no one else was cited, and hence, according to de Ravignan, the procedure was illegal as far as the rest of the community was concerned. However, they made no difficulty about it and from that moment considered themselves as no longer Jesuits. It was supposed that a great amount of money would be seized at the central house of the Society; but the hope was not realized; for only about $50,000 were found, and that sum had been collected to defray the expenses of the beatification of St. Francis Hieronymo. It really belonged to St. Peter's rather than to the Gesù. However, there was plenty of material in the gold and silver vessels of the chapels, the works of art, the valuable library, and the archives.

The same process was followed in the other Jesuit establishments of the city. The Fathers were locked up while the soldiers guarded the doors and swarmed

37

through the rooms and passage ways. The old and infirm were carried to the Roman College, and then sent back to the place whence they had been taken; in both instances on stretchers, when the victim was unable to walk.   One old Father was actually breathing his last during the transfer.   They were all suspended from their priestly faculties, and ordered to report every three months to the authorities with a certificate of their good behavior, signed by the parish priest.   They were ecclesiastical "ticket of leave men." Pretexts were multiplied to have many of them arrested. They were paraded through the streets in custody of a policeman, and after being put in the dock with common criminals were locked up or banished from the Papal States.

On August 17 at night-fall, the carriage of Cardinal Corsini drove to the Gesù. In it was the auditor of the congregation with a request to Father Ricci to meet the cardinal at the English College. The invitation was accepted in perfect good faith, although that very morning an offer made by the minister of Tuscany to take the General under his protection and thus secure him from arrest had been declined by Ricci. The freedom of the house was given to him on his arrival, but soon he was restricted to three rooms, and he then noticed that soldiers were on guard both inside and outside of the college. He was kept there for more than a month, during which time he was subjected to several judicial examinations; finally he was transferred to the Castle Sant' Angelo where he was soon followed by his secretary, Commolli, and the assistants, Le Forestier, Zaccharia, Gautier and Faure. They were all assigned to separate cells. The enemies of the Society now had the arch-criminal in their hands, the General himself, Father Ricci; and they could get from him all the secrets of the redoubtable organization which they had destroyed. His papers, both private and official, were in their possession. The archives of the Society were before them with information about every member of it from the beginning, as well as all the personal letters from all over the world written in every conceivable circumstance of Jesuit life. They were all carefully studied and yet no cause for accusation was found in them. The jailors seemed to have lost their heads and to have forgotten their usual tactics of forgery and interpolation.

The trial of Father Ricci was amazing both in its procedure and its length. There were no witnesses to give testimony for or against him, but he was brutally and repeatedly interrogated by an official named Andretti who was suggestively styled "the criminalist." The interrogatories have all been printed, and some of the questions are remarkable for their stupidity. Thus for instance, he was asked, " Do you think you have any authority since the suppression of the Society?" The answer was. " I am quite persuaded I have none." " What authority would you have if, instead of abolishing the Society, the Pope had done something else?" " What he would give me." " Are there any abuses in the Order?" To this he replied, " If you mean general abuses, I answer that, by the mercy of God there are none. On the contrary, there is in the Society a great deal of piety, regularity, zeal, and especially charity, which has shown itself in a remarkable way during these fifteen years of bitter trials." " Have you made any changes in the government of the Order?" " None." " Where are your moneys?" " I have none. I had not enough to keep the exiles of Spain and Portugal from starvation."

The result of this investigation which went on for more than two years was that nothing was found either against him or against the Society, and yet he was kept in a dungeon until he died. As the end was approaching Father Ricci read from his dying bed the following declaration:

" Because of the uncertainty of the moment when God will please to summon me before him and also in view of my advanced age and the multitude, duration, and greatness of my sufferings, which have been far beyond my strength, being on the point of appearing before the infallible tribunal of truth and justice, after long and mature deliberation and after having humbly invoked my most merciful Redeemer that He will not permit me to speak from passion, especially in this the last action of my life, nor be moved by any bitterness of heart, or out of wrong desire or evil purpose, but only to acquit myself of my obligation to bear testimony to truth and to innocence, I now make the two following declarations and protests:

"First, I declare and protest that the extinct Society of Jesus has given no reason for its suppression; and I declare and protest with that moral certainty which a well-informed superior has of what passes in his Order. Second, I declare and protest that I have given no reason, not even the slightest, for my imprisonment, and I do so with that sovereign certitude which each one has of his own actions. I make this second protest solely because it is necessary for the reputation of the extinct Society of which I was superior.

" I do not pretend in consequence of these protests that I or any one may judge as guilty before God any of those who have injured the Society of Jesus or myself. The thoughts of men are known to God alone. He alone sees the errors of the human mind and sees if they are such as to excuse from sin; He alone penetrates the motives of acts; as well as the spirit in which things are done, and the affections of

the heart that accompany such actions; and since the
malice or innocence of an external act depends on all
these things, I leave it to God Who shall interrogate
man's thoughts and deeds.

" To do my duty as a Christian, I protest that with
the help of God I have always pardoned and do now
sincerely pardon all those who have tortured and
harmed me, first, by the evils they have heaped on
the Society and by the rigorous measures they have
employed in dealing with its members; secondly, by
the extinction of the Society and by its accompanying
circumstances; thirdly, by my own imprisonment, and
the hardships they have added to it, and by the harm
they have done to my reputation; all of which are
public and notorious facts. I pray God, out of His
goodness and mercy, through the merits of Jesus
Christ, to pardon me my many sins and to pardon
also all the authors of the above-mentioned evils and
wrongs, as well as their co-operators. With this
sentiment and with this prayer I wish to die.

" Finally I beg and conjure all those who may read
these declarations and protests to make them public
throughout the world as far as in them lies. I ask
this by all the titles of humanity, justice and Christian
charity that may persuade them to carry out my will
and desire. (signed) Lorenzo Ricci."

The trial had been purposely prolonged. At each
session only three of four questions would be put to
the accused, although he constantly entreated the
inquisitors to proceed. Then there would be an
interruption of eight, ten and even twenty days or
more. At times the interrogations were sent in on
paper, until finally, Andretti, the chief inquisitor, said
that the case was ended and he would return no more.
Nevertheless he made his appearance a few days later.

" No doubt," says Father Ricci, "someone had told

him that the whole process was null and void; and I
pitied this honest man, advanced in age as he was, and
so long in the practice of his profession, who was now
told that he did not know the conditions necessary for
the validity of a process.   Those who gave him that
information should have warned him long before.
So he began again, going over the same ground in the
same way, and I gave him the same answers.   His
questions were always preceded by long formulæ to
which I paid no heed.   After each question, he made
me repeat my oath.   I asked him to let me know the
reason of my incarceration and could get no answer;
but, finally he uttered these words: ' Be content to
know that you have not been imprisoned for any
crime; and you might have inferred that from the fact
that I have not interrogated you about anything
criminal whatever.' "

As a necessary consequence of this exoneration by
the official deputed to try him, it follows that the
Order of which he was the chief superior was also
without reproach; for, if the numberless offences
alleged against the Society were true, it would have
been absolutely impossible for the General not to
have known them; and having this knowledge, he
would have been culpable and deserving of the severest
punishment, if there had been dissensions in the Order
and he had not endeavored to repress them; if lax
morality had been taught and he did not censure it;
if the Society had indulged in mercantile transactions
and he had not condemned such departures from the
law; if it had been guilty of ambition and he had not
crushed it.   Being the centre and the source of all
authority and of all activity in the Order, his knowledge
of what is going on extends to very minute details
and hence if the Order was guilty he was the chief
criminal.   But even his bitterly prejudiced judges

had declared him innocent and he was, therefore, to be set free.

At this juncture, the Spanish minister, Florida Blanca, intervened and in the name of Charles III warned the Pope not to dare to release him. The Bourbons were still bent on terrorizing the Holy See. The difficulty was solved by the victim himself who died on November 24, 1775. He was then seventy-two years of age. He was able to speak up to the last moment and was often heard to moan: "Ah! poor Society! At least to my knowledge you did not deserve the punishment that was meted out to you."

On the evening of the 25th, Father Ricci's remains were carried to the Church of St. John of the Florentines. The whole edifice was draped in black, and the coffin was placed on the bier around which were thirty funeral torches. A vast multitude took part in the services. The Bishop of Commachio, a staunch friend of the Society, celebrated the Mass. He came, he said, not to pray for the General but to pray to him. Another bishop exclaimed: "Behold the martyr!" In the evening, the corpse was carried to the Gesù. It should have arrived by 9 o'clock, but it reached the church only at midnight. To avoid any demonstration, the approaches to the church had been closed, and there were only five or six Fathers present. From Garayon's narrative it would appear that the uncoffined body was carried in a coach and was clothed in a very short and very shabby habit. The curé of the parish and two other persons were in the conveyance. Two other carriages whose occupants were unknown but who were suspected of being spies followed close behind. After the absolution, the body was placed in the coffin and laid in the vault beside the remains of Ricci's seventeen predecessors. The tomb was then closed and a scrap of paper was fixed on it, with the inscription: " Lorenzo Ricci, ex-General of the Jesuits, died at Castle Sant' Angelo, November 24, 1775."

After reciting these facts, Boero asks why the ex-General was kept in such a long and severe confinement? There is no answer, he says, except that such was the good pleasure of His Majesty Charles III. The Spanish minister, Moñino, had declared that such was the case. To let him out alive would have been an indirect condemnation of the pressure exerted by the court of Madrid in directing the course of the commission which had been expressly created to pass a sentence of death on the Society. The knowledge that the General and his assistants had issued alive from the dungeons of Sant' Angelo would have troubled the peace of Charles III and his fellow-conspirators; hence, in spite of the good will and the affection of the Sovereign Pontiff, Father Ricci, after two years imprisonment in Adrian's Tomb, was carried out a corpse. Those of his companions who survived were released, but were commanded by the judges to observe the strictest silence on what had passed during their captivity, or not to tell what questions had been put to them.

One of the victims showed his indignation at this excessive cruelty, and exclaimed, " Why should you require me to swear on the Holy Gospels not to speak of my trial, when you know very well that it con-sisted of two or three insignificant and ridiculous questions?" Another assistant was merely asked his name and birthplace, and no more. A third satis-fied the judges when he replied, " I have neither said nor done anything wrong." He was never interro-gated again. The secretary of the Society had been asked in what subterranean hiding-place he kept the treasures. He answered that there were no sub-terranean hiding-places, and no treasures. In that consisted his whole examination. He died shortly afterwards of sickness contracted in the prison and his death was for a long time concealed.

Father Faure inquired of one of his judges: " For what crime am I in jail?" " For none," was the reply, "but the fear of your pen, and especially the fear of having you write against the Brief. That is the only cause of your imprisonment." " By the same rule," retorted the prisoner, " you might send me to the galleys for fear I might steal, or to be hanged to prevent me from committing murder." He was the only recalcitrant, and he was so dreaded that during his incarceration he was ordered to keep his light burning all night, so that he might be watched. This was after they found a black spot on his bed. They thought it was ink. Father Ricci, however, contrived to keep an exact account of the questions that were asked. Carayon has published them in 'his " Documents inédits."

One of these redoubtable personages so rigidly kept in confinement was Father Romberg, the German assistant, who was eighty-two years of age. He became very feeble, and had a stroke of paralysis which kept him to his chair. When the governor of the Castle came with the judges and officials to tell him he was free, he thanked them effusively, but requested the favor of being left in his cell to die. " You see," said he, " I have two fine friends who are prisoners here, and they, out of charity, come regularly every morning and carry me in my chair to the chapel where I can hear Mass and go to Communion. If I leave this place, God knows if I should have the same help and the same consolation." This was a specimen of the men who made Charles III and Florida Blanca tremble. In spite of the protests of the Spanish minister, every one was set free on February 16, 1776, and Pius VI cancelled the order of the inquisitors who forbade their victims to hold any communication with their fellow-Jesuits.

The manner in which the Brief was executed outside of Rome varied with the mentality and morality of the nations to which it was sent. Much to the chagrin of the Sovereign Pontiff, it was enthusiastically acclaimed by all the Protestants and infidels of Europe. For, was it not a justification of all the hatred they had invariably heaped on the Society wherever it happened to be? They could now congratulate themselves that they had instinctively divined the malignant character of the Institute which it took centuries for the Church to discover, and they logically concluded that all the laudatory Bulls lavished on the Society by previous Pontiffs were intentional deceits or ignorant delusions. They might have argued contrariwise, but as it would have been against themselves they refrained. They were jubilant because the Sovereign Pontiff had slain their chief enemy, and they had a medal struck to commemorate the event.

In " Les Jésuites " by Böhmer-Monod (p. 278) we find the following: " Cultured Europe triumphed in the Suppression of the Order, and the people everywhere showed their approval. Here and there some pious devotees raised their voices in lamentation, but nowhere in Europe or elsewhere was there any serious opposition to the Brief. The Order had forfeited all esteem; and public opinion evinced no compassion for anything tragic that occurred in its fall. It remained quite indifferent to the atrocities of which Pombal was guilty. The injustices which certain Fathers suffered in various places were considered a just retribution or at least were regarded as necessary for progress of light and virtue." This is not very flattering to "cultured " Europe.

Apart from the self-stultifying utterances on this quotation, as for instance, that "the injustices suffered were a just retribution, or were at least regarded as necessary for the progress of light and virtue," and also that certain Fathers suffered in various places; whereas the same authors give 23,000 who suffered all over the world, it is an absolute contradiction with the facts of the case to say that " nowhere in Europe was there any serious opposition to the Brief " and that " they everywhere showed their approval and evinced no compassion for anything tragic that occurred in the fall."

In the first place, Frederick the Great in Prussia and Catherine II of Russia not only would not allow the Brief in their dominions, but forbade it under the severest penalties. Poland for a long time refused to receive it, and the Catholic cantons of Switzerland sent a remonstrance to the Pope. Moreover, although, even before the document was promulgated, the Fathers had secularized themselves of their own initiative, yet, the authorities would not allow them to give up the colleges. The other side of the picture was that in Naples, Tanucci not only forbade the Brief to be read under pain of death, but forbade all mention of it. In Portugal, of course, no opposition was made for there were no Jesuits to suppress, they were either dead or in prison or exile. It was, however, an occasion of public rejoicing, and the document was received with booming of cannon and ringing of bells, as if a victory had been won, but that governmental device did not extinguish in the heart of the suffering people a deep compassion for the victims of Pombal's " atrocities."

In Spain, it was absolutely prohibited to read it or speak about the Brief, because by its eulogy of the virtues of the members of the Society, it gave the

lie to the government, which insisted on the suppression
of the Society precisely because of the immorality of
its members. In France, its promulgation was forbidden for the very opposite reason, that is, because it
praised the Institute, which the politicians had declared
to be essentially vicious; though they admitted that
the individual Jesuits were irreproachable. Thus,
like Spain, France had been officially convicted by
the Brief of calumniating, plundering and annihilating
a great religious order. Voltaire, commenting on the
situation, suggested that there might be a sort of
national exchange by France and Spain. " Send the
French Jesuits to Spain," he said, " and they will
edify the people by observing the Institute, and send
the Spaniards to France where they will satisfy the
people by not observing it."

The most notable opposition to the Brief, occurred
in France. The whole hierarchy and clergy positively
refused to accept it, and the Archbishop of Paris,
Christopher de Beaumont, who had been especially
requested by the Pope to promulgate it, answered by
a letter which is unpleasant for a Jesuit to publish on
account of its tone; for the most profound affection
and reverence for the Holy See is one of the ingrained
and distinctive traits of the Society. However, it is
a historical document and is called for in the present
instance as a refutation of the statement that there
was no opposition to the Brief in Europe This famous
letter was dated April 24, 1774, that is more than
eight months after the Suppression. It is addressed
to the Holy Father himself and runs as follows:

" This Brief is nothing else than a personal and
private judgment. Among other things that are remarked in it by our clergy is the extraordinary, odious,
and immoderate characterization of the Bull " Pascendi
Munus " of the saintly Clement XIII, whose memory

will be forever glorious and who had invested the Bull in question with all the due and proper formalities of such documents. It is described by the Brief not only as being inexact but as having been ' extorted ' rather than obtained; whereas it has all the authority of a general council; for it was not promulgated until almost the whole clergy of the Church and all the secular princes had been consulted by the Holy Father. The clergy with common accord and with one voice applauded the purpose of the Holy Father, and earnestly begged him to carry it out. It was conceived and published in a manner as general as it was solemn. And is it not precisely that, Holy Father, which really gives the efficacity, the reality and the force to a general council, rather than the material union of some persons who though physically united may be very far from one another in their judgments and their views? As for the secular princes, if there were any who did not unite with the others to give their approbation, their number was inconsiderable. Not one of them protested against it, not one opposed it, and even those who, at that very time, were laying their plans to banish the Jesuits, allowed the Bull to be published in their dominions.

" But as the spirit of the Church is one and indivisible in its teaching of truth, we have to conclude that it cannot teach error when it deals in a solemn manner with a matter of supreme importance. Yet it would have led us into error if it had not only proclaimed the Institute of the Society to be pious and holy, but had solemnly and explicitly said: 'We know of certain knowledge that it diffuses abroad and abundantly the odor of sanctity.' In saying this it put upon that Institute the seal of its approbation, and confirmed anew not only the Society itself, but the members who composed it, the functions it exercised, the doctrines

it taught, the glorious works it accomplished, all of
which shed lustre upon it, in spite of the calumnies by
which it was assailed and the storms of persecution
which were let loose against it. Thus the Church
would have deceived us most effectively on that
occasion if it would now have us accept this Brief
which destroys the Society; and also if we are to suppose that this Brief is on the same level in its lawfulness and its universality as the Constitution to
which we refer. We abstract, Holy Father, from the
individuals whom we might easily name, both secular
and ecclesiastical who have meddled with this affair.
Their character, condition, doctrine, sentiment, not to
say more of them, are so little worthy of respect, as to
justify us in expressing the formal and positive judgment
that the Brief which destroys the Society of Jesus is
nothing else than an isolated, private and pernicious
judgment, which does no honor to the tiara and is
prejudicial to the glory of the Church and the growth
and conservation of the Orthodox Faith.

" In any case, Holy Father, it is impossible for me
to ask the clergy to accept the Brief; for in the first
place, I would not be listened to, were I unfortunate
enought to lend the aid of my ministry to its acceptance. Moreover, I would dishonor my office if I did
so, for the memory of the recent general assembly
which I had the honor to convoke at the instance of
His Majesty, to inquire into the need we have of the
Society in France, its usefulness, the purity of its
doctrines, etc., is too fresh in my mind to reverse my
verdict. To charge myself with the task you wish me
to perform would be to inflict a serious injury on
religion as well as to cast an aspersion on the learning
and integrity of the prelates who laid before the king
their approval of the very points which are now condemned by the Brief. Moreover, if it is true that the

Order is to be condemned under the specious pretext of the impossibility of peace, as long as the Society exists, why not try it on those bodies which are jealous of the Society? Instead of condemning it you ought to canonize it. That you do not do so compels us to form a judgment of the Brief which, though just, is not in its favor.

" For what is that peace which is incompatible with this Society? The question is startling in the reflection it evokes; for we fail to understand how such a motive had the power to induce Your Holiness to adopt a measure which is so hazardous, so dangerous, and so prejudicial. Most assuredly the peace which is irreconcilable with the existence of the Society is the peace which Jesus Christ calls insidious, false, deceitful. In a word what the Brief designates as peace is not peace; *Pax, pax et non erat pax.* It is the peace which vice and libertinism adopt; it is the peace which cannot ally itself with virtue, but which on the contrary has always been the principal enemy of virtue.

" It is precisely that peace against which the piety of the Jesuits in the four quarters of the world have declared an active, a vigorous, a bloody warfare; which they have carried to the limit and in which they have achieved the greatest success. To put an end to that peace, they have devoted their talents; have undergone pain and suffering. By their zeal and their eloquence they have striven to block every avenue of approach, by which this false peace might enter and rend the bosom of the Church; they have set the souls of men free from its thralldom, and they have pursued it to its innermost lair, making light of the danger and expecting no other reward for their daring, than the hatred of the licentious and the persecution of the ungodly.

" An infinite number of splendid illustrations of their courage might be adduced in the long succession of memorable achievements which have never been interrupted from the first moment of the Society's existence until the fatal day when the Church saw it die. If that peace cannot co-exist with the Society, and if the re-establishment of this pernicious peace is the motive of the destruction of the Jesuits, then the victims are crowned with glory and they end their career like the Apostles and Martyrs; but honest men are dismayed by this holocaust of piety and virtue.

" A peace which is irreconcilable with the Society is not that peace which unites hearts; which is helpful to others; which each day contributes an increase in virtue, piety and Christian charity; which reflects glory on Christianity and sheds splendor on our holy religion. Nor is there need of proving this, though proof might be given, not by a few examples which this Society could furnish from the day of its birth to the fatal and ever deplorable day of its suppression, but by a countless multitude of facts which attest that the Jesuits were always and in every clime, the supporters, the promoters and the indefatigable defenders of true and solid peace. These facts are so evident that they carry conviction to every mind.

" In this letter I am not constituting myself an apologist of the Jesuits; but I am placing before the eyes of Your Holiness the reasons which, in the present case, excuse us from obeying. I will not mention place or time, as it is an easy thing for Your Holiness to convince yourself of the truth of my utterance. Your Holiness is not ignorant of them.

" Moreover, Holy Father, we have remarked with terror, that this destructive Brief eulogizes in the highest way certain persons whose conduct never merited praise from Clement XIII, of saintly memory. Far from doing so, he regarded it always as his duty to set them aside, and to act in their regard with the most absolute reserve.

" This difference of appreciation necessarily excites attention, in view of the fact that your predecessor did not consider worthy of the purple those whom Your Holiness seems to design for the glory of the cardinalate. The firmness on one side and the connivance on the other reveal themselves only too clearly. But perhaps an excuse might be found for the latter, were it not for the fact which has not been successfully disguised that an alien influence guided the pen that wrote the Brief.

" In a word, most Holy Father, the clergy of France, which is the most learned and most illustrious of Holy Church, and which has no other aim than to promote the glory of the Church, does now judge after deep reflection that the reception of the Brief of Your Holiness will cast a shadow on the glory of the clergy of France; and it does not propose to consent to a measure which, in ages to come, will tarnish its glory. By rejecting the Brief and by an active resistance to it our clergy will transmit to posterity a splendid example of integrity and of zeal for the Catholic Faith, for the prosperity of the Church and particularly for the honor of its Visible Head.

" These, Holy Father, are some of the reasons which determine us, myself and all the clergy of this kingdom, never to permit the publication of such a Brief, and to make known to Your Holiness, as I do by this present letter, that such is my attitude and that of all the clergy, who, however, will never cease to unite in prayer with me to our Lord for the sacred person of Your Holiness. We shall address our humble supplications

38

to the Divine Father of Light that He may deign to diffuse it so abundantly that the truth may be discerned whose splendor has been obscure."

The Bishop of Quebec, Mgr. Briand, refused to promulgate the Brief, and he informed some of his intimate friends that he had no fear of excommunication in doing so, for the reason that he was in constant communication with Pope Clement XIV, who approved of his course of action. Associated with the bishop was Governor Carleton, who was interested in the matter for his own personal reasons. His rival, General Amherst, the conqueror of Quebec, was anxious to see the Jesuits driven out, so as to secure their property for himself. Carleton, on the contrary, proposed to keep it for future educational purposes. He could not seize it immediately, for the treaty at the conquest had guaranteed the protection of the Canadians in their religion. Hence he did not molest the Fathers, though he refused to allow any accession either of novices or former Jesuits to their ranks. The result was that they gradually died out. The last of all was the venerable Casot, who gave up the ghost in 1800 after having distributed all his goods to the poor. What was not available in that way he conveyed to religious communities or to churches. The relics of Brébeuf and Lalemant are now among the treasures of the Hotel-Dieu. The Jesuit College, which was opposite the present basilica cathedral, was occupied by soldiers, and was first known as the "Jesuit Barracks," and subsequently as the "Cheshire Barracks." Later it was a refuge for the poor, until at length Cardinal Taschereau ordered it to be demolished as unsafe. Thus the Brief was not executed in Canada. The Jesuits of New Orleans had been already expelled by Choiseul, and there was no one left to whom it could be read.

The suppression of the Society in what is now the
United States is of special interest to Americans,
though it possesses also a general value in the fact that
it furnishes the only account in English, as far as we
are aware, of what took place in Belgium some years
before as the prelude of the general suppression. This
is based on the highest authority, for it is the personal
narrative of John Carroll, the founder of the American
hierarchy. He had gone when a lad of fourteen to
St. Omers in French Flanders, and after his college
course entered the Jesuit novitiate at Watten about
six miles away, where he met several of his countrymen who were to distinguish themselves later in
the Jesuit mission of Maryland. They were Horne,
Jenkins, Knight, Emmot and Tyrer. There also was
the English Jesuit, Reeve, whose "Bible History"
was once an indispensable treasure in every Catholic
family.

On completing his novitiate, Carroll was sent for his
theology and philosophy to Liège, and was ordained
priest in 1769, after having proved his ability by a
brilliant public defense in theology. He then taught
at St. Omers and was subsequently made professor of
philosophy and theology to the scholastics at Liège.
He pronounced his four solemn vows as a Professed
Father on February 2, 1771, a little more than two
years before the suppression of the Society. As St.
Omer was in France the Jesuits were expelled from
it in 1764. That the occupants of the house were
English did not matter. International comity received
scant consideration in those days Every one was
driven out except Father Brown, who was then ninety-
four years of age. He was left there alone to die.
The others, under the guidance of Father Reeve, crossed
the frontier to Bruges where they had been invited
by the authorities to found a college.

Here begins a story told by Carroll of government duplicity which shows how largely the motive of plunder entered into the whole movement of the suppression. Belgium was then under the domination of Austria, and the government continually urged the Fathers to begin the erection of a college on a grand scale at that place. In all confidence that they would never be disturbed, they expended on the first set of buildings the sum of $37,000 a considerable amount of money in those days. They would have gone further but their money was exhausted.

While teaching there, Father Carroll was sent on a short tour through Europe as tutor to the young son of Lord Stourton, an English nobleman. He passed through Alsace and Lorraine, where the Jesuits were still protected; was welcomed at the University of Heidelberg, and finally reached Rome. There, though under the very eyes of the Pope, he was compelled to conceal his identity as a Jesuit and hence met none of his brethren. He saw everywhere not only infamous libels on the Society which were for sale in the streets, but books and pamphlets assailing the devotion to the Sacred Heart of Jesus, and ridiculing the ceremonies of the Mass. The overthrow of the Jesuits was the common topic of conversation and word from the King of Spain was momentarily expected. Henry Stuart, Cardinal of York, the last descendant of James II, was there at the time, but as he was a rancorous enemy of the Society, Father Carroll did not dare to present the young Catholic nobleman to him. He returned by the way of France and saw the ruins everywhere, and finally arrived at Bruges to take part in the tragedy as one of the victims.

The Brief was promulgated on August 16, and the superiors of the two colleges at Bruges, encouraged by the general expectation of the town that their status would not be effected, wrote a letter to the president of the council at Brussels, offering their services as secular clergy to continue the work of education. The rectors were invited to Brussels, and assured that they would be treated with respect, allowed to retain private property and be granted proper maintenance. Even after the reception of the Brief, the Bishop of Bruges assured them that in a few days the excitement would pass and everything would go on as usual. Austria, however, had already accepted and promulgated the Brief.

The first commissioners of the Suppression threw up the work in disgust. It was then handed over to a coarse young fellow named Marouex who was anxious to make a name for himself. He succeeded. Arriving at the college on September 20, he summoned the community to his presence and ordered the Brief and edict to be read. He then forbade anyone to leave the house, or to be allowed to enter, or to write any letters, or to direct the college, or to teach the pupils. He seized the account books and began a hunt for hidden treasures. Each member of the community was examined individually, put under oath, and ordered to produce everything he had, even family letters; "which explains," says Shea, "how there is no trace of Carroll's letters from his mother and kindred in America."

On October 14, Marouex, accompanied by a squad of soldiers, burst into the community rooms and ordered Fathers Angier, Plowden and Carroll to follow him. He would not even permit them to go to their rooms for a moment to get what they needed, but sent them under guard to wagons waiting outside, and hurried them off to the Flemish college, which had been already plundered. There they were locked up for several days without a bed to lie on. The

community was still there under lock and key.   Three
of them were kept as hostages and the rest were
ordered out of the country.   Thus did Maria
Theresa allow her beloved Jesuits to be treated, in
return for the benefits they had heaped on her empire
from the time when Faber and Le Jay and Canisius
and their great associates had saved it from destruction.

Thoroughly heartbroken, Carroll turned his steps
towards Protestant England. Before leaving the
Continent, he wrote the following pathetic letter to his
brother Daniel, who was in Maryland. Because of
Carroll's own personal character and his prominence
in American history, it is a precious testimonial of
love and affection for the Society, as well as a splendid
vindication of it for the world at large. It is dated
September 11, 1773.

" I was willing to accept the vacant post of prefect
of the sodality here, but now all room for deliberation
is over. The enemies of the Society and, above all,
the unrelenting perseverance of the Spanish and
Portuguese ministries, with the passiveness of the
court of Vienna have at last obtained their ends;
and our so long persecuted, and, I must add, holy
Society is no more. God's holy will be done and
may His Name be blessed for ever and ever! This
fatal blow was struck on July 21, but was kept secret
at Rome till August 16, and was only made known to me
on September 5. I am not, and perhaps never shall
be, recovered from the shock of this dreadful intelligence. The greatest blessing which in my estimation
I could receive from God would be immediate death,
but if He deny me this, may His holy and adorable
designs on me be wholly fulfilled.

" I find it impossible to understand that Divine
Providence should permit such an end to a body,

wholly devoted, and striving with the most disinterested charity to procure every comfort and
advantage to their neighbors, whether by preaching,
teaching, catechizing, missions, visiting hospitals,
prisons and in every other function of spiritual and
corporal mercy. Such have I beheld it in every part
of my travels, the first of all ecclesiastical bodies in
the esteem and confidence of the faithful, and certainly the most laborious. What will become of our
flourishing congregations with you and those cultivated by the German Fathers? These reflections
crowd so fast upon me, that I almost lose my senses.
But I will endeavor to suppress them for a few moments.
You see I am now my own master and left to my own
direction. In returning to Maryland, I shall have
the comfort of not only being with you, but of being
farther out of reach of scandal and defamation, and
removed from the scenes of distress of many of my
dearest friends whom I shall not be able to relieve.
I shall therefore most certainly sail for Maryland early
next spring if I possibly can."

At the time of the Suppression there were nineteen
Jesuits in Maryland and Pennsylvania; as it was then
three years before the Declaration of Independence,
they were still English subjects. On October 6,
1773, Bishop Challoner, the Vicar of London, though
Chandlery in his "Fasti breviores" says it was
Talbot, sent them the following letter:

"To Messrs the Missioners in Maryland and
Pennsylvania.

"To obey the order which I have received from
Rome, I notify to you, by this the Breve, of the total
dissolution of the Society of Jesus; and send withal a
form of declaration of your obedience and submission,
to which you are all to subscribe, as your brethren

have done here, and send me back the formula with the subscription of you all, as I am to send them up to Rome.

" Ever yours,

"Richard Deboren. V. Ap."

In passing, it may be remarked that as a missive from a Superior to a number of devoted priests against whom not a word of reproach had been ever uttered and whose lives were wrecked by this official act this communication of the vicar cannot be cited as a manifestation of excessive paternal tenderness.

The formula to which they were required to subscribe, was, in its English translation, as follows:

"We the undersigned missionary priests of the London District of Maryland and Pennsylvania, hitherto known as the Clerks of the Society of Jesus, having been informed by the declaration and publication of the Apostolic Brief issued on July 21, 1773, by our Most Holy Lord Pope Clement XIV, by which he completely suppresses and extinguishes the aforesaid Congregation and Society in the whole world, and orders the priests to be entirely subject to the rule and authority of the Bishops as part of the secular clergy, we the aforesaid, fully and sincerely, submit to the Brief, and humbly acquiescing to the complete suppression of the said Society, submit ourselves entirely as secular priests to the jurisdiction and rule of the above mentioned Bishop, the Vicar Apostolic."

In this document of the vicar there are some features which are worthy of consideration. The first is that it was not communicated personally to those interested but through the post — and it might have been a forgery. Secondly, it was not correct in saying that it was issued on July 21, 1773. It was signed on July 21 but issued or published only on August 16 of that

year, and it was not effective or binding until that
date. Thirdly, there was no mention of the renewal
of faculties to the superior whose ecclesiastical character had now been completely transformed from that
of a religious to a secular priest; and they were thus
obliged to presume that they were not suspended and
that their power of transmitting faculties was not
withdrawn. Fourthly, before the Suppression, the
vicar Apostolic had warned the Propaganda that he
could do nothing to aid the Maryland missioners,
and after the Revolution he refused absolutely to
have any communication with them. Thus, there
was no possibility of fulfilling the injunction of becoming
secular priests, as the Brief enjoined.

As far as the Jesuit habit was concerned there was no
difficulty, for there is no distinctive habit in the Society.
The Jesuits are ecclesiastically in the rank of " clerici
regulares," and can wear the garb of any secular
priest, just as they do, at present, in many parts of
the world. St. Francis Xavier once wore green silk,
and in our own days, the English Jesuit dress is rather
an academic gown than a cassock. Again in Maryland and Pennsylvania, there were at that time
no secular priests; the missionaries were all Jesuits,
and it would have been difficult to get any other
ecclesiastical attire. What they wore was, as a
matter of fact, used only in ecclesiastical functions.
An analogous obstacle presented itself in the name.
The people continued to recognize them as Jesuits,
and it would have been very imprudent to publicly
announce that they were no longer such. There are
several letters extant, however, in which the Jesuits
advise their friends to drop the S. J. in their correspondence, but that is not unusual even now. Exteriorly,
the life of those old Maryland Jesuits continued to be
precisely the same as it had always been.

Moreover they retained possession of their property, for unlike the Jesuits of Canada, Illinois and Louisiana, they held their estates by personal, not by corporate title; and regularly deeded their possession by will or transfer from one to another. In Maryland, it was impossible to do otherwise, for the English government did not recognize the Jesuits as constituting a legal association.

Indeed, Challoner informs Talbot that he considered the promulgation of the Brief as enjoined by the Pope would be fraught with serious danger, and hence he was convinced that the method adopted for the extinction of the Jesuits of England and her colonies was the only one possible and that the Pope would be so advised.

A lament from one of the Maryland missionaries may be of interest. Father Mosley is the writer. " I cannot think of it," he says, "without tears in my eyes. Yes, dear Sister, our Body or Factory is dissolved of which your two brothers are members; and for myself, I know I am an unworthy one when I see so many worthy, saintly, pious, learned, laborious missionaries dead and alive who were or who have been members of the same, for the last two ages. I know no fault that we are guilty of. I am convinced that our labors are pure, upright and sincere for God's honor and our neighbor's good. What our Supreme Judge on earth may think of our labors is a mystery to me. It is true he has stigmatized us through the world with infamy, and declared us unfit for our business or his service. Our dissolution is known through the whole world; it is in every newspaper, and I am ashamed to show my face. As we are judged unserviceable, we labor with little heart, and what is worse, by no Rule.

" To my great sorrow, the Society is abolished, and with it must die all the zeal that was founded and

raised on it. Labor for our neighbor is a Jesuit's
pleasure; destroy the Jesuit and labor is painful and
disagreeable. I must allow that what was my pleasure
is now irksome. Every fatigue I underwent caused a
secret and inward satisfaction; it is now unpleasant
and disagreeable. I disregarded this unhealthy climate,
and all its agues and fevers which have really paid me
to my heart's content, for the sake of my rule. The
night was as agreeable as the day; frost and cold as
a warm fire and a soft bed; the excessive heats as
welcome as a cool shade or pleasant breezes,
but now the scene is changed. The Jesuit is
metamorphosed into I know not what. He is a
monster; a scarecrow in my idea. With joy I impaired
my health and broke my constitution in the care of
my flock. It was the Jesuit's call; it was his whole
aim and business. The Jesuit is no more. He now
endeavors to repair his little remains of health and his
shattered constitution, as he has no rule calling him
to expose it.

"Joseph Mosley, S. J. forever, as I think and hope."

It must have been a very hard trial for the Jesuit
vicars Apostolic in the various foreign missions to be
the executioners of their own brethren in carrying out
this decree. One of these sad scenes occurred in
Nankin, where Mgr. Laimbeckhoven, S. J., was
vicar. He did not live to see the Restoration, for he
died in 1787.

CHAPTER XX

THE SEQUEL TO THE SUPPRESSION

Failure of the Papal Brief to give peace to the Church — Liguori and Tanucci — Joseph II destroying the Church in Austria — Voltaireanism in Portugal — Illness of Clement XIV — Death — Accusations of poisoning — Election of Pius VI — The Synod of Pistoia — Febronianism in Austria — Visit of Pius VI to Joseph II — The Punctation of Ems — Spain, Sardinia, Venice, Sicily in opposition to the Pope — Political collapse in Spain — Fall of Pombal — Liberation of his Victims — Protest of de Guzman — Death of Joseph II — Occupations of the dispersed Jesuits — The *Theologia Wiceburgensis* — Feller — Béauregard's Prophecy — Zaccaria — Tiraboschi — Boscovich — Missionaries — Denunciation of the Suppression in the French Assembly — Slain in the French Revolution — Destitute Jesuits in Poland — Shelter in Russia.

CLEMENT XIV did not give peace to the Church as he had hoped. On the contrary, distressing scandals were continually occurring in the Holy City itself under his very eyes. Infamous books and pamphlets directed against the Church were hawked about the streets, and actors and buffoons parodied the most sacred ceremonies in the public squares. Elsewhere the same conditions obtained. Tanucci who had governed Naples for over forty years was continuing his ruthless persecution of every thing holy, and enriching himself by the spoliation of ecclesiastical property. Even St. Alphonsus Liguori could not obtain from the Pope the recognition of the Redemptorists as a congregation because Tanucci opposed it. Doctrinal views leading to schism in the Church were openly advocated in the schools and universities of Austria, in spite of the entreaties and threats of the Sovereign Pontiff. Maria Theresa had proved feeble or false, and her son Joseph II was in league with the Bourbon princes in their work of destruction. In Portugal, Pombal was still raging like a wild beast; filling the schools with the disciples of Voltaire, flouting the papal nuncio, and keeping in dark and filthy dungeons the members of the detested Order which he had exterminated. The Philosophers and Jansenists were rejoicing in their triumph, and were suppressing all religious communities and seizing their property; the morality and orthodoxy of Poland were being rapidly corrupted; Catherine of Russia was creating bishops and establishing sees as the fancy prompted her, and Freemason lodges were multiplying all over Europe. Worst of all, the Pope's own household with but few exceptions kept aloof from him and were silent about what he had done, while many bishops of various countries of Europe and the entire episcopacy of France endorsed the sentiments expressed in the terrible letter of the Archbishop of Paris, denouncing the Suppression.

Ineffably shocked by all this, the Pope began to show signs of depression, and everyone was in consternation. St. Alphonsus Liguori, especially, was anxious about him and kept continually repeating: " Pray for the Pope; he is distressed; for there is nowhere the slightest glimmer of peace for the Church. He is praying for death, so crushed is he by the sorrows that are overwhelming the Church; he remains continually in seclusion; gives audience to no one; and attends to no business. I have heard things about him from those who are at Rome that would bring tears to your eyes." His mind was unbalanced, and one of his successors, Pius VII, related later what he had been told by a prelate who was present at the signing of the fatal Brief: " As soon as he had affixed his signature to the paper he threw the pen to one side and the paper to the other. He had lost his mind."

Before that, Pius had said the same thing to Cardinal
Pacca at Fontainebleau, when in an agony of remorse
for having signed the Concordat with Napoleon:
" I cannot get the cruel thought out of my mind.
I cannot sleep at night and I am haunted by the
fear of going mad and ending like Clement XIV."
Another writer who received his information from
Gregory XVI tells the same sad story (de Ravignan,
Clément XIII et Clément XIV, I, 452).　St. Alphonsus
Liguori was with the Pope when he died, but according
to a Redemptorist writer, it was " in spirit," and not
by bodily bilocation.　The end came in September
22, 1774, thirteen months after the unfortunate Brief
was issued.

Of course, when he died, the report went abroad
that the Jesuits had poisoned him, by administering
a dose of *aqua toffana*, but although no one has ever
found out what *aqua toffana* is or was, and as there
were no Jesuits in Rome at the time, the story was
nevertheless believed by many and was adduced as
a proof of the wisdom of the Pope in suppressing the
iniquitous organization.　The Jansenists even made a
saint of the dead Pontiff and circulated marvellous
romances about the incorruption of his body and the
miracles that were wrought at his tomb.

Cantù in his " Storia dei cent' anni " says that " the
Pope whose health and mind were grievously affected,
died in delirium, haunted by phantoms, and begging
for pardon.　It was claimed that he had been poisoned
by the Jesuits, but the truth is that the physicians
found no trace of poison in the body.　Had the Jesuits
possessed the power or the will to do so, one might
ask why they did not do it before and not after Clement
had struck them.　But passion often makes light of
common sense."　The post-mortem which was made
in the presence of a great many people showed that

the sickness to which he had succumbed arose from scorbutic and hemorrhoidal conditions from which he had been suffering for many years, and which were aggravated by excessive work and the system he had followed of producing artificial perspiration even in the heats of summer."

The poor Pope had exclaimed before he signed the Brief: " Questa soppressione mi darà la morte " (this suppression will kill me.) " After it," says Saint-Priest in his ' Chute des Jésuites,' " he would pace his apartments in agony, crying: ' Mercy! Mercy! They forced me to do it. *Compulsus feci.*' However, at the last moment his reason returned. He showed his indignation at a proposal made to him even then, to raise some of the enemies of the Society to the cardinalate and drove them from his bedside with loathing.

Bernis, the French ambassador at Rome, wrote to Louis XV that " the Vicar of Christ prayed like the Redeemer for his implacable enemies," and insinuated that he was poisoned. Knowing this d'Alembert warned Frederick II to be on his guard against a similar fate, but the king replied: " There is nothing more false than the story of the poisoning; the truth is that he was profoundly hurt by the coldness manifested by the cardinals and he often reproached himself, for having sacrificed an Order like that of the Jesuits, to satisfy the whim of his rebellious children." Becantini (Storia di Pio VI, i, 31) says: " Nowadays no one believes the story of the poisoning of Clement XIV. Even Bernis who first stood for it, afterwards disavowed it." Cancelleri one of the most distinguished savants of Italy denies the fact; so does Gavani, a bitter enemy of the Church and the Society. Finally, Salcetto the physician of the Apostolic palace, and Adinolfi the Pope's own doctor, in their official

report to the majordomo, Archinto, declare it to
have been an absolutely natural death and they
explain that the corruption which set in was due to
the excessive heat that prevailed at the time.

It was even said that the Pope had expressed to
the General of the Conventuals, Marzoni, a fear that
he had been poisoned. Whereupon Marzoni caused
the following statement to be published:

"I, the undersigned Minister General of the Order
of the Conventuals of St. Francis, fully aware that by
my oath I call the sovereign and true God to witness
what I say; and being certain of what I say, I now
without any constraint and in the presence of God who
knows that I do not lie, do by these words, which are
absolutely true, and which I write and trace with my
own hand, swear and attest to the whole universe,
that never in any circumstance whatever did Clement
XIV ever say to me either that he had been poisoned
or that he felt the slightest symptom of poison. I
swear also that I never said to any one soever that
the same Clement XIV assured me in confidence
that he had been poisoned or had felt the effects of
poison. So help me God.

"Given in the Convent of the Twelve Apostles at
Rome July 27, 1775.
"I, Bro. Louis – Maria Marzoni
"Minister General of the Order."

Thus Clement XIV, far from giving peace to the
Church, left a heritage of woe to his successor, Angelo
Braschi, who was elected Pope on February 15, 1775,
and took the name of Pius VI. The new Pope was
painfully conscious that an error had been committed
by suppressing an Order without trial and without
even condemnation, and that a reflection had been
cast upon a great number of Pontiffs who had been

unstinted in their praise of it, no one more so than
Clement's immediate predecessor. The act had also
given to the Jansenists a terrific instrument in the
implied approval of them by the Sovereign Pontiff.
They became more aggressive than ever and organized
their forces to introduce their doctrines into Italy itself.

By a curious coincidence the leader of the movement was of the same family as the General of the
suppressed Jesuits: Scipio Ricci, the Bishop of Pistoia.
Supporting him in the civic world was the Grand Duke
of Tuscany who was the brother of Joseph II of
Austria. Ricci convened the famous Synod of Pistoia,
on July 31, 1786. No doubt July 31 was chosen purposely; it was the feast of St. Ignatius. There were
247 members in attendance, all exclusively Jansenists
and regalists. The four Gallican Articles were endorsed
and among the measures was that of conferring the
right on the civil authority to create matrimonial
impediments. It advocated the reduction of all
religious orders to one; the abolition of perpetual
vows; a vernacular liturgy; the removal of all altars
but one from the church; etc. The Acts of the synod
were promulgated with the royal imprimatur. Indeed
Pius VI found himself compelled to condemn eighty-
five of the synod's propositions.

Worse than this was the Febronianism of Austria,
which went far beyond the Gallicanism of France or
Italy in its rebellious aggressiveness. It maintained
that the primacy of Rome had no basis in the authority
of Christ; that the papacy was not restricted to Rome,
but could be placed anywhere; that Rome was merely
a centre with which the individual churches could
be united; that the papal power was simply administrative and unifying and not jurisdictional; that the
papal power of condemning heresies, confirming episcopal elections, naming coadjutors, transferring and

39

removing bishops, erecting primatial sees, etc., all rested on the False Decretals. It was maintained that the Pope could issue no decrees for the Universal Church, and that even the decrees of general councils were not binding until approved of by the individual churches.

In vain Clement XIV had begged Maria Theresa to check the movement. She was absolutely in the power of her son Joseph II, whose very first ordinances forbade the reception of papal decrees without the government's sanction. The bishops, he ruled, were not to apply to the Pope for faculties; they could not even issue instructions to their own flocks without permission of the civil authority. He established parishes, assigned fast days, determined the number of Masses to be said, and sermons to be preached. He even decided how many candles were to be lighted on the altar; he made marriage a civil contract and abolished ecclesiastical ceremonies.

In the hope that a personal appeal might avail, the Pope determined to make a journey to Vienna to entreat the emperor to desist. He arrived there on March 22, 1782, and was courteously received by Joseph himself, but brutally by his minister, Kaunitz, who forbade any ecclesiastic to present himself in the city while the Pope was there. Pius remained a month in the capital and succeeded only in extracting a promise that nothing would be done against the Faith or the respect due the Holy See. How far the royal word was kept may be inferred from the fact that after accompanying the Pope as far as the Monastery of Marianbrunn Joseph suppressed that establishment an hour after the Pope had resumed his journey to Rome.

In Germany the three ecclesiastical Electors of Mayence, Treves and Cologne with the Archbishop of

Salzburg met in a convention at Ems in 1786, and attempted to curtail the powers of the Pope in dealing with bishops. That assembly was also strongly Jansenistic. Thirty-one of its articles were directed against the Pope. Pacca, the papal nuncio, was not even received by the Archbishop of Cologne, and three of the Elector bishops refused to honor his credentials. The famous " Punctation of Ems," which consisted of twenty-three articles, declared that German archbishops were independent of Rome, because of the " False Decretals." They pronounced for an abolition of all direct communication with Rome; all monasteries were to be subject to the bishops; religious orders were to have no superior generals residing outside of Germany; Rome's exclusive power of granting faculties was denied; Papal Bulls were binding only after the bishop of the diocese had given his *placet*; all Apostolic nunciatures were to be abolished, etc. In brief, the synod, or " Congress " as it was called, aimed at establishing a schismatical church. But the Pope's remarkable letter to the dissidents and the progress of the French Revolution, which was then raging furiously, prevented the application anywhere of the doctrines put forth at the meeting.

Spain, Sardinia, Venice and Sicily were all in this movement against the Church, and Ferdinand IV of Sicily claimed the right of appointment to all ecclesiastical benefices, as well as the power to nullify all Papal Briefs which had not received his approval.

Nor did the Brief of Suppression contribute to the political stability of the nations. In Naples, for example, Tanucci was flung from power when the young king married an archduchess of Austria; so that he disappeared from the scene three years after the suppression of the Society. In 1798 the Bourbons fled from Naples; the city was given over to a mob directed by an innkeeper called Michael the Madman; the Duke della Torre and his brother were burned alive in the public square; the Senate was dissolved; the palaces were pillaged; a republic was proclaimed and the whole Peninsula of Italy fell into the hands of the French.

Charles III of Spain died in 1788, and was succeeded by Charles IV, whom Arnado describes as more deficient in character and ability than his father. The rude Florida Blanca, who was so conspicuous for his brutality in terrorizing Clement XIV, was thrown out of office by the inept Godoy, who allied Spain with France against England, and brought on the disaster of Trafalgar. The king was driven from his throne and country by his rebellious son, Ferdinand, and then laid his royal crown at the feet of Napoleon Bonaparte. Since that time, the country has been in a ferment because its politics are filled with the ideas of the French Revolution and of English Liberalism.

In Portugal, retribution came at a rapid pace. Pombal fell from power in 1777 on the death of the king. He had been detected in a plot to have the young Prince of Beira succeed to the throne to the exclusion of Queen Maria. It was possibly with the same end in view that he had endeavored to start a war with Spain. He had seized Spanish posts in America, mobilized troops and fortified Lisbon, but hostilities were never declared. Queen Maria's first act at her accession was to open Pombal's dungeons. Eight hundred men of all classes issued from these sepulchres in which some of them had been for eighteen years without a trial. They were like ghosts; emaciated; hollow-eyed and ghastly; some were sightless, many were half-naked. Among them were sixty Jesuits. The populace were so infuriated at the horrible spectacle that Pombal feared to venture into the street. He might have been torn to pieces, and he was conducted under guard to his country estates. Father Oliviera, the confessor of the queen, was installed in court, and the venerable Father de Guzman issued the following statement to the public:

" At the age of eighty-one and at the point of appearing before the tribunal of Divine Justice, John de Guzman, the last assistant of the Society of Jesus, for the provinces and dominions of Portugal, would believe himself guilty of an unpardonable sin of omission, if, in neglecting to have recourse to the throne of Your Majesty where clemency and justice reign, he did not place at your feet, this humble petition in the name of six hundred subjects of Your Majesty, the unfortunate remnants of a wrong inflicted on them.

" He entreats Your Majesty by the Sacred Heart of Jesus Christ, by that tender love which Your Majesty bears to the August Queen, His mother, and to the illustrious King Don Pedro, to the princes and princesses of the royal family, that you would deign and even command that the trial of so many of the faithful subjects of Your Majesty, who have been branded with infamy in the eyes of the world, be now reviewed. They are groaning under the accusation of having committed outrages and crimes which the very savages would shrink from even imagining, and which no human heart could ever conceive. They lament and moan that they were condemned without even having been brought to trial, without being heard and without being allowed to make any defense. Those who have now issued from prison are all in accord in this matter, and unanimously attest, that during all the time of their imprisonment, they have not even seen the face of any judge.

" On his part, your suppliant, who is now making this appeal, and who for many years occupied a position where he could acquire an intimate knowledge of what was going on, is ready to swear in the most solemn manner, that the superiors and members of the Spanish assistancy of the Society of Jesus were without reproach. He and all the other exiles are ready to undergo sufferings more rigorous than any to which they have hitherto been subjected, if a single individual has ever been guilty of the least crime against the State.

" Moreover, your suppliant and his brethren, the chief superiors of the Society, have been examined in Rome, again and again, in the most searching manner, and have been declared innocent. Pope Pius VI, now gloriously reigning, has seen the minutes of those investigations, and Your Majesty will find in that great Pontiff an enlightened witness whose integrity nothing on earth can equal; and at the same time you will find a judge who could not commit a wrong without rendering himself guilty of an unparalleled iniquity.

" Deign, then, Your Majesty, to extend to us that clemency which belongs to you as does your throne; deign to hearken to the prayers of so many unfortunates, whose innocence has been proven, and who have never ceased in the midst of their sufferings to be the faithful subjects of Your Majesty; and who could never falter or fail an instant, in the love that they have from childhood entertained for the royal family."

This appeal had its effect. An enquiry was ordered, and in October 1780 a revision of the trial of the alleged conspirators of 1758 was begun. On April 3, 1781, the court announced that " all those, either living or dead, who had been imprisoned or executed in virtue of the sentence of January 12, 1759, were absolutely innocent." Pombal himself was put on trial, found guilty, and condemned to receive " an exemplary punishment." He escaped imprisonment on account of his age, but he died of leprosy on May 8, 1782. His corpse lay unburied until the Society which he had crushed was restored thirty-one years later to its former place in Portugal. One of its first duties was to sing a Requiem Mass over his remains. The details of the trial were suppressed at the request of the Pope, for the reason that too many prominent personages in the Church were implicated. There was another reason. The spirit of Pombal had so thoroughly impregnated the ruling classes that the report was withheld out of fear of a revolution. Indeed, the queen was so terrified by the danger that she lost her mind. Finally, in 1807 a French army occupied Lisbon and the royal family fled to Brazil. Since then Portugal which was once so great counts for very little in the political world.

It is unnecessary to refer to France, except to note that it was Choiseul who purchased Corsica and thus gave his country which he had helped to ruin an alien ruler: Napoleon Bonaparte, who put an end to the orgies of the Revolution by deluging Europe with French blood; who imprisoned the Pope; demolished the Bourbon dynasties wherever he could find them, and bound France in fetters which, in spite of its multiplied changes of government, it has never shaken off.

When Joseph II of Austria ended his lonely and unhappy existence in 1790, he saw in France the beginning of the wreck which his friend Voltaire had helped to effect; he did not live to see the execution of his own sister, Marie Antoinette, but enough had occurred to fill him with terror especially as the existence of his own monarchy was threatened; Belgium was lost; Hungary was in wild disorder, and other parts of the empire were about to rebel. Before he died he wrote his own epitaph. It was: " Here lies

Joseph II, who never succeeded in any of his under-
takings."

What became of the scattered Jesuits? The
scholastics and lay-brothers, of course, went back to
the world, but, in France, by a refinement of cruelty
they were declared by the courts to be incapable of
inheriting even from their own parents, because of
the vows they had pronounced on entering the Society.
That the vows no longer existed made no difference to
the lawmakers. As for the priests they were
secularized, and in many places were welcomed by
the bishops as rectors or professors in colleges and
seminaries. They were in demand, also, as directors
of religious communities and not a few became bishops.
Thus, in America, the first two members of the
hierarchy, Carroll and Neale, were old Jesuits, as was
Lawrence Graessel who had been named as Carroll's
successor but who died before the Bulls arrived.
Crétineau-Joly has a list of twenty-one bishops in
Europe alone. Others were called to episcopal sees,
but in hopes of the restoration of the Society they had
declined the honor.

Father Walcher was appointed imperial director of
navigation and mathematics by Maria Theresa; Cabral,
Lecci, and Riccati, were engaged by various governments in engineering works; Zeplichal was employed
by Frederick II in exploiting mines. The Theresian
College of Vienna became one of the best schools in
the world under their direction; and Breslau felt the
effects of their assistance, as did other colleges such
as the Oriental in Vienna, the University of Buda,
and the schools of Mayence, and of various cities in
Italy.

They must have been often amused at some of the
situations in which they found themselves. Thus,
for instance in 1784 the Parliament of Languedoc,

which had been one of the bitterest enemies of the
Society, met to arrange for the solemn obsequies of
the Jesuit Father Sesane "the friend of the poor,"
and the ecclesiastical authorities were busy taking
juridical information for his canonization. Again,
although not permitted to exist in Switzerland the
Council of Soleuse erected a statue in honor of the
Jesuit Father Crollanza, who all his life had shunned
honor and was conspicuous for his humility. On the
pedestal was the very delightful inscription:
" Pauperum patrem, ægrorum matrem, omnium
fratrem, virum doctum et humilimum, in vita, in morte,
in feretro suavitate sibi similem amabat, admirabatur,
lugebat Solodurum." In the same way, Maria Theresa
in an official document dated 1776 declared that
" moved by the consideration of the brilliant virtues,
the science, the erudition and the regular and exemplary
life of Jean-Theophile Delpini; and reflecting moreover on his apostolic labors in Hungary and the
Principality of Transylvania where to our great
consolation, he led a vast throng of Anabaptists back
to the true Faith, we have chosen and we hereby
appoint the said Theophile Delpini who has merited
much from the Church and the State, and who is
therefore very acceptable to us personally, to the
post of Abbot of Our Lady of Kolos-Monostros."

Parhamer obtained a similar distinction in Austria
and Carinthia. He was an advanced advocate of what
is now called social service, and he made use of his
position as confessor and friend of the Emperor Francis
I to establish useful popular institutions; among which
was an orphanage for the children of soldiers who had
died for their country. It was a sort of child's
Hôtel des Invalides. The discipline was exclusively
military, with drills, camp life, etc. Joseph II
wanted to make him a bishop but Parhamer asked

for two months to think it over and before the two
months had expired he was dead. That was as late
as 1786. Meantime, Marie Leczinska, the Queen of
France, would only have these prescribed Jesuits hear
her confession, and two Poles, Radomiviski and Buganski
were chosen for that office. On account of their nationality they could not be exiled from France. In Austria,
Father Walcher was kept busy building dykes to prevent
inundations. Father Cabral, a Portuguese, had to
harness the cataract of Velino, which had so long
wrought havoc in the city of Terni, and then he did the
same thing for his own country by confining the
Tagus to its bed. In doing so he did not remember
that his country had kept him in exile for eighteen
years. Ximenes made roads and bridges in Tuscany
and Rome. Riccati saved Venice from inundations by
controlling the Po, the Adige and Brenta, and by
order of Frederick II of Prussia Father Zeplichal
had to locate the metal mines of Glatz, and so on.
All this was over and above their ecclesiastical work
for which they were called on by every one, even by
the Pope who had suppressed them.

The famous astronomer, Maximilian Hell, was
another of the homeless Jesuits of that period; and as
it happened that from the beginning, astronomy had
always been in honor in the Society, there was a great
number of such men adrift in the world when their
own observatories were taken away from them. The
enthusiastic historian of the Society, Crétineau-Joly
has an extended list of their names as well as those
who were remarkable in other branches of science.

The "Theologia Wiceburgensis," which is so popular
in the modern Society, was composed by dispersed
Jesuits, and, according to Cardinal Pacca, "in the
difficulties that arose between the Papal nuncios and
the ecclesiastical Electors of Germany it was the

former Jesuits who appeared in the lists as the champions of the Holy See, to illumine and strengthen the minds of the faithful by their solid and victorious writings." François Xavier de Feller belonged to this period, and in the opinion of Gerlache, the historian of the Netherlands, " he exerted a great influence on the Belgian Congress of 1790." It was he who led the assault on Josephinism and Febronianism. With him in this fight was Francesco Antonio Zaccaria who compelled the author of the "Febronius" to acknowledge his errors. Guillaume Bertier revived the famous " Journal de Trévoux, " and Fréron made a reputation for the "Journal des Débats." Girolamo Tiraboschi wrote his "History of Italian Literature," Juan Andrés, his "Origin of All Literature," Francisco Clavigero continued his "History of Mexico" and Antoine de Berault-Bercastel, François De Ligny, Jean Grou, Giulio Cordara, wrote their various well-known works. Besides writing his still popular "Bible History" Reeve translated into Latin verses much of the poetry of Pope, Dryden and Young. The list is endless. A French-Canadian, Xavier du Plessis, was famous in the pulpits of France in those days, as was Nicholas de Beauregard, who in 1775 startled all France by an utterance he made when preaching at Notre-Dame.

" These philosophers," he exclaimed, " are striking at the king and at religion. The axe and the hammer are in their hands. They are only waiting for the moment to overturn the altar and the throne. Yes Lord, Thy temples will be plundered and destroyed, Thy feasts abolished, Thy name proscribed. But what do I hear? Great God! what do I see. Instead of the holy canticles which resounded beneath these consecrated vaults till now, I hear lascivious and blasphemous songs. And thou, the infamous divinity

of paganism, lascivious Venus, thou darest to come
to take the place of the living God, to sit upon the
throne of the Holy of Holies and receive the guilty
incense of thy worshippers." The vision was realized
eighteen years later.

The sermon caused a tumult in the church. The
preacher was denounced as seditious, and as a calumniator of light and reason. Even Condorcet wrote him
down as a *ligueur* and a fanatic. He continued preaching, nevertheless, and his old associates followed his
example. During one Lent, out of twenty of the great
preachers, sixteen were Jesuits.

Three of these former Jesuits especially attracted
attention at this time in the domain of letters and
science: Zaccaria, Tiraboschi, and Boscovich.

Francesco Antonio Zaccaria, whose name is sometimes written Zaccheria, was a Venetian who had
entered the Austrian novitiate in 1731, when he was
a boy of seventeen. He taught literature at Goritz,
but was subsequently sent to Rome where he became
very distinguished both for his eloquence and his
marvellous encyclopedic knowledge. In 1751 he was
appointed to succeed Muratori as the ducal librarian
at Modena, though Cardinal Quirini had asked for
him and the celebrated Count Crustiani subsequently
tried to bring him to Mantua. His fame was so great
that the most illustrious academies of Italy claimed his
name for their registers. In Rome he became the
literary historiographer of the Society, and had been
so excellent an aid for Clement XIII in the fight
against Gallicanism that the Pope assigned him a
pension. That was just before the Suppression of
the Society; when that event occurred he was deprived
of his pension, and after frequently running the risk
of being imprisoned in the Castle Sant' Angelo, he was
ordered not to attempt to leave Rome. When Pius VI

became Pope, Zaccaria's life became a little happier. His pension was restored and even increased; he was made Rector of the College of Clerical Nobles, and regained his old chair of ecclesiastical history in the Sapienza. He died in 1795 at the age of eighty-two. The " Biographie Universelle " says that, besides innumerable manuscripts, Zaccaria left one hundred and six printed books, the most important of which is the " Literary History of Italy " in 14 octavo volumes with supplements to volumes IV and V. His method of leading his readers through the literary labyrinth deserves no less praise than the penetration of his views, and the good taste of his criticism. Besides this literary work, he wrote on moral theology, scripture, canon law, history, numismatics, etc.

Girolamo Tiraboschi, who was born in Bergamo on December 28, 1731, went to the Jesuit school at Monza, and from there entered the Society. His first characteristic work, while teaching literature in Bergamo, was to re-edit the Latin-Italian dictionary of Mandosio. He made so many corrections that it was substantially a new work. When occupied as librarian in Milan, he discovered a set of valuable manuscripts about the suppressed Order of Humiliati. The publication of these MSS. filled up a gap in the annals of the Church, and made Tiraboschi's reputation in the world of letters. The Duke of Modena made him his librarian, the post formerly held by Zaccaria. Thanks to the munificence of the princes of Este, the library was a literary treasure house, and Tiraboschi conceived the idea of gathering up the riches around him and writing a good history of Italian literature; a task that seemed to be too much for one mind. The difficulty was increased by the jealousy of the various Italian states, so that an unbiased judgment about the merits of this army of writers called for a man with courage

enough to shut his ears to the clamors of local prejudice.
It supposed also a profound knowledge of ancient and
modern literature, a sufficient acquaintance with the
arts and sciences, and skill enough not to be overwhelmed by the mass of material he had to handle.
It took him eleven years to complete the work.

The Spaniards were irritated by the "History"
for they were blamed for having corrupted the literary
taste of Italy, and three Spanish Jesuits attacked
him fiercely on that score.   Nevertheless, the Academy
accepted a copy of the work in the most flattering
terms.   The Italians regarded it as a most complete
history of their literature and a monument erected to
the glory of their country.   He was made a knight
by the Duke and appointed counsellor of the principality.   While he was engaged in this work, the Society
was suppressed, and like Boscovich and Zaccaria,
he did not live to see its resurrection.   He died in
Modena on June 3, 1794.

Ruggiero Giuseppe Boscovich was a Dalmatian
from Ragusa, where he was born on May 18, 1711.
He was a boy at the Jesuit college of that town and
entered the Society at the early age of fourteen.
He was sent to the Roman College, where his unusual
literary and philosophical as well as mathematical
abilities immediately attracted attention.   He was
able to take the place of his professor in mathematics
while he was yet in his theological studies, and subsequently occupied the chair of mathematics with great
distinction for a generation.   His bent, however, was
chiefly for astronomy, and every year he issued a
treatise on one or another subject of that science.
Among them may be mentioned: the "Sun spots"
(1736); "The Transit of Mercury" (1737); "The
Aurora Borealis" (1738); "Application of the Tele-
scope in Astronomical Studies" (1739); "The Figure

of the Earth " (1739); " The Motion of the Heavenly Bodies in an unresisting Medium " (1740); " Various effects of Gravity " (1741); " The Aberration of the Fixed Stars " (1742); and numberless others. Foreign and Italian academies, among them Bologna, Paris and London admitted him to membership. It was he who first suggested the massive pillars of the college church of St. Ignatius as the foundation of the Observatory in Rome; but the Suppression of the Society prevented him from carrying out the plan. When the great dome of St. Peter's began to crack, he allayed the general alarm by placing iron bands around it. His advice was sought for the draining of the Pontine Marshes; he surveyed the Papal States by order of Benedict XIV and induced the Pope to withdraw the obsolete decree in the Index against the Copernican system.

When King John V of Portugal asked for ten Jesuit Fathers to make an elaborate survey of Brazil, Boscovich offered himself for the arduous task, hoping thus to make a survey in Ecuador, so as to obtain data for the final solution of the problem of the figure of the earth which was then exciting much attention in England and France, but the Pope kept him for the survey of Italy, which Boscovich did, and in 1755 he published a large quarto volume describing the work. In 1748, he had already revived Leibnitz's system of dynamism in the composition of bodies, a view which his fellow-Jesuits generally rejected. When this volume was issued, the publisher added a list of Boscovich's previous works. They amounted to sixty-six and he soon added three more quartos on " The Elements of Mathematics." He even wrote Latin poetry, mostly eulogies of the Pope and distinguished men, and published five volumes of verse on " The Defects of the Sun and the Moon."

Boscovich's advice was sought as an engineer for damming the Lakes which were threatening the city of Lucca; and he acquitted himself so well, that he was made an honorary citizen and his expenses were subsequently paid for his scientific exploration in Italy, France and England. He settled a dispute between his native town and the King of France. He journeyed with the Venetian ambassador to Constantinople to complete his archæological studies, but that journey seriously injured his health. He then accepted the appointment of professor of mathematics at the University of Pavia and helped to found the Observatory of Brera in Milan which with that of the Collegio Romano is among the most prominent in Italy. The London Academy wanted to send him to California in 1769 to observe the transit of Venus, but the opposition to the Jesuits, which was four years later to lead to their suppression, caused the invitation to be withdrawn. Louis XV then called him to France where he was made director of optics for the Navy with a salary of 8,000 francs. He retained this position until 1783, that is ten years after the Society of Jesus had gone out of existence. He then went to Italy to publish five more books, and at the age of eighty-six retired to the monastery of the monks of Vallombroso. On account of his great ability, or rather on account of his being a Jesuit, he was bitterly assailed by Condorcet and d'Alembert and other infidels of France.

Bolgeni, who died in 1811, was made penitentiary by Pius VI in recognition of his services against Jansenism and Josephinism. Unfortunately, however, he advocated the acceptance of some scheme of Napoleon, for which Pope Pius VII deposed him from his office and called Father Muzzarelli from Parma to take his place. In 1809 when Pius VII was exiled, Muzzarelli went with him to Paris or at least followed soon after. His work on the " Right Use of Reason in Religion " ran up to eleven volumes, besides which he produced other books against Rousseau, and several pious treatises, like the " Month of May," which has been translated into many languages.

Possibly a certain number of missionaries remained with their neophytes because they were too remote to be reached. Others, who owed no allegiance to the king who ordered the expulsion, paid no attention to it, as the Englishman King, for instance, who was martyred in Siam after the Suppression; or the Irishman O'Reilly, who buried himself, in the forests of Guiana with his savages; Poirot was kept at the court of Pekin as the emperor's musician; and Benoit constructed fountains for the imperial gardens, invented a famous waterclock, which spouted water from the mouths of animals, two hours for each beast, thus running through the twenty-four hours of the day; he made astronomical observations, brought out copper-plate engravings of maps and so on, and finally died of apoplexy in 1774, one year after Clement XIV had suppressed the Society. Hallerstein, the imperial astronomer, was also there waiting for news of the coming disaster.

B. N. in " The Jesuits; their history and foundation " (II, 274) and Crétineau-Joly both declare that there were four of the proscribed Jesuits in the Etats généraux which was convened in Paris at the opening of the Revolution: Delfau, de Rozaven, San-Estavan and Allain. Of course, the Rozaven in this instance was not the John Rozaven so famous later on. In 1789 John was only eighteen years of age. In the session of February 19, 1790, the famous Abbé Grégoire, who afterwards became the Constitutional Bishop of Loir-et-Cher, startled the assembly by crying out,

40

" Among the hundred thousand vexations of the old government, whose hand was so heavy on France, we must place the suppression of the celebrated Order of the Jesuits." The Deputy Lavie had also asked for justice in their behalf. The Protestant Barnave declared that " the first act of our new liberty should be to repair the injustices of despotism; and I, therefore, propose an amendment in favor of the Jesuits." "They have," said the next speaker, the Abbé de Montesquiou, " a right to your generosity. You will not refuse justice to that celebrated Society in whose colleges some of you have studied; whose wrongs we cannot understand, but whose sufferings were to be expected."

The sentiments of the speakers were enthusiastically applauded, but it was all forgotten as the terrible Revolution proceeded on its course. Jesuits like other priests were carried to the guillotine; but, as no records could now be kept, it is impossible to find out how many were put to death. We find out, however, from " Les martyrs " of Leclercq that in Paris alone there were eleven: DuPerron, Benoit, Bonnand, Cayx, Friteyre, du Rocher, Lanfant, Villecrohain, Le Gue, Rousseau, and Seconds. Crétineau-Joly adds to this list the two Rochefoucaulds; Dulau, who was Archbishop of Arles; Delfaux; Millou; Gagnière; Le Livec; another Du Rocher; Vourlat; Du Roure; Rouchon; Thomas; Andrieux and Verron; making in all twenty-five. In " Les crimes de la Révolution " there are two volumes of the names of the condemned in all parts of France, but as the ecclesiastical victims are merely described as " priests " it is impossible to find out how many Jesuits there were among them. The twenty-five, however, make a good showing for a single city. Probably the proportion was the same elsewhere.

The old Jesuits appear again for a moment in Spain, when in 1800 Charles IV recalled them. A pestilence was raging in Andalusia when they arrived, and they immediately plunged into the work of caring for the sick.   Twenty-seven Jesuits died in the performance of this act of charity; but the government soon forgot it and again drove into exile the men whom they had appealed to for help.   In Austria they remained in the colleges as secular priests.   At Fribourg, Lucerne and Soleure, the people insisted on their retaining the colleges.   In China, they clung to their missions until the arrival of the Lazarists in 1783.   In Portuguese India, even before the Suppression, they had been forcibly expelled, and the same thing occurred in South America wherever Portugal ruled.   The Spanish missions of both South and North America had likewise been wrested from them.   In Turkey the French ambassador, Saint-Priest, insisted on their staying at their posts in Constantinople, because of their success in dealing with the Moslems and schismatics.   As we have seen when missionaries were needed in the deadly forests of French Guiana, the government was shameless enough to ask the Portuguese Jesuits to devote themselves to the work; and the request was acceded to.   They were also entreated to remain in French India.

Speaking of Brazil, Southey says (III): " Centuries will not repair the evil done by their sudden expulsion. They had been the protectors of a persecuted race; the advocates of mercy, the founders of civilization; and their patience under their unmerited sufferings forms not the least honorable part of their character." What Southey says of Brazil applies to Paraguay, Chile and other missions.

Montucla in his " Histoire des mathématiques " tells us that Father Hallerstein, the president of the tribunal of astronomy in China hearing of the Suppression, died of the shock, as did his two dis-

tinguished companions. The story related by the
Protestant historian Christopher de Mürr in his
" Journal " is also illustrative of the general attitude
of mind in this trying conjuncture. Just before the
Suppression, he informs us, a French Government ship
left Marseilles for Pekin with four Jesuits on board.
One was a painter, another a physician and the two
others were mathematicians. All of them were to be
in the personal entourage of the Emperor of China.
They were Austrians from the Tyrol, but France,
which had expelled the French Jesuits a few years
before, was sending these foreign Jesuits to represent
her, and to promote the interests of science in the
Chinese court. They set sail in the month of July,
1773, and not a word was said to them about the general
Suppression, which Choiseul knew perfectly well would
soon take place. The Archbishop of Paris, de Beaumont, had warned them of what was in the air, but they
could not believe it possible and so they departed for
the Far East.

After a weary journey of four months, they arrived
at Macao. Meantime the Brief had been published,
and the Bishop of Macao, a creature of Pombal's made
haste to inform them of the fact. Had he held his
peace there would have been no difficulty about the
continuance of the journey to Pekin, and their subsequent standing at the court, for the Brief was not
effective until it was promulgated. But once they
knew it, the poor men were in a dilemma. Not to
heed the invitation of the Chinese emperor meant
death, if he laid hold of them; but, on the other hand,
to go to China without the power of saying Mass or
preaching, or hearing confessions, namely as suspended
priests, was unthinkable. For three days, the unfortunate wanderers studied the problem with aching
hearts, and finally determined to run the risk of capture

by the Chinese with its subsequent punishment of death. They stowed themselves away on separate ships and thus got back to Europe. Incidentally, it serves as a proof that the Jesuits did not go out to China to be mandarins, as some of their enemies alleged. They accepted what honors came to them, but only to help them in their apostolic work.

It was found out subsequently that these poor men would have had better luck had they continued on their journey to China instead of returning to Europe. The promulgation of the Brief and the observance of all the legal technicalities connected with its enforcement was next to impossible in China, and hence we find a letter of Father Bourgeois from Pekin to his friend Duprez in France, which bears the date May 15, 1775, announcing that " the Brief is on its way." It had been issued two years previously. Of course, Bourgeois is in tears over the prospective calamity, and tells his friend: " I have nothing now but eternity and that is not far off. Happy are those of Ours who are with Ignatius and Xavier and Aloysius Gonzaga and the numberless throng of saints who follow the Lamb under the glorious banner of the Name of Jesus."

Crétineau-Joly discovered another letter from an Italian lay-brother named Panzi, who writes eighteen months later than Bourgeois. It is dated November 11, 1776. In it he says " the missionaries had been notified of the Bull of Suppression (he does not state how), nevertheless they live together in the same house, under the same roof and eat at the same table." Apparently there had been a flaw in the promulgation of the " Bull " or Brief. The brother goes on to say, that " the Fathers preach, confess, baptise, retain possession of their property just as before. No one has been interdicted or suspended for the reason that

in a country like this it would have been impossible
to do otherwise. It is all done with the permission
of the Bishop of Nankin, to whom we are subject.
If the same course had been pursued here as in some
parts of Europe, it would have put an end not only
to the missions but to all religion, besides being a
great scandal to the Chinese Christians who could not
be provided for and who would have abandoned the
Faith.

" Thanks be to God, our holy Mission is going on
well and at present everything is very tranquil. The
number of converts increases daily. Father Dollières
brought over an entire tribe which lives on the
mountains two days' journey from Pekin. The
Emperor, so far, shows no signs of embracing the
Catholic Faith, but he protects it everywhere throughout his vast dominions, and so do the other great
men of the Empire. I am still at my work of painting.
I am glad I am doing it for God; and I am determined
to live in this holy mission until God wishes to take
me to himself."

About this time, the Fathers addressed a joint
letter to Cardinal de Bernis, the French ambassador
at Rome, who had been so conspicuous in wresting the
Brief of Suppression from Clement XIV and had
originated the calumny about the poisoning of the
Pope.

" Would your Eminence," says the document, " cast
a glance at the inclosed report on the present condition
of the French missions of China and the Indies which
has been asked for by the Holy Congregation of the
Propagation of the Faith. To these missions as you
know, his majesty has sent great amounts of money
and a large number of his subjects, knowing as he did
that the interests of France are bound up with those
of religion, and the advancement of the latter was

what he had chiefly in view. It will be gratifying to you to learn that the Chinese Emperor takes great pleasure in having these French missionaries employed in his palace; he frequently takes them with him on his journeys through the empire, and makes use of them to draw up maps of the country, which are of invaluable service to him. On the other hand, the missionaries, on account of the esteem in which they are held, use all their influence to prevent the persecution of Christians and have succeeded in obtaining favors for Europeans and especially for the Frenchmen who arrive at Canton, by protecting them from the annoyances to which they are exposed. Over and above this, several of the Fathers are in correspondence with the Paris Academy of Science, and also with the ministers of State, and are sending them the results of their astronomical observations, and of their discoveries in botany, natural history, in brief, whatever can contribute to the advancement of science and art.

" The king and his ministers, have in the past few years, accorded free transportation to the Fathers who are sent out here to the French missions of India, and deservedly so, for these missionaries have frequently rendered important service to France, and for that reason, the Supreme Council of Pondicherry has taken up their defense against the rulings of the Parliament of Paris, which sent officers out here to seize the little property we possess. The Pondicherry authorities would concede only that the Fathers might make a small change in their soutane and be called the " Messieurs les missionnaires de Malabar." It is in accordance with this arrangement that we continue to exercise our functions under the jurisdiction of the bishop. We are the only ones who understand the very difficult language of the country and there does not seem to be any reason why we should not be left as we are. Besides these two missions, there are two others in the Levant, one in Greece, the other in Syria. They have always been and still are under the protection of France. M. le Chevalier de Saint-Priest, who is ambassador to Turkey, said, on his arrival at Constantinople, that the king had explicitly recommended to him the French missions and ordered him to assure the Fathers of the continuance of his protection."

Of the missions in Hindostan it may be of use to quote here the utterance of M. Perrin of the Missions Etrangères, who went out to India three years after the destruction of the Jesuit Missions in those parts. "I cannot be suspected when I speak in praise of those Fathers. I was never associated with them. Indeed, they were already extinct as a body when Providence placed me in the happy necessity of having had to do with some of the former members. I belonged to an association which had protracted and sometimes very lively debates with the Jesuit Fathers, who might have regarded us as their enemies, if Christians are capable of entertaining that feeling; but I feel bound to say that, notwithstanding these discussions, we always held each other in the highest esteem, and I hereby defy the most audacious calumniator to prove that the Society of Jesus had ever to blush for the conduct of any of its Malabar missionaries either at Pondicherry or in the interior. All were formed and fashioned by virtue's hand and they breathed virtue back in their conduct and their sermons." (Voyage dans l'Indostan, II, 261.)

Among the French Jesuits in China, Father Amiot was conspicuous. Langlès, the French Academian who was ambassador in China, dedicated to him a translation of Holme's "Travels in China," in which the Jesuit is described as "Apostolic Missionary at Pekin,

Correspondent of the Academy of Inscriptions and Belles Lettres; an indefatigable *savant*, profoundly versed in the knowledge of the history of the sciences, the arts and the language of China and an ardent promoter of the Tatar-Manchou language and litterature." With Amiot was Father Joseph d'Espinha, who was president of the imperial tribunal of astronomy, and simultaneously administrator of the Diocese of Pekin. Fathers de Rocha and Rodrigues presided over the tribunal of mathematics, and Father Schelbarth replaced Castiglione as the chief painter of the emperor; there were other Jesuits also who evangelised the various provinces of the country under the direction of the Ordinary.

This condition of things lasted for ten years and it was only then that the question arose of handing over the work to the Lazarists. Thus in a letter of Father Bourgeois, of whom we have already spoken, he says: " they have given our mission to the Lazarist Fathers." The letter is dated November 15, 1783, namely ten years after the suppression of the Society. " They were to have come last year," continues the writer; " Will they come this year? They are fine men and they can feel sure that I shall do all in my power to help them and put them in good shape." It was not until 1785 that a Lazarist, Father Raux, took over the Pekin Mission, and in 1788, three years afterwards, Bourgeois was able to say to Father Beauregard who had contrived to remain in Paris in spite of the Revolution: " Our missionary successors are men of merit, remarkable for virtue, talent and refinement. We live together like brothers, and thus the Lord consoles us for the loss of our good mother, the Society, whom we can never forget. Nothing can tear that love out of our hearts, and hence every moment we have to make acts of resignation in the calamity that has fallen upon us. Meanwhile it is hard to say in our house whether the Lazarists live as Jesuits or the Jesuits like Lazarists."

The old and infirm Jesuits who were homeless and could find no ecclesiastical employment had much to suffer. They became pitiable objects of charity. Zalenski in "Les Jésuites da la Russie Blanche" (I, 77) gives an instance of it, in an appeal made to the King of Poland by one hundred and five of these outcasts, many of whom had been distinguished professors in the splendid colleges of the country. They had been granted a miserable pittance out of their own property in the way of a pension, but even that was often not forthcoming. After reminding His Majesty that this pension had been guaranteed them by the Church, by their country, and by the Sovereign Pontiff, and that the allowance was from their own property; and was due to them from the natural law; and also that the amount needed was every day decreasing, because of the great number among them who were dying, they asked him imploringly: "Will Poland, so long known for its humanity, be cruel only to us; will you permit us the Lord's anointed, the old teachers of the youth of Poland, to go begging our bread on the streets, with our garments in rags, and exposed to insults; will you permit that our tears and our cries which are forced from us by the grief and abandonment to which we are reduced should add to the affliction of our country; will you permit that our country should be accused of inhumanity and insulted because it withholds our pension? It is sad enough for us to have lost the Society, the dearest and nearest thing to our heart in this life, without adding this new suffering. Should you not have pity on our lot and grant us a pension? Do not bring us down to the grave with this new sorrow." Whether their prayers were answered or not we do not know. However, as Cardinal Pallavicini denounces the king as "impious and inert," it is very likely that the poor old men were left to starve.

Quite unexpectedly the Protestant Frederick the Great of Prussia and the schismatical Catherine II of Russia insisted on having what Jesuits they could get for educational work in their respective domains. As neither sovereign would permit the Papal Brief to be read in the countries which they governed, a number of the exiles in various parts of Europe flocked thither. Efforts were made to have the Brief promulgated in both countries, but without success; for Catherine as well as Frederick denied any right of the Pope in their regard; nor would either of them listen to any request of the Jesuits to have it published. They were told to hold their peace. Of course, they were condemned by their enemies for accepting this heterodox protection; but it has been blamed for almost everything, so they went on with their work, thanking God for the unexpected shelter, and knowing perfectly well that Clement XIV was not averse to the preservation of some of the victims.

CHAPTER XXI

THE RUSSIAN CONTINGENT

Frederick the Great and the " Philosophers "— Protection of the
Jesuits — Death of Voltaire — Catherine of Russia — The Four Cól-
leges — The Empress at Polotsk — Joseph II at Mohilew — Archetti
— Baron Grimm — Czerniewicz and the Novitiate — Assent of Pius
VI — Potemkin — Siestrzencewicz — General Congregation — Benislawski — "*Approbo; Approbo* "— Accession of former Jesuits. Gruber
and the Emperor Paul — Alexander I — Missions in Russia.

EVEN before the general suppression of the Society,
Frederick II of Prussia had given a shock to the
politicians of Europe and to his friends the *philosophes*
of France, by welcoming the exiled Jesuits into his
dominions and employing them as teachers. Hence
d'Alembert wrote to remonstrate; though at first
glance he appears to approve of the king's action,
his insulting tone when speaking of the Pope reveals
the animus of this enemy of God. It ran as follows:
" They say that the Cordelier, Ganganelli, does not
promise ripe pears to the Society of Jesus and that
. St. Francis will very likely kill St. Ignatius. It
appears to me that the Holy Father, Cordelier though
he be, would be very foolish to disband his regiment
of guards to please the Catholic princes. Such a
treaty would be very like that of the sheep and
the wolves; the first article of which was that the
sheep should deliver their dogs to the wolves. But in
any case, Sire, it will be a curious condition of affairs,
if while the Most Christian, the Most Catholic, the
Most Apostolic, and the Most Faithful kings are
destroying the grenadiers of the Holy See, your Most
Heretical Majesty should be the only one to protect
them." A little later he writes: " I am assured that

the Cordelier Pope needs a good deal of plucking at his sleeves to get him to abolish the Jesuits. I am not surprised. To propose to the Pope to destroy this brave troop is like asking Your Majesty to disband your body guards."

D'Alembert was playing double. He was as anxious as any one to bring about the Suppression, and on April 3, 1770, Frederick wrote him that, " The Philosophy which has had such vogue in this century is bragged about more brazenly than ever. But what progress has it made? 'It has expelled the Jesuits,' you tell me. Granted, but I will prove, if you want me to do so, that the whole business started in vanity, spite, underhand dealing and selfishness."

On July 7, 1770, Frederick wrote to Voltaire and said: " The good Cordelier of the Vatican lets me keep my dear Jesuits whom they persecute everywhere. I will guard the precious seed so that some day I may supply it to those who may want to cultivate this rare plant in their respective countries." Frederick had annexed Silesia which was entirely Catholic, while the part of Poland which was allotted to him at the time of the division had remained only half faithful. To gratify them and keep them at peace, he thought he could do no better than to ask the Jesuits to take care of the education of the youth of those countries, " let the *philosophes* cry out against it as they may." Hence, on December 4, 1772, he wrote to d'Alembert: " I received an ambassador from the General of the Ignatians, asking me to declare myself openly as the protector of the Order; but I answered that when Louis XV thought proper to suppress the regiment of Fitz-james (the Jansenists), I did not think I could intercede for that corps; and moreover, the Pope is well able to bring about such a reformation without having heretics take a hand in it."

A Jesuit named Pinto had, indeed, presented himself to Frederick to ask for his protection, but he had no warrant to do so. Someone in Rome had suggested it, and he was encouraged in his enterprise by Maria Theresa. When apprised of it, the General sent a very severe reprimand to the volunteer ambassador, and that disposed of Father Pinto. No more was heard of him.

Frederick showed himself a very vigorous protector of the Society. When the Brief was published he issued the following decree: "We, Frederick by the Grace of God, King of Prussia, to all and every of our subjects, greeting:

"As you have already been advised that you are not permitted to circulate any Bulls or Briefs of the Pope, without our approbation of the same, we have no doubt that you will conform to this general order, in case the Brief of the Pope suppressing the Society of Jesus arrives at any department within your jurisdiction. Nevertheless, we have deemed it necessary to recall this to your memory, and as, under the date of Berlin, the sixth of this month, we have resolved, for reasons prompting us thereto, that this annihilation of the Society which has recently taken place shall not be published in our states, we graciously enjoin upon you to take all necessary measures in your district to suppress the aforesaid Bull of the Pope; for which end you will, in our name, as soon as you receive this communication, issue an explicit order, under penalty of rigorous chastisement, to all ecclesiastics of the Roman Catholic religion domiciled in your territory not to publish the aforesaid Bull annulling the Society of Jesus. You are commanded to see carefully to the execution of this order, and to inform us immediately in case any high foreign ecclesiastics endeavor to introduce any Bulls of this kind into our kingdom surreptitiously."

This mandate had the effect of protecting the Jesuits who were in his dominions; for as canon law made the promulgation of the Brief an indispensable condition of the suppression, it followed that the Jesuits in Prussia could conscientiously continue to live there as Jesuits. Indeed, the king had previously notified the Pope that such would be his course of action, and an autograph dispatch to the Prussian representative at Rome, dated Potsdam, September 13, 1773, reads as follows: " Abbé Columbini: You will say to whomsoever it may concern, but without any ostentation or affectation, and indeed you will endeavor to find an opportunity to say naturally, both to the Pope and his prime minister, that with regard to the affair of the Jesuits, my resolution is taken to keep them in my States as they hitherto have been. I guaranteed in the treaty of Breslau the *statu quo* of the Catholic religion, and I have found no better priests than they under every aspect. You will add that as I am a heretic, the Pope cannot dispense me from the obligation of keeping my word nor from nullifying my obligation as an honest man."

The last phrase, of course, is very insulting, but there was no help for it. It was the king's. When d'Alembert heard of the letter, he revealed his true colors, and warned Frederick that he would regret it, reminding him that in the Silesian War, the Jesuits had been opposed to him; that is to say, the Silesian Jesuits were faithful to Silesia. Frederick replied, on Jan. 7, 1774: " You need not be alarmed for my safety. I have nothing to fear from the Jesuits; they can teach the youth of the country, and they are better able to do that than any one else. It is true that they were on the other side, during the war, but, as a philosopher, you ought not to reproach me for being kind and humane to every one of the human species, no matter what religion or society he belongs to. Try to be more of a philosopher and less of a metaphysician. Good acts are more profitable to the public than the most subtle systems and the most extravagant discoveries, in which, generally speaking, the mind wanders wildly without ever finding the truth. In any case, I am not the only one who has protected the Jesuits. The English and the Empress of Russia have done as much." This correspondence with d'Alembert continued for a year or so; and in 1777, when Voltaire was dying, the king wrote to advise him to think of his old school days at Louis-le-Grand. " Remember Father Tournemine, who was your nurse and made you suck the sweet milk of the Muses. Reconcile yourself with the Order which in the last century gave to France its greatest men." To all appearances Voltaire did not take the advice of his royal friend.

The politicans of Spain were particularly irritated at this action of Frederick, but he paid no attention to their anger. It is even said that the Pope ordered his nuncio at Warsaw to suspend all the Jesuits in Prussia from their ecclesiastical and pedagogical function and that a request was made to the King to have it done *pro forma*, with a promise to lift the ban immediately afterwards, a proposition which seems too silly to have ever been seriously made. But when Clement XIV died, Pius VI, after a few perfunctory protests, so as not to exasperate the other powers, let it be known that he was not dissatisfied with the status of the Jesuits in Prussia, and he not only wrote in that sense to Frederick, but encouraged him to continue his protection of the outcasts. Whereupon Frederick dispatched the following letter to the superior of Breslau. It is dated September 27, 1775:

" Venerable, dear and faithful Father: The new Pontiff having declared that he left to me the choice of the most suitable means to be employed for the conservation of the Jesuits in my kingdom, and that he would put no obstacle in my way by any declaration of irregularity, I have in consequence enjoined on my bishops to leave your Institute *in statu quo*, and not to trouble any of your members or to refuse ordination to any of your candidates to the priesthood. You will therefore conform to this arrangement and advise your confrères to do likewise."

Until the death of Bishop Bayer of Culm, who was the staunch friend of the Fathers, there was no cloud on the horizon; but he was succeeded by Bishop Hohenzotten, who belonged to the House of Brandenburg. He had been extremely friendly before his installation as bishop, but immediately afterwards he advised the king to secularize the Jesuits and to forbid the establishment of a novitiate. The king, however, would not yield any further than to permit of their dressing as secular priests, and until his death in 1786 they continued to live in community under the name of the " Priests of the Royal Institute." His successor was not so benignant, for he seized all the revenues of the houses and thus put an end to their existence in Prussia, and they, like their brethren elsewhere, took the road of exile. Some joined the secular clergy and others made their way to Russia.

More surprising still was the protection accorded to them by the terrible Empress Catherine II of Russia. Indeed, it was she who made it possible to preserve unbroken the link between the old and the new Society. On the other hand, not a few Pharisees have reproached the Society for having accepted the protection of this imperial tigress. For the same reason, they might have found fault with Daniel in the lion's den. He

41

could not get out of it; and, the animals were kinder than the humans above ground.

Catherine of Russia was not a Russian but a Prussian. Her name was Sophia Augusta of Anhalt-Zerbst. She and her unfortunate husband had been adopted by the czarina, Elizabeth, as her successors on the imperial throne of Russia, on condition that they would change their name and religion. There was no difficulty about either, especially the latter. According to Oliphant, Kohl, Döllinger and others who have described the state of the empire as it was about forty years later, sixteen millions or about one fourth of the entire population of Russia did not profess the Greek faith. The educated classes neither cared nor affected to care for the state religion. From the mercantile classes and most of their employees and the landed aristocracy all faith had departed. The peasants were divided into about fifty sects, and hatred and contempt for one another and the enmity of all of them for the Orthodox Church were extreme. No two Russian bishops had any spiritual dependence or connection with any other. They were simply paid officials of a common master who appointed, degraded or discarded them at pleasure. De Maistre who lived in Russia about that time says. " The words: " Oriental Church " or " Greek Church " have no meaning whatever." " I recognize," said Peter the Great, " no other legitimate Patriarch than the Pope of Rome. Since you will not obey him you shall obey me only. Behold your Pope." On that basis the Russian Church was built.

Strictly speaking the Jesuits were not entering Russia but merely staying in their old establishments which were still Polish, though geographically labelled Russia. Nevertheless, with Russia proper they had already a considerable acquaintance. Thus, as early as 1612, Father Szgoda had allowed himself to be taken by the Tatars to the Crimea, so as to evangelize the Cossacks. Later, Father Schmidt had appeared at the court of Peter the Great as chaplain of the Austrian embassy. In 1685, Father Debois brought a letter to the czar from the Pope Innocent III, and in 1687 Father Vota, encouraged by several Russian theologians of note, was bold enough to propose to Peter the Great a union with Rome. Peter's sister Sophia was favorable to the project and the moment seemed propitious, but a brace of fanatical monks backed by the patriarch, fiercely denounced the scheme and it was dropped. A school, however, was established at Moscow, but when Sophia died, Peter drove out the Fathers. In 1691, however, he returned to a better state of mind and permitted the Catholics of Moscow to build a church and to invite the Jesuits to take charge of it. But in 1719 he again expelled them, for he had conceived the idea of a Church of his own; not only independent of Rome but of Constantinople, and absolutely under his own control — a view it is said that was suggested to him by the French Jansenists whom he met in Paris on a visit there in 1717.

That ended all hopes of Catholicity in Russia, but in 1772 when Poland was dismembered, a large number of Catholics were added to the population of Russia and Catherine II, who had murdered her husband in order to be supreme in the State, addressed herself to the task of constituting these Russianized Poles into an independent Catholic Church. She found an ambitious Polish bishop, named Siestrzencewicz who entered into her views, and on May 23, 1774, by an imperial ukase she established the Diocese of White Russia. Zalenski, S. J., the author of " Les Jésuites et la Russie Blanche " is strong in his denunciation of Siestrzencewicz, as are Pierling and Markowitch, but Godlewski is more benignant and tries to excuse the bishop as a man who did indeed resort to questionable methods, but was striving to stave off an open persecution of the Catholics. Zalenski has the more likely view.

This name of " White " Russia is a puzzle to most people, as are the opposite descriptions of " Black " and " Red " Russia. Indeed Okolski, who wrote in 1646, has a book entitled " Russia Florida," a name not in accordance with the popular notions about that country. There is also a " Greater " and a " Little " and a " West " Russia. The geographical limits of White Russia may be found in any encyclopedia. It is the region in which are Polotsk, Vitebsk, Orsha, Mohilew, Motislave and Gomel, and is bounded by the rivers Duna, Dneiper, Peripet and Bug. It was Russia's share in the first spoliation of Poland, and had a population of 1,600,000. Moscow is not far to the east but St. Petersburg (Petrograd) is at a great distance to the north.

In 1772 Catherine made known her intention regarding the Jesuits whom she found teaching in the section of Poland which had passed under her sceptre. They were even to retain their four colleges of Polotsk, Vitebsk, Orsha and Dunaberg besides their two residences and fourteen missions. She needed them as teachers and as they were the first to declare their acceptance of the new conditions, and had thus set an example to their countrymen, she revoked the ancient proscription of Peter the Great against the Society in Russia proper, and also apprised the other provinces of Europe that she would be their guardian in the future.

When the Brief of Suppression was announced, the Fathers felt perfectly sure that, like Frederick II, she would not permit it to be promulgated, both because the Russian Church refused allegiance to Rome, and also because she had already bound herself by a promise to protect them. Nevertheless, through their superior, they addressed to her " Sacred Imperial Majesty " the following letter:

" It is to Your Majesty that we owe the privilege of professing publicly the Roman Catholic Religion in your glorious states, and of depending in spiritual matters on the Sovereign Pontiff who is the visible head of our Church. That is the reason why we Jesuits, all of whom belong to the Roman Rite, but who are most faithful subjects of Your Majesty, now prostrate before your august imperial throne, implore Your Majesty by all that is most sacred to permit us to render prompt and public obedience to the authority which resides in the person of the Sovereign Roman Pontiff and to execute the edict he has sent us abolishing our Society. By condescending to have a public proclamation made of this Brief of Suppression, Your Majesty will thus exercise your royal authority, and we by promptly obeying will show ourselves obedient both to Your Majesty and to the Sovereign Pontiff who has ordered this proclamation. Such are the sentiments and the prayers of all and each of the Jesuits, which are now expressed by me to Your Majesty, of whom I have the honor to be, with the most profound veneration and the most respectful submission, the most humble, the most devoted and the most faithful subject,

" Stanislas Czerniewicz."

" Her Sacred Majesty " absolutely refused to accede to the request. On the contrary she insisted that the Brief should not be proclaimed in her dominions. She showed them the greatest consideration and insisted that her nobles should imitate her example, so that it became the fashion for the dignitaries of the empire to visit the various Jesuit establishments; on their part, the Jesuits never failed to show their appreciation of such an honor in as splendid a fashion as possible. The most memorable of all such visits was one in which the " Semiramis of the North " was the central figure. Catherine left St. Petersburg, on May 20, 1780, and reached Polotsk ten days later. In her suite were Potemkin, Tchernichef, de Cobentzel, the Prince Marshal Borjantynski, and Prince Dolkowiouki. On her arrival, while surrounded by all the notables who had hastened to meet her, the Jesuits were pointed out to her and she graciously saluted them. In the evening, the college was splendidly illuminated in her honor, and on the following morning she came to the church, for she was burning with a desire to witness a Catholic ceremonial. After Mass she went through the house, and both at her arrival and departure the rector celebrated her glory in an epic poem.

From thence she set out for Mohilew where Joseph II of Austria awaited her. He had already visited the college at this place, and was received with proper honor by the rector and provincial. He made all sorts of inquiries about the reason why the suppressed Jesuits were permitted to exist in Russia, and the bishop told him laconically: " The people need them; the empress ordered it and Rome has said nothing." " You did well," replied the emperor, " you should not, and could not have done otherwise." With the emperor on this occasion appears the unexpected figure of one of the suppressed Jesuits: Father Francis Xavier Kalatai. He was his majesty's travelling companion, and has left a letter telling us what happened on this occasion.

" At Mohilew," he writes, " at the farthest extremity of the recently dismembered provinces of Poland, the

Jesuits still remain on their former footing. They are protected by the empress, because of their ability in training the youth of the country in science and piety. I asked to be presented to the superior when we visited the college and found him to be a very venerable old man. I questioned him and other members of the community on what they based their non-submission to the Brief of Suppression, and they replied in the same formula as the bishop: " Clementissima imperatrice nostra protegente, populo derelicto exigente, Roma sciente et non contradicente;" (i.e. on the protection of our most clement empress, the needs of the the abandoned people, and the knowledge and tacit consent of Rome). They then showed me a letter from the Pope expressing his affection for them, and exhorting them to remain as they were until new arrangements could be made. He insisted upon their receiving novices and admitting Jesuits from other provinces, who desired to resume with them the sweet yoke of Christ from which they had been so violently torn. The provincial added that all the Jesuits of Russia were willing to relinquish everything they had, at the first authentic sign of the will of the Pope, and that they waited only a canonical announcement to that effect. Thus, I found that the true spirit of the Society had kept its first fervor among these scattered remnants of it in Russia."

The empress arrived, after making fifty leagues a day on the trip from Polotsk; killing ten horses on the journey. The meeting of the two sovereigns was unusually splendid; ten thousand soldiers stood on guard in the city, and besides state receptions, there were theatrical performances, public sports, banquets and the rest. The Jesuits of other establishments paid their respects, and were presented to the empress by the governor. On the 12th of June, " Semiramis " left for St. Petersburg. Such a favor, of course, made the Jesuits still more popular and, at the same time, checked the papal nuncio, Archetti, who had not yet recovered from his failure to have the suppression made effective. Nevertheless, he still persisted in his efforts, in spite of the threats of the empress. But she never yielded.

Father Brucker writing in the " Etudes " (tom. 132, 1912, 558–59) gives a characteristic letter of the empress to Baron Grimm who was a friend and associate of Rousseau, Diderot, d'Alembert, Holbach and the rest. At that time, Grimm was the envoy of the Duke of Saxe-Gotha, at the court of France, and later on, Catherine's own plenipotentiary to Lower Saxony.

The letter is dated May 7, 1779 and runs as follows: " Neither I nor my *coquins en titre* (my honorable rogues) *les Jésuites de la R. Bl.* (the Jesuits of White Russia) are going to cause the Pope any worry. They are very submissive to him and want to do only what he wishes. I suppose it is you who wrote the article in the ' Gazette de Cologne ' about the hot house (the Jesuit novitiate). You say that I am amusing myself by being kind to them. Assuredly, you credit me with a pretty motive, whereas I have no other than that of keeping my word and seeking the public good. As for your grocers (the Bourbon kings) I make a present of them to you; but I know one thing, namely, they are not going to visit me and sing the song: ' Bonhomme! you are not master of your house while we are in it.' "

As early as 1776, that is only three years after the Suppression, the Jesuits of White Russia already numbered 145 members, and had twelve establishments: colleges, residences, missions, etc. In 1777 the question was discussed about opening a novitiate

and the Fathers had sufficient evidence that Pius VI
would be glad of it and that even Clement XIV had
not been averse. Moreover, the letter sent to Bishop
Siestrzencewicz had been found on examination not
to be the " formidable decree," as friends in Rome had
described it, for it left to him the right of creating and
renewing only " what he might find necessary."
Finally, as it was not couched in the usual form of
Apostolic documents, the superior, Father Czerniewicz, set aside his doubts and wrote both to the
bishop and to the firm friend of the Society, Governor
General Tchernichef, that he had determined to open
that establishment.

Tchernichef's support must have been very strong,
for when Father Czerniewicz arrived at Mohilew to
arrange matters with the bishop, he received from the
prelate a decree dated June 29, 1779, authorizing him
to carry out his purpose. This decree began with
the words: " Pope Clement XIV, of celebrated
memory, condescending to the desire of the Most
August Empress of the Russias, our Most Clement
Sovereign, had permitted the non-promulgation in
her dominions of the Bull 'Dominus ac Redemptor;'
and Our Holy Father Pope Pius VI, now happily
reigning, shows the same deference to the desires of Her
Imperial Majesty, by refraining from all opposition to
the retention of their habit, name and profession by
the Regular Clerks of the Society of Jesus, in the estates
of her Majesty, notwithstanding the Bull 'Dominus ac
Redemptor.' Moreover as the Most August Empress to
whom both we and the numerous Catholic churches in
her vast domains are under such grave obligations has
recommended to us both verbally and by writing
to do all in our power to see that the aforesaid Regular
Clerks of the Society of Jesus may provide for the
conservation of their Institute, we hasten to fulfil

that duty which is so agreeable to us and for which
we should reproach ourselves did we stint our efforts
in carrying it out. Hitherto, they have not had any
novitiate in this country, and, as their numbers are
gradually diminishing, it is evident that they cannot
exercise their useful ministry unless a novitiate is
accorded them."

In virtue of this permission, a novitiate was established at Polotsk on February 2, 1780, and ten novices
entered and began community life under the direction
of Father Lubowicki, On that occasion, according to
de Mürr, a formidable Latin poem of 169 hexameters
was composed by Father Michael Korycki in honor of
Bishop Siestrzencewicz. Thus was the house established; and in spite of the importunities of the Bourbon
ambassadors at Rome, the Sovereign Pontiff, Pius VI,
never gave utterance, either personally or through his
nuncio in Poland, to any public protest against it.
All the denunciations of the alleged " refractory
Jesuits " were either letters of private individuals or
secret official correspondence, written doubtless in
the name of the Pope, but indirectly, that is through
the channel of the secretaryship of State and the
nunciature; and never going outside the narrow diplomatic circle. Nor is there the slightest positive proof
that the Pope regarded the Jesuits of White Russia
except as religious.

" On the contrary," says Zalenski (I, 330), " Pius
VI knew very well, as did everyone else in Rome, that
Clement XIV had published the Brief of Suppression
in spite of himself, and only after four years of hesitation
and conflict with the diplomats. Moreover, Cardinals
Antonelli and Calini, eye-witnesses of what had
happened, represented to Pius VI in personal memorials
that the suppression was invalid. Pius himself had
belonged to that section of cardinals which disapproved

of the destruction, and, as has been already said, when he was Pope, he set free the prisoners of the Castle Sant' Angelo, rehabilitated their memory, and ordered Father Ricci to be buried with the honors due to the general of an Order. In brief, Pius VI, as both Frederick II and Tchernichef insisted, was really glad that the Society had been preserved, and his silence was an approbation of it. Indeed, he could not, as the Father of Christendom, exclude the Jesuits from the protection of the general law of the Church and regard them as suppressed and freed from their vows, before the Brief of Clement XIV had been properly made known to them by the ordinary of the diocese. Of course, their enemies systematically rejected this axiom although accepted both by common and canon law. They denounced it as " a vain subterfuge," and even the Apostolic nuncio, in one of his dispatches declared it to be such; but the Holy Father could not, in conscience, accept that view.

In February, 1782, Tchernichef, the great friend of the Society, fell from power, but his successor Potemkin showed himself even a more devoted defender. Fortunately, Father Benislawski, a former Jesuit, but now a canon, was very intimate with him and induced him to give his aid to the Society. As Bishop Siestrzencewicz had meantime become Archbishop of Mohilew, the fear was again revived that he would claim to be the religious superior of the Jesuits. Indeed, by sundry appointments to parishes, he began to reveal that such was his intention, and Archetti, the nuncio at Warsaw, urged him to persist in his attacks. To head off the danger, the Fathers had determined to proceed to the election of a Vicar General, and they obtained permission from the empress to that effect. She issued a ukase, on June 23, 1782, in which she said that the Jesuits were to be subject to the archbishop, in things that pertained to his rights and duties, but that he should be very careful not to interfere with any of the rules of the Order which were to remain intact "in as far as they agree with our civil constitutions." Siestrzencewicz was quite upset by this order, and not knowing that it had been obtained through the intervention of Potemkin, he asked the Prince Wiaziemski, who was then president of the Senate, to obtain a decree from that body subjecting the Jesuits to his jurisdiction. The Senate so ruled by a rescript dated September 12, 1781, but it was a very ill-advised proceeding on their part, for it set them in opposition both to the empress and the powerful Potemkin, besides making a rebel of the archbishop and a meddler of the nuncio.

While a spirited correspondence was going on between those two distinguished ecclesiastics about the matter, the Fathers met at Polotsk, on October 10, 1782, which happened to be the feast of St. Francis Borgia, to hold the twentieth congregation of the Society. Everything was done according to the rule which governs such assemblies, and Father Stanislaus Cerzniewicz, the vice-provincial, was chosen Vicar General of the Society. In the following session, it was decreed that for those who re-entered the Society, the years spent involuntarily and by compulsion, in the world, would count as so many years in religion. With this the congregation ended, because orders had come to Polotsk, for the Vicar General to report immediately to the Empress at St. Petersburg. Accordingly, after naming Father Francis Kareu, vice-provincial, he set out for the capital and was welcomed by Catherine with the words: "I defended you thus far, and will do so till the end."

The question now arose how would the archbishop receive the delegates of the congregation which had ignored his claim to control the internal affairs of the Society. The all-powerful Potemkin had attended to that. He had called the prelate to task for daring to oppose the explicit command of the empress, and warned him of the danger of such a course of action. As Siestrzencewicz was primarily a politician, he had no difficulty in modifying his views. Moreover, Canon Benislawski, who had studied him at close range and knew his peculiarities, had taken care to prepare him for the visit of the delegates. When they arrived, he received them with the greatest courtesy and sent a letter of congratulation to the newly-elected vicar. The future of the Society was thus assured. A successor to Father Ricci had been elected; a general congregation had convened and its proceeding had been conducted in strict conformity with the Constitution. Besides, a novitiate had been established, members of the dispersed provinces had been officially recognized as belonging to the Society; and all this had been done with the tacit consent of the Sovereign Pontiff.

Father Czerniewicz remained in St. Petersburg more than three months, during which time he was frequently summoned to discuss with the empress and Potemkin matters pertaining to education, but chiefly to make arrangements for negotiations in Rome, in order to obtain the Pope's express approval of the election. The matter called for considerable diplomatic skill, for in the Acts of the congregation, some very bold expressions had been employed which might cause the failure of the whole venture. Thus, it had declared that "the Brief of Clement XIV destroyed the Society outside of Russia;" and again, that "the Vicar was elected by the authority of the Holy See." The second especially was a dangerous assertion, since the papal nuncio, Archetti, regarded the election as illegal, and even a few of the Jesuits themselves were doubtful as to the correctness of the claim. There was fear, also, about the personal disposition of the Pope on that point.

To dispose of all these difficulties Catherine sent Benislawski as her ambassador to Rome, with very positive instructions not to modify them in any way whatever. He was not to stop at Warsaw, but might call on the nuncio, Garampi, at Vienna, and also on Gallitzin, the Russian ambassador. He was to go by the shortest route to Rome, to visit no cardinals there, but to present himself immediately to the Pope. In his audience, he was to make three requests. They were: first, the preconization of Siestrzencewicz as archbishop; second, the appointment of Benislawski himself as coadjutor; and third, the approbation of the Jesuits in White Russia, and especially the recognition of the Acts of the congregation. The refusal of anyone of them was to entail a rupture of negotiations with Russia.

On February 21, 1783, Benislawski arrived in Rome, and saw the Pope on the same day. He was received most graciously; his own nomination as bishop was confirmed; but, said the Pope: " Siestrzencewicz had no right to open the novitiate." " That was done," replied Benislawski, " by order of the empress." " Since that is the case," said the Pope, " I shall forget the injury done to me by the bishop." He then asked about the Jesuits and their General, and whether the election had been formally ordered by the empress." When assured upon the latter point, he answered, " I do not object." After an interview of two hours Benislawski withdrew.

At the second audience the attitude of the Pope was cold and indifferent, for the Bourbon ambassadors had influenced him meantime. Noticing the change, Benislawski fell upon his knees and asked the Pope's

benediction. " What does this mean?" he was asked.
" My orders are to withdraw immediately, if my
requests are not granted." That startled the Pope,
and he immediately changed his tone; he spoke kindly
to Benislawski and told him to put his requests in
writing. All night long the faithful ambassador
labored at his desk formulating each request and
answering every argument that might be alleged
against it. Zalenski gives the entire document (I,
386), which substantially amounted to this: " The
failure of the bishop to abolish the Society in Russia;
the establishment of the novitiate, and the election
of the General were all due to the explicit and positive
orders of Catherine. As she had threatened to persecute
the Catholics of Russia and to compel the Poles to
enter the Orthodox Church, it was clear that there
was no choice but to submit to her demands.

" With regard to the objection that the Bourbon
Princes would be angry at Catherine's support of the
Jesuits, Benislawski made answer, that, ' as the
empress had offered no objections to the suppression
of the Order in the dominions of those rulers, she
failed to see why they had any right to question her
action in preserving it. She owed those kings no
allegiance.' Secondly, the approval of the Society
would not be a reflection on the present Pope, who
had as much right to reverse the judgment of Clement
XIV, as Clement XIV had to reverse the judgment of
thirty of his predecessors. If none of the kings and
diplomats had blamed Clement for acting as he did,
why should they blame Pius VI for using his own right
in the premises? Moreover, the Brief was never
published in Russia, and there was not the slightest
prospect that it ever would be. Finally, the empress
had made a solemn promise not to harm her Catholic
subjects; but she was convinced that she could not

inflict a greater injury on them than to deprive their churches of priests and their schools of teachers who in her opinion were invaluable." As to the charge that the whole course of the empress was due to the suggestion of the Jesuits, Benislawski replied that " everyone knew they had petitioned her to have the Brief promulgated, and that she had told them they were asking what was not agreeable to her."

The next day the Pope read the statement, smiled and said, " You want to arrange this matter by a debate with me. But there can be no answer to your contention. Your arguments are irrefutable." Very opportunely, a letter arrived from the empress who expressed her willingness to receive a papal legate to settle the case of the Uniate Archbishop of Polotsk, and asking to have Benislawski consecrated in St. Petersburg. The letter was read to the Pope, in the presence of a number of Cardinals, to whom Benislawski was presented. The Holy Father then gave his assent to the preconization of the archbishop, and the consecration of Benislawski. " As to the third," he said, raising his voice: " Approbo Societatem Jesu in Alba Russia degentem; approbo, approbo" (that is I approve of the Society of Jesus, now in Russia; I approve, I approve). As the verbal utterances of Popes in public matters of the Church, have the same force as when they are in writing, and are designated by canonists and theologians as *vivæ vocis oracula*, Benislawski contented himself with this approval. Besides, fearing the machinations of the Bourbon politicians, he could not ask for more. He had won his case, and had received the Pope's assurance that the Society in Russia was not and never had been suppressed. No more was needed.

Against the immense majority of historians of every shade of opinion, Theiner in his " Pontificate of Clement

XIV " denounces this account of the embassy as " a fabrication of the Jesuit Benislawski," though Benislawski was not then a Jesuit, nor did he ever re-enter the Society. Besides, although Theiner characterizes the distinguished canonist whom the Pope had just made a bishop as " a liar " and " an intriguer," he admits at the same time that he was " a virtuous man " and " a pious priest." If the account of the audience had been untrue, the Pope would certainly have been compelled to denounce it; for it was published immediately in the Florence Gazette; and the falsifier would assuredly never have received his mitre. Nevertheless, to settle the matter definitely and to allay all doubts and suspicions, Benislawski, after he was installed as Bishop of Gadara, was invited to the second congregation of the Jesuits. It met at Polotsk, on July 25, 1785, and he there made the following declaration under oath:

" Having been sent to Rome by the Most Illustrious Empress of all the Russias to interview the Pope with a view of settling the difficulty about the Archbishopric of Mohilew and of the Co-adjutorship of that see, as well as to obtain from the Pope the approval of the Society of Jesus in White Russia, I represented to His Holiness the state of the Jesuits living there in conformity with the laws of their Institute, and I acquainted him with the fact that they had elected a General in obedience to the command of the Most Illustrious Empress. After having heard me, His Holiness kindly approved of the manner of life which the Jesuits were leading in White Russia, and ratified the election of the General, repeating three times, 'approbo, approbo, approbo.' I affirm under a most solemn oath, the truth of this verbal approbation; in confirmation of which I hereunto affix my seal and signature."

42

Theiner adduces three Briefs of Pius VI to offset this affidavit of Benislawski, but two of them antedate the episode at Rome; the third was issued a month later, and has nothing in common with the question at issue. Besides this, a few years subsequent to this approval, when Father Joseph Pignatelli, who may one day be among the canonized saints of the Church, asked permission of the Pope to go to White Russia "if the Society existed there," His Holiness answered: "Yes, it exists there; and if it were possible I would have it extended everywhere throughout the world. Go to Russia. I authorize you to wear the habit of the Jesuits. I regard the Jesuits there, as true Jesuits and the Society existing in Russia as lawfully existing." (Bonfier, Vie de Pignatelli, 196.)

As their status was now settled, the Fathers addressed themselves to the educational reform which the empress wanted to introduce into the schools of Russia. It consisted mainly in giving prominence to the physical sciences. They had no difficulty in complying with her wishes, and Father Gruber, who was an eminent physicist, immediately established a training-school for the preparation of future professors, and in March 1785, a number of Jesuit scientists were summoned by Potemkin to St. Petersburg.

On June 20, of that year, the Vicar General Czernie- wicz died. He was born in 1728, and had entered the Society at sixteen; af er teaching at Warsaw, he was called to Rome as secretary to Father Ricci; later he was substitute assistant of Poland. He was then sent to be rector of Polotsk, and was at that post when Clement XIV issued the decree of Suppression. At the congregation which was called on October 1, Father Lenkiewicz was elected to succeed him.

By this time, many of the old Jesuits were sending in their requests for admission. Among them were

such distinguished personages as the astronomer Hell;
two of Father Ricci's assistants, Romberg and Korycki
and others. All could not be received in Russia itself,
but wherever they were, in America, Europe, China,
the East and West Indies, etc., they were all gladly
welcomed back and their names were inscribed in the
catalogue. It is of especial interest for Americans to
find those of Adam Britt of Maryland and of several
who were sent from White Russia to the United States
when Carroll was empowered to re-establish the Society
in 1805. They are Anthony Kohlmann, Malevy, Brown,
Epinette and others. Those who, for one reason or
another, were unable to go to Russia in person, were
informed that they were duly recognized as Jesuits
and were given permission to renew their vows. This
arrangement was made especially for the ex-members
who had been appointed to bishoprics, or were employed
in some important function, such as royal confessors,
court preachers, scientists, etc., or again, who were
prevented by age and infirmity from making the long
and difficult journey.

In the " Catalogus mortuorum," or list of deceased
members, which covers the period between 1773 and
1814, Zalenski counts 268 who are *extra provinciam;*
all nations under the sun are represented. From
everywhere gifts were sent by former Jesuits. Thus,
Father Raczynski who had become Primate of Poland
gathered together at various auctions as many as
8000 Jesuit books and sent them to the College of
Polotsk. Others followed his example, and in 1815
the college library had 35,000 volumes on its shelves.
Other contributions came in the form of money. As
early as 1787, Polotsk had a printing-press, and
produced its own text-books, besides publishing a
number of works which were out of print. Fr. Gruber
kept at work forming a corps of able scientists, and

he even made many coadjutor brothers architects,
painters and skilled artificers in various crafts. The
institution soon became famous for its physical and
chemical laboratories, its splendid theatre, its paintings,
sculpture, etc. The minor colleges soon followed its
example, and the Jesuit churches resumed their customary magnificence. Sodalities were established, distant
missions were undertaken, and among the neighboring
Letts, Jesuit missionaries created a veritable Paraguay.

Catherine reigned for thirty-five years, and until
her death, as she had promised, she had never failed
to protect the Society. Her word alone counted in
Russia. She was alone on the throne for she had
murdered the czar, her husband, because of his repudia-
tion of her son Paul, and also because of her
natural intolerance of an equal. It is true that Father
Carroll, in far-away America, was lamenting that his
brethren had such a protectress, but that was beyond
their control. It can at least be claimed that they
had never yielded an iota in their duties as Catholic
priests. During the whole of her reign she kept her
unfortunate heir almost in complete seclusion. He
was confided to the care chiefly of Father Gruber,
who besides being a saint was a man of wonderful
ability. He was a musician, a painter, an architect, a
physicist and a mathematician. One of his oil paintings
adorns the refectory of Georgetown today; brought
over, no doubt, by some of the Polish Fathers. It is
very far from being the work of an amateur. Naturally,
therefore, Paul took to him kindly, and the affection
continued till the end. When on the throne, he
multiplied the colleges of the Society, enlarged the
novitiate, installed the Fathers in the University of
Vilna, and even persuaded the Grand Turk to restore
to the Jesuits their ancient missions on the Ægean
Archipelago.

The intimacy was so great that Gruber was supposed to be able to procure any favor from Paul and hence his life was made miserable by the swarm of suitors who beset him; but he was not foolish enough to forfeit the favor of the prince by being made a tool to further the selfish aims of the petitioners. He did, however, request the czar to ask the newly-elected Pope Pius VII for an official recognition of the Society in Russia. The Pope was only too willing to grant it, but the lingering hostility to the Jesuits, even in Rome itself, made it somewhat difficult. Indeed, a certain number of the cardinals pronounced very decidedly against it, and only yielded, when the Pope made them take all the responsibility of a refusal. He appointed a committee of the most hostile among them to report on the imperial request, thus bringing them face to face with the consequences of opposing the ruler of a great empire and converting him from a friend into a persecutor of the Church. Looking at it from that point of view, they quickly came to a favorable conclusion, and on March 7, 1801, the Bull " Catholicæ Fidei " was issued, explicitly re-establishing the Society of Jesus in Russia. It was the first great step to the general restoration throughout the world thirteen years later. The approbation arrived very opportunely, for sixteen days after its reception Paul I was assassinated.

At his accession, Alexander, though less demonstrative than Paul, showed his esteem for the Society to such an extent that when the General, Father Kareu, was at the point of death, the czar went in person to Polotsk to offer his condolence. This condescension was so marked that Father Gruber availed himself of the opportunity to solicit the publication of the Papal Bull which the turmoil consequent upon Paul's assassination had prevented from being officially proclaimed. The emperor made no difficulty about it, and issued a ukase to that effect. He even went further in his approval, for when Gruber was elected General in place of Father Kareu, he was summoned to St. Petersburg to occupy a splendidly equipped College of Nobles which Paul had established in the city itself. It was there that Gruber met the famous Count Joseph de Maistre who was at that time Ambassador of Sardinia at the imperial court. A deep and sincere affection sprung up between the two great men, and in the storm that, later on, broke out against the Society, de Maistre showed himself its fearless and devoted defender.

Catherine II had, in her time, attempted the colonization of the vast steppes of her empire, and Paul I had been energetic in carrying out her plans. Alexander I, also, was anxious to further the project which called for not a little heroism on the part of those who undertook it. Incidentally, it would relieve the government of considerable anxiety and worry; for as the new settlers came from every part of Germany, and professed all kinds of religious beliefs, it was considered to be of primary importance politically, to establish some sort of unity among them and to accustom them to Russian legislation and ways of life. The Jesuits were selected for the task, and in spite of the hardships and the isolation to which they were subjected, and in face, also, of the hatred and opposition of their enemies as well as the usually surly mood of the brutalized immigrants who had been driven out of their own country by starvation and oppression, order was restored within a year, and the government reported that these few priests had achieved what a whole army of soldiers could never have accomplished. The missions of Astrakhan were said to be similarly successful. But it appears in the light of subsequent events, that no solid or permanent results had been effected.

A glance at the map will show us that these two fields of endeavor were at the extreme eastern and western ends of Russia's vast empire. The Riga district is on the Baltic or, more properly, on the Gulf of Riga. Below it, are the now famous cities of Köningsberg and Dantzic. Astrakhan is on the Caspian Sea into which the great River Volga empties. On both sides of this river, as in the city itself, the Jesuits had established their mission posts. But from both the Baltic and the Caspian they had to withdraw, when driven out of Russia by Alexander in 1820.

The present condition of these two sections of the now dismembered empire is most deplorable. Indeed, as early as 1864 Marshall (Christian Missions, I, 74) says of them: " Let us begin with the Provinces of the Baltic. The Letts who inhabit Courland and the southern half of Livonia, though long normally Christians and surrounded by Lutherans and Russo-Greeks, sacrifice to household spirits by setting out food for them in their gardens or houses or under old oak trees. Of the Esthonians, Kohl says: ' The old practices of heathenism have been preserved among them more completely than among any other Lutheran people. There are many spots where the peasants yet offer up sacrifices.' Let us now accompany Mr. Laurence Oliphant down the Volga to the Caspian Sea. Everywhere his experience is uniform. The Kalmuks whom he discovered are still Buddhists. Near the mouth of the Volga he visits a large and populous village in a state of utter heathenism and apparently destined to remain so. At Sarepta near Astrakhan, the Moravians had attempted to convert the neighboring heathen but the Greek clergy prevented

them.   One tribe is made up of followers of the Grand
Lama; another of pagans; a third of Mahometans.
In the city of Kazan, once the capital of a powerful
nation, there are 20,000 Mahometans, and the immense
Tatar population of the entire region reaching as far
as Astrakhan has adopted a combination of Christianity,
Islamism and Shamanism, or are as out and out pagans
as they were before being annexed to the Russian
Empire."

Among these degraded peoples the Jesuits were at
work while they were directing their colleges at Polotsk,
St. Petersburg and elsewhere until 1814.

CHAPTER XXII

THE RALLYING

Fathers of the Sacred Heart — Fathers of the Faith — Fusion — Paccanari — The Rupture — Exodus to Russia — Varin in Paris — Clorivière — Carroll's doubts — Pignatelli — Poirot in China — Grassi's Odyssey.

WHILE the Society was maintaining its corporate life in Russia several contributory sources began to flow towards it from various parts of Europe. The most notable was the association that was formed under the eyes and with the approval of the wise and virtuous Jacques-André Emery, the superior of the Seminary of Paris, who himself had been trained in the Jesuit college of Macon. Under his guidance and very much attached to him, was a little group of seminarians consisting of Charles and Maurice de Broglie, sons of the celebrated Marshal of that name, both of whom bore the title of Prince; François Eléonore de Tournély, who was the animating spirit of the little association, and, omitting others, Joseph Varin who succeeded de Tournély as the guide of the growing community.

When the Revolution broke out, Varin yielding to his martial instincts, left the seminary and became a soldier in the royalist army; but Charles de Broglie kept the group together and under the direction of Pey, a distinguished canon of Paris, they plunged into the study of the spiritual life and continued to dream of an association which might in one way or another take up the work of the suppressed Society of Jesus. In 1791 they were compelled to seek a refuge in Luxembourg. Two years later, they fled to Antwerp, and

finally found themselves in the old Jesuit villa of
Louvain, which is still standing near the château of
the Duc d'Arenberg. There they were joined by de
Broglie's brother, Xavier, and by Pierre Leblanc,
both of whom had served for two years in the army
of the Prince de Condé. Varin joined them in that
year. He had been a soldier ever since the seminary
had closed, and had given up all idea of ever resuming
the soutane. But it happened that he was absent
from his regiment when a battle occurred, and in
disgust he had gone to Belgium to ask to be transferred
to another corps. While there, he fell into the hands
of his old seminary friends; in a few days his former
fervor returned and he was accepted as the sixth
member of what de Tournély had determined to call
" The Society of the Sacred Heart."

On the very day of Varin's entrance, he and five
associates started off on foot, with their bags on their
backs, to beg their way to Bavaria. It took them five
days to get as far as Augsburg, and there they remained,
though their intention was to establish themselves at
Munich. But the Bishop of Augsburg told them that
if they wanted to learn what the Society of Jesus was,
no better place could be found than the city in which
they then found themselves, for the memory of many
illustrious Jesuits was still fresh in the hearts of the
people. The bishop who gave them this welcome
hospitality was Clemens Wenzeslaus, who besides
being a prelate was a prince of Saxony and Poland.
Yielding to his advice, they took up their abode in
Augsburg where they were soon joined by two distinguished men who were afterwards to be conspicuous
in the reconstructed Society, Grivel, who was to be
sent to Georgetown in America as master of novices,
and the famous Rozaven, who was to save the Society
from wreck in the first general congregation held after

the Restoration, and who was subsequently to be the assistant General both of Fortis and Roothaan.

As they were all Frenchmen, they were necessarily debarred from apostolic work among the people whose language they could not speak. But that was providential, for they had thus a better opportunity to devote themselves to the study of the spiritual life. On March 12, 1796, Varin and some others were promoted to the priesthood, and about the middle of December, they were installed first at Neudorf and then at Hagenbrünn, near Vienna, as the invading armies of Moreau and Jourdan made Augsburg an unsafe place to live in. They were now sixteen in number and their close imitation of the Jesuit mode of life caused a sensation there, as Austria had only a short time before suppressed the Society.

De Tournély died on July 9, 1797, and Varin was elected in his place on the first ballot. The organization however, had not yet received the authorization of the Sovereign Pontiff, for as Napoleon held him a prisoner now in one place now in another, it was impossible to make any personal application for his approval of the new organization. Hence, a petition was drawn up, signed by twenty-five or thirty bishops asking the Holy Father's approbation. The answer came in the month of September 1798, assuring them that their project afforded him the greatest consolation, and with all his heart he gave them his blessing.

The establishment of this Society was not as has been said " the underhand work of the Jesuits," for Varin and his associates had as yet never met any member of the old Society, nor were they aware of the existence of any similar organization in Italy. Indeed, when a letter came from Rome, signed Nicolas Paccanari, announcing that he was their superior, and was such, " in virtue of an express wish of the Pope

to have the two communities united," the associates
regarded it as the abolition of their Society of the
" Fathers of the Sacred Heart," especially as this
unknown individual announced that he was then on
his way to Hagenbrünn to carry the plan into effect.

Nicolas Paccanari was a very curious personage.
He had no education whatever, and in his early life
had been engaged in various occupations which
scarcely seemed to fit him to be the founder of a
religious order. He was born near Trent, and had been
for some time a soldier, then a merchant on a small
scale, and when swindled by an associate, he took to
tramping from town to town, vending, as Guidée
says, " objects of curiosity," that is, he was an itinerant
peddler. He was a pious man, and as he belonged to
one of the guilds in the Caravita at Rome, he was
prompted by the spirit that prevailed in that famous
Oratory to do something more than usual for the glory
of God. He first thought of being a Carmelite, and
then the fancy seized him that he was destined to
resuscitate the Society of Jesus. Strangely enough,
although he was not even a priest, he was joined by
a doctor of the Sapienza and two French ecclesiastics,
Halnat and Epinette, the latter of whom entered the
Society and later taught philosophy at Georgetown
D. C. He was undoubtedly clever, and so plausible in
his speech that he won the confidence of the most
distinguished personages in Europe : cardinals and
noblemen and heads of religious orders, with the result
that he and his two friends made their vows on the
eve of the Assumption 1797, in the chapel of the
Caravita, and Paccanari was elected superior. He
succeeded even in seeing the Pope, who was then a
prisoner at Spoleto, and obtained his approval and
blessing. He called his organization " The Society of
the Fathers of the Faith of Jesus," which was shortened

later into "The Fathers of the Faith." In Böhmer-
Monod we find them styled "The Brothers of the
Faith."

Paccanari failed to arrive at Hagenbrünn for a
considerable time, for he had fallen into the hands of
the police and was kept a prisoner in Sant' Angelo.
His restless activity and constant change of abode had
attracted the notice of the authorities, and he was
suspected of being concerned in some political plot
against the Roman Republic, which the French had
just then set up in the Papal dominions. His associates
were arrested at the same time, and were not released
for four months. It was during this time of incarceration that Paccanari sent a second letter to Varin
more startling than the first. It announced that the
Fathers of the Sacred Heart had been received into
the Paccanari association, and that Father Varin was
appointed superior of the society in Germany. Such
a communication from a man whom they had not
even seen, made them conclude that they had to do
with a lunatic. Finally, in the month of February 1799,
a third letter arrived, clearing up what had been said
in the second. The explanation offered was that not
knowing if he would ever be let out of jail, and not
wishing that the privileges he had received from the
Holy See should lapse, he had as a precaution admitted
Varin and his associates into the Society of the Fathers
of the Faith.

When at last he was released, he started for Vienna,
and on his way, made it his business to see some of
the dispersed Jesuits who were in Parma and Venice.
They were very kind to him, procured him financial
assistance, but did not welcome him with the enthusiasm he expected. They had remarked that he never
spoke of uniting his associates with the Jesuits of
Russia. Paccanari was keen enough to divine their

reason, and he was therefore only the more eager to affiliate with the people at Hagenbrünn, for he had only twenty members of his own, not more than three of whom were priests. He reached Vienna on April 3, and was naturally received with some reserve, but when Cardinal Migazzi and the nuncio made known the desire of the Pope, all opposition ceased and the discussion of the mode of union began. The sessions lasted ten days and ended by the election of Paccanari as general. The Society of the Fathers of the Sacred Heart thus passed out of existence on April 18, 1799.

The house at Hagenbrünn at once took on a different aspect. There was less study, fewer exercises of piety, the recreations were immoderately prolonged, and the Fathers were actually compelled to take up a series of athletic exercises that made them think they were back in their college days. Of course this soon became intolerable, but little else could have been expected from a man like Paccanari, who was absolutely ignorant of the first elements of community life. What is still more curious is that he was not even yet tonsured; but he was, nevertheless, so wonderfully insinuating in his manner that he succeeded in persuading everyone outside of his own household that he was the man of the hour. The public praised him, but his subjects were exasperated at his opinionativeness, his despotism, his repeated absences from home, and above all by his avoidance of all association with the dispersed Jesuits. All that quickly convinced the Fathers of the Sacred Heart that a serious mistake had been made. It is true that on August 11, 1799, Paccanari made a formal announcement that his sole purpose was to amalgamate with the Jesuits of Russia, but it was tolerably clear that if he ever had any such intention it was rapidly vanishing from his mind. He began by founding several establishments in various parts of Europe, even Moravia being favored in this respect. In this distribution, de Broglie and Rosaven were dispatched to England, and Halnat, Roger and Varin to France.

After the example of the old Jesuits, the first work that Varin and his companions undertook when they arrived in Paris was the care of the hospitals of La Salpétrière and Bicêtre, the first of which had 6,000 patients and had not seen a priest in its wards for ten years. The government now admitted the folly of its previous methods of procedure, and sought the help of the ministers of religion. A tremendous transformation was immediately effected. Nor could it have been otherwise, for the zealous priests spent thirteen and fourteen hours a day there, going from bed to bed to comfort the patients.

It was Halnat who first discovered the existence of the venerable Father de Clorivière, a Jesuit of the old Society, who was to be the first provincial of France after the restoration. The pious Mlle. de Cicé, a niece of the Archbishop of Bordeaux, also comes into view at this period. She had been the directress of an association of ladies established by Father de Clorivière to supply as far as possible the place of the expelled nuns, in looking after the young girls of Paris. Varin became her spiritual guide and also directed Mlle. de Jugon, a remarkable woman, who subsequently married a wealthy nobleman; but at his death she resumed with great ardor the charitable works which had previously reflected such glory upon her piety and zeal.

Just at this time, an attempt was made to assassinate Napoleon. An "infernal machine," as it was called, was exploded under his carriage, and Mlle. de Cicé was suspected of knowing something about it, chiefly because of her association with the mysterious personages who had recently arrived in France — Varin and his companions. Indeed, although the good woman's holiness of life was vouched for by a great number of witnesses, chiefly the beneficiaries of her charity, she might have been condemned to death, had not Father Varin appeared in court, where he made a candid explanation of the character of his society, as having for its only purpose religion and charity, without any political affiliations whatever. His good temper at the trial was a happy offset to Father Halnat's outburst of anger which almost provoked an unfavorable verdict. Later Halnat applied for admission to the Society of Jesus, but it was thought unsafe to admit him.

At this juncture, there appears the figure of Madeleine-Sophie Barat, the foundress of the Ladies of the Sacred Heart, a title chosen at that time not to indicate any social distinction; indeed Madame Barat was from people in very ordinary circumstances, but the name "religious" was in disfavor at that turbulent period, and it was thought advisable not to obtrude unnecessarily the fact that she and her associates formed a community of nuns. They were merely *des dames pieuses*, who lived together for charitable and educational work. The name "dames" is an old title for nuns in England.

She was the sister of Father Louis Barat, who was one of the Fathers of the Faith, and when Varin was looking around for some capable woman to give the girls of Paris and elsewhere a Christian education, Barat suggested her as a possibility. He had taught her Latin, Greek, Spanish, Italian, and natural philosophy, besides subjecting her to a very rigid and somewhat harsh training in asceticism. She was then twenty years of age, and with her usual habit of submission, she and her three companions addressed

themselves to the task. This was in 1801. Before
1857, she had succeeded in establishing more than
eighty foundations in various parts of the world and
she is now ranked among the Beatified.

To Varin must also be accorded the credit of forming in the religious life another woman who is among
the Blessed; the Foundress of the Sisters of Notre-
Dame de Namur, Julie Billiart. Perhaps his prayers
had something to do with the restoration to health
of this remarkable woman, who had been a paralytic
and almost speechless for thirty-one years. She
recovered her youthful vigor in 1804, at the end of
a novena to the Sacred Heart, which had been suggested
by her confessor. She was then at Amiens, and
Varin united her and her companions into a teaching
community, and drew up the rules and constitutions
which they have undeviatingly adhered to ever since.
Indeed it was this very fidelity that gave them the
name of Notre Dame de Namur. For in the absence
of Varin a prominent ecclesiastic attempted to modify
their rule, whereupon the indignant women left Amiens
and emigrated in a body to Namur. That city has
ever since been regarded as their spiritual birthplace.
In the space of twelve years, namely between 1804
and 1812, this quondam paralytic founded fifteen
convents, and made as many as one hundred and
twenty journeys, some of them very long and toilsome,
in the prosecution of her great work for the Church.
Like the Ladies of the Sacred Heart, the Sisters of
Notre Dame de Namur have establishments all over
the world.

Meantime, a very marked difference had displayed
itself in the tone of the various members of the Fathers
of the Faith. Those who had been followers of
Paccanari had no idea whatever of the real nature of
religious life, whereas the disciples of Varin for the

43

most part were spiritual men and eager in the work of
perfection. How noticeable this was, is revealed in
a letter from Bishop Carroll in America. He had
asked for help from the new organization, and four
priests had been promised him, but only one arrived —
an Italian named Zucchi. Whether he lost his way or
not, or fancied he could follow his own guidance, he
went first to Quebec, but was promptly informed by the
government officials there that his presence was
undesirable. He finally reached Maryland, and Carroll
describes him in a letter to Father Plowden in England
as follows: " There is a priest here named Zucchi,
a *Romano di nascità*, a man of narrow understanding,
who does nothing but pine for the arrival of his companions. Meantime he will undertake no work.
From this sample of the new order, I am led to believe
that they are very little instructed in the maxims of
the Institute of our venerable mother, the Society.
Though they profess to have no other rule than ours,
Zucchi seems to know nothing of the structure of our
Society, nor even to have read the *Regulæ Communes*
which our very novices know almost by heart."

The bishop had also heard of the establishment of
one of the communities of women by Father Varin,
and that made him still more suspicious about the
genuineness of the Fathers of the Faith. " In one
point," he writes to Plowden, " they seem to have
departed from St. Ignatius, by engrafting on their
Institution a new order of nuns, which is to be under
their government."

The rupture in the ranks of the Fathers of the
Faith took place in 1803. In the preceding year,
Rozaven and Varin had gone to Rome and were there
confirmed in their suspicions that Paccanari was not
sincere in his protestations about his desire to join
the Jesuits in Russia. They were also shocked at the

lack of religious spirit in the Paccanarist house in
Rome. In the following year, Rozaven again returned
to Rome, and besides being confirmed in his conviction that Paccanari was working for the development
of an independent society, he was informed of certain
charges against the personal character of the man.
Paccanari's explanation of the accusations, far from
convincing Rozaven, only confirmed him in his opinion.
The result was that he obtained a private audience
with the Pope, and was authorized to sever his connection with the Fathers of the Faith.

To his amazement, he found on his return to London,
that his associates had already taken the matter in
hand for themselves and had applied to Father Gruber
in Russia, for admission to the Society. The petition
was granted, not, however to enter corporately but
individually, namely after each one's vocation had
been carefully examined. The application was to be
made to Father Strickland in England, who had been
a member of the old Society. With other candidates
from Holland and Germany, twenty-five new members
passed over to Russia.

It is very distressing to note that Father Charles
de Broglie, who with de Tournély had initiated the
whole movement, was not in this group. He and
three others remained in London as secular priests,
and unfortunately, his relations with a certain number
of refractory Frenchmen led him into the schism
known as La Petite Eglise. He persisted in his rebellion
as late as 1842, when he at last made his submission
to the Church.

Rozaven wrote from Polotsk to Varin, giving him
an account of what had happened to him in Rome,
insisting on the justifiableness of the act, and reminding
him that they had joined the Fathers of the Sacred
Heart, and subsequently the Fathers of the Faith, solely

for the sake of uniting with the Jesuits in Russia. As Paccanari had not only no intention of carrying out that purpose, but was doing everything in his power to prevent it, the duty of allegiance ceased, and so the Pope had decided. Forthwith, Varin, with the approval of all his subjects in France, notified Paccanari that they had severed all connection with his Society. Meantime however, they retained the name of Fathers of the Faith.

But this independence was not satisfactory to Varin. What was he to do? Should he disband his communities which were performing very effective work in France or wait for developments? The Apostolic nuncio at Paris, della Genga, decided that he should continue as he was till more favorable circumstances presented themselves. They had not long to wait. The emperor's uncle, Cardinal Fesch, had thus far protected them, but in 1807 Napoleon publicly and angrily reproached him for this patronage, and on November 1st ordered all the Fathers to report to their respective dioceses within fifteen days, under penalty of being sent to the deadly convict colony of Guiana. Fouché offered several positions of honor to Varin and on his refusal to accept them, drove him out of Paris. By this time, however, Varin was a Jesuit and was following the directions of the venerable Father Clorivière who had been empowered to receive him.

The secession of the Fathers of France and England was quickly imitated by the communities in other parts of Europe. Meanwhile Paccanari's conduct became a public scandal. A canonical process was instituted against him in 1808, and he was condemned to ten years' imprisonment. But when the French took possession of the city in 1809 and opened the prison doors, Paccanari disappeared from view, and no one ever knew what became of him.

While the work of the Fathers of the Faith was progressing in France and elsewhere, the saintly Pignatelli, who had been Angel Guardian of the Spanish Jesuits when they were expelled from their native land, was accomplishing much for the general establishment of the Society. After landing in Italy where the Jesuits were as yet unmolested, he had betaken himself, with the advice of the provincial to Ferrara, and there housed the exiles as best he could. He also established a novitiate in connection with the college which had been handed over to him; but all this was swept away when the Brief of Clement XIV suppressed the entire Society in 1773. Of course, the first thought of Pignatelli after this disaster was to join his brethren in Russia, and with that in view he wrote to Pope Pius VI, who had succeeded Clement XIV, asking him if the Jesuits whom Catherine II had sheltered, really belonged to the Society. The reply delighted him beyond measure, for it told him that he might go to Russia with a safe conscience and put on the habit of the Society. The Jesuits there really belonged to the Society for the Brief of Suppression had never reached that country. The Pontiff also added that he would restore the Society as soon as possible; and if he were not able to do so he would recommend it to his successor.

Pignatelli's joy knew no bounds, and he immediately prepared for his journey to the North, but the Providence of God kept him in Italy, for the Duke of Parma, though a son of Charles III of Spain, had resolved to recall the Jesuits to his Duchy, and for that purpose had written to Catherine II of Russia to ask for three members of the Society to organize the houses. The empress was only too glad to accede to his wish; on February, 1794, three Jesuits arrived in Parma and began their work at Calorno, just when Pius VI was passing through that city on his way to the prisons of France. The opportunity was taken advantage of to ask the august captive for authorization to open a novitiate and he most willingly granted the request. Panizzoni, who was then provincial of Italy, appointed Pignatelli as superior and master of novices. Unfortunately the Duke of Parma died, and the Duchy was taken over by France; however, the Jesuits were not molested for a year and a half, and during this time Pignatelli, who was exercising the office of provincial, succeeded in having the Society restored in Naples and Sicily. This was in 1804. But when Napoleon laid his hands on the whole of the peninsula an order was formulated for the expulsion of the Jesuits. Fortunately its execution was not rigorously enforced and colleges were established in Rome, Tivoli, Sardinia and Orvieto.

Meantime matters were progressing favorably in Russia, so much so that in 1803 Father Angiolini was sent as imperial ambassador to the Pope to solicit alms for the missions. When he appeared in Rome dressed as a Jesuit, he found himself the sensation of the hour. The Sovereign Pontiff received him with effusive affection and granted all that he asked. He remained there as procurator of the Society, and in the following year, was able to communicate to Father Gruber the pleasing news that, at the request of King Ferdinand, the Society had been re-established in the Two Sicilies. Father Pignatelli was made provincial, and as many as 170 of those who had survived after Tanucci had driven them out thirty-seven years previously came from the various places that had sheltered them during the Suppression to resume their former way of life. Several of them who had been made bishops asked the Pope for permission to return but all were refused except two, Avogado of Verona and Bencassa of Carpi.

The whole kingdom welcomed back the exiles with enthusiasm. The King came in person to open the Church which he had persistently refused to enter ever since the expulsion; at the first Mass he and the entire royal family received Holy Communion. He also gave the Fathers their former college, and endowed it with an annual income of forty thousand ducats. This example encouraged others; colleges were founded everywhere, and the number of applicants was so great that the conditions for admission to the Society had to be made as rigorous as possible. Unfortunately this happy condition of affairs did not last long, for in March 1806, Joseph Bonaparte replaced Ferdinand IV on the throne of Naples, and the Jesuits again took the road of exile. The Pope offered them a refuge in Rome, and when they protested that such a course would draw on him the wrath of Napoleon, he replied that they were suffering for the Church, and that he must receive them just as Clement XIII had done when they were exiled from Naples.

While these events were occurring in Italy and France, an opportunity was presented to the Jesuits of Russia to revive their old missions in China. Unfortunately it was frustrated. The story as told in the " Woodstock Letters " (IV, 113) is a veritable Odyssey, and is particularly interesting to Americans, for the reason that the principal personage concerned in what proved to be a very heroic enterprise became subsequently the President of Georgetown College: John Anthony Grassi.

Grassi was a native of Bergamo, and in 1799 entered the novitiate established by Father Pignatelli at Calorno. He thus received a genuine Jesuit training and escaped the influence of the establishments which Paccanari was inaugurating in Italy just as that time. From Calorno he was sent to Russia, and was made Rector of the College of Nobles which was dependent upon the establishment at Polotsk. Meanwhile, he was preparing himself for the missions of Astrakhan, and was already deep in the study of Armenian when the Chinese matter was brought to the attention of Father Gruber by a letter from a member of the old Society, who had contrived to remain in China ever since the Suppression. He was Louis Poirot. It appears that his ability as a musician had charmed the emperor, and thus enabled him to continue his evangelical work in the Celestial Empire.

Hearing of the establishment in Russia, he bethought himself of having the Jesuits resume their old place in China, evidently unaware that the Brief of 1801 expressly declared that the Society had been established "only within the limits of the Russian Empire." But not knowing this he availed himself of the return of a Lazarist missionary and wrote two letters; one to the Pope and another to the Father General in which he said: "I am eighty years of age and there is only one thing I care to live for. It is to see the Jesuits return to China." His letter to the General ends with a request to be permitted to renew his vows, "so as to die a true son of the Society of Jesus." Between the time he wrote this letter and its arrival in Europe, the limitation of the approval of the Society to Russia had been withdrawn, and Father Gruber immediately set about granting the venerable and faithful old man's request. Happily a solemn legation was just then to leave St. Petersburg for China, and the ambassador, Golowkin, was urged to take some Jesuits in his suite. The offer was gladly accepted, but it was decided that it should be better for the priests to go by the usual sea route than to accompany the embassy overland.

Father Grassi was considered to be the most available man in the circumstances, and he was told merely that he was to go to a distant post, and that his companions were to be Father Korsack, a native of Russia and a German lay-brother named Surmer, who happened to be a sculptor. On January 14, 1805, they left Polotsk, and travelling day and night, arrived at St. Petersburg on January 19. Only then were they informed that their destination was Pekin. On February 2 they started on sleds for Sweden. At the end of three days, they were all sick and exhausted, but kept bravely on till they reached the frontier where they found shelter in a little inn. Fortunately a physician happened to be there and he helped them over their ailments, so that in ten days they were able to resume their journey. They then started for Abo, the capital of Finland and from there crossed the frozen sea at top speed, till they reached the Island of Aland. On March 20 they traversed the Gulf of Bothnia in a mail packet, and landed safely on the shore of Sweden. On March 22 they were in Stockholm, but the Abbé Morrette, the superior of the Swedish mission to whom they were to present themselves was dead. An Italian gentleman, happily named Fortuna, who was Russian Consul at that place, took care of them and presented them to Alopeus, the Russian minister.

Alopeus dissuaded them from going to England as they had been directed, and suggested Copenhagen as the proper place to embark. Arrived there, they were informed that there was a ship out in the harbor, waiting to sail for Canton, but that the captain refused to take any passengers; whereupon they determined to follow their original instructions, and after a stormy voyage arrived at Gravesend on May 22. From there they went to London where they met Father Kohlmann.

The same misfortune attended them at London for although Lord Macartney, who had known the Jesuits in Pekin, did everything to secure them a passage to China, he failed utterly. Then acting under new instructions they set sail for Lisbon on July 29, but were driven by contrary winds to Cork in Ireland, where of course they met with the heartiest welcome from everyone especially from the bishop. They finally landed at Lisbon on September 28; passing as they entered the harbor, the gloomy fortress of St. Julian where so many of their brethren had been imprisoned by Pombal. They were befriended there by an Irish merchant named Stack, and also by the rector of the Irish College; but were finally lodged in an old dismantled monastery where they slept on the floor. Then, in the dress of secular priests, they presented themselves to the Apostolic nuncio who was very friendly to the Society, and who would have been a Jesuit himself had it not been for the opposition of his family. He warned them to be very cautious in what they did and said, and informed them that there were very few ships clearing for Macao.

While at Lisbon, they devoted themselves to the study of mathematics and astronomy, and after two months their friend, the Irish merchant, came to tell them that there was a ship about to sail. They hastened to advise the nuncio of it, but were then told that they could not go to China, without the Pope's permission, for the reason that the Society had been suppressed in that country. They also learned from a missionary priest of the Propaganda, that Rome was very much excited about their proposed journey; Father Angiolini who was then in Rome, wrote to the same effect. It was then March 1806. Not knowing what to do, they began a course of astronomy at the observatory of Coimbra, but unfortunately, the founder of the observatory, an ex-Jesuit, José Monteiro da Rocha, was very hostile to the Society; and even

went so far in his opposition that in a public oration
before the university he had praised Pombal extravagantly for having abolished the Order.

The wanderers remained at Coimbra for two months,
and then returned to Lisbon. On their way to the
capital they saw the unburied coffin of Pombal. On
June 4 a letter came from England which revived their
hopes, especially as it was followed by pecuniary
help from the czar; but soon after that, they received
news of the Russian embassy's failure to reach China,
and they also heard that the country of their dreams
was in the wildest excitement because a missionary
there had sent a map of the empire to Europe. The
imprudent cartographer was imprisoned and an imperial
edict announced that vengeance was to be taken on all
Christians in the empire. Who the poor man was we
do not know. It could not have been old Father
Poirot. He was merely a musician and not a maker
of maps. On December 2, 1806, the nuncio at Lisbon
was informed that the Pope quite approved of the
project of the Fathers and had urged his officials to
assist them to carry it out. The reason of this change
of mind on the part of the Holy Father is explained by
the fact that he was anxious to propitiate Russia.
Nevertheless, the nuncio advised them to wait for
further developments.

Another year went by, during which they continued
their studies and made some conversions. They had
also the gratification of being introduced to the Marchioness of Tavora, the sole survivor of the illustrious
house which Pombal had so ruthlessly persecuted.
Finally they were recalled to England, which they
reached on November 16 1807, after a month of
great hardship at sea. They were welcomed at
Liverpool by the American Jesuit, Father Sewall, who
was at that time sheltering four other members of the

Society in his house.   When the little community met
at table, they represented seven different nationalities
— American, English, French, German, Italian, Polish
and Belgian. Father Grassi remained in England,
chiefly at Stonyhurst until 1810, and on August 27
of that year set sail from Liverpool for Baltimore,
where he arrived on October 20.   He had thus passed
three years in England where community life had been
carried on almost without interruption from the time
of the old Society.   For although the Brief of Suppression had explicitly forbidden it, nevertheless
Clement's successor had authorized it as early as
1778, and had permitted the pronouncement of the
religious vows in 1803,— a privilege that was extended
to the Kingdom of Naples in 1804.   Arriving in the
United States, Father Grassi found that there had been
virtually no interruption of the Society's traditions in
this part of the world.   The Fathers had been in
close communication with Russia as early as 1805 and
were being continually reinforced by members of
the Society in Europe.   When the Bull of Re-establishment was issued there were nineteen Jesuits in the
United States.

CHAPTER XXIII

THE RESTORATION

Tragic death of Father Gruber — Fall of Napoleon — Release of the Pope — The Society Re-established — Opening of Colleges — Clorivière — Welcome of the Society in Spain — Repulsed in Portugal — Opposed by Catholics in England — Announced in America — Carroll — Fenwick — Neale.

IN 1805 the Society met with a disaster which in the circumstances seemed almost irreparable. During the night of March 25–26 its distinguished General, Father Gruber, was burned to death in his residence at St. Petersburg. His friend, the Count de Maistre, who was still ambassador at the Russian Court, hurried to the scene in time to receive his dying blessing and farewell. Gruber's influence was so great in Russia that it was feared no one could replace him. His successor was Thaddeus Brzozowski, who was elected on the second of September. Splendid plans, especially in the field of education had been made by Gruber and had been warmly approved of by the emperor, but they had to be set aside for more pressing needs. Napoleon was just then devastating Europe, and the very existence of Russia as well as of other nations was at stake. It is true that the empire was at peace with France, but at the rupture of the treaty of Amiens, Napoleon complained of the political measures of the cabinet of St. Petersburg, and the ambassadors of both countries received their papers of dismissal. The result was that a coalition of Russia, England, Austria and Sweden was formed to thwart the ambitions of Napoleon who was at that time laying claim to the whole Italian Peninsula. War was declared in 1805.

Austerlitz compelled the empire to accept Napoleon's
terms, but Prussia and Russia continued the fight
until the disasters at Jena, Eylau and Friedland.
Then the Emperor of Russia and the King of Prussia
met Napoleon on a raft anchored out in the Niemen,
where on the eighth and ninth of July peace was
agreed to.

At Erfurt, in 1808 Napoleon and Alexander drew
up what was known as the " Continental System," in
accordance with which, all English merchandise was
to be excluded from every continental nation. This
was followed by a defensive alliance of Austria and
England, and as Austria was Russia's ally, Alexander
again entered the fight against Napoleon, but the
victory of Wagram and the marriage of Napoleon
with the Austrian archduchess, Maria Louisa, changed
the aspect of affairs and the " Continental System "
was restored, but in so modified a form that war
broke out again, and in 1812 Napoleon began his
Russian Campaign. The battle of Smolensk opened
the way for him to Moscow, but when the conqueror
arrived he found the city in flames. He mistook it
for an act of surrender and Alexander purposely
detained him, discussing the terms of peace until
the winter set in. Then the conqueror decided to
return, but it was too late. On February 22, 1813,
Alexander sent out a call to all the kings of Europe to
unite against Napoleon and they eagerly responded.
He beat them at Lutzen and Bautzen, and in Silesia,
but in spite of his success he had to continue his retreat.
He won again at Dresden and Leipzig, but they pursued
him relentlessly, until at last the Rhine was reached.
Peace was offered in December 1813, but when its
acceptance was delayed, the Allies entered France, and
on March 3, 1814, laid siege to Paris. The city
surrendered on the following day.

Meantime Napoleon had released Pius VII from
captivity, not voluntarily, but as a political measure,
to propitiate the anger of the Catholics of the world,
who were beginning to open their eyes to the extent
of the outrage. Eighteen months previously he had
dragged the venerable Pontiff from Rome and hurried
him night and day over the Alps, absolutely heedless
of the age and infirmity of his victim, until at last the
Pope entered Fontainebleau a prisoner. According to
Pacca, it was a jail more than a palace. There by
dint of threats and brutal treatment Napoleon so
wore out the strength of the aged man that a Concordat
was signed which sacrificed some of the most sacred
rights of the Holy See. It was cancelled, indeed,
subsequently, but it almost drove the Pope insane
when he realized the full import of what he had been
driven to concede. "I shall die like Clement XIV,"
he exclaimed. But his jailer was heartless and it
was only after a year and a half of imprisonment, and
when the Allies were actually entering France as
conquerors, that he made up his mind to send the
Pontiff back to Rome. Had he done it with less
brutality he might even then, have succeeded in his
calculations, but only one attendant was sent to
accompany the prisoner. The cardinals were purposely
dismissed some days later in batches, and ordered to
go by different routes so as to prevent any popular
demonstration on the way.

Pacca overtook the Pope at Sinigaglia on May 12,
and on May 24, after a brief stay at Ancona, Loreto,
Macerata, Tolentino, Foligno, Spoleto, Terni and
Nepi, entered Rome. What happened at these places
deserves to be recorded, as it shows that the Faith
was not only not dead but had grown more intense
because of the outrages of which the Vicar of Christ
had been the object. At Ancona, for instance, Artaud

tell us, "he was received with transports of delight. The sailors in the harbor flocked around his carriage, unhitched the horses and with silken ropes of yellow and red drew it triumphantly through the city, while the cannon thundered from the ramparts, and the bells of every tower proclaimed the joy of the people. From the top of a triumphal arch the Pope gave his benediction to the kneeling multitudes, and then blessed the wide Adriatic. From there he went to the palace of the Picis for a brief rest. The next day he crowned the statue of the Blessed Virgin, Queen of All Saints, and then set out for Osimo escorted as far as Loreto by a scarlet-robed guard of honor. Entering Rome by the Porto del Popolo, his carriage was drawn by young noblemen, and he was met by a procession of little orphan children chosen from the Protectory of Providence. They were all clothed in white robes and in their hands they held golden palm branches which they waved above their heads, while their young voices filled the air with jubilant songs. When the crowd became too dense, the little ones knelt before him to present their emblems of peace, which he affectionately received, while tears rolled down his cheeks. At last, the city gates were reached and he proceeded along the streets lined on either side by kneeling multitudes who were overcome with joy at his return."

Almost the first official act of the Pope was to re-establish the Society. How that came about may be best told in the words of his faithful servant, Cardinal Pacca.

"While we were in prison together," says the illustrious cardinal, "I had never tired of adroitly leading the conversation up to this important matter, so as to furnish His Holiness with useful information if ever it happened that he would again ascend the

Chair of St. Peter. In those interviews he never
failed to manifest the greatest esteem and affection
for the Society. The situation in which we found
ourselves was remarkable, and it shows the admirable
Providence of God with regard to this celebrated
Society.

"When Barnabo Chiaramonte was a young Benedictine, he had teachers and professors in theology
whose sentiments were anti-Jesuit, and they filled his
mind with theological views that were most opposed
to those maintained by the Society. Everyone knows
what profound impressions early teaching leaves in the
mind; and, as for myself, I also had been inspired
from my youth with sentiments of aversion, hatred
and, I might say, a sort of fanaticism against the
illustrious Society. It will suffice to add that my
teachers put in my hands and ordered me to make
extracts from the famous ' Lettres Provinciales,' first
in French and then in Latin, with the notes of Wendrok
(Nicole) which were still more abominable than the
text. I read also in perfect good faith, ' La morale
pratique des Jésuites,' and other works of that kind
and accepted them as true.

"Who then would have believed that the first act
of the Benedictine Chiaramonte who had become
Pope, immediately after emerging from the frightful
tempest of the Revolution, and in the face of so many
sects, then raging against the Jesuits, should be the
re-establishment of the Society throughout the Catholic
world; or that I should have prepared the way for this
new triumph; or, finally, that I should have been
appointed by the Pope to carry out those orders
which were so acceptable to me and conferred on me
so much honor? For both the Pope and myself,
this act was a source of supreme satisfaction. I was
present in Rome on the two memorable occasions of

44

the Suppression and the Re-establishment of the
Society, and I can testify to the different impressions
they produced.   Thus, on August 17, 1773, the day
of the publication of the Brief ' Dominus ac Redemptor,' one saw surprise and sorrow painted on
every face; whereas on August 7, 1814, the day of the
resurrection of the Society, Rome rang with accla-
mations of satisfaction and approval.   The people
followed the Pope from the Quirinal to the Gesù, where
the Bull was to be read, and made the return of the
Pope to his palace a triumphal procession.

" I have deemed it proper to enter into these details,
in order to profit by the occasion of these ' Memoirs '
to make a solemn retraction of the imprudent utterances
that I may have made in my youth against a Society
which has merited so well from the Church of Jesus
Christ."

Some of the cardinals were opposed to the Restoration, out of fear of the commotion it was sure to excite.
Even Consalvi would have preferred to see it deferred
for a few months, but it is a calumny to say that he
was antagonistic to the Society.   As early as February
13, 1799, he wrote as follows to Albani, the legate at
Vienna: " You do me a great, a very great wrong,
if you ever doubted that I was not convinced that the
Jesuits should be brought back again.   I call God
to witness that I always thought so, although I was
educated in colleges which were not favorable to them,
but I did not on that account think ill of them.   In
those days, however, I did say one thing of them, viz.,
that although I was fully persuaded of their importance, I declared it to be fanatical to pretend that the
Church could not stand without them, since it had
existed for centuries before they existed, but when
I saw the French Revolution and when I got to really
understand Jansenism, I then thought and think now

that without the Jesuits the Church is in very bad straits. If it depended on me, I would restore the Society to-morrow. I have frequently told that to the Pope, who has always desired their restoration, but fear of the governments that were opposed to it made him put it off, though he always cherished the hope that he could bring it about. He would do it if he lived; and if he were unable he would advise his successor to do it as quickly as possible. The rulers of the nations will find out that the Jesuits will make their thrones secure by bringing back religion."

Of course, the thought of restoring the Society did not originate with Pius VII and Pacca. Pius VI had repeatedly declared that he would have brought it about had it been at all feasible. Even after the return of Pius VII to Rome, some of the most devoted friends of the Jesuits, as we have seen, thought that the difficulties were insuperable; but the Pope judged otherwise, and hence the affection with which the Society will ever regard him. Indeed, he had already gone far in preparing the way for it. He had approved of the Society in Russia, England, America and Italy. He had permitted Father Fonteyne to establish communities in the Netherlands; Father Clorivière was doing the same thing in France with his approval so that everyone was expecting the complete restoration to take place at any moment. The Father provincial of Italy had announced that the Bull would be issued before Easter Sunday 1814, although some of his brethren laughed at him and thought he was losing his mind. This did not disturb him, however, and in June, 1814 he knelt before the Sovereign Pontiff and in the name of Father General Brzozowski presented the following petition:

"We, the Father General and the Fathers who, by the benignity of the Holy See, reside in Russia and in Sicily, desiring to meet the wishes of certain princes who ask our assistance in the education of the youth of their realms, humbly implore Your Highness to remove the difficulty created by the Brief of Clement XIV and to restore the Society to its former state in accordance with the last confirmation of it by Clement XIII, so that in whatever country we may be asked for we may give to the princes above referred to whatever help the needs of their several countries may demand."

On June 17, Pius VII let it be known that he was more than eager to satisfy the wish of the petitioners; and a few days afterwards, when Cardinal Pacca said to him, " Holy Father, do you not think we ought to do what we so often spoke of? " he replied, " Yes; we can re-establish the Society of Jesus on the next feast of Saint Ignatius." Even Pacca was taken aback by the early date that was fixed upon, for there was not a month and a half to prepare for it.   The outside world was even still more surprised, and the enemies of the Society strove to belittle the Pontifical act by starting the report that it was not the old Society that was going to be brought back to life; only a new congregation was to be approved.   That idea took possession of the public mind to such an extent that Father de Zúñiga, the provincial of Sicily, brought it to the attention of the Sovereign Pontiff.   " On the contrary," said Pius, " it is the same Society which existed for two hundred years, although now circumscribed by some restrictions, because there will be no mention of privileges in the Bull, and there are other things which will have to be inserted, on account of circumstances in France and Spain and the needs of certain bishops."

The chief difficulty was in draughting the document. The time was very short and some of the cardinals were of opinion that the courts of Europe should be

consulted about it. But Pacca and the Pope both
swept aside that suggestion. They had had a sad
experience with the courts of Europe. Hence Cardinal
Litta, who when ablegate at St. Petersburg had asked
for the confirmation of the Society in Russia, was
chosen to draw up the Bull. He addressed himself
to the task with delight and presented to the Pope a
splendid defense of the Society which he declared
" had been guilty of no fault; " but when he added that
" the suppression had been granted by Clement XIV
unwillingly," and that " it was to be ascribed to the
wicked devices, the atrocious calumnies, and the impious
principles of false political science and philosophy
which, by the destruction of the Order, foolishly
imagined that the Church could be destroyed," the
language was found to be too strong and even Cardinal
di Pietro, who was a staunch friend of the Society,
protested vehemently against it. Indeed, di Pietro
went so far as to say that certain changes should be
made in the Institute before the Bull was issued.
Other members of the Sacred College were of the same
opinion, but did not express themselves so openly.
They were afraid to do so, because the popular joy was
so pronounced at the news of the proposed restoration
that anyone opposing it would run the risk of being
classed as an enemy.

As a compromise, the Pope set aside the Bull drawn
up by Litta and also the corrections by di Pietro, and
entrusted the work to Pacca. It was his draught that
was finally published. It makes no mention of any
change or mutilation of the Institute; neither does it
name nor abrogate any privilege; it is not addressed
to any particular State, as some wished, but to the
whole world; it does not reprehend anyone, nor does it
subject to the Propaganda the foreign missions which
the Society might undertake. Some of the " black

cardinals " such as Brancadoro, Gabrielli, Litta, Mattei and even di Pietro, asked for greater praise in it for the Society, while others wanted it just as Pacca had written it; Mattei objected to the expression " primitive rule of St. Ignatius," because the words would seem to imply that the Society had adopted another at some time in its history and he also wanted the reason of the restoration to be explicitly stated, namely: " the Pope's deep conviction of the Society's usefulness to the Church." His reason was that many had asked for it; but only some of his suggestions were accepted.

These details prevented the publication of the Bull on July 31, hence August 7, the octave of the feast was chosen.

A few extracts from it will suffice. Its title is " The Constitution by which the Society of Jesus is restored in its pristine state throughout the Catholic World." The preamble first refers to the Brief " Catholicæ fidei " which confirmed the Society in Russia and also to the " Per alias " which restored it in the Two Sicilies. It then says: " The Catholic world unanimously demands the re-establishment of the Society of Jesus. Every day we are receiving most urgent petitions from our venerable brothers, the archbishops and bishops of the Church, and from other most distinguished personages to that effect. The dispersion of the very stones of the sanctuary in the calamitous days which we shudder even to recall, namely the destruction of a religious order which was the glory and the support of the Catholic Church, now makes it imperative that we should respond to the general and just desire for its restoration. In truth, we should consider ourselves culpable of a grievous sin in the sight of God, if, in the great dangers to which the Christian commonwealth is exposed, we should fail to avail ourselves of the help which the special Providence of God now puts at our disposal; if, seated as we are in the Barque of Peter, we should refuse the aid of the tried and vigorous mariners who offer themselves to face the surges of the sea which threaten us with shipwreck and death. Therefore, we have resolved to do to-day what we have longed from the first days of our Pontificate to be able to accomplish, and, hence, after having in fervent prayer implored the Divine assistance, and having sought the advice and counsel of a great number of our venerable brothers, the cardinals of the Holy Roman Church, we have decreed, with certain knowledge, and in virtue of the plenitude of our Apostolic power, that all the concessions and faculties accorded by us to the Russian empire and the Two Sicilies, in particular, shall henceforward be extended in perpetuity to all other countries of the world.

" Wherefore, we concede and accord to our well-beloved son Thaddeus Brzozowski, at present the General of the Society of Jesus, and to the other members of the Society delegated by him, all proper and necessary powers to receive and welcome freely and lawfully all those who desire to be admitted into the Regular Order of the Society of Jesus, and that, under the authority of the General at the time such persons may be received into and assigned to one or many houses, or colleges or provinces, as needs be, wherein they shall follow the rule prescribed by St. Ignatius Loyola, which was confirmed by the Constitutions of Paul III. Over and above this, we declare them to possess and we hereby concede to them the power of devoting themselves freely and lawfully to educate youth in the principles of the Catholic religion; to train them in morality; to direct colleges and seminaries; to preach and to administer the sacraments in their place of residence, with the consent and approbation of the ordinary. We take under our protection and under our immediate obedience as well as that of the Apostolic See, all the colleges, all the houses, all the provinces, all the members of the Order, and all those who are gathered in their establishments, reserving nevertheless to Ourself, and to the Roman Pontiffs, our successors, to decree and prescribe whatever we consider it our duty to decree and prescribe as necessary to consolidate more and more the same Society, in order to render it stronger and to purge it from abuse, if ever (which may God avert) any may be found therein. And we exhort with our whole heart, in the name of the Lord, all superiors, rectors and provincials, as well as all the members and pupils of this re-established Order to show themselves in all places, faithful imitators of their Father. Let them observe with exactness the rule prescribed for them by their great founder, and let them follow with ever increasing zeal the useful admonitions and counsels which he has left for the guidance of his sons.

" Finally we earnestly recommend in the Lord this Society and its members to the illustrious kings and princes and temporal lords of the various nations, as well as to our venerable brothers, the archbishops and bishops and whosoever may occupy positions of honor and authority. We exhort them, nay we conjure them, not only not to suffer that these religious should be molested, in any manner, but to see that they should be treated with the benevolence and the charity which they deserve."

A difficulty now arose as to the person into whose hands the Bull was to be delivered. It was impossible for the General to be present, for he was unable to obtain permission of the emperor to take part in what concerned him more than any other member of

the Society — a condition of things which made it
evident that the residence of the next General had to
be in some other place than Russia. That, of course,
the czar would never permit and the expulsion of the
Society from Russia was from that moment a foregone conclusion. Angiolini, who was rather conspicuous in Rome at that time, possibly because he had
some years before arrived in the city as an envoy
from the Russian court, was first thought of. In
fact the Pope had already named him, but Albers
in his " Liber sæcularis " does not hesitate to say that
Angiolini sought the honor, and had succeeded in
enlisting the interest of Cardinal Litta in his behalf.
But he was known to be a man of impetuous character,
eager to be concerned in every matter of importance
and decidedly headstrong. The provincial was chosen,
therefore, to represent the General, and Angiolini was
consoled by being made consultor of the Congregation
of Rites. The difficulty seems almost childish, for
whatever prominence Angiolini possessed, it was
purely personal whereas that of Father Panizzoni was
official. It may be, however, that Angiolini's friendship for Rezzi, who attempted to wreck the Society
at the first congregation, had laid him open to suspicion.

At last the great day arrived. It was Sunday; and
all Rome was seen flocking to the Gesù. As early
as eight o'clock in the morning, as many as one hundred Jesuits along with the College of Cardinals were
waiting to receive the Pope. He arrived at last and
said Mass at the high altar. He then proceeded to
the chapel of the Sodality which was crowded with
bishops and most of the notables then in the city.
Among them were Queen Marie Louise of Bourbon, the
wife of Charles IV of Spain, with her niece and three
sons. It was Spain's reparation for the wrong it had
done the Society. Behind the cardinals, in a double

row were the Spanish, Italian and Portuguese Jesuits;
the youngest of whom was sixty years of age, while
there were others still who had reached eighty-six.
It is even asserted that there was present one old
Jesuit who was one hundred and twenty-six years old.
His name was Albert Montalto and he had been in
the Society for one hundred and eight years. He was
born in 1689, was admitted to the novitiate in 1706
and hence was sixty-four years old at the time of
the Suppression.

This beautiful fairy story is vouched for by Crétineau-Joly (V, 436), but Albers, in his " Liber sæcularis,"
tells us that there is no such name as Montalto or
Montaud in the Catalogue of 1773 or in Vivier's
" Catalogus Mortuorum Societatis Jesu."

When the Pope had taken his seat upon the throne,
he handed the Bull to Belisario Cristaldi, who in a
clear voice, amid the applause of all in the chapel,
read the consoling words which the Jesuits listened
to with tears and sobs. Then one by one some
hobbling up with the help of their canes, others leaning on the arms of the distinguished men present,
knelt at the feet of the Pontiff, who spoke to them all
with the deepest and tenderest affection. For them
it was the happiest day of their lives and the old men
among them could now sing their " Nunc dimittis."

Pacca then handed to Panizzoni a paper appointing
him superior of the Roman house, until the nomination arrived from Father General. The professed
house, the novitiate of Sant' Andrea and other properties
were also made over to the Society with a monthly
payment of five hundred scudi.

On entering the Gesù, the Fathers found the house
almost in the same condition as when Father Ricci
and his assistants left it in 1773, to go to the dungeons
of Sant' Angelo. It was occupied by a community

of priests, most of them former Jesuits, who had continued to serve the adjoining church, which, though despoiled of most of its treasures, still possessed the remains of St. Ignatius. Two years later, the novitiate of Sant' Andrea was so crowded that a second one had to be opened at Reggio. Among the novices at that place was Charles Emanuel, King of Sardinia, who had resigned his crown to enter the Society. He died there in 1819. In 1815 the Jesuits had colleges in Orvieto, Viterbo, Tivoli, Urbino, Ferentino, and Galloro, Modena, Forlì, Genoa, Turin, Novarra, and a little later, Nice. In Parma and Naples, they had been at work prior to 1814.

Just eight days before these happenings in Rome, an aged Jesuit in Paris saw assembled around him ten distinguished men whom he had admitted to the Society. It was July 31, the feast of St. Ignatius, and the place of the meeting was full of tragic memories. It was the chapel of the Abbaye des Carmes, where, in the general massacre of priests which took place there in 1792, twelve Jesuits had been murdered. In the old man's mind there were still other memories. Fifty-two years before, he and his religious brethren had been driven like criminals from their native land. Forty years had passed since the whole Society had been suppressed. He had witnessed all the horrors of the French Revolution, and now as he was nearing eternity — he was then eighty-five — he saw at his feet a group of men some of whom had already gained distinction in the world, but who at that moment, had only one ambition, that of being admitted into the Society of Jesus, which they hoped would be one day re-established. They never dreamed that seven days after they had thus met at the Abbaye to celebrate the feast of St. Ignatius, Pius VII who had returned from his captivity in France would, by the

Bull "Sollicitudo omnium ecclesiarum," solemnly re-establish the Society throughout the world.

The old priest was Pierre-Joseph Picot de Clorivière. He was born at St. Malo, June 29, 1735 and had entered the Society on August 14, 1756. He was teaching a class at Compiègne when Choiseul drove the Society out of the country, but though he was only a scholastic, it had no effect on his vocation. He attached himself to the English province, and after finishing his course of theology at Liège in Belgium, was professed of the four vows about a month after Clement XIV had issued his Brief of Suppression. The decree had not yet been promulgated in the Netherlands. Instead of going to England as one would expect, he returned to his native country as a secular priest, and we find him in charge of a parish at Paramé from 1775 to 1779. He was also the director of the diocesan College of Dinan, where he remained up to the time of the Revolution. Meantime, he was writing pious books and founding two religious congregations, one for priests, the other for pious women in the world. The former went out of existence in 1825. The latter still flourishes.

Having refused to take the constitutional oath, he was debarred from all ecclesiastical functions, and began to think of offering himself to his old friend and classmate at Liège, Bishop Carroll, to work on the Maryland missions; but one thing or another prevented him from carrying out his purpose, though on the other hand it is surprising that he could make up his mind to remain in France. His brother had been guillotined in 1793; his niece met the same fate later; his sister, a Visitation nun, was put in prison and escaped death only by Robespierre's fall from power; several of his spiritual followers had perished in the storm, but he contrived to escape until 1801, when, owing to his relationship with Limoellan, who was implicated in the conspiracy to kill the First Consul, he was lodged in jail. He was then sixty-nine years old.

During his seven years of imprisonment, he wrote voluminous commentaries on the Bible, chiefly the Apocalypse. He also devoted himself to the spiritual improvement of his fellow-prisoners, one of whom, a Swiss Calvinist named Christin, became a Catholic. As Christin had been an attaché of the Russian embassy he posted off to Russia when he was liberated in 1805, taking with him a letter from Clorivière to the General of the Society, asking permission for the writer to renew his profession and to enter the Russian province. Of course, both requests were granted. When he was finally discharged from custody in 1809, Clorivière wrote again to Russia to inform the General that Bishop Carroll wanted to have him go out to Maryland as master of novices. As for himself though he was seventy-five years of age, he was quite ready to accede to the bishop's request. The General's decision, however, was that it would be better to remain in France.

Meantime, Father Varin, the superior of the Fathers of the Faith, had convoked the members of his community to consider how they could carry out the original purpose of their organization, namely: to unite with the Jesuits of Russia, but no progress had been made up to 1814. In his perplexity, he consulted Mgr. della Genga who was afterwards Leo XII, and also Father Clorivière. But to his dismay, both of them told him to leave the matter in *statu quo*. This was all the more disconcerting, because he had just heard that Father Fonteyne, who was at Amsterdam, had already received several Fathers of the Faith. Whereupon he posted off to Holland, and was told that both della

Genga and Clorivière were wrong in their decision.
To remove every doubt he was advised to write
immediately to Russia, or better yet to go there in
person. He determined to do both. At the beginning
of June 1814, he returned to France to tell his friends
the result of his conference with Father Fonteyne,
but during his absence Clorivière had been commissioned by Father Brzozowski to do in France what
Fonteyne had been doing in Holland. That settled
everything, and on July 19, 1814, Fathers Varin,
Boissard, Roger and Jennesseaux were admitted
to the novitiate; and a few days later, Dumouchel,
Bequet, Ronsin, Coulon, Loriquet, with a lay brother
followed their example. On the 31st, St. Ignatius'
Day, they all met at the Abbaye to entreat the Founder
of the Society to bless this inauguration of the province
of France.

In virtue of his appointment Father Clorivière
found that he had now to take care of seventy novices,
most of whom were former Fathers of the Faith;
in this rapidly assembled throng it was impossible
to carry out the whole scheme of a novitiate training
in all its details. Indeed, the only " experiment "
given to the newcomers was the thirty-days retreat,
and that, the venerable old superior undertook himself. Perhaps it was age that made him talkative,
perhaps it was over-flowing joy, for he not only carried
out the whole programme but overdid it, and far
from explaining the points, he talked at each meditation during what the French call " five quarters of an
hour." But grace supplied what was lost by this
prolixity, and the community was on fire with zeal
when the Exercises were ended. How soon they
received the news of what happened on August 7,
in Rome, we do not know. But there were no happier
men in the world than they when the glad tidings came;

and they continued to be so even if Louis XVIII did not deign or was afraid to pay any attention to the Bull, and warned the Jesuits and their friends to make no demonstration. The Society was restored and that made them indifferent to anything else.

In Spain, a formal decree dated May 25, 1825, proclaimed the re-establishment of the Society, and when Father de Zúñiga arrived at Madrid to re-organize the Spanish province, he was met at the gate of the city by a long procession of Dominicans, Franciscans, and the members of other religious orders to welcome him. Subsequently, as many as one hundred and fifteen former Jesuits returned to their native land from the various countries of Europe where they had been laboring, and began to reconstruct their old establishments. Many of these old heroes were over eighty years of age. Loyola, Oñate and Manresa greeted them with delight, and forty-six cities sent petitions for colleges. Meanwhile, novitiates were established at Loyola, Manresa and Seville.

Portugal not only did not admit them, but issued a furious decree against the Bull. Not till fifteen years later did the Jesuits enter that country, and then their first work was to inter the yet unburied remains of their arch-enemy Pombal and to admit four of his great-grandsons into one of their colleges. Brazil, Portugal's dependency, imitated the bitterness of the mother country. The Emperor of Austria was favorable, but the spirit fostered among the people by his predecessor, Joseph, was still rampant and prevented the introduction of the Society into his domains, But, on the whole, the act of the Pope was acclaimed everywhere throughout the wold. So Pacca wrote to Consalvi.

Of course there was an uproar in non-Catholic countries. In England, even some Catholics were in arms against the Bull. One individual, writing in the " Catholic Directory " of 1815, considered it to be " the downfall of the Catholic religion." A congress in which a number of Englishmen participated was held a few years later at Aix-la-Chapelle to protest against the re-establishment of the Order. Fortunately it evoked a letter from the old Admiral Earl St. Vincent which runs as follows: " I have heard with indignation that Sir J. C. Hippisley, a member of Parliament, is gone to the Congress. I therefore beseech you to cause this letter to be laid before his Holiness the Pope as a record of my opinion that we are not only obliged to that Order for the most useful discoveries of every description, but that they are now necessary for the education of Catholic youth throughout the civilized world." With the exception of John Milner, all the vicars Apostolic of England were strongly opposed to the restitution of the Society in that country.

The United States was at war with England just then, and it happened that seventeen days before the Bull was issued Father Grassi and his fellow-Jesuits were witnessing from the windows of Georgetown College the bombardment of Washington by the British fleet. They saw the city in flames, and fully expected that the college would be taken by the enemy, but to their great delight they saw the forty ships on the following morning hoist their anchors and, one by one, drop down the Potomac. They did not, of course, know what was going on in Rome, but as soon as the news of the re-establishment arrived in America, Father Fenwick, the future Bishop of Boston, who was then working in St. Peter's Church, New York, wrote about it to Father Grassi, who was President of Georgetown. The letter is dated December 21, 1814 and runs as follows:

" Rev. and Dear Father,

Te Deum Laudamus, Te Dominum confitemur!
The Society of Jesus is then re-established! That
long-insulted Society! The Society which has been
denounced as the corrupter of youth, the inculcator
of unsound, unchristian and lax morality! That
Society which has been degraded by the Church
itself, rejected by her ministers, outlawed by her kings
and insulted by her laity! Restored throughout the
world and restored by a public Bull of the Sovereign
Pontiff! Hitherto cooped up in a small corner of
the world, and not allowed to extend herself, lest the
nations of the earth, the favorites of heaven, should
inhale the poison of her pestiferous breath, she is now
called forth, as the only plank left for the salvation of
a shipwrecked *philosophered* world; the only restorer of
ecclesiastical discipline and sound morality; the only
dependence of Christianity for the renewal of correct
principles and the diffusion of piety! It is then so.
What a triumph! How glorious to the Society! How
confounding to the enemies! *Gaudeamus in Domino,
diem festum celebrantes!* If any man will say after
that, that God is not a friend of the Society, I shall
pronounce him without hesitation a liar.

" I embrace, dear Sir, the first leisure moments after
the receipt of your letter, to forward you my congratulations on the great and glorious tidings you have
recently received from Europe — tidings which should
exhilarate the heart of every true friend of Christianity
and of the propagation of the Gospel; tidings particularly grateful to this country, and especially to the
College of which you are rector, which will hereafter
be able to proceed *secundum regulam et Institutum.*"

A word about this distinguished American Jesuit
may not be out of place here. He was born in the

45

ancestral manor of the Fenwicks, in old St. Mary's County, Maryland, and was a lineal descendant of Cuthbert Fenwick who was distinguished among the first Catholic colonists by his opposition to Lewger, Calvert's secretary, then assailing the rights of the Church in Maryland. When Georgetown College opened its doors, Benedict Fenwick and his brother Enoch were among its first students. After finishing the course, he took upon himself what his old admirer, the famous Father Stonestreet, calls "the painful but self-improving duties of the class room," and was professor of Humanities for three years. Later he began a course of theology at St. Mary's Seminary, Baltimore, but he left in order to become a Jesuit. The Fenwicks, both in England and America had been always closely identified with the Society, and when the news came that it was about to be resuscitated, Benedict and Enoch were chosen with four other applicants to be the corner stones of the first novitiate in the United States of North America. He was ordained on June 11, 1808, in Trinity Church, Georgetown, D. C., by the Jesuit Bishop Neale, coadjutor of Archbishop Carroll, and was immediately sent to New York with Father Kohlmann to prepare that diocese for the coming of its first bishop Dr. Concanen. Kohlmann himself had been named for the see, but the Pontiff had yielded to the entreaties of Father Roothaan not to deprive the still helpless Society of such a valuable workman; hence, Father Richard Luke Concanen, a Dominican, was appointed in his stead.

Kohlmann and Fenwick were welcomed with great enthusiasm in New York which had suffered much from the various transients who had from time to time officiated there. Several distinguished converts were won over to the faith, and an attempt was made to influence the famous free-thinker, Tom Paine, but the unfortunate wretch died blaspheming. It was Kohlmann and Fenwick who established the New York Literary Institute on the site of the present St. Patrick's Cathedral. It was successful enough to attract the sons of the most distinguished families of the city and merited the commendation of such men as the famous governor of New York, De Witt Clinton, and of Governor Thompkins who was subsequently Vice-President of the United States. At the same time, they were building old St. Patrick's, which was to become the cathedral of the new bishop. Bishop Concanen never reached New York, and when his successor Bishop Connolly arrived in 1814, Father Fenwick was his consolation and support in the many bitter trials that had to be undergone in those turbulent days. He was made vicar general and when he was sent to Georgetown to be president of the college in 1817, it was against the strong protest and earnest entreaties of the bishop, who, it may be said in passing, regretted exceedingly the closing of the Literary Institute,—a feeling shared by every American Jesuit. The reason for so doing is given by Hughes (History of the Soc. of Jesus in North America, I, ii, 945).

While Fenwick was in Georgetown, Charleston, South Carolina, was in an uproar ecclesiastically. The people were in open schism, and Archbishop Maréchal of Baltimore, in spite of his antagonism to the Society appealed to the superior of the Jesuits for some one to bring order out of the chaos. Fenwick was sent, and such was his tact, good judgment and kindness, that he soon mastered the situation and the diocese was at peace when the new bishop, the distinguished John England, arrived. Strange to say, Bishop England had the same prejudice as Bishop Concanen, against the Society; a condition of mind that may be explained by the fact that it had been suppressed by the highest authority in the Church, and that even educated men were ignorant of the causes that had brought about the disaster. But Fenwick soon disabused the bishop. Indeed, he remained as Vicar General of Charleston until 1822, and when he was recalled to Georgetown, Bishop England, at first, absolutely refused to let him go.

In a funeral oration pronounced over Fenwick, later by Father Stonestreet he said in referring to the Charleston troubles; " Difficulties had arisen between the French and Anglo-Irish portions of the congregation, each insisting it should be preached to in its own tongue; each restive at remaining in the sacred temple while the word of God was announced in the language of the other. The good Father, nothing daunted by the scene of contrariety before him, ascends the pulpit, opens his discourse in both languages, rapidly alternates the tongues of La Belle France and of the Anglo-Saxon, and by his ardent desire to unite the whole community in the bonds of charity, astonishes, softens, wins and harmonizes the hearts of all. A lasting peace was restored which still continues."

Bishop Cheverus, who was then at Boston, was subsequently called to France to be Archbishop of Bordeaux and cardinal. Father Fenwick, without being consulted, was appointed to the vacant see. In fact, the first news he had of the promotion was when the Bulls were in his hands, so that no means of protesting was possible. He was consecrated on November 1, 1825, and his friend Bishop England travelled all the way from Charleston to assist as one of the Consecrators. At that time the diocese of Boston was synonymous with New England, but it had only ten churches, two of which were for Indians. Fenwick, however, set to work in his usual heroic fashion. He was particularly fond of the Indians, and bravely

fought their battle against the dishonest whites.
As the red men were the descendants of the Abenakis
to whom the old Jesuits had brought the Faith, there
was a family feeling in his defense of them.   The same
sentiment of kinship prompted him to establish a
newspaper which he called " The Jesuit." It was
a defiance of the bigotry of New England, of which
there were to be many serious manifestations.   " The
Jesuit " was the pioneer of Catholic journalism in the
United States.

Bishop Fenwick was averse to the crowding of
Catholics in the large cities, and to segregate them
he established the exclusively Catholic colony of
Benedicta, but this scheme of a Paraguay in the woods
of Maine had only a limited success.   Prompted by
the same motive of love of the Society he visited
the place which Father Rasle had sanctified with his
blood when the fanatical Puritans of Massachusetts
put him to death in 1724.   Father Rasle was the
apostle of the Abenakis and had established himself
at what is now Norridgewock on the Kennebec.   Fenwick went there to pray.   Although it was in the
wilderness, he determined to make it a notable place
for the future Catholics of America; and over the
mouldering remains of Rasle and his brave Indian
defenders, he erected a monument, a shaft of granite,
on which an inscription was cut to record the tragedy.
It was too much for the bigotry that then reigned in
those parts, and the monument was thrown down;
but Fenwick put it in its place again; at a later date
when, in the course of time, it had fallen out of per-
pendicular, Bishop Walsh of Portland corrected the
defect and amid a great throng of people solemnly
reconsecrated it.

While he was Bishop of Boston, Fenwick made a
pious pilgrimage to Quebec; the city from which

the Jesuits of the old Society had started on their
perilous journeys to evangelize the Indians of the
continent. He saw there an immense building on
whose façade were cut the letters I. H. S. " What
is that?" he asked.   " It is the old Jesuit College, now
a soldiers' barracks," was the reply. His soul was
filled with indignation and he exclaimed in anger,
" The outrage that these men of blood should occupy
the house sanctified by the martyrs Jogues, Brébeuf,
Lalemant and the others." The good bishop was
unaware that the martyrs had never seen the building.
It was built after they had gone to claim their crowns
in heaven.

During his episcopacy Knownothingism reigned, and
in one of the outbreaks the Ursuline Convent in
Charlestown was attacked at midnight. The sisters
were shot at, the house was pillaged, the chapel desecrated and the whole edifice given over to the flames.
The blackened ruins remained for fifty years to remind
the Commonwealth of its disgrace, until finally the
remnants of the building, which it had cost so much to
erect, had to be removed to escape taxation. It was
Fenwick who founded Holy Cross College, in Worcester,
Massachusetts, an establishment which is the Alma
Mater of most of the subsequent bishops of New
England. It has also the singular distinction of being
the only Catholic College exempted by law from
receiving any but Catholic students. Fenwick is
buried there. He died on August 11, 1846, after an
episcopacy of twenty-one years.

Strange to say the Bull resurrecting the Society
was not sent to America until October 8, 1814, and
on January 5, 1815, Bishop Carroll wrote to Father
Marmaduke Stone, in England, as follows: " Your
precious and grateful favor accompanied by the Bull
of Restoration was received early in December and

diffused the greatest sensation of joy and thanksgiving, not only among the surviving and new members of the Society, but also all good Christians who have any remembrances of their services or heard of their unjust and cruel treatment, and have witnessed the consequences of their suppression. You may conceive my sensations when I read the account of the celebration of Mass by His Holiness himself at the superb altar of St. Ignatius at the Gesù; the assemblage of the surviving Jesuits in the chapel to hear the proclamation of their resurrection, etc."

On returning to America after the suppression of the Society in Belgium, Father Carroll had gone to live at his mother's house in Rock Creek, Maryland, for he no longer considered himself entitled to support from the funds of the Jesuits who still maintained their existence in the colonies. They had never been suppressed, whereas he had belonged to a community in the Netherlands which had been canonically put out of existence by the Brief. He spent two years in the rough country missions of Maryland and then went with Benjamin Franklin, Samuel Chase and his cousin Charles Carroll to Canada to induce the Frenchmen there to make common cause with the Americans against Great Britain. The Continental Congress had especially requested him to form a part of the embassy. The mission was a failure and the Colonies had themselves to blame for it; because two years previously they had issued an "Address to the English People" denouncing the government for not only attempting to establish an Anglican episcopacy in the English possessions, but for maintaining a papistical one on the banks of the St. Lawrence. Clearly it would have been impossible for the French Catholics who had been guaranteed the free exercise of their religion to transfer their allegiance to a country which considered that concession to be one of the reasons justifying a revolution.

When the war was over, Carroll and five other Jesuits met at Whitemarsh to devise means to keep their property intact in order to carry on their missionary work. They had no other resources than the produce of their farms, for their personal support. The faithful gave them nothing. At this conference they decided to ask Rome to empower some one of their number to confirm, grant faculties and dispensations, bless oils, etc. They added that, for the moment, a bishop was unnecessary. The petition was sent on November 6, 1783, and on June 7, 1784, Carroll was appointed superior of the missions in the thirteen states, and was given power to confirm. There were at that time about nineteen priests in the country and fifteen thousand Catholics, of whom three thousand were negro slaves. In 1786 Carroll took up his residence in Baltimore and was conspicuously active in municipal affairs, establishing schools, libraries and charities. Possibly it was due to him that Article 6 was inserted in the Constitution of the United States which declares that "no religious test shall ever be required as a qualification to any office or public trust under the United States;" and probably also the amendment that "this Congress shall make no laws respecting the establishment of religion or prohibiting the free exercise thereof." Its actual sponsor in the Convention was C. C. Pinckney of South Carolina.

Carroll was made Bishop of Baltimore by Pius VI on November 6, 1789, twenty-four out of the twenty-five priests in the country voting for him. He was consecrated on August 15, 1790, at Lulworth Castle, England by the senior vicar Apostolic of England, Bishop Walmesly. On the election of Washington to the presidency, he represented the clergy in a con-

gratulatory address to which Washington answered;
" I hope your fellow-countrymen will not forget the
patriotic part in the accomplishment of the Revolution
and the establishment of the government or the important assistance which they received from a nation in
which the Roman Catholic Faith is professed."

He convoked the first Synod of Baltimore in 1791.
There were twenty-two priests of five nationalities
in attendance. He called the Sulpicians to Baltimore in 1791; the first priest he ordained was Stephen
Badin, the beloved pioneer of Kentucky, and four
years later the famous Russian prince, Demetrius
Gallitzin. He also succeeded in having a missionary
for the Indians appointed by the government. He had
intended to have as his coadjutor and successor in
the see, Father Lawrence Grässel, who had been a
novice in the old Society and who at Carroll's urgent
request, had come out to America as a missionary.
Grässel, however, died before the arrival of the Bulls.
Father Leonard Neale, a Maryland Jesuit, was then
chosen and was consecrated in 1800. A year and
two months after the re-establishment of the Society,
namely on December 3, 1815, Carroll died. It was
fitting that this son of Saint Ignatius should be called
to heaven on the feast of the great friend and companion
of Saint Ignatius, Saint Francis Xavier.

Apropos of this, a note has been quoted by Father
Hughes (op. cit., Doc., I, 424) which is often cited as
revealing a change in Carroll's attitude toward the
Society after he became archbishop. Fr. Charles
Neale had written to him as follows, " It is equally
certain that I have no authority to give up any right
that would put the subject out of the power of his
superior, who must and ought to be the best judge
of what is most beneficial to the universal or individual
good of the members, of the Congregation." On

the back of the letter appear the words "Inadmissible Pretensions," said by Bishop Maréchal to have been written by Carroll.

Archbishop Carroll's attitude to the Society is clearly manifested in his letter of December 10, 1814, addressed to Father Grassi, which says: " Having contributed to your greatest happiness on earth by sending the miraculous bull of general restoration, even before I could nearly finish the reading of it, I fully expect it back this evening with Mr. Plowden's letter." It should not be forgotten that Carroll was heartbroken when the Society was suppressed and that he longed for death because of the grief it caused him. The words " Inadmissible Pretensions " noted on Neale's letter referred to a formal protest made by Father Charles Neale against a synodial statute of the bishops convened at Baltimore. Neale, indeed, desired to exercise the special privileges of the Society and to govern as was done in the old Society or as in Russia, a procedure which incurred the disapproval of the General.   Grassi writing to Plowden, in England, says: " He (Archbishop Carroll) considers Mr. Chas. Neale as a wrongheaded man, and persons who knew him at Liège and Antwerp are nearly of the same opinion." In brief, Neale's administration both as president of Georgetown and as superior of the mission was most disastrous (cf. Hughes, I, ii, passim).

Leonard Neale, like Carroll, was an American. He was born near Port Tobacco in Maryland in 1746, and with many other young Marylanders, was sent to the Jesuit College of St. Omer in France. After the Suppression he went to England, where he was engaged in parochial work for four years. From there he was sent to Demerara in British Guiana and continued at work in that trying country from 1779 to 1783. His health finally gave way, and he returned to Maryland and joined his Jesuit brethren. He distinguished himself in the yellow fever epidemic in Philadelphia, and remained in that city, for six years as the vicar of Bishop Carroll. In 1797 another epidemic of fever occurred and he was stricken but recovered. In 1798 he was sent to Georgetown College as president, and in 1800 while still president he was consecrated coadjutor of Archbishop Carroll. He continued his scholastic work until 1806, succeeding to the See of Baltimore in 1815. He was then seventy years old and in feeble health. He died at Georgetown on June 18, 1817. Bishop Maréchal who had been suggested to the Pope by Bishop Cheverus of Boston, had already been named for the See.

Bishop Maréchal was a Sulpician. He had left France at the outbreak of the French Revolution and after spending some years in America as a professor both at Georgetown and Baltimore, returned to his native country, but was back again in Maryland after a few years. Neale wanted him to be Bishop of Philadelphia, but the offer was declined, and he was made coadjutor of Baltimore with the right of succession. He was consecrated on December 14, 1817, and occupied the see until 1826. Unfortunately, the whole period from 1820 was marked by misunderstandings with the Society. In spite of this controversy, which was unnecessarily acrimonious at times, Archbishop Maréchal was anxious to have the Jesuit visitor Father Peter Kenny appointed Bishop of Philadelphia. (cf. Hughes, op. cit., Documents, for details of the controversies.)

CHAPTER XXIV

THE FIRST CONGREGATION

Expulsion from Russia — Petrucci, Vicar — Attempt to wreck the Society — Saved by Consalvi and Rozaven.

THE superiors-general who presided over the Society in Russia were Stanislaus Cerniewicz (1782–85), Gabriel Lenkiewicz (1785–98), Francis Kareu, (1799–1802), Gabriel Gruber, (1802-05), and Thaddeus Brzozowski, (1805–20). The first two were only vicars, as was Father Kareu when first elected, but by the Brief " Catholicæ Fidei " he was raised to the rank of General on March 7, 1801. His two successors bore the same title. Father Brzozowski lived six years after the Restoration. But those years must have been a time of great suffering for him. Over the rapidly expanding Society, whose activities were already extending to the ends of the earth, he had been chosen to preside but he was virtually a prisoner in Russia. It soon became evident that such an arrangement was intolerable and not only was there an exasperating surveillance of every member of the Order by the government, but even when Brzozowski himself asked permission to go to Rome to thank the Holy Father in person for the favor he had conferred on the Society by the Bull of Re-establishment, he was flatly refused. Hence it was resolved that when he died, a General had to be elected who would reside in Rome, no matter what might be the consequences in Russia.

The difficulty, however, solved itself. Though officially the head of the Orthodox Church, Alexander cared little for its doctrines, its practises or its tradi-

tions, and he set about establishing a union of all the
sects on the basis of what he considered to be the
fundamental truths of religion. He is even credited
with the ambition of aiming at a universal spiritual
dominion which would eclipse Napoleon's dream of
world-wide empire built upon material power.
Whether this was the outcome of his meditations,
— for after his fashion, he was a religious man,— or
was suggested to him by the Baroness Julia de Krudner,
who was creating a sensation at that time, as a revivalist,
cannot be ascertained. There is no doubt, however,
that he fell under her sway.

Mme. de Krudner had given up pleasures and
wealth to bring back the world to what she called the
principles of the primitive Church. She travelled
through Germany and Switzerland with about forty
of her admirers, who kept incessantly crying out:
" We call only the elect to follow us." She established
soup-kitchens wherever she went, and her converts
knelt before her, as this slim diet which they regarded
as a gift from heaven was doled out to them. Naturally this attraction worked first on the poor, but the
baroness soon reached the upper grades of society.
Her opportunity presented itself at Vienna, where
the allied sovereigns were in session to determine
the political complexion of the world, after they had
disposed of Napoleon. They did her the honor of
attending some of her meetings, and Alexander who
showed himself greatly interested, became the special
object of her attention. She styled him: " The
White Angel of God," while Napoleon was set down as
" The Dark Angel of Hell."

Such a serious writer as Cantù is of the opinion that
it was the baroness who drew up the scheme of the
Holy Alliance, in which the four monarchs agreed
to love one another as brothers; to govern their

respective states as different branches of the great family of nations, and to have Jesus Christ, the Omnipotent Word, as their Sovereign Lord. But immediately after making this pious pact they began to distribute among themselves the spoils of war. Prussia took Saxony; Russia, Poland; Austria, Northern Italy; and England, Malta, Helioland and the Cape. Thus was virtue rewarded.

At the suggestion of Galitzin, his minister of worship, Alexander had begun a devout course of Bible reading as a means of lifting himself out of the gloom into which he seemed to be plunged after the war. It had apparently some beneficial effect on him, and he became an enthusiastic advocate of the practise for all classes of people. The English Bible Society was to help the propaganda and the Catholic Archbishop of Mohilew and his clergy strongly supported the imperial project. Necessarily the Jesuits had to antagonize this wholesale diffusion of corrupt versions of the sacred text, and they endeavored to point out the folly of leaving its interpretation to ignorant people. The consequence was that they provoked the anger not only of the Bible Society and of the emperor, but also both of the Russian and partly of the Catholic clergy. The troublesome Siestrzencewicz, Archbishop of Mohilew, not only strongly favored the project but suggested to Galitzin that the attitude of the Jesuits furnished an excellent opportunity to get rid of them. There was another reason also why the blow was sure to fall. A Catholic Polish woman named Narychkine it is said had been dissociated from the czar by a refusal of absolution at Easter time. The confessor was the Jesuit, Father Perkowski, and, of course, as all his associates would have acted in the same way, the whole Society came under the ban.

Zalenski, in his "Russie Blanche," finds another reason for this loss of Alexander's favor. He was not only not a Romanoff but had not a drop of Russian blood in his veins, except through his father Paul, the alleged bastard son of Catherine before she became empress. He was aware that the Jesuits knew of this family stain, though not a word was ever uttered about it. It made him uncomfortable, nevertheless, and he was quite willing to rid himself of their presence.

As he had officially proclaimed that all religions were alike, many who had professed allegiance to the Greek Church under political pressure became materialists or atheists, and some distinguished women became Catholics. No attention was paid to the atheists, but these conversions to the Faith were blamed on the Jesuits, particularly on three French fathers, among whom was Rozaven. Count de Maistre, who was in St. Petersburg at the time, declares emphatically that they had nothing to do with it. The feeling against them, however, was very intense and only lacked an occasion to show itself. It came when a nephew of Galitzin, announced that he was going to become a Catholic. This was too much for the minister of worship to put up with and although the lad, who was a pupil of one of the Jesuit colleges, had let it be known that the Fathers had absolutely nothing to do with his project and that his resolution was only the result of his own investigations, he was not believed, and a ukase, dated December 25, 1815, was issued, proclaiming their expulsion from the country. This was seventeen months after the Re-establishment.

The decree called attention to the fact that " when the Jesuits were expelled from all the other nations of Europe, Russia had charitably admitted them and confided to their care the instruction of youth. In return, they had destroyed the peace of the Orthodox Church and had turned from it some of the pupils of their colleges. Such an act, said the document, explains why they were held in such abhorrence elsewhere. The ukase bubbles over with piety, deploring the " apostacies " that had taken place, and then goes on to state that: first, the Catholic Church in Russia is hereby re-established on the plan which had been adopted since the time of Catherine II until the year 1800; secondly, the Jesuits are to withdraw immediately from St. Petersburg; thirdly, they are forbidden to enter either of the capitals.

It is noteworthy that the decree of banishment is not stocked with calumnies like those issued by the Catholic courts of Europe. It was based purely on religious ground. Nor was the expulsion characterized by any exhibition of brutality as in Spain, Portugal and France; for although the police descended on the houses, in the dead of night, and drove out the occupants, an almost maternal care was taken against their suffering in the slightest degree on their way to the places of their exile. Of course, all their papers and books were seized but perhaps the Fathers were glad of it; for although, since Catherine's time, they had been brought into closest contact with the hideous skeletons of her court and those of her successors, no mention was made of any family scandal in the voluminous correspondence that had been so suddenly seized by the government. As regards the charge of proselytism, there is a letter from Father Brzozowski to Father de Clorivière, dated February 20, 1816, which stated that not only did none of the Fathers ever attempt to influence their pupils, but that during the thirteen years of the existence of the College of St. Petersburg, no Russian Orthodox student had been admitted to the Church. It goes on to say that for a long time the storm had been foreseen and that everyone was prepared for it.

Before the final blow came, Father Brzozowski petitioned the emperor at least to permit the Fathers to continue their labors in the dangerous mission of the Riga district, in the Caucasus, and on the banks of the Volga, in all of which places, their success in civilizing and christianizing the population had been officially recognized by the emperor. But the request was not granted, and in 1820, just as Father Brzozowski was dying, the Jesuits were ordered out of the empire, and all their possessions were confiscated. The loss was a grevious one in many respects, but it had its compensations. For, in the first place, it effectually settled the question of the General's residence. Secondly, as the Jesuits living in Russia were almost of every nationality in Europe and as many of them were conspicuous for their great ability in many branches of learning, a valuable re-inforcement was thus available for the hastily formed colleges in various parts of the world. Thirdly, the traditions of the Society had remained unbroken in Russia, and the example and guidance of the venerable men who were there to the number of 358 would transmit to the various provinces the true spirit of the Society. In any case Alexander's successor would have expelled them, for he was a violent persecutor of the Church, and, moreover, Freemasonry and infidelity had been making sad havoc with what was left of the religion of the nation.

Brzozowski when dying, had named as Vicar, Father Petrucci, the master of novices at Genoa, a most unfortunate choice; for Petrucci was not only old and ill, but was woefully lacking in wordly wisdom, and proved to be a pliant tool in the hands of designing men. His appointment went to show the impossibility

46

of directing the Society in pent-up Russia, where the
General could not be sufficiently informed of the
character of the various members of the Order. The
congregation was summoned for September 14, 1820,
but although there were already in Rome on August 2
seventeen out of the twenty-one delegates, Cardinal
della Genga wrote to Petrucci to say that the Pope
wanted the congregation to be delayed, because he
desired time for the arrival of the Polish Fathers who
represented a notable part of the Society.

As no one ever questioned the fact that the Polish
province, which alone had remained intact in the
general wreck, was a notable part of the Congregation
and of the Society, and as, moreover, the Polish
delegates would have no difficulty in reaching Rome
before September 14, everyone suspected that something sinister was being attempted. That Petrucci
and Cardinal della Genga were in league with each
other in this matter was clear from the fact that
Petrucci, without consulting any one of his colleagues,
immediately dispatched letters to all the provinces
announcing the prorogation of the congregation,
protesting meantime that the office of vicar was too
great for one of his age and infirmities. It was also
remarked that with the cardinal was a small group
of malcontents composed of Rizzi, Pancaldi, who was
only in deacon's orders, Pietroboni and a certain
number of Roman ecclesiastics, some of them prelates
who, like della Genga, did not of course belong to
the Society.

These conspirators kept the minds of the waiting
delegates in a feverish state of excitement by giving
out that there was a great fear, not only in the public
at large, but even in the papal court, that a Paccanarist
might be elected. Indeed there were already three
of them among the electors: Sineo, Rozaven and

Grivel, and hence it was desirable to delay the congregation until it would be sure that no others would
arrive. Over and above this, some of those recently
admitted to the Society maintained that only those who
belonged to the old Society or had been a long time
in Russia should be accepted as delegates. Doubts
were raised also as to whether those who had taken
their vows before the formal recognition of the Society
in Russia in 1801, or the recognition in Sicily in 1804,
were to be considered as Jesuits or as secular priests.

In brief, Rizzi and his associates had so filled the
minds of outsiders with doubts, that some prelates
and even a cardinal advised that the questions should
be submitted to the Pope for settlement. Finally, on
the day originally fixed for the congregation, namely,
September 14, Cardinal della Genga sent three letters
to the Fathers at Rome. In the first he said that the
Pope was convinced that the meeting of the delegates
should be postponed, and that he had given to the
Vicar, Petrucci, all the faculties of a regularly elected
General. The second letter was directed to the
assistants, who were informed that it was the wish
of His Holiness that all the irregularities which della
Genga declared existed in the congregation should be
remedied, and to that end, he had appointed a committee composed of himself, Cardinal Galiffi and the
Archbishop of Nanzianzum, together with Petrucci
and Rizzi to consider them. This committee, moreover,
was to preside at the election. The third letter
ordered that new assistants should be added to those
already in office, making seven in all, a thing absolutely
unheard of in the Society until then.

Rizzi and Petrucci were in high spirits when this
became known, but not so the other delegates, and
they determined to appeal directly to the Pope. Then
a doubt arose as to which cardinal was to present the

appeal. Mattei and Litta, the staunch friends of the
Society were dead and Pacca leaned slightly to Rizzi's
views. There remained Consalvi. To him Father
Rozaven wrote the appeal, but, two of the assistants
and Petrucci refused to sign it. Consalvi received the
petitioners with the greatest benignity, promised to
present the document to the Pope, and bade the
Fathers not to be discouraged. He explained the
situation to the Holy Father, who immediately approved
of the request, and issued the following order:
" Having heard the plea, We command that the
general congregation be convened immediately, and
that, as soon as possible, the General be elected, all
things to the contrary notwithstanding." " Everyone," wrote Rozaven, " was delighted, except of
course, Petrucci, the provincial of the Italian Province,
Pietroboni, and those who had been misled by Rizzi.

The congregation met on October 9. Twenty-four
professed Fathers were present and they elected Father
Aloysius Fortis as General. Petrucci protested the
legality of the election, but when the usual delegation
presented itself to the Pope, they were received most
cordially and he referred them to Consalvi for the decree
of " sanation," if any were needed.   " He is altogether
devoted to you," said the Pope, " and watches with
the greatest concern over your interests."   Now that
the congregation was regularly constituted, the Fathers
proceeded as quickly as possible to the punishment of
the conspirators. Both Petrucci and Pietroboni were
deposed from their respective offices as Vicar and
provincial, and other disturbers were expelled from the
Society;— the Pope highly approving of the action.
It was Cardinal Consalvi who had averted the wreck.

In view of the great cardinal's attitude in this matter,
it is distressing to find Crétineau-Joly declaring that
Consalvi acted as he did because he was a diplomat,

a man of the world rather than an ecclesiastic. He cared little for the Jesuits (il aimait peu les Jésuites) whom he regarded as adding a new political embarrassment to the actual complications in Europe, but he knew how to be just, and refused to be an accomplice in the plot (VI, 1). This is a calumny. We have the Pope's own words about Consalvi's concern for the Society, and in the " Memoirs " edited by Crétineau-Joly himself the exact opposite is asserted. Thus on page 56, we read: " he made the greatest number of people happy and in doing so was happier than they, because he was thus making them venerate the Church, his Mother." On page 11, he says that whenever Consalvi wrote about Napoleon " he placed himself in the presence of God in order to be impartial in judging his persecutor." On page 180: " He lived without any concern for wealth; he never asked or received any gifts. He realized what St. Bernard and Pope Eugenius III said of a Cardinal Cibo in their day: ' In passing through this world of money, he never knew what money was. He was prodigal in his benevolence and died virtually a poor man." These are not the traits of a " man of the world and a politician."

As for " his not liking the Jesuits," we find in those " Memoirs," which were finished in 1812, and consequently eight years before the meeting of the congregation, the following words (II, 305): " When Pope Pius VII returned to Rome in 1801, he received a letter from Paul I, the Emperor of Russia, asking for the re-establishment of the Jesuits in his dominions. The Pope was delighted to have the chance to gratify the Czar and also to perform a praiseworthy (louable) action;— for it was restoring to life an Institute which had deserved well of Christendom and whose fall had hastened the ruin of the Church, of thrones, of public order, of morality, of society. One can assert this without fear of being taxed with exaggeration or falsehood by honest and reasonable men and by those who are not imbued with a false philosophy or party spirit."

He then narrates how cautious the Pope had to be before granting Paul's request, " so as not," Consalvi says, " to arouse the antagonism of the enemies of the Society: the philosophers and haters of religion and of public order, who, as they had forced its condemnation from Clement XIV, would now employ all the machinery of the courts which had asked for the suppression to prevent its rehabilitation. The Pope succeeded, but a few years afterwards, when the Emperor of Austria asked for the Jesuits, his ministers brought about the failure of the project. They consented to accept the Jesuits, but in such a fashion and under such a form that they could no longer be Jesuits. The Pope would not consent to such conditions, and as the imperial court would not accept them as they were, the matter was dropped." In other words, Pope Pius VII and his great cardinal believed with Clement XIII that no changes should be made in their Institute. *Sint ut sunt aut non sint.* Let them be themselves or not at all. To assert that in the heart of the great champion of the Faith, Consalvi, there was little love for the Jesuits is to say what is contrary to facts.

The new General, Father Aloysius Fortis, was born in 1748 and was consequently seventy-two years of age when he was elected. In spite of his age, however, he was in vigorous health and governed the Society for nine years. He had been in the old Society for eleven years before the Suppression. In 1794 he was associated in Parma with the saintly Pignatelli, who twice foretold his election. He had been prefect of

studies in the scholasticate at Naples, and when the
Society was re-established he was named as Father
Brzozowski's vicar in Rome. In 1819 Pius VII
appointed him *Examinator Episcoporum*. Hence his
election was naturally gratifying to the Pope, and he
gave evidence of it by the joy that suffused his countenance when the formal announcement of the result
was made to him. The eagerness with which he affixed
his signature to the official document also testified to
his satisfaction. In the Professed House, the Fathers
acclaimed the choice with enthusiasm, as did the
throngs of people who had immediately flocked to
the Gesù to hear the announcement. They have chosen
a saint was the universal cry. The Emperor of Austria,
Francis I, Frederick, the Prince of Hesse, and Duke
Antony, who was soon to be King of Saxony, all
expressed their pleasure at the promotion of Father
Fortis.

The letter written by Antony is worth quoting.
" I have read with the greatest joy, in the public press,"
he said, " of the election of a man of whom it may well
be said he is *Fortis* by name and *fortis* by nature.
I am aware that his humility would prompt him to
differ with me, but I hoped that such would be the
choice, and now my desire has been fulfilled. God
who directed this election will give you that strength
which you think you lack to fulfill the duties of your
office. Now more than ever I commend myself to
the fervent prayers of yourself and your associates.
I have a claim on them, for ever since my earliest
youth, I have been most devoted to the Society, to
which I owe my religious training."

In the congregation, Father Fortis proposed a
resolution or a decree, as it is called, which is of
supreme importance, and which was, it is needless to
say, unanimously adopted. It runs as follows:

"Although there is no doubt that both the Constitutions given by Our Holy Founder and whatever in the course of time the Fathers have judged to add to them have recovered their force at the very outset of the restored Society, as it was the manifest wish of our Holy Father, Pius VII, that the Society re-established by him should be governed by the same laws as before the Suppression, nevertheless, to remove all anxiety on that score, and to put an end to the obstinacy of certain disturbers of the peace, this congregation not only confirms, but as far as necessary decrees anew, in conformity with the power vested in the General and the congregations by Paul III, and reaffirms that not only the Constitutions with the declarations and the decrees of the general congregations, but the Common Rules and those of the several offices, the Ratio Studiorum, the ordinations, the formulas and whatsoever belongs to the legislation of Our Society are intact, and it wishes all and each of the aforesaid to have the same binding force on those who live in the Society that they had before Clement XIV's Bull of Suppression."

Although Fortis was gentle and humble he admitted no relaxation, especially in the matter of poverty, and those who were unwilling to put up with the requirements, he allowed to leave the Order. "We want fruits," he used to say, "not roots." Again, in spite of his new dignity and of his great natural gifts he was always the same simple Father Fortis. He was such an ardent lover of poverty that he kept his clothes till they were threadbare and torn, and had to be stolen out of his room to be replaced by others more befitting his station. In 1821 he united into a vice-province the various members of the Society scattered through Belgium, Holland, Switzerland and Germany and gave it a name descriptive of its composition: "The Vice-Province of Switzerland and the German Missions." In 1823 the Province of Galicia was established. In it were many of the old Fathers of Russia, but the number was so great that many had to be sent to Italy, France and elsewhere. Sicily, especially, was benefited in this way. From the province thus established three others sprung in a short time: Germany, Belgium and Holland.

Father Fortis died on January 27, 1829. The grief for his loss was general and none felt it more keenly than the King of Saxony, who wrote another affectionate letter to express his sorrow. It is worthy of note that, although the royal family of Saxony is still Catholic, no one who has been trained in a Jesuit School is eligible there to any ecclesiastical office. It is a curious condition in a kingdom which in 1821 was ruled by a sovereign who exulted in the fact that he was a Jesuit alumnus.

Chief among the distinguished Jesuits in the congregation of 1820 was, without doubt, the Frenchman, John Rozaven. He was born at Quimper in Brittany, March 9, 1772. His uncle had belonged to the Society when it was suppressed in France in 1760, and had then become a parish priest at Plogonnec. While there, he was elected, in 1789, at the outbreak of the Revolution to be a representative at the Etats Généraux. He accepted the constitutional oath, but soon retracted. He had to atone for his treason to the Church, however, by being made the victim of his bishop, who, like him, had joined the schism but had not recanted. On account of this ill-feeling, Rozaven left the country, taking with him the future Jesuit, his nephew, who was living with him at that time. They both disappeared on the night of June 20, 1792, and on the 24th arrived at the Island of Jersey. From there they went to London and after a few months made their way to the Duchy of Cleves.

Hearing that there was a French ecclesiastical seminary at Brussels, young Rozaven entered it, was ordained sub-deacon, but was obliged to leave after six months, because of the arrival of the French troops. He and his uncle then took up their abode in Paderborn and lodged in an old Jesuit establishment where they lived for four years, at which time the young man was ordained priest and then left his uncle in order to join the Fathers of the Sacred Heart under Father Varin. When informed of the existence of the Jesuits in Russia, John applied for admission and was received on March 28, 1804. He was subsequently made prefect of studies and professor of philosophy in the College of Nobles at St. Petersburg. In the course of his ministerial work, he brought to the Faith the Princess Elizabeth Galitzin, well-known as one of the first of the Ladies of the Sacred Heart. The famous Madame Swetchine was another of his converts. He was the professor of the young Galitzin who had created such an uproar in St. Petersburg by his supposed part in the conversion.

At the death of Father General Brzozowski, Rozaven was sent as a delegate to the congregation and, as we have seen, it was his wisdom and courage that saved the Society from shipwreck on that occasion. He was elected assistant to the General, and, with the exception of one short visit to France, remained for the rest of his life in Rome. He was too valuable an aid for the General to be allowed even to be the official visitor to France although everyone there was clamoring for him. It was he who demolished the philosophical system of de Lamennais, and at the same time restrained the hotheads of the French provinces from accepting and teaching the new doctrine. His

" Examen of Certain Philosophical Doctrines " came
out in 1831, and although his office of assistant gave
him plenty of occupation, he taught theology, was a
member of several pontifical congregations, and heard
as many as 20,000 confessions a year. This immense
labor was made possible by his rising at half past three
in the morning, and by the clock-like punctuality
and system with which he addressed himself to the
various tasks of the day. In the cholera epidemic
of 1837, despite his sixty-five years of age, he plunged
into the work like the rest of his brethren and heard
23,000 confessions during the continuance of the plague.

When the Revolution of '48 broke out, Rozaven
remained at Rome more or less secluded, but at last,
when there was danger of his being taken to prison,
a friend of his, the Count Rampon, said: " You will
come to my château and I shall see that you are not
molested." The protection was accepted, and a few
nights after, a banquet was given at the château, to
which the French ambassador and several conspicuous
anti-Jesuit personages had been invited. When the
guests were seated it was remarked that there was an
empty place near the Count. " Are you waiting
for someone else?" they asked. " Yes," he said
" I have here a very remarkable old gentleman whom
I want to present to you. He is my friend and more
worthy of respect than anyone in the whole world."
Then leaving the room, he led Father Rozaven in by
the hand and said to his guests in a loud voice:
" Gentlemen, I have to present my friend, Father
Rozaven, who has deigned to accept my hospitality.
He is here under my protection and I place him under
yours. If, contrary to my expectation, hatred pursues
him into my house, the Count Rampon will defend his
guest to the last drop of his blood." Then making
a step backward, he swung open a door which revealed

a formidable array of muskets, pistols and swords which would be available if the contingency he referred to arose.   It is needless to say that Father Rozaven was treated with the most distinguished consideration, not only at the banquet but subsequently.

From there he went to Naples but, later, joined Father Roothaan in France.   When Pius IX returned to Rome, the Father General and his faithful assistant returned also.   But Rozaven had reached the end of his pilgrimage.   In 1851 he fell seriously ill and breathed his last on April 2, at the age of seventy-nine. He had put in thirty years of incessant work since the time he had fought so valiantly in the twentieth congregation.

Besides Rozaven, there was present at the twentieth congregation the distinguished English Jesuit, Charles Plowden.   He was born at Plowden Hall, Shropshire, in 1743, of a family which had not only steadfastly adhered to the Faith in all the persecutions that had desolated England, but had given several of its sons to the Society of Jesus and some of its daughters as nuns in religious orders.   He entered the Society in 1759, and was ordained in Rome three years before the Suppression.   He was in Belgium when the Brief was read and was kept in prison for several months.   After teaching at Liège, he returned to England where he was appointed chaplain at Lulworth Castle, and as such preached there at Bishop Carroll's consecration.   He had much to do with the establishment of Stonyhurst and was the first master of novices in England after the re-establishment, subsequently he was rector of Stonyhurst and provincial.   It was he who, with Fathers Mattingly and Sewall, called upon Benjamin Franklin in Paris to persuade him to crush the scheme of making the Church of the United States dependent upon the ecclesi-

astical authorities of France. He died at Jougne, in
France, on his way home from the congregation and
was buried with military honors, because his attendant
had informed the authorities of the little town that
the dead man had been called to Rome for the election
of a General. They mistook the meaning of the word
" General ", and so buried the humble Jesuit with all
the pomp and ceremony that usually accompany the
obsequies of a distinguished soldier.

On August 20, 1823, Pius VII, the great friend of the
Society, died and it was with no little consternation
that the Jesuits heard of the election of Leo XII. He
was the same Cardinal della Genga who had endeavored
to control the twentieth congregation and was supposed
to have revealed his attitude towards the Society
years before, when he advised Father Varin not to
attempt to form a union between the Fathers of the
Faith and the Jesuits in White Russia. Father
Rozaven, especially, had reason for apprehension, for
it was he who had thwarted della Genga's plans at
the election of Fortis; but the fear proved to be ground-
less, and Rozaven hastened to assure his friends in
France that in the three years that had intervened
since that eventful struggle, God had operated a
change in the mind of della Genga. As Sovereign
Pontiff he became one of the most ardent friends of the
Society.

CHAPTER XXV

A CENTURY OF DISASTER

Expulsion from Holland — Trouble at Freiburg — Expulsion and recall in Spain — *Petits Seminaires* — Berryer — Montlosier — The Men's Sodalities — St. Acheul mobbed — Fourteen Jesuits murdered in Madrid — Interment of Pombal — de Ravignan's pamphlet — Veuillot — Montalembert — de Bonald — Archbishop Affre — Michelet, Quinet and Cousin — Gioberti — Expulsion from Austria — Kulturkampf — Slaughter of the Hostages in the Commune — South America and Mexico — Flourishing Condition before Outbreak of the World War.

WHEN Pius VII restored the Society in 1814, he said it was because " he needed experienced mariners in the Barque of Peter which was tossed about on the stormy sea of the world." The storm had not abated. On the contrary its violence had increased, and the mariners who were honored by the call have never had a moment's rest since that eventful day when they were bidden to resume their work.

As early as 1816 the King of the Netherlands, William I, sent a band of soldiers to drive the Jesuits out of his dominions. He began with the novitiate of Destelbergen. Some of the exiles went to Hanover and others to Switzerland. The dispersion, however, did not check vocations. In 1819, for instance, Peter Beckx, who was then a secular priest in the parish of Uccle, never imagining, of course, that he was afterwards to be the General of the Society, entered the novitiate at Hildesheim. Before 1830 more than fifty applicants had been received. The figure is amazing, because it meant expatriation, paternal opposition, and a decree of perpetual exclusion from any public office in Holland. In spite of the law of banishment, however, a few priests succeeded in remaining in the country, exercising the functions of their ministry secretly.

In Russia, the Society, as mentioned above, had been cooped up in a restricted part of White Russia from 1815; on March 13, 1820, Alexander II extended the application of the decree of banishment to the entire country.

Then the storm broke on the Society in Freiburg, the occasion being a pedagogical quarrel with which the Jesuits had absolutely nothing to do. The people of the city were discussing the relative merits of the Pestalozzi and Lancaster systems for primary teaching; and to restore peace, the town council, at the bishop's request, closed all the schools. This drew down the public wrath on the head of the bishop, but as reverence for his official position protected him from open attack, someone suggested that the Jesuits were at the back of the measure. The result was that, at midnight on March 9, 1823, a mob attacked the Jesuit college, and clamored for its destruction. The bishop, however, wrote a letter assuming complete responsibility for the measure and the trouble then ceased.

After the fall of Napoleon, Talleyrand suggested to Louis XVIII to recall the Jesuits for collegiate work. But before his majesty had succeeded in making up his mind, the proposition became known and Talleyrand was driven from power in spite of a proclamation which he issued, assuring the public that he was always a foe of the Society. In the lull that followed, the Fathers were able to remain at their work, but four years afterwards, namely in 1819, they were expelled from Brest but continued to labor as missionaries in the remote country districts.

On May 15, 1815, they had been recalled to Spain by Ferdinand as a reparation for the sins of his ancestors

and their reception was an occasion of public rejoicing
— the Imperial College itself being entrusted to them.
They then numbered about one hundred, and in the
space of five years there were one hundred and ninety-
seven on the catalogue. They were left at peace
for a time, but in 1820 throngs gathered in the streets
around their houses, clamoring for their blood, and a
bill was drawn up for their expulsion. By a notable —
or 'was it an intentional?— coincidence the document bore the date of July 31, the feast of the Spanish
saint, Ignatius Loyola. The feeling against them was
so intense that three Fathers, who had been acclaimed
all over Spain for their devotion to the plague-stricken,
were taken out of their beds, thrown into prison and
then sent into exile. Meantime, Father Urigoitia
was murdered by a mob, near the famous cave of
St. Ignatius at Manresa. The Pope and king protested in vain. Indeed the king was besieged in his
palace and kept there until everything the rioters
demanded was granted; he remained virtually a
prisoner until the French troops entered Spain. In
1824 the Jesuits were recalled again, in 1825 the preparatory military school was entrusted to their care,
as was the College of Nobles at Madrid in 1827.

In 1828 new troubles began for the French Jesuits.
As they had been unable to have colleges of their own,
they had accepted eight *petits séminaires* which were
offered them by the bishops. This was before they
had become known as Jesuits, for to all outward
appearances they were secular priests. But, little by
little, their establishments took on a compound character. Boys who had no clerical aspirations whatever
asked for admittance, so that the management of
the schools became extremely difficult and, of course,
their real character soon began to be suspected by the
authorities. Investigations were therefore ordered of

all the *petits séminaires* of the country, though the
measure was aimed only at the eight controlled by
the Jesuits. As the interrogatory was very minute,
it caused great annoyance to the bishops, who saw in
it an attempt of the government to control elementary
sacerdotal education throughout the country, and
hence there was an angry protest from the whole
hierarchy, with the exception of one prelate who had
been a Constitutional bishop.

It was on this occasion that the younger Berryer
pronounced his masterly discourse before the " General
Council for the Defense of the Catholic Religion."
He established irrefragably the point of law that
" a congregation which is not authorized is not therefore prohibited "— a principle accepted by all the
French courts until recently. Apart from the ability
and eloquence of the plea, it was the more remarkable
because his father had been one of the most noted
assailants of the Society in 1826. The plea ended with
this remarkable utterance: " Behold the result of all
these intrigues, of all this fury, of all these outrages,
of all this hate! Two ministers of State compel a
legitimate monarchy to do what even the Revolution
never dreamed of wresting from the throne. One of
these ministers is the chief of the French magistracy,
and the guardian of the laws; the other is a Catholic
bishop, an official trustee of the rights of his brethren in
the episcopate. Both of them are rivals in their zeal
to exterminate the priesthood and to complete the
bloody work of the Revolution. Applaud it, sacrilegious and atheistic race! Behold a priest who
betrays the sanctuary! Behold a magistrate who
betrays the courts of law and justice!"

Berryer's chief opponent was the famous Count
de Montlosier whose " Memoire " was the sensation of
the hour. It consisted of four chapters: 1. The

47

Sodalities. 2. The Jesuits. 3. The Ultramontanes.
4. The Clerical Encroachments. These were described
as " The Four Calamities which were going to subvert
the throne." The Sodalities especially worried him,
for they were, according to his conception of them,
" apparently a pious assembly of angels, a senate of
sages, but in reality a circle of intriguing devils."
These sodalities or congregations, as they are called
in France, had assumed an importance and effectiveness
for good which is perhaps unequalled in the history of
similar organizations elsewhere. Their founder was
Father Delpuits, "whom it is a pleasure to name,"
said the eloquent Lacordaire, " for though others may
have won more applause for their influence over
young men, no one deserved it more."

When the Society was expelled from France in 1762,
Delpuits became a secular priest and was offered a
canonry by de Beaumont, the Archbishop of Paris.
He gave retreats to the clergy and laity and especially
to young collegians. During the Revolution, he was
put in prison and then exiled, but he returned to
France after the storm. There he met young Father
Barat, who had just been released from prison and
was anxious to join the Jesuits in Russia. Delpuits
advised him to remain in France where men of his
stamp were sorely needed and hence Barat did not
enter the Society until 1814.

In 1801, following out the old Jesuit traditions,
Delpuits organized a sodality, beginning with four
young students of law and medicine. Others soon
joined them, among them Laennec who subsequently
became one of the glories of the medical profession
as the inventor of auscultation. Then came two
abbés and two brothers of the house of Montmorency.
The future mathematician, Augustin Cauchy, and also
Simon Bruté de Rémur who, at a later date, was to be

one of the first bishops of the United States; Forbin-Janson, so eminent in the Church of France, was a sodalist, as were the three McCarthys, one of whom, Nicholas, became a Jesuit, and was regarded as the Chrysostom of France. The list is a long one. When Delpuits died in 1812, his sodalists erected a modest memorial above him, and inserted the S. J. after his name. That was two years prior to the re-establishment. A Sulpician then took up the work, but in 1814, he turned it over to Father de Clorivière who, in turn, entrusted it to Father Ronsin. Its good works multiplied in all directions, and branches were established throughout France. By the time Montlosier began his attacks, the register showed 1,373 names, though Montlosier assured the public that they were no less than 48,000. Among them were a great number of priests and even bishops, notably, Cheverus, the first Bishop of Boston and subsequently, Cardinal Archbishop of Bordeaux. The last meeting of the sodality was held on July 18, 1830. Paris was then in the Revolution and the sodality was suppressed, but rose again to life later on.

While this attack on the sodalists was going on, the Jesuits of course were assailed on all sides. The fight grew fiercer every day until the " Journal des Débats " was able to say: " The name Jesuit is on every tongue, but it is there to be cursed; it is repeated in every newspaper of the land with fear and alarm; it is carried throughout the whole of France on the wings of the terror that it inspires." As many as one hundred books, big and little, were counted in the Bibliothèque Nationale, all of which had been published in the year 1826 alone. They were the works not only of anonymous and money-making scribes, but of men like Thiers and the poet Béranger who did not think such literature beneath them. Casimir Périer

appeared in the tribune against the Society, and the
ominous name of Pasquier, whose bearer was possibly
a descendant of the famous anti-Jesuit of the time of
Henry IV, is found on the list of the orators.   Lamennais got into the fray, not precisely in defense of the
Jesuits, but to proclaim his ultra anti-Gallicanism;
thus bringing that element into the war.   Added to
this was the old Jansenist spirit, which had not yet
been purged out of France; indeed, Bournichon dis-
covers traces of it in some of the Fathers of the Faith
who had joined the Society.

Finally came the Revolution of 1830, during which
the novitiate of Montrouge was sacked and pillaged.
Other houses of France shared the same fate.   On
July 29 a mob of four or five hundred men attacked
St. Acheul, some of the assailants shouting for the
king, others for the emperor, others again for the
Republic, but all uniting in: " Down with the priests!
Death to the Jesuits! "   Father de Ravignan attempted
to talk to the mob, but his voice was drowned in the
crashing of falling timbers.   The bell was rung to call
for help, but that only maddened the assailants the
more.   De Ravignan persisted in appealing to them,
but was struck in the face by a stone and badly
wounded.   Then some one in the crowd shouted for
drink, and wine was brought out.   It calmed the
rioters for a while, but while they were busy emptying
bottles and breaking barrels, a troop of cavalry from
Amiens swept down on them and they fled.   The
troopers however, came too late to save the house.
It was a wreck and some of the Fathers were sent
to different parts of the world — Italy, Switzerland,
America or the foreign missions.   But when there
were no more popular outbreaks, many returned from
abroad and gave their services to the French bishops,
with the result that there never had been a period

for a long time which had so many pulpit orators
and missionaries as the reign of Louis-Philippe.

Pius VIII died on November 30, 1830, and it was
a signal for an uprising in Italy. Thanks to Cardinal
Bernetti, the Vicar of Rome, peace was maintained
in the City itself, but elsewhere in the Papal States,
the anti-Jesuit cry was raised. The colleges were
closed and all the houses were searched, on the pretext
of looking for concealed weapons. Meantime
calumnious reports were industriously circulated against
the reputations of the Fathers.

In the Spanish Revolution of 1820, twenty-five
Jesuits were murdered. In 1833 civil war broke out
between the partisans and opponents of Isabella and,
for no reason whatever, two Jesuits were arrested and
thrown into prison. One of them died after three
months' incarceration. Meanwhile threats were made
in Madrid to murder all the religious in the city.
The Jesuits were to be the special victims for they
were accused of having started the cholera, poisoned
the wells, etc. July 17, 1834, was the day fixed for
the deed, and crowds gathered around the Imperial
College to see what might happen.

The pupils were at dinner. A police officer entered
and dismissed them and then the mob invaded the
house. Inside the building, three Jesuits were killed;
a priest, a scholastic and a lay-brother. The priest
had his skull crushed in, his teeth knocked out and
his body horribly mangled. The scholastic was beaten
with clubs; pierced through the body with swords,
and when he fell in his blood, his head was cloven
with an axe. Four of the community disguised
themselves and attempted to escape but were caught
and murdered in the street. Three more were killed
on the roof; and two lay-brothers who were captured
somewhere else were likewise butchered. The rest

of the community had succeeded in reaching the chapel, and were on their knees before the altar, when an officer forced his way through the crowd and called for his brother who was one of the scholastics, to go with him to a place of safety. The young Jesuit refused the offer, whereupon the soldier replied: "Very well I shall take care of all of you." He kept his word and fifty-four Jesuits followed him out of the chapel and were conducted to a place of safety. The house, however, was gutted; unspeakable horrors were committed in the chapel; everything that could not be carried off was broken, and in the meantime a line of soldiers stood outside, not only looking on, but even taking sides with the rioters.

Evidently the times had passed when it was necessary to go out among the savages to die for the Faith. The savages had come to Madrid. Nor was this a conventional anti-Jesuit uprising; for on that hideous 17th of July, 1834, seventy-three members of other religious communities were murdered in the dead of night in the capital of Catholic Spain. Nevertheless Father General Roothaan wrote to his Jesuit sons: "I am not worried about our fourteen who have so gloriously died, for 'blessed are those who die in the Lord.' What causes me most anguish is the danger of those who remain; most of them still young, who are scattered abroad, in surroundings where their vocation and virtue will be exposed to many dangers." Nothing was done to the murderers, and before another year had elapsed, a decree was issued expelling the Jesuits from the whole of Spain; but as Don Carlos was just then in the field asserting his claim to the throne, a large number of the exiles from other parts of Spain, were able to remain at Loyola in the Pyrenees until 1840.

The Portuguese had waited for fifteen years after Pius VII had re-established the Society before consent-

ing to re-admit the Jesuits. Don Miguel issued a
decree to that effect on July 10, 1829, and the Countess
Oliviera, a niece of Pombal, was the first to welcome
them back and to place her boys in their college.
The Fathers were given their former residence in Lisbon
and, shortly afterwards, the Bishop of Evora established
them in their old college in that city. In 1832 they
were presented with their own college at Coimbra,
and on their way thither they laid in the tomb the
still unburied remains of their arch-enemy, Pombal,
which had remained in the morgue ever since March
5, 1872,— a space of half a century. It seemed
almost like a dream. Indeed it was little else, for
Dom Miguel, who was then on the throne, was deposed
by his rival, Dom Pedro, soon after, and on July 20,
1833 the Jesuits of Lisbon were again expelled. The
decree was superfluous, for in the early Spring, their
house had been sacked, and on that occasion the
inmates would have been killed had not a young
Englishman, a former student of Stonyhurst, appeared
on the scene. The four that were there he took
on his yacht to England, the others had already
departed for Genoa.

Hatred for the Society, however, had nothing to do
with it. The whole affair was purely political. Had
the Fathers accepted Dom Pedro's invitation to go
out among the people and persuade them to abandon
the cause of the deposed king, they would have been
allowed to remain. They were expelled for not being
traitors to their lawful sovereign. The Fathers of
Coimbra contrived to remain another year, but on
May 26, 1834, they were seized by a squad of soldiers
and marched off to Lisbon. Fortunately the French
ambassador, Baron de Mortier, interceded for them,
otherwise they would have ended their days in the
dungeons of San Sebastian, to which they had already

been sentenced. They were released on June 28, 1834, and sent by ship to Italy and from there, along with the dispersed Spaniards were sent by Father Roothaan to France and South America.

Switzerland, which is the land of liberty to such an extent that it will harbor the worst kind of anarchists, refused to admit the Jesuits, at least in some parts of it. There were seven Catholic Cantons, Uri, Schwyz, Unterwalden, Lucerne, Zug, Fribourg and Valais. These sections formed a coalition known as the Sunderbund. A war broke out between them and the other cantons, but the Sunderbund was defeated. The Jesuits were then expelled from the little town of Sion where they had an important school. In 1845 the people of Lucerne asked for a college, and though Father Roothaan refused, Pope Gregory XVI insisted on it. The expected happened. The Radicals arose in a rage and with 10,000 men laid siege to Lucerne. They were beaten, it is true, but that did not insure the permanency of the college. In 1847 the Sunderbund was again defeated, and in 1848 when the general European revolution broke out, the College of Fribourg was looted, and its collection of Natural History which was regarded as among the best on the Continent was thrown out in the street.

The rumblings of the storm began to be heard in France on May 1, the Feast of the Apostles Philip and James, Louis-Philippe's name-day. Someone in the Tuilleries said that the Jesuits were starting a conspiracy against the throne. Happily a distinguished woman heard the remark, and admitted that she was concerned in it, along with 300 other conspicuous representatives of the best families of France. It was a charity lottery and most of the conspirators had received a pot or basket of flowers for their participation in the plot.

When that myth was exploded, the "Journal des Débats" attacked de Ravignan for his wide influence over many important people in Paris, and though admitting his unquestioned probity, added "What matters his virtue, if he brings us the pest?" The word caught the popular fancy, but it brought out de Ravignan's famous reply: "De l'éxistence et de l'institut des Jésuites." It was received with immense favor, applauded by such men as Vatemesnil, Dupanloup, Montalembert, Barthélemy, Beugnot, Berryer and others. In this year 1844 alone, 25,000 copies were sold.

The root of the trouble was the university's monopoly of education; which was obnoxious even to many who cared little for religion. Catholics objected to it chiefly because Cousin, the Positivist, controlled its philosophy. Many of the bishops failed to see the danger until Father Delvaux published a digest of the utterances of many of the university professors on religious subjects. Then the battle began. On the Catholic side were such fighters as Veuillot, Montalembert, Cardinal de Bonald, Mgr. Parisis. Ranged against them were Michelet, Quinet, Sainte-Beuve and their followers. The battle waxed hotter as time went on; and the Jesuits soon became the general target. Cousin introduced the "Lettres Provinciales" in the course. Villemain in his Reports denounced "the turbulent and imperious Society which the spirit of liberty and the spirit of our government repudiate." Dupin glorified Etienne Pasquier, the old anti-Jesuit of the time of Henry IV; similar eulogies of the old enemy were pronounced in various parts of France; Quinet and Michelet did nothing else in their historical lectures than attack the Society, while Eugene Sue received 100,000 francs from the editor of the "Constitutionel" for his "Juif errant," which presented to the public the most grotesque picture of the Jesuits that was ever conceived. It was however, accepted as a genuine portrait.

The anti-Jesuit cry was of course the usual campaign device to alarm the populace. It was successful, chiefly because of the persistency with which it was kept up by the press, and, from 1842 till 1845, the book-market was glutted with every imaginable species of anti-Jesuit literature. Conspicuous among the pro-Jesuits were Louis Veuillot and the Comte de Montalembert. The royalist papers spoke in the Society's defense but feebly or not at all. Finally, a certain Marshall Marcet de la Roche Arnauld, who as a scholastic had been driven from the Society in 1824, and who had been paid to write against it, suddenly disavowed all that he had ever said. Crétineau-Joly also leaped into the fray with his rapidly written six volumes of the " History of the Society."

It would have been comparatively easy to continue the struggle with outside enemies, but in the very midst of the battle, the Archbishop of Paris, Affre, ranged himself on the side of the foe. He denied that the Jesuits were a religious order, for the extraordinary reason that they were not recognized by the State; their vows, consequently, were not solemn; and the members of the Society were in all things subject to the curé of the parish in which their establishment happened to be. He even exacted that he should be informed of everything that took place in the community, and if an individual was to be changed, His Grace was to be notified of it a month in advance. The archbishop, however, was not peculiar in these views. They were deduced from Bouvier's theology which was then taught in all the seminaries of France.

Of course, this affected other religious as well as the Jesuits, and, hence, when Dom Guéranger wanted to establish the Benedictines in Paris, the archbishop had no objection, except that "they had no legal existence in France." To this Guéranger immediately replied: "Monseigneur! the episcopacy has no legal existence in England, Ireland and Belgium, and perhaps the day will come when it will not have any in France, but the episcopacy will be no less sacred for all that." The great Benedictine then appealed to the Pope, and when the reply was handed to him, the Apostolic nuncio said: "It is not an ordinary Brief I give you, but an Apostolic Constitution." In it the archbishop was told by His Holiness that the French religious had not been destroyed because of the refusal of the government to give them a legal existence. His Grace had also received a communication from Father Roothaan, the General, who, after reminding him of the provision of canon law on the point at issue, warned him that if he persisted in his view the Jesuits would simply withdraw from his diocese.

Meantime the Pope had suspended the execution of the orders of the archbishop and shortly after, sent him the following severe admonition: "We admit, Venerable Brother, our inability to comprehend your very inconsiderate ruling with regard to the faculties for hearing confessions which you have withdrawn from the Jesuit Fathers, or by what authority or for what reason you forbid them either to leave the city or to enter it, without notifying you a month in advance; especially as this Society, on account of the immense services it has rendered to the Church, is held in great esteem by far-seeing and fervent Catholics and by the Holy See itself. We know also that it is calumniated by people who have abandoned the Faith and by those who have no respect for the authority of the Holy See and we regret that they will now use the authority of your name in support of their calumnies."

Of course the archbishop could do nothing else than obey. But he did not change his mind with regard to the objects of his hostility. Possibly he was constitutionally incapable of doing so. For he treated his cathedral chapter in the same fashion and we read in a communication from the French ambassador at Rome to Guizot who was then head of the Government that the canons of Paris had complained of being absolutely excluded from all influence or authority in the administration of the diocese. This note gives an insight into the methods of Gallicanism, which conceded that the disputes or differences of the clergy with the archbishop were to be passed upon by a minister of state even if he were a Protestant.

The trouble did not end there and the Parliamentary session of 1844 marked a very notable epoch in the history of the French province of the Society and of the Church of France. M. Villemain presented a bill which proposed to reaffirm and reassure the university's monopoly of the education of the country. It explicitly excluded all members of religious congregations from the function of teaching. It is true that there was not a single word in it about the Jesuits, nevertheless in the stormy debates that it evoked, and in which the most prominent men of the nation participated, there was mention of not one other teaching body. Almost the very first speaker, Dupin, pompously proclaimed that " France did not want that famous Society which owes allegiance to a foreign superior and whose instruction is diametrically opposed to what all lovers of the country desire" nor was it desirable that " these religious speculators should slip in through the meshes of the law." His last word was: " Let us be implacable." In the official Report, however, " implacable " became " inflexible." The ministerial and university organ, the " Journal des

Débats," admitted that such was the purpose of the bill.

Villemain fancied that he had silenced the bishops by leaving them full authority over the little seminaries. He was quickly disillusioned. From the entire hierarchy individually and collectively came indignant repudiations of the measure and none was fiercer than the protest of Mgr. Affre, Archbishop of Paris. He denounced the university as "a centre of irreligion" and as perverting in the most flagrant manner the youth of France. "You reproach us," he said, "with disturbing the country by our protests. Yes, we have raised our voices, but the university has committed the crime. We may embarrass the throne for the present, but in the university are to be found all the perils of the future." The excitement was so intense that the government actually put the Abbé Combalot in jail for an article he wrote against the bill, and the whole hierarchy was threatened with being summoned before the council of state if they persisted in their opposition.

Montalembert was more than usually eloquent in the course of the parliamentary war. To Dupin who exhorted the peers to be "implacable" he replied: "In the midst of a free people, we, Catholics, refuse to be slaves; we are the successors of the martyrs and we shall not quail before the successors of Julian the Apostate; we are the sons of the Crusaders and we shall not recoil before the sons of Voltaire."

There were thirty-five or forty discourses and twelve or fifteen of the speakers described the Society as "the detested congregation," while the members who admitted the injustice and the odious tyranny of the proposed legislation made haste to assure their constituents that they had no use for the Jesuits. Cousin consumed three hours in assailing them;

another member of the Dupin family saw " an appalling danger to the State in the fact that Montalembert could speak of them without cursing them, and that the peers could listen to him in silence, while he extolled the poisoners of the pious Ganganelli." Others insisted that the Jesuits had dragged the episcopate into the fight; even Guizot declared that " public sentiment inexorably repudiated the Jesuits and the other congregations, who are the champions of authority and the enemies of private judgment." The great man was not aware that the same reproach might be and is addressed to the Church.

The measure was finally carried by 85 against 51, but the heavy minority disconcerted the government and better hopes were entertained in the lower house to which Villemain presented his bill on June 10th. There it was left in the hands of Thiers, and it did not reach the Assembly, as a body, for an entire month. As the summer vacations were at hand, the *projet de loi* was dropped. Guizot then conceived the plan of appealing directly to the Pope to suppress the French Jesuits. He chose as his envoy an Italian named Rossi, who had been banished from Bologna, Naples and Florence as a revolutionist. After a short stay at Geneva, he made his way to France where, by Protestant influence, chiefly that of Guizot, he advanced rapidly to very distinguished and lucrative positions. The country was shocked to hear that an Italian and a Protestant should represent the nation at the court of the Pope from whose dominions he had been expelled, but Guizot intended by so doing, to express the sentiments of his government. It was an open threat. Rossi arrived in Rome and presented his credentials on April 11.

The French Jesuits who had been expelled from Portugal did not return to their native country; for

Charles X, discovering at last that the Liberals, as they called themselves, had played him false, resolved to have a thoroughgoing monarchical government; and, to carry out his purpose, made the inept Polignac prime minister. On July 25 he signed four ordinances, the first of which restricted the liberty of the press; the second dissolved parliament; the third diminished the electorate to 25,000. The next day, the press was in rebellion; Charles abdicated and sailed for England. Of course the Revolution was anti-religious and the Jesuits were the first sufferers. House after house was wrecked and the scholastics were gathered together and hurried off to different countries in Europe. Thus ended the first sixteen years of the Society's existence in France, after the promulgation of the Bull of Pius VII " Sollicitudo omnium ecclesiarum."

The first successor of Father de Clorivière as vice-provincial was Father Simpson. France was made a province in 1820, and on the death of Father Simpson, the new General, Father Fortis, appointed Father Richardot, who at the end of his three years' term asked to be relieved. In 1814 Godinot was appointed, because none of those who had been proposed for the office had been more than ten years in the Society. Godinot himself had been admitted only in 1810. He had been vice-provincial of the Fathers of the Faith, and eleven years after his admission, was directing the scattered Jesuit establishments in Switzerland, Belgium, Holland and Germany. In Switzerland, he had given the impulse to the college of Fribourg, which afterwards became so famous. It is worth noting that when he was a Father of the Faith he was a member of the community of Sion in Valais which enjoyed the exceptional privilege of being united as a body to the Society. Everywhere else each individual had to be admitted separately.

On April 14, the peers met to discuss a very exciting subject. A protest had come from Marseilles signed by 89 electors, against the books of Michelet and Quinet. Immediately Cousin was on his feet and ascribed it to the Jesuits. A few days later, another topic engrossed their attention. Dupin's " Manual of Ecclesiastical Law " had been condemned by Cardinal de Bonald, and more than sixty bishops concurred with him in prohibiting the book. At Rome, it was put on the Index, along with Cousin's " History of Philosophy." The anti-Catholics were in a fury, and on April 24, Cousin addressed the House. At the end of a three hour discourse which he began, unbeliever though he was, by protesting his respect for " the august religion of his country," he concluded by saying that " probably the action of the bishops was due to the Jesuits " and therefore he called for the enforcement of the law for their suppression. The question now arose, whether they could proceed to the suppression by force of law while the government actually had an envoy at Rome to dispose of the affair in a different fashion. It was decided that the non-authorized congregations would be suppressed, no matter what might be the outcome of Rossi's mission. Such a resolution was a gross diplomatic insult, but they cared little for that.

Meanwhile no news had come from Rossi. He had been left in the ante-chamber of the Pope until the Abbé de Bonnechose had succeeded in getting him an audience, a service which de Bonnechose had some difficulty in explaining when he was subsequently made a cardinal. A congregation of cardinals was named to discuss Guizot's proposition, and it was unanimously decided to reject it; and when Rossi asked what he had to do, he was told he might address himself to the General of the Society. To make it

easy for him, Lambruschini, the papal secretary of
state, proposed to Father Roothaan to diminish the
personnel of some of the houses which were too much
in evidence or remove them elsewhere. As for dissolution of the communities or banishment from
France, not a word was said.

Immediately Rossi despatched a messenger to Paris
with the account of what had been done, and twelve
days afterwards the " Moniteur " stated: " The
Government has received news from Rome that the
negotiations with which M. Rossi was entrusted have
attained their object. The congregation of the Jesuits
will cease to exist in France and will, of its own accord,
disperse. Its houses will be closed and its novitiates
dissolved." On July 15, Guizot was asked by the
peers to show the alleged documents. He answered
that " they were too precious to give to the public."
They have been unearthed since, and it turns out
that Guizot's notice in the " Moniteur " does not
correspond with the despatch of Rossi who merely
said, " the Congregation is going to disperse; " and
instead of saying " the houses will be closed," he
wrote: " only a small number of people will remain
in each house." In brief, the famous Guizot, so
renowned for his integrity, prevaricated in this instance,
and one of the worst enemies of everything Jesuitical,
Dibidous, who wrote a " History of the Church and
State in France from 1789 to 1870 " declares bluntly
that Guizot's note in the " Moniteur " was not only
a lie but " an impudent lie."

A great many militant Catholics in France were
indignant that Father Roothaan had not defied the
government on this occasion. Yet probably those
same perfervid souls would have denounced him, had
he acted as they wished. He knew perfectly well
that the government was only too anxious to get out

48

of the mess in which it found itself, and the little
by-play which was resorted to harmed nobody and
secured at least a temporary respite.

"To gain the support of the Catholics against the
anarchical elements which were everywhere revealing
themselves," says the Cambridge History (XI, 34)
" Guizot had tolerated the unauthorized Congregations. This had the immediate consequence of
concentrating popular attention upon those religious
passions whose existence the populace, if left to itself,
might have forgotten. Even the colleagues of Guizot,
such as Villemain and the editors of the "Journal des
Débats," the leading ministerial organ, began by declaring that they saw everywhere the finger of the
Jesuits. In each party, men's minds were so divided
on the subject of the Jesuits or rather that of educational liberty which was so closely linked with it,
that nothing of immediate gravity to the Government
would for the moment arise." Liberals, or rather
Republicans, such as Quinet and Michelet, in their
lectures at the Collége de France took up the alarm
and spread.it broadcast.

Bournichon in his " Histoire d'un Siècle," (II, 492)
calls attention to the fact that this attack was
apparently against the Jesuits, but in reality against
the Church. The " Revue Indépendante " did not
hesitate to make the avowal that " Jesuitism is only
a formula which has the merit of uniting all the popular
hatred for what is odious and retrograde in a degenerate
religion." Cousin started the hue and cry, in this
instance, and Thureau-Dangin in his " Histoire de
la monarchie de Juillet " (p. 503–10) says that " Quinet
and Michelet transformed their courses into bitter
and spiteful diatribes against the Jesuits. Both were
hired for the work, and did not speak from conviction."
" Quinet," says Bournichon (II, 494) " was quite

indifferent to religious matters and had passed for a
harmless thinker and dreamer up to that moment.
As for Michelet, he had obtained his position in the
Ecole Normale from Mgr. Frayssinous, yet he forgot
his benefactor, and maintained that not only the
Jesuits but Christianity was an obstacle to human
progress; paganism or even fetichism was preferable,
and Christ had to be dethroned."

Guizot removed Villemain from the office of Minister
of public instruction and reprimanded Michelet and
Quinet. Then Thiers seized the occasion to denounce
Guizot for favoring the religious congregations and
succeeded in defeating the minister's measure for
educational freedom. It was at this stage that Guizot
sent his envoy Rossi to Rome to induce Pope Gregory
XVI to recall the Jesuits so as to extricate the French
government from its difficulty. The Pope refused,
as we have seen, and Father Roothaan merely gave
orders to the members of the Society in France to
make themselves less conspicuous.

In 1847 Gioberti published his " Gesuita Moderno "
which unfortunately had the effect of creating in the
minds of the Italian clergy a deep prejudice against
the Society. Gioberti was a priest and a professor
of theology. He first taught Rosminianism, and then
opposed it. Under the pen-name of " Demofilo " or
the " People's Friend " he wrote articles for Mazzini
in the " Giovane Italia," and was the author of " Del
Buono " and " Del primato morale e civile degli
Italiani." His first attack on the Society appeared
in 1845 in the " Prolegomeni al Primato;" " Il Gesuita
Moderno," a large sized pamphlet full of vulgar invec-
tive, appeared in 1847. It was followed in 1848 by
the " Apologia del Gesuita Moderno." He was
answered by Father Curci. Deserting Mazzini, Gioberti espoused the cause of King Charles Albert, and

founded a society to propagate the idea of a federated
Italy with the King of Piedmont at its head. His
last book, " Rinnovamento civile d'Italia " showed
him to be the enemy of the temporal power of the
papacy. His philosophy is a mixture of pantheistic
ontology, rationalism, platonism and traditionalism.
Though a revolutionist, he denied the sovereignty
of the people. His complete works fill thirty-five
volumes.

Of course the Society felt the shock of the Italian
Revolution of 1848. Gioberti's writing had excited
all Italy and as a consequence the Jesuit houses
were abandoned. At Naples, the exiles were hooted
as they took ship for Malta; they were mobbed in
Venice and Piedmont. The General Father Roothaan
left Rome on April 28 in company with a priest and a
lay-brother, and as he stood on the deck at Genoa,
he heard the cry from the shore, " You have Jesuits
aboard; throw them overboard." There was nothing
surprising in all this, however, for Rossi, the Pope's
prime minister, was stabbed to death while mounting
the steps of the Cancelleria. On the following day,
the Pope himself was besieged in the Quirinal; Palma,
a Papal prelate, was shot while standing at a window;
and finally on November 24, Pope Pius fled in disguise to Gaeta.

In Austria, the Jesuits were expelled in the month of
April. The community of Innsbruck, which is in
the Tyrol, held together for some time, but finally
drifted off to France or America or Australia or elsewhere. The emperor signed the decree on May 7,
1848. It applied also to Galicia, Switzerland, and
Silesia, and the Jesuit houses all disappeared in those
parts.

What happened to the Jesuits in France in the
meantime? Nothing whatever. They had obeyed the

General in 1845, and had simply kept their activities
out of sight. They did not wait for the Revolution,
and hence although the "Journal des Débats,"
announced officially, on October 18, 1845, that "at
the present moment there are no more Jesuits in
France," there were a great many. Indeed, the
catalogues of 1846 and 1847 were issued as usual, not
in print, however, but in lithograph, and as if they
felt perfectly free in 1848, the catalogue of that year
appeared in printed form. Meantime de Ravignan
was giving conferences in Notre-Dame, and preaching
all over the country. The only change the Fathers
made was to transport two of their establishments
beyond the frontiers. Thus a college was organized
at Brugelette in Belgium and a novitiate at Issenheim.
The scholasticate of Laval continued as usual. What
was done in the province of Paris was identical with
that of Lyons. For a year or so the catalogues were
lithographed but after that they appeared in the
usual form.

For two years Father Roothaan journeyed from place
to place through France, Belgium, Holland, England,
and Ireland, and in 1850 returned to Rome. The
storm had spent itself, and the ruins it had caused
were rapidly repaired, at least in France, where the
Falloux Law, which was passed in 1850, permitted
freedom of education, and the Fathers hastened to
avail themselves of the opportunity to establish colleges throughout the country.

Elsewhere, however, other conditions prevailed.
In 1851 there was a dispersion in Spain; in 1859 the
provinces of Venice and Turin were disrupted and the
members were distributed through the fifteen other
provinces of the Society. In 1860 the arrival of
Garibaldi had already made an end of the Jesuits in
Naples and Sicily. The wreckage was considerable,

and from a complaint presented to King Victor Emmanuel by Father Beckx, it appears that the Society had lost three establishments in Lombardy; in Modena, six; in Sardinia, eleven; in Naples, nineteen, and in Sicily, fifteen. Fifteen hundred Jesuits had been expelled from their houses, as if they had been criminals, and were thrown into public jails, abused and ill-treated. They were forbidden to accept shelter even from their most devoted friends, and the old and the infirm had to suffer like the rest. Nor were these outrages perpetrated by excited mobs, but by the authorities then established in Sardinia, Sicily, Naples, Modena and elsewhere. " This appeal for justice and reparation for at least some of the harm done," said Father Beckx, " is placed, as it were, on the tomb of your ancestor Charles Emmanuel, who laid aside his royal dignity and entered the Society of Jesus as a lay-brother. He surely would not have embraced that manner of life if it were iniquitous." But it is not on record that Victor Emmanuel showed his appreciation of his predecessor's virtue by healing any of the wounds of the Society, whose garb Charles Emmanuel had worn.

The Jesuits of Venice had resumed work in their province, when in 1866 war was declared between Prussia and Austria. Sadowa shattered the Austrian forces, and though the Italians had been badly beaten at Custozzio, Venice was handed over to them by the treaty that ended the war. That meant of course another expulsion. Most of the exiles went to the Tyrol and Dalmatia. Then followed the dispersion of all the provinces of Italy except that of Rome.

The Spanish Jesuits had recovered somewhat from the dispersions of 1854, but, in 1868 just as the provincial congregations had concluded their sessions, a revolution broke out all over Spain. Many of the houses were attacked, but no personal injuries were inflicted. After a while, a provisional government was established at Madrid which held the mob in check but made no pretence to restrain the attacks on priests and nuns. Indeed, it inaugurated a bitter persecution on its own account. The minister of justice issued a decree which not only ordered the Jesuits out of all Spain and the adjacent islands within three days, but forbade any Spaniard to join the Society, even in foreign parts. Of course all the property was confiscated. That was probably the chief motive of the whole procedure. The outcasts for the most part went to France, and a temporary novitiate was established in the territory known as Les Landes. They returned home after some time, but were expecting another expulsion in 1912 when the great war was threatening. Possibly the hideous scenes enacted in Portugal in 1912 were deemed sufficient by the revolutionists for the time being.

The expatriation of the Jesuits and other religious from Portugal which was decreed by the Republican government, on October 10, 1910, six days after the bombardment of the royal palace and the flight of King Manuel, is typical of the manner in which such demonstrations are made in Europe. We have an account of it from the Father provincial Cabral which we quote in part.

" After the press had been working up the populace for three years to the proper state of mind by stories of subterranean arsenals in the Jesuit colleges; the boundless wealth of the Fathers; their affiliated secret organizations; their political plots, etc., the colleges of Campolide and San Fiel were invaded. The occupants were driven out and led between lines of soldiers through a howling mob to the common jail. Those who had fled before the arrival of the soldiers were pursued across the fields with rifles, and when caught were insulted, beaten and spat upon, and led like the others to prison.   They had to eat out of the dishes with their hands, and at night sentinels stood over them with loaded rifles and warned the victims that if they got up they would be shot.   Abandoned women were sent in among them, but those poor creatures soon withdrew.   The prisoners were then transferred to Caixas where they slept on the floor.   Twenty-three were confined in a space that could scarcely accommodate three.   They were kept there for four days, and were not allowed to leave the room for any reason whatever, and were told that they would be kept in that condition until they began to rot, and that then some of their rich friends would buy them off.   They were photographed, subjected to anthropometric examinations, and their finger prints taken, etc.   They were then expelled from the country and forbidden ever to return.   They had only the clothes on their backs, and had no money except what was given them by some friends; their colleges with their splendid museums and libraries were confiscated, and in this condition they set out, old and young, the sick and the strong, to ask shelter from their brethren in other lands.   It was almost a return to the days of Pombal.

In Germany the Kulturkampf began in 1870, and in 1872 a decree was signed by the Kaiser, on June 14, 1872, expelling all members of the Society, and with them the Redemptorists, Lazarists, Fathers of the Holy Ghost, and the Society of the Sacred Heart. Some of the Jesuits went to Holland; others to England and America.   Contrary to expectations, this act of tyranny did not harm the German province, for, whereas it then numbered only 775, it now (1920) has 1210 on its roll, of whom 664 are priests.

France had its horror in 1871, when on May 24 and 26, Fathers Olivaint, Ducoudray, Caubert, Clerc and de Bengy were shot to death by the Communists, who were then in possession of Paris. It was not, however, a rising against the Jesuits. There were fifty-seven victims in all: priests, religious and seculars, were immolated. At their head, was the venerable Archbishop of Paris, Mgr. Darboy. Again, on March 29, 1880, a decree issued by Jules Ferry brought about a new dispersion and the substitution of staffs of non-religious teachers in the Jesuit colleges. The law was not enforced, however, and little by little the Fathers returned to their posts. Then followed the law of Waldeck-Rousseau in 1901 against unauthorized congregations, which closed all their houses, for these religious declined to apply for authorization which they knew would be refused, or if not, would be used to oppress them. The communities were, therefore, scattered in various houses of Europe. The last blow was the summons sent to all parts of the world for every Frenchman not exempt from military service to take part in the great World War, as chaplains, hospital aids or common soldiers.

The simultaneity as well as the similarity in the methods of executing these multiplied expulsions show clearly enough that they were not accidental but part of a universal war against the Church. Thus, at the other ends of the earth, similar outrages were being committed. When, for instance, the Conservatives fell from power in Colombia, South America, in 1850, the Jesuits were expelled. They went from there to Ecuador and Guayaquil, but were left unmolested only for a year. In 1861 they were re-admitted, and soon had fifty mission stations and had succeeded in converting 10,000 natives to the faith. But Garcia Moreno who had invited them was assassinated, and forthwith they were expelled. A second time they were recalled, but remained only from 1883 to 1894, and from there they returned to Colombia where they are at present. In Argentina, whither they were summoned in 1836, their houses were closed in 1841. They entered Paraguay in 1848, where the old Society had achieved such triumphs, but were allowed to remain there only three years. They asked the Chilian government to let them evangelize the fierce Araucanian savages, but this was refused. At the death of the dictator Rosas in 1873, they again went to Argentina and have not since been disturbed. They have had the same good fortune in Chile.

A different condition of things, however, obtained in Brazil. In the very year that Rosas died in Argentina, 1873, the Jesuit College of Olinda in Brazil was looted and the Fathers expelled. The reason was not that the Jesuits were objectionable but that the bishop had suspended a young ecclesiastic who was a Freemason. The College of Pernambuco was wrecked by a mob, and one of the priests was dangerously wounded. Worse treatment was meted out to them when the Emperor, Don Pedro, was deposed in 1889. Since then, however, there has been comparatively no trouble.

Of course, when the Piedmontese broke down the Porta Pia the Jesuits had to leave Rome, where until then they had undisturbed. The novitiate of Sant' Andrea was the first to be seized; then St. Eusebio, the house of the third probation, and after that, St. Vitalis, the Gesù, and finally the Roman College. The occupants had three months to vacate the premises. The other religious orders whose general or procurator resided at Rome could retain one house for the transaction of business but that indulgence was not granted to the Jesuits. Their General was not to remain, and hence Father Peter Beckx, though then seventy-eight years old, had to depart with his brethren for Fiesole, where he was received in the family of the Counts of Ricasole

on November 9, 1873. From that place he governed
the Society until the year 1884, when he was succeeded
by Father Anthony Anderledy, who remained in the
same city until he died. Father Luis Martín, the
next General, returned to Rome in 1893, so that Fiesole
was the centre of the Society for twenty years.

As the chief representative of Christ on Earth is the
most prominent victim of these spoliations, and as
he has been frequently driven into exile and is at
present only tolerated in his own territory, the Society
of Jesus with the other religious orders cannot consider
it a reproach but rather a glory to be treated like him.
How does the Society survive all these disasters?
It continues as if nothing had happened, and one reads
with amazement the statement of Father General
Wernz at the meeting of the procurators held in
September and October 1910, when in a tone that is
almost jubilant he congratulates the Society on its
" flourishing condition." He said in brief:

" There are five new provinces; a revival of the
professed houses; new novitiates, scholasticates, ter-
tianships and courses in the best colleges for students of
special subjects; and a superior course for Jesuit
students of canon law in the Gregorian University.
Next year there are to be accommodations for 300
theologians (boarders) at Innsbruck, which institution
will be a Collegium Maximum for philosophy, theology
and special studies. The novitiate is to be moved to
the suburbs of Vienna. In the province of Galicia
sufficient ground has been bought to make the College
of Cracow similar to Innsbruck, and a beautiful
church is being built there. The province of Germany
though dispersed has built in Holland an immense
novitiate and house of retreats and the Luxemburg
house of writers is to be united to the Collegium
Maximum of Valkenburg. The Holland province

has more diplomated professors than any other in the
Society, and is about to build a new scholasticate.
Louvain is becoming more and more a house of special
studies. In England, the Campion house at Oxford
is continuing its success and there is question of moving
St. Beuno's. The Irish province is looking for another
site for the novitiate and juniorate, and is using the
University to form better teachers. Canada is looking
for another place for its novitiate and so are Mexico,
Brazil and Argentina, while Maryland is trying to put
its scholasticate near New York.

" Not much remains to be done in Spain. However,
Toledo has established a scholasticate in Murcia, and
Aragon is planning one for Tarragona. France is
dispersed, but it has furnished excellent professors
for the Biblical Institute and the Gregorian University.
In the mission of Calcutta, 130,000 pagans have been
brought to the Faith and in one Chinese mission,
12,000. The numbers could be doubled if there were
more workers." This was in 1910, and within a week
of this pronouncement, the expulsion in Portugal took
place; in 1914 the war broke out which shattered
Belgium and made France more wretched than ever.
What the future will be no one knows.

CHAPTER XXVI

MODERN MISSIONS

During the Suppression — Roothaan's appeal — South America — The Philippines — United States Indians — De Smet — Canadian Reservations — Alaska — British Honduras — China — India — Syria — Algeria — Guinea — Egypt — Madagascar — Mashonaland — Congo — Missions depleted by World War — Actual number of missionaries.

BESIDES its educational work, the Society of Jesus has always been eager for desperate and daring work among savages. At the time of the Suppression, namely in 1773 three thousand of its members were so employed; and the ruthless and cruel separation from those abandoned human beings was one of the darkest and gloomiest features of the tragedy. To all human appearances millions of heathens were thus hopelessly lost. Happily the disaster was not as great as was anticipated. In his " Christian Missions " Marshall says: — It would almost seem as if God had resolved to justify his servants by a special and marvellous Providence before the face of the whole world, and had left their work to what seemed inevitable ruin and decay only to show that neither the world nor the devil, neither persecution, nor fraud nor neglect could extinguish the life that was in it. And so when they came to look upon it, after sixty years of silence and desolation they found a living multitude where they expected to count only the corpses of the dead. Some indeed had failed, and paganism or heresy had sung its song of triumph over the victims; others had retained only the great truths of the Trinity and the Incarnation while ignorance and its twin sister, superstition, had spread a veil over their eyes, but still

the prodigious fact was revealed that in India alone
that there were more than one million natives who, after
half a century of abandonment, still clung with
constancy to the faith which had been preached to
their fathers, and still bowed the head with loving
awe when the names of their departed apostles were
uttered amongst them. Such is the astonishing conclusion of a trial without parallel in the history of
Christianity, and which if it had befallen the Christians
of other lands, boasting their science and civilization,
might perhaps have produced other results than
among the despised Asiatics. The natural inference
would be that besides this special Providence in their
regard these neophytes had been well trained by their
old masters (I, 246).

For a time, of course, there were some Jesuits who
lingered on the missions in spite of the government's
orders to the contrary. Thus we find a very distinguished man, a Tyrolese from Bolzano, who died at
Lucknow on July 5, 1785. His name was Joseph
Tiffenthaller and he had lived forty years in Hindostan.
His tombstone, we are told, may be still seen in the
cemetery of Agra where they laid his precious remains.
He was a man of unusual ability and besides speaking
his native tongue was familiar with Latin, Italian,
Spanish, French, Hindustanee, Arabic, Persian and
Sanscrit. He was the first European who wrote a
description of Hindostan. It is a detailed account of
the twenty-two Provinces of India, with their cities,
towns, fortresses, whose geographical situations were
all calculated by means of a simple quadrant. The
work contains a large number of maps, plans and
sketches drawn by himself and the list of places fills
twenty-one quarto pages. He also made a large
atlas of the basin of the Ganges, and is the author of
a treatise on the regions in which the rivers of India

rise; a map of the Gagra which Bernoulli calls "a work of enormous labor" is another part of Tiffen-thaller's relics.

In the field of religion he wrote books on "Brahmanism," "Indian Idolatry," "Indian Asceticism," "The religon of the Parsees and Mohammedanism with their relations to each other." He also published his astronomical observations on the sun-spots, on the zodiacal light, besides discussions on the astrology and cosmology of the Hindus, with descriptions of the flora and the fauna of the country. He was besides all that an historian, and has left us an account in Latin of the origin and religion of the Hindus, another in German of the expedition of Nadir Shah to India; a third in Persian about the deeds of the Great Mogul, Alam, and a fourth in French which tells of the incursions of the Afghans and the capture of Delhi, together with a contemporary history of India for the years 1757–64. In linguistics, he wrote a Parsee-Sanscrit lexicon and treatises in Latin on the Parsee language, the pronunciation of Latin, etc., He was held in the highest esteem by the scientific societies of Europe with which he was in communication. During the greater part of his life in India, the struggle was going on between the French and English for the possession of the Peninsula.

Of course he was not alone in India, at that time, for Bertrand tells us in his "Notions sur l' Inde et les missions" (p. 30) that "the Jesuits had a residence at Delhi as late as 1790", but, unfortunately, he could say nothing more about them. It is very likely, however, that when Pombal's agents attempted to crowd the 127 Jesuits who were at work in the various districts of Hindostan into a ship which had accommodations — and such accommodations — for only forty or fifty, many of them had perforce to be left behind, or perhaps failed to report at the place of embarcation. By keeping out of Goa, they could easily elude the pursuivants.   The jungle, for instance, was a convenient hiding place.   However, as they received no recruits the work went to pieces when the old heroes died, so that there were, most likely, no Jesuits there at the beginning of the nineteenth century.   It was just at this time, that England took possession of the greater part of Hindostan and, as a consequence, the country was soon swarming with Protestant parsons of every sect, eager to fill their depleted ranks with new converts from the East.

Marshall had been employed to report on their success, but as every one knows, the investigation brought him to the Church.   His researches furnish very reliable and interesting information about the conditions prevailing in those parts among the old proselytes of the Jesuits.   Quoting from the " Madras Directory " of 1857, he shows that in the Missions of Madura, founded by de Nobili, there were still 150,000 Catholics, and in Verapoli as many as 300,000, with an accession of 1000 converts from Mohammedanism every year.   Nor were these Hindus merely nominal Christians.   Bertrand who knew India thoroughly, writing in 1838, says of the Sanars: " One might almost say that they have not eaten of the tree of knowledge of good and evil with Adam, and that they were created in the days of original innocence. Among these Hindus there are numbers who when asked whether they commit this or that sin, answer: ' Formerly I did, but that is many years ago.   I told it to the Father, and he forbade me to do it.   Since then I have not committed it.'   We reckon more than 7000 Christians of this caste."   Father Garnier, S. J. wrote in the same year as follows: "The Christians of this country are, in general, well disposed and strongly attached to the Faith. The usages introduced among them by the Jesuits still subsist; morning prayer in common, an hour before sunrise; evening prayer with spiritual reading; catechism for the children every day given by a catechist; Mass on Sunday in the chapel. But in spite of these excellent practices there still remains much ignorance and superstition, and we shall have a good deal to do to form them into a people of true Christians before we turn our attention to the pagans. We shall do that when we are more numerous."

Of course these testimonies of Jesuits may be rejected by some people, but the Protestant missionaries in Hindostan, at that time, leave no room for doubt about the actual conditions. Buchanan, for instance, who was particularly conspicuous among his fellows and was greatly extolled in England says: " There are in India members of the Church of Rome who deserve the affection and respect of all good men. From Cape Commorin to Cochin, there are about one hundred churches on the seashore alone. Before each is a lofty cross which like the church itself is seen from a great distance. At Jaffna, on Sundays, about a thousand or twelve hundred people attend church and on feast days three thousand and upward. At Manaar they are all Romish Christians. At Tutycorin, the whole of the tribe, without exception, are Christians in the Romish Communion. Before they hoist sail to go out to sea, a number of boatmen all join in prayer to God for protection. Every man at his post, with the rope in his hands, pronounces the prayer."

One of these parsons who bore the very inappropriate name of Joseph Mullens and whose writing is usually a shriek against the Church says that " in 1854, the Jesuit and Roman Catholic missions are spread very widely through the Madras Presidency. At Pubna there is a population of 13,000 souls. It is all due to

49

the Catholic missionaries. I allow that they dress simply, eat plainly and have no luxuries at home; they travel much; are greatly exposed; live poorly, and toil hard, and I have heard of a bishop living in a cave on fifty rupees a month, and devoutly attending the sick when friends and relatives had fled from fear. But all that is much easier on the principles of a Jesuit who is supported by motives of self-righteousness than it is to be a faithful minister on the principles of the New Testament."

The bloody persecution of 1805 in China showed how fervent and strong those Christians were in their faith. Very few apostatized, though new and terrible punishments were inflicted on them. Dr. Wells Williams, a Protestant agent in China, says that " many of them exhibited the greatest constancy in their profession, suffering persecution, torture, banishment and death, rather than deny their faith, though every inducement of prevarication and mental reservation was held out to them by the magistrates, in order to avoid the necessity of proceeding to extreme measures." It came to an end only when it was discovered that Christianity had even entered the royal family, and that the judges were sometimes trying their own immediate relatives. In 1815, however, the very year that the Protestant missionaries arrived in China the persecution broke out again. Bishop Dufresse was one of the victims, and when the day of execution arrived he with thirty-two other martyrs ascended the scaffold. In 1818 many were sent to the wastes of Tatary, and 1823 when pardon was offered to all who would renounce their faith, after suffering in the desert for five years only five proved recreant. In the midst of all this storm one of the missionaries reported that he had baptized one hundred and six adults.

That a great many Chinese had remained faithful
Catholics during the long period which had elapsed
after the Suppression was manifested by a notable
event recorded by Brou in " Les Jésuites Missionaires."

" On November 1, 1903," he writes " a funeral
ceremony took place in Zikawei, a town situated about
six miles from Shanghai. It was more like the triumph
of a great hero than an occasion of mourning. The
people were in a state of great enthusiasm about it,
and assembled in immense throngs around the tomb
of the illustrious personage whose glories were being
celebrated. The object of these honors was Paul Zi
or Sin, a literary celebrity in his day, the prime minister
of an emperor in the long past, and one of the first
converts of the famous Father Ricci, whom he had
aided with lavish generosity in building churches and
in establishing the Faith in the neighborhood of
Shanghai.

" The celebration of 1903 was the third centenary
of his baptism, and all his relations or descendants
who were very numerous, had gathered at Zikawei
for the occasion. Among them, the Fathers discovered
a great number of Christians who had remained true
to the teachings of the Church during those 300 years;
and there were many others throughout the country
who resembled the Zi family in this particular. In
Paul's district, that is in the neighborhood of Shanghai,
there were, 60 years after the baptism of the great
man, as many as 40,000 Christians, and in 1683 the
number had risen to 800,000, but a century later the
persecutions had cut them down to 30,000 though
doubtless there were many who had succeeded in
concealing themselves."

With Cochin the Jesuits never had anything to do,
except that their great hero, de Rhodes, was its first

successful missionary in former days. It was at his suggestion that the Society of the Missions Etrangères was founded and took up the work which the Jesuits were unable to carry on alone.

About Corea, Marshall furnishes us with two very interesting facts. The first is that England had the honor of giving a martyr to Corea, the English Jesuit, Thomas King, who died there in 1788, that is fifteen years after the Suppression. Unfortunately the name "King" does not appear in Foley's "Records."

The second is vouched for by the "Annales" (p. 190) which relate that a French priest, known as M. de Maistre, had for ten years vainly endeavored to enter the forbidden kingdom and had spent 60,000 francs in roaming around its impenetrable frontier. He assumed all sorts of disguises, faced every kind of danger in his journeys from the ports of China to the deserts of Leao-tong, asking alternately the Chinese junks and the French ships to put him ashore somewhere on the coast. Death was so evidently to be the result of his enterprise that the most courageous seaman refused to help him. It required the zeal of an apostle to comprehend this heroism and to second its endeavors. Father Hélot, being a priest, understood what the Cross required of him, and as a member of a society whose tradition is that they have never been baffled by any difficulties or perils, felt himself at the post where his Company desired him to be. The Jesuit becomes the pilot of a battered ship, safely conducts his intrepid passenger to an unknown land, and having deposited him on the shore, looked after him for a while and returned to his neophytes with the consoling satisfaction of having exposed his life for a mission that was not his own.

From the Catalogues of the Society, we find that Louis Hélot was born on January 29, 1816. He was

a novice at St. Acheul, in 1835, and in the same house
there happened to be a certain Isidore Daubresse,
not a novice, however, but a theologian who was well-
known later on in New York. The master of novices
was Ambrose Rubillon who was subsequently assistant
of the General for France. By 1850 Hélot was in
China and spent the rest of his life hunting after souls in
the region of Nankin. He died sometime after 1864.
De Maistre succeeded in entering the country and we
find him waiting one Good Friday night to welcome
the first bishop who had three priests with him, one
of whom was a Jesuit.

Before the re-establishment the few Jesuits in White
Russia had kept up the missionary traditions of the
Society. Their missions extended all along the Volga
and they were at Odessa in 1800. In 1801, thanks to
the Emperor Paul's intercession, they had returned
to their ancient posts on the Ægean Islands, which
were in the dominions of the Grand Turk; by 1806 they
had reached Astrakhan; and in 1810 were in the Caucasus. Before Father Grassi came to America, he
was studying in St. Petersburg to prepare himself
for the missions of Astrakhan.

In America, in spite of the Suppression, the work
of the old Jesuits did not fail to leave its traces. Thus
in Brazil where Nobrega and Anchieta once labored,
over 800,000 domesticated Indians now represent the
fruit of their toil. Deprived during sixty years of
their fathers and guides and too often scandalized by
men who are Christians only in name, the native
races have not only preserved the Faith through all
their sorrows and trials, but every where rejected the
bribes and promises of heresy. In that vast region, which
stretches from the mouth of the San Francisco to the
Isthmus of Panama, watered by the mightiest rivers
of our globe, and including the district of the Amazon

with its 45,000 miles of navigable water communication, "the natives who still find shelter in its forests or guide their barks over its myriad streams," says a Protestant writer, " push their profession of the Catholic religion even to the point of fanaticism."

The Paraguayans of course could be counted upon not to forget their fathers in Christ. Both Sir Woodbine Parish and d'Orbigny testify that the effects of the preponderating influence of the monastic establishments are still visible in the habits of the generality of the people. One thing is certain, they say, and ought to be declared to the praise of the Fathers, that since their expulsion the material prosperity of Paraguay has diminished; many lands formerly cultivated have ceased to be so; many localities formerly inhabited present at this day only ruins. What ought to be confessed is this — that they knew how to engrave with such power, on their hearts, reverence for authority that even to this very hour the tribes of Paraguay beyond all those who inhabit this portion of America are the most gentle and the most submissive to the dictates of duty.

In " La Compañía de Jesús en las Republicas del Sur de America," Father Hernández tells us that there were three former Jesuits in Chile at the beginning of the nineteenth century: Father Caldera, Vildaurre and Carvajal. The first two died respectively in 1818 and 1822, the date of Carvajal's demise is not known, nor is there any information available as to whether or not they ever re-entered the Society. In the old Province of Paraguay, there was a Father Villafañe who was seventy-four years old in 1814. Hearing of the re-establishment, he wrote to the Pope asking to renew his vows when " in danger of death." The request, of course, was granted but he continued to live till the year 1830. Whether he waited till then

to renew his vows has not been found out. In that
same year there died in Buenos Aires an Irish Jesuit
named Patrick Moran. His name is inscribed not
only on the headstone over his remains, in the Recolta
graveyard, but on a slab inserted in the wall of the
church. He was probably a chaplain in some distinguished family or what was more likely exercising
his ministry in the Irish colony of that place.

Coming to the northern part of the hemisphere we
are told by Mr. Russell Bartlett that the Yaqui Indians
of Sonora, the fishermen and pearl divers of California
are invariably honest, faithful and industrious. They
were among the first to be converted by the Jesuits.
Originally extremely warlike, their savage nature was
completely subdued on being converted to Christianity,
and they became the most docile and tractable of
people. They are now very populous in the southern
part of Sonora.

Anyone who has visited the Abenakis at Old Town
in Maine, or La Jeune Lorette in Quebec, or Caughnawaga on the St. Lawrence, or the Indian settlements
at Wekwemikong and Killarney on Lake Huron will
testify to the excellent results of the teachings implanted
in their hearts by the old Jesuit missionaries who
reclaimed them from savagery.

A most remarkable example of this fidelity to their
former teachers was afforded by the Indians of Caughnawaga. They were mostly Iroquois from New York
who after their conversion to the Faith were sent or
went, of their own accord, to the Christian village
that was assigned to them above Montreal. Long
after the Suppression of the Society, namely in the
first third of the nineteenth century, a party of these
Indians headed by two chiefs with the significant
names of Ignace and François Régis tramped almost
completely across the continent, and without the aid

of a priest, for none could be got, converted an entire tribe to Christianity and did it in such wonderful fashion that the first white men who visited these converts were amazed at the purity, honesty, self-restraint and piety that reigned in the tribe. Over and over again, Ignace travelled down to St. Louis, thus making a journey of two thousand miles each time to beg for a Black Robe from the poor missionary bishop who had none to give him. The devoted Ignace, at last, lost his life in pursuance of his apostolic purpose. He fell among hostile Indians, and though he might have escaped, for he was dressed as a white man, he confessed himself an Iroquois and died with his people.

Father Fortis, the first General after the re-establishment of the Society, was rather averse to any missionary enterprise for the time being, because he judged that he had not as yet any available men for such perilous work. Father Roothaan, his immediate successor, was of a different opinion, and when in 1833, he appealed for missionaries the response was immediate. Hence Bengal was begun in 1834; Madura, Argentina and Paraguay in 1836, and the Rocky Mountains and China in 1840. In 1852 at the request of Napoleon III the penal colony of French Guinea was accepted as were the offers of Fernando Po in Africa and the Philippines from Queen Isabella of Spain.

The Spanish missions in Latin America were the least successful of any in the Society. The Fathers were debarred from any communication with the native tribes, even those formerly Christianized and civilized by them, or if permission were granted it was soon under some frivolous pretext or other rescinded, as we have mentioned above.

The Belgian Jesuits went to Guatemala in 1843, but only after considerable trouble was their existence assured by a government Act, in 1851. In 1871, however, they were expelled and withdrew to Nicaragua, from which they were driven in 1884. The Brazilian Mission was inaugurated by the Jesuits whom Rosas had exiled from Argentina. They were acceptable because priests were needed in the devastated Province of Rio Grande do Sul, which had been the theatre of an unsuccessful war of independence. Of course, the usual government methods in vogue in that part of the world were resorted to.

The suppression of the Society wrought havoc in the Philippines, and we are told that in 1836 as many as 6000 people were carried off into slavery by Mohammedan pirates, a disaster that would have probably been prevented had the missionaries been left there. They would have made soldiers out of the natives as they did in Paraguay. It was only in 1859 that they returned to that field of work. They resumed their educational labors in Manila and at the same time evangelized Mindanao with wonderful success. In 1881 there were on that island 194,134 Christians and in 1893, 302,107. Inside of thirty-six years, the Fathers had brought 57,000 Filipinos to the Faith and established them in Reductions as in Paraguay. Great success was also had with the Moros, who were grouped together in three distinct villages. The Spanish War brought its disturbances, but little by little the Jesuits recovered what they had lost and there are at present 162 members of the province of Aragon at work in the Islands.

In the United States, the native races have largely disappeared except in the very far West. With the remnants, the Jesuits are, of course, concerned, and perhaps the most reliable official estimate of the success they have achieved was expressed by Senator Vest during the discussion of the Indian Appropriation Bill before the United States Senate in 1900:

"I was raised a Protestant," he said; "I expect to die one. I was never in a Catholic church in my life, and I have not the slightest sympathy with many of its dogmas; but above all I have no respect for the insane fear that the Catholic Church is about to overturn this Government. I should be ashamed to call myself an American if I indulged in any such ignorant belief. I said that I was a Protestant. I was reared in the Scotch Presbyterian Church; my father was an elder in it and my earliest impressions were that the Jesuits had horns and hoofs and tails, and that there was a faint tinge of sulphur in the circumambient air whenever one of them crossed your path. Some years ago I was assigned by the Senate to examine the Indian schools in Wyoming and Montana. I visited every one of them. I wish to say now what I have said before in the Senate and it is not the popular side of the question by any means, that I did not see in all my journey a single school that was doing any educational work worthy of the name educational work, unless it was under the control of the Jesuits. I did not see a single Government school, especially day schools where there was any work done at all. The Jesuits have elevated the Indian wherever they have been allowed to do so without the interference of bigotry and fanaticism and the cowardice of politicians. They have made him a Christian, have made him a workman able to support himself and those dependent on him. Go to the Flathead Reservation in Montana, and look at the work of the Jesuits and what do you find? Comfortable dwellings, herds of cattle and horses, self-respecting Indians. I am not afraid to say this, because I speak from personal observation, and no man ever went among these Indians with more intense prejudice than I had when I left the city of Washington to perform that duty.

Every dollar you give to the Government day schools might as well be thrown into the Potomac under a ton of lead." (Congressional Records, Apl. 7, 1900, p. 7. 4120.)

The most conspicuous of the missionaries among the North American Indians is Father Peter de Smet. He was born in Dendermonde on the Scheldt, and was twelve years old when the booming of the cannons of Waterloo startled the little town. He came out to Maryland in 1821 and after remaining for a short time at Whitemarsh in the log cabin which then sheltered the novices of the Province of Maryland, set out on foot with a party of young Jesuits for the then Wild West. They walked from Whitemarsh to Wheeling, a distance of 400 miles, and then went in flat boats down the Ohio to Shawneetown and from there proceeded again on foot to St. Louis. It was a journey of a month and a half.

His first work was among the Pottawotamis, and then he was sent to the wonderful Flatheads, whom the Iroquois from Caughnawaga had converted. From that time forward his life was like a changing panorama. In the story, there are Indians of every kind who come before us. Gros Ventres and Flatheads and Pottawotamis, and Pend d'Oreilles and Sioux; their incantations and cannibalism and dances and massacres and disgusting feasts are described; there are scenes in the Bad Lands and mountains and forests; there are tempests in the mid-Pacific and more alarming calms; there are councils with Indian chiefs, and interviews with Popes and presidents and kings and ambassadors and archbishops and great statesmen and Mormon leaders, always and exclusively in the interests of the Church. The great man's life has been written in four volumes by two admiring Protestants, and another biography has lately come from the pen of a

Belgian Jesuit. In them appears an utterance from Archbishop Purcell about the hero, which deserves to be quoted. " Never," he says, "since the days of Xavier, Brébeuf, Marquette and Lalemant has there been a missionary more clearly pointed out and called than Father de Smet." Thurlow Weed, one of the most conspicuous American statesmen of the day, said of him: " No white man knows the Indians as Father de Smet nor has any man their confidence to the same degree." Thomas H. Benton wrote to him in 1852: " You can do more for the welfare of the Indians in keeping them at peace and friendship with the United States than an army with banners."

Again and again he was sent by the government to pacify the Indians. His mission in 1868 was particularly notable. Sitting Bull was on the warpath and was devastating the whole regions of the Upper Missouri and Yellowstone. They were called for a parley, and de Smet went out alone among the painted warriors. He held a banner of the Blessed Virgin in his hand and pleaded so earnestly with them to forget the past, that they went down into the very midst of the United States troops and signed the treaty of peace that brought 50,000 Indians to continue their allegiance to the government. De Smet in his journeys had crossed the ocean nineteen times and had travelled 180,000 miles by sailing vessels, river barges, canoes, dogsleds, snow shoes, wagons, or on horseback or on foot. " We shall never forget," said General Stanley of the United States Army — and this eulogy of the great man will suffice — " nor shall we ever cease to admire the disinterested devotion of Reverend Father de Smet who at the age of sixty-eight years did not hesitate, in the midst of the summer heat, to undertake a long and perilous journey across the burning plains, destitute of trees and even of grass, having none but

corrupted and unwholesome water, constantly exposed
to scalping by Indians, and this without seeking
honor or remuneration of any sort but solely to arrest
the shedding of blood, and save, if it might be, some
lives and preserve some habitations."

In Canada, the Indian reservation of La Jeune
Lorette, which was established in the early days by
Father Chaumonot, is now directed by the secular
clergy of Quebec. The Caughnawaga settlement near
Montreal was, of course, lost to the Society at the time
of the Suppression, but of late years has been restored
to its founders. The Canadian Jesuits also look after
the Indians of Lakes Huron and Superior. Their latest
undertaking is in Alaska which began by a tragedy.

The saintly Bishop Charles John Seghers, who was
coadjutor to the Bishop of Oregon, had himself transferred to the See of Vancouver in order to devote his
life to the savages of Alaska. In 1886 when he asked
the Jesuits to come to his assistance, Fathers Tosi
and Robaut were assigned to the work. In July, the
bishop, the two Jesuits and a hired man started over
the Chilcoot Pass for the headwaters of the Yukon.
It was decided that the two Jesuits should spend the
winter at the mouth of the Stewart River, while the
Bishop with his man hastened to a distant post to
forestall the members of a sect, who contemplated
establishing a post at the same place. During the
terrible 1,100 mile journey the servant became insane
and in the dead of night killed the bishop. The result
was that new arrangements had to be made and Father
Tosi was made prefect Apostolic in 1894. His health
soon gave way under the terrible privations of the mission and he died in 1898, although only fifty-one years of
age. He was succeeded by Father René of the Society
who resigned in 1904, and the present incumbent Father
Crimont, S. J., took his place.

The condition of Alaska has greatly changed since the advent of the missionaries. The discovery of placer gold deposits with the influx of miners robbed a portion of Alaska of its primitive isolation. The invading whites had to be looked after, and hence there are resident Jesuit priests at Juneau, Douglas, Fairbanks, Nome, Skagway, St. Michael and Seward. A great number of posts are attended to from these centres. The Ten'a Indians and Esquimaux are the only natives whom the missionaries have been able to evangelize thus far. There is a training-school for them at Koserefsky, where the boys are taught gardening, carpentry and smithing of various kinds, and the girls are instructed in cooking, sewing and other household arts. This work is particularly trying not only because of the bodily suffering it entails, but because of the awful monotony and isolation of those desolate arctic regions. Some idea of it may be gathered from a few extracts taken from a letter of one of the missionaries. It is dated May 29, 1916.

" The Skúlarak district of 15,000 square miles, depending on St. Mary's Mission," says the writer, " is as large as a diocese. It has seventy or eighty villages. The whole country along the coast is a vast swamp covered with a net work of rivers, sloughs, lakes and ponds. There is only one inhabitant to every ten or twelve square miles. There is no question of roads except in winter and then as everything is deep in snow, it is impossible to tell whether one is going over land or lake or river. When we started the thermometer registered 28° below zero, Fahrenheit. We had nine dogs; but two were knocked out shortly after starting. Eleven hours travelling brought us to our first cabins. We rose next morning at five, said Mass on an improvised altar and set out southward. At noon we stopped for lunch, which consisted of frozen bread and some tea from our thermo bottle. It was only at seven o'clock that we reached a little 'village' of three houses at the foot of the Kusilwak Mountains, which are two or three thousand feet high. They served as a guide to direct our course." At another stage of the journey he writes: " At sundown as we lost all hope of reaching any village we made for a faraway clump of brushwood intending to pass the night there. It is full moon and its rays light up an immaculate white landscape, there is a bright cloudless sky, and everything is so still that you cannot even breathe without a plainly audible sound."

What kind of people was he pursuing? Not very interesting in any way. " I came upon a new style of native dwelling, a low-roofed miserable hovel about twelve feet square; in the centre, a pit, about two and a half feet deep, was the sink and dumping ground for the refuse of the house. There we had to descend if we wanted the privilege of standing erect. That is where I placed myself to perform a baptism of the latest arrival of the family whom the mother held on her lap squatted on the higher ground which served as a bed. The habits of the natives cannot be described." " Our dogs were so exhausted," he says in the course of his narrative, "that they lay down at once without waiting to have their harness taken off. We fed them their ration of dry fish, they curled up in the snow and went to sleep. As for ourselves we tried to build a fire but could not succeed in boiling enough of melted snow for even a cup of tea; a box of sardines, the contents of which were so frozen that I had to chop them up with the prong of a fork constituted my royal supper. A hole was soon dug in the snow, by using the snow shoes for a shovel and a few sticks thrown in to prevent direct contact with the snow. I opened my bag of blankets, put on my fur parkey and tried to keep the blankets around me to keep from freezing. After a couple of hours I felt my limbs getting numb, and I was compelled to crawl out and look around for a hard mound of snow where I began to execute a dance that would baffle the best orchestra. I jigged and clogged around for fifteen or twenty minutes, and feeling I was alive again sought my blankets once more, but the cold was too intense and I could only say a few prayers and make a peaceful application of the meditation ' de propriis peccatis.'

" Another time, after fruitlessly scanning the horizon for a sign of a village, we found ourselves compelled to pass the night in the open air. This time I constructed a scientific Pullman berth for myself. Selecting the leeward side of an ice block, I dug a trench in the snow, using the fire-pan as a shovel. I hewed out the pillow at the head and made the grave (indeed it looked like one) about two feet wide and two deep and my exact length. Stretching my cassock over it, with the snow shoes as a supporting rack, I crawled into it and passed a tolerably comfortable night, though I awoke dozens of times from the violent coughing that had stuck to me since my stay in Tumna. So it went on till April 8. We had been three weeks on the road. Never had the trip to Tumna lasted so long. This was due to the fact that the dogs were exhausted and we had to walk back for about 250 miles in the snow."

The missionaries of the old Society would recognize this light hearted modern American apostle as their brother.

Another example in a region which is the very opposite of Alaska will convince the skeptic that the modern Jesuit retains the old heroic spirit of the missions. This time we are in the deadly swamps and forests of British Honduras and the apostle there is Father William Stanton of the Missouri province. As a scholastic he was teaching the dark skinned boys of Belize and incidentally gathering numberless specimens of tropical flora and fauna for the Smithsonian Institute in Washington. From there he went to the other end of the earth and was put at scientific work in the Observatory at Manila. He was the first American priest ordained in the Philippines, and his initial ministerial work was to attend to the American soldiers, who were dying by scores of cholera. After that we find him again in Honduras, no longer in college but in the bush with about 800 Maya Indians, whose language he did not know but soon learned. He was still a naturalist but first of all he was absorbed in the care of the lazy and degraded Indians. His hut was made of sticks plastered with mud and thatched with palm leaves and he was all alone.

"Roads! Roads!" he writes, "they are simply unspeakable. It's only a little over nine miles from Benque Viejo to Cayo but it took me five hours to do it on horseback. Rain and the darkness caught me. It was so dark I could not see my horse's head but my Angel Guardian brought me through all right. . . . The only beasts that bother me are the garrapatas (ticks). I have to spend from an hour and a half to two hours picking them out of my flesh and my whole body is thickly peppered with blotchy sores where they have left their mark. But one can't expect to have everything his own way in this life even in the paradise of Benque. By the way, before I forget, would you try to send me a wash basin or bowl of glazed metal. I have nothing but the huge tin dishpan of the kitchen to wash my face in. It's a little inconvenient to scour the grease out every time I want to wash and I don't want to fall into real Spanish *costumbres*." His table was a packing case, his chair a box of

50

tinned goods, his bed four ropes and a mat woven of palm leaves. He had one cup, plate and saucer.

" I have forty stations to get around to, and I haven't a decent crucifix, or ciborium, and only one chalice. I am not squealing for my house but for the Lord's. My good little mud house is a palace, even if the pigs and goats of the village do break in now and then to make a meal off one's old boots or the scabbard of one's machete. My bush church is fine; same architecture as my house, only larger. In ch rch, the men stand around the walls, while the women and children squat on the clay floor and the babies roll all over, garbed only in angelic innocence."

Of one of his journeys he writes: " I have just returned from a river trip, after being away from home thirty-one days moving about from place to place among my scattered people on the river banks and in the bush. My health was good until last week when I got a little stroke from the heat, followed by several days' fever which put me on my back for four days, but I am now myself again. Fortunately I had only three more days' journey, and with the help of my two faithful Indians I arrived safely at Benque." These " three days," though he does not say so, were days of torture, and his Indians wondered if they could get him back alive. " I am now back as far as Cayo, arriving at 1.30 this morning. Everything is flooded with mud and water. I must get a horse and get out to Benque today, as I hear Father Henneman is down with fever. I have ten miles more to make, and over a terrible road through the bush, with the horse up to his belly in mud and water most of the time; but with the Lord's help I hope to be safe at home before night. I have been away only a week, having made some hundred and sixty miles on horseback, the whole of it through a dense jungle. I had to cut

my way through with my machete, for the rank vege-
tation and hanging lianas completely closed the narrow
trail."

He had gone out to visit a village and crossed a ford
on the way. The river was high and the current
strong. His horse was swept off his feet and Father
Stanton slipped out of his saddle and swam beside
the animal. Some quarter of a mile below there was
a dangerous fall in the river, but they managed to reach
the bank a hundred feet above the fall. He caught
hold of a branch, but it broke and he was swept down
the stream. With a prayer to his Guardian Angel he
struck out for the deepest water and went over the fall.
Some Indians near the bank saw the bearded white
man go over the roaring cataract and they thought
he was a wizard, but he went safely through, and then
with long powerful strokes (he was a marvellous
swimmer) he made for the bank. Then waving his
hand to the startled Indians, he cut his way with his
machete through the bush to look for his horse.
Another time we find him returning after what he
calls a "stiff trip," soaking wet all the time, for he
had to swim across a swift river with boots and clothes
on, he was all day in the saddle, was caught one night
in the jungle in a swamp, pitch dark, knee deep in
the mud — "Clouds of mosquitos and swarms of fiery
ants had taken their fill of me," he writes, "while the
blood sucking vampire bats lapped my poor horse.
We got out all right and I had the consolation of
being told by an Indian that three big tigers (jaguars)
had been killed near the place last month."

On April 13, 1909, he says: "Just at present I am
flat on my back with an attack of something, apparently
acute articular rheumatism." He felt it, the first
time while he was working in the garden. "I simply
squirmed on the ground and screeched like a wild

Indian." And yet he starts off to Belize on horseback
to see the doctor, which meant a distant journey of
four days, and he had to sleep in the bush one night.
From Belize he returned by water in a "pitpan,"
a freight boat for shallow rivers that can easily upset
in the slightest current. That meant eight weary
days without room even to stretch himself out at night;
with no awning in the day to shield him from the sun
and frequently drenched by torrential rains. In
September he is following his horse through the mud
of the jungle. In October he was sent for again by
the doctor at Belize, and returns a second time to his
mission which meant eight days in the forest alone.

Finally, Father Stanton was ordered home to St.
Louis, and it was found that his whole body was
ringed around with a monstrous growth of cancer.
He died in intense agony, but never spoke of his
sufferings. In his delirium he was talking about
Honduras. Only once he said " I am so long a-dying."
He finally expired on March 10, 1910. He had just
completed his fortieth year, but his missionary work
was equal to anything in the old Society.

When the Jesuits resumed work in China in 1841 they
found that all over the country there were great
numbers of natives who had kept the Faith in spite
of the bitter persecutions to which they had been
subjected during the absence of the missionaries.
The Province of Kiang-nan, the capital of which is
Nankin, and the city where Ricci began his apostolic
labors, welcomed back the great man's brethren.

Kiang-nan is a territory half the size of France.
In the west and south-west it is hilly, but the rest
of it is an immense plain watered by the Yang-tse-
Kiang and by countless lakes, streams and canals.
It is marvellously fertile and furnishes a double crop
every year. The rivers swarm with fish, and the

land with human beings. In it are many large cities
such as Shanghai with its 650,000 inhabitants; Tchen-
Kiang with 170,000, Odi-si with 200,000 and so on.
Nankin is the residence of the viceroy, and was formerly
the " Capital of the south," and the rival of Pekin,
but later it had only 130,000 people within its walls.
At present, however, it is reviving and is credited with
three or four hundred thousand inhabitants. Before
the Jesuits arrived, the country had been cared for
by other religious orders, chiefly the Lazarists and the
Fathers of the Missions Etrangères.

In the neighborhood of Shanghai, there were 48,000
Catholic Chinese who dated back through their
ancestors to the time of the Jesuit missionaries of the
seventeenth century. Perhaps four thousand more
might have been found in the rest of the province,
but they were submerged in the mass of 45,000,000
idolaters. The outlook on the whole was consoling,
for the vicar Apostolic, Mgr. de Besi, had founded
a seminary, which before 1907 furnished more than
one hundred native priests. The work of the Holy
Childhood was enthusiastically carried on, with the
result that in the years 1847–48, 60,963 names appear
on the baptismal registers. In 1849 the Jesuits had
establishments at Nankin, Ousi and along the Grand
Canal. That year, however, was made gloomy by
floods, famine and sickness. Nevertheless the trials
had the good result of compelling the erection of
orphanages where the Faith could be taught without
difficulty. In 1852 the revolt against the Manchu
dynasty broke out, and in 1853 Nankin and Shanghai
were sacked. Everything Christian disappeared in the
general carnage; but in 1855 the imperial troops with
the aid of the French Admiral Laguerre entered
Shanghai, but Nankin and the provinces remained
in the hands of the rebels.

Certain ecclesiastical changes also occurred at that time. Pekin and Nankin disappeared as dioceses, and the province of Kiang-nan became a vicariate Apostolic, whose administration was entrusted to the Jesuits of Paris under Mgr. Borgniet. He was appointed in 1856. The vicariate of South-Eastern Tche-ly was given to the province of Champagne and Mgr. Languillat began his work there with three Fathers and 9,475 old Christians, the descendants of the neophytes of Pekin.

In 1860 the Chinese war broke out and the Taipings availed themselves of it for another rising. The English and French, who were fighting the emperor, held different opinions about what to do with the rebels, and finally contented themselves with defending Shanghai; leaving the rest of the country to be ravaged at will. Father Massa was thrown into prison and was about to be executed, but contrived to make his escape. His brother Louis, however, was put to death at Tsai-kia-ouan, along with a crowd of orphans whom he was trying to protect. In 1861 Father Vuillaume was killed at Pou-tong and others were robbed, taken prisoners and ill-treated. In 1862 an epidemic of cholera broke out in the province and lasted two years; the vicar Apostolic, Mgr. Borgniet, sixteen religious and four hundred of the faithful succumbed to the pestilence. In the following year six more Jesuits died. At this time General Gordon was beginning his great career. He was then only a major but he reorganized the imperial army, crushed the rebels and took Nankin. This gave a breathing spell to the missionaries; but in 1868, the Taipings were out again, under another name, and anarchy reigned for an entire year.

In the mean time the cities of Shanghai and Zikawei had relatively little to suffer, and the end of the war gave the missionaries the right to build churches, to exercise the ministry everywhere, and even to be compensated for the destruction of their property. But the rights were merely on paper, and fourteen or fifteen years of quarrels with every little mandarin in the country followed. Nevertheless the work went on. At Zikawei, for instance, schools were established, a printing-establishment inaugurated, and in 1872 the observatory which was soon to be famous in all the Orient was begun. Progress was also made at Shanghai. Of course the usual burnings and plunderings, with occasional massacre of groups of Christians continued, but not much attention was paid to these disturbances until 1878, when the Church at Nankin was set on fire, and Sisters of Charity, priests, and Christians in general, among whom was the French consul, were all ruthlessly murdered. The imperial government then took cognizance of the outbreak, and eleven alleged culprits were put to death. That helped to calm the mob, and evangelical work was resumed, so that Kiang-nan, which had 70,685 Christians in 1866 counted over 100,000 in 1882. In the year 1900 there were 124,000 of whom 55,171 were adults. There were also 50,000 catechumens preparing for baptism. The number of priests had grown to 159, of whom 42 were Chinese. The 940 schools had an attendance of 18,563 children

The Boxer uprising was the most formidable trial to which the mission has so far been subjected. It was organized in the court itself by Toan, the emperor's uncle, General Tong-Fou-Siang and the secretary of state, Kangi-i, and its rumblings were heard for years before the actual outbreak. In Se-tchouan, a third of the churches were destroyed, villages set on fire, missionaries thrown into prison and many Christians massacred. A priest and his people were burned in the church at Kouang-toung; and at Hou-pe, another was put to death. These outrages were as yet local, but there was every evidence that a general conspiracy was at work for the expulsion of all foreigners from the empire. Finally the Boxers, or *Grand Sabres*, declared themselves, and by order of the viceroy, Yu-heen, 360 Christian villages were destroyed. That was only a beginning. Tche-ly suffered most. It was the stronghold of the rebels. In the autumn of 1899 there were conflagrations and riots everywhere. In 1900 the northern part of the mission was in flames, and forty-five Christian centres were reduced to ashes, but there were few, if any, apostacies, although thousands were put to death in the most horrible fashion. On June 20 Fathers Isore and Andlauer were murdered at the altar. On July 20 Fathers Mangin and Denn were killed, and on April 26, 1902, after peace had been concluded, Father Lomüller with his catechist and servant suffered death.

In this storm, five missionaries had been killed; Mgr. Henry Bulté died of exhaustion; 5,000 Christians had disappeared from the country; 616 churches had been destroyed along with 381 schools and three colleges. But that the blood of martyrs is the seed of the Church was shown by the fact that there are now more Christians in the district than there were before the persecution. The churches have been rebuilt; priests and catechists are more numerous; the seminary is crowded, and schools and pupils and teachers are at work, as if nothing had happened. The exact figures may be found in Brou's " Jésuites missionaires au xix siécle." Shanghai and Zikawei form the center of the Vicariate of Kiang-nan. In Shanghai are a cathedral and three parish churches which provide for a Catholic population of 9,724. There are three hospitals; an orphanage with trade schools; six schools; a home for the aged; conferences of St. Vincent de Paul. At Zikawei there is a scholasticate of the Society; a grand and little seminary; a meteorological and magnetic observatory; a museum of natural history; a college with 266 students, of whom 105 are pagans; a printing-house; a bi-weekly publication, and the beginnings of a university which it is hoped will head off the tendency of the natives to go for an education to Japan or to the Japanese schools founded in China itself.

When Gregory XVI sent the Jesuits to China, it was thought that from there it would be easy for them to go to Japan to resume the work in which they had so distinguished themselves in former times. Eighty years have passed since then, and only lately, a few Jesuits have shown themselves in that country. The Fathers of the Missions Etrangères have occupied the ground and have succeeded in establishing a complete hierarchy of five bishops and have won praise for themselves by their work in missions and parishes, in polemics and conferences. A school has been attempted and an American Jesuit has lately been placed on the staff of the University of Tokio. Only that and nothing more. What the future has in store, who can tell?

It was a happy day for the new Society when in 1841 it was ordered by Gregory XVI to undertake the missions of Hindostan; the country sanctified by the labors of Francis Xavier, de Nobili, de Britto, Criminali and a host of other saintly missionaries. No work could be more acceptable. The chief obstacle in the way of success was the protectorate which Portugal exercised over the churches of the Orient. In Catholic times its kings had the right not only to nominate all the bishops of the East, but to legislate on almost the entire ecclesiastical procedure within its

dominions. Not even a sacristan could be sent to
the Indies without the official approval of the Portuguese government. Such a state of things was bad
enough in Catholic times, but when the politics of
Portugal were in the hands of infidels and enemies of
the Church, it could not possibly be tolerated, no
matter how persistent was the claim that the right
still adhered to the crown. Another abnormality in
the pretence was that the country no longer belonged
to Portugal but was to a very great extent English
and hence if there were to be any dictation it should
come from the government of that country.

The first act of the Pope was to create a number of
vicars Apostolic who were to be independent of the
Archbishop of Goa. This started a war which lasted
sixty years. It was called the Goanese schism, or the
fight of the double jurisdiction. The vicar Apostolic
of the Calcutta district was Robert St. Leger, an
Irish Jesuit, who came to India with five members of
the Society after his appointment on 15 April, 1834.
St. Leger's jurisdiction was disputed by a number of
the adherents of Goa and he retired in December, 1838.
The Jesuits with him had begun a college, which was
enthusiastically supported by his successor, Bishop
Jean-Louis Taberd. Unfortunately he died suddenly
in 1840, and the same encouragement was not given
by Dr. Patrick Carew, the third vicar, with the result
that the college which had begun to prosper was
closed. In 1846 the Jesuits left Calcutta, but in 1860
they were recalled by Mgr. Oliffe, the successor of Dr.
Carew.

The missionaries came under the leadership of
Father Depelchin, who when he had finished his work in
Calcutta was later to add to his glory by founding the
mission of the Zambesi in Africa. They found everything in ruins. Out of a population of 2,300,000 in

the city and suburbs, there were no more than seven
or eight thousand Catholics, many of whom were
Tamouls from Madras. Only a few of the faithful
were in easy circumstances and their influence in the
city amounted to nothing. There was no help for it,
therefore, but to resuscitate the College of St. Francis
Xavier, which had been suppressed fourteen years
before. It had no furniture and its library consisted
of a few books with the covers off. The college was
opened nevertheless and had, on the first day, eighty
students on the benches. When Bishop Oliffe died
there was a dreadful possibility of the appointment of
a Goanese bishop, which, for the Jesuits, meant packing up a second time and leaving Calcutta. An
appeal was therefore made to Rome and Father
Auguste Van Heule was named, but he died in 1865
shortly after his arrival, and in 1867, Bishop Walter
Steins was called over from Bombay to take his place.
By this time the college had 350 students; a new
building and another situation were imperative, but
Depelchin was equal to the task, and before he left
Calcutta for Africa he had 500 students on the roster.

The initial work of the missionaries was the development of the colleges but they subsequently addressed
themselves to the evangelization of the whole population of the city and suburbs, and to-day they have
six parishes with a population of 13,000 souls, who are
provided with schools, hospitals, asylums and the
like. The native population, the Bengalis as they are
called, were found to be hopeless. Contact with the
whites has made them skeptical in religion, and morally
worse than they had been originally. The only
Christian Hindoos in Calcutta are Tamouls from
the South.

Not finding the Bengalis apt for evangelization,
they sought out their countrymen, the Ourias in the

Delta of the Ganges. Their home had the unhappy distinction of being called " the famine district," the dreadful calamity being caused either by too much water or by none. In 1866 there was a drought that withered all the crops, and then came inundations that covered 68,000 acres of land, swept away hundreds of villages, and diminished the population by half a million. Orphans, of course, abounded, and in 1868 an asylum was built for them in Balasore, which served also as an evangelical centre for missionary expeditions into the interior. But this venture was not very successful, for only about 1,600 conversions resulted after years of hard labor. The Ourias, it was found, had all the bad qualities of their friends the Bengalis. Perhaps also the movement was halted because their territory was a sort of Holy Land for Hindooism. Every year 500,000 pilgrims arrived there to pray at the shrine of Vishnu, and idolatry of all kinds, from the bloody ancestral fetichism to the refined cult of the Vedas and undiluted Brahmanism, took root and flourished there. Hence a mission was begun among the Orissas still further south.

Better than anywhere else one can see at close range among the Ourias how formidable are the moral, intellectual, social and historical obstacles that oppose the progress of Christianity in Hindostan. To add to the difficulty, Protestantism with its jumble of sects had established itself there and claimed at this time 15,000 adherents. But when cholera swept over the land in 1868, the Protestant missionaries fled and many of the native converts came over to the priests who, of course, did not imitate their non-Catholic rivals in deserting their charges. Father Goffinet especially distinguished himself in this instance, going everywhere in his narrow canoe and lavishing spiritual and corporal aid on the victims. In 1873 he was joined by Father

Delplace, who went still nearer the sea. Others
followed, lived in the huts of the natives, satisfied their
hunger with a few handfuls of rice varied by a fish on
Sundays to break the monotony of the diet, with the
result that, in three years, there were thirty Catholic
missions between the Hoogly and the Mutlah with
3,000 converts in what had been previously a stronghold of Hindoo Protestantism.

In the same year, Father Schoff went north of Calcutta to Bardwan —" The Garden of Western Bengal."
He kept away from the rich, and devoted himself to the
dregs of the populace. Over and over again the
superiors doubted if it were worth while, but to-day
the Haris, who were previously so degraded, live in
pretty villages, and the order, piety and honesty for
which they are noted make one forget the ignorance,
debauchery and dishonesty of the past. A group of
over 5,000 Catholics may be found there at the present
time.

In these parts, the caste system prevails in all its
vigors but if you go still further west into the heart of
the Province of Chota-Nagpur you come upon a half-
savage people, the offscouring of humanity who have
been driven into the hills and forests by the conquering
Aryans of the plains. They are the Ouraons of
Dravidian origin; small, black as negroes, filthy,
often wrapped in cow-dung and tattooed all over the
body, but nevertheless light-hearted, robust and proud
of their ability to perform hard work. With them also
lives a more ancient race known as the Koles: men
of broad flat faces which recall the Mongolian type.
They are probably the aborigines. Their religion is
grossly elementary — a vague adoration of the Supreme
Being, superstition and ancestor worship; but with a
shade of the pride that characterizes the horrible caste
system of the Hindoos. The German Lutherans had

essayed to convert them. Fifty rupees were paid for each adhesion, and fifty ministers devoted themselves to this apostolate. They are credited with having disbursed 3,700,000 francs by the year 1876. Then came the Anglicans who claimed 40,000 of them. In 1869 Father Stockman arrived and opened a mission at Chaibassa. In 1873 he had only a group of thirty converts. Nine years later, he had succeeded in baptising only 273, but by 1885 there were four residences in Chota-Nagpur with one out-mission. Five priests were engaged in the task.

The progress of the work, however, was comparatively slow until the young Father Constant Lievens made himself the champion of the natives in the courts. This gave it a phenomenal impulse. For years, these poor mountaineers had been cruelly exploited by Hindoo traders from Calcutta. As soon as the natives had contrived to cultivate a bit of land they were loaded down with taxes and enforced contributions, haled before the magistrates and flung into jail to rot. Unfortunately the police regulations were all in favor of the aggressors. Hence there were incessant riots and massacres, and when the English authorities tried in good faith to remedy matters, they could find no one among these poor outcasts fit to hold any position of responsibility. The Lutherans presented themselves and promised protection for those who would join the sect, and many went over to them, but the government disapproved of these unworthy tactics, as calculated only to make things worse in the end. It was like the temptation on the mountain.

At this point Father Lievens stepped into the breach. He could speak all the languages: Bengali, Hindoo, Mundari and Ouraon; and he then plunged into a study of the laws and customs of the land; an apparently inextricable maze, but in less than a year he was master of the whole legal procedure then in force. Thus armed, he appeared in court whenever a victim was arraigned, and almost invariably won a verdict in his favor. His reputation spread, and the victims of the sharks flocked to him from all sides. He argued for all of them, without however, omitting his ministerial occupation of preaching, teaching, composing canticles, helping the needy, and seeking out souls everywhere. He cut out so much work for his associates that his superiors were in a panic. But he succeeded. The native Protestants came over in crowds, and there was a flood tide of conversions to the Faith. It cost him his life, indeed, for he died in 1892, overcome by his labors and privations, but he had started a great movement and two years after his death, the flock had grown from 16,000 to 61,312, with more than 2,566 catechumens preparing for baptism. To-day the district is absolutely unlike its former self. Sacred canticles have taken the place of the old pagan chants and immoral dances are unknown. Even the pagans who are in the majority do not dare to perform certain rites of theirs in public.

In a district of Chota-Nagpur other than that in which Lievens labored, the conversions are still more pronounced. Six missionaries are at work, and their catechumens number more than 25,000. They offered themselves in spite of the fact that the Rajah was in a rage with his subjects about it; beat many of them unmercifully, and flung them into jail. Indeed the English government had to intervene to stop him. If there were a sufficiency of priests, there would be no difficulty in converting the whole countryside. The last accounts available tell us that the inhabitants of fifteen villages have declared themselves Christians, and cut off their hair to let the world know that they have renounced idolatry. Fifty years ago there were in all Western Bengal only a few thousand Catholics. In 1904 there were 106,000; in the following year, 119,705; in 1906, 126,529. Chota-Nagpur alone has another 102,000 and the number could be doubled if twenty new missionaries were on the spot. Western Bengal has now 27 churches, 346 chapels, 124 schools and two great colleges. Working there, are 101 priests, 55 scholastics and 27 coadjutor brothers of the Society, along with 34 Christian Brothers and 158 Sisters.

When Bishop Steins left Bombay, his successor Mgr. Jean-Gabriel Meurin built the college already planned, and called it St. Francis Xavier's. The undertaking was a difficult one, for the schismatical Goanese numbered 40,000 out of the 60,000 Catholics in the city, and their ecclesiastical leaders were not only indifferent to the project but refused to contribute anything to carry it out, just as if it had been a Moslem or a heretical establishment. The people, however, were better minded. Every one, Catholic, heathen and heretic, was eager to build the college, for Bombay was proud of being a great intellectual centre; and hence when the government promised to double what could be collected, the enthusiasm was general and money poured in. The Observatory still bears the name of the rich Parsee who built it.

The Bombay mission included Beluchistan up to the frontiers of Afghanistan; its southern limit was the Diocese of Poona. In this vast territory were native villages, military posts, Anglo-Indian settlements, Indo-Portuguese, and pure Hindoos. There were only about 33,000 Christians to be found in this amalgam, excluding the 70,000 people of the Goanese allegiance. Four colleges were erected in the various districts of this territory, but, unlike the great establishments of Bombay and Calcutta, they were exclusively Catholic. They gave instructions

respectively to 500, 690, 298, and 306 pupils. The
girls of the two dioceses were also provided for and the
high school population exceeded 10,000. The great
advantage of this scheme was that it ate very rapidly
into the schism through the children of the insurgents.

The Carmelites had been in Mangalore; but found
it too hard to hold out against the Calvinists from
Bâle who, in 1880 had twenty stations, sixty-five
schools and an annual budget of half a million; consequently they begged the Holy See to call in the Jesuits.
When the new missionaries arrived in December, 1879,
the Carmelites went out to meet them in a ship hung
with flags and bunting and, on landing, presented them
to the enthusiastic multitude waiting on the shore.
The college of St. Aloysius was immediately begun and
opened its classes with 150 students. Thus it happened
that the greatest part of St. Francis Xavier's territory
had come back to the Society; German Jesuits being
in Bombay, Belgians in Calcutta, French in Madura
and Italians in Mangalore. In the latter mission
out of a population of 3,685,000 there are to-day only
93,000 Catholics, but there were 1,500 Christian
students in St. Aloysius' college in 1920. It might be
noted that Mangalore has acquired a world wide
reputation for its leper hospital which was founded
by Father Müller, formerly of the New York province.
In that district also there are more native priests than
in any other part of India. They number 60 all told
and take care of about 32 parishes. They are not
pure-blood, however, for they bear distinctively Portuguese names, such as Coelho, Fernandes, Saldanha
and Pinto. This growth of the native clergy is encouraging, but it would be a mistake to regard them as
useful for spreading the Faith. They make relatively
very few conversions. They leave that to outsiders.

51

They merely hold on to what has been won for them by others.

In 1884, the college of Negapatam was transferred to Trichinopoly, the reason being that in the latter there was a Catholic population of 20,000. Of course, the Anglican educators of the city tried to prevent the move but failed. The college at one time had 1,800 pupils, and although there was a drop to 1,550 in 1905, because of new rivals in the field, the latest accounts place the attendance at 2,562. St. Xavier's high school in Tuticorin, in the Madura mission had 563 pupils in 1920, and St. Mary's erected in 1910 in the very heart of Brahmanism has 441. In Trichinopoly, the discipline and work of the students have attracted much attention, but especially the enterprise of the sodalists, who have formed twenty groups of catechists and are engaged in giving religious instruction to 700 children. Most notable, however, is the success of the college in overthrowing the caste barriers. Indeed the missionaries of the old days would look with amazement at the grouping in the class rooms of Brahmins, Vellalans, Odeayans, Kallans, Paravers and twenty other social divisions down to the very Pariahs, all studying in the same house and eating at the same table. There were walled divisions, at first; then screens; then benches, and now there is only an imaginary line between the grades which formerly could not come near each other without contamination.

Among these castes, the Brahmins display the greatest curiosity about things Christian, but like the rich young man in the Gospel when they hear the truth they turn sadly away. " Why did God permit me to meet you," said one of them, " if I am going to suffer both here and hereafter?" One of them at last yielded and took flight to the ecclesiastical seminary at Ceylon. When the news spread abroad, priests from the pagodas and professors from the national schools came to the college and stormed against the other catechumens but without avail. Another Brahmin declared himself a Christian the next year; three in 1896, three in 1897, four in 1898, six in 1899 and two in 1900. They all have a hard fight before them; for they are thrown out of their caste and are disinherited by their families. Two of these converts died, and there is a suspicion that at least one was poisoned. Already 60 Brahmins have been baptized and India is in an uproar about it. To those who know the country, these conversions are of more importance than that of a thousand ordinary people and it is almost amusing to learn that the well-known theosophist leader, Annie Besant, hastened back to India to denounce the Catholic Church for its effrontery. The incident, it is true, gave a new life to idol-worship but possibly it was the last gasp before death.

The Madura district had been taken over by the Fathers of the Foreign Missions, after the Jesuits had been suppressed in 1773. When the Pope, Pius VII, re-established the Society, insistent appeals were made by those devoted and overtaxed missionaries to have the Jesuits resume their old place in that part of the Peninsula. The petition was heeded and the Jesuits returned to Madura in 1837. They were confronted by a frightful condition of affairs. In spite of the heroic labors of their immediate predecessors, there were scandals innumerable, and a large part of the population had lapsed into the grossest superstition and idolatry. The missionaries were well received at first, but a fulmination from Goa incited the people to rebellion. Moreover their labors were so crushing that four of the Fathers died of exhaustion in the year 1843 alone. Little by little however a change of feeling began to manifest itself, and as early

as 1842, there were 118,400 Catholics in the mission,
many of them converts from Protestantism and
paganism. In 1847 Madura was made a vicariate
Apostolic under Mgr. Alexis Canoz, a year after the
Hindo-European college was established at Negapatam.

Madura has another great achievement to its credit.
The English government had put an end to the suttee:
the frightful and compulsory custom of widows flinging
themselves on the funeral pyres of their husbands
who were being incinerated. The prohibition was
universally applauded but the Fathers started another
movement. It was against the enforced celibacy of
widows, some of whom had been married in babyhood,
often to some old man, and were consequently obliged
to live a single life after his death. The moral results
of such a custom may be imagined. It was difficult
at first to convince a convert that it was a perfectly
proper thing for him to marry a widow, but little by
little the prejudice was removed. Of course there are
orphanages, old people's homes, Magdalen asylums,
maternity hospitals, industrial schools, and other
charitable institutions in prosperous Madura.

The work among the lower classes in the country
districts is of the most trying description. There is
no place for the itinerant missionary to find shelter in
the villages except in some miserable hut. Indeed,
1,853 of these hamlets out of 2,035 have no accommodations at all for the priest, who perhaps has travelled
for days through forests to visit them. Moreover,
though the people have their good qualities and a great
leaning to religion, they are fickle, excitable, ungrate-
ful, unmindful as children at times, and hard to manage.
In certain quarters, especially in the south, conversions
are multiplying daily. The movement began as early
as 1876, after a frightful famine that swept the country,
and in one place the Christian population grew in

fifteen years from 4,800 to 68,000. In 1889 around Tuticorin whole villages came over in a body. In December, 1891, 600 people were clamoring for baptism in one place, and they represented a dozen different castes. In 1891 one missionary was compelled to erect thirty-two new chapels. " I said we have 75 new villages; " writes another, " if we had priests enough we could have 75 more."

In 1920, there were in the Diocese of Trichinopoly besides the bishop, Mgr. Augustine Faisandier, 119 Jesuit priests of whom 28 are natives. There are a number of native scholastics. Besides this group there are 27 natives studying philosophy and theology in the seminary at Kandy. Add to this 32 Brothers of the Sacred Heart, an institute of Indian lay religious, who assist the missionaries as catechists and school teachers; 75 nuns in European and 346 in Indian institutions; and 75 oblates or pious women who devote themselves to the baptizing of heathen children; and you have some of the working corps in this prosperous mission. The Catholic population was 267,772 in 1916. There are 1,100 churches and chapels, 2,620 posts, a school attendance of 27,378 children, and 7 Catholic periodicals.

The missions in Mohammedan countries were particularly difficult to handle, because Turkey is a veritable Babel of races, languages and religions. There are Turks, and Syrians, and Egyptians and Arabians, along with the Metualis of Mount Lebanon and the Bedouins of the desert. There are Druses, who have a slender link holding them to Islamism; there are idolaters of every stripe; there are Schismatical Greeks, who call themselves Orthodox and depend on Constantinople; and there are United Greeks or Melchites who submit to Rome; Monophysite Armenians, and Armenian Catholics; and Copts also of the same divided allegiance. Then come Syrian Jacobites and United Syrians, Nestorians, Chaldeans, Maronites, Latins, Russians, with English, German and American Protestants, and to end all, the ubiquitous Jews. The missionaries who labor in this chaos are also of every race and wear every kind of religious garb. What will be the result of the changes consequent upon the World War no one can foretell. There is nothing to hope for from the Jews or Mohammedans; and only a very slight possibility of uniting the schismatics to Rome, or of converting the Protestants who have nothing to build on but sentiment and ingrained and inveterate prejudice. There is plenty to do, however, in restraining Catholics from rationalism and heresy; in lifting up the clergy to their proper level, by imparting to them science and piety; forming priests and bishops for the Uniates; promoting a love for the Chair of Peter; and all the while not only not hurting Uniate susceptibilities, but showing the greatest respect for the jealous autonomy of each Oriental Church.

Before the Suppression, the missions of the Levant were largely entrusted to the Jesuits of the province of Lyons. The alliance of the Grand Turk with the kings of France assured the safety of the missionaries and hence there were stations not only at Constantinople, but in Roumelia, Anatolia, Armenia, Mingrelia, Crimea, Persia, Syria, Egypt and in the Islands of the Ægean Sea. The work of predilection in all these places was toiling in the galleys with the convicts, or in the lazar houses with the plague-stricken. Between 1587 and 1773, more than 100 Jesuit missionaries died of the pest. In 1816, that is two years after the re-establishment of the Society, the bishops of the Levant petitioned Rome to send back the Jesuits. Thanks to Paul of Russia, they had resumed their old posts in 1805 in the Ægean, where one of the

former Jesuits, named Mortellaro, had remained as
a secular priest, and lived long enough to have one of
the Fathers from Russia receive his last sigh and hear
him renew his religious vows.   This was the beginning
of the present Sicilian Jesuit missions in the Archipelago.
The Galician province has four stations in Moravia,
and the Venitian has posts in Albania and Dalmatia.

In 1831 Gregory XVI ordered the Society to undertake the missions of Syria; but at that time Mehemet
Ali of Egypt was at war with the Sultan, and the
Druses and Maronites were butchering each other at
will. Finally, in the name of the Sultan, Emir
Haidar invited the Fathers to begin a mission at
Bekfaya on the west slope of Mount Lebanon and
about 10 miles west of Beirut.   Simultaneously Emir
Beckir, who was an upholder of Egypt, established
them at Muallakah, a suburb of Zahlé on the other
side of the mountain.   At Hauran, on the borders
of the desert, they found a Christian population in the
midst of Druses and Bedouins.   They were despised,
ill-treated and virtually enslaved.   They had no
churches and no priests, were in absolute ignorance
of their duties as Christians, and were stupefied to
find that Rome had come so far to seek them.   The
work of lifting them up was hard enough, but it was
a trying task to be commissioned by Rome to settle
the disputes that were continually arising between
Christian, Orthodox, and Turk, and even between
ecclesiastical authorities. Father Planchet was the
chief pacificator in all these wrangles, and for his
punishment was made delegate Apostolic in 1850,
consecrated Bishop of Mossul in 1853, and murdered
in 1859 when about to set out for Rome.

Father Planchet was a Frenchman; with Father
Riccadonna, an Italian, and Brother Henze, a Han-
overian, he went to Syria in 1831, at the joint request

of the Melchite bishop, Muzloum, Joseph Assemani, the procurator of the Maronite patriarch and the Maronite Archbishop of Aleppo, Germanus Harva. A hitherto unpublished document recently edited by Father Jullien in " La Nouvelle Mission en Syrie " gives a detailed account of the journey of this illustrious trio from Leghorn to Syria.

" The vessel was called ' The Will of God,' and the voyage was," says Riccadonna " an uninterrupted series of misfortunes,— fevers, faintings, rotten water, broken rigging, shattered masts, wild seas, frightful tempests, a sea-sick crew and escapes from English, Turkish and other cruisers on the high seas. When they came ashore the cholera was raging throughout the country." The narrative is full of interest with its picturesque descriptions of the people, their habitations, their festivals, their caravans, their filth, their fanaticism and the continually recurring massacres of Christians. The travellers journeyed to Beirut and Qamar and Bagdad and Damascus, and give vivid pictures of the conditions that met them in those early days. The medical ability of the lay-brother was of great service. He was the only physician in the country, with the result that, according to Riccadonna, each stopping place was a *probatica piscina*, every one striving to reach him first. " In Arabia," says the Relation, "as in the plains of Ba'albek, there is nothing but ignorance and sin. There are sorcerers and sorceresses in every village; superstitions of every kind, lies, blasphemies, perjury and impurity prevail. It is a common thing for Christians to bear Mussulman names and to pray to Mahomet. They never fast, and on feast days never go to Mass. Of spiritual books or the sacraments they know nothing; clan and personal vengeance and murder are common, and sexual immorality indescribable." Such was the state of these countries in 1831.

In 1843 the mission, which until then depended on the general, was handed to the province of Lyons. In that year a seminary for native priests was begun at Ghazir, in an old abandoned castle bought from an emir of the mountains. It began with two students, but at the end of the year there were twenty-five on the benches, and in that small number, many Rites were represented. A college for boys soon grew up around it, and a religious community of native nuns for the education of children was established. The latest account credits the Sisters with nearly 4,000 pupils.

New posts were established at Zahlé and ancient Sidon and also at Deir el Qamar. The prospects seemed fair for the moment, for had not the French and Turks been companions in arms in the Crimea? But in 1860 the terrible massacres in Syria began as a protest of the ultra-Mussulmans against the liberal concession of Constantinople to the Christians. In the long list of victims the Jesuits counted for something; for on June 18, four of them were butchered at Zahlé and a fifth at Deir el Qamar. In that slaughter eight thousand Christians were killed; 560 churches destroyed; three hundred and sixty villages devastated and forty-two convents burned. Three months later the Turkish troops from the garrison at Damascus butchered eight thousand five hundred people, four prelates, fifty Syrian priests, and all the Franciscan Friars in the city. They levelled to the ground three thousand eight hundred houses and two churches, and would have done more; but the slaughter was stopped when the Algerian Abd-el-Kader arrived on the scene. They still live on a volcano. Preceding and during the war of 1914, massacre of the Christians continued as usual.

Armenia is the Ararat of Scripture. Little Armenia, in which the Jesuits are laboring, is an irregular strip of territory that starts from the Gulf of Alexandretta and continues on towards the Black Sea. Its principal towns are Adana, Cæsarea, Civas, Tokat, Amasia, and Marswan, about two or three days' journey from each other. The country is mountainous, without railroads or other means of transport. The highways are infested with brigands; and the climate is excessively hot and excessively cold. The difficulties with which the Church has to contend in this inhospitable region are first, the government which is Turkish; second, the secret societies which are continually plotting against their Turkish masters; and third, the American Protestant sects which are covering the country with churches, orphan asylums, schools and dispensaries, and flooding it with anti-Catholic literature, and money. In 1886 all the schools were closed by the Turks, but when the French protested they were reopened. In 1894 two of the priests died while caring for the cholera victims and that helped to spread the Faith, for, of course, there are never any parsons on the scene in such calamities. Under Turkish rule also, massacres are naturally chronic, but Brou informs us that on such occasions the Protestants suffer more than the Catholics; for the latter are not suspected of being in the secret revolutionary societies, while the others are known to be deeply involved.

The population of this region consists of 500,000 Christians, of whom 14,000 are Protestants and 12,000 Catholics. The rest are Monophysite schismatics. In the mission besides the secular priests there are 57 Jesuits and 50 teaching sisters from France. There are 22 schools with 3,309 pupils, but only 504 of these

children are Uniate Catholics. They are what are
called Gregorians, for the tradition is that Armenia
was converted to the Faith by St. Gregory the Illuminator. There are few conversions, but the schismatics
accept whatever Catholic truth is imparted to them.
They believe in the Immaculate Conception; pray for
the dead; love the Pope; say their beads; and invoke
the Sacred Heart. For them the difference between
Romans and Gregorians is merely a matter of ritual.
In several places, however, whole villages have asked
to be received into Roman unity. As a people they
look mainly to Russia for deliverance from the
Turk, but neither Turk nor Russian now counts
in the world's politics and no one can foresee the
future.

Father Roothaan had long been dreaming of sending
missionaries to what until very recently has been called
the Unknown or Dark Continent, Africa. Hence
when the authorities of the Propaganda spoke to him
of a proposition, made by an ecclesiastic of admitted
probity, about establishing a mission there, Roothaan
accepted it immediately, and in the year 1846 ordered
Father Maximilian Ryllo with three companions to
ascend the Nile as far as possible and report on the
conditions of the country. Ryllo was born in Russia
in 1802 and entered the Roman province in 1820.
After many years of missionary work in Syria, Malta
and Sicily he was made rector of the Urban College in
Rome on July 4, 1844, and was occupying that post
when he was sent by Father Roothaan to the new
mission of Central Africa.

In 1845 Ryllo was at Alexandria in search of "the
eminent personage" who had suggested the mission
and had been consecrated bishop *in partibus*, for the
purpose of advancing the enterprise. But the "eminent personage" was not to be found either there or

in Cairo. Hence after waiting in vain for a month,
Ryllo and his companions started for Khartoum
which was to be the central point for future explorations. After a little rest, they made their way up the
White Nile. They were then under the equator, and
had scant provisions for the journey, and no means of
protection from the terrible heat, and, besides, they
were in constant peril of the crocodiles which infested
the shores of the river. The first negro tribes they
met spoke an Arabic dialect, so it was easy to
understand them. The native houses were caves in
the hillsides, a style of dwelling that was a necessity
on account of the burning heat. Their manner of
life was patriarchal; they were liberal and kind, and
seemed to be available foundation stones for the future
Church which the missionaries hoped to build there.
Satisfied with what they had discovered, they returned
to Khartoum, but when they reported in due time to
Propaganda, the mission was not entrusted to them.
It was handed over to the Congregation of the Missionaries of Verona.

In 1840 the Jesuits went to Algeria. The work was
not overwhelming. They were given charge of an
orphan asylum. But unfortunately though they had
plenty of orphans they had no money to feed them.
Nevertheless, trusting in God, Father Brumauld not
only did not close the establishment, but purchased
370 acres of ground, in the centre of which was a pile
of buildings which had formerly been the official baths
of the deys of Algiers. In 1848 the asylum sheltered
250 orphans. Fr. Brumauld simply went around the
cafés and restaurants and money poured into his hat,
for the enterprise appealed to every one. He even
gathered up at the hotels the left-over food and brought
it back to the motherless and fatherless little beggars
whom he had picked up at the street corners. They were

filthy, ragged and vicious, but he scraped them clean and clothed them, taught them the moral law and gave them instructions in the useful trades and occupations. Marshal Bougeaud, the governor, fell in love with the priest and when told he was a Jesuit, replied " he may be the devil himself if you will, but he is doing good in Algeria and will be my friend forever." One day some Arab children were brought in and he said to Father Brumauld " Try to make Christians out of these youngsters. If you succeed they won't be shooting at us one day from the underbrush."

The Orphanage stood in the highroad that led to Blidak and permission was asked to get in touch with natives. Leave was given Father Brumauld to put up a house which served as café for the Arabs. It had a large hall for the travellers and a shed for the beasts. Next to it was a school the upper part of which gave him rooms for his little community. It was a *zaoui* for the Christian marabouts, a meeting place for the French and natives, and a neutral ground where fanaticism was not inflamed but made to die out. All the governors, Pelissier, the Duc d'Aumale, Mac-Mahon, Admiral de Guéydon and General Chanzy were fond of the Father and encouraged him in his work. One day General d'Hautpoul praised him for his success, and advised him to begin another establishment. The suggestion was acted on immediately. The government was appealed to and soon a second orphanage was in operation at Bouffarik further South. Finally, as the number of Arab orphans was diminishing in consequence of better domestic conditions, Brumauld asked why he could not receive orphans from France? Of course he could, and he was made happy when 200 of them were sent as a present from Paris. There would be so many gamins less in the streets of the capital.

Meantime, residences and colleges were being established in the cities of Al-Oran, Constantine and Algiers, but when at the instance of the bishop, Father Schimbri opened a little house in the neighborhood of Selif and was ingratiating himself with the natives, the authorities demanded his immediate recall. Later, when the bishop solicited leave to begin a native mission he was denounced in Paris for influencing minors, because he had asked some Lazarists to teach a few vagabond Arab children; but the government, whose disrespect for religion was a by-word with the natives, had no scruple in building Moslem schoolhouses, allowing a French general to pronounce an eulogy of Islamism in the pulpit of a mosque. While it forbade religious processions, it provided a ship to carry Arabian pilgrims to Mecca. It was so scrupulously careful of the Moslem conscience that it forbade the nuns to hang up a crucifix in the hospital when these holy women were nursing sick Mohammedans.

In 1864 there were Jesuit chaplains in two of the forts, and from there they ventured among the natives with whom they soon became popular. That was too much to put up with, so they were ordered to discontinue, because, forsooth, they were attacking the right of freedom of conscience. The result of this governmental policy was that in the revolt of the Kabyles in 1871 the leaders of the insurgents were the Arab students who had been given exclusively lay and irreligious instructions in Fort Napoleon. Father Brou says (viii, 218) that MacMahon who was governor of the colony was opposed to Cardinal Lavigerie's efforts to Christianize the natives, but that Napoleon III supported the cardinal, who after his victory, installed the Jesuits in the orphanage and also made Father Terasse novice master of the community

of White Fathers, which was then being founded;
two others were commissioned to put themselves in
communication with the tribes of the Sahara and when
they reported that everything was favorable the new
Order began its triumphant career. That was in 1872.
When Vice-Admiral de Guéydon was made governor
he willingly permitted the cardinal to employ Jesuits as
well as White Fathers in the work among the Kabyles,
but de Guéydon was quickly removed from office and
the old methods of persecution were resumed. When
the year 1880 arrived and the government was busy
closing Jesuit houses, the single one left to them in
Algeria was seized.

Portugal graciously made a gift to Spain of the
Island of Fernando Po in the Gulf of Guinea. Brou
calls it " an island of hell," with heat like a lime-kiln,
and reeking with yellow fever. It was inhabited by
a race of negroes called Boubis, who were dwarfs, with
rickety limbs, malformed, tattooed from head to foot,
smeared with a compound of red clay and oil, speaking
five different dialects, each one unintelligible to
speakers of the others; they had been charged with
poisoning the streams so as to get rid of the Portuguese
and were trying to kill the Spaniards by starvation.
It cannot have been brotherly love that suggested
this Portuguese present. To this lovely spot Queen
Isabella of Spain invited the Jesuits in 1859, and they
accepted the offer. They lived among the blacks,
unravelled the tangle of the five dialects and won
the affection of the natives. Their success in civilizing
these degraded creatures was such that whenever a
quarrel broke out in any of the villages the governor
had only to send his staff of office and peace descended
on the settlement. In other words the missionaries
had made Fernando Po a Paraguay. This condition

of things lasted twelve years, but when Isabella descended from her throne the first act of the revolutionists was to expel the Jesuits from the mission.

Leo XIII had ordered the General, Father Beckx to begin a seminary at Cairo. It was opened with twelve pupils. Three years afterwards occurred the Turkish massacre of Damascus and Libanus and the bombardment of Alexandria by the English. In consequence of all this the seminarians fled to Beirut, and after the war a college was begun at the deserted establishment of the Lazarists at Alexandria. Cairo was near by, but there was such an antagonism between the two cities that two distinct colleges with different methods and courses had to be maintained. Cairo was Egyptian in tone; Alexandria was French. Meanwhile, a mission was established on the Nile at Nineh which was some distance south of Cairo. In this mission the young priests trained at Beirut were employed, and they proved to be such excellent apostles that Leo XIII made three of them bishops and thus laid the foundation of the United Coptic hierarchy. In 1905 there were 20,000 United Copts in Egypt, four-fifths of whom had been reclaimed from the schism. This is all the more remarkable because the Protestants had spent enormous amounts of money in schools, hospitals, and asylums.

Madagascar was originally called the Island of St. Lawrence, because it was first sighted on the festival day of the great martyr by Diego Diaz, who with Cabral, the Portuguese discoverer, was exploring the Indian Ocean in the year 1500. A Portuguese priest was massacred there in 1540; in 1585 a Dominican was poisoned by the natives, and in the seventeenth century two Jesuits came from Goa with a native prince who had been captured by the Portuguese. Their benevolence toward the prince secured them permission to preach Christianity for a while, but when their influence began to show itself, they were, in obedience to a royal order, absolutely avoided by the natives so that one starved to death; the other succeeded in reaching home. The Lazarists came in 1648, but remained only fourteen months, two of their number having died meantime. Other attempts were made, but all ended in disaster to the missionaries. Nothing more was done until the middle of the nineteenth century. In 1832 Fathers de Solages and Dalmond were sent out, but they had been anticipated by the Protestant missionaries who, as early as 1830, had 32 schools with 4,000 pupils. De Solages soon succumbed and Dalmond continued to work on the small islands off the coast until 1843, when he returned to Europe to ask Father Roothaan to send him some Jesuits. Six members of the Society together with two Fathers of the Holy Ghost responded to the call, but they could get no farther than the islands of Nossi-Bé or St. Mary's and Réunion, or Bourbon as it was called.

The Queen Ranavalo, who was a ferocious and bloodthirsty pagan, had no use for any kind of evangelists, Protestant or Catholic, but there was a Frenchman named Laborde in the capital, who was held in high esteem by her majesty, because he was a cannonfounder, a manufacturer of furniture and a maker of soap. Besides these accomplishments to recommend him, he had won the esteem of the heir-apparent. Incidentally Laborde put the prince in relation with the missionaries off the coast. A short time afterwards, there appeared in the royal city another Frenchman who could make balloons, organize theatrical representations, and compound drugs. He was accepted in the queen's service. He was a Jesuit in disguise. His name was Finaz, and he continued to remain at Tananarivo until 1857, when the violence of the queen, who was insanely superstitious, brought about an uprising against her which was organized by the Protestant missionaries. She prevailed against the rebels, and as a consequence all Europeans were expelled from the island, and among them Father Finaz. He could congratulate himself that he had at least learned the language and made himself acquainted with the inhabitants.

Four years later (1861), the queen died, and King Radama II ascended the throne; whereupon six Jesuits opened a mission in Tananarivo. They soon had 2 schools with 400 pupils and numberless catechumens, but their success was not solid, for the Malgassy easily goes from one side to another as his personal advantage may dictate. Radama was killed, and then followed a forty years' struggle between the French and the English to get control of the island. The English prevailed for a time and, in 1869, Protestantism was declared to be the state religion. The number of evangelists multiplied enormously, but they were merely government agents and knew next to nothing about Christian truth or morality. The confusion was increased, when to the English parsons were added American Quakers and Norwegian Lutherans. The Evangelical statistics of all of them in 1892 were most imposing. Thus the Independents claimed 51,033 and the Norwegians 47,681, with 37,500 children in their schools. The names were on the lists, but the school-houses were often empty, and in the interim between the different official visits of the inspectors often no instruction was given. Against this the Catholics had only 22 chapels and 25 schools, and they were mostly in the neighborhood of Tananarivo.

France was subsequently the dominant influence in Madagascar but, as in the mother country religion was tabooed, there was little concern about it in the colonies. When the Franco-Prussian war showed the weakness of France, the respect for the alleged religion of France vanished, especially when a crusade began against the Catholic schools. Nevertheless the faithful continued to grow in number, and in 1882 they were reckoned at 80,000 with 152 churches, 44 priests, 527 teachers and 2,000 pupils. War broke out in 1881, and the missionaries were expelled but returned after hostilities ceased, and found that their neophytes, under the guidance of a princess of the royal blood, had held firmly to their religion, notwithstanding the closing of the schools and the sacking of the churches. After these troubles, conversions increased, and in 1894 there were 75 Jesuit priests in the island; and, besides the primary schools which had increased in number, a college and nine high schools as well as a printing house and two leper hospitals were erected. Added to this, an observatory was built and serious work began in geographical research, cartography, ethnography, natural history, folklore and philology.

Just at the height of this prosperity, a persecution began. The missionaries were expelled, their buildings looted, and the observatory wrecked. In 1896 the bishop counted 108 of his chapels which had been devastated, but in 1897 General Galieni arrived, and the queen vanished from the scene. After that the faith prospered, and in the year 1900 alone there were 94,998 baptisms. In 1896 Propaganda divided Madagascar into three vicariates: one entrusted to the Lazarists; another to the Fathers of the Holy Ghost; and a third to the Jesuits of the provinces of Toulouse and Champagne. In the Jesuit portion, the latest

statistics give 160,080 Christians and 170,000 catechumens, with 74 priests, 8 scholastics and 11 lay-
brothers. The chief difficulty to contend with is the
gross immorality of the people who are, in consequence,
almost impervious to religious teaching, and at the same
time easily captured by the money that pours into the
country from England and Norway. The French
officials, of course, cannot be expected to further the
cause of Catholicity.

In 1877, when Bishop Ricards of Grahamstown in
South Africa asked the Jesuits to accept the Zambesi Mission, Father Weld ardently took up the
work, and in April, 1879, Father Depelchin, a
Belgian, started from Kimberly, with eleven companions for Matabeleland, over which King Lo Benguela
ruled. It was a five months' journey and the
missionaries did not arrive at the royal kraal until
September 2. But as the prospects of conversion of
the much-married king and his followers were not
particularly bright, only one part of the expedition
remained with Lo Benguela, while two others struck
for the interior. There several of the strongest
missionaries sickened and died. The work went on,
however, for ten weary years when the king told them
to stop teaching religion and show the people how
to till the soil. Otherwise they must go. They
accepted the offer, of course, for it got them a better
means of imparting religious instruction.

Then a quarrel broke out between the British, the
Portuguese, the Boers and Lo Benguela for the possession of Mashonaland. The British as usual won
the fight, but when Cecil Rhodes came to the kraal,
to arrange matters, Lo Benguela ordered all the whites
out of his dominion and the Fathers withdrew. A
new difficulty then arose between the English and
Portuguese, and the mission was divided between

Upper and Lower Zambesi, the latter being assigned
to the Portuguese Jesuits.   There was trouble with
the natives of both sections for some time, and then
the Anglo-Boer war broke out, so that for twenty-five
years very little apostolic progress was made.   In
Upper Zambesi or Rhodesia, as it is called, there are at
present 40 Jesuit priests and 24 brothers, and 3 missionaries of Mariannhill, with 115 nuns, 20 churches
or chapels, and 30 schools of which 26 are for natives,
and about 5,000 Catholics.   Naturally speaking the
result scarcely warrants the outlay but the purpose is
supernatural and intelligible only from that point of
view.   In Lower Zambesi, which was given to the
Portuguese Jesuits, there have been no troubles because
it is garrisoned by Portuguese soldiers; the four stations in that district with their thirty-five Fathers
were doing splendid work when the Portuguese revolution occurred; the Jesuits were then expelled, but
twenty-six Fathers of the Divine Word took their
place.

The early days of the Zambesi mission evoked
splendid manifestations of the old heroic spirit of
the Society.   Thus we read of one of the missionaries, a
Father Wehl, who was separated from his companions
and wandered for twenty-six days in the bush, luckily
escaping the wild beasts and finally falling into the
hands of some Kaffirs who were about to put him to
death, when he was saved by the opportune arrival of an
English gold-hunter.   But starvation and disease had
shattered his health and his mind was gone.   Six
months afterwards he died.

Meantime his two companions Father Law and
Brother Hedley found shelter among the natives, but
had to live in a clay hut which was a veritable oven.
They both fell sick of fever; little or no food was given
them, and they slowly starved to death.   They lay

along side of each other, neither being able to assist his companion, and when finally the Father breathed his last, all the poor lonely brother could do was to place a handkerchief on the face, but when he removed the covering in the morning, he found that the rats had been eating the flesh. The dead missionary lay there for some time because the superstitious natives would not touch the corpse; when finally a rope was tied around it, they dragged it out of the hut and left it in the forest. For three weeks after this horrible funeral the poor brother had to fight off the rats that were attacking himself; at last the chief took pity on him and had him carried on a litter to a band of other missionaries who were approaching. When his friends saw him they burst into tears. He had not changed his clothes for five months and they were in tatters. His whole body was covered with sores and ulcers and the wounds were filled with vermin. He was in a state of stupor when he arrived, but strange to say he recovered. His dead companion, the priest, had been a naval officer, and was a convert to the Faith and the grandson of one of the lord chancellors of England.

The Congo mission was organized by the Belgium Jesuits in 1885, under the auspices of Leopold II of Belgium, who had established the Congo Free State. His majesty requested the Fathers to assist him, but he gave them no financial aid whatever, though he was pointedly asked to do so. The Congo Free State begins 400 miles from the Atlantic ocean and extends to Central Africa. Leopold's plan was to abolish slavery within the boundaries of this domain; then to make the adult male population his soldiers, and meantime to place the orphans and abandoned children in asylums which the missionaries would manage. Some of these establishments were to be supported from the public revenues, others by charity. The whole hope of the mission was in these orphanages, for nothing could be expected from the adult population. The boys were to be taught a trade and then married at the proper time. These households were to be visited and supervised by the missionaries.

It was an excellent plan, but it was opposed by the Belgian anti-clericals, who objected to giving so much power to priests. A number of English Protestants also busied themselves in spreading calumnies about these settlements and brought their accusations to court, where sentence was frequently given without hearing the accused. The charges were based on alleged occurrences in three out of the forty-four mission stations. The persecution became so acute that the Jesuits appealed to the king and received the thanks of his majesty and the government for the work they had performed, but the calumnies were not retracted, until May 26, 1906, when a formal document was issued by the Free State declaring that it greatly esteemed the work performed by the Catholic missionaries in the civilization of the State. In the following year on May 22, it added: " Since it is impossible to do without the missionaries in the conversion of the blacks, and as their help is of the greatest value in imparting instruction, we recommend that the mission be made still more efficacious by granting them a subsidy for the upkeep of their institutions. At the beginning of 1913, the Jesuits had seven stations and forty missionaries. In spite of all this, however, the work of systematic calumniation still continues.

The great war of 1914 brought absolute ruin on all the missions of Asia and Africa. Thus France called to the army every French priest or lay brother who was not crippled by age and infirmity, and made him fight in the ranks as a common soldier or a stretcher bearer in the hospital or on the battlefield. This was

the case not only with the Jesuits, but with other
religious orders and the secular priesthood. Nor was
this call to the colors restricted to those who were in
the French colonies; it affected all priests or brothers
of French birth who were laboring in Nigeria, Sierra
Leone, Belgian Congo, Angola, Zambesi, Canada, Haiti,
the United States or South America. Sixty priests
or brothers had to leave Japan. Out of forty-three
missionaries of the Society of African Missions who
were in Egypt, half had to leave. Of the twenty-two
who were on the Ivory Coast sixteen were mobilized.
Indeed, four bishops were summoned to the ranks,
Mgrs. Moury of the Ivory Coast, Terrien of Benin,
Perros of Siam, and Hermel of Haiti. There were at
the outbreak of the war thirty-five Jesuits from the
Levant in the army, besides others from Madagascar,
Madura and China.

CHAPTER XXVII

COLLEGES

Responsibility of the Society for loss of Faith in Europe. The Loi Falloux — Bombay — Calcutta — Beirut — American Colleges — Scientists, Archæologists, Meteorologists, Seismologists, Astronomers — Ethnologists.

THE Society of Jesus is frequently charged with being responsible for the present irreligious condition of the Latin nations, of France in particular, because, having had the absolute control of education in the past, it did not train its pupils to resist the inroads of atheism and unbelief.

In the first place, the charge is based on the supposition that the Society had complete control of the education of Catholic countries, which is not the case. Thus, for instance, Montesquieu, one of the first and most dangerous of the assailants of the Church in the eighteenth century, was educated by the Oratorians. As much as thirty-seven years before the French Revolution, namely, in 1752, Father Vitelleschi, the General of the Society, addressed the following letter to the Jesuits throughout the world:

" It is of supreme importance that what we call the *scholæ inferiores* (those namely below philosophy and theology) should be looked after with extreme solicitude. We owe this to the municipalities which have established colleges for us, and entrusted to us the education of their youth. This is especially incumbent upon us at the present time, when such an intense desire for scholastic education everywhere manifests itself, and has called into existence so many schools of that kind. Hence, unless we are careful, there is danger of our colleges being considered unnecessary. We must not forget that for a long time there were almost no other Latin schools but ours, or at least very few; so that parents were forced to send their sons to us who otherwise would not have done so. But now in many places, many schools are competing with ours, and we are exposing ourselves to be regarded as not up to the mark, and thus losing both our reputation and our scholars. Hence, our pupils are not to be detained for too long a period by a multiplication of courses, and they must be more than moderately imbued with a knowledge of the Classics. If they have not the best of masters, it is very much to be feared that they will betake themselves elsewhere and then every effort on our part to repair the damage will be futile."

In the second place, after the year 1762, that is twenty-seven years before the Revolution, there were not only no Jesuit colleges at all in France, but no Jesuits, and consequently there was an entire generation which had been trained in schools that were distinctly and intensely antagonistic to everything connected with the Society. Furthermore, it is an undeniable fact, provable by chronology, that the most conspicuous men in that dreadful upheaval, namely, Robespierre, Desmoulins, Tallien, Fréron, Chenier and others were educated in schools from which the Jesuits had been expelled before some of those furious young demagogues were born. Danton, for instance, was only three years old in 1762; Marat was a Protestant from Geneva, and, of course, was not a Jesuit pupil; and Mirabeau was educated by private tutors. The fact that Robespierre and Desmoulins were together at Louis-le-Grand has misled some into the belief that they were Jesuit students, whereas the college when they were there had long been out of the hands of the Society. The same is true of Portugal and Spain. The Society

had ceased to exist in Portugal as early as 1758, and in
Spain in 1767.

Far from being in control of the schools of France,
the whole history of the French Jesuits is that of
one uninterrupted struggle to get schools at all.
Against them, from the very beginning, were the
University of Paris and the various parliaments of
France, which represented the highest culture of the
nation and bitterly resented the intrusion of the Society
into the domain of education.

Not only is this true of the period that preceded but
also of the one that followed the French Revolution.
It was only in 1850, namely seventy-seven years after
the Suppression of the Society, that the Jesuits, in
virtue of the *Loi Falloux*, were permitted to open a
single school in France. The wonder is that the incessant confiscations and suppressions which followed
would permit of any educational success whatever.
Nevertheless, in the short respites that were allowed
them they filled the army and navy with officers who
were not only conspicuous in their profession but, at
the same time, thoroughgoing Catholics. Marshal
Foch is one of their triumphs. Indeed it was the superiority of their education that provoked the latest
suppression of the Jesuit schools in France.

It is this government monopoly of education in all
the Continental countries that constitutes the present
difficulty both for the Society of Jesus and for all the
other teaching orders. Thus after 1872, the German
province had not a single college in the whole extent
of the German Empire. It could only attempt to do
something beyond the frontiers. It has one in Austria,
a second in Holland, and a third in Denmark. Austria
has only one to its credit; Hungary one and Bohemia
another. The province of Rome has one; Sicily two,
one of which is in Malta, and Malta is English terri-

tory; Naples had three and Turin four, but some of these have already disappeared. All the splendid colleges of France were closed by Waldeck-Rousseau in 1890. Spain has five excellent establishments, but they have no guarantee of permanency. Belgium has thirteen colleges, packed with students, but the terrible World War has at least for a time depleted them. Holland has three colleges of its own. England four, and Ireland three.

The expulsions, however, have their compensations. Thus when the Jesuits were expelled from Germany by Bismarck, the English government welcomed them to India, and the splendid college of Bombay was the result. Italy also benefited by the disaster. Not to mention other distinguished men, Father Ehrle became Vatican librarian, and Father Wernz, rector of the Gregorian University and subsequently General of the Society. In South America, the exiles did excellent work in Argentina and Ecuador. The Jesuits of New York gave them an entrance into Buffalo, and from that starting-point they established a chain of colleges in the West, and later, when conditions called for it, they were assimilated to the provinces of Maryland, New York and Missouri, thus greatly increasing the efficiency of those sections of the Society.

When driven out of their country, the Portuguese Jesuits betook themselves to Brazil, where their help was greatly needed; the Italians went to New Mexico and California; and the French missions of China and Syria benefited by the anti-clericalism of the home government; for Zikawei became an important scientific world-centre and Beirut obtained a university. The latter was, until the war broke out, a great seat of Oriental studies.

The most imposing institutions in Beirut, a city with a population of over 150,000, made up of Mussulmans,

Greeks, Latins, Americans and Jews, are those of the
Jesuits. They maintain and direct outside of Beirut
192 schools for boys and girls with 294 teachers and
12,000 pupils. There is, in the city, a university with
a faculty of medicine (120 students) founded in 1881
with the help of the French government; its examinations are conducted before French and Ottoman
physicians and its diplomas are recognized by both
France and Turkey. The university has also a seminary (60 students) for all the native Rites. Up to
1902 it had sent out 228 students including three
patriarchs, fifteen bishops, one hundred and fifteen priests
and eighty-three friars. Its faculty of philosophy and
theology grants the same degrees as the Gregorian
University in Rome. Its faculty of Oriental languages
and sciences, founded in 1902, teaches literary and con-
versational Arabic, Hebrew, Syriac, Coptic and Ethi-
opic; the comparative grammar of the Semitic languages;
the history and geography of the Orient; Oriental
archæology; Græco-Roman epigraphy and antiquities.
Its classical college has 400 pupils and its three primaries
600. A printing-house, inaugurated in 1853, is now
considered to be the foremost for its output in that
part of the world. Since 1871 it has published a
weekly Arabic paper, and since 1898 a fortnightly
review in the same language, the editors of which
took rank at once among the best Orientalists. Besides
continually adding to their collection of philological
papers, they contribute to many scientific European
reviews. (The Catholic Encyclopedia, II, 393.)

There are Jesuit colleges, also, throughout India,
such as the great institutions of Bombay and Calcutta
with their subsidiary colleges, and further down the
Peninsula are Trichinopoly, all winning distinction
by their successful courses of study. Indeed the first
effort the Society makes in establishing itself in any

part of the world, where conditions allow it, is to organize a college. If they would relinquish that one work they would be left in peace.

An interesting personage appears in connection with the University of Beirut: William Gifford Palgrave. It is true that one period of his amazing career humiliated his former associates, but as it is a matter of history it must needs be told.

He was the son of an eminent English Protestant lawyer, Sir Francis Palgrave, and had Jewish blood in his veins. He was born in 1826, and after a brilliant course of studies at Oxford began his romantic career as a traveller. He went first to India and was an officer of Sepoys in the British army. While there, he became a Catholic, and afterwards presented himself at the novitiate of Negapatam as an applicant for admission. Unfortunately his request was granted, and forthwith he changed his name to Michael Cohen, as he said to conceal his identity. This was a most amazing mask; for Palgrave would have escaped notice, whereas everyone would immediately ask, who is this Jesuit Jew? How he was admitted is a mystery, especially as he proclaimed his race so openly.

After his novitiate he was sent to Rome to begin his theology — another mystery. Why was he not compelled to study philosophy first like everyone else? Then he insisted that Rome did not agree with his health, and he was transferred to Beirut to which he betook himself, not in the ordinary steamer, but in a sailing vessel filled with Mussulmans. On the way, he picked up Arabic. Inside of a year, namely in 1834, he was made a priest and given charge of the men's sodality which he charmed by his facility in the use of the native tongue; in the meantime he made many adventurous journeys to the interior to convert the natives, but failed every time. In 1860 he was sent to France for his third year of probation under the famous Father Fouillot, whom he fascinated by his scheme of entering Arabia Petrea as its apostle. He succeeded in getting Louis Napoleon to give him 10,000 francs on the plea that he would thus carry out the scheme of the Chevalier Lascaris whom Napoleon Bonaparte had sent to the East.

At Rome, he found the Father General quite cold to the proposition, and when he had the audacity to ask Propaganda for permission to say Mass in Arabic, he was told: " Convert your Arabs first and then we shall see about the Mass." The brother who was to go with him fell ill, and the General then insisted that he should not attempt the journey without a priest as companion; whereupon Palgrave persuaded the Greek Bishop of Zahlé to ordain one of the lay professors of the college, after a few days' instruction in moral theology. Fortunately this improvised priest turned out well, and he became His Beatitude Mgr. Geraigri, patriarch of the Greek Melchites.

In 1862 the travellers set out by way of Gaza in Palestine, Palgrave as a physician, the other as his assistant. They covered the entire Arabian peninsula and were back again in Beirut at the end of fourteen months. Palgrave had made no converts, and was himself a changed man. Even his sodalists remarked it. What had happened no one ever knew. In 1864 he was sent to Maria-Laach in Germany, where the saintly Father Behrens wrestled with him in vain for a while, but he left the Society and passed over to Protestantism, securing meanwhile an appointment as Prussian consul at Mossul. In the following year he published an account of his travels and the book was a European sensation. In it he made no secret of his having been a member of the Society, which he says was

" so celebrated in the annals of courageous and devoted philanthropy. The many years I spent in the East were the happiest of my life." In 1884 he was British consul at Montevideo and remained there till 1888 when he died.

For twenty years he seemed never to have been ashamed of his apostasy, but three or four years before his death the grace of God found him. The change was noticed on his return from a trip to England. He had become a Catholic again. He went to Mass and received Holy Communion. Although a government official, he refused to go to the Protestant Church even for the queen's jubilee, in spite of the excitement caused by his absence. He died of leprosy. A Jesuit attended him in his last sickness, and he was buried with all the rites of the Church. These details are taken from a recent publication by Father Jullien, S. J., entitled "Nouvelle mission de la Compagnie de Jésus en Syrie " (II, iii.)

The great difficulty that confronts educators of youth in our times, is state control. In the United States it has not yet gone to extremes, but every now and then one 'can detect tendencies in that direction. Meantime the Society has developed satisfactorily along educational lines. According to the report of October 10, 1916 (Woodstock Letters, V 45), there were 16,438 students in its American colleges and universities. Of these 13,301 were day scholars and 3,137 boarders. There were 3,943 in the college departments, 10,502 in the high schools and 1,416 in the preparatory. Besides all this, there were commercial and special sections numbering 737. The total increase over the preceding year was 523.

The Maryland-New York provinces had 1,848 students of law, 341 of medicine, 127 of dentistry, 122 of pharmacy. Missouri had 786 students of law,

643 of medicine, 776 of dentistry, 245 of pharmacy, 126 of engineering, 530 of finance, 240 of sociology, 425 of music, 43 of journalism, and 61 in the nurse's training school. New Orleans had a law school of 81 and California one of 232 students.

It is sometimes urged as an objection to Catholic colleges that they give only a Classical education, and are thus not keeping pace with the world outside. To show that the objection has no foundation in fact, it would be sufficient to enter any Jesuit college which is at all on its feet, and see the extensive and fully equipped chemical and physical laboratories, the seismic plants and in some cases the valuable museums of natural history which they possess. If it were otherwise, they would be false to all their traditions; for the Society has always been conspicuous for its achievements in the natural sciences. It has produced not only great mathematicians and astronomers, but explorers, cosmographers, ethnologists, and archæologists. Thus, for instance, there would have been absolutely no knowledge of the aborigines of North America, their customs, their manner of life, their food, their dress, their superstitions, their dances, their games, their language had it not been for the minute details sent by the missionaries of the old and new Society to their superiors. In every country where they have been, they have charted the territories over which they journeyed or in which they have labored, described their natural features, catalogued their fauna and flora, enriched the pharmacopeia of the world with drugs, foodstuffs and plants, and have located the salts and minerals and mines.

That this is not idle boasting may be seen at a glance in Sommervogel's "Bibliothèque des écrivains." Thus the names of publications on mathematics fill twenty-eight columns of the huge folio pages. Then

53

follow other long lists on hydrostatics and hydraulics, navigation, military science; surveying; hydrography and gnomics; physics, chemistry and seismology call for thirty columns; medical sciences; zoology, botany, geology, mineralogy, paleontology, rural economy and agriculture require eight. Then there are two columns on the black art. The fine arts including painting, drawing, sculpture, architecture, music, equitation, printing and mnemonics take from column 927 to 940.

According to this catalogue, the new Society has already on its lists one hundred and sixty-four writers on subjects pertaining to the natural sciences: physics, chemistry, mineralogy, zoology, botany, paleontology, geography, meteorology, astronomy, etc. The names of living writers are not recorded. Nor does this number include the writers who published their works during the Suppression, as de Mailla, who in 1785 issued in thirteen volumes a history of China with plans and maps, the outcome of an official survey of the country — a work entrusted by the emperor to the Jesuits. Father de Mailla was made a mandarin for his share of the work.

The extraordinary work on the zoology of China by the French Jesuit, Pierre Heude, might be adduced as an illustration of similar work in later times. He began his studies in boyhood as a botanist, but abandoned that branch of science when he went to the East. While laboring as a missionary there for thirty years he devoted every moment of his spare time to zoology.

He first travelled along all the rivers of Middle and Eastern China to classify the fresh-water molluscs of those regions. On this subject alone he published ten illustrated volumes between 1876 and 1885. His treatise " Les Mollusques terrestres de la vallée du Fleuve Bleu " is today the authority on that subject.

He then directed his attention particularly to the systematic and geographical propagation of Eastern Asiatic species of mammals, as well as to a comparative morphology of classes and family groups, according to tooth and skeleton formations. His fitness for the work was furthered by his extremely keen eye, his accurate memory, and the enormous wealth of material which he had accumulated, partly in the course of his early travels and partly in later expeditions, which carried him in all directions. These expeditions covered chiefly the eight years from 1892 to 1900. They took him to the Philippines which he visited three times; to Singapore, Batavia, the Celebes, the Moluccas, New Guinea, Japan, Vladivostock, Cochin-China, Cambodia, Siam, and Tongking. He carried on his work with absolute independence of method. He contented himself with the facts before him and sought little assistance from authorities; nor did he fear to deduce theoretical conclusions from his own observations which flatly contradicted other authorities. He continued his scientific work until shortly before his death which occurred at Zikawei on January 3, 1902. (The Catholic Encyclopedia, VII, 308.)

Albers in his " Liber Sæcularis " maintains that " in the cultivation of the natural sciences, the restored Society won greater fame than the old," and that " a glance at the men whom the Italian provinces alone have produced would be sufficient to convince the doubter. Angelo Secchi, of course, stands out most prominently, and a little later Father Barello, who with the Barnabite Denza established the Meteorological Observatory of Malta. Giambattista Pianciani was regarded with the greatest veneration in Rome because of his vast erudition as a scientist, as were Caraffa, Mancini and Foligni for their knowledge of mathematics. Marchi was the man who trained the illustrious de Rossi, as an archæologist, and also the Jesuit Raffaele Garrucci whose "Monumenta delle arte cristiane primitive nella metropoli del Cristianesimo" laid the foundations of the new study of archæology. The writings of Father Gondi and Francis Tongiorgi have also contributed much to advancement in those fields of knowledge.

Faustino Arévalo was one of the exiles from Spain at the time of the Suppression. He was born at Campanario in Estremadura in 1747, and entered the Society in 1761. Six years afterwards he was deported to Italy by Charles III. In Rome he won the esteem and confidence of Cardinal Lorenzano, who proved to be his Mæcenas by bearing the expense of Arévalo's learned publications. He was held in high honor in Rome, and was appointed to various offices of trust, among them that of pontifical hymnographer and theologian of the penitenziaria, thus succeeding the illustrious Muzzarelli. When the Society was restored, he returned to Spain and was made provincial of Castile. One of his works was the "Hymnodia hispanica," a restoration of ancient Spanish hymns to their original metrical, musical and grammatical perfection. This publication was much esteemed by Cardinal Mai and Dom Guéranger. It was accompanied by a curious dissertation on the Breviary of Cardinal Quignonez. He also edited the poems of Prudentius and Dracontius and those of a fifth century Christian of Roman Africa. Besides this, he has to his credit four volumes of Jouvancy's "Gospel History," the works of Sedulius and St. Isidore and a Gothic Missal. He stands in the forefront of Spanish patristic scholars, and has shed great lustre on the Church of Spain by his vast learning, fine literary

Colleges 837

of his fatherland.

The founder of the science of archæology, according
to Hurter, was Stefano Antonio Morcelli. He was
a member of the old Society and re-entered it when
it was restored. Even before the Suppression, which
occurred twenty years after his entrance, he had
established an archæological section in the Kircher
Museum of Rome. When he found himself homeless,
in consequence of the publication of the Brief of
Clement XIV, he was made the librarian of Cardinal
Albani. He refused the Archbishopric of Ragusa and
continued his literary labors in Rome. His first
publication was " The Style of Inscriptions." In the
town of Chiari, his birthplace, to which he afterwards
withdrew, he founded an institution for the education
of girls, reformed the entire school system, devoted
his splendid library to public use, and restored many
buildings and churches. Meantime his reputation as
master of epigraphic style increased and he was placed
in a class of his own above all competitors. Besides
his many works on his special subject, he gave to the
world five volumes of sermons and ascetic treatises.
When the Society was re-established he again took his
place in its ranks, and died in Brescia in 1822 at the
age of eighty-four. Hurter classifies him as also
a historian and geographer.

Nor was Morcelli an exception. Fathers Arthur
Martin and Charles Cahier are still of great authority
as archæologists, chiefly for their monograph in which,
as government officials, they described the Cathedral
of Bourges; and likewise for their " Mélanges arché-
ologiques," in which the sacred vessels, enamels and
other treasures of Aix-la-Chapelle and of Cologne are
discussed. They also wrote on the antique ivories

of Bamberg, Ratisbon, Munich and London; on the Byzantine and Arabian weavings; and on the paintings and the mysterious bas-reliefs of the Roman and Carlovingian periods. Their works appeared between 1841 and 1848.

A very famous Jesuit archæologist died only a few years ago, and the French government which had just expelled the Jesuits erected a monument at Poitiers to perpetuate his memory. He was Father Camille de la Croix. He was a scion of the old Flemish nobility and was born in the Château Saint-Aubert, near Tournai in Belgium, but he passed nearly all his life in France, and hence Frenchmen considered him as one of their own. He got his first schooling in Brugelette, and, when that college was given up, went with his old masters to France. In 1877 we find him mentioned in the catalogue as a teacher and writer of music. Three years later, the French provinces had been dispersed by the government, and he was then docketed as an archæologist at the former Jesuit college of Poitiers.

De la Croix's success as a discoverer was marvellous. Near Poitiers he found vast Roman baths, five acres in extent, whose existence had never even been suspected. There were tombs of Christian martyrs; a wonderful crypt dating from the beginning of the Christian era; a temple dedicated to Mercury, with its sacred wells, votive vases etc. At Sauxay, nineteen miles from Poitiers, he unearthed the ruins of an entire Roman colony; a veritable Pompeii with its temple of Apollo, its theatres, its palaces, its baths etc. He had the same success at Nantes, Saint-Philibert, and Berthouville; — the French government supplying him with the necessary funds. The " Gaulois " said of him that " in his first ten years he discovered more monuments than would have made twenty archæologists famous." Meantime he lived in a wooden cabin, on the banks of the Clain, and there he died at the age of eighty, on April 14, 1900; and there also the French government built his monument. At the dedication, all the scientific men of the country were present, and the King of Belgium sent a representative.

Although the well-known François Moigno severed his connection with the Society, it was only after he had achieved greatness while yet in its ranks. He entered the novitiate on September 2, 1822, when he was eighteen years of age. He made his theological studies at Montrouge, and in his spare moments devoted himself to the study of the natural sciences. At the outbreak of the Revolution of 1830, he went with his brethren to Brieg in Switzerland, where he took up the study of languages, chiefly Hebrew and Arabic. When the troubles subsided in France he was appointed professor of mathematics in Paris at the Rue des Postes, and became widely known as a man of unusual attainments. He was on intimate terms with Cauchy, Arago, Ampère and others. He was engaged on one of his best known works: "Leçons de calcul différentiel et de calcul intégral" and had already published the first volume when he left the Society. He had been a Jesuit for twenty-one years. He was then made chaplain of Louis-le-Grand, one of the famous colleges owned by the Jesuits before the Suppression, and became the scientific editor of "La Presse" in 1850; of "Le Pays" in 1851, and in the following year, founded the well-known scientific journal "Cosmos," followed by "Les Mondes" in 1862, editing meanwhile "Les Actualités scientifiques." As a matter of fact, it was the Society that had formed him and enabled him to publish his greatest works.

The German, Father Ludwig Dressel, who was for many years the director of the Polytechnic in Quito, is well-known for his treatises on geology, chemistry and physics. Kramers, in Holland, is the author of three volumes on chemistry. In entomology, Father Erich Wasmann is among the masters of today, and has written a series of works which have elicited the applause of the scientific world, especially his " Die moderne Biologie und die Entwicklungstheorie." (Modern Biology and the Theory of Evolution.) The writings of Bolsius on biology won for him a membership in the scientific societies of Russia, Belgium, Italy and Holland.

The first meteorological society, the " Palatina," was founded by Father Johann Hemmer in 1780, and it is noteworthy that nearly all its contributors were members of the various religious orders of Austria-Hungary, Italy and France. Its scope was not restricted to the study of meteors, for it accepted papers on ethnology, linguistics, etc. Hence we find Father Dobrizhoffer writing to it from Paraguay, Joseph Lafitaux from Canada, Johann Hanxleden, the Sanscrit scholar from Hindostan, and Lorenzo Hervás. Hanxleden and his colleague Roth were the pioneers in Sanscrit. The former was the first European to write a Sanscrit grammar and to compile a Malabar-Sanscrit-Portuguese dictionary. Hervás was one of the Jesuits expelled from Mexico, and after the Suppression was made prefect of the Quirinal Library by Pius VII. While there, he worked in conjunction with several of his former brethren in the compilation and composition of scientific works, mostly of an ethnological character. He also wrote a number of educational works for deaf mutes.

The Observatory of Stonyhurst dates back to 1838-39, when a building consisting of an octagonal center-piece with four abutting structures was erected in the middle of the garden. But it was not until 1845

that a 4-inch Jones equatorial was mounted in its
dome. Meteorological observations were begun as
early as 1844, and magnetic in 1856 by Father Weld.
In 1867 an 8-inch equatorial was set up. The chief
workers were Fathers Stephen Perry, Walter Sidgreaves
and Aloysius Cortie. All three were members of
the Royal Astronomical Society and were frequently
chosen to fill official positions. Father Perry achieved
special prominence. He was the director from 1860 to
1862, and again from 1868 till his death in 1889. He
was a member of more scientific expeditions than
any other living astronomer. He was at Cadiz for
the solar eclipse in 1870; he was sent as astronomer
royal in 1874 for the transit of Venus to Kerguelen
or Desolation Island, and for another observation to
Madagascar in 1882. In 1886 he observed a total
eclipse at Carriacou in the West Indies. For the
eclipse of 1887 he was sent to Russia, and for that
of 1889 to Cayenne. On the latter expedition he was
attacked by a pestilential fever and died on board
the warship " Comus" off Georgetown, Demerara,
after receiving the last sacraments from a French
Abbé resident in Georgetown. Father Perry was
buried there in the cathedral cemetery. His death
was that of a saint, and a touching account of it has
been left by his assistant, a Jesuit lay-brother.

Father Perry's prominence in the scientific world
may be judged by the honors bestowed upon him.
He was a Fellow of the Royal Society and a member
of the Council; also a member and Fellow of the
Royal Astronomical Society and, shortly before he
died, he had been proposed as Vice-President. At the
time of his death he held the post of President of the
Liverpool Astronomical Society. He was a Fellow
of the Royal Meteorological Society, a member of the
Physical Society of London, and an associate of the

Papal Academy of the Nuovi Lincei, the oldest
scientific society in Europe. He belonged also to the
Societé Géographique of Antwerp, and had received
the degree of Doctor of Science *honoris causa* from the
Royal University of Ireland. For several years before
his death, he served on the committee of the council
on education, as well as on the committee for compar-
ing and reducing magnetic observations, for which
work he had been appointed by the British Association
for the Advancement of Science, a body of which he was
a life-member. In 1887 and 1889 he attended at
Paris the meetings of the Astrographic Congress for
the photographic charting of the heavens.

In the " Monthly Notices " of the Royal Astronomical
Society (L, iv) the following resolution appears on
the occasion of his death: " The Council having heard
with the deepest regret of the death of the Rev. S. J.
Perry while on the Society's expedition to observe
the total eclipse at the Salut Islands, desire to put
on record their sense of the great loss which astronomy
has suffered by the death of so enthusiastic and capable
an observer, and to offer to his relations and to his colleagues at Stonyhurst the expression of their sincere
sympathy and condolence on this sad event." The
list of his scientific papers covers twelve pages of his
biography. Father Cortie, his associate in the Stonyhurst Observatory, says of him: " His death was
glorious, for he died a victim to his sense of duty
and his zeal for science. Truly he may lay claim to
the title of ' martyr of science,' and a part of the
story of the eclipse of December 22, 1889, will be the
account of how Father Perry was carried from a sick
bed to take his last observation."

Besides the Observatories in Granada and Oña the
Spanish Jesuits have another near Tortosa. The
main object of the latter is the study of terrestrial

magnetism, seismology, meteorology, study of the sun, etc. It has five separate buildings and a valuable periodical regularly published by the observers.

The Zo-se Observatory near Zikawei in China is in charge of the French Fathers. The Observatory is about 80 feet in length. It has a library of 20,000 volumes with numerous and valuable Chinese manuscripts. They have another station in Madagascar, which is 4,600 feet above sea-level, and consequently higher by 100 metres than the Lick Observatory in California. When the Jesuits were expelled from Madagascar, the Observatory was demolished by the natives who thought it was a fortress. It was rebuilt later at the expense of the French government and the director, Father Colin, was made a corresponding Member of the French Academy. In 1890, 1895, 1898 and 1899 the observers were honored by their home government with purses of considerable value, one being of 6,000 and another of 3,000 francs.

There are other observatories at Calcutta, Rhodesia, Feldkirch, Louvain, Oudenbosch (Holland), Puebla (Mexico), Havana, Woodstock and other Jesuit colleges in the United States; these are attracting notice principally by their seismograhical reports. The most conspicuous of all these North American observatories is that of Georgetown which was founded in 1842–43, about the same time as the Naval Observatory. It was built under the direction of Father Curley, whose determination of the longitude of Washington in conjunction with Sir G. B. Airy, the Astronomer Royal of Greenwich, England, was made by observing a series of transits of the moon, and was later shown by the electric telegraph to have been correct to within the tenth of a second. Fathers De Vico, Sestini and Secchi labored at Georgetown.

Secchi's " Researches in Electrical Rheometry " was published in 1852 by the Smithsonian Institute. It was his first literary contribution to science. Sestini's drawings of the sun spots were published by the Naval Observatory. In 1889 Father Hagen, then the director, published his " Atlas stellarum variabilium." In 1890 Father Fargis solved the question of " the personal equation " in astronomical observations by his invention of the Photochronograph. It had been attempted by Father Braun in Kalocsa (Hungary) and by Repsola in Königsberg, but both failed. Professors Pickering and Bigelow in the United States had also given it up, but Father Fargis solved the difficulty by a fixed photographic plate and a narrow metal tongue attached to the armature of an electric magnet. It has proved satisfactory in every test.

In Sommervogel's " Bibliothèque " the list of the astronomical works written by Secchi covers nineteen pages quarto, in double columns. He was equally active in physics and meteorology and his large meteorograph described in Ganot's " Physics " merited for him the Grand Prix (100,000 francs) and the Cross of the Legion of Honor at the Paris Universal Exposition in 1867. It was conferred upon him by the hand of the Emperor Napoleon, in the presence of the Emperors of Russia and Austria and the Kings of Prussia and Belgium. The Emperor of Brazil sent him a golden rose as a token of appreciation.

The " Atlas stellarum variabilium " by Father Johann Hagen is according to " Popular Astronomy " (n. 81, p. 50) the most important event in the star world. Ernst Harturg (V. J. S., vol. 35) says: " It will without doubt become in time an indispensable requisite of the library of every observatory just as the Bonn maps have become." Father Hagen has also won distinction in the mathematical world by his

" Synopsis der höheren Mathematik," in four volumes quarto.

The seismological department of Georgetown, under Father Francis A. Tondorf, has attained an especial prominence in the United States. Its equipment is of the latest perfection, and its earthquake reports are those most commonly quoted in the daily press of America.

Important in their own sphere are the books " Astronomisches aus Babylon " by Fathers Joseph Epping and Johann Nepomuk Strassmaier, and " Die babylonische Mondrechnung " by Epping. F. K. Ginzel (in V. J. S., vol. 35.) expresses the following opinion of them: " It is well known that the investigations made by the Jesuit Father Epping, in conjunction with the Assyriologist Father Strassmaier, upon many Babylonian astronomical bricks have had as a consequence that the scientific level upon which the history of astronomy had formerly placed the Babylonians must be taken considerably higher. Epping's investigations now receive a very valuable extension through the labor of Father Kugher of Valkenburg, Holland. From the communications received concerning Kugher's work the importance of his book to the history of astronomy may be inferred."

" Die Gravitations-Constante " (Vienna, 1896), by Father Carl Braun of Mariaschein, Bohemia, represents about eight years of patient work, and according to Poynting (Proc. of the Royal Soc. Inst. of Great Britain, XVI, 2) " bears internal evidence of great care and accuracy. He obtained almost exactly the same result as Professor Boys with regard to the earth's mean density. Father Braun carried on his work far from the usual mechanical laboratory facilities and had to make much of the apparatus himself. His patience and persistence command our highest admiration."

With regard to the " Kosmogonie vom Standpunkte christlicher Wissenschaft," by Father Braun, Dr. Foster says: (V. J. S., vol. 25) " this problem, mighty in every aspect, is treated from all points of view with clearness and impressiveness. One could hardly find at this time in any other book all the essential features of a theory of the sun collected together in such a directive manner."

Perhaps the famous phrase of St. Ignatius, *Quam sordet tellus quum cælum aspicio*, had something to do with the Society's passion for astronomy. " How sordid the earth is when I look at the sky." His sons have been looking at the sky from the beginning not only spiritually but through telescopes, and many of them have become famous as astronomers. This is all the more notable, because star-gazing was only a secondary object with them. They were first of all priests and scientific men afterwards. As early as 1591 Father Perrerin, in his " Divinatio astrologica," denounced astrology as a superstition although his Protestant friend, the great Kepler, did not admit the distinction between it and astronomy. The book of Perrerin's went through five editions. Father de Angelis published in 1604 five volumes entitled " In astrologos conjectores " (Against astrological guessers). As late as 1676, the work was still in demand, for illustrious personages like Rudolph II, Wallenstein, Gustavus Adolphus, Catherine de' Medici and even Luther and Melanchthon with a host of others were continually having their horoscopes taken.

Another eminent worker was Father Riccioli, of whom we read: " If you want to know the ancient follies on this point consult Riccioli." (Littrois in " Wunder des Himmels," 1886, 604.) The implication might be that Riccioli approved of them, but the reverse is the case, for, as Thomas Aquinas furnishes a list of

every actual and almost every possible theological
and philosophical error, but after each adds *videtur
quod non*, which he follows up by a refutation, so
does Riccioli in his Astrology. He was a genius. He
became a Jesuit when he was sixteen, and for years
never thought of telescopes. He taught poetry,
philosophy and theology at Parma and Bologna,
and took up astronomy only when his superiors assigned
him to that study. Being an Italian, he did not like
Copernicus or Kepler. They were from the Protestant
North and had refused to accept the Gregorian Calendar. He admitted, indeed, that the Copernican
system was the most beautiful, the most simple, the
best conceived, but not solid, so he made one of his
own, but did not adhere to it tenaciously.

Appreciating the deficiencies of the astronomy of the
ancients, he composed the famous "Almagestum
novum," which placed the whole science on a new
basis. Beginning by the measurement of the earth, he
produced, though he made mistakes, the first meteoro-
log-system. His lunar observations revealed 600 spots
on the moon, which is fifty more than had been found
by Hevelius. His collaborator, Grimaldi, the greatest
mathematician of his age, made the maps. His remarks
on libration fill an entire volume, and the writer in
the "Biographie universelle" gives him the credit of
experimenting on the oscillations of the pendulum before
Galileo. His health was always poor, but he worked
like a giant. His "Almagestum" consists of 1500
folio pages, and is described as a treasure of astronomical erudition. Lalande quotes from it continually.
His "Astronomia reformata" is in two volumes
folio, and he has twelve folio volumes on geography
and hydrography. Its learning is astounding. Thus,
for instance, in the second part of his "Chronologia"
there is a list of the principal events from the creation

to the year 1688, along with the names of kings, patriarchs, nations, heresies, councils, and great personages, which was really collateral matter.

What the Jesuit astronomers accomplished in China from the time of Ricci down to Hallerstein in 1774 has been continued there to the present day. The first government observatory in Europe was erected in the University of Vienna, then in the hands of the Jesuits. There were others at Vilna, Schwetzingen and Mannheim. Twelve other private ones had been built in the various European colleges of the Society. The establishment of these observatories was providential, for when the Society was suppressed they afforded occupation and support to a great number of dispersed Jesuits, who remained in charge of them during their forty years of homelessness and kept alive the old spirit of the Order in its affection for that particular study. As in the old Society this work is still a matter of private enterprise. As far as we are aware there is only one observatory where a government assists, the Observatory of Manila, in which the employees are salaried by the United States government. The equipment itself, however, was provided by the Jesuits, who reduced their living expenses to the minimum in order to build the house and buy the instruments.

On the other hand, the number of actual Jesuit observatories in the strict sense of the term already rivals that of the old Society. The Roman establishment which had been made famous by Scheiner, Gottignes, Asclepi, Borgondius, Maire and Boscovich was continued during the Suppression by the secular priest Calandrelli. In 1824 Leo XII restored it to the Society, and Father Dumouchel took charge of it with De Vico as an assistant. The latter's reputation was European. He was known as the Comet Chaser, for he had discovered eight of them. The well-known

five and a half years periodic comet bears his name.
He succeeded Dumouchel as director in 1840, and was
holding that office when the Revolution of 1848 drove the
Jesuits from Rome. He was received with great
enthusiasm in France by Arago, and in England he
was offered the directorship of the Observatory of
Madras but he preferred to go to Georgetown in the
United States. Being called to London on business,
he died there on November 15, 1848, at the age of 43.
Herschel wrote his obituary in the "Notices of the
Astronomical Society."

Secchi had gone with De Vico to Georgetown, but was
recalled to Rome in 1849 by Pius IX, and given
charge of the observatory. He was born at Reggio in
1818, and, after studying in the Jesuit college there,
entered the Society at the age of sixteen. He began
as a tutor in physics and continued at that work when
he went to Georgetown. Astronomy had as yet not
appealed to him, but in Washington he met the famous
hydrographer, meteorologist and astronomer, Maury,
and a deep affection sprang up between them, and
Secchi dedicated one of his books to his American
friend. His appointment to the Roman Observatory in
1859 was due to the recommendation of De Vico, and
in two years his brilliant success as an observer attracted
the attention of the scientific world. He began by a
revision of Struve's "Catalogue of Double Stars,"
which necessitated seven years' strenuous work, and
he was able to verify 10,000 of the entries. Meantime
he was studying the physical condition of Saturn,
Jupiter, Mars and the four great moons of Jupiter.
In 1852 the moon became the special object of his
investigations, and his micrometrical map of the great
crater was so exact that the Royal Society of London
had numerous photographs made of it. In 1859 he
published his great work "Il quadro fisico del sistema

54

solare secondo il piu recenti osservazioni." The study
of the sun spots was his favorite task, and his expedition
to Spain in 1860 to observe the total eclipse established
the fact that the red protuberances around the edge of
the eclipsed sun were real features of the sun itself and
not optical illuminations or illuminated mountains of
the moon. He began the " Sun Records " in Rome,
and they are kept up till this day. No other observatory
has anything like them. All this, with his inventions,
and the study of the spectroscope, heliospectroscope
and telespectroscope, besides the mass of scientific
results which he arrived at, has put him in the very
first rank of astronomers. He was equally conspicuous
as a meteorologist and a physicist. When the Piedmontese took Rome, Secchi was offered the rank of
senator and the superintendency of all the observatories
of Italy if he would leave the Society. Of course he
scoffed at the proposal; but his authority in Italy was
so great that the invaders did not dare to expel him
from his observatory. He died in 1878.

Clerke says of him: " The effective founders of
stellar photography were Father Secchi, the eminent
Jesuit astronomer of the Collegio Romano, and Dr.
Huggins with whom the late Professor Mullen was
associated. The work of each was happily made to
supplement that of the other. With less perfect
appliances, the Roman astronomer sought to render
his work extensive rather than precise; whereas, at
Upper Tulse Hill, searching accuracy over a narrower
guage was aimed at and attained. To Father Secchi
is due the merit of having executed the first spectroscope
view of the heavens. Above 4000 stars were all
passed in review by him and classified according to the
varying qualities of their light. His provisional
establishment (1863–7) of four types of stellar spectra

has proved a genuine aid to knowledge, through the facilities afforded by it for the arrangement and comparison of rapidly accumulating facts. Moreover it is scarcely doubtful that these spectral distinctions correspond to differences in physical conditions of a marked kind."

" I saw the great man," said one who was in the audience of the splendid hall of the Cancelleria, " when he was giving a course on the solar spectrum. The vast auditorium was crowded with a brilliant throng in which you could see cardinals, archbishops, monsignori and laymen, all representing the highest religious, diplomatic and scientific circles. Though an Italian, Secchi spoke in French that was absolutely perfect. Everyone was enthralled, but what captivated me was the gentleness and even deference with which he spoke to the men who were adjusting the screens. He almost seemed to be their servant and I could not help saying to myself, ' Oh! I love you.' I saw him later in the street. It was in the turbulent days of the Italian occupation. He was walking alone; his head slightly bowed. Suddenly the cry was heard: ' Death to the Jesuits!' and an excited mob was seen rushing towards him. He stood still; grasped the stout stick in his hand, glared at them; and they fled. I never saw anything like it. I loved him before. I adored him now." In brief, Secchi was a great man in the eyes of the world, but he was a greater religious. Indeed it is said that when his superiors told him to apply himself to mathematics he burst into tears. He wanted to be a missionary. He was such, while being at the same time one of the most distinguished men in the scientific world.

The Manila Observatory in the Philippines, strictly speaking, began its meteorological service in 1865, though observations had been made many years previously. In 1881 it was officially approved by the Spanish government and in 1901 by that of the United States. The meteorological importance and efficiency of the Manila Observatory overshadows its astronomical, for the reason that it is situated in the eastern typhoon path. Astronomy, however, is by no means neglected. From 1880 up to the present time it has rendered very valuable services to the world. First, the official time was given to the city of Manila and, after the American occupation, it was extended to all the telegraph stations throughout the islands. Secondly, about one hundred ship chronometers are annually compared and rated at the Observatory free of charge.

In 1894 Father José Algué began to complete the astronomical equipment and erected a new building at the cost of $40,000, equipping it with instruments of the latest and best type. Three years later he was given charge of the whole establishment, and is now rendering immense and indispensable service to the shipping interests of the Far East by his weather predictions. His barocyclonometer is carried on every ship in those waters. In 1900 he was sent to Washington by the United States government to supervise the printing of his immense work entitled " El Archipiélago Filipino," and he gave later to the World's Fair at St. Louis one of its remarkable exhibits,— a relief map covering a great expanse on the ground and representing every island, river, bay, cape, peninsula, volcano, village and city of the Archipelago. Previous to his appointment in Manila Father Algué had worked for several years in the Georgetown Observatory.

In the matter of the theological teaching it will suffice to note that the Collegium Germanicum was given back to the Society in 1829 and entrusted to Father Aloysius

Landes as rector. The German government for some time forbade German students to attend its classes, but in 1848 there were 251 on the roster. Since it opened its doors to the present day, it has given to the Church 4 cardinals, 4 archbishops, 11 bishops, 3 coadjutor bishops, 1 vicar Apostolic, besides a number of distinguished professors, canons and priests.

A very notable recognition of the Society in the field of education was given by Pius IX, when he confided to it the government of the college known as the Pium Latinum. The distinguished ecclesiastic who suggested it was the Apostolic prothonotary, José Ignacio Eyzaguirre, a Chilian by birth. The college was founded in 1858 to prepare a body of learned priests for the various countries of South America. In 1908 at its golden jubilee it could show a record not only of distinguished priests but of a cardinal, Joachim Arcoverde de Albuquerque Cavalcanti, and of 30 bishops, though it began with only 15 students. The house that first sheltered them was extremely small, but the Pope saw to it that they had a larger establishment. While urging the bishops of Latin America to support it liberally — for having been Apostolic delegate in Chili no one knew better than he the urgent necessity of such a school — he himself was lavish in his gifts of money, books, vestments, etc. In 1867 a part of the old Jesuit novitiate was purchased from the Government, and although in 1870 the Jesuits were expelled from Rome those in the Pio Latino were not disturbed. In 1884 a new site was found near the Vatican and on the banks of the Tiber where there is now a splendid college with a capacity of 400 students. In 1905 Cardinal Vives y Tuto published an Apostolic Constitution which gave the title " Pontifical " to the college and confided the education *in perpetuum* to the Society.   This Constitution had been asked for by the Latin American Bishops during the Council, it was promised by Leo XIII, and finally realized by Pius X.   When formally handed over to the Jesuits there were 104 alumni present. The trust was accepted in the name of Father General by Father Caterini, provincial of the Roman province.

CHAPTER XXVIII

LITERATURE

Grammars and Lexicons of every tongue — Dramas — Histories of Literature — Cartography — Sinology — Egyptology — Sanscrit — Catholic Encyclopedia — Catalogues of Jesuit Writers — Acta Sanctorum — Jesuit Relations — Nomenclator — Periodicals — Philosophy — Dogmatic, Moral and Ascetic Theology — Canon Law — Exegesis.

THE literary activity of the Society has always been very great, not only in theological, philosophical and scientific fields, but also in those that are specifically designated as pertaining to the *belles lettres*. Thus, under the heading "Linguistics," in Sommervogel's "Bibliotheca" we find treatises on philology, the origin of language, grammatical theories, a pentaglottic vocabulary, a lexicon of twenty-four languages, the first language, etc. Then come the Classics. Under "Greek," there are two huge pages with the names of various grammars; besides dictionaries, exercises and collections of old Greek authors. Under "Latin," we find four pages of grammars and lexicons; some of the latter giving the equivalents in Portuguese, Tamul, Chinese, French, Polish, Brazilian, Bohemian, Syrian, Armenian and Japanese. After that we have: "Elegances," "Roots," "Ancient and Modern Latin," "Anthologies," "Pronunciations," "Medullas" etc. Six pages are devoted to grammars and dictionaries of European languages, not only the ordinary ones but also Basque, Bohemian, Celtic, Croat, Illyrian, Wend, Provençal, Russian and Turkish. The Asiatic languages follow next in order: Annamite, Siamese, Arabian, Armenian, Georgian, Chinese, Cochinese, Hebrew, Hindustanee, Japanese, Persian, Sanscrit and Syrian; with two columns of Angolese, Caffre, Egyptian, Ethiopian, Kabyle and Malgache grammars. The Malgache all bear the dates of the late nineteenth century, and there is an Esquimaux Grammar by Father Barnum dated 1901.

The tongues of most of the North and South American Indians are represented; the dictionaries of the South American Indians were all written by the Fathers of the old Society.

The books devoted to the study of eloquence are appalling in their number. They are in all languages and on all sorts of subjects, sacred and profane. There are panegyrics, funeral orations, coronation speeches, eulogies, episcopal consecrations, royal progresses, patriotic discourses, but only occasionally does the eye catch a modern date in the formidable list of sixty-three folio pages.

Latin poetry claims fifty-seven pages for the titles of compositions or studies. Poetry in the modern languages is much more modest and requires only as many columns as the ancients demanded pages. The English list is very brief; the Italian very long; and while the ancient Jesuits seemed to have little fear of breaking forth into verse, the modern worshippers of the Muse, except when they utter their thoughts in Malgache, or Chouana or Tagale or Japanese, are very cautious.

Pious people perhaps may be scandalized to hear that the Jesuits of the old Society wrote a great deal for the theatres; it was not, however, for the theatres of the world, but for the theatres of their colleges. Hence in the chapter entitled " Theatre," after a number of treatises on " The Restriction of Comedies," " Théatre des Grecs," " Liturgical Drama," " Reflections on the Danger of Shows," " The mind of St. Paul, St. Thomas Aquinas and St. Francis de Sales on Plays;"

etc., we come face to face with the titles of plays that crowd and blacken by their close print no less than ten huge folio pages. They are contributed by the Jesuits of all countries. Germany especially was very prolific in this kind of literature, claiming as many as four pages of titles; England furnishes only seven dramas in all, three of which are modern. Three of the ancient plays had for their author no less a personage than the Blessed Edmund Campion. They were entitled "The Sacrifice of Isaac," "The Tragedy of King Saul," while Southwell credits him with "Nectar et Ambrosia," which was acted before the emperor. All these were written in 1575, when he was professor of rhetoric in Bohemia.

Belgium has a long list to its credit, and among the dramatists appears the very eminent Ignace Carbonelle, but only as the author of the text of a Cantata for the jubilee of Pius IX in 1877. In France occurs the name of Arsène Cahours, who wrote many tragedies and even a vaudeville, which he called "L'enterrement du Père Simon, le brocanteur." Longhaye's well-known college plays are on the list.

There are many oratorios, but it is feared that the timid will be scandalized to hear that an entire column is required for the names of the authors of *ballets*. One of the writers is no less a personage than the distinguished historian Jouvancy. The ballets are interludes; there was no impropriety in these dances, however, for no female characters appeared, and the college boys for whom they were written had to do all the dancing themselves.

"Many of these dramas," says Father Schwickerath quoting Janssen, "were exhibited with all possible splendor, as for instance those given at La Flèche in 1614 before Louis XIII and his court. But it seems that nowhere was greater pomp displayed than at

Munich where the court liberally contributed to make
the performances especially brilliant. In 1574 the
tragedy ' Constantine ' was played on two successive
days, and the whole city was beautifully decorated.
More than one thousand actors took part in the play.
Constantine entered the city in a triumphal chariot
surrounded by four hundred horsemen in glittering
armor. At the performance of ' Esther ' in 1577,
the most splendid costumes and gems were furnished
from the treasury of the Duke; and at the banquet of
King Assuerus one hundred precious dishes of gold
and silver were used."

Those old Jesuits seemed to be carrying out the
famous order of La Mancha's Knight when the ordinary
stage was too small: " Then build a house or act it
on the plain;" or as a recent writer declares " Like
Richard Wagner in our days, the Jesuits aimed at and
succeeded in uniting all the arts within the compass
of the drama. The effect of such plays was like those
of the Oberammergau Passion Play, ravishing, over-
powering. Even people ignorant of the Latin tongue
were captivated by these representations and the
concourse of people was usually very great. In 1565
' Judith ' was acted before the court in Munich and
then repeated in the public square. Even the surrounding walls and roofs of the houses were covered with
eager spectators. In 1560 the comedy ' Euripus '
was given in the courtyard of the college at Prague
before a crowd of more than eight thousand people.
It had to be repeated three times and was asked for
again and again."

The early German parsons denounced these dramas
as devices for propagating idolatry, but on the other
hand a very capable critic Karl von Reinhardstottner
says: " In the first century of their history the Jesuits
did great work in this line. They performed dramas

full of power and grandeur, and though their dramatic
productions did not equal the fine lyrics of the Jesuit
poets Balde and Sarbiewski, still in the dramas of
Fabricius, Agricola and others, there is unmistakable
poetic spirit and noble seriousness. How could the
enormous success of their performances be otherwise
explained? And who could doubt for a moment that
by their dramas they rendered great service to their
century; that they advanced culture, and preserved
taste for the theatre and its subsidiary arts? It would
be sheer ingratitude to undervalue what they effected
by their dramas."

Goethe was present at a play given in 1786 at Ratisbon. It was during the Suppression, but happily the
Jesuit traditions had been maintained in the college.
He has left his impressions in writing: " This public
performance has convinced me anew of the cleverness
of the Jesuits. They rejected nothing that could
be of any conceivable service to them, and they knew
how to wield their weapons with devotion and dexterity.
This is not cleverness of the merely abstract order; it
is a real fruition of the thing itself; an absorbing interest
which springs from the practical uses of life. Just as
this great spiritual society had its organ-builders,
its sculptors, its gilders so there seem to be some who
by nature and inclination take to the drama; and as
their churches are distinguished by a pleasing pomp,
so these prudent men have seized on the sensibility
of the world by a decent theatre." (Italien Reise, Goethe
Werke, Cotta's Ed. 1840 XXIII p. 3-4.)

Tiraboschi began his literary work when a young
professor in Modena by editing the Latin-Italian
dictionary of Monza, but he made so many corrections
that it was practically a new work. Subsequently he
was appointed librarian at Milan, and by means of
the documents he discovered, wrote a " History of

the Humiliati," which filled up a gap in the annals of the Church. While librarian in the ducal library at Modena, he began his monumental work on the " Storia della letteratura italiana." This history extends from Etruscan times to 1700, and required eleven years of constant labor to complete it.

Hurter tells us " Michael Cosmas Petrus Denis was a most celebrated bibliographer, whose almost innumerable works must be placed in the category of humanistic literature." He entered the Society in Upper Austria on October 17, 1747, and taught rhetoric for twelve years in the Theresian College for Nobles, where he won some renown by his poetry. At the time of the Suppression of the Society, to which he ever remained grateful and attached, he was given charge of the Garelli Library and devoted himself to the study of literature and bibliography. His public lectures attracted immense throngs from far and near. He was promoted to be royal counsellor by Emperor Leopold and was made custodian of the Imperial Library. By that time he was a European celebrity. De Backer in his " Bibliotheca " mentions ninety-three of his publications. Hurter classifies as the most important the " Denkmale der christlichen Glauben- und Sittenlehre." His poems which he signed " Sined," which was Denis spelled backward, won him the name of Bard of the Danube, and helped considerably to promote the study of German in Austria. He was one of a group of poets whose chief aim was to arouse German patriotism. Ossian was their ideal and inspiration, and Denis translated the Gaelic poet into German (1768–69), and in addition he published two volumes of poems just one year before the Suppression. Naturally these patriotic effusions in verse by a Jesuit attracted considerable attention. Denis died in Vienna on 20 September, 1800.

Father Baumgartner has won a high place in the domain of letters by his large work entitled " History of the Literature of the Entire World." Besides this he has to his credit three volumes on " Goethe," another on " Longfellow;" a fifth on " Vondel," a sixth entitled " Ausflüge in das Land der Seein " and a seventh called " Island und die Faröer."

Of Father Faustino Arévalo, the distinguished hymnographer and patrologist, we have spoken above.

Geographical themes appealed to many writers both of the old and the new Society, and also to those of the intervening period. The subjects relate to every part of the world. There is, for instance, " The German Tyrol " by the Italian Bresciani; " The Longitude of Milan " by Lagrange; " The Geography of the Archipelago " by F. X. Liechtlé. This archipelago was the West Indies. His brother Ignatius executed a similar work on the Grecian Islands. He went to Naxos in 1754, and died there in 1795. " Chota-Nagpur " is described in 1883, " Abyssinia " in 1896, and the " Belgian Congo " in 1897. Veiga writes of the " Orinoco " in 1789, and Armand Jean of the " Polynesians " in 1867. There is no end of maps such as " Turkestan and Dzoungaria," " China and Tatary," " The Land of Chanaan," " Paraguay," " Lake Superior," " The Land between the Napo and the Amazons." The famous maps of Mexico by Father Kino have been reproduced by Hubert Bancroft in his " Native Races."

Joseph de Mayoria de Mailla's great work called " Toung-Kian-Kang-mou," which is an abstract of the Chinese annals, was sent to France in 1737, but was not published until 1785. He was the first European to give the world a knowledge of the classic historical works of the Chinese. His work is of great value for the reason that it provides the most important foundation for a connected history of China. He sent along with it many very valuable maps and charts — the result of his work in making a cartographical survey of the country; the part assigned to him including the provinces of Ho-nan, Kiang-hinan, Tshe-Kiang, Fo-Kien and the Island of Formosa. As a reward for his labor the emperor made him a mandarin, and when he died at the age of seventy-nine very elaborate obsequies were ordered by imperial decree.

Father Joseph Fischer, a professor at Feldskirch, is known in all the learned societies of the world for his " Die Entdeckungen der Normannen in America " and also for his " Cosmographiæ introductio " of Martin Waldseemüller, on whose map the name " America " first appeared. The maps and studies of old Huronia by Father Jones have been published by the Canadian Government.

John Baptist Belot, who died in 1904, won a reputation as an Orientalist, as did his associate Father Cheiko by his " Chrestomathia Arabica," in five volumes, and also by his Arabic Lexicon. Their fellow-worker Father Lammens is now a professor in the Biblical Institute in Rome. As they lived a considerable time in Syria they have a distinct advantage over other Europeans in this particular study.

Andrew Zottoli is an authority as a sinologist. The misfortune of being exiled from Italy in 1848 gave him the advantage, which he would not otherwise have had, of becoming proficient in Chinese, for he lived fifty-four years in Kiang-nan. Besides his Chinese catechism and grammar, he has published a complete course of Chinese literature in five volumes, and a universal dictionary of the Chinese language in twelve.

To this list may be added what a recent critic called the monumental work of the illustrious Father Beccari, known as " Scriptores rerum ægyptiacarum." It

consists of sixteen volumes, and includes the entire
period of Egyptian history from the sixteenth to the
nineteenth century. In this category, Father Strassmaier represents the Society by his works on Assyri-
ology and cuneiform inscriptions. With him is Father
Dahlman whose " Das Mahabharata als Epos und
Rechtbuch," " Nirvana," " Buddha," and " Mahab-
hatara Studien " have won universal applause.

Luigi Lanzi, the Italian archæologist, was born at
Olmo near Macerata in 1732, and entered the Society
in 1749. At its Suppression, the Grand Duke of
Tuscany made him the assistant director of the
Florentine Museum. He devoted himself to the study
of ancient and modern literature, and was made a
member of the Arcadians. The deciphering of monuments, chiefly Etruscan, was one of his favorite
occupations and resulted in his writing his " Saggio
di lingua etrusca " in 1789. Four years later he
produced his noted " History of Painting in Italy." His
other works included a critical commentary on Hesiod's
" Works and Days," with a Latin and an Italian translation in verse; three books of " Inscriptiones et carmina,"
translations of Catullus, Theocritus and others, besides
two ascetic works on St. Joseph and the Sacred Heart
respectively. He died in 1810 four years before the
Restoration.

Angelo Mai is one of the very attractive figures at the
beginning of the nineteenth century. He had studied
at the seminary of Bergamo and had as professor,
Father Mozzi, a member of the suppressed Society.
When the saintly Pignatelli opened the novitiate at
Parma in 1799, Mozzi joined him and young Angelo
who was then seventeen years old went there as a
novice. He was sent to Naples in 1804 to teach
humanities, but was obliged to leave when the French
occupied the city. He was then summoned to Rome,

and ordained a priest. While there, he met two
exiled Jesuits from Spain: Monero and Monacho, who
besides teaching him Hebrew and Greek, gave him
his first instructions in paleography, showing him how
to manipulate and decipher palimpsests. In 1813
he was compelled by the order of the duke to return
to his native country, and was appointed custodian
of the Ambrosian Library at Milan. There he made
his first great discoveries of a number of precious
manuscripts, which alone sufficed to give him an important place in the learned world. In 1819 at the
suggestion of Cardinals Consalvi and Litta, the
staunchest friends of the Society, Pius VII appointed
him librarian of the Vatican, with the consent of the
General.

From all this it is very hard to understand how Mai
is generally set down as having left the Society.
Albers says so in his " Liber sæcularis," Hurter in his
" Nomenclator," as does Sommervogel in his " Bibliotheca," and his name does not appear in Terrien's
list of those who died in the Society. In spite of all
this, however, the expression "left the Society" seems
a somewhat cruel term to apply to one who was
evidently without reproach and who was asked for
by the Sovereign Pontiff. He was made a cardinal
by Gregory XVI, a promotion which his old novice
master Father Pignatelli had foretold when Angelo
was summoned to be librarian at Milan. He continued
his work in the Vatican and gave to the world the
unpublished pages of three hundred and fifty ancient
authors which he had discovered.

Father Hugo Hurter calls Francesco Zaccaria of the
old Society the most industrious worker in the history of literature. This praise might well be applied to
himself if it were only for his wonderful " Nomenclator
literarius theologiæ catholicæ." It is a catalogue of the

names and works of all Catholic theological writers
from the year 1564 up to the year 1894. Nor is it merely
a list of names for it gives an epitome of the lives
of the authors and an appreciation of their work
and their relative merit in the special subject to which
they devoted themselves; it thus covers the whole
domain of scholastic, positive and moral theology,
as well as of patrology, ecclesiastical history and the
cognate sciences such as epigraphy, archæology and
liturgy. It consists of five volumes with two closely
printed columns on each page. The last column in
the second volume is numbered 1846. After that come
fifty-three pages of indexes and a single page of *corri-
genda* in that volume alone. It is worth while noting
that there are only six errors in all this bewildering mass
of matter; there are, besides, three additions, not to the
text, but to the index, from which the names of three
writers were accidentally omitted.

So condensed is the letterpress that only a dash
separates one subject from another. Nevertheless,
thanks to the ingenious indexes, both of persons
and subjects, the subject sought for can be found
immediately. Finally, between the text and the indexes
are two marvellous chronological charts. By means of
the first, the student can follow year by year the
growth of the various branches of theology and know
the names of all the authors in each. The second
chart takes the different countries of Europe — Italy,
Spain, Portugal, France, Belgium, Germany, England,
Poland and Hungary — and as you travel down the
years in the succeeding centuries you can see what
studies were most in favor in different parts of the
world and the different stages of their history. Not
only that, but a style of type, varying from a large
black print, down to a very pale and small impression,
gives you the relative prominence of every one of the

vast multitude of authors. Such a work will last to the end of time and never lose its value, and how Father Hurter, who was the beloved spiritual father of the University of Innsbruck, whose theological faculty he entered in 1858, and who, besides publishing his unusually attractive theology and editing fifty-eight volumes of the Fathers of the Church, could find time and strength to produce his encyclopedic " Nomenclator " is almost inconceivable.

In the year 1907, the scheme of a Catholic Encyclopedia was launched in New York. The editors chosen were Dr. Charles Herbermann, for more than fifty years professor of Latin and the most distinguished member of the College of the City of New York; Mgr. Thomas Shahan, the rector of the Catholic University at Washington, and later raised to the episcopal dignity; Dr. Edward A. Pace, professor of philosophy in the same university; Dr. Condé Benoist Pallen, a well-known Catholic publicist, and Father John J. Wynne of the Society of Jesus.

The scope of the work is unlike that of other Catholic encyclopedias. It is not exclusively ecclesiastical, for it records all that Catholics have done not only in behalf of charity or morals, but also in the intellectual, and artistic development of mankind. Hence, while covering the whole domain of dogmatic and moral theology, ecclesiastical history and liturgy, it has succeeded in giving its readers information on art, architecture, archeology, literature, history, travel, language, ethnology, etc., such as cannot be found in any other encyclopedia in the English language. Only the most eminent writers have been asked to contribute to it, and hence its articles can be cited as the most recent exposition of the matters discussed. It appeared with amazing rapidity, the whole series of sixteen volumes being completed in nine years. To it is

added an extra volume entitled " The Catholic Encyclopedia and its Makers," which consists of photographs
and biographical sketches of all the contributors.

The encyclopedia has proved to be an immense
boon to the Church in America. The chief credit of
the publication is generally accorded to Father John
Wynne, who is a native of New York. It was he who
conceived it, secured the board of editors, and, as his
distinguished associate, Bishop Shahan, declared with
almost affectionate eagerness at a public session of
the faculty and students of the ecclesiastical seminary
of New York: " it was he who encouraged and sustained
the editors by his buoyant optimism in the perilous
stages of its elaboration." This information may be
helpful abroad to show that the Society in America
is doing something for the glory of God and the salvation of souls. The apostolic character of the work is
further enhanced by the fact that funds are being
established in various dioceses to enable each seminarian
to become the personal owner of the entire set from
the very first moment he begins his studies. The
effect of such an arrangement on the ecclesiastical
mind of the century is inestimable. It is also being
placed by the Knights of Columbus and by rich
Catholics in battleships and the United States' military
posts, as well as in civic libraries and club houses.

The first catalogue of Jesuit writers was drawn up
by Father Ribadeneira in 1602–1608. Schott and
Alegambe continued the work in 1643, and Nathaniel
Bacon or Southwell, or Sotwel, as he was called on
the Continent, published a third in 1676. Nothing
more, however, was done in that line by the old Society,
and it was not until the twenty-first congregation, at
which Father Roothaan presided, that a postulatum
was presented asking for the resumption of this valuable
work. Something prevented this from being done for

the time being, and it was not until 1853 that the work was undertaken by the two Belgians, Augustine and Aloys de Backer.

Up to 1861 a series of seven issues appeared, but as by that time the number of names had increased to ten thousand, a new arrangement had to be made, and in 1869 the work appeared in three large folios. In 1885, on the death of Augustine de Backer, Charles Sommervogel took up the work. Providentially he was well equipped for the task, for although he had been continually employed at other tasks, sometimes merely as a surveillant in a French college, he had contrived to pub lish in 1884 a "Dictionnaire des ouvrages anony meset pseudonymes des religieux de la Compagnie de Jésus." He began by recasting all that his predecessors had done, and it was only after four years that he had published the first volume. Others, however, followed in quick succession, and in 1900 the ninth volume appeared. The tenth volume, an index, was unfinished at the time of his death, but has since been completed by Father Bliard. Besides his articles in the " Etudes," he had also put into press a " Table méthodique des Mémoires de Trévoux," in three volumes, a "Biblio theca Mariana S. J." and a " Moniteur bibliographique de la Compagnie de Jésus." He had intended to publish a revised edition of Carayon's, " Bibliographie historique," but was prevented by death.

As far back as 1658, Pope Alexander VIII did not hesitate to declare that " no literary work had ever been undertaken that was more useful or more glorious " than the " Acta Sanctorum " of Father Bollandus and his associates, nor did the learned Protestants of those days refrain from extolling the scientific spirit in which the work was being conducted. The " Acta," which began in the middle of the seventeenth century and which is still going on, reads like a romance. The account of it by De Smedt tells us how the first writers had only a garret for a library, and were forced to pile their books on the floor; how Cardinal Bellarmine denounced the work as chimerical; how the Carmelites were in a rage because Papebroch denied that Elias was the founder of their order; how the Spanish Inquisition denounced the work and condemned the thirty volumes as heretical, and how finally it reached its present status.

The Bollandists did not immediately feel the blow that struck the rest of the Society of Jesus in 1773. Indeed, the commissioners announced that the government was satisfied with the labors of the Bollandists and was disposed to exercise special consideration in their behalf. In 1778 they removed to the Abbey of Caudenberg in Brussels, and the writers received a small pension. In 1788 three new volumes were published. Meantime Joseph II had succeeded Maria Theresa, and the sky began to darken. On October 16, 1788, the government decided to stop the pension of the writers, and their books and manuscripts which the official inspectors denounced as "trash" were ordered to be sold. After a year, the Fathers made an offer to the Premonstratensian Abbot of Tongerloo to buy the books and manuscripts for what would be equivalent now to about $4,353; the money, however, was to be paid to the Austrian government and not to the owners of the library. Happily the writers found shelter in the monastery with their books and, though the Brabantine Revolution disturbed them for a time, they continued at their work unmolested until 1794, when they issued another volume.

It was fortunate that they had succeeded in putting that volume into print, for that very year the French invaded Belgium and both Premonstratensians and Bollandists were obliged to disperse. Some of the

treasures of the library were hidden in the houses
of the peasants, and others were hastily piled into
wagons and carried to Westphalia, with the only
result that could be anticipated — the loss of an
immense amount of most valuable material; a certain
number of the books were returned to the abbey, and
left there in the dust until 1825. As there was no
hope, at that time, of the Bollandists ever being able
to resume their work, the monks disposed of most of
the library treasure at public auction, and, what was
not sold, was given to the Holland government and
incorporated in the library of the Hague. The manuscripts were transported to Brussels and deposited in
the Burgundian Library. They are still there.

In 1836 a hagiographical society in France under
the patronage of Guizot and several bishops proposed
to take up the work of the Bollandists and an envoy
was sent to purchase the documents from the Belgian
government. The proposition evoked a patriotic storm
in the little country, and a petition was made to the
minister of the interior, de Theux, imploring him to
lose no time in securing for his native land the honor
of completing the work, and to entrust the task to the
Jesuit Fathers, who had begun it and carried it on
for two centuries. The result was that on January
29, 1837, the provincial of Belgium appointed four
Fathers who were to live at St. Michel in Brussels.
The government gave them an annual subsidy of six
thousand francs, but this was withdrawn in 1868
by the Liberals and never restored, though the Catholics
have been in control since 1884.

There are more than one hundred volumes to the
credit of the writers up to the present time, sixty-five
of which are huge folios. What they contain may be
learned from the most competent of all authorities,
Charles de Smedt, the Bollandist director, who wrote

the most complete and scientific account of the
Bollandist collection for the Catholic Encyclopedia.
It is sufficient to state that in the opinion of the most
distinguished and capable scholars in the field, the
work of the later Bollandists is in no wise inferior to
the work of their illustrious predecessors of the seventeenth and eighteenth centuries.

In reviewing a recent publication of a Bollandist
work, the scholarly " American Historical Review "
(July, 1920) has this to say: " It is to be hoped that
a more widely diffused knowledge of what the
Bollandists have been doing for human learning,
historical and literary, may bring American aid to fill
the gaps in their resources caused by the devastations
of war. It is a pleasure to know that the Princeton
University Press intends to issue an English translation
of Father Delehaye's admirable book, which gives an
account of the labors of the Bollandists from 1638
down to the present day."

It has been said that the Jesuits had a way of keeping
their most brilliant members before the public eye while
sending their inferior men to the missions to be eaten
by the savages. That this is not an accepted opinion
in America is evidenced by the publication of what
are called the " Jesuit Relations," in seventy-two
volumes, by a firm in Cleveland, Ohio, whose members
had no affiliation with Catholics or Jesuits, and whose
venture involved immense financial risks. " The Jesuit
Relations and Allied Documents " is the title of
the work. The subsidiary title is " Travels and
Explorations of Jesuit Missionaries in New France,
1610–1791. The Original French, Latin and Italian
Texts, with English Translations and Notes, illustrated
by Portraits, Maps and Facsimiles."

The editor is Reuben Gold Thwaites, Secretary of
the State Historical Society of Wisconsin. In his

preface he says: " American historians from Shea and Parkman down have already made liberal use of the ' Relations,' and here and there antiquarians and historical societies have published fragmentary trans- lations. The great body of the ' Relations ' and their allied documents however have never been Englished; hence these interesting papers have never been accessible to the majority of historical students. The present edition offers to the public for the first time an English rendering side by side with the original.

" The authors of the journals which form the basis of the ' Relations ' were for the most part men of trained intellect, acute observers, and practiced in the art of keeping records of their experiences. They had left the most highly civilized country of their times to plunge at once into the heart of the wilderness and attempt to win to the Christian Faith the fiercest savages known to history. To gain these savages it was first necessary to know them intimately, their speech, their habits, their manner of thought, their strong points and their weak. These first students of American Indian history were not only amply fitted for their task but none have since had better opportunity for its prosecution. They performed a great service to mankind in publishing their annals, which are for historian, geographer and ethnologist our best authorities.

" Many of the ' Relations ' were written in Indian camps amid a chaos of distractions. Insects innumer- able tormented the journalists; they were immersed in scenes of squalor and degradation, overcome by fatigue and lack of proper sustenance, often suffering from wounds and disease, maltreated in a hundred ways by hosts, who at times, might more properly be called jailers; and not seldom had savage superstition risen to such heights that to be seen making a memorandum was certain to arouse the ferocious enmity of the band. It is not surprising that the composition of these journals is sometimes crude; the wonder is that they could be written at all. Nearly always the style is simple and earnest. Never does the narrator descend to self-glorification or dwell unnecessarily upon the details of his continual martyrdom. He never complains of his lot, but sets forth his experiences in matter of fact phrases.

" From these writings we gain a vivid picture of life in the primeval forests. Not only do these devoted missionaries — never in any field has been witnessed greater personal heroism than theirs — live and breathe before us in these ' Relations,' but we have in them our first competent account of the Red Indian when relatively uncontaminated by contact with Europeans. Few periods of history are so well illuminated as the French régime in North America. This we owe in a large measure to the existence of the Jesuit Relations."

" The existence of these Relations," to use Mr. Thwaites' expression, is due to the scholarly modern Jesuit, Father Félix Martin, the founder and first rector of St. Mary's College at Montreal, who in 1858 induced the Quebec government to reprint the old Cramoisy editions of the seventeenth and eighteenth centuries. It was Martin who developed in Gilmary Shea, then a Jesuit scholastic in Montreal, the historical instinct; and gave to Parkman much if not all of the information that made that author famous, in spite of the bigotry or lack of comprehension that sometimes reveals itself in his pages. Martin's first publication consisted of three double columned, closely printed and bulky octavos in French. He never dreamed that the interest in the book would grow until the splendid edition of Thwaites in seventy-two volumes would signify to the scientific world the value of these docu-

ments " written in canoes or in the depths of the
forests," as Thwaites says, "a decade before the landing of the Plymouth Pilgrims."

While these " Relations " about the Canada missions were being published Father Le Gobien began to
issue his " Lettres sur les progrès de la religion de la
Chine," which ultimately developed into the well-
known " Lettres édifiantes et curieuses " describing
missionary enterprises all over the world. During
the Suppression they were issued in twenty-six duo-
decimo volumes. An Austrian Jesuit began in 1720
to translate some of these letters, entitling his work
" Neue Welt Bott." It soon became independent of
the " Letters " and appeared in five volumes folio.
It is still being published.

A certain number of periodicals are published by
the Society, the most important of which are the
" Civiltà Cattolica," the " Etudes," the " Stimmen aus
Maria-Laach " and the " Razón y Fe."

The " Civiltà " was begun in 1850 by express order
of Pius IX. Its first editors were Fathers Curci,
Bresciani, Liberatore, Taparelli, Oreglia, Piccirillo,
and Pianciani, a staff which would insure the success
of any publication. Its articles are of the most serious
kind, dealing with questions of theology, philosophy,
sociology and literature. Its first issue of 4,200 copies
appeared at Naples; later it was published at Rome.
In 1870 the staff was transferred to Naples, but returned
in 1887 to Rome. It is published every fortnight, and
at present has a circulation of over 12,000 copies.
It is under the direct control of the Pope, and unlike
other Society publications of the same kind it is not
connected with any house or college. It has received
the highest commendations from Pius IX and from
Leo XIII.

In 1856 the " Etudes " was begun by the Jesuits in France under the editorship of Daniel Gagarin and Godfroy. In character it closely resembles the " Civiltà." The troubles of 1876 caused its suspension for almost a year, but the various dispersions of the French provinces have not affected it, except perhaps in the extent of its circulation. It is published at Paris, but was at one time issued from Lyons. From a monthly it has developed into a fortnightly review in latter years.

The German Fathers have their monthly " Stimmen aus Maria-Laach," the first number of which appeared in 1865. The defense of the Syllabus called it into being. When the Kulturkampf drove the editors from Maria-Laach, they migrated to Tervuren in Belgium. There they remained until 1880, when they went to Blijenbeck in Holland. In 1910 we find them at Valkenburg, Holland, attached to the Scholasticate. The ability of the staff has placed the " Stimmen " on a very high plane as a periodical.

The monthly " Razón y Fe " was begun by the Spanish Fathers in 1901, and " Studies " by the Irish Jesuits in 1912. This latter, however, admits contributors who are not of the Society. The same may be said of the " Month " (London), the weekly "America" (New York), the " Irish Monthly " (Dublin) and a number of minor periodicals. There are also publications for private circulation, such as the " Woodstock Letters," the " Letters and Notices "; " Lettres Edifiantes " of various provinces of the Society, most of which are printed in the scholasticates, and convey information about the different works of the Society in different parts of the world. They are largely of the character of the ancient " Relations des Jésuites " of the old French Fathers and are of great value as historical material. Finally the American " Messenger of the Sacred Heart " publishes a monthly edition of 350,000, besides millions of leaflets to promote the devotion. There are fifty-one editions of the "Messenger" published in thirty-five different languages.

The reason why the Society has not succeeded in producing since the Restoration any theologians like Suárez, Toletus and others, is the same that prevented Napoleon Bonaparte from winning back his empire when he was a prisoner on St. Helena. Conditions have changed. Suárez, de Lugo, Ripalda and their brilliant associates passed their lives in Catholic Spain which gloried in universities like Salamanca, Valladolid or Alcalá. There those great men wrote and taught; Bellarmine and Toletus labored in Rome and Lessius in Louvain; whereas the Jesuit theologians in our day have been not only debarred from the great universities but robbed of their libraries, sent adrift in the world and compelled to seek not for learned leisure but for a roof to shelter them. They were expelled from France in 1762, and were never allowed to open a school even for small boys until 1850. At present they are permitted to shed their blood on the battle field for their country from which they have been driven into exile. They were banished from Italy repeatedly, and have never secured a foothold in Germany since 1872; they do not exist in Portugal and any moment may see them expelled from Spain. In England and Ireland Catholics were not emancipated until 1829, and it is only grudgingly that the government allows Ireland to have a university which Catholics can safely frequent, and even there no chair of Catholic theology may be maintained with the ordinary revenues. In America everything is in a formative state and what money is available has to be used for elementary instruction, both religious and secular, of the millions whom poverty and persecution have driven out of Europe. It is very doubtful if Suárez and his great associates would have written their splendid works in such surroundings.

As the eye travels over Hurter's carefully prepared chronological chart, it catches only an occasional gleam of the old glory, when the names of the Wiceburgenses, Zaccaria, Mai, Muzzarelli, Arévalo and Morcelli make their appearance in the late sixties of the nineteenth century. But those were the days of the French Revolution and of its subsequent upheavals. The Church itself was in the same straits between 1773 and 1860, and its number of great theologians of any kind is extremely small. Thus, abstracting from the Jesuits, we find in 1773 only Flórez, the Augustinian, who wrote ecclesiastical history; in 1782 the erudite Maronite Assemani, who is classed as a moralist; in 1787 St. Alphonsus Liguori; and in 1793 the Benedictine Gerbert, who is also a moralist. The Barnabite Gerdil appears under date of 1802 as an apologist, and from that year up to 1864 there is no one to whom Hurter accords distinction in any branch of divinity. Perhaps the reason is that the century was in the full triumph of its material civilization and that men derided and despised the dogmatic teachings of religion.

A study of Hurter's " Nomenclator " is instructive. In 1774, the year after the Suppression, there are only four publications by Jesuit authors; in 1775 there are nine; and then the number begins to grow smaller. In 1780 the figure rises to ten, and it is somewhat remarkable that in 1789 and 1790, the first years of the French Revolution, seventeen writers appear. The stream then dribbles along until 1814, the year of the Restoration, when we find only one book with the letters S.J. after the name of its author. The next year there is none.

The Jesuit who illumines the darkness of that period is Thaddeus Nogarola, whom Hurter describes as " a member of the most noble family of Verona." He was born on 24 December, 1729. Consequently he was eighty-five years of age at the time of the Restoration. He wrote on sanctifying grace; and in 1800 he and another Jesuit had a fierce theological battle on the subject of attrition, in which he defended his position with excessive vehemence. In 1806 he had issued his great treatise against Gallicanism. His doughty antagonist re-entered the Society in 1816. He had expressed himself very vigorously on the subject of the Napoleonic oath in France and his books were prohibited in the Cisalpine Republic.

In 1816 four books were published; but the number continues small and 1823 is credited with none. In 1824, there were two publications, one of them by Arévalo, the eminent patrologist, who composed the hymns and lessons of the feast of Our Lady Help of Christians. It is a very sad list from 1826 to 1862, with its succession of ones and zeros. Only three names of any note appear: Kohlmann in 1836, Loriquet in 1845, and de Ravignan in 1858. That period of almost forty years had seen the revolutions of 1830 and 1848, and there was no stability for any Jesuit establishment. Finally, however, in 1862 came Pianciani, Taparelli and Bresciani; and in 1865 and 1866 Tongiorgi and Gury, respectively. It was only then that the Society was able to begin its theological work after its redintegration. The space is not great between 1862 and the present time, but since then there have been Perrone and the great Bollandist and theologian, Victor de Buck, who appeared in 1876; Edmund O'Reilly in 1878; Ballerini and Patrizi in

1881; Kleutgen in 1883; and in 1886 Cardinals Franzelin and Mazzella.

During that period there was no end of confiscations and expulsions, even of those who were not engaged in educational work. Thus the German Jesuits acquired the old Benedictine Monastery of Maria-Laach in 1863 on the southwest bank of a fine lake near Andernach in the Rhineland. There they organized a course of studies for the scholastics as well as a college of writers. Among them were the learned Schneeman, Riess and others who began the great work of the church Councils and the " Philosophia Lacensis," besides publishing the Jesuit " Stimmen." How long were they there? Only ten years. The Kulturkampf banished them from their native land and they had to continue their labors in exile. This has been the story of the Society in almost every European country and in the Spanish Republics of South America and Mexico. In spite of all this, however, Hurter's chart shows that from 1773 to 1894 there have been no less than four hundred Jesuit theologians who published works in defense of the doctrines of the Church, and some of them have achieved prominence.

In philosophy, for instance, there was Taparelli who died in 1863. He was the first rector of the Roman College, when it was given back to the Society by Leo XII. He taught philosophy for fifteen years at Palermo, and in 1840 issued his great work which he called " A Theoretical Essay on Natural Rights from an historical standpoint." It reached the seventh edition in 1883 and was translated into French and German. Next in importance is his " Esame critico degli ordini rappresentativi nella società moderna." Besides his striking monographs on " Nationality," " Sovereignty of the People," " The Grounds of War," he wrote a great number of articles in the " Civiltà " on matters of political economy and social rights.   His first great work was in a way the beginning of modern sociology.   Palmieri issued his " Institutiones Philosophiæ " in 1874, and at the very outset won the reputation of a great thinker, even from those who were at variance with his conclusions and mode of thought.

In the same branch Liberatore was for a long time preëminent, and his " Institutiones " and " Composito humano " went through eleven editions.   Cornoldi's " Filosofia scolastica specolativa " was also a notable production. Lehmen's " Lehrbuch " reached the third edition before his death in 1910.   Boedder is well-known to English speaking people because of his many works written during his professorship at St. Beuno's in Wales. Cathrein's " Socialism " has been translated into nine different languages, and his " Moral Philosophy " has enjoyed great popularity. Pesch's position is established; his last work, " Christliche Lebens-philosophie," reached its fourth edition within four years. Kleutgen who is perhaps the best known of these German Jesuits, was called by Leo XIII " the prince of philosophers " and is regarded as the restorer of Catholic philosophy throughout Germany.   In Spain, Father Cuevas has written a " Cursus completus philosophiæ " and a " History of Philosophy." Mendive's " Text-book of Philosophy " in Spanish is used in several universities, but the writer who dominated all the rest in that country is admittedly Urráburu, who died prematurely in 1904.   His " Cursus philosophiæ scholasticæ," brings up the memory of the famous old philosophers of earlier ages.

It is not only edifying but inspiring to hear that the Venerable Father de Clorivière occupied himself while in prison in the Temple at Paris during the Revolution

in writing commentaries on the Sacred Scriptures.
He was over seventy years of age and was expecting
to be summoned to the guillotine at any moment,
but he had plenty of time to write, for his imprisonment lasted five years. Sommervogel credits him with
commentaries on "The Canticle of Canticles," "The
Epistles of St. Peter," "The Discourse at the Last
Supper," "The Animals of Ezechiel," "The Two
Seraphim of Isaias," besides Constitutions for the
religious orders he had founded, lives of the saints,
novenas, and religious poems. He also translated
"Paradise Lost" into French. Evidently the commentary written in a prison cell cannot have measured
up to the scientific exegesis of the present day, but
perhaps for that reason it reached the soul more
readily. In any case, the Scriptural students of the
modern Society made an excellent start with a saint
and a virtual martyr.

Francis Xavier Patrizi distinguished himself as an
exegete. He was one of the first to enter the Society
after the Restoration, and was so esteemed for his
virtue and ability that he came very near being elected
General of the Society. His first publication on
"The Interpretation of the Holy Scriptures" appeared
in 1844. He translated the Psalms word for word
from the Hebrew. His works are packed with erudition, of scrupulous accuracy in their citations, and of
most sedulous care in defending the Sacred Text against
the Protestants of the early days of the nineteenth
century. The "Cursus Scripturæ" of the Fathers of
Maria-Laach: Cornely, Knabenbauer, Hummelauer,
and others, is a monument of erudition and labor
and is without doubt the most splendid triumph of
exegesis in the present century.

In 1901, the Sovereign Pontiff appointed and approved
a Biblical Commission for the proper interpretation and

defense of Holy Scripture. It consists of five cardinals and forty-three consultors. Among the distinguished men chosen for this work we find Fathers Cornely, Delattre, Gismondi, von Hummelauer, Méchineau, and Prat. One of the duties with which the commission was charged was the establishment of a special institute for the prosecution of higher Biblical Studies. In 1910 Father Fonck, its first rector, began the series of public conferences which was one of the assigned works of the Institute. It publishes the "Biblical Annals." The French Fathers in Syria are very valuable adjuncts to this institute, because of their knowledge of Oriental languages. One of them, Father Lammens, was for years the editor of "Bachir," an Arabic periodical.

When Father John Carroll went to England to be consecrated Bishop of Baltimore, he probably met at Lulworth Castle, where the ceremony took place, a French Jesuit of the old Society who had found shelter with the Weld family during the Revolution and was acting as their chaplain. He was Father Grou, a man of saintly life. It was while he was in England that he wrote " La Science de crucifix " the " Caractère de la vraie dévotion," " Maximes spirituelles," " Médita- tion sur l'amour de Dieu," " L'intérieur de Jésus et de Marie," " Manuel des âmes intérieures," " Le livre du jeune homme." These works were frequently reprinted and translated.

It is very interesting to find that, before the expul- sion from France, Father Grou had been an ardent student of Plato and had even published eight books about the great philosopher. He also wrote an answer to La Chalotais' attack on the Society. Sommervogel mentions another book written by him in conjunction with Father du Rocher. It is entitled " Temps Fabuleux," an historical and dogmatic treatise on the true religion.

Among the other noted ascetical writers were Vigitello, author of " La Sapienza del cristiano," Mislei, who wrote " Grandezze di Gesù Cristo" and " Gesù Cristo e il Cristiano," Hillegeer, Dufau, Verbeke, Vercruysse, de Doss, Petit, Meschler, Schneider and Chaignon, whose " Nouveau cours de méditations sacerdotales " has gone through numberless editions; Watrigant has made extensive studies on the " Exercises;" Ramière's " Apostolat de la Prière " made the circuit of the world and gave the first impulse to the League of the Sacred Heart. Coleridge's " Life of Our Lord," consisting of thirty volumes, is a mine of thought and especially valuable for directors of religious communities.

In 1874 Father Camillo Tarquini was raised to the cardinalate for his ability as a canonist. His dissertation on the Regium placet exequatur made him an international celebrity. With him high in the ranks of canonists are Father General Wernz, Laurentius, Hilgers, Beringer, Oswald, Sanguinetti, Ojetti, Vermeersch, and the present Assistant General Father Fine.

Stephen Anthony Morcelli, who is eminent as a historian and is regarded as the founder of epigraphy, was born in Trent, in the year 1737. He made his studies in the Roman College, and there founded an academy of archæology. At the Suppression he became the librarian of Cardinal Albani. He re-entered the restored Society. He was then eighty-four years of age. He had no superior as a Latin stylist. His " Calendar of the Church of Constantinople," covering a thousand years, his " Readings of the Four Gospels " according to various codices, and his notes on " Africa Christiana " are of great value. Possibly the Portuguese Francis Macedo might be admitted to this list of famous authors. It is true that he left the Society but as he had been a member for twenty-eight years it deserves some credit for the cultivation of his remarkable abilities. Maynard calls him the prodigy of his age. Thus at Venice in 1667 Macedo held a public disputation on nearly every branch of human knowledge, especially the Bible, theology, patrology, history, literature and poetry. In his quaint and extravagant style he called this display the literary roarings of the Lion of St. Mark. It had been prepared in eight days. On account of his success, Venice gave him the freedom of the city and the professorship of moral philosophy at the University of Padua. In his " Myrothecium morale " he tells us that he had pronounced three hundred and fifty panegyrics, sixty Latin harangues, thirty-two funeral orations, and had composed one hundred and twenty-three elegies, one hundred and fifteen epitaphs, two hundred and twelve dedicatory epistles, two thousand and six hundred heroic poems, one hundred and ten odes, four Latin comedies, two tragedies and satires in Spanish, besides a number of treatises on theology such as " The Doctrines of St. Thomas and Scotus," " Positive theology for the refutation of heretics," " The Keys of Peter," " The Pontifical Authority," " Medulla of Ecclesiastical History," and the " Refutation of Jansenism." The Society made him great but failed to teach him humility.

In most theological libraries which are even moderately equipped one sees long lines of books on which the name of Muzzarelli appears. They are of different kinds; ascetical, devotional, educational, philosophical and theological, and many of them have been translated into various languages. He belonged to the old Society, entering it only four years before the suppression. He was then twenty-four years of age. As he was of a noble family of Ferrara, he held a benefice in his native city at the time of his banishment, and a little later, the Duke of Parma made him rector of the College of Nobles. Pius VII called him to Rome and made him theologian of the Penitentiaria, which meant that he was the Pope's theologian. When the Society was re-established in Naples, he asked permission to join his brethren there, but the Pope refused. It was just as well, for Napoleon's troops soon closed the establishment. When Pius VII was carried off a prisoner in 1809, Muzzarelli was also deported. He never returned to Rome, but died in Paris one year before the Restoration of the Society. He was not however forgotten in his native city, which regarded him as one of its glories. Among his works were several of an ascetic character such as " The Sacred Heart," " The Month of Mary," and also a "Life of St. Francis Hieronymo."

There were also a few modern Jesuits who were conspicuous in moral theology. First, in point of time was Jean-Pierre Gury, who was born in Mailleroncourt on January 23, 1801. He taught theology for thirty-five years at Annecy and at the Roman College. He died on April 18, 1866. His work was adopted as a text-book in a number of seminaries, because of its brevity, honesty and solidity. It is true that his brevity impaired his accuracy at times, as well as the scientific presentation of questions, but his successors such as Seitz, Cercia, Melandri and Ballerini filled up the gaps by the help of the decisions of the Congregations and the more recent pronouncements of the Holy See. Besides his " Moral Theology " he also published his " Casus conscientiæ." That made him the typical " Jesuit Casuist," and drew on him all the traditional hatred of Protestant polemicists, especially in Germany. His work did much to extirpate what was left of Jansenism in Europe.

Antonio Ballerini held the chair of moral theology in the Roman College from 1856 until his death in 1881. In the cautious words of Hurter he was " almost the prince of moralists of our times." Besides his " Principi della scuola Rosminiana " he wrote his remarkable " Sylloge monumentorum ad mysterium Immaculatæ Conceptionis illustrandum," and in 1863 issued his " De morali systemate S. Alphonsi M. de Ligorio." In 1866 appeared his " Compendium theologiæ moralis." The style was somewhat acrid, and sharp, especially in the controversy it provoked with the out-and-out defenders of St. Alphonsus. His annotations were a mine of erudition and revealed at the same time a very unusual intellectual sagacity and correctness of judgment. His book, on the whole, exercised a great influence in promoting solid theological study; and its denunciation of the frivolous reasons on which many opinions were based and the unreliableness of many quotations decided the tone of subsequent works by other authors. Following Ballerini were other Jesuits such as Lehmkuhl, Sabbetti, Noldin, Genicot and Palmieri, who won fame as moralists.

Palmieri was not only a theologian, a moralist and a philosopher, but an exegete. He taught Scripture and the Oriental languages in Maastricht for seven years, and in 1886, published a Commentary on the Epistle to the Galatians and another on the historicity of the Book of Judith. He was among the first to sound the alarm about Loisy's heterodoxy and he wrote several books against the Modernistic errors. His reputation rests chiefly on his dogmatic theology; every two years, from 1902, he issued treatises that immediately attracted attention for their brilliant originality and exhaustive learning. He died in Rome on May 29, 1909. " This superlatively sagacious man," says Hurter, " blended Gury and the super-

abundant commentaries of Ballerini into one continuous text, injecting, of course, his own personal views
into his seven great volumes, with the result that it
is a positive pleasure to read him. The wonderful
theological acumen manifested in this, as in his
other works apparently restored him to favor with
Leo XIII, who disliked some of his philosophical
speculations. Hence, when Father Steinhüber was
made cardinal, Palmieri was appointed to succeed him
as theologian of the Penitentiaria.

Besides all this, Palmieri gave a delightful revelation
of his affectionate character as a devoted son, when
he wrote, at the request of his mother, a Commentary
of Dante. Ojetti says that " he brought all the pro-
fundity of his philosophy and theology to his task
and produced a work which astonished those who
were able to appreciate the depth of the thought and
the scientific erudition employed in the exposition of
each individual canto."

The great Perrone was born in Chieri in 1794 and entered the Society on December 14, 1815, one of the first
novices after the Re-establishment. He began his
career as professor of dogma at Orvieto, and from thence
was transferred to Rome, where he remained until the
outbreak of the Revolution in 1848. After a three
years' stay in England he resumed his place at the
Roman College. He was consultor of various congregations, was conspicuous as the antagonist of
Hermes, and also in the discussion that ended in the
dogmatic definition of the Immaculate Conception.
His " Prælectiones theologiæ " in nine volumes reached
its thirty-fourth edition, while its " Compendium "
saw fifty-seven.

Carlo Passaglia is another great theological luminary.
He entered the Society in 1827, and when scarcely
thirty years old was teaching at the Sapienza and

was prefect of studies at the Collegium Germanicum. The Gregorian University then claimed him, and, in 1850, he took a leading part in preparing the definition of the dogma of the Immaculate Conception on which he wrote three large volumes. Other great works are to his credit, but his historico-linguistic method met with criticism. It was said he substituted grammar for dogma. Passaglia left the Society, however, in 1859. Pius IX gave him a chair in the Sapienza; there he came in contact with an agent of Cavour and under his influence wrote his book " Pro causa italica." It was placed on the " Index," and Passaglia fled to Turin, where he taught moral philosophy until his death and edited a weekly called " Il Medicatore," which welcomed articles from discontented priests. He also published a daily paper called " La Pace," as well as " Il Gerdil," a theological review. He was suspended from his priestly functions, dressed as a layman, and was temerarious enough to criticise the Syllabus. The Bishop of Mondovi tried to reconcile him with the Church, but he did not retract until a few months before his death. Hurter calls him " an illustrious professor of dogma who was carried away by politics, left the Society, assailed the Temporal Power, and by his sad defection cast a stain on his former glory. His quotations from the Fathers are too diffuse, and although his work on the Immaculate Conception displays immense erudition it crushes the reader by its bulk."

Carlo Maria Curci also brought grief to his associates in those days. He had acquired great fame for his defense of the rights of the Pope against the Liberal politicians of the Peninsula, but unfortunately, soon after, became a Liberal himself and left the Society. He returned again, however, shortly before his death which occurred on June 19, 1891. He was one of the first contributors to the " Civiltà " and was, besides, a remarkable orator. His " Nature and Grace," " Christian Marriage," " Lessons from the two books of the Machabees and the Four Gospels," and " Joseph in Egypt " were the most notable of his writings.

Josef Wilhelm Karl Kleutgen was a Westphalian. He entered the Society on April 28, 1834, at Brieg; to avoid difficulties with the German Government he became a naturalized Swiss, and for some time went by the name of Peters. In 1843 he was professor of sacred eloquence in the Collegium Germanicum, and subsequently was named substitute to the Secretary of Father General, consultor of the Congregation of the Index, and collaborator in the preparation of the Constitution " De fide catholica " of the Vatican Council. He wrote the first draft of Pope Leo's Encyclical " Æterni Patris " on the revival of Scholastic theology and philosophy. His knowledge of the writings of the Angelic Doctor was so great that he was called *Thomas redivivus*. His first work " Theologie der Vorseit " and his " Philosophie der Vorseit " against Hermes, Hirscher, and Günther were declared to be epoch-making. The writing of these books coincided with a remarkable event in his life, namely suspension from his priestly office for his imprudence in allowing a community of nuns under his direction to honor as a saint one of their deceased members. He went into seclusion consequently but at the opening of the Vatican Council he was recalled by Pius IX to take part in it. All his works excel in solidity of doctrine, accuracy and brilliancy of exposition and nobility of style.

Johann Franzelin was a Tyrolese. He entered the Society on 27 July, 1834, but passed most of his life outside of his country. He studied theology in Rome, and became such an adept in Greek and Hebrew that he occupied the chair when the professor was ill. He had to leave the city in the troublous times of 1848, but on his return he gave public lectures in the Roman College on Oriental languages. In 1857 he began his career as professor of dogma and his immense erudition caused him to be called for in many of the Roman congregations. In 1876 Pius IX created him cardinal. His theological works are known throughout the Church for their solidity, erudition and scrupulous accuracy. His dignity made no change in his simple and laborious life. He continued until the end of his days to wear poor garments, occupied two small rooms in the Novitiate of Sant' Andrea, rose at four every morning and spent the time until seven in devotional exercises. He kept up his penitential practises till death came on 11 December, 1886.

CHAPTER XXIX

THE SOVEREIGN PONTIFFS AND THE SOCIETY

Devotion, Trust and Affection of each Pope of the Nineteenth and Twentieth Centuries manifested in their Official and Personal Relations with the Society.

THE restored Society, like the old, has been the recipient of many favors from the Sovereign Pontiffs. Pius VI would have immediately undone the work of Clement XIV, had it been at all possible; and Pius VII faced the wrath of all the kings and statesmen of Europe by issuing the Bull that put back the Society in the place it had previously occupied in the Church.

The election of Leo XII, who succeeded Pius VII on September 28, 1823, had, at first, thrown consternation among the members of the Order, because of his previous attitude as Cardinal della Genga. He had been associated with its enemies and had uttered very harsh words about the Society, but it soon became evident that it was all due to the impression which the plotters had given him that they were fighting against the influence of Paccanarism in certain members of the congregation. When he became Pope, he understood better the facts of the case and became one of the warmest friends the Society ever had.

On May 7, 1824, he recalled the Fathers to the Roman College and gave them a yearly revenue of 12,000 scudi, besides restoring to them the Church of St. Ignatius, the Caravita Oratory, the museum, the library, the observatory, etc. He entrusted to them the direction of the College of Nobles; assigned to them the Villa of Tivoli; set apart new buildings for the Collegium Germanicum, and on July 4, 1826, he established them in the College of Spoleto, which he had founded for the teaching of humanities, philosophy, civil and canon law, theology and holy Scripture; for all of which he had provided ample revenues.

In the same year he issued the celebrated Bull " Plura inter," restoring the ancient privileges of the Society and adding new ones. This list of spiritual favors fills seven complete columns. " Everyone is aware," he said in the Bull, " how many and how great were the services performed by this Society, which was the fruitful mother of men who were conspicuous for their piety and learning. From it we expect still more in the future, seeing that it is extending its branches so widely even before it has taken new root. For not only in Rome but in Transalpine countries and in the remotest regions of the world, it is affectionately received, because it leaves nothing undone to train youth in piety and the liberal arts, in order to make them the future ornaments of their respective countries."

On July 27, he increased the revenues of the College of Beneventum, and on October 11, of the same year, he told the people of Faenza that he could not, just then, give them a Jesuit College because of the lack of funds, but that he would meet their wishes as soon as possible. The very month before his death, he sent encouraging words to the Fathers in England, who were harassed by all sorts of calumnious accusations, and told the Bishop of Thespia that " the English scholastics could be ordained *sub titulo paupertatis*, and had a right to the same privileges as other religious orders in England." Finally, he would have appointed Father Kohlmann Bishop of New York and Father Kenny to the See of Dromore, had not the General persuaded him not to do so. The same thing occurred in the case of Father Pallavicini who was named for the See of Reggio in Calabria. Pope Leo XII died on February 10, 1829, a few days after the demise of Father Fortis, who was his affectionate and intimate friend.

The name of his successor, Pius VIII, was Francis Xavier Castiglione — a good omen for the brethren of the great Apostle.   Indeed, brief though his pontificate was, he always made it clear that the Society was very dear to him. " I have always let it be known," he said to the Fathers who had presented themselves to greet him at his accession, "and I shall avail myself of every occasion to declare that I love the Society of Jesus. From my earliest childhood that feeling was deep in my heart, and I have always profoundly venerated St. Ignatius and St. Francis Xavier. I bear, all unworthy as I am, the name of Xavier. I have been taught by the most distinguished Jesuits, and I know how much good they have done for the Church, so that as the Church cannot be separated from the Pope, he cannot be separated from the Society. These are sad days and there never was witnessed greater audacity and hate. Impiety has never employed greater cunning against the truth. Perhaps very soon other grievous wounds will be inflicted on the Church; but together we shall fight the enemies of God. Return to your provinces, therefore, and arouse in your brethren the same ardor that is in your hearts. Preach and teach obedience and integrity of life in your schools, in your pulpits, by voice and pen, and with all your soul. May God second your efforts. Meantime keep always unshaken in the assurance that I shall always be, before all, your most tender and devoted Father."

On December 2, 1829, accompanied by Cardinals Somaglia and Odescalchi he went to the Gesù, and after praying at the altar of St. Francis Xavier, published the beatification of Alphonsus Liguori, the founder of the Redemptorist Order. He lavished favors on the Germanico-Hungarico and the College of Nobles; and when Charles Augustus von Reisach, a student of the Collegium Germanicum who was very young at the time, was named rector of the Propaganda, the Pope said to those who referred to it: " Never mind; he is young but he has studied in the best of schools and every one praises him for the maturity of his character, his irreproachable life and his fitness for the office."

When this devoted friend of the Society died, Cardinal Cappellari, the learned Camaldolese monk, ascended the pontifical throne and took the name Gregory XVI. Fifteen days afterwards all Italy was in the throes of Revolution. The Carbonari were in control, and as usual the Society felt the first blow. On February 17th, at the same hour, the colleges of Spoleto, Fano, Modena, Reggio, Forlì and Ferrara were attacked and the masters and pupils thrown out in the street. A decree of banishment was issued, but the people arose in their wrath, suppressed the insurrection and the Fathers were re-instated.

When peace was restored, the Pope gave a notable illustration of his esteem for the Society. He summoned all the religious of the various orders in Rome to the Gesù to make the Spiritual Exercises. A short time afterwards, at the instance of the Propaganda, he entrusted to it the administration of several colleges and formulated the concessions in the most eulogistic of terms, declaring among other things that a long and happy experience from the very beginning of the Institute until the present time, and in divers parts of the world, had shown the Holy See the incontestable aptitude of the Fathers for directing both clerical and secular schools. The same conviction, he said later, also prompted him to give them the Illyrian College.

The cholera which was sweeping over Europe finally reached Rome. The Pope had already established ambulances and hospitals in various parts of the city, and his appeal to the religious sentiments of the people prevented the frightful orgies which had disgraced London, Madrid and Paris when similarly afflicted. Cardinal Odescalchi, soon to be a Jesuit, was especially conspicuous in tranquillizing the populace, and a solemn ceremony in which the entire city participated is especially worthy of note, since it was intended by the Sovereign Pontiff to be an official announcement that while the pestilence lasted, the Jesuit Fathers were to be the principal channel of the Papal charities. The miraculous picture of the Blessed Virgin was carried in procession from St. Mary Major's to the Gesù and, in spite of the stifling heat, the Pope himself, surrounded by his cardinals, the clergy and the principal civil officials, accompanied the picture through the kneeling multitudes in the streets, and placed it on the altar in the Jesuit church, which thus became the prayer centre for the city while the pestilence lasted.

On August 23, 1837, it struck the city at the same moment in several places. Two princesses were its first victims, but the Pope in person went wherever the harvest of death was greatest, and his example inspired every one to emulate his devotion. Naturally members of the Society did their duty in those terrible days when 9,372 people were attacked by the disease and more than 5,000 perished. By the month of October the plague had ceased.

Cardinal Odescalchi, who had won the affection of the people of Rome by his heroic devotion to them at this crisis, astounded them in the following year by the renunciation of the exalted dignities which he enjoyed in the Church and in the State, for he was a prince — in order to assume the humble garb and subject himself to the obedience of the Society of Jesus. The Pope and the cardinals endeavored to dissuade him from taking the step, pleading the interests of the Church, but he persisted, and on the day of his admission, December 8, 1838, he wrote to Father Roothaan to say that he could not describe the happiness that he felt, and he requested the General to deal with him as he would with the humblest of his subjects. He was then fifty-two years old. He died at Modena, on August 17, 1841, and had thus been able as one of its sons to celebrate the third centenary of the Society, which occurred in 1840. There was little if any public declaration, however, of this anniversary, for Father Roothaan had sent a reminder to all the provinces that the dangers of the time made it advisable to keep all manifestations of happiness and of gratitude to God within the limits of the domestic circle.

In 1836 an imperial edict in answer to a popular demand permitted the Jesuits to establish schools anywhere in the limits of the Austrian empire and to follow their own methods of teaching independently of university control. The emperor and empress honored by their presence the first college opened in Verona. Other cities of Italy invited the Fathers to open schools, and Metternich, who is sometimes cited as their enemy, allowed them to install themselves at Venice, where a remnant of antagonism had remained, ever since the time of Paolo Sarpi; but by St. Ignatius Day in 1844 that had all vanished and the patriarch, the doge, the nobility, the clergy and the people united in giving the Fathers a cordial welcome.

In the Island of Malta, which had become a British possession, the inhabitants sent a letter of thanks to

Lord Stanley, the secretary of State, for having granted them a college of the Society. The letter had 4,000 signatures. The Two Sicilies welcomed the Society in 1804 and restored to it the Professed house, along with the Collegium Maximum and the old churches; other establishments were begun elsewhere in the kingdom. After the Jesuits had been expelled by the Carbonari in 1820 the usual reaction occurred and they were soon back at their posts. The cholera of 1837 gave them a new hold on the affection of the people, and for the moment their position in the kingdom appeared to be absolutely secure.

During the fifteen years of his pontificate, Gregory XVI published no less than fifteen rescripts in favor of the Society. On March 30, 1843, he empowered Georgetown College in Washington to confer philosophical and theological degrees. In the following year he restored the Illyrian College, which Gregory XIII had established at Loreto, and gave it to the Society together with the Villa Leonaria. At the request of Cardinal Franzoni, the prefect of the Propaganda, he turned over the Urban College to the Society, and in the rescript announcing the transfer he said: " Whereas the Congregation of the Propaganda was convinced that the instruction of the young clerics who are to be sent to foreign parts to spread the light of the Gospel and to cultivate the vineyard of the Lord could not be better trained for such a task than by those religious who make it the special work of their Institute to form youth in piety, literature and science, and who always strive intensely in whatever they undertake to promote the greater glory of God; and whereas, from the very establishment of the Society of Jesus, the Church has had daily experience of the aptitude of the Fathers of the Society in the education of youth both in secular and clerical pursuits in all

57

parts of the world; and whereas the testimony which
even the enemies of the Holy See and of the Church
are compelled by the evidence of things to pay to the
Society of Jesus for the excellent education which the
youth of their colleges receive, we do therefore assent
most willingly to the petition of the lord cardinal of
the Congregation of the Propaganda."

On October 11, 1838, a chair of canon law was
erected in the Roman College. In the following year
on March 5, the Pontiff gave the Society the College
of Fermo, and on September 28, the College of Camerino.
In brief, there was no end of the spiritual favors which
Gregory XVI bestowed on the Society through its
General, Father Roothaan, whom he honored with his
most intimate friendship.

Pius IX succeeded Gregory XVI, and although he
greatly esteemed Rosmini, who was attacked for his
philosophical views by the Jesuits, chiefly by Melia,
Passaglia, Rozaven and Ballerini, that did not affect
the great Pontiff's affection for the Society. Hence
when the procurators at their meeting of 1847 presented
themselves to His Holiness to protest against the
charge that they were averse to his governmental
policies, he assured them that he was well aware of
the calumnious nature of the accusation. He repeated
the same words in 1853 to the electors of the twenty-
second general congregation, and in 1860, when Garibaldi expelled the Jesuits from the Two Sicilies, Pope
Pius not only welcomed the refugees to Rome, but,
when they arrived, went in person to console them.
" Let us suffer with equanimity," he said, "whatever
God wishes. Persecution always brings courage to
Catholics. What you have suffered is passed. What
is to come who knows? It is splendid," he said as
he withdrew, " to see that even when you are scourged
you do not cease to work."

Not only did he comfort them verbally, but he issued as many as one hundred and thirty-two briefs and Bulls, in each of which some favor was conferred on the Society. He beatified seventy-seven Jesuits and canonized three of them. He gave the College of Tephernatum to the Society and endowed it richly. In 1850 he ordered Father General, who was hesitating because of the difficulty of the work, to establish the " Civiltà Cattolica." In 1851 he built and endowed a college at Valiterno, and gave them another at Sinigaglia. He entrusted to them the Collegium Pio-Latinum Americanum, a confidence in their ability which was reaffirmed in 1908 by Pius X when he said: " For fifty years this college has been of singular advantage to the Church by forming a learned body of holy bishops and distinguished ecclesiastics."

As for Leo XIII, he was during his entire life intimately associated with the Society. " You Jesuits have enjoyed the great privilege," he once said to a Father of the Roman Province, " of having had saints for Generals. I knew Father Fortis; he was a saint. I knew Father Roothaan intimately; he was a saint. I was long acquainted with Father Beckx; he was a saint. And now you have Father Anderledy."

On February 25, 1881, he gave to the college at Beirut in Syria the power of conferring degrees in philosophy and theology. Four years later when there was question of a new edition of the third volume of the Institute, and Father Anderledy had asked His Holiness to re-affirm the ancient privileges of the Society, Leo XIII replied with the Brief " Dolemus inter," which is regarded by the Society as one of its great treasures. After expressing his sorrow for the persecution which it was just then suffering in France, the Pope says: " In order that our will with regard to the Society of Jesus may be more thoroughly understood, we hereby declare that each and every Apostolic letter which concerns the establishment, the institution and confirmation of the Society of Jesus and which has been published by our predecessors, the Roman Pontiffs, beginning with Paul III of happy memory, up to our own time either by briefs or Bulls, and whatever is contained in them or follows from them and which either directly or by participation with other religious orders has been granted to the Society and has not been abrogated or revoked in whole or in part by the Council of Trent and other Constitutions of the Apostolic See, namely, its privileges, immunities, exemptions and indults, we hereby confirm by these letters, and fortify them by the strength of our Apostolic authority and once more concede. . . Let these letters be a witness of the love which we have always cherished and still cherish for the illustrious Society of Jesus which has been most devoted to Our Predecessors and to Us; which has been the fruitful mother of men who are distinguished for their holiness and wisdom, and the promoter of sound and solid doctrine, and which, although it suffered grievous persecution for justice sake, has never ceased to labor with a cheerful and unconquerable courage in cultivating the vineyard of the Lord. Let this well-deserving Society of Jesus, therefore, which was commended by the Council of Trent itself and whose accumulated glory has been proclaimed by Our Predecessors, continue in spite of the multiplied attacks of perverse men against the Church of Jesus Christ to follow its Institute in its fight for the greater glory of God and the salvation of souls. Let the Society continue in its efforts to bring to pagan nations and to heretics the light of truth, to imbue the youth of our times with virtue and learning, and to inculcate the teachings of the Angelical doctor in our schools of philosophy and theology. Meantime, embracing this Society of Jesus, which is most beloved by Us, We impart to its Father General and his vicar and to all and each of its members our Apostolic benediction."

On the occasion of his golden jubilee in 1888, he showed his esteem for the Society by canonizing Peter Claver, and when the Fathers went to express their gratitude for this mark of affection, he replied that the Society had always been dear to the Sovereign Pontiffs, considering it as they did to be a bulwark of religion, and a most valiant legion that was always ready to undertake the greatest labors for the Church and the salvation of souls. To himself personally it had always been very dear. He had shown this affection as soon as he was made Pope, by making a cardinal of Father Mazzella, whose virtue and doctrine he held in the highest esteem, and by employing Cardinal Franzelin as long as he lived in the most important and most secret negotiations. Neither of whom ever waited for the expression of his wish. A mere suggestion sufficed. He then began to speak of his boyhood in the College of Viterbo, where he had learned to love the Jesuit teachers, and he went on to say that his affection had increased in the Roman College under such eminent masters as Taparelli, Manera, Perrone, Caraffa and others whom he named. He spoke enthusiastically of Father Roothaan, and then reverting to Blessed John Berchmans whom he had canonized, he told how his devotion to the boy saint began in his early college days of Viterbo.

In 1896 he showed his approval of the Society's theology by giving it the Institutum Leoninum at Anagni, and in the *Motu proprio* which he issued on that occasion, he said: " To the glory which the Society acquired even in its earliest days among learned men, by its scientific achievements and the excellent work it accomplished in doctrinal matters, must be added the art which is so full of cleverness and initiative of instilling knowledge and piety in the hearts of their scholars. Such has been their reputation throughout their history, and we recall with pleasure that we have had the opportunity of studying under the most distinguished Jesuits. Hence, as soon as by the Providence of God we were called to the Supreme Pontificate, we asked more than once that young men, especially those who were to consecrate themselves to the Church, should be trained by the members of the Society, both in our own city and in distant countries of the world. We recall especially in this connection their work among the Basilians of Galicia and in the Xaverian Seminary which we established at Kandy in the East Indies. Hence, wishing to inaugurate an educational institution in our native city of Anagni, we cast our eyes upon the members of the Society and in neither case have we been disappointed."

The mention of the Ruthenian Basilians refers to an extremely delicate work entrusted to the Jesuits. Something had gone wrong in the Basilian province of Ruthenia, and at the request of the bishops and by command of the Pope, a number of Galician Jesuits took up their abode in the monastery of that ancient and venerable Order, and after twelve years of labor restored its former fervor. One scarcely knows which deserves greater commendation: the prudence and skill of those who undertook the difficult task or the humility and submission of those who were the objects of it. When the end had been attained, the Jesuits asked to be relieved of the burden of direction and government, and far from leaving any trace of resentment behind them, it was solemnly declared by a general congregation of the Basilian monks that the

link of affection which had been established between
the two orders was to endure forever.   The second
apostolic work alluded to by the Pope in this Brief of
1897, was the Pontifical Seminary for all India which
he had built on the Island of Ceylon and entrusted to
the Belgian Jesuits.

In 1887, he had established a hierarchy of thirty
dioceses in the Indies, and as a native clergy would
have to be provided, an ecclesiastical seminary was
imperative.   The Propaganda was therefore commissioned to erect the buildings and provide for the
maintenance of the teachers, and in virtue of the command 250 acres of land were bought in 1892 near the
city of Kandy on the Ampitiya Hills.   Father Gros-
jean, S. J., was appointed superior and began his
work in a bungalow.   It took five years before any
suitable structures could be provided.   The course of
studies included three years of philosophy and four
years of theology.   There is now a staff of eleven professors and they have succeeded in overcoming a difficulty which seemed at first insurmountable, namely,
the grouping together under one roof of a number of
men who were of different castes and of different races.
The bishops held off for a time, and in the first year
only one diocese sent its pupils; three years later, seven
were represented and now there are one hundred seminarians from all parts of India.   They are so well
trained that it is a rare thing for them not to satisfy
their bishops when they return as priests.   " The
project of the great Pontiff, Leo XIII," says the Belgian chronicler, " seemed audacious but the results
have justified it."

The Fathers found another friend in Pius X.   They
knew him when he was Bishop of Mantua, and he not
only frequented their house but used to delight to
stand at the gate distributing the usual dole to the poor.

He enjoyed immensely the joke of the coadjutor brother
who said. "Bishop Sarto (*sarto* means tailor) will
make a fine garment for the Church when he is Pope;"
though the holy prelate never dreamt of any such honor
in those days or even when he was Patriarch of Venice.
When he went to his new see, he took his Jesuit confessor with him, and there, as at Mantua, he was at
home with the community and found particular delight
in talking to the brothers. When Farther Martín
lost his arm in consequence of an operation for sarcoma, the Pope gave him permission to celebrate
Mass. "I tried it myself to see if it were possible,"
he said "and I found it could be done without much
difficulty, so I give permission to Father General to
offer the Holy Sacrifice, provided another priest assists
him." When the new General, Father Wernz, and
his associates presented themselves to the Pope after
the election, he thanked God for having given him the
Society, which he described as "a chosen body of
soldiers, who were skilled in war, trained to fight,
and ready at the first sign of their leader." He gave
a further proof of the trust he had in them by putting
into their hands the Pontifical Biblical Institute, which
was part of the general purpose he had in view when,
in 1901, he organized the Biblical Commission already
described.

Apart from the esteem manifested by the Sovereign
Pontiffs for the Society itself as a religious order, their
personal regard for each successive General is worthy
of note. Thus Pius VII, on being informed of the
election of Father Brzozowski as General, immediately
expressed his gratification by letter "that the Society
had chosen a man of such merit and virtue." Leo XII,
as we have said, lived on the most intimate and affectionate terms with Father Fortis. Only his brief
career as Pontiff prevented him from giving more

positive proofs of his affection. The same may be said
of Pius VIII, whose term was even shorter than that of
Leo XII. During that time, however, he lavished
favors on the Society. Gregory XVI made Father
Roothaan his intimate friend and gave him any favor
he asked, and Pius IX expressed the wish that " the
Society would elect a General of equal prudence and
wisdom, and who, like Roothaan, would be a man
according to the heart of God." The amiable Father
Beckx was always welcomed by Pius IX and their
intercourse with each other was almost one of famil-
iarity. When the General was on his death-bed, Leo
XIII said to the Roman provincial: " I am deeply
moved by the illness and suffering of Father Beckx
for whom I have always entertained a great regard and
even a filial affection. I most willingly send him
my blessing; tonight in his pain and agony, I shall be
at his side in spirit and aid him with my prayers."

In Father Beckx's successor, Father Anderledy,
Leo XIII had absolute confidence. So too, Father
Martín's return to Rome from Fiesole was made an
occasion of great rejoicing for the Pope, who used to
ask Cardinal Aloysius Massella good humoredly:
" Why don't you give up your office and be a Jesuit?"
When Father Martín presented himself for an audience
in times of trouble, Leo would say to him affectionately:
" Come here, Father General and sit beside me so that
we can talk over our sorrows; for your sufferings are
mine."

Of course, affection was almost expected from Pius X,
and when Father Martín returned to Rome with his
health slightly improved, his reception by the Pope
was like that of a son coming from the grave to the
arms of his father. Later on he kept himself informed
about Father Martín's suffering and prayed for him
several times every day. " We cannot spare such

men " was his expression; and when at last the General died, the Pope was deeply affected. " He was a man of God," was his exclamation, " A saint! A saint! A saint! " At the election of Father Wernz, Pius X spoke of the great good he had done to the whole Church by his profound learning as teacher in the Gregorian University. " There was scarcely any part of the world," he said, " where his merit was not acknowledged. He was known to all as the possessor of a great, solid and sure intelligence; of vast erudition which found expression in his learned treatises on the Law of Decretals, and which won the applause of all who were versed in canon law."

Another mark of this esteem for the Society, though an unwelcome one, was the elevation of so many of its members to ecclesiastical dignities by the Sovereign Pontiffs. First, in point of time, was the selection of John Carroll to be the founder of the American hierarchy. It was all the more notable because Challoner, the Vicar Apostolic of London, had repeatedly said that there was no one in America who measured up to the height of the episcopal dignity. The sequel proved that the Pontiff was wiser than the Vicar. We have already called attention to the fact not generally known that there was another Jesuit appointed to the See of Baltimore; though he never wore the mitre. He died before the Bulls arrived. His name was Laurence Grässel, and he had been a novice in the Society in Germany at the time of the Suppression. Carroll describes him as " a most amiable ex-Jesuit." Shea records the fact that " the Reverend Laurence Grässel, a learned and devoted priest, of whose sanctity tradition has preserved the most exalted estimate, revived the missions in New Jersey which had been attended by the Reverend Messrs. Schneider and Farmer." (Vol. II.)

Leonard Neale, who succeeded Archbishop Carroll in the See of Baltimore, was a Jesuit priest in Liège at the Suppression. Before returning to his native country, he spent four years in England and four more in Demerara. In Philadelphia, when vicar general of Bishop Carroll, he was stricken with yellow fever while administering to the sick during the pestilence. Later he was made president of Georgetown College, and in 1801 was appointed Coadjutor of Baltimore. The successor of the illustrious Cheverus in the See of Boston was Benedict Fenwick, who had entered the Society in Maryland eight years before Pius VII re-established it throughout the world. The first Bishop of New York also would have been a Jesuit, Anthony Kohlmann, had not Father Roothaan, entreated the Pope to withdraw the nomination.

Anthony Kohlmann was born at Kaisersberg in Alsace, July 13, 1771. The outbreak of the French Revolution compelled him to leave his country when he was a young man and betake himself to Switzerland to continue his interrupted studies. He completed his theological course and was ordained a priest in the College of Fribourg. In 1796 he joined the Congregation of the Fathers of the Sacred Heart, and labored for two years in Austria and Italy as a military chaplain. We find him next at Dillingen in Bavaria as the director of an ecclesiastical seminary. By this time the Fathers of the Faith, Paccanari's organization, had united with those of the Sacred Heart, and Kohlmann was dispatched to Berlin and subsequently to Amsterdam as rector of a new college in that place.

As soon as he heard that the Jesuits in White Russia had been recognized by the Pope, he applied for admission, and entered the novitiate at Duneburg on 21 June, 1803, and in the following year was sent to Georgetown as assistant-master of novices.

While holding that position he travelled extensively through Pennsylvania and Maryland to look after several groups of German colonists who had settled in those states.   When the ecclesiastical troubles of New York were at their height, Bishop Carroll selected Kohlmann to restore order.   With him went Father Benedict Fenwick and four scholastics.   He was given charge of that whole district in 1808.   There were about fourteen thousand Catholics there at the time: French, German and Irish.   In 1809 he laid the corner stone of old St. Patrick's, which was the second church in the city.   He also founded the New York Literary Institution as a school for boys, on what is now the site of the present cathedral, but which then was far out of town.   In 1812 he began a nearby school for girls and gave it to the Ursuline nuns, who had been sent from Ireland for that purpose.

Father Kohlmann rendered a great service to the Church by the part he took in gaining a verdict for the protection of the seal of Confession.   He had acted as agent in the restitution of stolen money when the owner of it demanded the name of the thief.   As this was refused, he haled the priest to court, but the case ended in a decision given by the presiding Judge, DeWitt Clinton, that " no minister of the Gospel or priest of any denomination whatsoever shall be allowed to disclose any confession made to him in his professional character in the course of discipline enjoined by the rules or practices of such denomination."   This decision was embodied in a state law passed on December 10, 1828.   His controversy with Jared Sparks, a well-known Unitarian, brought his reply entitled " Unitarianism, theologically and philosophically considered."   It is a classic on that topic.

As mentioned above, Kohlmann was designated Bishop of New York, but at the entreaty of the General of the Society, the Pope withdrew his name. In 1815 he returned to Georgetown as master of novices, and in 1817 was appointed president of the college. In 1824 he was called to Rome as professor of theology in the Gregorian University and occupied that post for five years. Among his students were the future Pope Leo XIII, Cardinal Cullen of Dublin, and Cardinal McCloskey of New York. Both Leo XII and Gregory XVI held Kohlmann in the highest esteem and had him attached to them as consultor to the staffs of the College of cardinals and to several important congregations such as that of Extraordinary Ecclesiastical Affairs; of Bishops and Regulars; and the Inquisition. He died at Rome in 1836, in consequence of overwork in the confessional.

It might be of interest to quote here a passage from the " Life of John Cardinal McCloskey " by Cardinal Farley: " About this time Father McCloskey suffered the loss of a very dear and devoted friend, Father Anthony Kohlmann, S. J. As pastor of St. Peter's, Barclay Street, he had been the adviser of the young priest's parents in New York for many years. He had seen him grow up from childhood, and had been his guide and friend in Rome. It is therefore but natural that he should express himself feelingly on the death of this holy man, as in this letter addressed to the Very Rev. Dr. Power:

Rome, April 15, 1836.
' Very Rev. dear Sir:
' It is truly with deep regret that I now feel it my duty to acquaint you with the news which, if not already known to you, cannot but give you pain. Our venerable and most worthy friend, Father Kohlmann, is no more. He has been summoned to another world, after a warning of only a few days. On Friday,

the 8th. inst., he was as usual in his confessional. During the course of the day he was seized with a violent fever which obliged him to take to his bed, and on Sunday morning, about five o'clock, he was a corpse.   On Monday, I had the melancholy pleasure of beholding him laid out in the Church of the Gesù, where numbers were assembled to show respect for his memory, and to view for a little time his mortal remains. His sickness was so very short that death effected but little change in his appearance.   He seemed to be in a gentle sleep, such calmness and placidity.   His countenance seemed to have lost nothing of its usual fulness or even freshness.   And such was the composure of every feature, that one could hardly resist saying within himself: He is not dead, but sleepeth.   His loss as you may well conceive, is deeply regretted by the members of his Order here as well as by all who knew him.

'As for myself, I feel his death most sensibly, having lost in him so prudent a director, so kind a father and friend.   You also, Very Reverend and dear Sir, are deprived by his death of a most active and valuable friend in Rome.'"

In Hughes's "History of the Society of Jesus in North America" (I, pt. ii, 866) there is a quotation from the "Memoirs" of Father Grassi which refers to Father Kohlmann and calls for consideration.   He is described by the odious name of Paccanarist.   As a matter of fact, Kohlmann joined the Fathers of the Sacred Heart in 1796, three years before Paccanari was even heard of.   In April 1799, by order of the Pope, the Fathers of the Sacred Heart were amalgamated with Paccanari's Fathers of the Faith, but from the very beginning there was distinct cleavage between the two sections; and in 1803 when it became evident

that Paccanari had no intention of uniting with the
Jesuits in Russia, Kohlmann was one of the first to
separate from him and was admitted to the Society
in that year. If he was a " Paccanarist," then so
were Rozaven and Varin.

We are also informed that Kohlmann was an ex-Capuchin.   It is strange, however, that Guidée makes no
mention of it in his historical sketches of the Fathers of
the Sacred Heart.   Moreover, if he ever were a member
of that Order, it must have been for an extremely
brief period; for he was born in 1771, and at the outbreak of the French Revolution which swept away
all religious communities he was only eighteen years
of age.   We find him then finishing his theological
studies at Fribourg where the Jesuits had been conspicuous before the Suppression, and he was ordained
a priest in 1796, when he was twenty-five years old.
Immediately afterwards, he joined the Fathers of the
Sacred Heart.   So that if he ever had been a Capuchin
it must have been at a very early age; and in any
case he did not leave his Order voluntarily.   It had
been swept out of existence in the general storm.

Grassi tells us also that, out of pity for the distressed
religious who had been thrown out of their homes at
that time, the General of the Society had asked the
Pope to lift the ban against the Society's receiving
into its ranks the members of other Orders — a policy
which it had always pursued, both out of respect for
the Orders themselves, and because a change in such
a serious matter would imply instability of character
in the applicant.   Father Pignatelli was deputed to
submit the cause to His Holiness, and Grassi is in
admiration at the sublime obedience of Pignatelli in
doing what he was told; but it is hard to imagine why
he should be so edified.   The Professed of the Society
make a special and solemn vow of obedience to the

Pope and admit his decision without question. Even when the Pope suppressed the entire Society they defended his action. Where is there anything heroic in being merely the messenger between the General and the Pope? In any case Kohlmann's admission to the Society was with the full approval of both the Sovereign Pontiff and the General, even if he had been a Capuchin, which is by no means certain.

We are also informed that the authorities in Rome were surprised that Kohlmann was admitted to his last vows before the customary ten years had elapsed, but there are many such instances in the history of the Society, and the General in referring to it may have been merely asking for information. Finally with regard to the alleged worry about Kohlmann's appointment as Vicar General of New York; it suffices to say that the office is of its nature temporary, and cannot well be classified as a prelacy; especially as there was only one permanent church structure in the entire episcopal territory that stretched between the Hudson River and Lake Erie, and the clergy was largely made up of transients.

At the time that Father Kohlmann was mentioned for the See of New York, Father Peter Kenny was proposed for that of Dromore in Ireland. Foley in his " Chronological Catalogue of the Irish Province S. J. " gives a brief account of this very distinguished man, who like Kohlmann was for some time identified with the Church in the United States.

He was born in Dublin, July 7, 1779, and entered the Society at Hodder, Stonyhurst, September 20, 1804. He died in the Gesù at Rome, November 19, 1841. When a boy he attracted the notice of Father Thomas Betagh, the last of the Irish Jesuits of the old Society, who was then Vicar General of Dublin, and was sent to Carlow College. Even in early youth he was remarkable for his extraordinary eloquence. When a novice he was told to come down from the pulpit, his fellow-novices being so spell-bound that they refused to eat. At Stonyhurst, he wrote a work in mathematics and physics. In 1811 he was Vice-President of Maynooth College. He purchased Clongowes Wood in 1814, and in 1819 was sent as visitor to the Jesuit houses of Maryland. He was made vice-provincial of Ireland in 1829, and again came to America in 1830, where he remained for three years and then installed Father McSherry as the first provincial of the American province. His retreats in Ireland are still enthusiastically referred to and quoted. In 1809 when he was finishing his theology in Palermo, Father Angiolini wrote to Father Plowden " Father Kenny is head and shoulders over every one. He has genius, health, zeal, energy, success in action and prudence to a remarkable degree. May God keep him for the glory and increase of the Irish Missions! " God did so and the missions of America also profited by his genius and virtue.

Later on, Father Van de Velde was made Bishop of Chicago, but he continually petitioned Rome to be allowed to return to the Society; while Father Miège after twenty-four years of the episcopate and without waiting to celebrate his silver jubilee became a Jesuit again and spent his last days at Woodstock, where he met Father Michael O'Connor, who had resigned the See of Pittsburg in order to assume the habit of St. Ignatius. His brother before being made Bishop of Omaha asked to enter the Society but he was told " Be a bishop first like your brother and afterwards a Jesuit." One of the most distinguished Jesuits of New York, Father Larkin, had to flee the country to avoid being made Bishop of Toronto, and Father William Duncan of Boston would have occupied

58

the See of Savannah had not he entered the Society.

The same thing is true of the cardinalate. An unusually large number of Jesuits have been raised to that dignity in the hundred years of the new Society, in spite of the oath they have taken to do all in their power to prevent it, an oath which they have all most faithfully kept, yielding only because they were bidden to do so under pain of sin.

Camillo Mazzella entered the Society in 1857, and when the scholasticate at Woodstock in Maryland was opened, he was made prefect of studies. He was called to Rome in 1878 to take the place of Franzelin in the Gregorian University. In 1886 he was created Cardinal deacon and ten years later Cardinal priest, while in 1897 he was appointed Cardinal bishop of Palestrina. Camillo Tarquini was made cardinal because of his prominence as a canonist; Andreas Steinhüber's learning and his great labors as Vatican librarian won for him the honor of the purple, while Louis Billot after teaching dogmatic theology at Angers and the Gregorian University was named Cardinal deacon of Santa Maria in Via Lata on November 27, 1911. But much greater consolation has been afforded to the new Society by the canonization of its saints than by the choice of its members for the cardinalate. One is a recognition of the intellectual ability and personal virtue; the other is an official, though indirect, approval of the Institute.

At the very time that Pombal, Choiseul and Charles III were crushing the Society in their respective countries, Rome as if in condemnation of the act was jubilant with delight over the heroic virtue of the Italian Jesuit, Francis Hieronymo; and people were asking each other how a Society could be bad when it produced such a saint? In an issue of the " Gazette " of distant Quebec at that time we find a bewildered Protestant Englishman who was the journal's correspondent at Rome asking himself that question. The political troubles of the period caused the proceedings of the canonization to be suspended, but Gregory XVI, who succeeded Leo XII, canonized Francis on the Feast of the Blessed Trinity, 1839. Pius IX beatified Canisius, Bobola, Faber, de Britto and Berchmans, with Peter Claver, the apostle of the negroes, and the lay-brother Alphonso Rodríguez, besides placing the crown of martyrdom on the throng of martyrs in Japan, Europeans and natives alike, as well as upon Azevedo and his thirty-nine Portuguese associates who were slaughtered at sea near the Azores.

Leo XIII beatified Antonio Baldinucci and Rudolph Aquaviva with his fellow-Jesuits who were put to death at Salsette in Hindostan, besides raising to the honors of sainthood Peter Claver and Alphonso Rodríguez, and also placing John Berchmans in the same category, thus re-affirming the sanctity of the rules of the Society, for the realization of which the holy youth had already been beatified. The canonization of Alphonso is also notable because it was by Leo XII, whose name Leo XIII had adopted, that the humble porter of Minorca was raised to the first honors of the altar. Finally, Pius X showed his love for the Society and his approval of the rule by beatifying the three martyrs of Hungary whom scarcely anybody had ever heard of before: Mark Crisin, Stephen Pongracz and Melchior Grodecz. There is also under consideration the beatification of the great American apostles Jogues, Brébeuf, Lalemant, Daniel, Chabanel, Garnier, Goupil and Lalande, five of whom died for the Faith in Canada, and three in what is now the State of New York.

The new Society has not failed to add new names to this catalogue of honor of prospective saints. They are Joseph Pignatelli, who died in 1811; Father Joseph de Clorivière, 1820; Paul Cappelari, 1857; and Paul Ginhac, 1895. Five Jesuits were put to death at Paris in 1871 by the Communards: namely Pierre Olivaint, Anatole de Bengy, Alexis Clerc, Léon Ducoudray, and Jean Caubert.

Between 1822 and 1902, forty-four others have given glory to the Society either by the heroic sanctity of their lives, or by shedding their blood for the Faith. Besides these, there are thirty-five Jesuits who have been put to death in various parts of the world. They are: four Italians, Ferdinando Bonacini and Luigi Massa in 1860; Genaio Pastore in 1887 and Emilio Moscoso in 1897; four Germans: Anthony Terorde in 1880; Stephen Czimmerman, Joseph Platzer and Clemens Wigger who were killed by the Caffirs in 1895-6. The French can boast of 12 namely: Bishop Planchet in 1859; Edouard Billotet; Elie Jounès, Habib Maksoud, and Alphonse Habeisch who were killed in Syria in 1860; Martin Brutail in 1883; Gaston de Batz in 1883; Modeste Andlauer, Léon Mangin, Remi Isoré, and Paul Denn, who met their death in the Boxer Uprising in 1900; Léon Müller was killed by the Boxers two years later. Sixteen Spaniards were put to death: Casto Hernández, Juan Sauri, Juan Artigas, José Fernández, Juan Elola, José Urrietta, Domingo Barreau, José Garnier, José Sancho, Pedro Demont, Firmin Barba, Martín Buxons, Emanuel Ostolozza, Juan Ruedas, Vincente Gogorza, who were massacred in Madrid in 1834.

CHAPTER XXX

CONCLUSION

Successive Generals in the Restored Society — Present Membership, Missions and Provinces.

As we have seen, the first General of the Society elected after the Restoration was Father Fortis, who died on January 27, 1829. On June 29 of that year Father John Roothaan was chosen as his successor on the fourth ballot. As in the previous election, Father Rozaven was the choice of many of the delegates.

John Philip Roothaan, the twenty-first General of the Society, was born at Amsterdam on November 23, 1785, and finished his classical studies in the Atheneum Illustre under the famous Jakob van Lennep. When he had made up his mind to enter the Society in White Russia in 1804, his distinguished teacher, though a Protestant, gave him the following letter of introduction: " I am fully aware of how in former times the Society distinguished itself in every branch of knowledge. Its splendid services in that respect can never be forgotten, and I am, therefore, especially pleased to recommend this young man whose merit I most highly appreciate. May he be enriched with all your science and your virtues, and I trust to see him again in possession of those treasures which he has gone so far to seek."

The praise was well merited, for, even at that early period of his life, Roothaan had mastered French, Polish, Latin, Greek and Hebrew. He studied philosophy at Polotsk, and in 1812 was ordained priest. After the expulsion he went to Switzerland in 1820, and taught rhetoric there for three years. As socius to the provincial, he made the tour of all the Jesuit houses in Germany, Switzerland, Belgium and Holland three times, and afterwards was appointed rector of the new college in Turin. As General, his chief care was to strengthen the internal life of the Society. His first eleven encyclicals have that object in view. His edition of the " Exercises " is a classic. In 1832 he published the " Revised Order of Studies," adapting the Ratio to the needs of the times; and he increased the activities of the Society in the mission fields. But his long term of office was one uninterrupted series of trials. His enforced visit to the greater number of the houses has already been told in a preceding chapter.

Among the many things for which the Society is profoundly grateful to Father Roothaan is the very remarkable publication of the " Exercises of St. Ignatius." According to Astrain, " the autograph was in rough and labored Castilian," for it must be remembered that the saintly author was a Basque. " The text," he tells us, " arrests the attention," not by its elegance but, " by the energetic precision and brevity with which certain thoughts are expressed. The autograph itself no longer exists. What goes by that name is only a quarto copy made by some secretary, but containing corrections in the author's handwriting. It has been reproduced by photography. Two Latin translations were made of it during the lifetime of St. Ignatius. There remain now, first the *versio antiqua* or ancient Latin translation, which is a literal version, probably by the saint himself; second, a free translation by Father Frusius, more elegant and more in accordance with the style of the period. It is commonly called the 'Vulgate.' The *versio antiqua* bears the date, Rome, July 9, 1541. The 'Vulgate' is later than 1541 but earlier than 1548, when the two versions were presented to Paul III for approval. He appointed three examiners, who warmly praised both versions, but the Vulgate was the only one printed. It was published in Rome on September 11, 1548, and was called the *editio princeps*.

" Besides these two translations, there are two others. One is the still unpublished text left by Blessed Peter Faber to the Carthusians of Cologne before 1546. It holds a middle place between the literal document and the Vulgate. The second was made by Father Roothaan, who, on account of the differences between the Vulgate and the Spanish autograph, wished to translate the Exercises into Latin as accurately as possible, at the same time making use of the *versio antiqua*. His intention was not to supplant the Vulgate, and on that account he published the work of Frusius and his own in parallel columns (1835)."

Father Roothaan was succeeded as General by Father Beckx, who was born in 1795 at Sichem, near Diest, the town that glories in being the birthplace of St. John Berchmans. He entered the Society at Hildesheim in 1819, after having been a secular priest for eight months. In 1825 he was appointed chaplain of the Duke of Anhalt-Köthen, who had become a Catholic after visiting the home of one of his Catholic friends in France. Anhalt-Köthen is in Prussian Saxony, and there were only twenty Catholics in the entire duchy when Beckx arrived there. Before four years had passed, the number had grown to two hundred. In 1830 he was sent to Vienna and for a time was the only Jesuit in that city. In 1852 he was made provincial of Austria and had the happiness of leading back his brethren to the beloved Innsbruck as well as to Lenz and Lemberg. In the following year he was elected General, and occupied the post for thirty-four years. He used to say that at the time he entered into office the province of Portugal consisted of one

Jesuit and a half. The one was in hiding in Lisbon, and the " half " was a novice in Turin. Even now they number only three hundred. All the houses have been seized by the Republican government and the Fathers, scholastics and brothers expelled from their native land in the usual brutal fashion.

During Father Beckx's term of office eighty Jesuits were raised to the honors of the altar. All but three of them were martyrs. In spite of this the Society was expelled from Italy in 1860; from Spain in 1868; and from Germany in 1873, at which time the General and the assistants left Rome, where, after the Piedmontese occupation, it was no longer safe to live. They took up their abode at Fiesole and there the curia, as it is called, remained until after the death of Father Beckx's successor. In 1883 the age and infirmities of the General made the election of a vicar peremptory, and Father Anderledy was chosen. Father Beckx died at the age of ninety-two, and one who saw him in the closing years of his life thus writes of him: " This holy old man who has attained the age of nearly ninety years, so modest, so humble, so prudent, always the same; always amiable, with the glory of thirty years' government and of interior martyrdom inflicted upon him by the mishaps of the Society, was a spectacle to fill one with admiration. His angelic mien delighted me. With how great charity he received me in his room! With what deference! His poor cassock was patched. He is as punctual at the exercises as the most vigorous. In spite of his old age he observes all the laws of fasting and abstinence. At a quarter past five he commences his Mass and spends considerable time kneeling before the Blessed Sacrament. God grant us many imitators of his virtues."

Father Anderledy was a Swiss. He was born in the canton of Valais in 1819, and entered the Society at

Brieg in 1838. He was sent to Rome for his theological studies and it is reported that he was such a pertinacious disputant that old Father Perrone said to him one day: "Young man, cease or I shall get angry." In the disturbances of 1847, he was on his way to Switzerland when he was halted by a squad of furious soldiers who asked him " Are you a Jesuit?" " What do you mean by a Jesuit?" he asked. When the conventional answer was given, he angrily demanded " Do you take me for a scoundrel?" and they let him pass. In 1848 he was sent to America and was ordained at St. Louis by Archbishop Kenrick and then put in charge of a German parish at Green Bay, Wisconsin, a place teeming with memories of the old Jesuit missionaries: Marquette, Allouez and others. On his return to Europe, he went through Germany preaching missions and winning a reputation as a great orator, although working in conjunction with the famous Father Roh. He was made rector of the College of Cologne and, subsequently, professor at the scholasticate of Maria-Laach. In 1870 he was called to Rome to be made German assistant, and in 1883 he was elected vicar to Father Beckx with the right of succession. He was particularly zealous as General in promoting the study of theology and philosophy, and in training men in the physical sciences. During his administration, the Society increased from 11,840 members to 13,275, but he was very much adverse to the establishment of new provinces. The creation of Canada as an independent mission was all he would grant in that direction. He died at Fiesole on 18 January, 1892.

Luis Martín García, or, as he is commonly called, Father Martín, who succeeded Father Anderledy, was the fifth Spanish General of the Society. He was born on 19 August, 1846, at Melgar de Fermamental, a small town about twenty-five miles north-west of Burgos, and was already a seminarian in his second year of theology when he began to think of becoming a religious. To be a Jesuit, however, was at first as abhorrent to him as becoming a Saracen. But his ideas on that point began to clarify when he heard his very distinguished professor Don Manuel González Peña, who had been a theologian in the Vatican Council, discourse enthusiastically and on every occasion, about the glories of Suárez, Toletus, Petavius, Bellarmine and the other great lights of the Society. The impression was heightened by some letters from the Philippine Jesuits which had fallen into his hands, and Crétineau-Joly's history also contributed to his change of views. A conversation with the Jesuit superior of the residence at Burgos, and the departure of a brilliant fellow-student for the novitiate, completed the disillusionment and he was admitted at Loyola on 13 October, 1864.

In 1870, when the Society was expelled from Spain, he went with the other scholastics to Vals in France, and later to Poyanne. In the latter place he remained as minister and professor of dogmatic theology until 1880, and when the religious were expelled from France he returned to Spain and was made superior of the scholasticate which had been opened in Salamanca. He was charged also with the duty of teaching theology and Hebrew. In 1886 he opened the house of studies at Bilbao, and in the same year he was made provincial of Castile. Previous to that he had been the editor of "The Messenger of the Sacred Heart" for a year. In 1891 he was summoned to Rome by Father Anderledy, to analyze and summarize the reports sent in by all the provinces on the proposed *quinquennium* of theology and a new arrangement of studies. On the death of Father Anderledy he was made Vicar General.

He was then only forty-five years of age. His appointment coincided with the outbreak of an epidemic of influenza of which he was very near being a victim. Singularly enough, it was this same disease that carried him off thirteen years later, supervening as it did on the terrible sarcoma from which he had long been suffering.

As Vicar he convoked the general congregation, assigning September 23 as the date and choosing Loyola in Spain as the place of meeting. It was the first time in the history of the Society that the convention took place outside of Rome, with the exception of the meetings in Russia during the Suppression. The reason for the decision was that the Pope let it be known that it would not be possible to remain in session in Rome for any considerable period, though he suggested that they might elect the General in Rome and then continue the congregation elsewhere. After long deliberation by the assistants, it was determined not to separate the election from the other proceedings. As for the place of meeting, Loyola was chosen, though Tronchiennes in Belgium had been offered. The choice of Spain was determined by the vote of the assistant who had no Spanish affiliations. Father Martín was elected general on 2 October, and the sessions continued until 5 December.

In this congregation, Father Martín called the attention of the delegates to the fact that no Jesuit had ever addressed himself to the task of writing the complete history of the Order; an abstention, it might be urged, which ought to acquit them of the accusation of unduly praising the Society. Father Aquaviva had indeed commissioned Orlandini to begin the work, but the distinguished writer not only got no further then the Generalate of St. Ignatius but did not even publish his book. Saechini his continuator had to see to the publication; his own contributions appeared in 1615 and 1621. Jouvancy was then called to Rome to finish the second half of the fifth section which had by that time appeared, but he did not advance beyond the year 1616. He had bad luck with it even in that small space, for certain opinions appeared in it about the rights of sovereigns which were not acceptable to the Bourbon kings, and the book was forbidden in France by decrees of Parliament, dated 25 February and 25 March, 1715. Finally, Cordara, an Italian, assumed the task and wrote two volumes, which though exquisitely done embraced not more than seventeen years of Father Vitelleschi's generalate (1616-33), and only one volume was published then. More than one hundred years elapsed before the second appeared. It was edited by Raggazzini in 1859.

It was high time, Father Martín declared, that something should be done to remedy this condition of affairs and that a history of the Society should be written on a scale commensurate with the greatness of the subject, and in keeping with the methods which modern requirements look for in historical writing. As the undertaking in the way it was conceived would have been too much for any one man, a literary syndicate was established in which Father Hughes was assigned to write the history of the Society's work in English-speaking America, Father Astrain that of the Spanish assistancy, Father Venturi the Italian, Father Fouqueray the French, Father Dühr and Father Kroess the German. This work is now in progress. Those who are engaged on it are men of unimpeachable integrity. Meantime an immense number of hitherto unpublished documents are being put in the hands of the writers. As many as fifty bulky volumes known as the " Monumenta historica Societatis Jesu," consisting of the chronicles of the houses and provinces, the intimate correspondence of many of the great men of the Society, such as Ignatius, Laínez, Borgia etc., have been printed, and sent broadcast through all the provinces. Nor is this mass of material jealously guarded by the Jesuits themselves. It is available to any sincere investigator.

As the Congregation had expressed the desire that the residence of the General and his assistants at Fiesole be closed, and that if the political troubles would permit it he should return to Rome, Father Martín, after consulting with the Pope, who granted the permission with some hesitation, established himself at the Collegium Germanicum on 20 January, 1895. The public excitement that was apprehended did not occur. The papers merely chronicled the fact but made no ado about it whatever. Father Martín had much to console him, during his administration, as, for instance, the beatification of several members of the Society, but he had also many sorrows such as the closing of all the houses in France by the Waldeck-Rousseau government and the deplorable defections of some Jesuits in connection with the Modernist movement.

In 1905 the first symptoms of the disease that was to carry him off in a short time declared themselves. In that year, four cancerous swellings developed in his right arm. He had submitted to the painful cutting of two of them without the aid of anesthetics. The operation lasted two hours and a half, and he maintained his consciousness throughout. A little later, the other swellings showed signs of gangrene and the amputation of the arm was decided upon, but in this instance he submitted to chloroform. He rallied after the operation and in spite of his crippled condition was permitted by the Pope to say Mass.

His strength had left him, however, and on 15 February, 1906 he was attacked by influenza and he died on 18 April at the age of sixty. At his death the Society numbered 15,515 members.

Father Martín's successor was Francis Xavier Wernz who was born in Würtemberg in 1842. When the Society was expelled from Germany in 1872, he went to Ditton Hall in England to complete his studies, after having spent the greater part of a year in the army ambulance-corps, during the Franco-Prussian War of 1870. He taught canon law for several years at Ditton Hall, and in 1882 was a professor at St. Beuno's in Wales. From there he was transferred to the Gregorian University in Rome, where he lectured from 1883 to 1906. In September of the latter year, he was elected General, in which post he lived only eight years. Previous to his election, he had issued four volumes of his great work on canon law. Two others were published later, one of them after his death. The end of his labors came on 19 August, 1914. He was then in his seventy-second year and had passed fifty-seven years in the Society. It was during this generalate that the provinces of Canada, New Orleans, Mexico, California and Hungary were erected.

Father Wladimir Ledochowski was elected to the vacant post on 11 February, 1915. He was then only forty-nine years of age. He entered the Society in 1889, and in 1902, shortly after his ordination, was made provincial of Galicia, while in 1906 he was elected as assistant to Father Wernz. He is the nephew of the famous Cardinal Ledochowski, whom Bismarck imprisoned for his courageous championship of the rights of Poland.

The new Society like the old has not failed to produce saints and at the present moment the lives of a very considerable number of those who have lived and labored in the century that has elapsed since the restoration are being considered by the Church as possible candidates for canonization.

The number of Jesuits who were under the colors as soldiers, chaplains or stretcher bearers or volunteers in the World War of 1914-1918 ran up to 2014,—a very great drain on the Society as a whole, which in 1918 had only 17,205 names on its rolls, among whom were very many incapacitated either by age or youth or ailment for any active work.   Of the 2014 Belgium furnished 165, Austria 82, France 855, Germany 376, Italy 369, England 83, Ireland 30, Canada 4 and the United States 50.   Of the 83 English Jesuits serving as chaplains, 5 died while in the service, 2 won the Distinguished Service Order, 13 the Military Cross, 3 the Order of the British Empire, 21 were mentioned in despatches, 2 were mentioned for valuable services and 4 received foreign decorations, — a total of 45 distinctions.

France calls for special notice in this matter.   From the four French provinces of the Society 855 Jesuits were mobilized.   Of these 107 were officers, 3 commandants, 1 lieutenant-commander, 13 captains, 4 naval lieutenants, 22 lieutenants, 50 second-lieutenants, 1 naval ensign, and 5 officers in the health services. The loss in dead was 165 Jesuits, of whom 28 were chaplains, 30 officers, 36 sub-officers, 17 corporals and 54 privates.   The number of distinctions won is almost incredible.   The decoration of the Légion d'honneur was conferred on 68, the Médaille militaire on 48, the Médaille des épidémies on 4, the Croix de guerre on 320, the Moroccan or Tunisian medal on 3, while 595 were mentioned in despatches, and 18 foreign decorations were received: in all 1,056 distinctions were won by the 855 Jesuits in the French army and navy (The Jesuit Directory, 1921).   " What party or group or club or lodge," says a sometime unfriendly paper, the " Italia," " can claim a similar distinction?" Another of their distinctions is that Foch, de Castelnau, Fayolle, Guynemer and many more French heroes were trained in Jesuit schools. Finally, the French Jesuits performed this marvellous service to their country in spite of the fact that the government of that country had closed and confiscated every one of their churches and colleges from one end of France to the other, and by so doing had exiled these loyal subjects from their native land. To add to the outrage, they were summoned back when the war began, and not one of them failed to respond immediately, returning from distant missions among savages at the ends of the earth or from civilized countries that were more hospitable to them than their own for the defense of which they willingly offered their lives. Now, when the war is over, they have no home to go to.

In 1912, two years before the War, the Society had on its rolls 16,545 members. At the beginning of 1920 it had 17,250 members: 8,454 priests, 4,819 scholastics, 3,977 lay-brothers. The Society is divided into what are called assistancies. The Italian assistancy, which is composed of the provinces of Rome, Naples, Sicily, Turin and Venice, numbers in all 1,415 members. The frequent dispersions and confiscations to which this section has been subjected account for the small number. Thus, the Roman province has only 354, and Sicily has but 223. In the assistancy there are 748 priests, but the prospects of the increase of this category is the reverse of encouraging, for there are only 308 scholastics. The lay-brothers number 359. What has acted as a deterrent in Italy has, paradoxically, acted in a contrary sense in the German assistancy. Several of these provinces have been dis-

persed, but they aggregate as many as 4,329 members.
Belgium is a strong factor in this large number, for
it totals 1,279, of whom 672 are priests; the Germans,
who have no establishment in their own country,
but are scattered over the earth, have a membership
of 1,210, of whom 664 are in Holy Orders. Austria
has 356 on her register, Poland 464, Czecho-Slovakia
114, Jugoslavia 113, Hungary 212, while Holland has
as many as 581.

The Waldeck-Rousseau Associations Law of 1901
not only confiscated every Jesuit establishment in
France but denied the Society the right even to possess
property. Nevertheless, unlike Italy the provinces of
Champagne, France, Lyons and Toulouse show 2,758
names in their catalogues for 1920. They have 1,647
priests with 583 scholastics to draw on. The Spaniards
are grouped in the provinces of Aragon, Castile, Mexico,
and Toledo, to which has been added the Province of
Portugal. This combination has 1,760 to its credit.
Possibly the figures would have been larger had not
the Revolution of 1901 brought about the exile of
the Jesuits. The English assistancy which until
recently included the United States, has now 1,622
members of whom 793 are priests and 544 scholastics:
England 750, Canada 472 and Ireland 400. The
assistancy of America has 2,892 members of whom 1,230
are priests with a future supply to draw on of 1,214
scholastics. The contingent of scholastics exceeds that
of any other assistancy by more than a hundred. The
province of California has 485 members, Maryland-
New York, 1,080; Missouri, 1,022 and New Orleans, 305.

Besides its regularly established houses the Society
has missions scattered throughout the world. Thus,
in Europe its missionaries are to be found in Albania;
in Asia, they are working in Armenia, Syria, Ceylon,
Assam, Bengal, Bombay, Poona, Goa, Madura, Man-

galore, Japan, Canton, Nankin, and South East Tche-ly. In Africa, they are in Egypt, Cape Colony, Zambesi, Rhodesia, Belgian Congo, and Madagascar, Mauritius and Réunion; in America, they are working in Jamaica and among the Indians of Alaska, Canada, South Dakota, the Rocky Mountains, the Pimeria, and Guiana; finally in Oceania, they are toiling in Celebes, Flores, Java, and the Philippines. To these missions 1,707 Jesuits are devoting their lives in direct contact with the aborigines.

INDEX

936 Index

Roh, 921
Roman College, 69
Romberg, Assistant, 585
Roothaan, John, 398, 667, 706
Rosas, 762
Rosmini, 898
Rossi, Giovanni Battista de, 836
Rossi, Guizot's envoy, 750
Rosweyde, 370
Roth, 840
Rozaven, 625, 719 et seq., 898
Rubillon, Ambrose, 773
Russia, 841
Russian Church, 642
Ruthenia, 902
Ryllo, Maximilian, 811sq.

S

Sabbetti, 886
Sacchini, 369, 923
Sacred Heart, Fathers of the, 666–668
Sacred Heart, Ladies of the, 672 sq.
St. Acheul, 740
St. Bartholomew Massacre, 272
St. Beuno's, 764
St. Clement's Island, 339
Sainte-Beuve, 283 sq., 745
Saint-Germain-des-Pres., Chapel, 58
St. Julian, Castle, 469–472
Saint-Jure, 381
Saint Kitts, 306–310
St. Michel, Brussels, 870
St. Omers, 407
St. Sulpice, Society of, 244
St. Vincent, Admiral, 704
Saints, 914–5
Salamanca, 21
Saldanha, 421–2
Salmeron, Alphonsus, 21, 45
Salsette, 170, 229
Salvatierra, 222, 321
Sancian, Island of, 84
Sanguinetti, 883
San Sebastian, prison, 743
Sant' Andrea, 762
Santel, 360
Sarbiewski, 359
Sardinia, 504, 758
Sarpi, 112, 220sq.
Sault Ste. Marie, 338
Saxony, 718
Scaramelli, 381
Schall, Adam, 254–261, 372
Scheiner, 848
Scholastics, 485
Schreiner, Christopher, 371
Science, 248–250, 631, 371, 834sq.
Scientia media, 215
Scotch Doctor, 38
Scotland, 40, 150
Secchi, 371, 835
Secret Members, of Jesuit Order, 35
Secularization, 600sq.
Sedeno, 333
Sedlmayer, 372
Segneri, 364
Segura, 54
Seminaries, 44, 65–67
Sequiera, 185
Sestini, 843sq.
Seven Years War, 425, 482sq.
Sewall, 732, 683
Shea, Gilmary, 873
Sherwin, 144
Shin-toism, 166
Shogun, 175

Siam, 234
Sicily, 504
Sidgreaves, Walter, 841
Sierra Leone, 824
Siestrzencewicz, 643
Sigismond, King of Poland, 35, 122, 208
Silesia, 637
Silverira, 85
Simpson, 751
Sin (Mandarin), 256
Sin, Paul, see Zi, 771
"Sined," 860
Sioux, 779
Sirmond, 354
Si-Senoussi, Sheik and Jesuit Constitutions, 35
Sixtus V, Pope, p. 7, 111, 202, 180, 206–209, 556–558
Skarga, 367
Slingsby, Francis, 149sq.
Smet, Peter de, 779–81
Smolensk, 686
Smyrna, 239
Sobieski, John, 394, 397, 404
Sodalities, 68, 297, 738
Sollicitudo omnium ecclesiarum, 694–6
Sommervogel, 868
Sorbonne, 216–7, 290
Soto, 115
Sotwel, 867
Sousa, 87–8
Southey, 90
Southwell, 147–8, 358
Spain, 36, 43, 202–14, 51–3
Sparks, 908
"Speculum Jesuiticum," 273
Spee, von, 117, 361sqq.
Spinola, 185
Spiritual Exercises, 13–15, 381, 918sqq.
Squillace, 428 507
Stanislaus Kostka, St., 48, 382, 418
Stanton, Father, 785–8
Staritza, 124
Statistics, 418–9, 550, 777, 800sqq.
Steinhüber, 887
Steins, 795
Stephens, 141sqq.
"Stimmen aus Maria Laach," 874sqq.
Stone, 710
Stonestreet, 706
Stonyhurst, 500, 732
Strada, 36, 53, 56, 359
Strassmaier, 845, 863
Stritch. See Bathe
Stuart, Henry. See York, Cardinal of
Suárez, 21, 116, 281, 379, 390, 395, 416, 486, 876
Suau, 52sqq.
Sulpicians, 713
Superior, Lake, 336
Suppression, 442–603
Surin, 381, 395
Suttee, 804
Sweden, 120–24, 404, 681, 685
Swetchine, 730
Switzerland, 346, 587, 617, 728, 734, 740
Syria, 240, 632, 806–9, 929

T

Tamburini, 417–8, 575
Tamil, 231, 362
Tanucci, 421, 506 et seq.
Tapparelli, 874
Tartary, 244, 770
Tegakwitha, 337–8

Press of
J. B. Lyon Company
Albany, N. Y.